EXPLORATIONS IN ANTHROPOLOGY: READINGS IN CULTURE, MAN, AND NATURE

THOMAS Y. CROWELL COMPANY NEW YORK, ESTABLISHED 1834

MORTON H. FRIED

explorations in anthropology

READINGS IN CULTURE, MAN, AND NATURE

 Published simultaneously in Canada by Fitzhenry & Whiteside, Ltd., Toronto.

LIBRARY OF CONGRESS CATALOGING IN PUBLICATION DATA

Fried, Morton Herbert, 1923– comp.
Explorations in anthropology.

Includes bibliographies.
1. Anthropology—Addresses, essays, lectures.

I. Title. GN29.F76 301.2′08 73–1265

ISBN 0-690-28252-4

Cover design and typography by Herman Strohbach

Manufactured in the United States of America

1 2 3 4 5 6 7 8 9 10

Cover and title page photographs: Charles Gatewood and Napoleon A. Chagnon.

Part title pages: p. 1–Marino Marini, *Dancer*, The Joseph H. Hirshhorn Collection; p. 11–UPI Photo; pp. 73 and 441–Courtesy of the American Museum of Natural History; p. 163–Barbara J. Price; p. 247–Karoo Ashevak, Courtesy of American Indian Arts Center.

PREFACE

Another book of readings in anthropology!

It was Jim Bergin of the Thomas Y. Crowell Company who, having seen Marvin Harris's *Culture, Man, and Nature* into print, approached me with the outrageous notion of adding yet another collection of readings to the sizeable total already available. Why did I do it?

Let me begin with a quote from the essay in this anthology by Professor Delmos J. Jones. Jones claims, rather ascerbically, that "the field of anthropology as a whole was dull and uncreative in the 1960's" (see p. 456). I like Jones's article very much, but I must say that I don't agree with him about that. Of course, I'm not sure about the "as a whole" bit, but it seems to me that everything I think of "as a whole" was compounded of ups and downs—politics at all levels, the economy, the arts, letters, sports, and certainly sex. Actually, anthropology is not the sort of field in which great breakthrough discoveries occur. Our knowledge is cumulative and although some sharp insights have considerable impact, progress is slow. But there have been numerous important changes in anthropology over the past several years sufficient to warrant gathering some of them together in a volume such as this.

The purpose of this book is not primarily to present a pandisciplinary view of the latest contributions. Instead my intention has been to convey some of the basic information comprising the contemporary discipline of anthropology; my method has been to permit a variety of anthropological specialists to speak for themselves in generally uncut essays devoted to particular topics. Because the editorial task is complicated by things that often have nothing to do with matters of intellectual substance, there are many interesting topical developments not found in these pages. On the other hand, I think that objective comparison of the contents of this book with those of others presently available, including my own two volume *Readings in Anthropology* (N.Y., Thomas Y. Crowell, 2nd ed., 1968), will show not only a number of specific changes in information, but, more significantly, a rather different overall mood and direction.

The difference that I refer to is manifested also in comparing Marvin Harris's *Culture, Man, and Nature* (N.Y., Thomas Y. Crowell, 1971) with other texts. The essence of the difference can be summed up in one much abused word—relevance. Harris deliberately set about the task of communicating the basic concepts and some of the basic data of anthropology in the context of our present world and its most pressing problems. While *Explorations in Anthropology* is a completely autonomous venture, I have tried to accomplish much the same end as did Harris, although our viewpoints are not necessarily the same. The use of the title of the Harris text as the subtitle of mine is, however, a calculated act of homage.

There are four things, in particular, that I would like to mention about this collection. First, although there is certainly no originality in the stress on the "four field" nature of anthropology, there is importance in its continuation. As time goes by and everything grows more complicated, pressures mount for earlier and earlier specialization in the educational process. Those of us who teach anthropology, particularly in graduate courses, know the strength of centrifugal tendencies among the subfields. But various essays between these covers offer proof of the vitality and utility of a unified concept of the science of culture. The work of the best contemporary physical anthropologists is comprehendable only in a matrix comprising literally all of anthropology. Similarly, the kind of archeology represented particularly by Price in this volume is literally impossible without nourishment from the discipline at large. Linguists and cultural anthropologists, too, make active use of the broadly construed setting and the details supplied by anthropology. Most important, this condition does not apply merely to those with professional interests in anthropology. The larger audience we serve recoils from increasingly arcane specialization and its often esoteric attempts at communication. To the extent that we can locate our specialized contributions within broader frameworks of a science of humankind and culture we can maintain dialogue and perform genuine educational functions.

To introduce my second point, let us reconsider the subtitle of this book and dwell for a moment on that word "nature." Neither "man" nor "culture" exists outside of some natural environment, no matter how changed, degraded, or polluted. Despite the banality of this concept, anthropology for quite a long period paid only the most obvious attention to man's interactions with nature. Recently, however, the ecological approach has been growing in popularity and effectiveness, often in quiet ways despite sometimes faddish associations. The contents of this volume reflects the strength of ecological orientations in anthropological work, pervading not merely studies of economic and social organization but penetrating the analysis of religious and other ideological systems. It is evident, at least to the editor, that the interest in ecological approaches increases anthropology's interaction with a great variety of other sciences and disciplines while simultaneously reasserting the integrity of the "four field" approach.

This is not the place for a discussion of the advisability or the possibility of an anthropology built upon and confined to problems of conspicuous current social weight. The questions involved are by no means hypothetical, for the limiting case is before us in the recent history of anthropology and sociology under Maoism, echoes of which can be heard on campuses in the United States. It is not necessary to go to such an extreme to face the problem of relevance in undergraduate instruction. For most professors their discipline is a thing of vital interest and value in itself, it needs no justification through contributions to the solution of current social ills. A different conception of relevance is involved. Indeed, anthropology and the disciplines lying closest to it are rarely seen by their practitioners as offering solutions to problems of that sort, although many believe that these disciplines can bring the kind of illumination that might aid in ameliorating them. This, in turn, is viewed with hostility and contempt by those who think, to cite Delmos Jones again, "that enough research has already been done, period. People with this attitude think that action is what is needed now." Obviously, a book such as this cannot be "action"; but a deliberate attempt has been made to tie much of the basic materials it purveys to some of the major problem areas of our society. The editor thinks it has a pretty fair relevance quotient and is proud of it.

Which takes us to the fourth point I would like to make about this book. However it may be rated on the previous three, the volume breaks new ground in this last point—the attention it pays to anthropological self-criticism. For the most part, this is not of the methodological variety, of which anthropology has an abundance. Thus, we find little in these pages about the emic-etic controversy, or the debate about structuralism, or crises of sampling. The criticism I refer to has to do primarily with anthropologists' relations with people and with the culture that sponsors their field. It may be that the relatively heavy weight of attention given this subject in Part Eight will dismay some of my colleagues, but I think that most will welcome it as overdue. One of the great strengths of anthropology has been its iconoclasm. Anthropologists have turned critical eyes on their own society and culture for some time. Now the focus is drawing ever closer to home and the precincts of the discipline itself are breached. While some students may suffer a crisis of confidence when confronted with such material, I think that most will react otherwise, gratified to encounter honesty and the stirrings of change.

Once again it is time to thank those whose labor made this volume possible. I am particularly grateful to the authors whose contributions comprise the book. Some of them went out of their way to revise or edit their papers; I am in their debt.

Thanks are due to Susan Bass and Jim Bergin of the Thomas Y. Crowell Company for assistance both spiritual and practical, including timely reminders of swift approaching deadlines. Lillian Lent moved the project along. Martha Fried and Nancy Fried offered helpful advice and criticism and Elman Steven Fried volunteered to do the book cover, but built some spaceship models instead. Many friends made extremely helpful suggestions. Once again I discovered that I was faced by far more articles of excellence than the book could hold. To all who helped, I am grateful. Thank you, thank you all.

June, 1972 MORTON H. FRIED

CONTENTS

PREFACE v

HEY! A WORD TO STUDENTS xiii

ONE THE FIELDS OF ANTHROPOLOGY 1

[1] **Anthropology as a Behavioral and Social Science**
The Behavioral and Social Sciences Survey, Anthropology Panel 3

TWO EXPLORATIONS IN HUMAN EVOLUTION 11

[2] **Evolutionary Theory in Biology** Ernst Mayr 13

[3] **Mendelian and Chemical Genetics** Alexander Alland, Jr. 20

[4] **A Gene by Any Other Name** 32

[5] **Primate Studies and Human Evolution** Sherwood L. Washburn 34

[6] **The Seed-Eaters: A New Model of Hominid Differentiation** Clifford J. Jolly 47

[7] **The Single Species Hypothesis** Milford H. Wolpoff 57

[8] **The Origin of Man** C. Loring Brace 67

THREE EXPLORATIONS IN RACE 73

[9] **Racial Classifications: Popular and Scientific** Gloria A. Marshall 75

[10] **The Population as a Unit of Research** Nigel A. Barnicot 84

[11] **Statement on Race and Racial Prejudice** 88

FOUR CULTURE AND ANTHROPOLOGY 93

[12] **The Concept of Culture and the Science of Man** Morton H. Fried 95

[13] **The Concept of Culture and the Culture of Poverty** Eleanor Burke Leacock 99

FIVE ASPECTS OF LINGUISTICS 113

[14] **The General Properties of Language** Noam Chomsky 115

[15] **The Logic of Nonstandard English** William Labov 124

[16] **Language and Communication** John J. Gumperz 150

SIX ASPECTS OF THE ARCHEOLOGICAL RECORD 163

[17] **The Emergence of Man the Tool-maker** J. Desmond Clark 165

[18] **Neanderthal—Worthy Ancestor** Ralph S. Solecki 182

[19] **The Origins of Agriculture: A Reconsideration** E. S. Higgs and M. R. Jarman 188

[20] **The Discovery of the First Civilization** Glyn Daniel 200

[21] **Prehispanic Irrigation Agriculture in Nuclear America** Barbara J. Price 211

SEVEN EXPLORATIONS IN CULTURAL ANTHROPOLOGY 247

[22] **An Ecological Approach in Cultural Anthropology** Andrew P. Vayda 249

[23] **Population Anthropology: Problems and Perspectives** Moni Nag 254

[24] **Economic Anthropology and Anthropological Economics** Marshall Sahlins 274

[25] **The Origin of the Family** Kathleen Gough 289

[26] **Kinship Concepts** Hope Jensen Leichter and William E. Mitchell 304

[27] **Anthropology and Political Science: Courtship or Marriage?** Ronald Cohen 321

[28] **Yanomamö Social Organization and Warfare** Napoleon A. Chagnon 334

[29] **On Peasant Rebellions** Eric R. Wolf 366

[30] **Culture and Personality** Anthony F. C. Wallace 373

[31] **Urban Anthropology** Peter C. W. Gutkind 394

[32] **The Sacred in Human Evolution** Roy A. Rappaport 403

[33] **Myth Charter in the Minority-Majority Context** John L. Gwaltney 421

[34] **Contemporary Arts in Non-Western Societies** Jacqueline Delange Fry 430

[35] **The Role of Music in Western Apache Culture** David P. McAllester 436

EIGHT ANTHROPOLOGY LOOKS AT ITSELF 441

[36] **As Others See Us** Nancy Oestreich Lurie 443

[37] **Towards A Native Anthropology** Delmos J. Jones 448

[38] **Skeletons in the Anthropological Closet** William S. Willis, Jr. 459

[39] **A Closing Word** Morton H. Fried 475

GLOSSARY 489

HEY! A WORD TO STUDENTS

Zinjanthropus, diastema, phoneme, Pliocene, Clactonian, kula, potlatch, kiva, Chuckchee, Hopi, Arapeshmundugumoraztecazandetrobriandaruntabagandahaida. . . . The students of introductory anthropology often feel they are drowning in a sea of unfamiliar words and concepts. A whole field that they may have approached with curiosity and anticipation begins to flounder in a mess of trivia. One of the main problems has to do with the absence of clearcut indications of relative significance. How should a student who is only beginning the study of anthropology know if it is more important to remember the names of the interstadial periods of Pleistocene glaciation in Europe, or the designations given certain bones that often are recovered in paleontological excavations?

The problem is complicated by the interposition of examinations and the cultural institution known as grading. In the face of such procedures, students must warp their own inclinations and interests in learning the new material to what they believe will be expected of them by the instructor. Some students who are remarkably successful at this are equally adept at jettisoning the freight of one semester's work to make room for the next. It is also common for students to concentrate on details without concern for deeper meanings or connections.

Unfortunately, a collection of articles such as this can play into the worst syndromes of the kind just described. Take, for example, the brilliant synopsis of the evolution of civilization in nuclear America by Barbara Price (selection 21). It is full of terms that few, if any, student readers have ever encountered before. What shall an intelligent student do about it?

Speaking as a Grand Inquisitor who still remembers life among the catechized, I urge the student reader approaching these essays to relax and optimize enjoyment, if that is possible. Instead of grubbing at every new detail, the object should be to get the biggest ideas being discussed. Hopefully, the brief introductory statements preceding the essays will assist you in that task, so please take advantage of the headnotes and let them orient you to what follows. If you follow the main arguments and understand them, agreement or disagreement notwithstanding, then some of the supporting data should also stick in your mind. What is more, these data will probably be more deeply implanted as a consequence of their attachment to a meaningful theoretical framework.

Although some of the articles in the book are of a review kind, attempting to summarize portions of the field, most are not. Instead, with various degrees of passion, they make points that are of great concern to their authors. When you read such selections it may help to keep in mind the question, "Why did the author write this particular piece?" If you really can't answer that after reading the article, you had better discuss it with your instructor or section leader and with other students. The same applies to articles that irritate or offend you or just seem wrong.

I suppose all professionals regard their own fields as intrinsically interesting, but as I attempted to show in the Preface, anthropology has so much to offer that is fresh and different and exciting that I think it is in a class by itself. It would be horrible if the length or complexity of some of the stuff in this book turned you off. Among the objectives of the editor was the desire to stimulate and excite you about anthropology. If you think I could have done a better job, why not write to me at the Department of Anthropology, Columbia University, New York, N.Y., 10027 and tell me how?

MORTON H. FRIED

ONE
THE FIELDS OF ANTHROPOLOGY

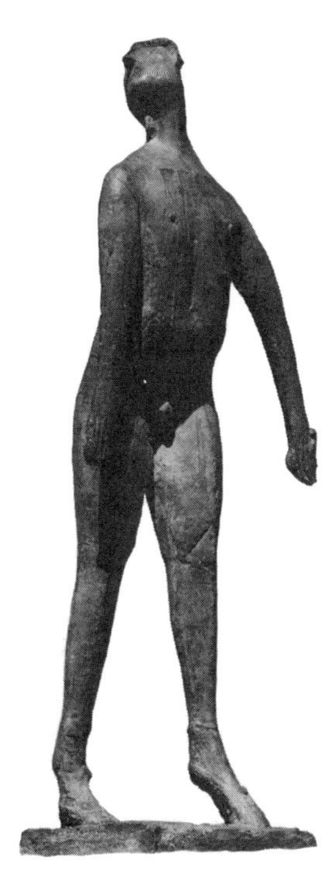

1

ANTHROPOLOGY AS A BEHAVIORAL AND SOCIAL SCIENCE

THE BEHAVIORAL AND SOCIAL SCIENCES SURVEY, ANTHROPOLOGY PANEL

One fairly consistent aspect of anthropology is controversy. Anthropologists tend to be contentious and to love disputation. They even argue about the name of their discipline. One focus of dissatisfaction is with the implicit emphasis on man, not merely for the unfortunate sexist connotation, but because it slurs over the fact that anthropology is interested in much more than the human animal. Much stress is placed upon the understanding and analysis of culture and a number of anthropological specialties have been developed to deal with different features and characteristics of culture, its varying structures and aspects.

The continuous development of subdisciplinary specializations within anthropology has had various effects. One result has been a kind of crisis of identity for the field as growing numbers of interested people, some professionals and some not, have wondered where anthropology left off and some other discipline began. Nor did such questions arise merely in familiar boundary areas, as between anthropology and history, or sociology, or geography. Now there are anthropologists who are most at home in discussion with economists, others who seek out political scientists, or psychologists, or even mathematicians. Perhaps the most serious questions arise in terms of preparing the most serious students. Shall they be given unlimited access to courses in nonanthropological fields and disciplines at the cost of mastering clearly anthropological subject matters, methods, and theories? What may be regarded as the substantive, methodological, and theoretical core of anthropology?

The problems just suggested were framed with regard to anthropology, but they exist among all disciplines. In recognition of this, two committees—the Committee on Science and Public Policy of the National Academy of Sciences and the Problems and Policy Committee of the Social Science Research Council—initiated a "Survey of the Behavioral and Social Sciences" in 1967. BASS, as it came to be called, created a number of panels of distinguished scientists, each concerned with one particular discipline or set of problems. Questionnaire-derived data were added to other knowledge and the reviews and appraisals conducted by the panels were summarized in a series of reports. Our first selection comes from one of these, the report dealing with anthropology, edited by Allan H. Smith and John L. Fischer. It sets the stage for all that follows by surveying the present layout of the discipline of anthropology, indicating major subdisciplines and also discussing the relations between anthropology and various fields that anthropology interacts with.

▼△▼△▼

Anthropology, as one of the component disciplines of the behavioral and social sciences, has a distinctive history that produces a sense of identity among those who call themselves anthropologists. At the same time, it covers a diverse set of interests overlapping in many ways with its neighboring disciplines, including biological sciences and the humanities. A defining structure is provided by the four commonly recognized subfields: *social-cultural anthropology,* sometimes called ethnology; *archaeology,* to be distinguished from classical archaeology, which tends to be manned by classical scholars; *linguistic anthropology;* and *physical anthropology.* A fifth subfield, less uniformly recognized as a separable component, is *applied anthropology.* The structure of the field as it exists, particularly in the United States, can best be understood by looking at these subfields.

SOURCE: *Anthropology* © 1970, Allan H. Smith and John L. Fischer (eds.), pp. 20–30, Chapter 2. Reprinted by permission of Prentice-Hall, Inc., Englewood Cliffs, N.J.

The Four Major Subfields

The expression *social-cultural anthropology* is used here to indicate the panel's belief that an effort to distinguish sharply between social and cultural anthropology is futile. There are those who would hold to a distinction, with social anthropology limited to interpersonal relations and social groups and cultural anthropology concerned with custom, tradition, and values. However, customs and values involve interpersonal relations, and traditions are passed on through organized social groups. Hence we prefer to treat the two subfields as one, with further internal specializations. More anthropologists acknowledge social-cultural anthropology as their special area of competence than any of the other three major subfields.

Archaeology is the branch of anthropology that involves the excavation and study of the material remains of former cultures. It is the second most populous subfield. Archaeology is really a variety of social-cultural anthropology in its broadest sense, since it is the study of past societies and cultures through their abandoned material remains. Obviously it is easier to find out about some things (such as subsistence techniques) than others (such as language or details of religious ceremonies) through archaeological investigation, but in principle, archaeologists are committed to understanding the implications of their data as fully as possible and some surprisingly detailed and plausible inferences may be made from the information available to them.

There is really no fundamental difference between exploring an Indian mound or an ancient Greek ruin, but as a result of the social history of scholarship the archaeological work of classical antiquity tends to be done by classical scholars, while the study of smaller cultures or the cultures of prehistory is done by anthropologists. These uncertainties as to which discipline belongs where are common to many fields of scholarship; thus when anthropologists study villages on the edge of a large industrial city, or a city ward, or various institutions of the city itself, it is hard to distinguish between their work and that of some sociologists. Increasingly we may expect many of the investigations to become multidisciplinary.

Linguistic anthropology is a branch of the larger field of linguistics, which is concerned with human language in all its aspects. Anthropologists came into this field early because many of the tribes they studied had languages that were little known, and in order to make headway in studying their cultures it was necessary to master the language. A grammar and dictionary of the language were often byproducts, but scientific interest went much farther than improving communication with the native users of the language. Languages provide invaluable data for studying the history of peoples; the ways in which languages can differ from one another and the universal features all have in common are of great theoretical interest for the light they shed on the nature of the human mind and of human culture. Linguistic anthropology can be considered a specialized branch of cultural anthropology because language involves customary behavior shared by a community or society. The skills and expertnesses required are such, however, that a specific subfield has developed.

Physical anthropology, essentially a subdivision of human biology, involves the study of the bodily characteristics of men as influenced by heredity and environment. Because of the strong evolutionary interest, much of this research deals with the remains of the most ancient human ancestors, including the anthropoids as man's nearest relatives. However, living and recent populations are also studied, and the behavioral patterns of apes, monkeys, and other primates may be investigated for the light they shed on the biological development of mankind.

This grouping of somewhat disparate subjects under the banner of anthropology is in part a response to a special historical situation: the rapid acculturation and disintegration of many American Indian tribes during the formative period of American anthropology before and after the turn of the century. In their field research the early anthropologists encountered small neglected groups of people, apparently about to lose their identity, who were the last representatives of formerly flourishing native societies. The investigators felt an obligation to science to record all possible information about these vanishing groups: a complete naturalistic description of physique, language, customs, traditions, and even a little of the local archaeology if possible.

Interrelations Among the Subfields

The tendency toward specialization commonly leads to the creation of new disciplines. Thus statistics branches off from mathematics and biochemistry separates itself from general chemistry. The different interests of anthropologists with unlike specialties have not resulted in a dismemberment of anthropology, however, because each of the subfields continues to become relevant to the others in newly discovered ways.

There are two major ways in which the data from two or more of the four major subfields are used jointly: (1) in the study of origins of human phenomena, i.e., in tracing the picture of *historical development* from early times to the present and the temporal relations of one human group to another; and (2) in the study of *function* or *process*, i.e., in the study of the operation of culture, of how human groups survive, of the causal relations of various human phenomena interacting within the present or over a relatively short period of time.

Whether in the investigation of historical development or in the study of the functional operation of a culture, anthropologists tend to prefer a "holistic" approach, rather than a piecemeal one. Such an approach—looking at the society and culture in all its aspects as a whole—is obviously facilitated by the choice of small nonliterate societies for study. With such an approach, it is not hard to see why the various anthropological specialties soon come into relation to each other.

In research on the origins of human groups, each of the major subfields of anthropology can provide its own kind of evidence as to the historical relation between two or more groups. Social-cultural anthropology examines oral traditions and attempts to separate fantasy from historical fact. Even more important is the analysis of the comparative content of cultures: how many customs do they have in common? how many beliefs? in what detail? Not all customs are of equal usefulness in the study of ethnic origins. Those customs which are specific adaptations to the geographical environment are not to be expected in a closely related ethnic group living in a different environment. On the other hand, customs that can vary somewhat more freely in relation to the natural environment, such as styles of art or decoration of utensils, religious beliefs and practices, or details of social and political organization, are likely to be especially useful in testing the common origin of two ethnic groups and in measuring the relative distance of their relationship. In archaeology, the main emphasis in testing common origin and measuring separation is on durable artifacts. Where pottery is present the techniques of making and decorating pottery are particularly useful in providing a cultural index, since archaeologists have identified a surprising number of technical variations which characterize precisely the pottery of a culture. Archaeologists also have a variety of ways to date objects—by noting their position in a sequence of deposits or by examining certain kinds of objects for chemical and physical changes that proceed at a measurable rate after manufacture or deposition in an archaeological site.

Linguistic anthropologists are able to identify languages of common origin where they can show that certain words and grammatical processes are shared by two or more languages and where there are regular correspondences between the sounds of two languages in related words. The linguistic anthropologist for the most part studies unwritten languages, so, unlike the linguist dealing with the major Old World languages, he has no old documents to tell him what his language was like centuries earlier. However, by the study of variants in existing languages and by comparing related languages, it is possible to reconstruct the family tree of cognate languages, to distinguish which related words have been in the languages for a long time and which are recent borrowings, and even to reconstruct much of a fairly remote ancestral language.

The physical anthropologist has a variety of methods to measure the biological relationship of two or more human populations, alive or dead. With living populations especially, a number of serological and biochemical tests (such as blood groups and other characteristics of known genetic origin) determine precisely which of a series of known alternant genes an individual possesses and what the frequency of each of these is in the population of which he is a member. In addition to these biochemical tests, physical anthropologists have long used measurements and other direct observations of the human skeleton and other bodily parts to determine how similar two populations are physically and to estimate the amount of common ancestry and the date of their separation.

While any one of the subfields of anthropology can in its own right provide data for inferring the historical connections between ethnic groups, the results are obviously sounder and more convincing if the contributions of more than one subfield can be compared and integrated into a single statement about the ethnic groups under consideration. Collating cultural similarities in surviving recent cultures with the traces of earlier cultures in the archaeological record, relationships between languages, and biological similarities in modern and archaeological populations yields a rather full picture of the development of an ethnic group, at least within recent millennia.

That the four subfields of anthropology can be coordinated in the search for human and ethnic origins does not imply much about possible causal or functional relationships between the objects of study in the different subfields. The search for origins merely assumes that ethnic groups change gradually in all respects —cultural, linguistic, and biological—and that groups that are similar in any of these respects are more closely related than dissimilar groups. Many anthropologists, however, are interested in functional relationships between the subfields of anthropology; some phenomenon in one subfield, say social anthropology, will have some clear connection with something in another subfield, say dialect and style in linguistics. Functional relationships involving all possible pairs of the four subfields of anthropology are under study.

Applied Anthropology as a Fifth Subfield

Applied anthropology is best considered a fifth subfield in its own right, although it parallels the four other subfields and possesses elements from each. During the past two decades, a good deal of research has been directed toward using standard anthropological data to solve practical problems. New methods of fact-gathering, a fresh body of data collected with these methods, and the identification of new research areas mark this subfield. Applied physical anthropology is contributing to an understanding of the biological aspects of race, to medicine, and even to the design of specialized clothing and advanced equipment (like supersonic planes and space vehicles) where the limitations and maximum possibilities of the human organism are crucial and must be fully understood. Archaeology is discovering new data about those cultural activities of prehistoric societies that caused fundamental and damaging changes to the physical environment and therefore yield lessons of practical importance for contemporary man. Cultural anthropology is providing technical guidelines to ease the transition of nonindustrial societies under Western influence to a more complex level of socioeconomic organization, of former colonial areas to independent nations, of societies with traditional explanations of disease causation to principles of modern scientific medicine, and so on. Applied cultural anthropology is likewise developing procedures by which action programs of international and governmental agencies (e.g., UNESCO and the Peace Corps) may be evaluated in terms of basic design and their success in attaining announced objectives. Linguistic anthropology is producing the language information, technical and practical, that is necessary to encourage the advance of literacy in societies with unwritten languages.

Applied anthropology, if carefully fostered and kept tightly scientific in methodology, offers great promise to those anthropologists who elect to make a professional commitment to improving man's lot. At the same time, the potential for a rich backflow of raw data to the more strictly scientific aspects of the discipline cannot be overlooked. Hypotheses drawn from "pure" data are ordinarily difficult to examine experimentally, but they may sometimes be tested in the field under nearly experimental conditions by anthropologists in a position to observe the effects on societies of administrative action with specific, practical objectives in mind. This field of anthropology is certain to receive increased research emphasis during the coming decades until, it may be predicted, it becomes a unit of major dimensions within the discipline.

The preceding paragraph suggests a revealing contrast between applied anthropology and other applied fields. In general, the "practitioners" of a field, those who apply its findings to practical problems, contribute little to the growth of the knowledge of that field. Distinctions like those between physician and medical researcher, politician and political scientist, and social worker and sociologist come readily to mind. The facts noted above reveal, however, that the applied anthropologist fails to fit in a parallel dyad against the cultural and other anthropologists. He does not need to lose his role as an anthropological scientist in order to be able to serve the needs of a developing society.

Relationships Between Anthropology and Other Behavioral Sciences

Up to this point we have considered the subdivisions of anthropology and their interrelationships. It is now appropriate to consider the relations between anthropology and various related disciplines, including the other social and behavioral sciences, the humanities, the biological sciences, and the physical sciences.

In colleges and universities anthropology has often been grouped in a single department with sociology or in a general department of social sciences including perhaps economics, political science, and psychology as well. There is obviously much in common between social anthropology and sociology: both are concerned with explaining how societies work and how they keep going. In practice, there has tended to be a working division in which sociologists study large modern societies, especially their own, and anthropologists study small underdeveloped societies, especially remote foreign ones. However, a majority of practitioners of both disciplines would probably deny these limitations on their data. Many anthropologists have worked in large modern societies, at any rate, and the proportion doing so is likely to increase. We may doubt whether it is possible to produce a generally accepted definition of the two disciplines that would separate them unequivocally in all cases, nor is it perhaps desirable to do so. However, we may cite several differences in emphasis that, when taken together, will differentiate the majority of social anthropologists from the majority of sociologists. One important difference is in methodological emphasis: the sociologist typically engages in the extensive, large-scale study of some rather precise questions; he is greatly concerned about the adequacy of his sample of subjects or respondents, or the accuracy of the data of others which he uses in secondary analysis. In contrast, the anthropologist typically conducts a more intensive clinical study of individuals as exemplars of sociocultural process; he is interested in many questions and he is willing to large extent to let his subjects or "informants" (a good word in anthropology, not the same at all as "informers" in politics) decide what they want to talk about; he is more concerned with establishing an intimate relationship with a few people who will talk with him freely and frankly than with selecting a representative sample. Both types of study obviously have their uses: work with informants produces much rich information, but some check is desirable to know how representative it is.

Social anthropology also has a substantial overlap of interest with economics, considered as the study of the production and distribution of goods. While not all societies have a fully developed monetary economy, all societies do have scarce goods and some means of exchange. Anthropologists are interested in exploring the range of production and distribution systems in human societies and in understanding the particular system in the society being studied at a given time. Most anthropologists are not scientifically interested in the operation of the economy of our own society; the typical nonanthropological economist, on the other hand, is extremely interested in the operation of our own economy. He will not ordinarily show much interest in the operation of greatly different economic systems.

Social anthropology has another substantial overlap of interest with political science. In contrast to the dominant trend in sociology, political scientists, like anthropologists, are interested in relationships between societies, both international relations and interethnic relations within nations. If the economy—the production and distribution of goods—is one tie that holds all societies together, the political system—the system of control of the legitimate use of force—is another major tie. No social system can be understood without the investigation of both of these major ties. The interests of social anthropologists contrast with those of political scientists, even when they study the same societies. The social anthropologist usually does not restrict himself as closely as the political scientist to the local political system. Moreover, the work of the political scientist in foreign areas often is concerned mainly with problems of modernization policy: how fast and to what extent can modern democratic practices be introduced into the area? The anthropologist is likely to have less of a commitment to find how the society might be changed and is inclined instead to wonder simply how the political system works and what its ties are with the past. If the system does change, will it become more or less like ours?

Social anthropology and linguistic anthropology both have overlapping interests with parts of psychology, itself a very diverse discipline. Social-cultural anthropologists, in their work with informants, have obvious close ties with clinical psychology and psychiatry. Both are trying to understand individuals in detail and in depth, although the anthropologist is studying the individual as an exemplar of his culture, while the psychiatrist or clinical psychologist usually takes the culture for granted and tries to understand the deviations that single an individual out from other participants in his culture. Ideally, the anthropologist ought to know enough about clinical psychology to be able to distinguish the idiosyncratic components in his data from the cultural. In fact, practitioners of both disciplines probably tend to make the expected errors of interpretation from time to time: a clinical psychologist is likely at times to interpret some standard belief or practice of a client from a different ethnic group as an individual neurotic symptom, while an anthropologist is likely at times to exaggerate the cultural significance of some individual aberrations.

A final social science which has an important degree of overlap with social-cultural anthropology is geography. Geographers share with anthropologists the tendency to specialize in a particular part of the world. Geographers, like cultural anthropologists, are interested in the use men make of their physical and natural environment and the modifications they bring about in it. However, geographers are typically more focused on the items of culture with which they are mainly concerned. Geographers are primarily concerned with human activities and objects that modify the natural environment or involve some transaction with it: farming, mining, architecture and city planning, highways, waterways, railways. The interests of the cultural anthropologist overlap, but are somewhat broader, for he is also interested in aspects of culture not very closely conditioned by the environment, such as language, literature and the arts, religion.

Relationships Between Anthropology and Other Fields of Scholarship

There is little point in making up a catalog of all the interrelationships between anthropology and fields of scholarship outside the behavioral and social sciences, except to point to a few areas in which the affiliations have been particularly close.

A number of areas bring anthropologists and humanists together, such as the study of art, music, and religion. A particularly noteworthy field is that of folklore. The folklorist of modern society is interested in the anonymous oral literature and art of recent culture. The discipline of folklore in the United States has been a union between humanists who moved into the area from the study of literature and cultural-social anthropologists who moved into it from the study of the traditional oral literature of primitive societies.

Many of the linguistics departments springing up in our universities have come into being through a union of linguistic anthropologists with classical linguists and other language specialists, often from the foreign language departments of the universities moving in this direction. Their common interests require no documentation.

Prehistory and recorded history merge into each other, so that the archaeological anthropologist's interest in prehistory merges with the classical archaeologist's interest in civilizations with a recorded history and with the historian's interest in understanding the march of events. Anthropology, under the influence of the concept of evolution, is the most historical-minded discipline within the social sciences, outside history itself, and in its time perspective exceeds our usual conception of history.

Physical anthropology is very closely related to other sciences of human biology, particularly anatomy, genetics, and evolution, but the interest merges also with comparative psychology (particularly in the evolution of behavior and the social behavior of animal aggregates). Some anthropologists work in medical schools, in which the social-cultural interests may be as relevant as the biological ones.

These few paragraphs merely hint at the many interrelationships. Modern science requires specialization because of the complex skills required of the scientist. At the same time, the specialist must be ready to "look aside," and to draw, through collaborative effort, on the expertness of many others besides himself—often those from disciplines other than his own. Because of its interest in all aspects of the societies it studies, anthropology, perhaps more than other sciences, needs to keep itself open to all available information.

TWO

EXPLORATIONS IN HUMAN EVOLUTION

2

EVOLUTIONARY THEORY IN BIOLOGY

ERNST MAYR

In popular opinion the concept of evolution tends to be primarily associated with the biological sciences. Yet, to some extent, evolutionary notions about the growth of culture and society developed as early or even earlier than those addressed to biological species. Furthermore, certain physical phenomena other than biological are now approached in the context of evolutionary theory appropriate to such events as the evolution of galaxies, stars, or elements. Thus it can be said that there are varieties of evolutionary theory adapted to each discriminated major level of phenomena—inorganic, organic, and superorganic (cultural).

During the past century or so, successive advances in evolutionary theory in the biological realm have been so conspicuous and productive that key concepts derived from biological evolution theory have been eagerly applied to both inorganic and cultural phenomena, although not always with positive results. Difficulties in the cultural applications have stemmed from imperfect knowledge or representation of biological theory, or from the unbalanced emphasis on one or very few factors. It therefore seems essential that all those interested in anthropology, whether in its physical or cultural aspects, be well grounded in the modern "synthetic" theory of evolution.

Those who know the work of Ernst Mayr will not be surprised that we turn to him to obtain a suitable statement, brief, sharp, and accurate. Those encountering this distinguished scientist for the first time will quickly detect the agile and undogmatic mind at work. It will be noted that for Mayr nothing is taken for granted. He has attacked static concepts and lazy ways of thought. For example, he has played a major role in forcing scientists to reconsider approaches to populations and species that depended to a large degree on stereotyping. Emphasis was laid on a model or archetype, and variation was often neglected. Mayr's attack on "typological thinking," as he calls it, helped create an intellectual climate that brought beneficial theoretical and methodological changes to disciplines, such as archeology, that were rather remote from Mayr's own special competence. Other portions of anthropology have also benefited from the considered use of theories of biological evolution.

A final introductory comment. The Lamarckism referred to in this selection (and in selection 6 by Clifford Jolly) has to do with a category of evolutionary theories in which adaptation is the result of more or less direct interaction between organisms and environments. In what Mayr recognized as "true Lamarckism," the evolutionary force is largely internal to the evolving organism, a drive toward perfection that is part of the creature's makeup. What Mayr calls "Geoffroyism" is more like what most people think of when the name Lamarck is raised. This is no surprise since it is named for Geoffroy St. Hilaire, a close colleague of Lamarck for many years. St. Hilaire was particularly taken with the theory that organs evolved with use or disuse, an element usually thought of as Lamarckian. As we will see in the selection that follows, this is only one of the strands that entered evolutionary thought and not the most useful at that.

▼△▼△▼

The theory of evolution is quite rightly called the greatest unifying theory in biology. The diversity of organisms, similarities and differences between kinds of organisms, patterns of distribution and behavior, adaptation and interaction, all this was merely a bewildering chaos of facts until given meaning by the evolutionary theory. There is no area in biology in which that theory does not serve as an ordering principle. Yet this very universality of application has created difficulties. Evolution shows so many facets that it looks alike to no two persons. The more different the backgrounds of two biologists, the more different

---

SOURCE: *Populations, Species, and Evolution,* Ernst Mayr, Cambridge, Mass.: The Belknap Press of Harvard University Press, Copyright, 1963, 1970 by the President and Fellows of Harvard College. Pp. 1–9, Chapter 1. Reprinted by permission of publisher and author.

their attempts at causal explanation. At least, so it was, until the 1930's, when the many dissenting theories were fused into a broad unified theory, the "modern synthesis." But even it has grown and matured since then.

Many of the earlier evolutionary theories were characterized by heavy emphasis, if not exclusive reliance, on a single factor (Table 1). The modern synthetic theory selected the best aspects of the earlier hypotheses and combined them in a new and original manner. In essence a two-factor theory, it regards the diversity and harmonious adaptation of the organic world as the result of a steady production of variation and of the selective effects of the environment.

TABLE 1. THEORIES OF EVOLUTIONARY CHANGE

- A. Monistic (single-factor explanations)
  - 1. Ectogenetic: changes directly induced by the environment
    - (a) Random response (for example, radiation effects)
    - (b) Adaptive response (Geoffroyism)
  - 2. Endogenetic: changes controlled by intrinsic forces
    - (a) Finalistic (orthogenesis)
    - (b) Volitional (genuine Lamarckism)
    - (c) Mutational limitations
    - (d) Epigenetic limitations
  - 3. Random events ("accidents")
    - (a) Spontaneous mutations
    - (b) Recombination
  - 4. Natural selection
- B. Synthetic (multiple-factor explanations)
  - 1b + 2a + 2b = most "Lamarckian-type" theories
  - 1b + 2b + 2c + 4 = some recent "Lamarckian" theories
  - 1b + 3 + 4 = late Darwin, Plate, most nonmutationists during first three decades of 20th century
  - 3 + 4 = early "modern synthesis"
  - 1a + 2c + 2d + 3 + 4 = recent "modern synthesis"

Attempting to explain evolution by a single-factor theory was the fatal weakness of the pre-Darwinian and most nineteenth-century evolutionary theories. Lamarckism with its internal self-improvement principle, Geoffroyism with its induction of genetic change by the environment, Cuvier's catastrophism, Wagner's evolution by isolation, De Vries' mutationism, all tried to explain evolution by a single principle, excluding all others. Even Charles Darwin occasionally fell into this error, yet on the whole he was the first to make a serious effort to present evolutionary events as due to a balance of conflicting forces. The current theory of evolution—the "modern synthesis," as Huxley (1942) has called it—owes more to Darwin than to any other evolutionist and is built around Darwin's essential concepts. Yet it incorporates much that is distinctly post-Darwinian. The concepts of mutation, variation, population, inheritance, isolation, and species, still quite nebulous in Darwin's day, are now far better understood and more rigorously defined.

The development of the modern theory was a slow process. Evolutionary biology was at first in the same situation as sociology, psychology, and other vast fields still are today: the available data were too voluminous and diversified to be organized at once into a single comprehensive theory. Looking back over the history of the many false starts gives a valuable insight into the process of theory formation. One important lesson is that some sets of data may not have significance until certain concepts are clarified or principles established. For instance, the true role of the environment in evolution could not be understood until the nature of small mutations and of selection was fully comprehended. Polygenes could not be analyzed and understood until the laws of inheritance had been clarified with the help of conspicuous mutations. The process of speciation (multiplication of species) could not be understood until after the nature of species and of geographic variation had been clarified. Discussions of variation among early evolutionists were utterly confused because they failed to make a clear distinction between geographical "variety" (geographical race) and individual variety. The analysis of quantitative characters was futile until the principles of particulate inheritance were fully understood.

Genetics, morphology, biogeography, systematics, paleontology, embryology, physiology, ecology, and other branches of biology, all have illuminated some special aspect of evolution and have contributed to the total explanation where other special fields failed. In many branches of biology one can become a leader even though one's knowledge is essentially confined to an exceedingly limited area. This is unthinkable in evolutionary biology. A specialist can make valuable contributions to special aspects of the evolutionary theory, but only he who is well versed in most of the branches of biology listed above can present a balanced picture of evolution as a whole. Whenever a narrow specialist has tried to develop a new theory of evolution, he has failed.

The importance of eliminating erroneous concepts is rarely given sufficient weight in discussions of theory formation. Only in some cases is it true that the new, better theory vanquishes the old, "bad" one. In many other instances it is the refutation of an erroneous theory that vacates the field for new ideas. An excellent illustration of this is Louis Agassiz's neglect of what seem to us most convincing evolutionary facts because they were inconsistent with his well-organized, harmonious creationist world view. Darwin, who had started the voyage of the *Beagle* with views similar to those of Agassiz, began to think seriously about evolution only after he had found overwhelming evidence that was completely irreconcilable with the creationist explanation of the diversity of animals and plants. Or, to cite another example, as long as spontaneous generation and the instantaneous conversion of one species into another were universally accepted, even for higher animals and plants, there was no room for a theory of evolution. By insisting on the fixity of species, Linnaeus did more to bring about the eclipse of the concept of spontaneous generation than did Redi and Spallanzani, who disproved it experimentally. Indirectly, Linnaeus did as much to prepare the ground for a theory of evolution as if he had proposed such a theory himself.

More important for the development of the synthetic theory than the rejection of ill-founded special theories of evolution was the rejection of two basic philosophical concepts that were formerly widespread if not universally held: preformism and typological thinking. *Preformism* is the theory of development that postulates a preformed adult individual in miniature "boxed" into the egg or spermatozoon, ready to "unfold itself" during development. The term evolution is derived from this concept of unfolding, and this connotation continued well into the post-Darwinian period. It was perhaps the reason Darwin did not use the term "evolution" in his *Origin of Species*. Transferred from ontogeny to phylogeny, evolution meant the unfolding of a built-in plan. Evolution, according to this view, does not produce genuine change, but consists merely in the maturation of immanent potentialities. This, for instance, was Louis Agassiz's theory of evolution (Mayr 1959b). Some of the orthogenic and finalistic theories of evolution are the last remnants of this type of thinking. Mutationism was the most extreme form of reaction to these orthogenetic concepts. The current theory compromises by admitting that genotype and phenotype of a given evolutionary line set severe limits to its evolutionary potential (Table 1, A2c, d), without, however, prescribing the pathway of future evolutionary change.

Typological thinking is the other major misconception that had to be eliminated before a sound theory of evolution could be proposed. Plato's concept of the *eidos* is the philosophical codification of this form of thinking. According to this concept the vast observed variability of the world has no more reality than the shadows of an object on a cave wall, as Plato puts it in his allegory. Fixed, unchangeable "ideas" underlying the observed variability are the only things that are permanent and real.

Owing to its belief in essences this philosophy is also referred to as *essentialism* and its representatives as *essentialists* (typologists). Most of the great philosophers of the seventeenth, eighteenth, and nineteenth centuries were influenced by the idealistic philosophy of Plato and the modifications of it by Aristotle. The thinking of these schools dominated the natural sciences until well into the nineteenth century. The concepts of unchanging essences and of complete discontinuities between every *eidos* (type) and all others make genuine evolutionary thinking well-nigh impossible. I agree with those who claim that the essentialist philosophies of Plato and Aristotle are incompatible with evolutionary thinking:

> The assumptions of population thinking are diametrically opposed to those of the typologist. The populationist stresses the uniqueness of everything in the organic world. What is true for the human species, that no two individuals are alike, is equally true for all other species of animals and plants . . . All organisms and organic phenomena are composed of unique features and can be described collectively only in statistical terms. Individuals, or any kind of organic entities, form populations of which we can determine the arithmetic mean and the statistics of variation. Averages are merely statistical abstractions; only the individuals of which the populations are composed have reality. The ultimate conclusions of the population thinker and of the typologist are precisely the opposite. For the typologist, the type (*eidos*) is real and the variation an illusion, while for the populationist the type (average) is an abstraction and only the variation is real. No two ways of looking at nature could be more different (Mayr 1959a:2).

The replacement of typological thinking by population thinking is perhaps the greatest conceptual revolution that has taken place in biology. Many of the basic concepts of the synthetic theory, such as that of natural selection and that of the population, are meaningless for the typologist. Virtually every major controversy in the field of evolution has been between a typologist and a populationist. Even Darwin, who was more responsible than anyone else for the introduction of population thinking into biology, often slipped back into typological thinking, for instance in his discussions on varieties and species.

Clarification of Evolutionary Concepts

A comparison of current evolutionary publications with those of only twenty or twenty-five years ago shows what great conceptual progress has been made in this short period. Since much of this volume is devoted to reporting this progress, I will barely mention some of these advances in this introductory discussion. Our ideas on the relation between gene and character have been thoroughly revised and the phenotype is more and more regarded not as a mosaic of individual gene-controlled characters but as the joint product of a complex interacting system, the total epigenotype (Waddington 1957). Interactions and balances among opposing forces are stressed to an increasing extent. Virtually every component of the phenotype is recognized as a compromise made in response to opposing selection pressures.

The realization that the DNA of the chromosomes carries a program of information has led to great clarification. The phenomena of ontogeny and physiology are now interpreted as manifestations of the decoding of the information embodied in the genotype. Phylogeny, on the other hand, and all the phenomena involving evolutionary change are considered the production of ever-new programs of information.

Let me cite some other advances in our understanding. Natural selection is no longer regarded as an all-or-none process but rather as a purely statistical concept. Isolation has been revealed as a dual phenomenon, either the separation of populations by environmental barriers or the maintenance of the genetic integrity of gene pools by isolating mechanisms. The environment is restored to its place as one of the most important evolutionary factors, but in a drastically different role than it held in the various "Lamarckian" theories. The new role of the environment is to serve as principal agent of natural selection.

Open Problems

The development of the evolutionary theory is a graphic illustration of the importance of the *Zeitgeist*. A particular constellation of available facts and prevailing concepts dominates the thinking of a given period to such an extent that it is very difficult for a heterodox viewpoint to get a fair hearing. Recalling this history should make us cautious about the validity of our current beliefs. The fact that the synthetic theory is now nearly universally accepted is not in itself proof of its correctness. It will serve as a warning to read with what scorn the mutationists (saltationists) in the first decade of this century attacked the contemporary naturalists for their belief in gradual changes and in the immense importance of the environment. It never occurred to the saltationists that their own typological and antiselectionist interpretation of evolution could be much further from the truth than the late Darwinian viewpoint of their adversaries. Mutations do not guide evolution, nor are their effects on the phenotype always sufficiently drastic to be visible. Recombination makes far more new phenotypes available for selection than does mutation, and the kinds of mutations and recombinations that can occur in a given organism are severely restricted. These statements are entirely consistent with the synthetic theory, but they may be quite startling to those who are unaware of the modern developments and who are still fighting the battle of the last generation.

The essentials of the modern theory are to such an extent consistent with the facts of genetics, systematics, and paleontology that one can hardly question their correctness. The basic framework of the theory is that evolution is a two-stage phenomenon: the production of variation and the sorting of the variants by natural selection. Yet agreement on this basic thesis does not mean that the work of the evolutionist is completed. The basic theory is in many instances hardly more than a postulate and its application raises numerous questions in almost every concrete case. The discussions throughout this volume are telling testimony of the truth of this statement.

Modern research is directed primarily toward three areas: evolutionary phenomena that do not yet appear to be adequately explained by the synthetic theory, such as stagnant or explosive evolution; the search for various subsidiary factors that, although inconspicuous on casual inspection, exercise unexpected selection pressures; and, perhaps most important, the interplay among genes and between genotypes and environment resulting in the phenotype, the real target of natural selection.

Most contemporary arguments concern the relative importance of the various interacting factors. One will get highly diverse answers if one asks a number of contemporary evolutionists the following questions:

How important are random events in evolution?

How important is hybridization in evolution?

What is the effect of interpopulation gene flow?

What proportion of new mutations are beneficial?

What proportion of genetic variability is due to balanced polymorphism?

Other areas in which there is still wide divergence of opinion are the importance of phenotypic plasticity, the pathway to adaptation, evolutionary mechanisms in higher and lower organisms, the origin of sexuality, and the origin of life. It must be stressed, for the benefit of nonevolutionists, that none of the arguments going on in these areas touches upon the basic principles of the synthetic theory. It is the application of the theory that is sometimes controversial, not the theory itself. And with respect to application we still have a long way to go. There are vast areas of modern biology, for instance biochemistry and the study of behavior, in which the application of evolutionary principles is still in the most elementary stage.

The Major Areas of Evolutionary Research

Important contributions to our understanding of the evolutionary process have been made by virtually every branch of biology. During the past one hundred years most of the research has been concerned with a number of discrete areas, progress within which has been unequal:

The fact of evolution,
The establishment of phylogenies,
The origin of discontinuities (speciation),
The material of evolution,
Rates of evolution,
Causes of evolution,
The evolution of adaptation.

The amount of attention given to each of these areas has changed with time. To establish unequivocally the fact of evolution was after 1859 the first concern of the young science of evolutionary biology. The study of phylogeny soon became predominant, at least in zoology. Indeed, even today there still are some zoologists to whom the term "evolution" signifies little more than the determination of homologies, common ancestors, and phylogenetic trees. The interest of most evolutionary biologists, however, has shifted to a study of the causes and mechanisms of evolutionary change and to an attempt at determining the role and relative importance of various factors. The different responses to these factors displayed by different types of organisms are also receiving increasing attention. Evolutionary biology is beginning to become truly comparative.

Each branch of evolutionary biology occupies a special niche and is uniquely qualified to illuminate some special problem. The geneticist is mainly concerned with the individual, the stability or mutability of loci, the modification of the phenotype, the interaction of parental genes in the production of the phenotype and the effect of this interaction on fitness, in short, all the problems concerning the gene and its interaction with other genes and with the environment. The development of population genetics led to an expansion of the geneticist's field of interest from the gene to the gene pool of the population.

The contribution of genetics to the understanding of the process of evolution has not yet been evaluated objectively. The assumption made by some geneticists, that it was quite impossible to have sensible ideas on evolution until the laws of inheritance had been worked out, is contradicted by the facts. Everyone admits that Darwin's evolutionary theories were essentially correct; yet his genetic theories were about as wrong as they could be. Conversely, the early Mendelians, the first biologists (except for Mendel himself) who truly understood genetics, misinterpreted just about every evolutionary phenomenon. Some of their contemporaries among the naturalists, on the other hand, though they did not understand genetics and even believed in some environmental induction (Geoffroyism), presented a remarkably correct picture of speciation, adaptation, and the role of natural selection. It would be going too far to claim that it is immaterial whether one believes the De Vriesian or the Lamarckian theory of the source of genetic variation, yet it is true that it is less important for the understanding of evolution to know how genetic variation is brought about than to know how natural selection deals with it. Replacing the erroneous belief in blending inheritance with the theory of particulate inheritance is the greatest single contribution of genetics. This advance has been the basis of all subsequent developments. . . .

The study of long-term evolutionary phenomena is the domain of the paleontologist. He investigates rates and trends of evolution in time and is interested in the origin of new classes, phyla, and other higher taxa. Evolution means change and yet it is only the paleontologist among all biologists who can properly study the time dimension. If the fossil record were not available, many evolutionary problems could not be solved; indeed, many of them would not even be apparent.

The taxonomist, who deals primarily with local populations, subspecies, species, and genera, is concerned with the region that lies between the areas of interest and competence of the geneticist and of the paleontologist, overlapping with both but approaching problems in the area of overlap from a somewhat different viewpoint. The species, the center of the taxonomist's interest, is one of the important levels of integration in the organic world. Neglect of this level in much of our biological curriculum is puzzling. We do not even have a special term for the study of the species, corresponding to cytology, the study of cells; histology, the study of tissues; and anatomy, the study of organs. Yet the species is not only the basic unit of classification, but also one of the most important units of interaction in ecology and ethology. The origin of new species, signifying the origin of essentially irreversible discontinuities with entirely new potentialities, is the most important single event in evolution. Darwin, who devoted so much of his life to the systematics of species, fully appreciated the significance of this level, as he made clear in the choice of title for his classic *On the Origin of Species.*

References

HUXLEY, J. 1942. *Evolution, The Modern Synthesis.* London: Allen & Unwin.

MAYR, E. 1959a. "Darwin and the Evolutionary Theory in Biology." In *Evolution and Anthropology: A Centennial Appraisal.* Anthropology Society, Washington. pp. 3–12.

——— 1959b. "Agassiz, Darwin and Evolution." *Harvard Library Bull.* 13:165–194.

WADDINGTON, C. H. 1957. *The Strategy of Genes.* London: Allen & Unwin.

3

MENDELIAN AND CHEMICAL GENETICS

ALEXANDER ALLAND, JR.

Anthropology can exist in the absence of strong evolutionary theory, but the scientific character of anthropology is vitally related to the development of such theory. In the light of this relationship we understand the impact of Darwinism on the anthropology of the nineteenth century and the continued influence of developments in evolutionary theory at present. The basic contribution of Charles Darwin has been epitomized by Julian Huxley in the form of three observations and two deductions. The resulting paradigm looks like this:

O_1 All organisms have the biological capacity to reproduce at greater than arithmetic rates of increase.

O_2 Despite this capacity, species populations tend to be fairly stable in numbers.

D_1 Since it is evident that far fewer organisms survive to reproductive age than are potentially available, it follows that there is a struggle for survival.

O_3 All organisms show some degree, however minute, of individual variation.

D_2 There is a process of natural selection.

As is so well known, Darwin's contribution was made in ignorance of the actual mechanisms of biological heredity. Actually, it was not merely knowledge of genetics that the Darwinian theory of evolution lacked. Indeed, the present version of evolutionary doctrine, although based on the great Darwinian contribution, has gone far beyond nineteenth-century understandings and is now often called "the synthetic theory of evolution." The word "synthetic" refers to the fact that modern evolutionary theory synthesizes three main inputs: the basic Darwinian concepts of adaptation and selection (modified by modern ecological knowledge); the Mendelian and post-Mendelian knowledge of genetics; and the use of mathematical-statistical methods for computing relations and probability. As for the term "theory," this is sometimes misunderstood as implying uncertainty that evolution has really taken place. As innumerable scientists have noted, however, there is no longer any question that evolution has occurred and still goes on in man as well as throughout the phenomenological universe. The questions are about the precise mechanisms, prediction, and controllability. As a matter of fact, the major mechanisms have been established for some time. They include mutation, selection, drift (i.e., random loss of genes through chance), and migration (i.e., genetic recombination following population movement).

Quite evidently, no current discussion of biological evolution can reasonably proceed unless informed by a certain minimum comprehension of genetics. One of the clearest presentations of the materials of genetics for a basically anthropological audience is the source of the reading that follows.

I. Mendelian Genetics

Probably since the earliest domestication of plants and animals man has used certain genetic principles without fully understanding them. Species were improved by breeding selectively only those animals which carried desirable traits and by disposing of those animals which did not. Thus, even today the life expectancy of a good egg-laying chicken is considerably higher than her less bountiful sisters.

To understand how selective breeding actually works, one must understand how and in what frequency specific characteristics pass from parent to offspring. Traits do not always appear to pass in orderly fashion. Two parent animals, each with the same trait, might transfer it to all their progeny while two other parents, again with the same trait, might transfer it with a frequency of only 50 per cent. On the other hand, an entire generation of siblings

SOURCE: Adapted and condensed from *Evolution and Human Behavior* by Alexander Alland, Jr. Garden City: Natural History Press. Chapters 2 and 3.

might differ considerably from either parent. Until the reasons for this variation were understood it was difficult to predict what the outcome of any specific cross might actually be.

A set of simple but elegantly controlled experiments conducted by the Abbé Mendel in the 1860s solved this basic problem and opened up the entire field of genetics. Unfortunately Mendel's work, although published in 1866, was ignored by the scientific community until 1900. The development of genetics, which progressed rapidly after this date, was tremendously important to evolutionists, for it provided a central concept of evolutionary theory: an explanation of the mechanisms of variation and continuity.

The science of genetics which Mendel founded is tremendously powerful, for its theories can be tested and verified in the laboratory through the replication of experiments under controlled conditions. Thus, with the development of genetics a laboratory science was added to the natural-historical approach of the early evolutionists.

Mendel's experiments were carried out on the common pea plant. In his search for order in the transmission of genetic material, Mendel chose pea plants displaying seven classes of easily observable traits, each with two variants. Among these were: height (tall vs. short); seed color (green vs. yellow); and seed texture (smooth vs. wrinkled). Mendel was careful to choose plants of pure strain, which when crossed with like plants bred true consistently, i.e. yellow plants produced 100 per cent yellow offspring, short plants produced 100 per cent short offspring, etc. Plants with various combinations of these three classes of traits were then crossed (tall, green, wrinkled, with short, yellow, smooth, for example) to produce a filial or F_1 generation. Members of this generation were again crossed to produce still another filial or F_2 generation. After the completion of each cross, the frequencies of the resulting traits were carefully recorded and analyzed statistically.

Segregation

Mendel's first concern was with traits of a single class. In these experiments he found that one trait in each class would fail to appear in the F_1 generation. A yellow crossed with a green, for example, would yield an F_1 generation with 100 per cent yellow-seeded plants. Furthermore, when F_1 plants were crossed with each other, the green color would reappear in 25 per cent of the F_2 offspring; the other 75 per cent would, of course, be yellow (Figure 1).

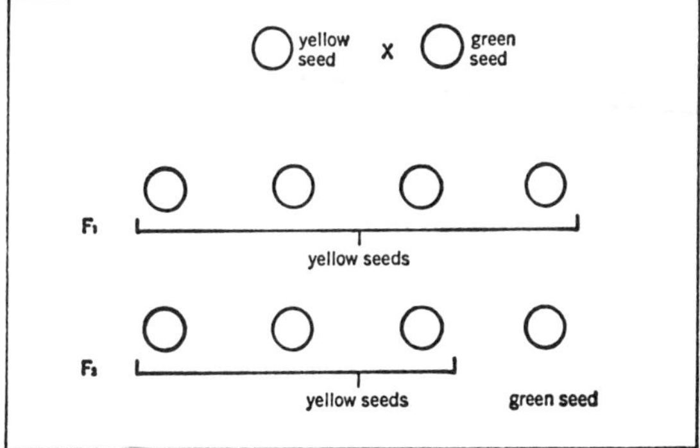

Figure 1. A cross of yellow with a green seed; the yellow trait is dominant here and masks the green color in the F_1 generation. In the F_2 generation the green color reappears in 25 per cent of the plants because no yellow component is present.

It appeared that the yellow was able to mask the green, at least in the F_1 generation. Mendel accounted for this fact by suggesting that some traits were *dominant* over others. The reappearance of the green color in the F_2 occurred because in 25 per cent of these plants no yellow component was present. The green component had "segregated out." Traits which could be masked in this way were said to be *recessive.* Mendel also found that in no case did a cross between green and yellow, tall and short, or smooth and wrinkled produce an intermediate form. Traits might be masked, but they never blended (Figure 2).

The reason for the specific frequency of the recessive trait in the F_2 generation can easily

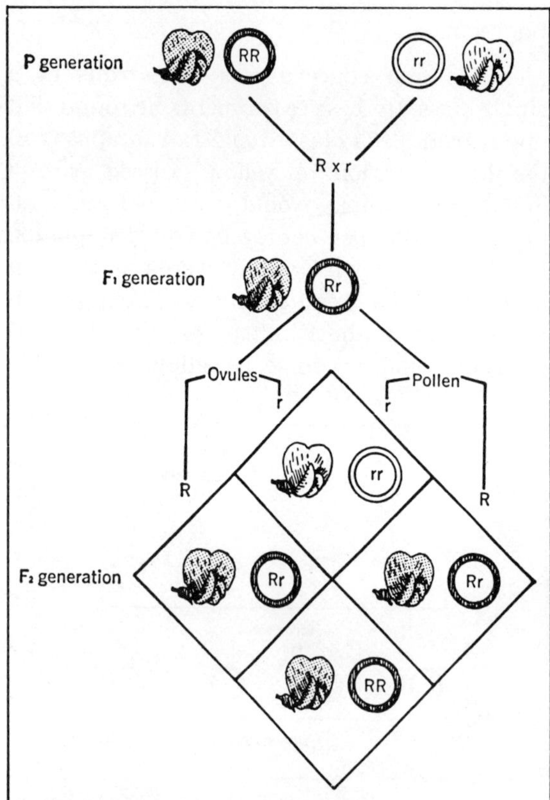

Figure 2. Mendel's law of segregation. A cross of a purple-flowered strain and a white-flowered strain of peas in which traits might be masked by the dominant component (purple) but never combine to form an intermediate form.

be accounted for by considering the simple permutations and combinations possible when two pure types are crossed. Each parent plant, quite obviously, will contribute a genetic unit, or gene, for the trait in question. Just as obviously, this must mean that the offspring will contain two units (one from each parent) for the trait. Different units of the same trait class —tall vs. short in the class of height, for example—are called *alleles*. Every plant contains two units for each trait, only one of which will be donated to a particular offspring. These units are donated at random. This means that either one has as good a chance as the other to turn up in the offspring. Now if we cross two pure strain plants of opposite type—a yellow with a green, for example—we can represent the cross as YY (yellow parent) × gg (green parent). All of the offspring will then be Yg, since all possible permutations and combinations yield four identical products (Yg, Yg, Yg, Yg). All the offspring will be yellow if the yellow allele is dominant over the green allele. Now if we cross any two of the F_1 plants (Yg × Yg) we should expect the following results: YY, Yg, Yg, gg. Twenty-five per cent of our offspring will be gg or green (Figure 3). In order to simplify the notation system in genetics, the letter symbolizing the dominant is used to represent both dominant and recessive alleles, the dominant in upper-case and the recessive in lower-case letters. Thus our F_2 cross would be written as follows: Yy × Yy. The result would be written YY, Yy, Yy, yy with the yy standing for the 25 per cent green-seeded offspring.

When the two units of a particular gene are identical (YY or yy), the organism is said to be *homozygous* for that trait. When the two units are different alleles as in Yy, the organism is said to be *heterozygous* for that trait. Heterozygotes are also referred to as *hybrids*.

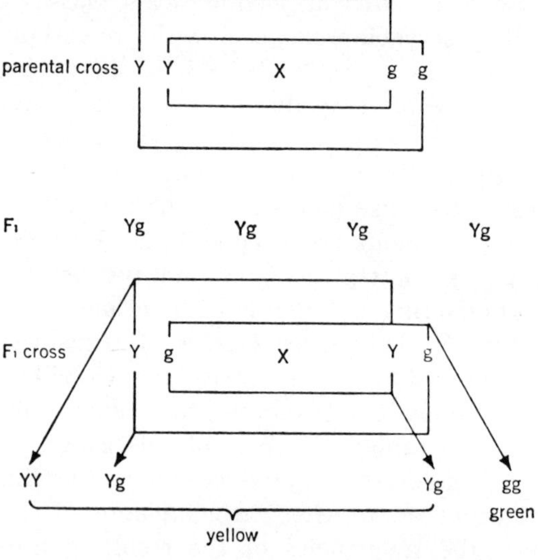

Figure 3. A cross of two pure strains of opposite type, again illustrating Mendel's law of segregation.

Independent Assortment

Mendel's experiments revealed another genetic regularity which he named the law of independent assortment. This law is concerned with the relationships among classes of traits (height and color, for example) rather than between traits of a single class. When Mendel crossed F_1 hybrids, he found that these various classes recombined at random in the F_2 generation. Thus, if you begin with only tall yellow and short green plants, you will eventually derive tall green and short yellow plants as well.

Tracing out such an experiment, we might begin with tall yellow, pure-strain plants and cross them with short green, pure-strain plants. This can be symbolized as TTYY × ttyy. In the F_1 generation, we should expect to end up with 100 per cent tall yellow hybrids. The permutations and combinations possible would yield only TtYy plants. Now, if we cross two hybrid tall yellow plants:

TtYy × TtYy

we will end up not only with short green and tall yellow plants, but also with tall green and short yellow plants. Apparently the alleles for height and color become separated and rearranged in a process of genetic recombination. If they are unhooked and recombine at random, then we should expect the four types to emerge in the following frequencies:

9 tall yellow
3 tall green
3 short yellow
1 short green

If we begin with a large enough sample, this will indeed be the end result.

To understand how this recombination operates and why it results in the expected frequency, it is necessary to draw out the possible allelic contributions which each parent could theoretically make to the offspring. Obviously each parent can donate with equal frequency the following pairs of alleles (remember that each parent donates one allele for each trait): TY, Ty, tY, or ty. If these possible alleles are charted (Figure 4), it will be easy to determine the frequencies of the expected phenotypes. Note that all but the double-recessive (short green) type ttyy will have more than one genotype (or genetic configuration) in the phenotype. Thus the nine tall yellow plants will have the following genotypes:

	TY	Ty	tY	ty
TY	TYTY	TyTY	tYTY	tyTY
Ty	TYTy	TyTy	tYTy	tyTy
tY	TYtY	TytY	tYtY	tytY
ty	TYty	Tyty	tYty	tyty

= a total of 9 tall yellow plants: 4 TYty 2 TYTy
2 TYtY 1 TYTY

Figure 4. An example of Mendel's law of independent assortment, showing that class of traits (for example, height and color) become separated and rearranged during genetic recombination.

TYTY (fully homozygous)
TYTy (homozygous for height, heterozygous for color)
TYtY (heterozygous for height, homozygous for color)
TYty (heterozygous for both traits)

Chromosomes

When one realizes that many thousands of traits contribute to the makeup of an organism, it should not be difficult to realize also the amount of potential variation present when genetic traits follow the law of independent assortment (Figure 5). There is, however, a restriction on the law which limits variation to a considerable degree. If all genes actually existed as independent units, like separate beads in a box, variation would be totally dependent on the laws of chance. Genes are, however, actually more like strings of beads,

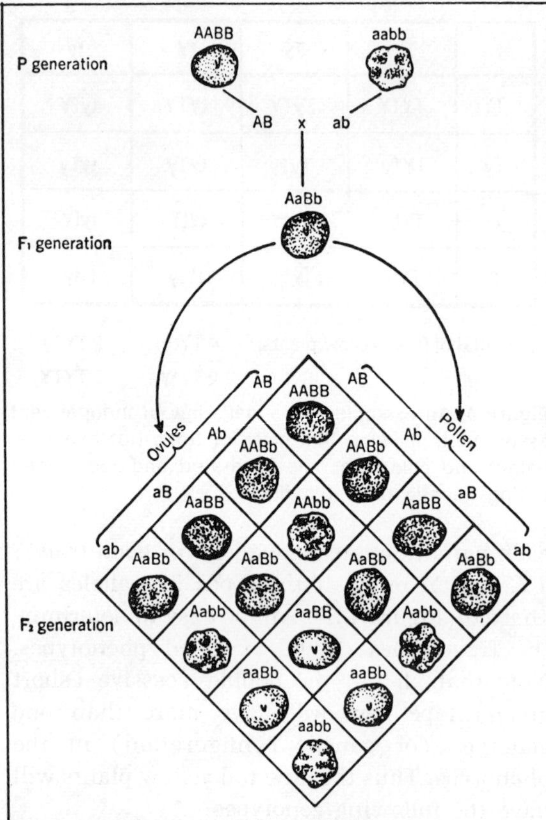

Figure 5. Another example of Mendel's law of independent assortment, in which strains of peas with yellow and smooth seeds and with green and wrinkled seeds are crossed. A and a represent yellow and green, and B and b smooth and wrinkled surfaces, respectively.

although, as we shall see later, neither analogy is particularly appropriate. At any rate, genes do not exist as totally independent units. They are linked together on chemical chains called *chromosomes*. Every cell contains several of these chromosomes, and their number depends on the particular species under consideration. Humans have forty-six chromosomes, and some species of fruit flies eight. The number of chromosomes is not dependent upon the size or relative primitiveness of the organism. Some one-celled animals (the protozoa), for example, are thought to have between forty and one hundred chromosomes. These genetic chains can be seen as a mechanism of continuity preserving, at least to some extent, stable combinations of genes, preventing them from completely sorting out during the reproductive process. As we shall see later, they do not prevent reassortment completely, but it should be obvious at this point that free assortment occurs only among genes on different chromosomes. Mendel was extremely lucky. Every one of the traits he used in his experiments occurred on a different chromosome, and therefore acted independently of every other unit. This is why they followed the law of independent assortment.

Codominance

But Mendel's luck was even greater than this. For not only can the law of independent assortment be violated by chromosome linkage, but the fact that genes are independent units (unit characters) can also *appear* to be violated, although this is actually not the case, at least in the chemical sense. Everyone knows, I think, that there are certain crosses in which it is possible to combine what appear to be two variant forms of a trait class. In certain species of plants, for example, it is possible to cross white- and red-flowered plants and produce an F_1 generation with pink flowers. When this occurs, the genes in question are said to be *codominant*. It is easy to prove, however, that even in the case of codominant genes blending of the genes themselves has not occurred. If the F_1 hybrids are crossed, the F_2 generation will contain white and red flowers as well as some pink ones. Let us see how this happens. We shall let R stand for Red and W for White (since there is no recessive gene, we shall not use a lowercase letter). The F_1 pink flowers will all be heterozygous RW. Now if we cross two of these we shall get the following results:

$$\text{RW} \times \text{RW}$$
$$\text{RR } 25\% \text{ (RW } 25\% \text{ WR } 25\% \text{) } = \text{RW } 50\% \text{ and WW } 25\%$$

When we read these phenotypes it should be obvious that we end up with 25 per cent white, 50 per cent pink, and 25 per cent red flowers. There has been no blending of genes.

Polygenes

There is another case of blending inheritance, however, which is more complicated. This kind of blending occurs when instead of one gene (and two or more alleles) for a trait, there are several genes at different places (*loci*) on a chromosome or even on different chromosomes. Such traits are said to be *polygenetic*.

Let us now imagine a case in which height is dependent upon three gene loci. Assuming that there are dominant and recessive alleles for each locus, a number of possible genetic combinations will produce different heights in an F_1 generation which is the result of a hybrid cross. If the tall genes are dominant over the short genes, then the tallest individuals would have at least one dominant gene at each locus. On the other hand, thc shortest individuals would be homozygous recessive at all three loci. Between these extremes there would be a distribution or range of heights. The situation would be more complicated with codominant genes at each locus. In such a case the tallest individual would have to be homozygous tall at each locus (six tall alleles) and each short gene present would have some effect on total height. The existence of polygenetic traits is demonstrated through breeding experiments which show a range of variation within a particular trait class, providing, of course, that environmental variation is accounted for. In many instances, particularly in humans, with whom controlled breeding is impossible to achieve, it is difficult if not impossible to determine if a particular range of variation is due to a polygenetic effect or to environmental variation affecting the total phenotype.

While the polygenetic effect appears to violate the principle of unit characters, because a series of genes modify each other, it is not difficult to prove that the principle of unit characters is a universal phenomenon in genetics. This has been demonstrated again and again in breeding experiments in which masked genes reappear (i.e. show their effects) in the expected frequencies in the proper generation (Figure 6).

red AABB x white aabb

(AB) (ab)

medium AaBb x medium AaBb

	(AB)	(Ab)	(aB)	(ab)
(AB)	AABB red	AABb dark	AaBB dark	AaBb medium
(Ab)	AABb dark	AAbb medium	AaBb medium	Aabb light
(aB)	AaBB dark	AaBb medium	aaBB medium	aaBb light
(ab)	AaBb medium	Aabb light	aaBb light	aabb white

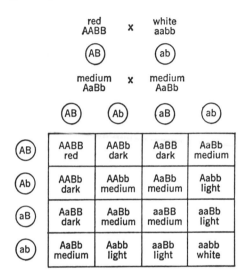

Figure 6. Cross between a wheat variety with red kernels with another having white kernels. This is another example of inheritance dependent on multiple genes.

Gene Modification

A further complication of the polygenetic effect results from the fact that some genes may not only have an additive effect, but can also modify or suppress the action of others. This phenomenon is known as *epistasis*. A gene which can suppress the effect of another gene at a different locus is said to be epistatic to that gene. (The suppression of a recessive gene by a dominant allele at the same locus is a special case and is not called epistasis.) The suppressed gene is said to be hypostatic to the suppressor gene. A clear example of this effect is found in Siamese cats. The seal-point Siamese has a normal gene for dark color at one locus and a pair of recessive alleles at another which modify the full expression of that color. The blue-point Siamese has the same suppressor gene, plus still another gene at a different locus which modifies the color gene and dilutes its effect. Such a gene is known as a *dilutant.* When either type of Siamese cat is crossed to a pure non-Siamese which is homozygous dominant at the suppressor locus, all the offspring will display non-Siamese coloration. All these offspring are, however, hybrid carriers of the recessive suppressor gene. If these cats are then crossed to pure Siamese (this is known as a *back cross*) 50 per cent of their offspring (in the F_2 generation) will be Siamese in coloration. Furthermore, since the suppression depends upon a recessive gene and therefore homozygosity, all cats which look Siamese will produce 100 per cent Siamese-looking offspring when bred to each other. A non-Siamese × Siamese cross at the suppressor locus would look like this:

PARENTAL GENERATION	SS × ss
F_1	Ss, Ss, Ss, Ss (no Siamese)
F_1 CROSS	Ss × Ss
F_2	SS, Ss, Ss, ss (25% Siamese)

Albinism in animals (white mice and humans, for example) is usually due to the epistatic effect of a suppressor gene on a normal color locus. The genes responsible for color are hypostatic to the gene for albinism.

It is also possible for genes at several loci to modify each other in such a way as to produce new variations of a trait. These combinations can be produced by genes which complement each other or by what is known as the additive effect. A typical case of the latter is provided by summer squash. One type of sphere-shaped squash (genotype aaBB) mated to another sphere-shaped squash (genotype AAbb) will yield an F_1 generation of disc-shaped hybrids (AaBb). The hybrid cross will produce nine discs, six spheres, and one fully recessive (aabb) elongate type.

It would be most convenient if the majority of genetic traits were caused by genes at a single locus, but this is not the case. The simple rules which Mendel discovered, however, remain as the basis for the study of variation. Each time a breeding experiment yields a significant departure from expected frequencies, this departure must be accounted for by a modification of theory. This modification must then be tested through further experimentation. This is how such phenomena as epistasis and the additive effect were discovered.

Sexual Recombination

Mendel's discoveries were based on the fact that in sexually reproducing species, hereditary material from each parent is combined in the genetic structure of the offspring.

Furthermore, it has been demonstrated that each parent donates exactly one half his or her normal chromosome number to each member of the succeeding generation. Since there are always two loci per trait, and since these loci are located along the length of the chromosome, it should be obvious that the full genetic complement of an individual is made up of homologous pairs of chromosomes. The alleles on these chromosomes may differ (they may be heterozygous) or they may be chemically identical (homozygous), but each set contains paired loci which control the same group of traits.

Sexual union produces a combination of genetic material from each parent. Both the sperm of the male and the egg of the female carry one of the two homologues of each chromosome. These specialized sexual cells or *gametes* unite to form a *zygote,* which will, by virtue of the combination, contain the normally paired sets of chromosomes. In the human there are forty-six pairs of chromosomes, and consequently twenty-three single chromosomes in each gamete. Forty-six is the *diploid,* or zygotic number; twenty-three is the *haploid,* or gametic number.

The process of gametic formation and recombination in the zygote is one of the most important events in the evolutionary process, for it produces genetic continuity between generations. But each parent also provides a source of variation. We have seen, for example, that two parents with different combinations of traits can produce even further differences in their offspring through the recombination of trait elements. Tall green plants crossed with short yellow plants produce not only the parental types, but also short green and tall yellow plants.

If two populations of the same species are separated for several generations, long enough for genetic divergence to occur, and are then brought together, new combinations can be produced. It is possible that some of these combinations might have a higher selective advantage than preexisting types. Even within a fairly stable population, sexual combination can produce a tremendous array of variation which can be played upon by selective forces. This type of variation and recombination requires no change in the basic chemical structure of the genes themselves, and is therefore quite different from chemical changes in the genes.

. . . . .

II. Chemical Genetics

Every living organism is a self-regulating system. This means that a definite structure exists which consists of interlocking and interacting units capable of carrying out necessary processes and of maintaining these processes within a specific normal range. In addition to maintaining the activities of the system, the organism must build and repair these units. Evolution has produced dynamic systems of great complexity. Even the "simplest" organisms must complete an astronomical number of chemical reactions merely to maintain their structural integrity. The metabolic process, for example, which converts materials absorbed from the environment into energy and necessary cellular structures requires several thousand enzymes for its successful operation. The absorption and synthesis of basic material includes the uptake of simple chemicals which are combined into more complex molecules, as well as the uptake of complex molecules which must be broken down to be rebuilt according to a specific architecture. The absorption of these chemicals must be a highly selective process, and their resynthesis must proceed according to a determined sequence.

Each individual living system has a finite existence. The continuation of a species depends upon reproduction. While single-celled organisms need only reproduce exact copies of themselves, multicellular organisms face additional problems. The uniting of two gametes is only the first step in the formation of any complex animal or plant. From worm to man, what begins as a simple cell capable of replication through mitosis must differentiate into the specialized cells which constitute and control the organs of nervous and muscular function, circulation, absorption, and excretion. The architect and engineer of organismic structure is the hereditary material which controls the heritage of a species and directs the operation of each individual organism.

DNA

The major hereditary unit is a long *polymere* (or chemical chain) known as *deoxyribonucleic acid* (Figure 7). Its core consists of sugar-phosphate molecules linked together in parallel chains. A series of bases is attached to one side of each chain. These are *adenine, cytosine, thymine,* and *guanine* (Figure 8). While the sugar-phosphate links are identical in structure, the sequence of bases may vary along the DNA molecule. These bases serve as connecting units between the two sugar-phosphate chains. The base sequence on one chain controls the base sequence on the other, because the hydrogen bonds which unite the base pairs can occur only between thymine and adenine, on the one

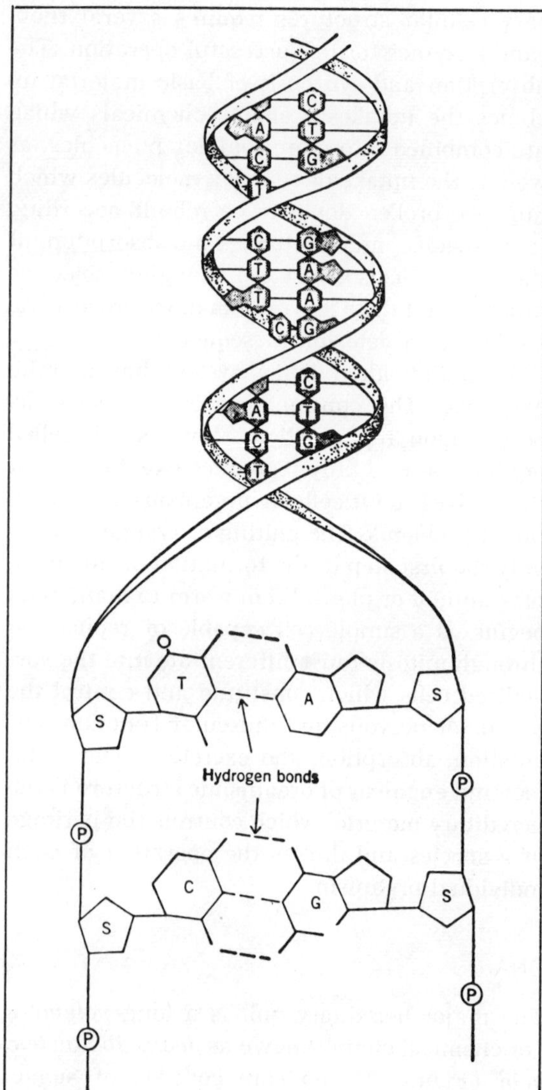

Figure 7. A schematic diagram of the Watson-Crick model of the DNA molecule.

hand, and cytosine and guanine on the other. If one chain contains the sequence adenine, adenine, adenine, thymine, the other chain must contain the opposite sequence—thymine, thymine, thymine, adenine. If one chain has adenine, cytosine, guanine, the opposite chain will have thymine, guanine, cytosine, and so on. The two sugar-phosphate chains united by hydrogen bonds at the base pairs make up the complete DNA molecule. Structurally this molecule appears to coil around itself in a double helix. Models of DNA have a superficial resemblance to the common pond algae *Spirogyra*.

DNA is the primary constituent of chromosomes and is now accepted as the basis of gene activity. The major function of genes in the nonreproducing cell is the production of enzymes which regulate cellular structure and function through their initiation and control of chemical reactions. Gene activity also controls the differentiation of structure which occurs in multicellular organisms. Again this process is carried out through enzymatic activity. Genes not only produce these enzymes, they also regulate their production so that only appropriate reactions occur at specific times. This control mechanism, which is only partially understood, is important because it lies at the basis not only of self-regulation, but also of differentiation in organisms all of which contain exactly the same genes in every cell. It is this regulatory mechanism which makes it possible for an undifferentiated zygote to develop into the total organism made up of an array of highly specialized organs.

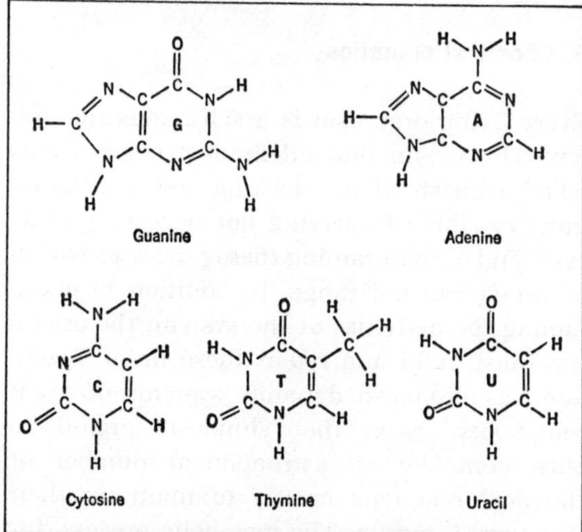

Figure 8. The bases of DNA and RNA (uracil being substituted for thymine in RNA).

There is strong evidence that the arrangements of bases on the DNA molecule act as code units in enzyme synthesis. Adenine, thymine, cytosine, and guanine are the four letters of the code. These letters are used to spell out any one of twenty amino acids used in the synthesis of proteins. If we assume that the code uses the smallest possible number of letters to spell out the entire twenty-word vocabulary, we shall find that only three letters are necessary for any one amino acid. A consideration of all the possible permutations and combinations of the four letters into three-letter words or triplets yields a total of sixty-four. Some amino acids can be coded by more than one triplet and some triplets spell out nonsense words, which may act as "punctuation marks" separating genetic messages from one another.

The active coding of amino acids comes off only one of the two sugar-phosphate chains. The other chain does not participate in the production of enzymes. This should immediately raise the question of why there should be two sugar-phosphate chains on the DNA molecule, if one is sufficient for coding. This is a legitimate question, because natural selection has a tendency to favor the simplest solution to problems. The simpler a system is, the less likely that it will contain errors. Simple systems also require less energy. The answer to this question lies in the reproductive function of DNA, and I shall discuss this before returning to the as yet incomplete explanation of protein synthesis.

Chromosome Reproduction

Microscopic examination of either miotic or mitotic cells reveals a duplication of chromosomes in the nucleus. Since DNA is the major element in these structures, it would appear that DNA itself is duplicated during the process of cell division. If one measures the quantity of DNA prior to the reproductive phase and again before cell division is complete, it is found to be double the original quantity. Thus cytological and chemical evidence both point to the duplication of DNA as a major step in reproduction. Looking again at the DNA molecule, let us imagine that prior to reproduction it uncoils and separates into two chains. Each chain will now consist of sugar-phosphate links plus one set of bases arranged lineally down the molecule. If the nucleus is able to produce new single sugar-phosphate links with attached bases, the separated but still complete single strands of DNA could function as templates for the formation of sister chains. Each old DNA strand could combine with a new strand to reconstitute a complete molecule. The two original strands of the old DNA molecule would then give rise to two complete DNA molecules identical in structure to the original (Figure 9).

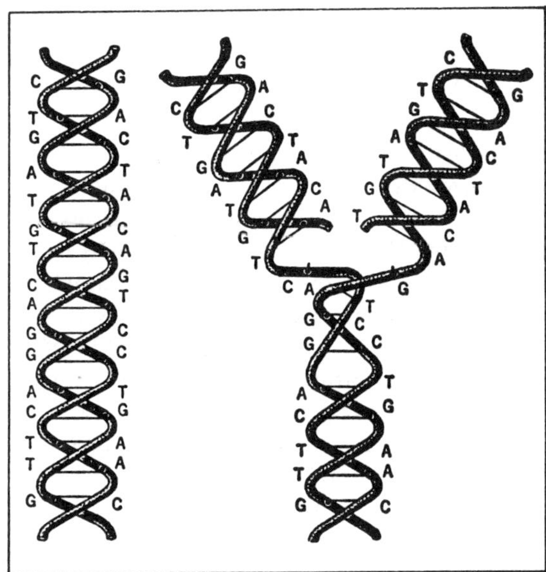

Figure 9. The double-helix model of the gene and chromosome structure (*left*) and of its replication (*right*) as suggested by the Watson-Crick hypothesis.

Sophisticated experiments have demonstrated that this is very likely what happens in both mitosis and meiosis. Sister chromatids appear to be the result of this process. The double strands of DNA are powerful mechanisms of continuity in the reproduction of like units.

DNA is nuclear material, and although it participates in the synthesis of cellular substances, it must do so in combination with another related molecule which is able to transmit messages from the chromosomes in the nucleus to the cytoplasm of the cell. This substance, *ribonucleic acid* or *RNA*, occurs in at least two forms, each of which has a particular function in the protein-building process. Like DNA, this molecule contains four bases linked to a sugar-phosphate chain, but the base *uracil* is substituted for thymine (Figure 8). RNA is not implicated in the reproduction of genes, and it need not occur as a double chain. The fact that RNA occurs as a single strand is further evidence for the specific relationship between double-strand structure and the reproduction of genetic units.

One form of RNA, known as S or *messenger RNA*, carries a DNA code message through the nuclear membrane to special areas in the cytoplasm known as *ribosomes*. It is at the ribosomes that synthesis takes place. Units of messenger RNA are sent out by activated portions of the DNA molecule which act as protein code units. These molecules break away from the DNA and pass out to the ribosomes, where they act as templates for *transfer RNA*. The latter type of RNA has an amino-acid-bearing capacity. Short strands of transfer RNA pick up amino acids appropriate to their base code and line up on the messenger RNA to form the precoded protein unit. When the process is complete—that is, when the protein has been fully organized—the newly formed molecule is released by the RNA and is ready to take part in cellular activity. In this particular scheme (Figure 10), DNA acts as the architect for protein synthesis, messenger RNA as the blueprint, and transfer RNA as the construction engineer.

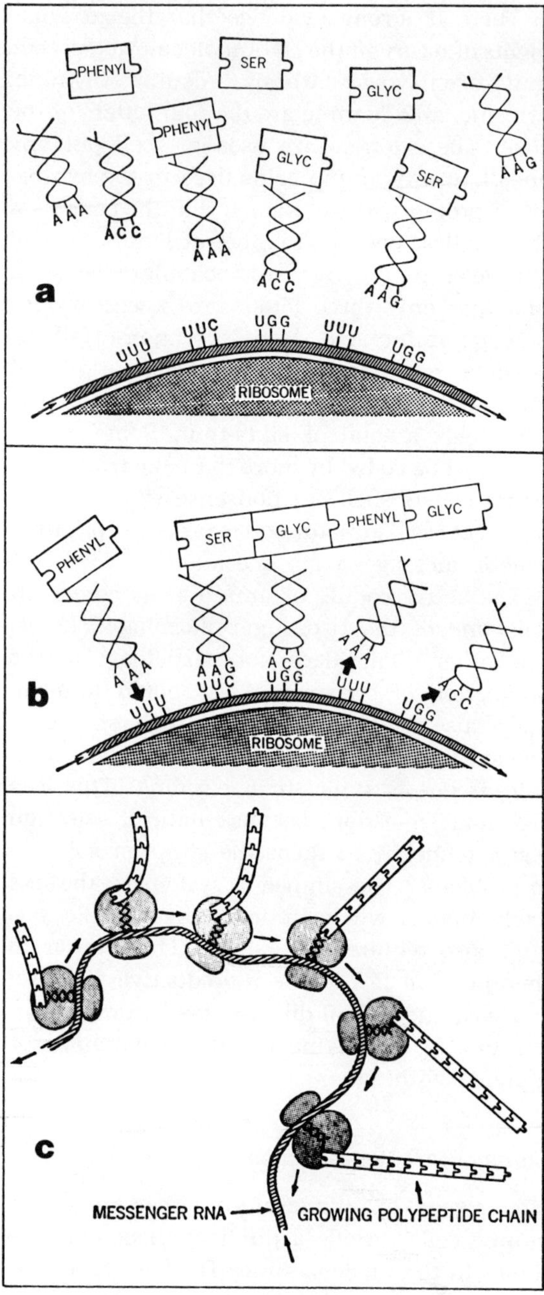

Figure 10. The messenger RNA (a) contains a sequence of base pairs complementary to those of the DNA strand that it "copied." The newly formed messenger RNA then moves from the nucleus of the cell to the cytoplasm where it attaches itself (b) to a ribosome. The transfer RNAs (c), joined to their

Gene Mutations

Gene mutations, which actually change the structure of the synthesized protein molecule, particular amino acids, gather along the messenger RNA on the ribosome. The order in which they assemble is presumably dictated by a matching of the sequence of bases along the ribosome and in one area of the transfer RNA molecule. As the amino acids form a peptide chain, the transfer RNA molecules are released. The same messenger RNA (c) molecule is usually "read" by a number of ribosome units simultaneously. (From Curtis)

are thought to be changes in the basic code unit of DNA. If only one code word of a DNA message is changed, the resulting protein will be significantly altered. If the alteration occurs on an active site of the protein—that is, a portion of the protein which enters into chemical reactions—the change can effect an entire enzymatic process and therefore alter any phenotypic traits which are the outcome of such activity.

A particularly well-documented example of a mutation on the chemical level is provided by the fatal disease known as *sickle-cell anemia.* Normal hemoglobin contains 574 amino acids arranged in two sets of paired units known as *beta* and *alpha* chains. In normal hemoglobin, the sixth amino acid in the beta chain is *glutamic acid.* Figure 11 shows how a single change in the DNA code can cause a substitution of *valine* for the glutamic acid. This leads to abnormal *hemoglobin S* and the pathological condition sickle-cell anemia (Figure 12). The change in hemoglobin structure affects the oxygen-transporting function of the red cell. The sickle-cell gene acts as a partial recessive, and although heterozygotes show some effects of the disease they are able to live, reproduce, and act as carriers of the mutant gene.

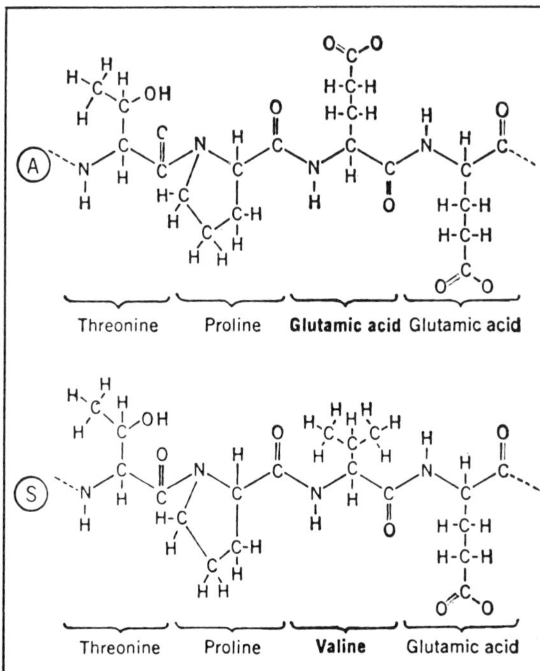

Figure 11. Corresponding sections of the molecules of hemoglobins A and S. The glutamic acid in A is replaced by valine in S.

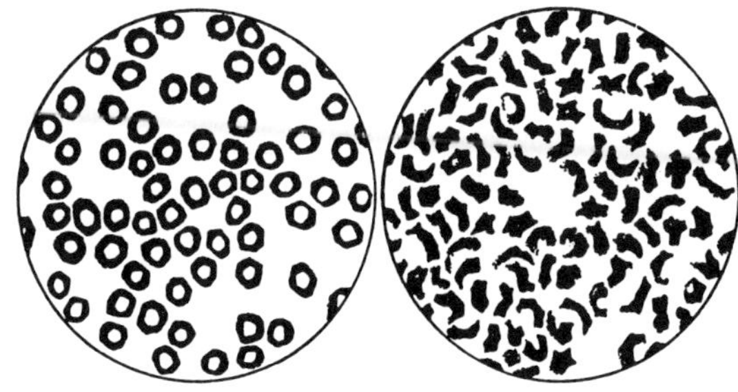

Figure 12. Phenotype produced by sickle-cell hemoglobin (Hb S), on the *right,* as compared with normal erythrocytes, *left.*

Changes in the chromosome through deletion and duplication also alter the chemical composition of the total DNA strand, and so it is not surprising that such aberrations have their effect on the organism. Less obvious is the fact that changes in the position of a segment of a chromosome through inversion or translocation can also affect gene activity. This fact strongly suggests that the behavior of any one segment of DNA can be influenced by associated parts of the chromosome. Thus, even on the molecular level one could say that environment is intimately related to the operation of heredity.

4

A GENE BY ANY OTHER NAME

Few areas of scientific knowledge are changing so rapidly as that including genetics. No matter how conscientiously composed, articles that attempt to summarize current understandings quickly fall out of date in certain details. It is for that reason the next piece has been included. The reader, even forearmed by his scrutiny of Alland's masterful summary (see selection 3), may fail to absorb all the points in the next selection, but its message, and reason for being included in this volume, is to be found in its final sentence.

▼△▼△▼

What is a gene? The answer to this apparently simple question seems to be of increasing uncertainty. A geneticist would no doubt argue that a gene is a segment of genetic material which can be delineated by the *cis/trans* test; that is to say, it must be an intact length of DNA. A biochemist might well be content to say that a gene is responsible for the synthesis of a particular protein. Both these viewpoints come to a common focus, of course, with the elaboration of the one gene–one enzyme concept into the definition that a gene is a segment of DNA (or on occasion RNA) which codes for a polypeptide chain.

But the concept of the gene now seems to encompass a wider range of structures; even a cursory glance at the literature will reveal references to structural genes, regulator genes, genes which code proteins, genes which code for RNA only. It seems, indeed, according to this more nebulous concept, as though any distinct section of the genetic material which has some defined function can be classed as a gene; this function need not be the specification of a protein.

But so generous a definition must inevitably mean that genes are destined to be divided into different functional categories. The most obvious distinction is between genes which are at least transcribed into RNA and regions of the genome which are sites of recognition for regulator molecules. Examples of such recognition sites are of course the promotors and operators of bacterial operons, which need not be transcribed into RNA or translated into protein; it is the sequence of DNA itself which is of functional significance for the cell. Perhaps a distinct term—such for example as a regulon—should be coined to describe such loci.

For in lieu of some such description, confusion will continue as to just what is meant by a regulator gene. This term is most properly used to describe a gene which codes for a protein which has as its function regulating the expression of other genes. Such is the *i* gene which codes for the repressor of the lactose operon. The distinction between this gene and the structural genes of the operon (which code for various enzymes) lies in the different types of function of the proteins for which they code; the two classes of gene are nicely distinguished by describing one as regulator and the other as structural.

Although genes in what has become the traditional sense must be translated into protein before the DNA sequence of nucleotide base pairs has any significance for the cell, some segments of DNA have fulfilled their function when they have been transcribed into RNA. Species such as ribosomal RNA and transfer RNA are themselves end products and are not translated into protein.

This distinction is subtle, for the transcription of DNA into RNA does not depend on the subsequent fate of the RNA. But distinguishing

SOURCE: "A Gene by Any Other Name," *Nature New Biology,* 230 (April 14, 1971): 194. Reprinted by permission of publisher.

between genes which code for proteins and genes which code only for RNA sequences is not merely pedantic, for the organization of these two types of DNA sequence may not be quite the same in the genome. Those sequences of DNA which code for ribosomal RNA are often clustered in one region of the genome; genes coding proteins are rarely organized in this manner. And if the way in which the synthesis of messenger RNA is balanced against that of ribosomal RNA by the cyclic AMP and ppGpp control systems in bacteria is anything to go by, there may be some feature to distinguish the two types of gene; possibly they are controlled by different types of promotor.

It is easier to make this distinction theoretically than it is to define a practical test for two types of gene. But can a firm distinction at least be drawn between regulator loci whose significance is that they are recognized by regulator molecules and those genes which are transcribed, no matter whether they are subsequently translated? Even in this instance, the lines of demarkation must be a little blurred, for it seems likely that the operator DNA sequence of the lactos operon of *Escherichia coli* may be transcribed onto the beginning of the polycistronic RNA which represents the operon, although this may not be needed for its function.

The definition of the cistron by genetic analysis is valid equally for genes coding proteins or coding (say) ribosomal RNA; in each case the *cis/trans* test will reveal that the functional coding unit must be a single stretch of DNA. But according to this definition of the cistron, the operator locus (or the promotor locus) can be considered to be part of any one of the structural genes of the operon, because it affects them only when it is located on the same piece of DNA.

Although genes can be divided into those which code for proteins, those which are transcribed into RNA but not translated into protein, and those whose functional significance does not demand that they are even transcribed, it is therefore difficult, perhaps even impossible, to devise a simple test which would define the types of function to which identifiable segments of genetic material are put. But it is perhaps some compensation for this confusion that looking at the gene in wider terms means that it must be defined in a way which Mendel himself would doubtless have appreciated; it seems that a gene must simply be described as a unit factor of inheritance.

5

PRIMATE STUDIES AND HUMAN EVOLUTION

SHERWOOD L. WASHBURN

There are several ways in which the general fact of the evolution of man from nonhominid animals can be demonstrated. By pursuing such clues, we can also improve our knowledge of the steps by which this evolution occurred, filling the gaps in our understanding with details of higher and higher probability. Among the major sets of studies that our comprehension of human evolution rests on are those that supply direct evidence of past developments, mainly the increasingly abundant supply of fossils of various kinds, portions of skeletal remains of creatures long dead, whose varieties, and species, and genera may be extinct. There are also sources of indirect evidence of evolutionary events, trends, and processes. Among these are the relatively molar (larger-scale) studies in such fields as comparative anatomy and physiology which, contrasting selected structures, organs, or organ systems of existing creatures, offer insights into or data for theories of evolutionary connections among existing bioforms. Similarly, there are molecular (smaller-scale) studies in genetics and biochemistry, particularly those that relate to a variety of serological (blood) factors and immunological reactions, that throw light on the probable length of time that has elapsed since the ancestors of two or more living bioforms separated from a common gene pool. Yet, as Washburn's essay makes clear, the study of evolution may be confused or misconstrued when only separate, often minor, traits are compared. It is always necessary, as much as possible, to deal with traits in the setting of the whole organism, considering the ethology and the ecological setting of the creature and the population as well.

In the selection that follows, one of our most respected and innovating physical anthropologists puts it all together and, with a minimum of technical detail, gives us his informed view of human evolution in the context of the evolution of the primates most closely related to us. Such a picture cannot be synthesized without conflict, no matter how distinguished the scientist attempting it. Thus, for example, when Sherwood Washburn declares flatly that he considers the problem of the relationships between man, the African apes, and the Old World monkeys to be settled, indicating further his opinion that apes and man share a long period of common ancestry after both separated from the Old World monkeys, he is deliberately controverting the opinion of other contemporary investigators of comparable reputation. Students should not get upset by the fact that the leading authorities differ. Science is a process whereby competing explanations are evaluated, hopefully with a minimum of preconception and emotional bias. Unfortunately, there is not space in a book such as this to adequately present a spectrum of alternative views, but the discerning reader will find numerous clues in several selections that follow.

▼△▼△▼

One hundred years ago it seemed clear to Darwin that man's closest relatives were the apes (Pongidae). In the introduction to the *Descent of Man* (1871:390) he stated, "Nor shall I have occasion to do more than allude to the amount of difference between man and the anthropomorphous apes; for Prof. Huxley, in the opinion of most competent judges, has conclusively shown that in every visible character man differs less from the higher apes, than these do from lower members of the same order of Primates." Huxley (1863:86) had stated, "It is quite certain that the Ape which most nearly approaches man, in the totality of its organization, is either the Chimpanzee or the Gorilla . . ." But this common nineteenth-century point of view came progressively under attack. During the first half of this century

---

SOURCE: *Nonhuman Primates and Medical Research,* Geoffrey H. Bourne (ed.). New York: Academic Press, Inc. This paper is part of a program on primate behavior supported by the United States Public Health Service (Grant No. MH 08623).

nearly every major group of living primates has been claimed as the one most closely related to man. At the present time responsible scientists regard the separation of the line leading to man as being from 5 to 50 million years ago. In examining sources, such as Flower and Lydekker (1891) or Weber (1928), it appears that, in addition to progress (new data and clarification of issues) scientists have produced confusion, especially in taxonomy. As Simpson has written (1945:181), "The peculiar fascination of the primates and their publicity value have almost taken the order out of the hands of sober and conservative mammalogists and have kept, and do keep, its taxonomy in turmoil. Moreover, even mammalogists who might be entirely conservative in dealing, say, with rats are likely to lose a sense of perspective when they come to the primates, and many studies of this order are covertly or overtly emotional." Or, again, on page 185, "With closer approach to man in the zoological system, the confusion bequeathed to us by swarms of students, of all degrees of competence and shades of judgment, becomes increasingly greater."

Although the taxonomic confusion and the multitude of theories on human origins are undoubtedly due in part to the situation which Simpson describes, there are other causes. The fossil record of monkeys and apes is exceedingly scanty, being composed largely of teeth and fragments of jaws. Romer (1968:161) has complained of this situation, "So great has been this concentration on dentition that I often accuse my 'mammalian' colleagues, not without some degree of justice, of conceiving of mammals as consisting solely of molar teeth and of considering that mammalian evolution consisted of parent molar teeth giving birth to filial molar teeth and so on down through the ages." Comparative anatomy provides a vastly greater amount of information than the fossil record; but there is no agreement on how the information is to be used. With access to the same information, scientists may conclude either that man is particularly closely related to the African apes or that no creatures properly classified as apes (Pongidae) could have been in the ancestry of man. The problem with the interpretation of the fossils is the fragmentary nature of the evidence. The problem with comparative anatomy is lack of rules in the use of a vast amount of descriptive information. These problems are vividly presented in the controversies between LeGros Clark (1964) and Zuckerman (1966) over the interpretation of *Australopithecus*.

It is my belief that study of the contemporary primates can supplement the fossil record, bringing order into the study of comparative anatomy and clarifying the behavioral stages in the origin and evolution of man. Recent developments have settled some of the fundamental issues, opening the way for a reconsideration of comparative anatomy, behavior, and the fossil record. Perhaps we can now see why Huxley was right, where subsequent comparative anatomy went wrong, and why there are major problems in interpreting the fossil record.

New Methods

An essential element in traditional paleontology and comparative anatomy was the judgment of the scientist. In the quotations from Simpson one reads that, "the sober and conservative mammalogists" are "likely to lose a sense of perspective." The closer the approach to man in the classification system, the more likely the scientist is to become emotional. In such a situation, methods which are not so dependent on the scientist's personal judgment are needed.

Quantitative methods have been developed that are not dependent on the judgment of the scientist performing the tests. The results of some of these are given in Table 1. It can be seen from the table that (whether the comparison is on the basis of DNA, sequence of amino acids, or immunological difference) man and chimpanzee are far more similar than man and Old World monkey. In sharp contrast to the situation in paleontology or comparative anatomy, the conclusion is the same, regardless of which method of comparison was used or in which laboratory the tests were performed. Wilson and Sarich (1969) have reviewed the evidence (albumin, transferrin, DNA, hemoglobin) and conclude that, of the contemporary primates, man is most closely related to the African apes (chimpanzee and gorilla). In fact the similarity is so great that the methods either fail to distinguish man and chimpanzee, or just make the distinction (Goodman, 1968). Man and chimpanzee differ no more than various species of macaques.

The results of the new information may be briefly summarized. Man is particularly closely related to the African apes. The order of similarity among the apes is African apes, orangutans, gibbons. The Old World monkeys form a natural group (Cercopithecidae) which is much less similar to man. Far less similar are New World monkeys and still further removed are various groups of prosimians. In short, the latest quantitative information agrees with the preevolutionary *scala naturae* (Napier and Napier, 1967:4–5), and with common opinion in the latter half of the nineteenth century. Neither Darwin nor Huxley would find the conclusions surprising, but they are contrary to many later theories that demand a great antiquity for a separate human lineage or which have suggested that the nearest living relative of man is a tarsier, monkey, at least not an ape.

The importance of the recent studies is not that they suggest radical changes in primate classification. They do not. The phylogenetic tree derived from the DNA hybridization experiments (Kohne, 1970) would have caused no particular comment in 1870. The general arrangement of the primates is what many scientists believed then. The new information bases the groupings of the primates on techniques which can be replicated, results which are not dependent on the judgment of the person performing the tests. The importance of this may be illustrated in the case of man, where emotions are strongest and where all the difficulties noted by Simpson (1945) are at their greatest. The remarkable similarity of man and the African apes certainly comes as a surprise to those who have been using the traditional comparative methods, whether paleontological or anatomical. Probably, the great majority of theories of human origins (those suggesting an early Miocene or earlier separation of the human line, a separation of more than 20 million years) are not compatible with the molecular data. Probably, even the "sober and conservative" scientists are going to be proven wrong. But the essential issue is not who is right or wrong, but that methods have been developed which will settle many of the controversies of the last one hundred years.

TABLE 1. EVOLUTIONARY DISTANCE BETWEEN MAN AND CHIMPANZEE AND MAN AND RHESUS MONKEY.

	MAN-CHIMP	MAN-MONKEY	
DNA	2.5%	10.1%	(Kohne, 1970)
Hemoglobin	0	15 Mut. dist.	(Reviewed by Wilson and Sarich, 1969)
Fibrinopeptides	0	7 Mut. dist.	(Doolittle and Mross, 1970)
Albumin	7	35 ID units	(Wilson and Sarich, 1969)
Transferrin	3	30 ID units	(Wilson and Sarich, 1969)
Carbonic anhydrase	4	50 ID units	(Nonno, Herschmann, and Levine, 1969)
Albumin	0.0	3.7	(Goodman, 1968)
Transferrin	0.0	3.7	(Goodman, 1968)
Gamma globulin	0.19	3.4	(Goodman, 1968)

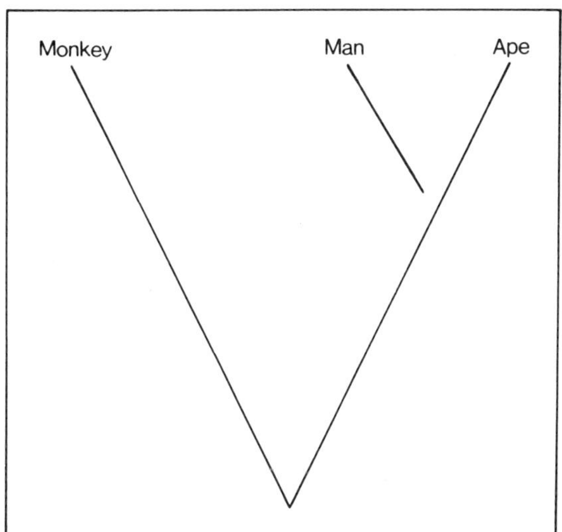

Figure 1. Relation of Old World Monkeys (Cercopithecidae), Man (Hominidae), and Apes (Pongidae).

I regard the problems of the relationship between man, the African apes, and Old World monkeys as now settled. The phylogenetic relationships appear to be of the kind shown in Figure 1, in which man and the African apes share a long period of common ancestry after the separation of the monkey and ape lineages.

The problems of the construction of a phylogenetic tree from molecular and immunological data of the contemporary primates have been discussed fully elsewhere (Sarich, 1970), and lie beyond the scope of this paper. However, there are two criticisms that have been raised so often that brief comments are needed here. The first is that the rates of evolution for different parts of animals or for different proteins are different, so that it is impossible to relate degree of morphological or biochemical difference to time. But the number of differences in the sequence of amino acids in hemoglobin between horse and man is 43, horse and chimpanzee 43, horse and macaque 43 (Wilson and Sarich, 1969). There is no evidence of greatly differing rates, as would be expected, from what is known of morphological evolution. It might be expected that the rate of change would correlate with length of generation, rather than with geologic time. But the distance, measured in immunological distance units (albumin), between carnivores and various primates is man 173, chimpanzee 173, tarsier 155, *Propithecus* 150, *Ateles* 172, Colobinae 177, Cercopithecinae 174 (Sarich, personal communication). The amount of change is not identical, but is surprisingly (to a morphologist) comparable. There is no indication that the amount of change is proportional to generation time.

The construction of the phylogenetic tree from the DNA, sequence data, and immunological information seems fully justified. That man is most closely related to the African apes may now be considered a fact. The determination of an evolutionary time scale from the same data is much more controversial. Theoretically, since there can be only one correct answer to an historical, phylogenetic problem, it should be possible to construct a phylogeny from one regularly evolving molecule and check the historical picture with another molecule. In my opinion this will be possible, and the time of separation of the major groups of primates will be determined from the molecular information. At the moment, albumin is the only protein that has been studied extensively enough so that the internal consistency of the evolutionary picture can be determined. The main outline of the phylogenetic picture derived from albumin agrees with the information from other molecules, but additional information is needed. At present determination of the rate of evolution of any protein involves major assumptions on the process of evolution, the rate of change, and the estimates of time necessary to calibrate the molecular clocks. In short, the main outlines of the primate phylogenetic tree are determined on the basis of molecular information which is quantitative, countable, and which may be replicated by different scientists. The determination of time scales still involves a much greater degree of personal judgment.

As far as the origin of man is concerned, the problem of man's relation to the apes is the same as that of the interrelations among the macaques—the creatures being compared are so close that the methods are at the limit of their usefulness. As shown in Table 1 (see p. 36), there are no differences in the sequence of amino acids in hemoglobin or fibrinopeptides, and very small differences in albumin, transferrin, or carbonic anhydrase. An accurate analysis of the differences between man, chimpanzee, and gorilla requires a more rapidly evolving molecular or more sensitive method of analysis.

At the present time, a separation of the lines leading to man and ape of less than 5 million years would be very difficult to reconcile with the fossil record. A separation of more than 10 million years is, probably, not compatible with the molecular and immunological data.[1] The rapid discovery of fossils and the greatly increased effort in biochemical taxonomy will undoubtedly narrow these limits in the near future.

Field Studies

The field studies support the indications from the molecular data that the behavior of chimpanzees is far more similar to that of man than is the behavior of Old World monkeys. (Chimpanzees are stressed only because there are more data, not because I regard them as necessarily closer to man than gorilla.) Van Lawick-Goodall (1968, 1970) describes extensive object use by chimpanzees; they use sticks in termite "fishing," poking, exploring, agonistic displays, and hitting other animals. They use leaves for cleaning and getting water. They throw rocks in aggressive interactions. Chimpanzees play with objects under natural conditions, and this wise use of objects offers a great contrast to the very limited use of objects by the baboon in the same area.

Chimpanzees hunt small mammals and the males may cooperate in this activity over a considerable distance. The female bears her first infant around eight or nine years and infants are spaced at more than three years. The whole situation is far closer to that of man than that of monkey, for which the comparable figures would be three to four years for first infant and subsequent infants spaced at approximately yearly intervals. The ape infant is much more dependent on its mother than is the case in monkeys. The female gorilla carries her infant for the first six weeks (Schaller, 1963). The importance of the field studies in reconstructing human evolution is discussed by Jay (1968).

Since the African apes are knuckle-walkers, the implications of this mode of locomotion for human evolution have been discussed elsewhere (Washburn, 1968a).

It was the behavioral similarity between man and ape that led Yerkes to develop the chimpanzee as a laboratory animal (Yerkes and Yerkes, 1929; and Yerkes, 1943; Bourne, 1971). Hodos (1970) has shown the importance of considering the actual phylogenetic relations of animals when making neural and behavioral comparisons, and Reynolds (1966) has stressed the importance of the chimpanzee in the reconstruction of the evolution of human behaviors.

Anatomy

Traditional comparative anatomy had two objectives: to describe the differences among

[1] It is difficult to relate time in millions of years to the traditional divisions of the age of the mammals. The end of the Miocene is variously estimated from 13 to 5.5 million years ago (Berggren, 1969). More radiometric dates are needed. If the short Pliocene dates are correct, a separation of man and ape lines on the order of 6 to 8 million years ago might be late Miocene and would make it far easier to reconcile the apparent discrepancies between the different lines of evidence.

animals, and to interpret the information in terms of evolution.[2] But the role of anatomy is changed if the major phylogenetic problems are settled by the molecular and immunological information. To take an extreme example, suppose that all the recent information had supported the theory that, of the contemporary primates, man's nearest living relative was the tarsier. Then the similarities of the apes and man would have to be accounted for on the basis of convergent evolution, and one would look at the writings of Wood Jones (1929) and Clark (1934) to see how they had arrived at this conclusion by anatomical means. Clark later changed his mind and his way of using the anatomical information (1955, 1959).

A less extreme case would be to suppose that the differences between man, apes, and monkeys (Hominidae, Pongidae, and Cercopithecidae) had proved to be approximately equal, suggesting that the three groups had diverged at more or less the same time, possibly in the Oligocene. This is the belief of many scientists, and this would also involve a very large amount of parallel evolution to account for the similarities of apes and man. The late separation of man and African ape suggests a very different interpretation of the anatomical data. The anatomical similarities are due to long, common ancestry and to recent separation. The point is simply that, if the historical, phylogenetic questions are settled, then all comparative anatomy can contribute is to the understanding of the history. The molecular information tells nothing about the structures and functions of the animals being compared, and the fossils are only bones. The comparative anatomical information is essential in the understanding of what happened in our evolutionary history. It is no longer essential in establishing phylogeny, and it is quite useless in arriving at estimates of time.

The historian of science undoubtedly will be able to find many reasons why so many scientists departed from the view that man's closest living relatives are the African apes, the view of the *scala naturae*, of Darwin and Huxley, of DNA. Some of the reasons are clear and it is essential to understand them, if anatomy is to be used to further the understanding of human evolution. In the earlier studies scientists considered the major anatomical systems of the whole animal. Huxley (1863) was concerned with proportions, bones, muscles, viscera, the brain, etc. This was the common practice of that time, and, if this is the nature of the information fed into the human computer, the arrangement of the primates will be essentially that given by DNA, molecular biology, and immunochemistry.

But in the succeeding era, particularly the first half of the present century, an enormous amount of descriptive anatomical information was collected. The general view of the whole animal was replaced by detailed studies of particular parts. Ruch's *Bibliographia Primatologia* (1941) gives some notion of the vast quantity of information that was accumulated in this way. Since the human mind could not possibly grasp the totality of the information, conclusions were drawn from each specialized investigation, the hope being that ultimately all the different lines of anatomical evidence would yield definitive conclusions. The history of comparative anatomy of the primates shows that this was not the case. There is more disagreement now than in 1890.

---

[2] This paper is concerned only with the primates and particularly with human evolution. Obviously, a major problem with the use of comparative anatomical information in evolutionary studies is that it is limited to the contemporary primates. Scientists may agree on the anatomical facts but disagree on their interpretation. With access to precisely the same information one may conclude that man's ancestors could not have been brachiators (Straus, 1968) or that this is the most reasonable interpretation of the evidence, both on the basis of the anatomy and on the fact that man still locomotes in that way under appropriate circumstances (Washburn, 1968b). The application of statistical methods does not remove the problem because the evolutionary issue is not the difference between two contemporary forms but the difference of each from a common ancestor some millions of years ago.

The reason that the traditional anatomical studies did not build toward generally acceptable conclusions are briefly these. First, the greater the detail with which two animals are compared, the more differences will be found between them. Continued study of the primates led to taxonomic splitting because, as time went on, more and more differences could be enumerated. This has been particularly true in the case of man, in which the early studies stress the general similarity with the apes and the later ones emphasize detailed differences. If the phylogenetic position of the animals being compared has been settled by other information, such as fossils and immunology, then the additional anatomical information enriches the understanding of what happened in the history of the primates. But if the anatomical information is being used to measure differences (with no control from other sources), then the greater the differences appear to be, the greater the separation will be. For example, in a general way the arm of man and the arm of the African apes seem very similar, but detailed studies have led to the conclusion that man's ancestors could not have been brachiators (Straus, 1968) or knuckle-walkers (Tuttle, 1969). The basic problem is that the more detailed the study, the more relatively minor structures become the basis for judgment, and, at least at present, there is no method for separating fundamental similarities from minor differences. For example, Napier (1970) stresses the intermembral index, but Schultz (1969) the relation of the limbs to trunk height. According to the intermembral index, man's arms are short, but according to trunk height, they are very long. The choice of the comparative standard determines the result, and, even when many measurements have been taken, the personal judgment of what was worth measuring is the most important factor in determining the result of the comparisons. In summary, rather than clarifying the origin of man, the vast increase of information on the nonhuman primates led to a proliferation of theories of human origins. Competent scientists with access to the same anatomical information select, describe, and evaluate so differently that a wide variety of conclusions may be reached. The increasing quantity of anatomical information has not brought agreement on the major questions of human evolution, *or even on how the information is to be used.*

But, if the phylogenetic questions are regarded as settled by DNA, sequence data, and immunochemistry, then the anatomical information may be evaluated and used effectively. The quantity of anatomical information cannot change the phylogeny, and it can only be used to help in the understanding of the adaptive reasons for the evolutionary history. For example, since the phylogeny shows that man and the apes shared a long time of common ancestry after their lineage had separated from that of the monkeys, much of the similarity of man and the apes in arms, trunk viscera, teeth, etc., may be accounted for by that long period of common adaptation to arboreal life. Differences may be accounted for by events after the various lineages separated. It can no longer be said that some anatomical difference is so great that there can have been no period of common ancestry after the separation of ape and monkey ancestral lines. If one regards the phylogenetic problems as settled, then the role of comparative anatomy is limited and determined. It can increase the understanding of the evolutionary events, but it cannot change the interpretation of the events.

It should be stressed that there is only one correct answer to a phylogenetic problem. At the present time there may be uncertainties, but ultimately all lines of evidence must accord with one history, with what actually happened. Once the phylogeny is settled, then all the different lines of anatomical evidence (proportions, muscles, viscera, etc.) must be understood in terms of that history. It becomes meaningless to conclude that of the contemporary apes, man is closest to the orangutan in the shoulder and to the African apes in the hand.

Counting the Differences

If the phylogeny is settled, differences may be evaluated and the problems of counting differences reduced. For example, in comparing man and the great apes, similarities in the arm and trunk are the result of the long, common arboreal adaptation, while differences in the pelvis and legs are the result of uniquely human adaptations. A list composed of items from different adaptive complexes is not useful because the items have very different historical and adaptive meanings. The listed items may be recent or old, correlated or not, of great adaptive importance or not. Even recent lists embody these difficulties (Mayr, 1970: 377), and the evaluation of the characters used in the comparisons still presents major problems. For example, to what extent is the shape of the human palate the result of the evolution of the dentition and to what extent may differences in the teeth and palate be evaluated and counted separately? It is my belief that this kind of problem can be settled by experiments and study of the contemporary primates.

Adaptive Complexes

The importance of adaptation in determining the course of evolution has been central in the synthetic theory of evolution (Dobzhansky, 1970; Mayr, 1970). How much the classic Darwinian position will have to be modified is now being debated. Even if non-Darwinian evolution has been important at the molecular level, the evolution of adaptive complexes was under the control of selection.[3] If this is the case, at least at some stage in comparisons, the complexes must be compared. This position is the same as that of LeGros Clark. As I see the matter, when he urges the study and comparison of "total morphological patterns," rather than isolated measurements or anatomical items, he is making the same point (Clark, 1955: 15). The morphological patterns and the adaptive complexes are the same, and the advantage of calling them adaptive is that it clarifies how they are to be identified and helps in interpreting them. For example, the differences in the size of the canine teeth between man and apes have been discussed for more than a century, and have recently been reviewed by Kinzey (1970). But the variations in the canine teeth appear very differently if considered primarily as a dental problem, or as part of an adaptive pattern. In the great apes the large canines are present in the males only (Washburn and Avis, 1958). They are part of the anatomy of fighting, and this complex includes canines, first lower premolars, sex differences in body size, size of muscles of mastication, size of neck muscles, callosities on head (gorilla) or cheek (orangutan), mane that erects, and agonistic displays. The sex differences in aggression are mediated by hormones (Goy, 1970) and practiced in patterns of play (reviewed by Dolhinow and Bishop, 1970). In the skull, the related differences appear in the size, shape of palate and nasal aperture, brow ridge, postorbital constriction, sagittal crest, and nuchal crest. Seeing the

[3] Even here it is important to distinguish selection as a guiding principle in research from a belief that all structures must be determined in detail by selection. Obviously, the same function (lateral orbital wall in New and Old World monkeys, for example) may be based on a different arrangement of the bones. It may be that, even with adaptation similar and selection constant, there may be more random variation in structures than has recently been supposed. Perhaps, the Darwinian and non-Darwinian models are not as different as they appear to be at first sight.

canine as part of the adaptive complex (total morphological pattern) of bluffing and fighting leads to an almost entirely different view of the problem than measuring teeth only. Traditionally the kinds of information that are combined in the understanding of the anatomy of aggression were relegated to many separate studies, and field studies are necessary in learning how to identify adaptive complexes.

The importance of considering adaptive complexes may be illustrated by current classifications of primate locomotion. The apes are labeled brachiators, yet the field studies show that the African apes rarely swing below branches (Schaller, 1963; van Lawick-Goodall, 1968). The anatomy must correlate with all the behaviors, not with one part of the total pattern, no matter how dramatic that may be. What is needed is a behavior profile: how the animals sleep, climb up or down, move through the branches or on the ground, feed, etc. From this point of view the African apes are nest sleepers, reaching climbers,[4] knuckle-walkers. The chimpanzees are primarily tree feeders and the gorillas ground feeders. Brachiation (swinging under branches) is seen in chimpanzees and young gorillas, and it may be shown experimentally in cages (Avis, 1962), but it is only a small part of the locomotor pattern. The complexity and diversity of the behaviors actually seen in the field situation change the interpretation drastically from what seemed reasonable on the basis of anatomy and observations under restricted conditions.

The Old World semibrachiators sleep sitting on callosities, climb and run quadrupedally, and this appears to be a most misleading label both behaviorally and anatomically (Ripley, 1967).

The lorises and pottos, called hangers, are slow-moving quadrupeds, the most extreme in their grasping adaptation of any of the primates (Grand, 1967).

In most mammals, feeding is not related to locomotor adaptations, but in the primate the two are closely interrelated. This is because the animals must hold and move while feeding, and this requires adaptations, especially in a large animal. For example, gibbons hang and feed for a large part of their active hours (Carpenter, 1940, 1964; Ellefson, 1968). This unique method of feeding probably accounts for much of the anatomy that has been attributed to brachiation. The long thumb and great toe are adaptations that allow a small animal to grasp a large branch or tree in climbing. The many limitations and consequences of the gibbon feeding-locomotor adaptations have been considered elsewhere (Washburn *et al.*, in press). They include size of reproductive group, sexual activity, territorial behavior, vocalizations, temperament, and socialization. Clearly, the kind of adaptive complexes that the field work is revealing are very different and much more complex than the traditional anatomical entities.

If anatomy is organized in terms of adaptive behavioral complexes, it is possible to relate these complexes to what the animals actually do, to a behavioral profile. Then this information may be related to ecological conditions and

---

[4] I think that the similarities in the arms and trunk of gibbons, great apes, and man are the result of reaching in many directions while climbing and feeding. Mobility in holding and feeding may have been particularly important. The importance of swinging under branches as a method of locomotion has been exaggerated (frequently by me!). The anatomy of climbing-feeding makes brachiation possible and, under appropriate circumstances, the great apes may brachiate, but only in the case of gibbons does it account for a large percentage of the locomotor activity. Elsewhere I have reviewed the anatomy of this kind of climbing-reaching-feeding and stressed that many of the detailed actions are common to the apes and man (Washburn, 1968b). Stressing the problems of arboreal feeding, in addition to those of locomotion, Avis (1962) suggests unexpected correlations of anatomical characteristics. For example, the prehensile tail of some New World monkeys is a feeding adaptation, in addition to its being used in some locomotor activities, in sleeping, stabilizing, and some social activities. The tail performs the same functions as the hand, or hand and foot, in gibbon and orangutan. From this point of view, there is no adaptation among the New World primates that closely approximates the climbing-feeding adaptation in the Pongidae.

to the social life of the animals (Campbell, 1963, 1966; Napier and Napier, 1970:xiv; Crook, 1970). Then it will be possible to approach problems of comparison and evolution in terms of complex behavioral systems. If, in studying human evolution, the goal is to understand the sequence of adaptive behaviors that led to *Homo sapiens*, then typological classifications and isolated anatomical detail are of limited utility. The adaptive behaviors that lead to the reproductive success of populations are complex, and their bases cut across the traditional methods of analysis. A major goal in the study of the contemporary primates is to learn how adaptation may be usefully applied to the problems of evolution.

Paleontology

If the main outlines of the phylogeny of the primates are now settled by the molecular and immunological data, this in no way reduces the importance of paleontology, the direct evidence from times past. For example, the whole controversy over the antiquity of anatomically modern man was based on the Piltdown forgery (Weiner, 1955) and paleontological mistakes, such as the Galley Hill skull (Oakley, 1964a). Without a fossil record it would not be possible to show that the large size of the human brain was very late in human evolution, long after the manufacture of stone tools (Howell, in press; Holloway, 1970). The calibration of any molecular clock requires some point of agreement between the fossil record and the molecular information. Potassium-argon and other methods of radiometric dating have revolutionized the whole time perspective on human evolution (Oakley, 1964b; Clark, 1970). The distribution and ecology of ancestral forms can only be determined from the fossil records.

Knowledge of the structure and behavior of the contemporary primates is necessary both in the interpretation of the fossils (both reconstruction and taxonomy) and in showing the limits of inferences that may be drawn from the fragmentary specimens. For example, there have been numerous attempts to deduce the diet of fossil primates from the dentition. It has been claimed that the large kind of *Australopithecus* (*Australopithecus robustus, A. boisei, Paranthropus,* possibly including *Meganthropus*) was a vegetarian and the small one (*A. africanus,* possibly including *Homo habilis*) was a meat eater. Yet among the contemporary primates, both chimpanzee and gorilla have been dissected. In addition to their dentitions the anatomy was known, and both species have been kept in captivity and have bred, so a very considerable amount was known about the animals and their dietary needs. Still no one guessed the degree of difference in the diets of the two species. Field studies have shown the chimpanzee is primarily a fruit eater (van Lawick-Goodall, 1968) and the gorilla primarily a ground feeder (Schaller, 1963). Even on the basis of a very large amount of information, chimpanzee termiting and hunting were not anticipated. One rule for the interpretation of the fossils might be that conclusions should not be drawn from teeth alone that cannot be drawn from extensive knowledge of whole contemporary animals. The difficulty of drawing dietary conclusions from teeth alone is probably particularly great in the primates which eat a wide range of foods, so that the degree of insect-eating, meat-eating, or various kinds of vegetarian adaptation may vary locally.

The importance of field studies in interpreting primate evolution is not limited to studies of the primates themselves. Sutcliffe (1970) has shown that hyenas do collect bones and do produce fragments that are very similar to those claimed to be the tools of the australopithecines. Schaller (1967) has shown the importance of the leopard and tiger as predators on primates. The van Lawicks (1971) have described the problems of scavenging, and have shown that hunting is an easier way for primates, such as baboons and chimpanzees, to obtain some meat. Ecological reconstruction depends on knowledge of the behaviors of the contemporary animals as well as the associations of the fossils.

The events of primate evolution cannot be interpreted without the fossil record, but freedom to interpret the record has now been sharply limited by the molecular and immunological information. Within these limitations a knowledge of the structure and behaviors of the contemporary primates, and at least of some other mammals, is essential to the interpretation of the fossil record.

Parallelism

Many paleontologists have thought that the lineage leading to man separated from that leading to the apes in the Oligocene, something on the order of 25 to 30 million years ago. According to some, the separation between the lineages of the great apes is nearly as ancient (Pilbeam, 1970). There is agreement that the ancestral monkeys and apes of the Oligocene were small quadrupedal forms, and the great separations of the ancestral lines of orangutan, chimpanzee, gorilla, and man would mean that all the anatomical similarities between these forms must be due to parallel evolution. The problem of detailed anatomical parallelism is recognized by Lewis (1969) who, on the basis of a very careful study of the wrist joint, concludes that the joint of man is particularly similar to that of the African apes and that the similarities are too detailed to be due to parallel evolution. The degree of difference between Lewis and Pilbeam clearly shows the necessity for considering the way anatomical and paleontological facts are interpreted. Competent scientists with access to the same information disagree and, as indicated earlier, the disagreements are greater than they were one hundred years ago.

Parallel evolution means that natural selection has been similar so that a common ancestral group, although divided into two or more reproductively isolated groups, evolved in a similar way. If evolution has been parallel, the similarities between two groups will be due to the events that took place after the separation, in addition to those due to the original common ancestry. Parallelism has certainly occurred, and the problem is to decide the importance of the process in particular cases. One method is to examine the detail of the similarity. This is the method used by Lewis in the case of the wrist joint, and the basis is the belief that parallel evolution may cause similarity, *not* identity. For example, the spider monkey may brachiate and in the length of arms (Erikson, 1963) and some other proportions *Ateles* parallels the gibbons. The shoulder shows some parallel features, but the hand without a thumb, the wrist, the long, prehensile tail, the teeth, and the immunological data (Sarich, 1970) show that the locomotor similarities are due to parallel evolution.

The basic principle in separating parallel evolution from similarity due to genetic similarity is that the parallel evolution is due to selection. Therefore, it is unlikely that selection will cause parallel evolution in many different adaptive systems at the same time. In the example cited above, selection has led to some similarities in the arms of spider monkey and gibbon, but the spider monkey has the most prehensile tail of all the primates and the gibbon the shortest tail (Schultz, 1969). The spider monkey retains three premolar teeth, but the reduction to two in the gibbon's ancestors had taken place by the Oligocene. In the case of man and the African apes the molecular and immunological information shows that the similarities are due to common ancestry, not to parallel evolution.

As shown in Table 1 (see p. 36), the molecular and immunological information shows that man and ape are similar in ways that are not related to locomotor adaptations. If the anatomical similarities were due to parallel evolution and man, African ape, and monkey had been separated for approximately an equal period of time, then the immunological differences between man and ape should be approximately equal to those between man and monkey.

In summary, paleontology and comparative anatomy can help us to reconstruct the events that led to man. They can help in understanding the events that took place during the long period in which man and apes shared common ancestors. They can no longer be used to deny the existence of such a period.

Conclusions

With the recent advances in molecular biology and immunology, studies of human evolution have swung through a whole circle. Starting with the notion that man was particularly close to the African apes, many other theories were advanced stressing the uniqueness and great antiquity of the human lineage. The new information shows that man shared a long period of common ancestry with the apes, and particularly with the African apes.

Studies of behavior, especially the field studies, strongly support the similarity between man and ape.

Comparative anatomy leads to the same conclusions, provided the anatomy is used to help in the understanding of adaptive complexes. If anatomical topics are investigated separately, almost any conclusions may be drawn from the vast amount of heterogeneous information.

The evidence of the fossils is essential for any understanding of the events of the past, but the conclusions that may be drawn from the fossils are limited by the other kinds of evidence. Particularly the molecular and immunological evidence may not be dismissed by unsupported appeals to parallel evolution.

The diversity of the contemporary primates offers many opportunities to enrich the understanding of behavior, adaptation, and the process of primate evolution. The issues are being clarified by new techniques, field studies, behavioral anatomy, and the increasingly rapid discovery of fossils. Some of the old problems are already settled and we may hope for the solution of many more in the near future.

References

AVIS, V. 1962. *Southwestern J. Anthrop.* 18:119.

BERGGREN, W. A. 1969. *Nature* 224:1072.

BOURNE, G. H. 1971. *The Ape People.* New York: Putnam.

CAMPBELL, B. 1963. In *Classification and Human Evolution* (S. L. Washburn, ed.), pp. 50–74. Chicago: Aldine.

——— 1966. *Human Evolution: An Introduction to Man's Adaptations.* Chicago: Aldine.

CARPENTER, C. R. 1940, 1964. *Naturalistic Behavior of Nonhuman Primates.* University Park: Pennsylvania State University Press.

CLARK, J. D. 1970. *The Prehistory of Africa.* London: Thames and Hudson.

CLARK, W. E. L. 1934. *Early Forerunners of Man.* Baltimore: William Wood and Co.

——— 1955. *The Fossil Evidence for Human Evolution.* Chicago: University of Chicago Press.

——— 1959. *The Antecedents of Man.* Edinburgh: Edinburgh University Press.

CROOK, J. H. 1970. In *Social Behaviour in Birds and Mammals* (J. H. Crook, ed.), pp. 103–66. London: Academic Press.

DARWIN, C. 1871. *The Descent of Man.* New York: Random House (Modern Library edition).

DOBZHANSKY, T. 1970. *Genetics of the Evolutionary Process.* New York: Columbia University Press.

DOLHINOW, P. J., and BISHOP, N. 1970. In *Minnesota Symposia on Child Psychology* (J. P. Hill, ed.), pp. 141–98. Minneapolis: University of Minnesota Press.

DOOLITTLE, R. F., and MROSS, G. A. 1970. *Nature* 225: 643.

ELLEFSON, J. O. 1968. In *Primates: Studies in Adaptation and Variability* (P. C. Jay, ed.), pp. 180–99. New York: Holt.

ERIKSON, G. E. 1963. In *The Primates* (J. Napier and N. A. Barnicot, eds.), pp. 135–64. London: Zoological Society of London.

FLOWER, W. H., and LYDEKKER, R. 1891. *Mammals, Living and Extinct.* London: Adam and Charles Black.

GOODMAN, M. 1968. In *Taxonomy and Phylogeny of Old World Primates with References to the Origin of Man* (B. Chiarelli, ed.), pp. 95–107. Turin: Rosenberg & Sellier.

GOY, R. W. 1970. In *The Neurosciences, Second Study Program* (F. O. Schmitt, ed.), pp. 196–207. New York: Rockefeller University Press.

GRAND, T. I. 1967. *Am. J. Phys. Anthrop.* 26:207.

HODOS, W. 1970. In *The Neurosciences, Second Study Program* (F. O. Schmitt, ed.), pp. 26–39. New York: Rockefeller University Press.

HOLLOWAY, R. L. 1970. *Nature* 227:199.

HOWELL, F. C. (in press). In *Perspectives on Human Evolution* (S. L. Washburn and P. Dolhinow, eds.), Vol. II. New York: Holt.

HUXLEY, T. H. 1863. *Man's Place in Nature.* Ann Arbor: University of Michigan Press (Ann Arbor Paperbacks edition, 1959).

JAY, P. C., ed. 1968. *Primates: Studies in Adaptation and Variability.* New York: Holt.

JONES, F. W. 1929. *Man's Place among the Mammals.* New York: Longmans, Green & Co.

KINZEY, W. 1970. Paper presented at meeting of American Anthropological Association, San Diego.

KOHNE, D. E. 1970. *Quarterly Rev. Biophys.* 3:327.

LEWIS, O. J. 1969. The Hominoid Wrist Joint. *Am. J. Phys. Anthrop.* 30:251–67.

MAYR, E. 1970. *Populations, Species and Evolution.* Cambridge: Harvard University Press.

NAPIER, J. 1970. *The Roots of Mankind.* Washington, D.C.: Smithsonian.

NAPIER, J. R., and NAPIER, P. H. 1967. *A Handbook of Living Primates.* New York: Academic Press.

——— (eds.). 1970. *Old World Monkeys.* New York: Academic Press.

NONNO, L. *et al.* 1969. *Archives Biochem. and Biophys.* 136:361.

OAKLEY, K. 1964a. The Problem of Man's Antiquity. London: Bull. British Museum (Natural History).

——— 1964b. *Frameworks for Dating Fossil Man.* Chicago: Aldine.

PILBEAM, D. 1970. *The Evolution of Man.* New York: Funk and Wagnalls.

REYNOLDS, V. 1966. *Man* 1:441.

RIPLEY, S. 1967. *Am. J. Phys. Anthrop.* 26:149.

ROMER, A. S. 1968. *Notes and Comments on Vertebrate Paleontology.* Chicago: University of Chicago Press.

RUCH, T. C. 1941. *Bibliographia Primatologica.* Springfield: C. C. Thomas.

SARICH, V. M. 1970. In *Old World Monkeys* (J. R. Napier and P. H. Napier, eds.), pp. 175–226. New York: Academic Press.

SCHALLER, G. 1963. *The Mountain Gorilla.* Chicago: University of Chicago Press.

——— 1967. *The Deer and the Tiger.* Chicago: University of Chicago Press.

SCHULTZ, A. H. 1969. *The Life of Primates.* London: Weidenfeld and Nicolson.

SIMPSON, G. G. 1945. The Principles of Classification and A Classification of the Mammals. *Bulletin of the American Museum of Natural History,* 85:i–xvi, 1–350.

STRAUS, W. L., Jr. 1968. In *Medicine, Science and Culture* (S. G. Stevenson and R. P. Multhauf, eds.), pp. 161–67. Baltimore: The Johns Hopkins Press.

SUTCLIFFE, A. J. 1970. *Nature,* 227:5263:1110–1113.

TUTTLE, R. H. 1969. Knuckle Walking and the Problem of Human Origins. *Science,* 166:953–61.

VAN LAWICK-GOODALL, J. 1968. The Behaviour of Free-Living Chimpanzees in the Gombe Stream Reserve. *Animal Behaviour Monographs* 1, 3, 161–311.

——— 1970. In *Advances in the Study of Behaviour.* (D. S. Lehrman *et al.,* eds.), Vol. 3, pp. 195–249. New York: Academic Press.

VAN LAWICK, H., and VAN LAWICK-GOODALL, J. 1971. *Innocent Killers.* Boston: Houghton Mifflin.

WASHBURN, S. L. 1968a. In *Changing Perspectives on Man* (B. Rothblatt, ed.), pp. 191–206. Chicago: University of Chicago Press.

——— 1968b. *The Study of Human Evolution.* Eugene: University of Oregon Press.

——— and AVIS, V. 1958. In *Behavior and Evolution* (A. Roe and G. G. Simpson, eds.), pp. 421–36. New Haven: Yale University Press.

——— *et al.* (in press). *Social Adaptation in Nonhuman Primates.*

WEBER, MAX. 1928. *Die Säugetiere.* Jena (Germany): Gustav Fischer.

WEINER, J. S. 1955. *The Piltdown Forgery.* London: Oxford University Press.

WILSON, A. C., and SARICH, V. M. 1969. *Nat. Acad. Sci.* 63:1088.

YERKES, R. M. 1943. *Chimpanzees.* New Haven: Yale University Press.

——— and YERKES, A. W. 1929. *The Great Apes.* New Haven: Yale University Press.

ZUCKERMAN, S. 1966. *J. Royal Coll. Surg. Edinburgh* 11:87.

THE SEED-EATERS: A NEW MODEL OF HOMINID DIFFERENTIATION

CLIFFORD J. JOLLY

On close scrutiny of most particular explanations of hominid evolution we find marked discrepancies between these explanations and evolutionary theory as currently understood. One set of problems commonly associated with such discrepancies has to do with the separation of the hominid from the pongid line. The selection that follows makes a special effort to view this differentiation, and to analyze the data on the australopithecines in terms of constant and critical attention to relevant aspects of evolutionary theory. In doing so, another vital subject is aired. For some years now, dominant in the lay view of human evolution has been a notion that *Homo sapiens* is descended from an aggressive, meat-eating hunter. The positing of such an ancestor has been useful in supporting the view that man is an innately combative creature, doomed by biological and psychological inheritance to participation in war and fierce competition. The opinions presented in this article, carefully based on data of which only a portion are here reprinted, offer us a very different interpretation. It is still much too early to attempt a conclusion about this vital matter, which has obvious significance for our own lives and for the future of our species. Nonetheless, it should be clear that those who take a dim view of the human capacity for peaceful coexistence do not have the full support of science, at least insofar as the material on human evolution is concerned.

The Jolly essay is interesting also because of other challenges it contains. The reader will soon find several points at which objections are raised to some of the interpretations found, for example, in the preceding piece by Washburn. More broadly, we can see that even now the study of evolution is laden with instances of avoidance of basic problems of the origins of specific hominid features (e.g., fully erect posture, bipedalism, large brain). Sometimes such problems are treated in an essentially Lamarckian way (see selection 2, by Ernst Mayr). Clifford Jolly wrote this article specifically to confront problems of this kind.

Unfortunately, due to limitations of space it was necessary to delete from this reprinting a long section (pp. 9–19) of the original article. The omitted portions comprised a discussion of parallelisms and divergences between hominid adaptations and those of the grassland baboon, *Theropithecus.*

▼△▼△▼

Despite years of theorising, and a rapidly accumulating body of fossil evidence, physical anthropology still lacks a convincing causal model of hominid origins. Diverse lines of evidence point to a later common ancestry with the African pongids than with any other living primate, and studies of hominid fossils of the Basal and Early Lower Pleistocene (Howell 1967) have elucidated the complex of characters which at that time distinguished the family from African and other Pongidae (Le Gros Clark 1964). It is also possible to argue that the elements of the complex form a mutually reinforcing positive feedback system. Bipedalism frees the forelimb to make and use artefacts; regular use of tools and weapons permits (or causes) reduction of the anterior teeth by taking over their functions; the elaboration of material culture and associated learning is correlated with a cerebral reorganisation of which increase in relative cranial capacity is one aspect. Bipedalism is needed to permit han-

SOURCE: "The Seed-Eaters: A New Model of Hominid Differentiation Based on a Baboon Analogy," *Man*, n.s. 5 (1970): 5–26. Reprinted by permission of Royal Anthropological Institute of Great Britain and Ireland and author.

NOTE: This article is a revised and expanded version of a paper read in the Department of Vertebrate Palaeontology, Yale Peabody Museum, on February 14, 1969. The helpful comments of Drs. Colin Groves, David Pilbeam, Elwyn Simons, and Alan Walker on this and other occasions are gratefully acknowledged.

dling of the relatively helpless young through the long period of cultural conditioning, and so on.

Preoccupied with the apparent elegance of the feedback model, we tend to forget that to demonstrate the mutual relationship between the elements is not to account for their origin, and hence does not explain *why* the hominids became differentiated from the pongids, or why this was achieved in the hominid way. From their very circularity, feedback models cannot explain their own beginnings, except by tautology, which is no explanation at all. In fact, the more closely the elements of the hominid complex are shown to interlock, the more difficult it becomes to say what was responsible for setting the feedback spiral in motion, and for accumulating the elements of the cycle in the first place. Most authors seem either to avoid the problem of origins and causes altogether (beyond vague references to 'open country' life), or to fall back upon reasoning that tends to be teleological and often also illogical. This article is an attempt to reopen the problem of origins by examining critically some of the existing models of hominid differentiation, and to suggest a new one based on a fresh approach.

Previous Models of Hominid Differentiation

Direct fossil evidence for the use of 'raw' tools or weapons is necessarily tenuous, and that for the use of fabricated stone artefacts appears relatively late (Howell 1967). Nevertheless, as Holloway has pointed out (1967), the currently orthodox theory regards these elements as pivotal in the evolution of the hominid adaptive complex, probably antedating and determining the evolution of upright posture, and certainly in some way determining the reduction of the anterior teeth, the loss of sexual dimorphism in the canines, and the expansion of the cerebral cortex (Bartholomew & Birdsell 1953; Washburn 1963; DeVore 1964). A variant of this theory, proposed by Robinson (1962), sees bipedalism as the primary adaptation (of unknown origin), from which tool-using developed and hence anterior dental reduction.

Holloway (1967) rejects the orthodox, tool-and-weapon-determinant model, partly on the grounds that it postulates no genetic or selectional mechanism for anterior dental reduction, and thus implies Darwin's 'Lamarckian' notion of the gradual loss of structures through the inherited effects of disuse. It seems a little carping to accuse Washburn and his colleagues of Lamarckism because they omit to make explicit their view of the selective factors involved. These are in fact stated by Washburn in his reply to Holloway (Washburn 1968): natural selection favours the reduction of canines after their function has been subsumed by artificial weapons since this reduces the chance of accidental injury in intra-specific altercations. Since, as we shall see, orthodox natural selection is adequate to explain the reduction of teeth to an appropriate size following a change of function, it is hard to see why Washburn should avoid the Scylla of Lamarckism only to fall into the Charybdis of altruistic selection. Why should natural selection favour the evolution of a structure that is of no benefit to its bearer, for the benefit of other, unrelated, conspecifics? Even if we swallow altruistic selection, a basic illogicality remains. If the males use artificial weapons to fight other species, why should they bite one another in intra-specific combat? If they do not, then the size of their canines is irrelevant to the infliction of any injury, accidental or otherwise. In any case, the best way to avoid accidental and unnecessary intra-specific injury, of any kind, is to evolve unambiguous signals expressing threat and appeasement without resort to violence. The ability to make and recognise such signals is of advantage to *both* parties to the dispute, and therefore can be favoured by orthodox natural selection, is independent of the nature of the weapons used, and is found in the majority of social species, including both artefact-using and non-artefact-using higher primates.

We may now consider the underlying proposition that it was artefact use, which, by making the canine redundant as a weapon, and the incisors as tools, led to their reduction. It is known that hominoids with front teeth smaller than those of living or fossil Pongidae were widespread at the close of the Miocene period: *Oreopithecus* in southern Europe and Africa (Hürzeler 1954, etc.; Leakey 1967), and *Ramapithecus* (probably including *Kenyapithecus*) in India, Africa, and perhaps southern Europe and China (Simons & Pilbeam 1965). If the theory of artefactual determinism is to be applied consistently, regular tool- and weapon-making has to be extended back into the Miocene, and also attributed to Hominoidea other than the direct ancestor of the Hominidae, whether one considers this to be *Ramapithecus*, *Oreopithecus*, or neither. Simons (1965) regards *Ramapithecus* as too early to be a tool-*maker*, but he and Pilbeam (1965) suggest that it was a regular tool-*user*, like the savannah chimpanzee (Goodall 1964; Kortlandt 1967). This is eminently likely, but is no explanation for anterior dental reduction since the chimpanzee has relatively the largest canines and incisors of any pongid, much larger than those of the gorilla, which has never been observed to use artefacts in the wild. To explain hominid dental reduction on these grounds, therefore, we presumably have to postulate that the basal hominids were much more dependent upon artefacts than the chimpanzee, without any obvious explanation of why this should be so. One would also expect signs of regular tool-making to appear in the fossil record at least as early as the first signs of dental reduction, rather than twelve million years later. The more artefactually sophisticated the wild chimpanzee is shown to be, of course, the weaker the logic of the tool/weapon determinant theory becomes, rather than the other way about, as its proponents seem to feel.

Clearly, some other explanation is needed for anterior tooth reduction, at least at its inception. Recognising this, Pilbeam and Simons (1965) and Simons (1965) regard tool-use by *Ramapithecus* as compensation rather than cause for anterior tooth reduction, adopting as a causal factor Mills's (1963) suggestion that upright posture leads to facial shortening, and that canine reduction would then follow to avoid 'locking' when the jaw is rotated in chewing. The main objection to this scheme (Holloway 1967) is that there is no logical reason why facial shortening should follow upright posture. Indeed, if brachiation is counted as upright posture, then it clearly does not. (Among extinct Madagascan lemurs, for instance, the long-faced *Palaeopropithecus* was a brachiator, the very short-faced *Hadropithecus* a terrestrial quadruped (Walker 1967).) Nor does a reduced canine accompany a short face in, for instance, *Hylobates* or *Presbytis*. Furthermore, the explanation extends only to the canines, and does not account for the fact that incisal rather than canine reduction distinguishes the known specimens of *Ramapithecus* from small female Pongidae.

The same criticism applies to the model proposed by Holloway (1967), who finds an explanation of canine reduction in hormonal factors associated with the adoption of a hominid way of life:

> . . . Natural selection favoured an intragroup organisation based on social cooperation, a higher threshold to intragroup aggression, and a reduction of dominance displays . . . a shift in endocrine function took place so that natural selection for reduced secondary sexual characters (such as the canines) meant a concomitant selection for reduced aggressiveness within the group (1967:65).

Thus, reduced canine dimorphism is apparently attributed to a pleiotropic effect of genetically-controlled reduction in hormonal dimorphism, itself favoured by the 'co-operative life' of hunting.

This argument is vulnerable on several counts. First, there is no obvious reason why even *Homo sapiens* should be thought less hormonally dimorphic than other catarrhines; in structural dimorphism the 'feminised' canine of the male is a human peculiarity, but humans are rather more dimorphic in body-mass than chimpanzees, and much more dimorphic than any other hominoid in the development of epigamic characters, especially on the breast and about the head and neck, which can only be paralleled, in Primates, in some baboons. Equally, there seems little to suggest that human males are any less competitive and aggressive among themselves than those of other species; the difference rather lies in the fact that these attributes are expressed in culturally-determined channels (such as vituperative correspondence in the *American Anthropologist*) rather than by species-specific threat gestures or physical assault, so that expression of rage is postponed and channelled, not abolished at source. It seems unlikely that the basal hominids had departed further than modern man from the catarrhine norm. In fact, an elaboration of dominance/subordination behaviour, and thus an intensification of the social bond between males, is often attributed to a shift to 'open-country' life (Chance 1955; 1967).

Second, the hypothesis that the canines which are disclosed when a male primate yawns are functioning as 'organs of threat' is not unchallenged; Hall (1962) found that in Chacma baboons yawning appeared in ambivalent situations where it could more plausibly be interpreted as displacement. The size of the canines 'displayed' by a male in a displacement yawn would be of no consequence to his social relations or his Darwinian fitness.

Third, and most trenchant, we must critically examine the assumptions, accepted by 'orthodox' opinions as well as by Holloway, that an increase in meat-eating beyond that usual in primates would follow 'open-country' adaptation, and that the peculiarities of the hominids ultimately represent adaptations to hunting. The first of these assumptions is perhaps supported by the fact that chimpanzees living in savannah woodland have been seen catching and eating mammals (Goodall 1965), while those living in rain-forest have not. The flaw lies in the second part of the argument, and is like that in the artefact-determinant theory; the more proficient a hunter the non-bipedal, large-canined, large-incisored chimpanzee is found to be, the less plausible it becomes to attribute the origin of converse hominid traits to hunting. Moreover, the hunting and meat-eating behaviour of the chimpanzee does not, to the unbiased eye, suggest the selective forces that could lead to the evolution of hominid characters. Neither weapon-use nor bipedalism is prominent. Prey is captured and killed with the bare hands, and is dismembered, like other fleshy foods, with the incisors. Thus, if a population of chimpanzee-like apes becomes adapted to a hunting life in savannah, there is absolutely no reason to predict incisal reduction, weapon-use, or bipedalism. On the contrary, it is most difficult to interpret the hominid characters of the australopithecines functionally as adaptations to life as a carnivorous chimpanzee. Incisal reduction would make for less efficient processing of all fleshy foods, including meat. A change from knuckle-walking, which can be a speedy and efficient form of terrestrial locomotion, to a mechanically imperfect bipedalism (Washburn 1950; Napier 1964) would scarcely improve hunting ability, especially since a knuckle-walking animal can, if it wishes, carry an artefact in its fist while running (cf. illustration in Reynolds & Reynolds 1965:382). Once these characters existed as preadaptations in the basal hominids, they may well have determined that when hunting was adopted as a regular activity, it was hunting of the type that we now recognise as distinctively human, but to use this as an explanation of their first appearance is inadmissibly teleological.

This view is supported by the absence of fossil evidence for efficient hunting before the latter part of the Lower Pleistocene. It seems most unlikely that the hominid line would become partially and inefficiently adapted to hunting in the Miocene, only to persist in this transitional phase until the Lower Pleistocene (becoming, meanwhile, very specialised dentally, but no better at hunting or tool-making!), when a period of rapid adaptation to hunting efficiency took place. Perhaps recognising this, adherents of the 'predatory chimpanzee' model tend to situate the hominid-pongid divergence in the late Pliocene, and regard all known fossils of basal Pleistocene Hominidae as representative of a short-lived transitional phase of imperfect hunting adaptation (Washburn 1963). This is a view that is intrinsically unlikely, and difficult to reconcile with the fossil evidence of Tertiary hominids. The obvious way out of the dilemma is to set aside the current obsession with hunting and carnivorousness, and to look for an alternative activity which is associated with 'open-country' life but which is functionally consistent with the anatomy of basal hominids.

Impressed by the bipedal charge of the mountain gorilla, and his tendency to toss foliage around when excited, two authors (Livingstone 1962; Wescott 1967) have suggested that therein might lie the origin of human bipedalism and the other elements of the hominid complex. The objection to this notion is again that it is illogical to invoke the behaviour of living apes to explain the origin of something that they themselves have not developed; if upright display leads to habitual bipedalism, why are gorillas still walking on their knuckles? Conversely, if homonid bipedalism were initially used solely in display, why should they have taken to standing erect between episodes? Even if we grant that the savannah is more predator-ridden than the forest (a view often stated but seldom substantiated, even for the recent, let alone the Tertiary), it is difficult to believe that attacks were so frequent as to make defensive display a way of life.

The occasional bipedalism, tool- and weapon-use, and meat-eating of the pongids are useful indicators of the elements that were probably part of the hominid repertoire, ready for elaboration under particular circumstances. To explain this elaboration, however, we must look *outside* the normal behaviour of apes for a factor which agrees functionally with the known attributes of early hominids. As we have seen, 'hunting' is singularly implausible as such a factor. The object of this article is to suggest an alternative, based initially on the observation that many of the characters distinctive of basal hominids, as opposed to pongids, also distinguish the grassland baboon *Theropithecus* from its woodland-savannah and forest relatives *Papio* and *Mandrillus*, and are functionally correlated with different, but no less vegetarian, dietary habits.

* * * * *

A New Model of Hominid Differentiation: Phase 1, the Seed-eaters

The anatomical evidence seems to suggest that at some time during the Tertiary, the populations of Dryopithecinae destined to become hominids began to exploit more and more exclusively a habitat in which grass and other seeds constituted most of the available resources, while trees were scarce or absent. However, the great majority of contemporary tropical grasslands and open savannahs (especially those immediately surrounding patches of evergreen rain-forest in all-year rainfall areas) are believed to be recent artefacts of burning and clearance by agricultural man (Rattray 1960; Richards 1952; Hopkins 1965; White *et al.* 1954). Under climatic climax conditions the vegetation of the seasonal rainfall tropics would almost always include at least one well-developed tree stratum, ranging from semi-deciduous forests through woodlands to *sahel* where paucity of rainfall inhibits both herb and tree strata (Hopkins 1965).

What, then, would have been the biotope of the grain-eating, basal hominids? The obvious answer is provided by the areas of treeless edaphic grassland which exist, even under natural conditions, within woodland or seasonal forest zones, wherever local drainage conditions cause periodic flooding, and hence lead to perpetual sub-climax conditions by inhibiting the growth of trees and shrubs (Richards 1952; Sillans 1958). These areas range in extent from hundreds of acres, like the bed of the seasonal Lake Amboseli, to a network of strips interlaced with woodlands (*dambos*) (Ansell 1960; Michelmore 1939; Sillans 1958). Edaphic grasslands produce no tree-foods, but support a rich, all-year growth of grasses and other herbs, and are the feeding-grounds for many grass-eating animals (Ansell 1960). The remains of Villafranchian hominids are often found in deposits formed in such seasonal waters, as is Pleistocene *Theropithecus* (Jolly in press), adding some circumstantial evidence that this was their preferred habitat. Seasonality in rainfall, producing a fluctuating water-level, is important to the development of edaphic grasslands, since perennial flooding leads to a swamp-forest climax. While there is little evidence for catastrophic desiccation in the tropics of the kind demanded by some models of hominid differentiation, there are indications that a trend towards seasonality persisted through the Tertiary, especially in Africa (Moreau 1951).

The first stages of grain-feeding adaptation probably took place in a *dambo*-like environment, later shifting to wider floodplains. The change from a fruit (or herbage)-centred diet to one based upon cereals would lead, by the evolutionary processes discussed, to the complex of small-object-feeding, seed-eating, terrestrial adaptations (see Figure 1). Other grassland resources obtainable by individual foraging or simple, *ad hoc* co-operation like that seen in the woodland chimpanzee, would also be utilised. Such items as small animals, vertebrate and invertebrate, leafy parts of herbs and shrubs, and occasional fruits and tubers would be qualitatively vital, if only to supply vitamins (especially ascorbic acid and B_{12}), and minerals, and could easily be accommodated by jaws adapted to grain-milling.

The ability to exploit grass-seeds as a staple is not seen in other mammals of comparable size, though it is seen in birds and rodents, presumably because the agile hand and hand-eye co-ordination of a higher primate is a necessary pre-adaptation to picking up such small objects fast enough to support a large animal. With these preadaptations, and the adaptive characters of jaws, teeth and limbs, the basal hominids would have faced little competition in the exploitation of a concentrated, high-energy food (a situation which would hardly have existed had they, as the 'hunting' model demands, started to eat the meat of ungulates in direct competition with the Felidae, Canidae, Viverridae, and Hyaenidae). They would thus have attained a stable, adaptive plateau upon which they could have persisted for millions of years, peacefully accumulating the physiological adaptations of a terrestrial, 'open-country' species. There is no reason to suppose that they would show radical advances in intellect, social organisation, material and non-material culture, or communication, beyond that seen in one or other of the extant higher primates. The 'third ape', in Simons's phrase, remained an ape, albeit a hominid ape.

Phase 2, 'Human' Hominids

We do not therefore need to invoke late, 'human' characteristics in teleological explanation of initial hominid divergence. However, Phase 1 hominids would be uniquely preadapted to develop such features following a further, comparatively minor, ecological shift. The latter may have involved the increasing assumption by the adult males of the role of providers of mammal meat, with the equally important (but often neglected) corollary that the females and juveniles thereby became responsible for collecting enough vegetable food for themselves *and* the hunters. The adult males would per-

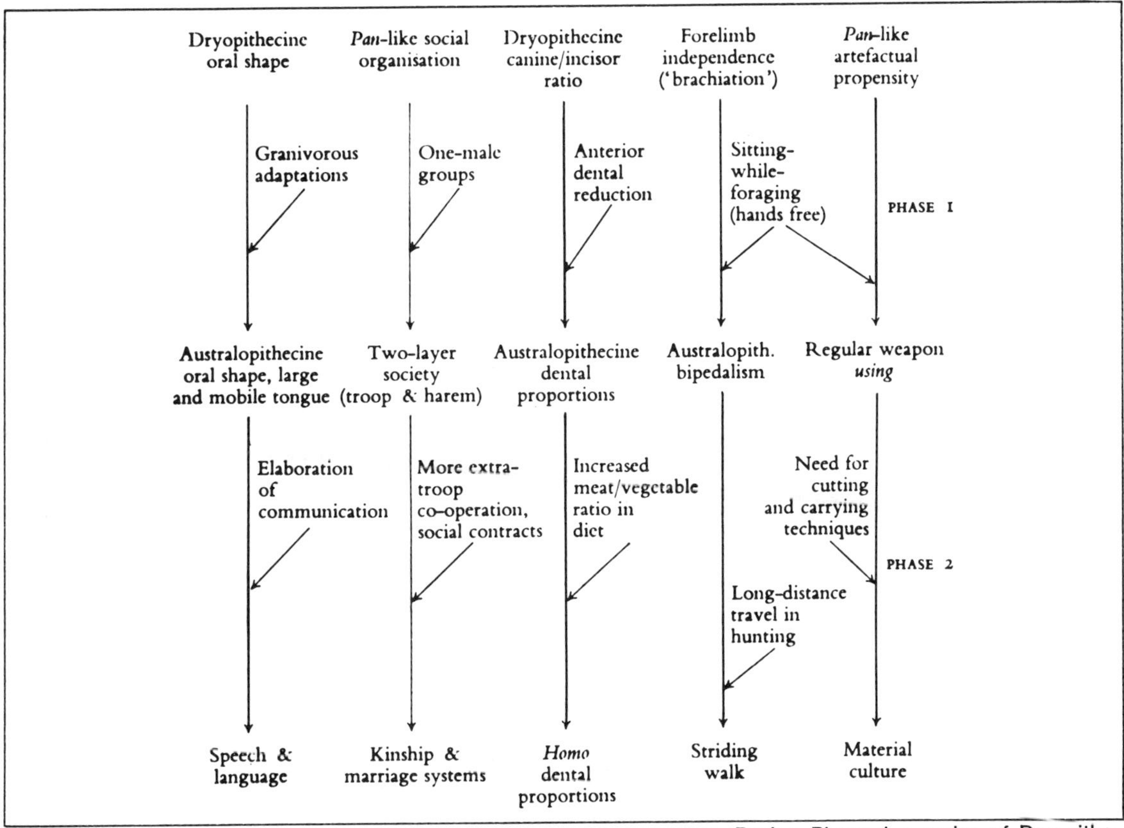

Figure 1. A model of the development of the major hominid characters. During Phase 1 a series of Dryopithecine heritage characters (top line) is modified by the functionally-determined requirements of the sedentary seed-eating complex (second line), producing the characters of evolved Phase 1 hominids (line three). These are the preadaptive heritage characters of Phase 2, which determine the fact that adaptation to the demands of a hunting way of life (fourth line) takes the form of the human traits listed in the bottom line. The illogicalities of previous models tend to arise from omitting the vital second line, inserting the elements of the hunting complex in its place, and invoking feedback.

haps be behaviourally predisposed to hunting by an existing role as 'scouts' (Reynolds 1966). This is as inherently likely in a species adapted to exploiting patches of seeding grasses as it is in the fruit-eating chimpanzee which Reynolds uses as a model of a pre-hominid hominoid. The environmental change prompting the inception of hunting need have been only slight; perhaps an intensification of seasonality in a marginal tropical area which would put a premium on exploiting meat as an additional staple instead of an occasional treat. The dietary change would be small; an increase in the ratio of one high-energy, concentrated food (meat) to another (grain), which would be reflected dentally in a moderate reversal of the Phase 1 back-tooth dominance in favour of the incisal breadth needed to tear meat. The major impact of the change would be upon culture and society rather than upon diet itself. To a female, collecting vegetable food for herself and her mate, there would be great advantage in developing techniques for more rapid harvesting, for carrying the day's booty, and for preparing it by a less laborious means than chewing. On the male side, there would be a premium on the development of cutting-tools for preparing the kill for transport back to the band. The skilful hands, upright posture, and reduced anterior dentition acquired as part of the Phase 1 complex would predispose the hominids to solve these problems of adaptation by the development of their hominoid artefactual propensity into true material culture, a solution which could not be predicted on the basis of the 'hunting chimp' model (see Figure 1). In both sexes the division of labour would involve constantly postponing feeding for the sake of contributing to the communal bag, and, in males, the impulse to dominate would likewise have to be controlled in the interests of the hunt. The need for co-operation between local bands may have led to the elaboration of truly human kinship systems, in which rights to females are exchanged.

All these factors, and others, were probably related to the evolution of complex forms of symbolic communication (largely, thanks to the seed-eating mouth, in the form of speech rather than gesture), language, ritual, and intellect. Thus the beginning of true hunting and the division of labour would initiate a second period of quantum evolution in hominid history, which we are still experiencing. The effects of this step upon human physical and behavioural evolution have been examined at length by others (e.g. Washburn & Lancaster, 1968), and are beyond the scope of this article. The point to be emphasised here is that this second, distinctively human phase is most comprehensible when it is built upon a firm base of preadaptations which had their initial significance in the seed-eating complex, not upon a chimpanzee-like or semi-human condition. By distinguishing the elements of the Phase 1 adaptive plateau, those of the Phase 2 'hominisation process' are thrown into relief.

After some populations had shifted into the Phase 2 cycle, there is no reason why they should not have existed sympatrically with other hominid species which continued to specialise in the Phase 1 niche.

The Fossil Record in the Light of the New Model

The new model must now be compared with the fossil record, both to test its compatibility and to relate its events to a timescale.

A medium-sized *Dryopithecus* of the Miocene is a reasonable starting-point for hominid differentiation, and increased seasonality in the Middle-to-Upper Miocene and Lower Pliocene makes it likely that Phase 1 differentiation began at that time. The fragmentary Upper Miocene specimens referred to *Ramapithecus* (Simons 1965), though representing only jaws and teeth, are of precisely the form to be expected in an early Phase 1 hominid: narrow, uprightly-placed and weak incisors, broad, large and mesio-distally crowded cheek-teeth, set in a short but very robust mandibular corpus. Recent work has shown (D. Pilbeam, personal communication) that the molar enamel is thicker than that of contemporary Dryopithecinae, though thinner than that of later hominids, and that the wear-gradient from anterior to posterior molars is steeper. In the Fort Ternan specimen the canine crown is small, but still conical, like that of a Mid-Pleistocene *Theropithecus* female of comparable size. The material is as yet insufficient to show whether or not the male canine was yet 'feminised'; this is immaterial to the argument that by Fort Ternan times the Hominidae had entered a granivorous niche in edaphic grasslands. Tattersall's recent (1969) appraisal of the habitat of the Siwalik *Ramapithecus* is consistent with this hypothesis. He describes forested country crossed by watercourses which at the latitude of the Siwaliks must have fluctuated with a seasonal rainfall, resulting in *dambo*-like conditions. The very incompleteness of the *Ramapithecus* material enables predictions to be made to test the seed-eating model. We may predict that the mandibular ascending ramus of *Ramapithecus* will be found to be relatively vertical, its postorbital constriction narrow, supraorbital ridge projecting and face concave in profile; the post-cranial skeleton should show a short ilium and short, stout phalanges, but also rather long arms and short, stout legs.

Among the Early Pleistocene hominids, the 'robust' australopithecines show exactly the combination of characters to be expected from long-term Phase 1 adaptation. Indeed, a major advantage of the two-phase model is that it makes sense of the apparent paradox of these hominids. Their specialisations (such as 'superhuman' incisal and canine reduction) are related to the seed-eating complex, while their apparent primitiveness (represented by characters like relatively small cranial capacity and comparatively inefficient bipedalism (Napier 1964; Day 1969; Tobias 1969)) is simply *absence* of Phase 2 specialisations.

Robinson (1962; 1963) is one of the few to see the robust australopithecines as representative of a primitive stage of hominid evolution, rather than a late and 'aberrant' line, and to recognise that basal hominids are unlikely to have been more carnivorous than pongids. He therefore comes closest to the present scheme, but does not solve the paradox of *robustus* by recognising the significance of *small-object* vegetarianism to the characters of Phase 1 adaptation. Recent discoveries suggest that robust australopithecines have a time-span in Africa running into millions of years; this would be compatible with our model of Phase 1 differentiation leading to an adaptive plateau, but not with schemes which see all australopithecines as incompetent and transient hunters, nor those that see the robust group as a late 'offshoot'.

The population represented by the specimens called *Homo habilis* (Leakey *et al.* 1964) fit the model as early, but clearly differentiated Phase 2 hominids, as their describers contend, with a dentition in which the trend to back-tooth dominance has been partially reversed, a cutting-tool culture, and increased cranial capacity. At several African sites there is evidence of contemporary and sympatric Prase 1 (*robustus*) hominids, as predicted by the model.

If this interpretation is correct, there would seem ample justification for referring *habilis* to the genus *Homo*, on the grounds of its departure along the path of Phase 2 adaptation.

The 'gracile' australopithecines (excluding *habilis*) might fit into one of three places on the model (and, conceivably, different populations referred to this species do in fact fit in different places). Possibly they are evolved Phase 1 hominids whose apparently unspecialized dental proportions might be attributed to an allometric effect of smaller size, as in *Theropithecus*. This interpretation, however, is unlikely, mainly because the size-difference between the robust and gracile groups seems insufficient to account for their divergences in shape by allomorphosis alone. Alternatively, they might be a truly primitive (Phase 1) stock from which both robust australopithecines and Phase 2 hominids evolved. This view has been widely espoused, and if dental proportions were all, it would be most plausible. However, the known *africanus* specimens are probably too late and too cerebrally advanced to be primitive. Most likely, they are at an early stage of Phase 2 evolution, with their osteodontokeratic culture, perhaps improved bipedalism, and some cerebral expansion beyond that seen in the *robustus* group (Robinson 1963). In this case their anterior dentition could be seen as secondarily somewhat enlarged from the primitive condition. This interpretation would favour sinking *Australopithecus* in *Homo*, while retaining *Paranthropus* for the evolved Phase 1 forms, as Robinson suggested.

* * * * *

The nature of an evolutionary model, concerned with unique events, is such that it cannot be tested experimentally. Its major test lies in its plausibility, especially in its ability to account for the data of comparative anatomy, behaviour, and the fossil record inclusively, comprehensively, and with a minimum of subhypotheses. It should also provide predictions which are in theory testable, as with a more complete fossil record, thus enabling discussion to move forward from mere assertion and counter-assertion. An evolutionary model which is designed to account for nothing beyond the data from which it is derived, may be entertaining, but has about as much scientific value as the *Just so stories*.

While none of the previous models of hominid differentiation is without plausibility, none is very convincing. Too few of the elements of the hominid complex are accounted for, and too often the end-products of hominid evolution have to be invoked in teleological 'explanation.' On the other hand, the nature of the causal factors invoked, especially behavioural ones, is often such as to make the hypothesis untestable.

The model presented here is based upon the nearest approach to an experimental situation that can be found in evolutionary studies, the parallel adaptation to a closely similar niche by a related organism. While based initially upon diet, and dental characters, it also accounts for hominid features as diverse as manual dexterity, shelfless mandible and epigamic hair, and for features of the fossil record such as the apparent paradox of *Paranthropus*, and the fact that hominid (or pseudohominid) dentitions apparently preceded tools by several million years. On the other hand, there seem to be no major departures from logic or from the data. It is therefore suggested that the two-phase model, with a seed-eating econiche for the first hominids, should at least be considered as an alternative working hypothesis against which to set new facts and fossils.

References

ANSELL, W. F. H. 1960. *Mammals of Northern Rhodesia*. Lusaka: Government Printer.

BARTHOLOMEW, G. A. & J. B. BIRDSELL 1953. Ecology and the protohominids. *Am. Anthrop.* 55:481–98.

BRACE, C. L. 1963. Structural reduction in evolution. *Am. Naturalist* 97:39–49.

CHANCE, M. R. A. 1955. The sociability of monkeys. *Man* 55:162–5.

——— 1967. Attention structure as the basis of primate rank orders. *Man* (N.S.) 2: 503–18.

CLARK, W. E. LE GROS 1964. *The fossil evidence for human evolution* (2nd edn). Chicago: Univ. Press.

CROOK, J. H. & J. S. GARTLAN 1966. Evolution of primate societies. *Nature, Lond.* 210:1200–3.

DAY, M. H. 1969. Femoral fragment of a robust Australopithecine from Olduvai Gorge, Tanzania. *Nature, Lond.* 221:230–3.

——— & J. R. NAPIER 1964. Hominid fossils from Bed I Olduvai Gorge, Tanganyika: fossil foot bones. *Nature, Lond.* 201:967–70.

DEVORE, I. 1964. The evolution of social life. In *Horizons in anthropology* (ed.) S. Tax. Chicago: Univ. Press.

GOODALL, J. 1964. Tool-using and aimed throwing in a community of freeliving chimpanzees. *Nature, Lond.* 201:1264–6.

——— 1965. Chimpanzees of the Gombe Stream Reserve. In *Primate behavior: field studies of monkeys and apes* (ed.) I. DeVore. New York: Holt, Rinehart & Winston.

HALL, K. R. L. 1962. The sexual, agonistic and derived social behaviour patterns of the wild chacma baboon, *Papio ursinus*. *Proc. zool. Soc. Lond.* 139:283–327.

HOLLOWAY, R. L. JR. 1967. Tools and teeth: some speculations regarding canine reduction. *Am. Anthrop.* 69:63–7.

HOPKINS, B. 1965. *Forest and savanna.* Ibadan, London: Heinemann.

HOWELL, F. C. 1967. Recent advances in human evolutionary studies. *Quart. Rev. Biol.* 42:471–513.

HÜRZELER, J. 1954. Zur systematischen Stellung von *Oreopithecus*. *Verh. naturf. Ges. Basel* 65:88–95.

KORTLANDT, A. 1967. Experimentation with chimpanzees in the wild. In *Progress in primatology* (eds.) D. Starck *et al.* Stuttgart: Gustav Fischer.

LEAKEY, L. S. B. 1967. Notes on the mammalian faunas from the Miocene and Pleistocene of East Africa. In *Background to evolution in Africa* (eds.) W. W. Bishop & J. D. Clark. Chicago: Univ. Press.

———, P. V. TOBIAS & J. R. NAPIER 1964. A new species of the genus *Homo* from Olduvai Gorge, *Nature, Lond.* 202:3–9.

LIVINGSTONE, F. B. 1962. Reconstructing man's Pliocene pongid ancestor. *Am. Anthrop.* 64:301–5.

MICHELMORE, A. P. G. 1939. Observations on tropical African grasslands. *J. Ecol.* 27:283–312.

MILLS, J. R. E. 1963. Occlusion and malocclusion in primates. In *Dental anthropology* (ed.) D. R. Brothwell. Oxford: Pergamon Press.

MOREAU, R. E. 1951. Africa since the Mesozoic with particular reference to certain biological problems. *Proc. zool. Soc. Lond.* 121:869–913.

NAPIER, J. R. 1964. The evolution of bipedal walking in the hominids. *Arch. Biol.* (*Liège*) 75:Suppt, 673–708.

PILBEAM, D. R. & E. L. SIMONS 1965. Some problems of Hominid classification. *Am. Sci.* 53:237–59.

RATTRAY, J. M. 1960. *The grass cover of Africa.* New York: FAO.

REYNOLDS, V. 1966. Open groups in hominid evolution. *Man* (N.S.) 1:441–52.

——— & F. REYNOLDS 1965. Chimpanzees in the Budongo forest. In *Primate behavior: field studies of monkeys and apes* (ed.) I. DeVore. New York: Holt, Rinehart & Winston.

RICHARDS, P. W. 1952. *The tropical rain forest: an ecological study.* Chicago: Univ. Press.

ROBINSON, J. T. 1962. The origins and adaptive radiation of the Australopithecines. In *Evolution und Hominization* (ed.) G. Kurth. Stuttgart: Gustav Fischer.

——— 1963. Adaptive radiation in the Australopithecines and the origin of man. In *African ecology and human evolution* (eds.) F. C. Howell and F. Bourlière (Viking Fd Publ. Anthrop. 36). Chicago: Aldine.

SILLANS, R. 1958. *Les savanes de l'Afrique centrale.* Paris: Editions P. Lechevalier.

SIMONS, E. L. 1965. The hunt for Darwin's third ape. *Med. Opinion Rev.* 1965 (Nov.):74–81.

——— & D. PILBEAM 1965. Preliminary revision of the Dryopithecinae. *Folia primat.* 3:81–152.

TATTERSALL, I. 1969. Ecology of the north Indian *Ramapithecus. Nature, Lond.* 221:451–2.

TOBIAS, P. V. 1969. Cranial capacity in fossil Hominidae. Lecture, American Museum of Natural History, May 1969.

WALKER, A. C. 1967. Locomotor adaptations in recent and fossil Madagascan lemurs. Thesis, University of London.

WASHBURN, S. L. 1950. Analysis of primate locomotion. *Cold Spr. Harb. quart. Symp. Biol.* 15:67–77.

——— 1963. Behavior and human evolution. In *Classification and human evolution* (ed.) S. L. Washburn (Viking Fd Publ. Anthrop. 37). Chicago: Aldine.

——— 1968. On Holloway's 'Tools and teeth'. *Am. Anthrop.* 70:97–101.

——— & C. S. LANCASTER 1968. The evolution of hunting. In *Man the hunter* (eds.) R. B. Lee and I. DeVore. Chicago: Aldine.

WESCOTT, R. W. 1967. Hominid uprightness and primate display. *Am. Anthrop.* 69:78.

WHITE, R. O., S. V. VENKATAMANAN & P. M. DABADGHAO 1954. The grassland of India. *C. R. int. Congr. Bot.* 8:46–53.

7

THE SINGLE SPECIES HYPOTHESIS

MILFORD H. WOLPOFF

The study of human evolution involves times so long gone and a data language so often abstruse that most laymen fail to see in it anything relevant to our time and our problems. We have already observed, however, that theories of human evolution can have startling significance for the present, as when it is asserted that our species has evolutionarily inherited propensities for warfare and competition. It is interesting to note that the following selection takes a further crack at this theory and offers further support of Jolly's contrary view (see selection 6).

But this is not the main reason for reprinting the Wolpoff article. Instead, consider that science, supposedly value-free, may be used wittingly or unwittingly to spread myths that may play vital roles in the organization and validation of contemporary society. One of the most distressing facts of modern life is that genocide, no matter how narrowly defined, has occurred in our own time. It was also a prominent feature of several preceding centuries, including the nineteenth, which managed to produce a sanctifying dogma for the process. Unfortunately and inaccurately the doctrine is known as Social Darwinism; in essence it asserts that the fittest survive, and it identifies as unfit those who are poor, lacking in modern technology, or disinterested in commercial competition. Such a doctrine legitimizes the near destruction of the American Indians and of various minority peoples elsewhere in the world, including some in China and the Soviet Union, as well as the total elimination of certain populations in Tasmania, Brazil, and elsewhere.

What has this to do with the technical article on human evolution that follows? Everything.

SOURCE: Adapted and condensed with permission of the author and the Royal Anthropological Institute from "Competitive Exclusion among Lower Pleistocene Hominids: The Single Species Hypothesis," *Man*, 6 (1971):601–14.

One of the ways in which Social Darwinism has been vindicated and made to seem scientifically unavoidable is by having a genocidal scenario projected into the past. If it can be argued that the evolution of the human species to its present preeminence was based upon genocide past, then there is justification, albeit hard, cold, and "scientific," for genocide present. The "two species hypothesis" is precisely such an argument. Basically, it asserts that in such-and-such a period of human evolution there were two species of contemporary, competing forms which fought it out, the victor being our ancestor. Actually, there have been several uses of such a doctrine. One of these we catch a glimpse of in later selections—the Neanderthals are sometimes set quite apart from the main stream of evolving humanity and are seen as being destroyed by higher types such as "Cro-Magnon." Similarly, the evolutionary events of a much earlier period have been interpreted in such a way as to reinforce the unfortunate political realities of our own time. Thus, the australopithecines are sometimes viewed as contemporaries of a more advanced population of hominids (*Homo habilis?*) which destroyed them. In another view the australopithecines comprised two distinct lineages, one gracile (delicately bodied), the other robust, with inevitable competition and conflict and the triumph of one.

The Wolpoff article leads us through the maze of argumentation and shows how weak is the contention of two species. Once again the article has been extensively cut so that little of the technical documentation remains. Nonetheless, what remains is sufficient to alert the reader to the substantial flaws in one of the most subtle kinds of presentation of the idea that human evolution and progress rests on competition and conflict.

▼△▼△▼

As early as 1950, Ernst Mayr suggested applying the competitive exclusion principle to early hominid evolution. As a result, the single species hypothesis emerged. Other authors, such as Schwalbe (1899; 1913), Weinert (1951), and Weidenreich (1943), interpreted hominid evolution within the framework of (what we would now describe as) a single evolving polytypic lineage, based purely on morphological considerations. Mayr, however, was the first to give this interpretation a theoretical basis in the synthetic theory.

The single species hypothesis rests on the nature of the primary hominid adaptation: culture (structured learned behaviour). Because of cultural adaptation, all hominid species occupy the same, extremely broad, adaptive niche. For this reason, allopatric hominid species would become sympatric. Thus the competitive exclusion principle can be legitimately applied. The most likely outcome is the continued survival of only one hominid lineage.

The Origin of Bipedal Locomotion

As Mayr originally claimed and as Washburn has often stressed (1951; 1960; 1963), one of the primary hominid morphological adaptations centres about bipedal locomotion. Other distinctive hominid characteristics not related to diet either arise from this adaptation, or form secondary adaptations.

What selective pressures lead to bipedalism? What selective advantages did bipedalism confer on very early hominids? Many answers to these questions have been proposed. For instance, Hewes (1961) suggests food transport across the savanna as the primary adaptive advantage of bipedal locomotion, and L. S. B. Leakey points to the ability to see over tall grass (personal communication). While these suggestions obviously form part of an adaptive explanation, by themselves they simply do not explain the presence of an adaptive advantage strong enough to compensate for the loss of quadrupedal mobility (Washburn 1951:69; Pfeiffer 1969:43–53; Oakley 1959:443); nor do they take sufficient account of the concomitant dangers due to predators in a savanna existence (Bramblett 1967). As Brace (1962: 607) put it: 'It would seem that a weaponless biped trudging over the savanna with a load of ripe meat would be an exceedingly poor bet for survival'.

Thus the use of tools as a means of defence appears to be critical. A dependence upon tools both in offensive and defensive behaviour explains the selective advantage of bipedal locomotion: the hands are freed during locomotion so that a tool or weapon is available at all times. The question of availability at all times is crucial, for the great apes can both produce and carry tools (Goodall 1964). However, tool use in chimpanzees differs from human tool use in one important respect: chimpanzees do not regularly use their tools as weapons, nor do they depend upon tools as a means of defence (Goodall 1964). Still, the established use of tools by these pongids as part of their normal way of life makes it likely that the ancestors of the earliest hominids were also capable of this behaviour.

Since the ability to make and use tools as a learned and ecologically important type of behaviour is not restricted to hominids, the unique hominid *dependence* upon tools for defence is all the more revealing. Faced with a predator, a hominid who knew how to use a club for defence but did not have one available was just as dead as one to whom the notion never occurred. The advantage of carrying weapons continuously probably provided the greatest impetus to the morphological changes transforming bipedal locomotion from a possibility to an efficient form of movement.

All the relevant australopithecine skeletal material known indicates a completely bipedal stance (Lovejoy *et al.* in press). . . .

Since the living African apes are capable of prolonged bipedal locomotion *without* all the morphological adaptations demonstrated for the australopithecines, the presence of such a total morphological pattern in the australopithecines most likely indicates habitual bipedalism in the same sense that modern man is habitually bipedal, although not necessarily in the same detailed way.

The pre-australopithecine hominids could be described as primates with the morphological and behavioural capabilities of living apes, using these capabilities in order to adapt to a way of life similar to that of baboons. The australopithecines themselves show the morphological consequences of this adaptation. The special fracturing of the battered baboon skeletal material at australopithecine-bearing sites such as Taung and Makapansgat suggests competition between these ecologically similar primate species.

The Meaning of Reduced Canines

According to this hypothesis, the reduced canines found in even the earliest australopithecines indicate a replacement of the canine defensive function (Washburn & Avis 1958: 425) by regularly employing implements as a means of defence, as Darwin suggested a century ago.

In this regard, it is important to establish that both gracile and robust australopithecines have reduced canines. Specifically, the canines of both australopithecine types are not significantly different in size from each other, or from those of *Homo erectus*. . . . In the mandible as well as the maxilla, both gracile and robust australopithecines are *not significantly different* from *Homo erectus*. . . . In fact, they are not significantly different from each other. . . . Apparently, australopithecine canines were already reduced to Mid-Pleistocene hominid size.

Australopithecines were small to moderate-sized creatures. The most recent body size estimation for STS 14 (one of the smallest specimens) is 42–43 inches, weighing between 40 and 50 pounds (Lovejoy & Heiple 1970). The Olduvai tibia suggests a height of 56 inches (Coon 1963:285). No estimates for the robust australopithecines have exceeded 200 pounds, and the small size of the femur heads of SK 82 and 97 (Napier 1964) suggests considerably less for at least some. Others were larger, as a comparison of Swartkrans mandibles shows (Wolpoff 1971*b*, fig. 1); the size range at this site alone was extensive. A similar size range occurs for postcranial material from East Rudolf (R. E. F. Leakey 1971).

Graciles and robusts overlapped considerably. Robinson indicates that male gracile and female robust australopithecines were approximately equal in robustness and stature (1970: 1219). A small body weight for many of the specimens is suggested by the size of the bones and joint surfaces. All the joints through which the weight of the body passes are very small: often smaller, in fact, than the joints in very small *Homo sapiens* (Broek 1938). . . .

There is every indication that early Pleistocene savanna primates of this size range would not lack natural predators, and would thus require a means of defence. The robust australopithecines have been compared to gorillas. Gorilla males, however, weigh between 300 and 400 pounds (Napier & Napier 1967) and do not live on savanna. The necessity of maintaining an adequate means of defence for a savanna-dwelling lower Pleistocene primate in the australopithecine size range is suggested by the fact that savanna-dwelling baboons of this time period were characterised by large projecting canines coupled with a body size sometimes exceeding that of male gorillas (R. E. F. Leakey 1969; Freedman 1957; von Koenigswald 1969; L. S. B. Leakey & Whitworth 1958).

The Evidence for Tool Use

Chimpanzees have been observed both walking erect and using tools. This indeed is part of their normal repertoire. The common ancestors of pongids and hominids were probably also capable of such behaviour. In view of the complex morphological and neurological prerequisites of primate tool use, and its transmission, and the very different adaptive patterns of the living hominid and pongid species now capable of such activity, it is unlikely that tool use arose in parallel after the lineages separated.

Given this reconstruction of pre-divergence behavioural capability, we must ask why the lineage separation occurred. The single species hypothesis rests on the *assumption* that the *dependence* upon tools as a means of defence allowed the savanna-forest niche divergence to occur, and thus formed the basis for this split. The resulting adaptation allowed effective hominid utilisation of savanna resources: first seeds and roots (Jolly 1970), and later scavenged game (Dart 1957; 1964; M. D. Leakey 1967). Pongids, on the other hand, became better adapted to a forest niche than their dryopithecine ancestors.

What were australopithecine tools like? The earliest dated implements, at this time, come from deposits on the east side of Lake Rudolf (M. D. Leakey 1970*b*), Kenya. These deposits are associated with a date of at least 2·6 million years (Fitch & Miller 1970). On the other hand, I believe, the earliest direct evidence of hunting activity, as opposed to scavenging or single kill sites (of possibly already incapacitated animals) derives from sites near the top of Bed I in Olduvai Gorge, *at least 1·5 million years later*. If tools were invented by 'killer ape' ancestors as a means for gathering animal protein (Ardrey 1961), archaeology indicates that these early hominids were not very good at it, because most early tools are simple cutting edges and digging implements (L. S. B. Leakey 1960): there are no hunting tools. Such implements could be interpreted as part of a dietary adaptation based on scavenging and gathering roots (unobtainable for baboons). Thus, Jolly's seed-eater hypothesis seems supported. *Homo erectus* is apparently the earliest hominid to show the dental reduction commensurate with significant meat-eating.

Unfortunately, the implements first used for defence were probably simple clubs of wood and bone. Their use is only occasionally, and often indirectly, shown (Dart 1957). To ask which came first, defensive implements or tools for cutting while scavenging and digging while gathering, is a 'chicken and egg' type of question. They are both part of the same adaptive complex: the hominid ecological equivalent of savanna-adapted baboons.

The early dependence on implements as a means of defence allowed an effective savanna adaptation, and consequently led to the differentiation of the hominid stock, necessitating bipedal locomotion and consequently providing its selective advantage. Culture, in this context, can be viewed as an adaptation to insure the effective transmission of tool use from generation to generation. Selection acted to modify the hominid morphology in the direction of producing a more efficient culture-bearing animal, allowing both the structuring and the transmission of survival-oriented kinds of learned behaviour.

Any bipedal small-canined hominid population should not only have been culture-bearing, but indeed should have been dependent upon culture for its survival. African archaeology offers support for the first part of this contention, for tools have been associated with all the earliest known bipedal hominids. . . . In numerous cases the evidence directly associates *both* gracile and robust australopithecines with the use and manufacture of stone tools. More often than not, most of these seem associated with scavenging activity. Australopithecine scavenging has been adequately demonstrated from the body part distribution at both Makapansgat (Dart 1957) and Olduvai Bed I (M. D. Leakey 1967).

Culture and Competitive Exclusion

Man has adapted *culturally* to the physical environment, and has adapted *morphologically* to effectively bearing culture. Thus culture, rather than any particular morphological configuration, is man's primary means of adaptation. His morphological evolution has been consistently directed by selection for a more effective culture-bearing creature. Culture plays the dual role of man's primary means of adaptation, as well as the niche to which man has morphologically adapted. In this sense, all hominids occupy the same adaptive niche.

The fact that culture is an integral part of man's adaptive pattern suggests that cultural evidence is as important as osteological evidence in reconstructing hominid evolutionary history.

Although culture may have arisen as a defensive survival mechanism, once present, it opened up a whole new range of environmental resources. Culture acts to multiply, rather than to restrict, the number of usable environmental resources. Because of this hominid adaptive characteristic implemented by culture it is unlikely that different hominid species could have been maintained. Mayr (1950) originally applied Gauss's principle (1934) of competitive exclusion to the understanding of hominid evolution. As he interprets the principle:

> the logical consequence of competition is that the potential coexistence of two ecologically similar species allows three alternatives: (1) the two species are sufficiently similar in their needs and their ability to fulfil these needs so that one of the two species becomes extinct, either (*a*) because it is 'competitively inferior' or has a smaller capacity to increase or (*b*) because it has an initial numerical disadvantage; (2) there is a sufficiently large zone of ecological nonoverlap (area of reduced or absent competition) to permit the two species to coexist indefinitely (1950:68).

There are two conditions that must be met for closely related species to coexist sympatrically: (1) they must be able to tolerate the hazards occurring in the area of overlap; (2) they must differ from each other in such a manner that they do not enter into a 'struggle for existence' in which one succeeds at the expense of the other.

In culture-bearing hominids, it is particularly difficult to meet these conditions. For the separation of two species, a fortuitous isolation of part of the parent species must occur over sufficient time for genetic isolating mechanisms to become established. If this separation were to have occurred before the hominid differentiation, then culture presumably arose independently in each lineage, as shown by both the archaeological evidence and by the same morphological evidence for bipedalism found in both gracile and robust australopithecines. On the other hand, a separation after the hominid differentiation is questionable for exactly the same reasons that sympatry itself is questionable (Mayr 1963:66).

Even if two separate hominid lineages could have arisen, how could they have been maintained for an appreciable length of time? One of the advantages afforded by culture is the great ecological diversity in the utilisation of a broad ecological base which it allows. In consequence, hominids tend to spread over a broad range, occupying areas where only *some* resources are available at a given time. That is, hominids can utilise more resources than are ever available at one place. Thus, the australopithecines spread over the Old World tropics and semi-tropics from South Africa to Java, occupying a large variety of climatic habitats and living sites. Synchronic culture-bearing hominid species could not help but become sympatric (Cain 1953) in a number of different areas. Related species are more likely to be found in similar habitats than are unrelated ones (Williams 1947; Bagenal 1951). The sympatric hominid species would then be in competition for *different* resources in *different* areas of overlap. For the total range of each species, the overlapping resource base would necessarily be extensive.

With competition occurring in different areas for different resources between species each able to utilise a broad ecological base, subsequent adaptation *could not reduce competition*. New adaptations would have to be learned. Rather than narrowing the range of utilised environmental resources for each species, such further adaptation would probably broaden this range by increasing the capacity to learn how to utilise additional resources, and thus *increase* the amount of real competition for the whole species. That is, competition would most likely cause each hominid species to develop the ability to utilise a wider range of resources and thus increase the amount of competition. One surely must succeed at the expense of the other.

Application to the Lower Pleistocene

Most authors now apply the results of competitive exclusion in interpreting Mid-Pleistocene and more recent hominids, recognising only one synchronic hominid species. The single species hypothesis is primarily applied here to hominid origins, predicting the valid application of competitive exclusion in interpreting earlier hominid remains.

There are excellent reasons to believe that culture played a crucial role in australopithecine survival, in and apart from the logic dictated by the single species hypothesis. Mann (1968), for instance, has been able to demonstrate that the rate of australopithecine development and maturation was delayed, as in modern man, rather than accelerated as in modern chimpanzees. Based on molar eruption timing, Mann showed that australopithecine children took as long to mature as do our own. If selection for increased learning capacity, associated with cultural behaviour, resulted in delayed maturation in Lower Pleistocene hominids, it must have been operative *before* the Pleistocene.

Similarly, McKinley (1971) demonstrated that australopithecines (graciles and robusts) followed a 'human' model of short birth spacing. In baboons, gorillas and chimpanzees, successive births are spaced apart by the length of child dependency. Thus in slow maturing chimpanzees, he calculated an average birth interval of 4·6 years from data given in Goodall (1967), the only available source. In man the maturation timing is about half as fast, so the corresponding period of child dependency is close to eight years. Human births, however, are not spaced by this period, but rather can be as close together as one to two years. This seems primarily due to the influence of complex social factors on the effect of child dependency. The result is highly adaptive to rapid population expansion. Australopithecines follow the human model of delayed maturation timing. The corresponding birth spacing, following the chimpanzee model but based on the delayed maturation rate, is close to eight years. However, the average time between births calculated by McKinley (1971), three to four years in the robusts and four to five years in the graciles, is less. Social behaviour, far more complex than that evinced by baboons, acted to *shorten* the effects of child dependence in australopithecines, although Mann's work shows that this period of dependence was *longer* for them than it is in modern pongids. In both cases, the evidence clearly indicates extensive australopithecine adaptation to social-cultural behaviour. This suggests that such behaviour was adaptively important prior to the Lower Pleistocene.

Is the conclusion that gracile and robust australopithecines are members of the same hominid lineage really so unlikely? Authors other than myself have demonstrated greater differences among groups of anatomically modern *Homo sapiens* (Bielicki 1966; Brace 1963*a*; 1963*b*; 1967*a*; 1967*b*; Buettner-Janusch 1966; Dart 1955*a*; LeGros Clark 1947; Oppenheimer 1964). Variation among all australopithecines appears on a par with variation in both gorillas and chimpanzees (Wolpoff 1970*b*; Remane 1959; Schultz 1937; 1954; 1963; 1968; 1969*a*). As Campbell has pointed out (1969), this interpretation fits the established pattern of both gracile and robust groups of people in Africa from the Lower Pleistocene to the present.

The synchronous occurrence of both gracile and robust australopithecines has been demonstrated in east Africa from terminal Pliocene well into the lower Pleistocene (Arambourg & Coppens 1967; 1968; Coppens 1970; Arambourg *et al.* 1967; 1969; Howell 1968a; 1968b; 1969; Patterson & Howells 1967; R. E. F. Leakey 1970a; 1970b; 1971; L. S. B. Leakey 1960). The available evidence indicates that social and cultural behaviours acted as evolution-orienting factors over the time span.

If the graciles and the robusts truly are separate lineages, there can by definition have been no gene flow between them. Given the facts that (1) they were supposed to be adapting quite differently, and that (2) they were synchronic for at least two million years (Howell 1969), one would expect non-overlapping differences in adaptively differentiated features to have occurred. Conversely, if this expectation were not permissible it would be impossible to test the hypothesis suggesting that the gracile and robust australopithecines were two different lineages. At that point, the question of separate australopithecine species would become unanswerable, and hence phylogenetically meaningless.

The interpretation of separate australopithecine lineages yields two testable predictions: 1) One expects non-overlapping sets of differences between the two lineages which indicate different adaptations, and consequently separate total morphological patterns; 2) One expects these differences to become greater through time.

The first prediction is best approached by directly testing the dietary hypothesis (Robinson 1956; 1963*a*; 1963*b*). Do graciles and robusts evince different dietary adaptations? The robusts are supposed to be adapted to a far more vegetarian diet than the graciles. Consequently, the grinding area of their cheek teeth should be considerably greater. The predicted difference in grinding area is fundamental to the dietary hypothesis. Without it, the demonstrable differences between graciles and robusts can only be related to size. Actually, the size difference complicates comparison of the cheek teeth. The robusts should have larger teeth corresponding to their larger size (Robinson 1963*b*), and at the same time they should also have larger teeth because of their more vegetarian diet. In sum, they should have *much* larger cheek teeth than do the graciles, . . . [yet] in both absolute and percentage differences, gracile and robust australopithecines are considerably closer together than numerous modern populations, in some cases living side by side. While [this does] not mean that the graciles and the robusts are identical to each other, the [data] clearly indicate extensive similarity in an adaptive complex which is supposed to show significant difference.

In posterior grinding area, a sample of 318 gorillas and robust australopithecines are within 5 percent of each other, although the smallest gorillas have at least double the maximum body mass estimated for robust australopithecines, and the larger specimens have three to four times the mass. The presence of a robust australopithecine-sized posterior grinding area in a species considerably larger, restricted to a primarily vegetarian diet, gives indication of the diet of the robusts. Jolly (1970) has argued that hominids arose from a savanna-based primate adapted to the extensive mastication involved in small object feeding. Given this tooth size comparison with the much larger gorillas, adapted to a forest foliage diet, the dietary part of Jolly's 'seed eaters' hypothesis seems substantiated.

According to Robinson's dietary hypothesis, gracile australopithecines are supposed to have reduced posterior dentitions because of their presumed more omnivorous diet. Actually, the graciles have posterior summed grinding areas completely within the range of variation of gorillas, in spite of the likelihood that their body side was between one-quarter and one-eighth gorilla size. Most estimates give robusts about double the average weight of graciles. If even approximately true, the graciles have relatively *larger* posterior teeth. Is it really so likely that the graciles had a more omnivorous diet than the robusts? Or rather, in keeping with Jolly's hypothesis that early hominids appear to be dentally adapted to a heavily masticated diet, does it not appear more probable that *both* the smaller graciles and the larger robusts subsisted on a diet of scavenged game, small objects and roots.

The second prediction is also questionable. Robust specimens from Omo (for instance L7–125) and Olduvai are considerably *more* extreme than robusts from apparently younger sites such as Swartkrans and Kromdraai. I do not conclude that there is a trend from greater to lesser robustness in the robusts (although this is possible), both because the earlier sample size is too small and because the range of variation in the later specimens is almost great enough to include the earlier ones. Certainly, however, there is no indication of the reverse tendency, as is predicted from the interpretation of separate lineages. This observation also directly contradicts the character displacement hypothesis suggested by Schaffer (1968).

With the increasing amount of data accumulated, numerous workers have come to recognise the intensive intergradation and overlap of gracile and robust australopithecines both in terms of individual specimens and in terms of entire sites such as Kromdraai and Makapansgat where 'intermediate' populations could be represented (LeGros Clark 1947; Brace 1963*a*; 1963*b*; 1967*a*; Campbell 1969; Dart 1955*a*; 1964; Buettner-Janusch 1966; Simons 1968; Mann 1970; Wolpoff 1968; 1970*a*; 1970*b*; 1971*a*). Indeed, one of those most familiar with the actual specimens has recently concluded:

> The distinction between these two lines should not be overstated: it is suggested that gene exchange between the two lines might have been possible. Such hybridizing effects might have aided the 'toning down' of the extremely robust earlier *A. boisei* into the later less robust *A. robustus;* and secondly, might account for a number of *A. robustus* features in the otherwise *A. africanus* forms of Makapansgat (Tobias 1969:311–12).

This description can only refer to subspecies within the same species.

There are certainly differences between what I have referred to as gracile and robust australopithecines, just as there is a difference between Bushmen and Bantu, or Norwegians and Lapps, or Lowland and Mountain gorillas. These differences can be extensive. One would never confuse crania of Bushmen and Bantu with each other, whether a single cranium or a much larger sample was involved. Different *types*, however, are not necessarily different *species*. If a sampling of australopithecine mendelian populations were available, I believe that we would characterise some as gracile, some as robust, and still others as intermediate. Thus a plausible interpretation of australopithecine variation refers the differences between them to sub-species level. This interpretation fits the predictions of the single species hypothesis.

The single species hypothesis is concerned with consequences of the pongid-hominid lineage separation. As such, it presents a way of approaching early hominid interpretations which would otherwise be untestable. While Jolly's 'seed eaters' hypothesis deals with the consequences of how early hominids *subsisted* on the savanna, this hypothesis considers the consequences of how they *defended* themselves. The two views are not contradictory.

The single species hypothesis is grounded in the synthetic theory, and fits the available evidence. Those who believe it to be invalid must not only demonstrate the unequivocal value of their proposed refutations, but must also replace the hypothesis with one which fits the evidence better.

References

ARAMBOURG, C. & Y. COPPENS 1967. Sur la découverte dans le Pléistocène inférieur de la vallée de l'Omo (Éthiopie) d'une mandibule d'Australopithécien. *C. r. Acad. Sci.* Ser. D 265:589–90.

——— 1968. Découverte d'un Australopithécien nouveau des gisements de l'Omo (Éthiopie). *S. Afr. J. Sci.* 64:58–9.

———, J. CHAVALLON & Y. COPPENS 1967. Premiers résultats de la nouvelle mission de l'Omo (1967). *C. r. Acad. Sci.* Ser. D 265:1891–6.

———, ——— & ——— 1969. Résultat de la nouvelle mission de l'Omo (2e campagne 1968). *C. r. Acad. Sci. Ser.* D. 268:759–62.

ARDREY, R. 1961. *African genesis.* New York: Bell.

BAGENAL, T. B. 1951. A note on the papers of Elton and Williams on the genetic relations of species in small ecological communities, *J. An. Ecol.* 20:242–5.

BIELICKI, T. 1966. On 'Homo habilis.' *Curr. Anthrop.* 7:576–8.

BRACE, C. L. 1962. Comment on 'Food transport and the origin of hominid bipedalism.' *Am. Anthrop.* 64:606–7.

——— 1963*a*. Review of *Evolution and hominisation* (ed.) G. Kurth. *Am. J. Phys. Anthrop.* 21:87–91.

——— 1963*b*. Review of *Ideas on human evolution* (ed.) W. W. Howells. *Hum. Biol.* 35:545–8.

——— 1967*a*. *The stages of human evolution.* Englewood Cliffs: Prentice-Hall.

——— 1967*b*. Environment, tooth form and size in the Pleistocene. *J. dent. Res.* 46:809–16.

BRAMBLETT, C. A. 1967. Pathology in the Darajani baboon. *Am. J. phys. Anthrop.* 26:331–40.

BROEK, A. J. P. v.d. 1938. Das Skelett einer weiblichen Efe-Pygmäe. *Z. Morph. Anthrop.* 40:121–69.

BUETTNER-JANUSCH, J. 1966. *The origins of man.* New York: Wiley.

CAIN, A. J. 1953. Geography and coexistence in relation to the biological definition of the species. *Evolution* 7:76–83.

CAMPBELL, B. G. 1969. Early man in southern Africa. *S. Afr. archaeol. Bull.* 24:212.

CLARK, W. E. LEGROS 1947. Observations on the anatomy of the fossil Australopithecinae. *J. Anat.* 81: 300–33.

COPPENS, Y. 1970. Les restes d'hominides des séries inférieures et moyennes des formations pliovillafranchiennes de l'Omo en Éthiopie. *C. r. Acad. Sci.* Ser. D 271:2286–9.

COON, C. S. 1963. *The origins of races.* New York: Alfred A. Knopf.

DART, R. A. 1955*a*. *Australopithecus prometheus* and *Telanthropus. Am. J. phys. Anthrop.* 13:67–96.

——— 1957. *The osteodontokeratic culture of Australopithecus prometheus* (Transvaal Mus. Mem 10). Pretoria: Transvaal Museum.

——— 1964. The ecology of the South African manapes. *Monogr. biol.* 14:49–69.

DAY, M. H. 1969. Femoral fragment from a robust australopithecine from Olduvai Gorge, Tanzania. *Nature, Lond.* 221:230–3.

FITCH, F. J. & J. A. MILLER 1970. Radioisotopic age determinations of Lake Rudolf artifact site. *Nature, Lond.* 226:226–8.

FREEDMAN, L. 1957. The fossil Cercopithecoidea of South Africa. *Ann. Transvaal Mus.* 43:121–262.

GAUSS, G. F. 1934. *The struggle for existence.* Baltimore: Williams & Wilkins.

GOODALL, J. 1964. Tool-using and aimed throwing in a community of freeliving chimpanzees. *Nature, Lond.* 201:1264–6.

——— 1967. Mother–offspring relations in free-ranging chimpanzees. In *Primate ethology* (ed.) D. Morris. Chicago: Aldine.

HEWES, G. W. 1961. Food transport and the origin of hominid bipedalism. *Am. Anthrop.* 63:687–710.

HOWELL, F. C. 1968*a*. Review of *Olduvai Gorge*, vol. 2, *The cranium and maxillary dentition of Australopithecus (Zinjanthropus) boisei* by P. V. Tobias. *Am. Anthrop.* 70:1028–30.

——— 1968*b*. Omo research expedition. *Nature, Lond.* 219:576–82.

——— 1969. Remains of Hominidae from Pliocene Pleistocene formations in the lower Omo basin, Ethiopia. *Nature, Lond.* 223:1234–9.

JOLLY, C. J. 1970. The seed-eaters: a new model of hominid differentiation based on a baboon analogy. *Man* (N.S.) 5:1–26.

KOENIGSWALD, G. H. R. VON 1969. Miocene Cercopithecoidea and Oreopithecoidea from the Miocene of east Africa. In *Fossil vertebrates of Africa* (ed.) L. S. B. Leakey, London: Academic Press.

LEAKEY, L. S. B. 1960 *Adam's ancestors* (4th edn.). New York: Harper.

——— & T. WHITWORTH 1958. *Notes on the genus* Simopithecus, *with a description of a new species from Olduvai* (Coryndon Mem. Mus. Occ. Pap. 6). Nairobi: Coryndon Memorial Museum.

LEAKEY, M. D. 1967. Preliminary survey of the cultural material from Beds I and II, Olduvai Gorge, Tanzania. In *Background to evolution in Africa* (eds) W. W. Bishop & J. D. Clark. Chicago: Univ. Press.

——— 1970*b*. Early artifacts from the Koobi Fora area. *Nature. Lond.* 226:228–30.

LEAKEY, R. E. F. 1969. New Cercopithecoidea from the Chemeron Beds of Lake Baringo, Kenya. In *Fossil vertebrates of Africa,* vol. I (ed.) L. S. B. Leakey. London: Academic Press.

——— 1970*a*. Fauna and artifacts from a new Plio-Pleistocene locality near Lake Rudolf in Kenya. *Nature, Lond.* 226:223–4.

——— 1970*b*. In search of man's past at Lake Rudolf. *Nat. Geogr.* 137:712–33.

——— 1971. Further evidence of Lower Pleistocene hominids from East Rudolf, North Kenya. *Nature, Lond.* 231:241–5.

LOVEJOY, C. O. & K. G. HEIPLE 1970. A reconstruction of the femur of *Australopithecus africanus. Am. J. phys. Anthrop.* 32:33–40.

——— in press. Proximal femoral anatomy of *Australopithecus. Nature, Lond.*

LOVEJOY, C. O., K. G. HEIPLE & A. H. BURSTEIN in press. The gait of *Australopithecus. Am. J. phys. Anthrop.*

MCKINLEY, K. R. 1971. Survivorship in gracile and robust australopithecines: a demographic comparison and a proposed birth model. *Am. J. phys. Anthrop.* 34:417–26.

MANN, A. E. 1968. The paleodemography of *Australopithecus*. Ph.D. Thesis, University of California, Berkeley. (Ann Arbor, University Microfilms 69–3652.)

——— 1970. 'Telanthropus' and the single species hypothesis: a further comment. *Am. Anthrop.* 72:607–9.

MAYR, E. 1950. Taxonomic categories in fossil hominids. *Cold Spring Harbor Symp. Quant. Biol.* 15:108–18.

——— 1963. *Animal species and evolution.* Cambridge: Belknap Press.

NAPIER, J. R. 1964. The evolution of bipedal walking in the hominids. *Arch. Biol.* 75:673–707.

——— & P. H. NAPIER 1967. *A handbook of living primates.* London: Academic Press.

OAKLEY, K. 1959. Tools makyth man. *Smithsonian Report* 1958:831–45.

OPPENHEIMER, A. M. 1964. Tool use and crowded teeth in Australopithecinae. *Curr. Anthrop.* 5:419–21.

PATTERSON, B. & W. W. HOWELLS 1967. Hominid humeral fragment from the Early Pleistocene in Northwestern Kenya. *Science* 156:64–6.

PFEIFFER, J. E. 1969. *The emergence of man.* New York: Harper & Row.

REMANE, A. 1959. Die primitivsten Menschenformen (*Australopithecinae*) und das Problem des tertiaren Menschen. *Naturwiss. Vereins für Schleswig-Holstein* 29:310.

ROBINSON, J. T. 1956. *The dentition of the Australopithecinae.* (Transvaal Mus. Mem. 9) Pretoria: Transvaal Museum.

ROBINSON, J. T. 1963*a*. Australopithecines, culture and phylogeny. *Am. J. phys. Anth.* 21:595–605.

——— 1963*b*. Adaptive radiation in the australopithecines and the origin of man. In *Classification and human evolution* (ed.) Sherwood L. Washburn. Chicago: Aldine.

——— 1970. Two new early hominid vertebrae from Swartkrans. *Nature, Lond.* 225:1217–19.

SCHAFFER, W. M. 1968. Character displacement and the evolution of the hominidae. *Am. Natur.* 102:559–71.

SCHULTZ, A. H. 1937. Proportions, variability and asymmetries of the long bones of the limbs and the clavicles in man and apes. *Hum. Biol.* 9: 281–328.

——— 1954. Bemerkungen zur Varibilität und Systematik der Schimpanzen. *Säugetierkundl. Mitteil.* 2:159–63.

——— 1963. Age changes, sex differences, and variability as factors in the classification of primates. In *Classification and human evolution* (ed.) S. L. Washburn, Chicago: Aldine.

——— 1968. The recent hominoid primates. In *Perspectives on human evolution* 1 (eds) S. L. Washburn and P. C. Jay.

——— 1969*a*. The skeleton of the Chimpanzee. In *The chimpanzee* 1, *Anatomy, behaviour, and diseases of chimpanzees* (ed.) G. H. Bourne. Baltimore: University Park.

SCHWALBE, G. 1899. *Studien über Pithecanthropus erectus Dubois. Z. Morph. Anthrop.* 1:1–240.

——— 1913. Kritische Besprechung von Boule's Werk: 'L'homme fossile de La Chapelle-aux-Saints' mit eigenes Untersuchungen. *Z. Morph. Anthrop.* 16: 527–610.

SIMONS, E. L. 1968. Assessment of a fossil hominid. *Science* 160:672–5.

TOBIAS, P. V. 1969. The taxonomy and phylogeny of the australopithecines. In *Taxonomy and phylogeny of the Old World primates with reference to the origin of man* (ed.) B. Chiarelli. Torino: Rosenberg & Sellier.

WASHBURN, S. L. 1951. The analysis of primate evolution with particular reference to the origin of man. *Cold Spring Harbor Quant. Biol.* 15:67–78.

——— 1960. Tools and human evolution. *Sci. Am.* 203:63–75.

——— 1963. Behaviour and human evolution. In *Classification and human evolution* (ed.) S. L. Washburn. Chicago: Aldine.

——— & V. AVIS 1958. Evolution of human behavior. In *Evolution and behavior* (eds) A. Roe and G. C. Simpson.

WEIDENREICH, F. 1943. The 'Neanderthal Man' and the ancestors of 'Homo sapiens'. *Am. Anthrop.* 45:29–48.

WEINERT, H. 1951. *Stammesentwicklung der Menschheit.* Braunschweig: Vieweg & Sohn.

WILLIAMS, C. B. 1947. The generic relations of species in small ecological communities. *J. An. Ecol.* 16: 11–18.

WOLPOFF, M. H. 1968. 'Telanthropus' and the single species hypothesis. *Am. Anthrop.* 70:477–93.

——— 1970*a*. *Metric trends in hominid dental evolution* (Case West. Reserve Stud. Anthrop. 2).

——— 1970*b*. The evidence for multiple hominid taxa at Swartkrans. *Am. Anthrop.* 72:576–607.

——— 1971*a*. Interstitial wear. *Am. J. phys. Anthrop.* 34:205–28.

——— 1971*b*. Is the new composite cranium from Swartkrans a small robust australopithecine? *Nature, Lond.* 230:398–401.

8

THE ORIGIN OF MAN

C. LORING BRACE

Professor Brace's overview of the main steps in the physical evolution of ourselves during the past few million years needs little in the way of specific introduction, particularly for those who have already encountered the views of physical anthropologists like Washburn, Jolly and Wolpoff (see selections 5, 6, and 7). The Brace presentation is neatly synthetic, clear, and forthright. Introducing it, however, offers an opportunity to deal critically with recent announcements of new findings that seem seriously to question the general view that Brace here presents.

Richard Leakey received considerable press coverage when he announced in November, 1972, that he had discovered at Lake Rudolf in Kenya, a skull which, when reconstructed by Maeve Leakey, warranted the designation *Homo sapiens.* The newsworthiness of this assertion hinges on the dating of the fossil, which is placed more than two and a half million years into the past. If Leakey is correct, present understanding of the course of human evolution requires extensive revision. For one thing, the fossils of *Homo erectus,* lying much closer to our own time, would likely lose significance as probable human ancestors. Like *Gigantopithecus,* the various populations of *H. erectus,* including the Chinese, Indonesian, African, and European finds, would all be relegated to some abortive evolutionary side road leading to extinction.

Years ago, human paleontology was torn by the scandal of Piltdown Man, an outright hoax that was exposed when sophisticated dating techniques revealed anomalies. Clearly the new Leakey find is not of that kind. Perhaps the strongest things about it, as a matter of fact, are its genuineness as a fossil and its dating. But there are other fossils whose failure

SOURCE: "The Origin of Man," *Natural History Magazine,* 79 (1970):46–49.

to hold center stage may offer instructive comparisons. One of these, *Oreopithecus bamboli,* remains an important fossil, but is no longer generally considered a direct human ancestor, and is placed at a greater remove from the main hominid line. A major source of difficulty and misinterpretation was the fact that *Oreopithecus* was found in a seam of lignite—a kind of coal—hence badly crushed and pressed out, something like Charlie Chaplin's watch in *Modern Times,* where Charlie fell into the big machine.

In another case, Swanscombe, a fossil comprising several distinct cranial segments became the basis of a controversial theory of ancient *sapiens* presence. This arose from reconstructions that gave a fairly large cranial capacity. But relatively small shifts in the placement of the individual fragments could result in wide differences in reconstruction.

That is precisely the point of the present case. According to newspaper accounts (the scientific descriptions are not yet available), the number of fragments involved in Richard Leakey's ancient *H. sapiens* is way beyond the number constituting Swanscombe. Even though some of the fragments may be quite large, the possibility of error is much greater than was the case with Swanscombe. The notion of using *one* fossil, a very dubious one at that, to challenge a structure based upon extensive fossil populations is ludicrous. If Leakey is right, he will be confirmed by future discoveries. I think he is wrong and I think his leap will turn into a pratfall. The new find is probably another australopithecine, perhaps with a larger cranium than any other yet discovered, but an australopithecine none the less. *Homo erectus* can rest peacefully in his grave. Remember that you read this first right here.

▼△▼△▼

More than a century ago when Darwin published *On the Origin of Species,* it was authoritatively assumed by those who had not read the book that he was chiefly concerned with the origin of man. He actually mentioned the word *man* only once in the epoch-making work, and then in a cryptic sentence on the last page. But such is the strength of popular assumption that the title has been consistently misquoted. The popular press still refers to his book as *The Origin of the Species,* and *the* species is assumed to be man. This example typifies man's timeless fascination with himself, as well as his propensity for repeating misinformation about himself—a universal quality that may have been best summed up by the acerbic Ambrose Bierce early in the twentieth century when he defined man as "an animal so lost in rapturous contemplation of what he thinks he is as to overlook what he indubitably ought to be."

But what, then, is man? What was he in the past, and what has allowed him to survive to the present? If these questions are answered, we can then contemplate, perhaps with alarm, the basis for what is to come.

Central to any definition of man, and the key to his evolutionary success, is a phenomenon not immediately visible when specimens of the creature are scrutinized. This phenomenon is what the anthropologist calls culture. It includes not only the high points of art, music, and literature, but also all those things that result from the cumulative efforts of other people and previous generations. Tools, the traditions regulating their use, vital information, and language itself—all are included in the concept culture. Man is not just an animal that possesses culture, but an animal that cannot survive without it. Men could not exist if each had to discover anew the control of fire, the manufacture of clothing and shelter, the sources of edible sustenance, and the guidelines for workable interpersonal relationships, to say nothing of the mechanics, electronics, chemistry, and physics on which human life depends today. These elements of culture are a cumulative continuation of simpler counterparts in the past.

In the beginning our ancestors, like other animals, must have been faced with the problem of surviving without the aid of culture. So much of culture is perishable or intangible that there is no way to determine when culture as a cumulative phenomenon began. Nonperishable cultural elements have an antiquity of about two million years in Africa. The cultural tradition of which they are a part continues without break, expanding to occupy the tropical and temperate parts of the Old World around 800,000 years ago, and ultimately developing into all the cultures in the world today.

From this we postulate an African origin for all mankind. The existence of crude stone tools in Africa a million and a half to two million years ago allows us to suppose the existence of culture at that time. Our guess suggests that the possessor of this culture could not have survived without it; therefore, he deserves the designation *man*—however primitive and crude he might have been.

We further postulate that culture existed a long time before the initial appearance of recognizable stone tools. This is speculation, but not idle speculation, because we could not otherwise account for the transformation of ape to man. Although small in quantity, supporting evidence exists in the form of skeletal material. Fossilized remains, including skulls, jaws, teeth, and a few other skeletal pieces have been found in association with the oldest known stone tools both in Olduvai Gorge in East Africa and in the Transvaal of South Africa. Since the discovery of these fossils in 1924, argument has continued over their status —ape? man? human ancestor? extinct side line? Brain size was within the range of that for the large modern anthropoid apes, but these early hominids walked erect on two feet as does modern man. Molar teeth were of gorilloid size, but the canines did not project beyond the level of the other teeth.

Despite continuing arguments over whether the balance of traits was on the human or simian side, it is apparent that the survival of these early hominids depended on a distinctly non-apelike adaptation. Bipedal locomotion did not enable hominids to escape predators by rapid flight. Neither could these hominids seriously threaten to bite a potential predator. Contrast this with such modern ground-dwelling primates as baboons and gorillas where the enlarged canine teeth of the males represent formidable defense weapons. We can guess that these early hominids depended for survival on something not visible in their anatomy, and our guess is that they used hand-held tools.

Possibly they defended themselves with the crude hunks of worked stone found at the sites where their skeletal remains have been discovered, but more likely they relied on pointed sticks. To use a rock as a defensive weapon requires close contact with the attacking creature, while the defender probably preferred to face his tormentor from the far end of a pointed stick. Not only is the pointed stick a simple and effective weapon—devisable with a minimum of manufacturing effort—but it can also double as a digging tool. Edible roots and bulbs are a substantial part of the diet of baboons that live today in the savanna, an environment typical of the areas inhabited by the earliest hominids. The addition of a simple digging stick of the kind used by the surviving hunting and gathering human groups—and probably by the early hominids—could easily double the baboons' food supply.

The huge, worn molars of the early hominids indicate that they relied on gritty, uncooked vegetables for subsistence. Unlike any other primates, their canine teeth are functionally indistinguishable from their small incisors. Assuming that the remote hominid ancestor had enlarged canine teeth like all other primates, then the creatures associated with the stone tools in East and South Africa two million years ago belonged to a line in which the selective pressures needed to maintain large canines had been suspended for a long time. Cultural means of defense must have existed long before the earliest stone tools.

Within the last three years jaws and teeth have been found in southwestern Ethiopia that are so like the Olduvai and Transvaal finds that they must be related. Their antiquity, however, extends back nearly four million years, and no stone tools are associated with them. The canine teeth in the fragmentary remains are not enlarged, leaving us to infer that defensive weapons must have been used some four million years ago—two million years before the earliest stone tools existed.

Reliance on hand-held weapons for defense (and perhaps also for food getting) did not automatically convert apes into men, but it altered the forces of selection so that evolution in the human direction was a consequence. For one thing, occupation with tool wielding reduced the locomotor role of hands. Legs and feet, as a result of natural selection, assumed the entire burden of locomotion. Tools usurped the defensive role of canine teeth, and, with an accumulation of mutations, these teeth were reduced. The vast majority of mutations interfere with the development of the structures that depend on their control, but usually these "deleterious mutations" are eliminated by selection. When selection is reduced or suspended—as when tools reduced the defensive role of teeth—the reductive mutations simply accumulate in the ongoing gene pool of the population. The structure controlled by the genes—the canine teeth, for example—eventually fails to achieve the full development once characteristic of the remote ancestral population.

Early in hominid development, when defensive weapons were not well developed, those charged with the task of defense, the males, must have been substantially more rugged than those less concerned with defensive activities, the females. Among terrestrial primates where a culture with weapons plays no defensive role, males tend to be much larger and stronger than females. Baboons, gorillas, and other ground-dwelling primates are good examples. Fossil fragments hint that this must have been the case for the earliest hominids as well. The difference in robustness of specimens from the early levels of Olduvai Gorge, the Transvaal, and now from Omo in southwest Ethiopia has led some scholars to suggest that two different species of hominid—one small and slender, the other large and robust—shared the same habitat. However, now that we can demonstrate a time span of nearly three million years for the early hominids, it makes better ecological and evolutionary sense to explain the differences in size as sexual dimorphism—male-female difference—in a single species of early hominid.

The taxonomy of these earliest hominids continues to be debated. Genera such as *Australopithecus*, *Paranthropus*, *Zinjanthropus*, *Homo*, and others have been suggested, and even more species tentatively recognized. Whatever the taxonomic designation, these early hominids, except for their reliance on learned behavior and on hand-held tools for defense and food getting, lived more like apes than humans.

The evidence from Olduvai Gorge in East Africa shows that crude stone tools were added to the limited cultural repertoire toward the end of this long early hominid phase—a period I prefer to call the australopithecine stage. These tools belong to the incipient part of a tradition of butchering large animals in the Middle Pleistocene. At the end of the Lower Pleistocene, however, they occur mainly with the fossilized remains of immature animals. We can guess that this records the beginning of the adaptive shift that was largely responsible for the development of *Homo sapiens*, a shift related to the development of hunting as a major subsistence activity.

In the Middle Pleistocene, somewhat less than a million years ago, man emerges as a major predator. This adaptation is unique among the primates, and it is not surprising that many of the physical, behavioral, and physiological characteristics that distinguish man from his closest animal relatives are related to this adaptation. While we cannot make direct behavioral or physiological tests on fossils, we can make inferences based on their anatomy, on their apparent ecological adaptation, and on conditions observable in their modern descendants.

Anthropologists generally agree that the men of the Middle Pleistocene are properly classified as *Homo erectus*. The first specimen to be discovered was classified in the genus *Pithecan-*

thropus at the end of the nineteenth century. While we no longer accept this generic designation, pithecanthropine remains a convenient, nontechnical term for Middle Pleistocene hominids.

Brain size was twice that of the preceding australopithecines and two-thirds that of the average modern man. With the absence of a specialized predatory physique, natural selection probably encouraged the evolution of intelligence. While brain size had increased, the size of the molar teeth had reduced, although they were still quite large by modern standards. This reduction may have been related to the shift from a rough vegetable diet to one with a large proportion of meat. Meat, needing only to be reduced to swallowable pieces, requires far less mastication than starches, which begin the process of conversion to simple sugars by mixing with salivary enzymes through extensive chewing.

Evidence, although fragmentary, also suggests that bipedal locomotion in its modern form was perfected at this time, the Middle Pleistocene. While man's mode of locomotion may not be speedy, it requires an expenditure of relatively little energy. To this day, primitive hunters employ the technique of trotting persistently on the trail of an herbivore until it is brought to bay, often many days later.

Several correlates of this hunting life are suggested. Man, reflecting his primate heritage, is relatively night-blind and must, therefore, confine his hunting activities to the daytime. A tropical mammal (and physiologically man is still a tropical mammal) pursuing strenuous activities in broad daylight is faced with the problem of dissipating metabolically generated heat. The hairless human skin, richly endowed with sweat glands, is unique among terrestrial mammals of much less than elephantine size, and I suggest that this developed under the selective pressures of regular big game hunting early in the pithecanthropine stage.

The elimination of the hairy coat by natural selection left the skin exposed to the potentially damaging effect of the ultraviolet component of tropical sunlight. The obvious response was the development of the protective pigment melanin. Consequently the Middle Pleistocene ancestors of all modern men were probably what in America today is called black.

The conversion of this being into what is technically known as *Homo sapiens* requires only the further expansion of the brain from the pithecanthropine average of 1,000 cubic centimeters (actually well within the range of modern variation) to the average today of 1,400 cc. Fragmentary fossil evidence suggests that this transition had taken place by the beginning of the Upper Pleistocene, about 120,000 years ago. Men at that time—referred to as Neanderthals—still had an archaic appearance. In general these early representatives of *Homo sapiens* were more muscular and robust than their modern descendants—particularly the males. Jaws and teeth were large, especially the front teeth, which, from their wear patterns, evidently served as all-purpose tools.

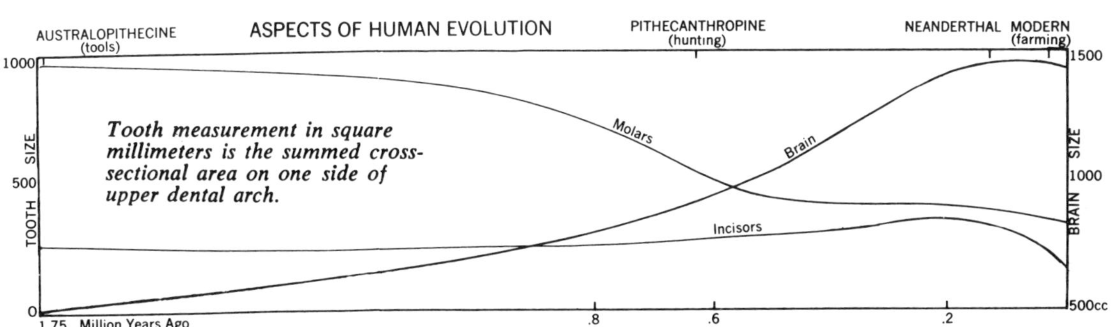

Since the first appearance of *Homo sapiens* in his Neanderthal form, human evolution has been characterized by a series of reductions. Whenever human ingenuity made life easier, there was a relaxation of the forces of selection, and these reductions followed. More effective hunting techniques lessened the burden on the hunter's physique, and an eventual reduction in muscularity was the result. Manipulating tools lessened the stress on the anterior teeth, and the consequent reduction of these and their supporting bony architecture converted the Neanderthal face into modern form. In parts of the world where manipulative technology is a late phenomenon, such as aboriginal Australia, faces and teeth have remained large. Where clothing was developed for survival in northern climes, the significance of protective skin pigment was lessened, and the consequent reduction produced the phenomenon that is euphemistically called white.

The only thing that has not been reduced is the number of human beings. We cannot even guess at the population density of the australopithecines. Throughout the Middle Pleistocene, the archeological record suggests a fairly constant population for the hunting pithecanthropines. Evidently the population increased dramatically with the Neanderthal form of *Homo sapiens*. The diversification of food resources and the increase in cultural complexity that accompanied the first appearance of modern *Homo sapiens* just under 35,000 years ago also signaled another sharp jump in population. This set the stage for the tremendous population growth made possible by the development of agriculture after the end of the Pleistocene 10,000 years ago.

Thus did *Homo sapiens* emerge—a manifestation of ecological imbalance, literally shaped by the consequences of his own impact upon the world. His fate, too, will be shaped by his future impact on the world—the result of his numbers and his actions. Malthus sounded the alarm nearly two centuries ago, but few listened to his warning. One who did was Ambrose Bierce, who added to his definition of man that "his chief occupation is extermination of other animals and his own species, which, however, multiplies with such insistent rapidity as to infest the whole habitable earth. . . ."

THREE
EXPLORATIONS IN RACE

RACIAL CLASSIFICATIONS: POPULAR AND SCIENTIFIC

GLORIA A. MARSHALL

Now that you have considered the probability that neither yours or anyone else's ancestors were white, in the conventional United States sense of the term (see p. 72), let us confront some other aspects of the concept of race applied to our own species. Indeed, one of most difficult things about *race* is to convince people that it is a concept rather than a hard and fast reality "out there." One sees physical differences and the leap to the notion of the existential reality of race follows almost without thought. It is very much like the idea, so widespread and so little challenged until relatively recent times, that the earth was flat. It is sometimes difficult to believe that the idea that earth was flat was held so fiercely, that people lost their lives for thinking otherwise.

But one of the very interesting things about the concept of race, both popular and scientific, is its fluid and changing character. This is beautifully brought out in the selection that follows, the first of several dealing with this "four letter word that hurts."

▼△▼△▼

I

Many scholars in the biological sciences agree that all typological divisions of mankind into discrete racial groups are to some extent arbitrary and artificial. Despite this widespread agreement, there appear to be two divergent views regarding the utility of the concept of race in studies of human biology. On the one hand, there are scholars who maintain that race as a statistically defined unit can and should be utilized in the description and analysis of intraspecific variation (1). According to this view, the concept of race is applicable to clusters of populations, each of which can be genetically defined.

On the other hand, there are scholars who argue that in view of the arbitrariness of racial classifications, there can be little or no justification for the continued use of the race concept. Scientists who hold this view consider that the analysis and description of intraspecific variation in human and nonhuman populations can be most fruitfully pursued without reference to the concept of race (2). Jean Hiernaux (3) has stated this position as follows:

> If any racial classification is arbitrary, for what purpose can it be of any use? Why spend so much time and effort building a classification, knowing that many others, not any worse, could be opposed to it, and that it runs the risk not only of being useless but also harmful by conveying the erroneous impression that it makes generalization possible?

Some of the anthropologists and biologists who favor continued use of the race concept have maintained that racial classifications are useful if they reflect the phylogenetic development of the species (4). That such a purpose is necessarily served by *any* racial classification is noted by Ehrlich and Holm (5), who caution that "there is no basis for assuming, without extensive genetic study, that any population or any taxonomic group is an evolutionary unit." On the same issue, Hiernaux (6) has argued that it would be extremely difficult to

SOURCE: *Science and the Concept of Race,* Margaret Mead, Theodosius Dobzhansky, Ethel Tobach, and Robert E. Light (eds.). New York: Columbia University Press. 1968. pp. 149–64. Reprinted by permission of the publisher and author.

I wish to thank Karen Kerner for her assistance in the research on which this paper is based. I also wish to thank Miss Kerner, along with Robert LeVine, Joyce Riegelhaupt, Edward Riegelhaupt, Harold Conklin, Marvin Harris, Samuel Sutton, and David Feingold for their helpful comments at various stages in the preparation of this paper.

derive a phylogenetic tree from data on contemporary human populations since the species did not split into groups which were "exposed to different evolutionary forces and events under complete or effective genetic isolation," and he goes on to state:

> The general picture [of human evolution] is not one of isolated groups differentiating in circumscribed areas. Mixture occurred many times in many places between the most various populations brought into contact by human mobility. The tendency toward high adaptive specialization was balanced again and again by migration, and by man's power to transform his environment. Even if we could reconstruct the intricate succession of mixtures that contributed to each living population, the final picture would look like a reticulum more than a tree, and a reticulum defies dichotomizing subdivision.

It is not only the study of human variation that has led to a reappraisal of the utility of the concept of race for the analysis of intraspecific variation. Examination of the characters used in subspecific classifications of butterflies led N. W. Gillham (7) to conclude:

> In view of the prevailing discordance of geographical patterns followed by different variates, racial partition of butterfly species is not only arbitrary, but it must also necessarily weight some variates and ignore others, without regard for the biological significance of any of them. The best that can be hoped for now is an analysis of variation by individual characters, avoiding arbitrary subdivision of the species. Such analysis will eventually yield a less distorted picture of species formation than that to which the artificial subspecies now inevitably leads.

The debate regarding the relevance of the concept of race for the analysis and description of intraspecific variation has important implications for all sciences concerned with the study of mankind. However, it does not appear that this debate has had widespread impact on professionals in the fields of medicine, psychology, sociology, history, or political science. Moreover, the investigations and publications of many scholars in these and other fields often deal with populations that are termed "races" even though the distinctive attributes of these populations have no proven biological significance.

What is often unrecognized or ignored is the fact that the "races" about which many scientists speak and write are those perceived and delineated by particular groups of people who interact in given sociopolitical contexts. Comparative studies of these popular racial typologies show them to vary from place to place; studies of popular racial classifications also show them to vary from one historical period to another. In no instance are these classifications referable to competent genetic studies; rather, they are "concocted by human beings to explain or render intelligible their observations" (8). Whereas most scholars today acknowledge that it is necessary to make a distinction between popular and technical conceptions about human biology, they do not necessarily avoid confusion of the two. Hence, many scientists persist in the use of the term race to describe groups whose racial statuses are determined, and whose racial characteristics are defined, by sociopolitical expediencies.

This paper attempts to document the variability in the criteria upon which popular racial classifications are based and to show that scientific discussions of race often reflect and reinforce popular notions about human variation. It also intends to show that both scientific and popular conceptions about race are usually influenced by sociopolitical considerations. Many of the points raised in this paper have been discussed in various contexts by anthropologists and by scholars in other fields. That they must be repeated here indicates the difficulties involved in communicating on the subject of race.

II

Most laymen and many scientists in the United States hold that there are three "major races":

Caucasian (white), Negro (black), and Mongolian (yellow). This typology has a scientific basis; it is a revision of that proposed by J. F. Blumenbach, a distinguished anatomist and physician of the eighteenth century (9). But in some parts of the country Chinese Americans and other peoples from Asia are sometimes classed as "white" (10). However, almost nowhere in the United States is there any doubt that there are at least two "major races": namely, the Negro race and the white race.

In the United States, it is popularly held that descent is the basis upon which individuals are assigned to racial groups. However, Marvin Harris (11) has argued that it is a rule of *hypodescent* which governs the assignment of many individuals to the two major races distinguished by Americans. A rule of hypodescent operates when individuals whose parents belong to different "races" are assigned to the one that is politically subordinate. In America, individuals who have no known or acknowledged African ancestry constitute a politically and economically superordinate group. From this group has come the rule that individuals of both European and African parentage must be assigned to the politically subordinate group that is referred to as the Negro race.* "Thus, first generation children of interracial marriages in the United States are uniformly Negroes, when it is absolutely certain that such children have received half of their hereditary endowment from one parent and half from the other" (11).

Even though the operation of the rule of hypodescent results in the application of the term Negro to American populations any of whose ancestors came from Africa, there is considerable ambiguity regarding the racial classification of peoples whose ancestors were European and Asian or African and Asian. Moreover, there does not appear to be popular consensus concerning the racial affiliation of people whose ancestors were African and European but who speak a language other than English. In New York, populations who speak Spanish are not usually referred to as belonging to the "Negro race" or to the "white race," but are simply designated as "Spanish," "Cuban," "Puerto Ricans," or "peoples of Puerto Rican descent." In many contexts, these appellations are used as if they were equivalent to the racial designations currently in use. Were the same people to speak only American English, they would be classed as Negro or as white, depending on the particular observer's perception of physical and behavioral "racial" cues.

Clearly, the popular racial typologies in America are not based on any competent genetic studies. It is also evident that observable phenotypical characteristics are often totally irrelevant in the assignment of individuals to the racial groups. There are Negroes who "can pass for white"; there are whites who "could pass for Negroes."

The popular American conceptions about race contrast sharply with those of contemporary Brazil, where descent plays a negligible role in establishing racial identity. Marvin Harris (12) has shown that full siblings whose phenotypes are markedly different are assigned to different racial categories. Harris's studies also indicate that more than forty racial categories are utilized in Brazil and that there are hundreds of racial terms constructed of combinations of these. In addition, there are alternative meanings for the same term, as well as a lack of consensus concerning the assignment of any particular term to a given individual (13). Moreover, Harris points out that there is "a high frequency of passing out to other categories in conformity with the achievement of socioeconomic success" (12). Phenotypical attributes such as skin color, hair form, and nose or mouth shape enter into Brazilian racial classifications, but no combination of these variants is predictive of the "race" to which a person will be assigned since socioeconomic

* In fact, it might be more accurate to say that it is known or demonstrable sub-Saharan African ancestry or "black African" ancestry which governs the assignment to the "Negro race," since the populations of North Africa are not usually termed Negro.

position is one important determinant of racial status.

In Japan, skin color does not necessarily enter into popular racial classifications. The Burakumin or "outcastes" are popularly believed to be racially distinct from ordinary Japanese. They were formerly termed Eta—a word written with the characters for "defilement abundant"—and were officially emancipated in 1871 but remain a minority group set apart from other Japanese by low socioeconomic status and by residential segregation.

The Eta are Japanese who descended from the lowest stratum in a hierarchical social system which existed in the earliest known period of Japanese history and was formalized by edict in the seventh century A.D. (14). At that time, the Imperial House created two major categories: the free and the base. Included in the latter category were peasants, certain artisan guilds, and slaves. By the tenth century, most of the formalized class distinctions had become meaningless; social differences between the free and the unfree were no longer observable, and most of the base guilds were free.

It was during this period that Buddhism became accepted throughout Japan, and the Buddhist beliefs fused with indigenous Shinto beliefs concerning the avoidance of impurity. According to Donoghue (14):

> The syncretic religious concepts that evolved associated the taking of life with ritual impurity, and the guilds whose livelihood depended upon animal slaughtering were physically and morally isolated from the "legitimate" society. The outcastes became known as Eta.

The Eta formed small enclaves on the outskirts of towns and villages, where they were joined by other marginal social groups such as beggars, criminals, vagabonds, and entertainers.

In Japan, some theories on the history of the outcastes suggest that they originated from a people different from the ancestors of the socially acceptable Japanese. One theory holds that the outcastes are descendants of the aboriginal inhabitants of the Japanese isles. Another theory maintains that they are descendants of Korean war captives brought to Japan in the late sixteenth century; a third considers the Eta to be the offspring of Negritoes of the Philippines (15).

Most Western scholars regard the outcastes as physically identical to other Japanese. However, in the 1920s and 1930s a number of Japanese scholars described the Eta as a distinct race, and today many laymen still regard the outcastes as racially distinct from other Japanese. The outcastes' "distinctive racial heritage" is allegedly manifest in their behavior and appearance. Outcastes are popularly considered to be dirty; they are likened to hoodlums and gangsters. They are said to be afflicted with venereal diseases, tuberculosis, and leprosy (14). They are said to have one rib bone missing, to have distorted sexual organs, and to have defective excretory systems. Since they are animals, dirt does not stick to their feet when they walk barefooted (16).

The data on popular racial classifications current in the United States, in Brazil, and in Japan indicate that any expedient set of physical and/or behavioral attributes may be taken as the basis for such classifications. In these and other popular racial taxonomies, there often is a fusion and/or confusion of behavioral and physical attributes, leading to the perpetuation of the notion of the inheritance of cultural characteristics.

The assignment of individuals to the various racial categories recognized in different societies is often based on perceived behavioral differences rather than on demonstrable physical differences. Even where physical differences exist between the "races" delineated, laymen usually make no attempt to ascertain the biological significance of these differences! Moreover, the physical and behavioral attributes which are perceived as characteristic of a group are usually "explained" as being racial in origin.

Despite the recognition by many scholars that popular racial classifications should not serve as a basis for scientific discussions of human variation and related topics, many scientific studies are based on these classifications. Moreover, many scholars provide support for these nonscientific classifications by stating or implying that the popularly and/or politically defined "races" can be distinguished on the basis of biologically relevant criteria.

"Scientific" justification for the classification of the Eta as a race was provided by Kikuchi Sanya, whose book on the outcastes was written "from an anthropological point of view." Ninomiya (17) summarizes Kikuchi's thesis as follows:

> There are many peculiarities of the *Eta*, such as (*a*) practice of eating meat when the Japanese proper despise it; (*b*) reddish tinge in eye color; (*c*) prominence of the cheek-bone; (*d*) non-Mongolian type of the eyes; (*e*) dolichocephalic head; (*f*) shortness of stature; and (*g*) shortness of the neck.

In the 1930s, a professor of anthropology at Tokyo Imperial University also was of the opinion that "the *Eta* are not of the Mongolian type," although he did not "make this as a definite conclusion" (17).

It is hardly necessary to document the fact that many scholars in the United States conduct research and write books which imply that the "white race" and the "Negro race" are genetically defined entities. It will suffice to point out that virtually all scholars who write about "race and intelligence" assume that the "races" which they study are distinguished on the basis of biologically relevant criteria. So accepted is this fact that most scholars engaged in such research never consider it necessary to justify their assignment of individuals to this or that "race" (18).

Even when scholars in the biological sciences devise or utilize racial classifications, these are generally no more than refinements of typologies used by laymen. Scientific racial typologies are usually based on presumptions about or intuitions regarding the distribution of genetic characteristics. The manifest bases for these typologies are variations in arbitrarily chosen phenotypical characteristics. Yet it is well known that the relationship between genotype and phenotype is not simple and that the effects of the operation of environmental forces on the phenotype are not genetically transmitted. Moreover, even when scientists make a serious attempt to base their racial typologies on genetic variants, they do not squarely face the problem that there should be some biologically relevant justification for the choice of the characters on whose variation the "races" are defined (19).

It cannot be expected that the difficulties inherent in the construction of racial classifications will be appreciated by laymen when these problems are not often acknowledged by the scientists themselves. Normally, the layman who reads the literature on race and racial groupings is justified in assuming that the existent typologies have been derived through the application of theories and methods current in disciplines concerned with the biological study of human variation. Since the scientific racial classifications which a layman finds in the literature are not too different from popular ones, he can be expected to feel justified in the maintenance of his views on race.

It is not surprising, therefore, that scientific discourses on race serve to buttress the popular belief that discrete racial groups exist among mankind or that scientific racial typologies serve to legitimize popular racial classifications. On the one hand, scientists often base their studies of "racial differences" on popularly and/or politically defined races. On the other hand, they often take popular racial classifications as a point of departure for the construction of their own typologies, which, on close examination, appear just as spurious as those utilized by laymen (20).

III

The literature on racial typologies of earlier historical periods in America further indicates that both scientific and popular racial classifications reflect prevailing sociopolitical conditions. Significant changes in the political status of some ethnic groups in America have led to reappraisals of their "racial" statuses and of the "racial" characteristics by which they were defined.

In contemporary America, there are a number of populations of European origin who comprise the "white race." Even though some laymen subdivide this race on the basis of the national origin or religious affiliation, most Americans agree that there is essentially one "white race." That scientists concur in this opinion is illustrated by the fact that no present-day study that proposes to compare races would compare Americans who came from Ireland with those who came from England. But this was not always the case. Barbara Solomon's book, *Ancestors and Immigrants* (21), which deals with racial ideologies in New England between the 1850s and 1920s, demonstrates that "white" people who are now regarded as members of one "race" were formerly divided into several "races." In the second half of the nineteenth century and the early decades of the twentieth century, various American scholars published works which divided and redivided peoples now termed white or Caucasian into the following "races": Anglo-Saxons, Celts, Teutons, Jews, and southern Europeans or "brownish races." Scandinavians were regarded as a branch of the Teutonic "race," and Teutons and Anglo-Saxons were regarded as cousins, "racially" speaking.

Between the 1830s and 1870s the industrial expansion of New England brought waves of immigrants from Europe to Boston and the surrounding areas. Most were from Ireland. In the early phases of immigration, the self-styled Brahmins, who comprised the New England aristocracy, decried the "racial inferiority" of these Irish immigrants. In the 1840s and 1850s many prominent New Englanders shared C. E. Norton's apprehensions about the "sudden influx of people so long misgoverned . . . [and] of a race foreign to our own" (22). Charles F. Adams, Jr. remarked that "the Irish race," being "quick of impulse, sympathetic, ignorant, and credulous . . . have as few elements in common with native New Englanders as one race of men well can have with another" (23).

By the 1870s, the Irish, representative of the so-called Celtic race, gained dominance in some service industries in Boston and nearby mill towns; by the 1880s, they wrested the political leadership of Boston from the old New England aristocracy. The political supremacy of the Brahmins having been challenged, various academicians from this aristocracy sought to prove that the increased influx of members of the Celtic and other "inferior races" undermined the chances for the survival of democratic institutions which were Teutonic in origin and transmitted "through the blood."

During the 1870s, Francis A. Walker, a noted social scientist who was to become a university president, was a leading spokesman for those who were alarmed by the rising power of the alien Celts. The census of 1880 confirmed Walker's suspicions that the birth rate among the urbanized immigrant populations was exceeding that of the native Anglo-Saxons, and he became obsessed by the "fecundity of the foreign elements in the United States." During the 1880s Walker wrote many articles on the evils of immigration and used his academic affiliations to appeal to younger scholars to support his thesis that the arival of foreigners in the United States had caused a "shock to the principle of population among the native element." By the end of the 1880s, "the happy ideal of assimilation, which [John] Fiske had spread over the land, disintegrated under Walker's cogent proofs, and, for old New Englanders, immigration became a matter of racial preservation" (24).

Support for New England raciology had come from academic circles in Europe. During the latter half of the nineteenth century one of the most influential books was *The Races of Men*, written in 1850 by Robert Knox, a professor of anatomy at the Edinburgh College of Surgeons, which proclaimed that all of civilization depended on race. To the Celts, Knox attributed the following characteristics: "furious fanaticism; a love of war and disorder; a hatred for order and patient industry; no accumulative habits; restless, treacherous, uncertain; [one need only] look at Ireland" (25). Knox saw the American Know-Nothing riots as a prelude to the inevitable conflict between Saxons and Celts. He said that "the war of race will some day shake the Union to its foundation. They never will mix—never commingle and unite" (25).

Edward A. Freeman, an Oxford historian, was another scholar who favored racial explanations of history. In 1881 when Freeman made a lecture tour of the United States, he proposed that "the best remedy for whatever is amiss in America would be if every Irishman should kill a Negro and be hanged for it" (26).

During the late nineteenth and early twentieth centuries, the appeals to limit European immigration were increasingly based on racial as well as economic arguments. The Immigration Restriction League of Boston, founded in 1894, was in the forefront of the battle to ensure that the Anglo-Saxon-Teutonic racial strains would not be overwhelmed by "Slav, Latin, and Asiatic races, historically downtrodden, atavistic, and stagnant" (27).

Solomon points out that historians, economists, sociologists, and physical scientists synthesized the earlier diffuse Teutonist sentiments into a pseudoscientific ideology of racial superiority. These academicians were influenced by the League's opinions; in turn, Brahmin restrictionist views were reinforced by the scholars' presentations. The Eugenics movement, which crystallized in America in the early twentieth century, argued that the influx of alien races had increased the rate of "insanity, imbecility, and feeblemindedness" in the population of the United States.

By the early twentieth century, however, less attention was being paid to the inferiority of the Celts than to that of the southeastern Europeans, who, according to the Eugenicists, "had hereditary passions which were unalterable, regardless of public schools and economic opportunities in the United States" (28). Restrictions on the immigration of these undesirables would be the initial step in the creation of a race of supermen in America.

The Anglo-Saxon, Teutonic, southern European, Jewish, and other "races" defined during this period of American history were considered immutable; the characteristics which distinguished them were endowed by heredity. As might be predicted, these "racial" characteristics were as often behavioral as physical. Despite the alleged immutability of these "races" and of the characteristics attributed to them, New Englanders did in fact change their evaluation of the so-called "races of Europe."

Between the 1830s and 1890s, the Celts were described as ignorant, shiftless, credulous, impulsive, and mechanically inept; they were inclined toward drinking and related crimes. By the 1890s, when the Irish were the political leaders of the hub of New England and large numbers of southern Europeans were coming to the United States, the Irish had become tolerated aliens. The shift in attitude toward the Celtic race reflected the change in the political situation. The Irish were said to have "a remarkable race trait of adaptability which explained the achievement of the more intelligent and prosperous of the Boston group." Moreover, the Irish "above all races [had] the mixture of ingenuity, firmness, human sympathy, comradeship, and daring that [made them] the amalgamator of races" (29).

That there were no proven biologically significant differences among the "races of Europe" did not prevent New Englanders from perceiving European immigrant populations as separate races. So-called racial differences were said to be manifest in life-styles; racial affiliation could be determined by listening to individuals speak or by hearing their names. In any case, even without perceptible clues, the relative backwardness of the immigrants was "proof" of their inferior intellectual capabilities and characters, both of which were reputedly determined by "racial" heritage.

IV

Solomon's *Ancestors and Immigrants*, Gossett's *Race: The History of an Idea in America*, Stanton's *The Leopard's Spots* (30), and Curtin's *Image of Africa* (31) provide abundant documentation for the statement that at various historical periods, racial typologies and/or ideologies have reflected prevailing sociopolitical conditions. Historically, both scientific and lay concepts of race have served to support the economic and political privileges of ruling groups who regarded themselves as superior by virtue of phylogenetic heritage rather than because of the accidents of culture history.

From the preceding discussion it should be apparent that popular racial classifications are based on a wide range of emotional, political, and other evaluative criteria that are not relevant to the biological study of human variation. The differences in popular racial typologies become apparent when one shifts in time or place from one society to another. Therefore, it is obvious that there can be no justification for the elevation of any popular racial classification to the status of an analytic system in science.

Studies which purport to demonstrate the genetic basis for this or that behavioral characteristic observed among persons who make up popularly defined races are essentially nonscientific and should be labeled as such. Hence, to presume to study the genetic basis for some behavioral attribute of the "Negro race" in America is to ignore the fundamental difficulty of defining that "race." It is entirely probable that any biogenetically significant division of Americans would include some groups comprised of *both* so-called Negroes and so-called whites. But to isolate such groups would violate the folk theory that there is a pure white race and a Negro race which includes some so-called racial hybrids.

In conclusion, it must be made clear that this paper is not aimed at the deprecation of the study of human variation. The directions for future research into the genetics of human variation have been indicated by various writers, including the contributors to the volume entitled *The Concept of Race*, edited by Ashley Montagu. The isolation of those genetic characters that constitute the most variable array of features in mankind, the determination of the characters that admit of biologically significant clusterings of breeding populations, the study of the relationship between genotype and phenotype, including the investigation of genetic characters as they are represented in different life stages of individuals—these are some of the problems which have to be pursued.

These problems can and should be studied without reference to race, which has never been and never will be a primarily biological concept. The history of the use of the race concept by scientists and laymen alike makes it apparent that race could probably never be accepted as a purely statistical concept. Race is a biopolitical concept, the continued use of which will serve only to obfuscate the problems entailed in the study of human variation. As Livingstone (32) has pointed out:

> Just as Galileo's measurements and experiments paved the way for Newton's laws of motion, which totally replaced the Aristotelian laws of motion concerned as they were with describing the nature of bodies and their "essences," our newer genetic knowledge and the measurement of gene frequencies will replace the studies on the nature or essence of race and the mathematical theory of population genetics will replace the Linnaean system of nomenclature.

Notes and References

1 This is the position taken by a number of contributors to this symposium. It is exemplified by Theodosius Dobzhansky in *Mankind Evolving* (New Haven, Yale University Press, 1965), 266–69. It also appears to be the view of William Boyd, *Genetics and the Races of Man* (Boston, Little, Brown and Co., 1950), and of C. S. Coon, S. M. Garn, and J. B. Birdsell in *Races* (Springfield, Ill., C. C. Thomas, Publisher, 1950).

2 This point of view is represented by a number of contributors to the volume *The Concept of Race*, edited by Ashley Montagu (New York, The Free Press, 1964). For critical examination of the theoretical and methodological problems involved in racial classifications, see especially the articles by Jean Hiernaux, "The Concept of Race and the Taxonomy of Mankind," 29–45; Frank B. Livingstone, "On the Nonexistence of Human Races," 46–60; Paul R. Ehrlich and Richard W. Holm, "A Biological View of Race," 153–79; and Nigel A. Barnicot, "Taxonomy and Variation in Modern Man," 180–227.

3 HIERNAUX, in *The Concept of Race*, 40.

4 See, for example, S. L. WASHBURN, "The Study of Race," in *The Concept of Race*, 242–60.

5 EHRLICH and HOLM, in *The Concept of Race*, 175; see also 154–55, 161–62, and 177–78.

6 HIERNAUX, in *The Concept of Race*, 41–42.

7 N. W. GILLHAM, "Geographic Variation and the Subspecies Concept in Butterflies," *Systematic Zoology*, 5 (1956), 110–20, quoted by Ehrlich and Holm, in *The Concept of Race*, 167.

8 LIVINGSTONE, in *The Concept of Race*, 56.

9 See THOMAS F. GOSSETT, *Race: The History of an Idea in America* (Dallas, Southern Methodist University Press, 1963), 37–39, 69–70, and 80.

10 *New York Times*, October 20, 1966, p. 21, reported that "Chinese-American public school children in Boston have been officially declared white by the School Committee ['the official city agency in charge of Boston's public schools'] in the latest phase of the controversy over racial imbalance in schools." One week later, it was reported that the Massachusetts State Board of Education had rejected the ruling of the Boston School Committee, and that Chinese-American children who had been classed as white would be reclassified as nonwhite. *New York Times*, October 27, 1966, p. 40.

11 MARVIN HARRIS, *Patterns of Race in the Americas* (New York, Walker and Co., 1964), 56.

12 MARVIN HARRIS, "Race," in *International Encyclopedia of the Social Sciences*, 1968. 13:263–68.

13 MARVIN HARRIS and RUTH MARTINEZ, "Referential Ambiguity in the Calculus of Brazilian Racial Identity," unpublished manuscript.

14 This account of the history of the Eta is based upon JOHN DONOGHUE, "An Eta Community in Japan: The Social Persistence of Outcaste Groups," *American Anthropologist*, 59 (1957), 1000–17. For additional data on this group, see GEORGE DE VOS and HIROSHI WAGATSUMA, eds., *Japan's Invisible Race: Caste in Culture and Personality* (Berkeley, The University of California Press, 1966).

15 See SHIGEAKI NINOMIYA, "An Inquiry Concerning the Origin, Development, and Present Situation of the *Eta* in Relation to the History of Social Classes in Japan," *Transactions of the Asiatic Society of Japan*, Second series, Vol. 10 (1933), 47–154.

16 KIKUCHI SANYA, *Eta-Zoku ni Kansuru Kenkyù* (A Study Concerning the *Eta* Race, Tokyo, 1923), cited in Ninomiya, *An Inquiry*, 56.

17 NINOMIYA, *An Inquiry*, 56.

18 This is exemplified by the comments of AUDREY M. SHUEY in her book, *The Testing of Negro Intelligence* (Lynchburg, Va., J. P. Bell Co., 1958), and by comments of the authors whose studies are reviewed by Shuey.

19 For a discussion of the methodological problems involved here, see HIERNAUX, 30–40 and EHRLICH and HOLM, 160–61 and 163–64 in *The Concept of Race*.

20 For a sample of scientific racial typologies, see those summarized in Dobzhansky, *Mankind Evolving*, 256–66.

21 BARBARA SOLOMON, *Ancestors and Immigrants* (Cambridge, Harvard University Press, 1956).

22 CHARLES ELIOT NORTON, "Goldwin Smith," *North American Review*, 205 (1864), 536, quoted in Solomon, *Ancestors*, 12.

23 CHARLES FRANCIS ADAMS, *Three Episodes of Massachusetts History* (Boston, Houghton, Mifflin and Co., 1892), Vol. II, 957, quoted in Solomon, *Ancestors*, 29.

24 SOLOMON, *Ancestors*, 69–79.

25 ROBERT KNOX, *The Races of Men* (Philadelphia, 1850), 26–27 and 177, quoted in Gossett, *Race*, 96.

26 EDWARD A. FREEMAN, *Lectures to American Audiences* (Philadelphia, 1882), quoted in Gossett, *Race*, 109.

27 SOLOMON, *Ancestors*, 111.

28 *Ibid.*, 151.

29 *Ibid.*, 154.

30 WILLIAM STANTON, *The Leopard's Spots* (Chicago, University of Chicago Press, 1960).

31 PHILIP D. CURTIN, *The Image of Africa* (Madison, University of Wisconsin Press, 1964).

32 LIVINGSTONE, in *The Concept of Race*, 55.

10

THE POPULATION AS A UNIT OF RESEARCH

NIGEL A. BARNICOT

Although Marshall, in the previous selection (9), concluded by identifying race as a biopolitical concept likely to serve only as a deterrent to meaningful scientific studies of human variation, she did not by any means wish to deny the utility of truly scientific studies of human variability. This leads quite neatly to the next selection, which concerns itself precisely with such researches. One of the first things that you will note it does is remove the concept and the word "race" from the discussion. Settling down to the much more manageable term "population," Barnicot sketches the kinds of productive studies we may look forward to, as well as some that are already under way.

▼△▼△▼

The Population as a Unit for Research

It is generally agreed that all living men belong to a single species, *Homo sapiens;* but this species, like most animal ones, is not geographically uniform but is differentiated into local variant populations which are interfertile and not sharply distinguishable from each other. During the last two centuries many classifications of mankind into races, sub-races, and other categories have been devised, and most of them have been based on a few easily visible external features such as skin colour, head shape, and hair form. Certain Asiatic peoples, for example, are grouped together in the Mongoloid race, which is characterized by lightly pigmented skin, straight hair, a rounded skull, a flat face with prominent malar bones, and a distinctive conformation of the eye region. In some peoples of south-east Asia and in American Indians, however, some of these diagnostic features are infrequent or absent while others are developed only to a slight extent in the individual. Such groups do not fit comfortably into so simple a classificatory scheme.

Although these formal classifications express certain genuine features of human variation they do so in an artificial and even misleading manner. They tend to give the impression that the human species is naturally partitioned into discrete, discontinuous groups, whereas in studying the geographical distribution of physical characters we commonly find gradual changes as we pass from one region to another rather than sharp boundaries and abrupt transitions. A mere list of diagnostic characters also tends to obscure the fact that all populations are very variable. In the case of quantitative characters such as stature or skin colour, which can be measured on a continuous scale, there is often much overlapping between the ranges of variation of different populations and the distinctions between them are most appropriately described in statistical terms as differences in the average values. In dealing with a discrete attribute, such as a particular blood-group variant, it is often found that it is present in many populations but that they differ in the frequency of its occurrence. The essentially statistical nature of many population differences means that to assign an individual to one group or another is often a matter of probability. It is true that if we select the most contrasted populations for comparison there may be little or no doubt in assigning each person to his appropriate group, but in many instances sorting would be much less certain.

As for the word 'race' itself, it has had a stormy and often disreputable career, and many

SOURCE: *Human Biology: An Introduction to Human Evolution, Variation and Growth,* G. A. Harrison, J. S. Weiner, J. M. Tanner, and N. A. Barnicot. New York: Oxford University Press, 1964. pp. 191–96. Reprinted by permission of The Clarendon Press, Oxford.

anthropologists and human geneticists prefer to avoid it. In zoology it is sometimes used to denote sub-specific groups, but even here its application is not clearly defined. It is a term which carries a strong implication that the differences in question are genetical, but this is sometimes not explicitly stated and often in fact not known. In the human context biological and cultural differences, whether political, linguistic, or religious, are often referred to indiscriminately as 'racial', and this leads to misunderstanding and confusion; it is an easy step to the fallacious view that associated differences of physique and culture have the same causes. In its worst manifestations the word is associated with semi-mystical 'racist' doctrines which assert the innate superiority of certain peoples and seek to justify discrimination and oppression.

In discussing group variation in man we prefer to use the word 'population' even at the risk of monotony. It is conveniently neutral, not in itself specifying or implying how the group is distinguished. In practice the members of a population which we wish to study biologically may live in a particular region, speak a certain language, form a political unit such as a nation or tribe, constitute a distinct social class, or share a common religious faith. Naturally, in many instances, these and other criteria which might be used are not mutually exclusive. As biologists we are often interested in so-called 'genetic isolates', the members of which are more likely to mate with one another than with outsiders. Both social and geographical factors may contribute to the formation and maintenance of such groups. One problem in field research is to collect a population sample in the way best fitted to the work in hand, and this will generally require an adequate knowledge of the way a society is organized. The aim should be to state clearly the criteria on which sampling was based so that the identity of the material is established with the least possible ambiguity. For some purposes it might suffice to label a sample 'Indian' or 'Hindu', but in the long run it is likely to be more useful to say exactly where the subjects came from and to which of the many Indian communities and caste-groups they belonged.

Aims of Comparative Population Studies

A great deal of comparative work on human populations has been, and still is, concerned with problems of historical relationship. The most direct evidence about the past comes from remains found by archaeologists, but, with rare exceptions, these consist only of skeletons and variations in the perishable soft parts, often so striking in living peoples, are irretrievably lost. The fossil evidence, outlined in earlier chapters, shows that at least by the close of the Pleistocene, some 10,000 years ago, *H. sapiens* was the sole remaining hominid species and had a wide geographical range extending to all the continental areas with the possible exception of Australia. There are indications of local variation, but the material is insufficient to trace the emergence of present-day forms in any detail. In studying subspecific variation abundant material is certainly needed so that the range of variability of each population can be assessed and proper statistical comparisons can be made. We may well be led astray if we attach too much importance to single specimens.

Living populations, on the other hand, offer plenty of material and a much wider range of physical characters for study. We may reasonably hope, following established principles of comparative anatomy, to infer something about their ancestral relationships by careful and detailed comparisons. Since the physical link between successive generations lies in the transmission of genes it is clear that the genetical composition of populations is crucial for this kind of analysis. The present pattern of phenotypic variation must be due in part to gene frequency changes brought about by the evolutionary processes already discussed in the previous chapter, and in part to the immediate effects of the environment acting on the individual. Many of the more obvious variations which have been studied by anthropologists have unfortunately proved too complex for detailed genetical analysis. We do not know, for example, whether dark-skinned populations in different parts of the world owe their pronounced pigmentation to the same genes, so that phenotypic resemblances in this respect may not necessarily indicate close genetic relationship. In the last few decades, however, an increasing number of simply inherited and relatively common variants have been discovered, and these are especially favourable for precise comparison of populations at the genetic level. Even so, it is always important to remember that the presence of a particular gene is inferred from an examination of the phenotype, and the precision of the identification depends on the available methods for detecting a specific effect to which this gene gives rise. It is a very common experience in genetics to find that what at first appeared to be a single inherited condition has proved on close scrutiny to include two or more different entities with somewhat different genetical antecedents. Any interpretation of the geographical distribution of a variant is likely to need modification if it is found not to be genetically identical in different regions.

In using genetic data from living populations for historical reconstructions it is generally assumed that the frequencies of the relevant genes have remained stable or at least have changed only slowly in relation to the timescale which is being considered. A segment of a population which split from a larger unit and migrated elsewhere might therefore be expected to retain in the pattern of its gene frequencies an indication of its origins. In the event of intermixture between two or more populations the gene frequencies to be expected in the hybrid group can be predicted if those of the parent populations are known and if the proportions in which they contributed to the cross can be specified. Although in some instances the genetic constitution of populations can plausibly be interpreted in terms of earlier migrations and intermixtures, these processes alone do not explain how initial differences of gene frequency were established. To account for these we must invoke the action of natural selection or of chance fluctuations of gene frequency.

It cannot be assumed that even characters like the blood groups, which on a superficial view may seem trivial and unlikely to influence fitness, are really selectively neutral. It is clear that in order to assess the value of various genes as historical markers we need to know much more about the rates of frequency change which can be expected under various conditions. Since gene frequencies can be changed by natural selection an initial resemblance between two populations, due to a common origin, might in time be obscured by the action of selective forces. Conversely, the occurrence of an identical gene in two or more populations might not be indicative of ancestral relationship since it might have arisen independently in each by mutation and have reached appreciable frequencies as a result of some selective advantage.

In principle the problem of the nature and magnitude of selective effects on various genes is open to investigation in populations as we find them today. It will not be easy, however, to detect very small differences of fitness which might none the less produce significant gene frequency changes if they were to operate for a sufficiently long period of time; nor must we forget that there may well have been selective agencies at work in the past which no longer act today and are lost to observation and experiment.

It would clearly be unwise to base far-reaching historical speculations on the distribution of any one genetical character. It is desirable to examine as many as possible so as to gain as wide a view as we can of overall resemblances and so as to check any hypothesis in the light of diverse evidence. The genes which have so far been characterized and used in this kind of research are a somewhat heterogeneous and arbitrary collection, in the discovery of which chance has often played a large part. There has probably been a tendency, however, to hit on ones associated with some deleterious effect, since these are more likely to be detected in medical investigations.

Archaeological or cultural evidence and sometimes historical records may be helpful in reaching an explanation of biological facts, but they must be used with due caution. Similarities of language or other aspects of culture can provide useful clues and suggest worthwhile lines of research, but they are not necessarily reliable guides in the interpretation of biological events. Isolation may result in the retention of archaic features of language but in some circumstances a language may die out and be replaced by an alien tongue. Political forces can weld biologically heterogeneous groups into new social units and customs and inventions can diffuse from one population to another with little or no biological intermixture. Written records, even when they are available, often lack the kind of detail which the biologist needs, while verbal traditions tend to merge rapidly into myth and fable.

It should not be assumed that the value of comparative population research rests solely on its contribution to historical problems. In genetical work the mapping of the geographical distribution of a gene is a natural extension of other studies; it may provide hints as to the selective forces which govern its frequency and these may not be negligible from the medical standpoint. By extending genetical investigations to a wide variety of populations new variants may be discovered which are too infrequent elsewhere to be readily detected or fully studied. If two or more genes are found to occur together in relatively high frequency in a certain region this may greatly facilitate work on linkage or on interaction between them.

Men live in a very wide range of habitats and are exposed to very varied climates, diets, and pathogenic factors. Controlled laboratory experiments on man are expensive and difficult to organize and therefore tend to be short in duration, and the only way to study the long-term effects of these influences may be by examining populations which are habitually exposed to them.

The comparative method is also important in epidemiology, a branch of medical science which deals with the factors affecting disease incidence in populations. Starting with the enumeration of cases and fluctuations of incidence over the years, it goes on to look for correlations with climate, diet, domestic crowding, and a host of other factors which may have a bearing on causation. From demography and population statistics it soon leads into many ramifications of human ecology in which the comparison of peoples living in contrasted conditions plays an important part.

11

STATEMENT ON RACE AND RACIAL PREJUDICE

The editor's work on this book was interrupted in the spring, 1972, when he was summoned to a courtroom to be a witness in the suit of a high school teacher who had been fired for bringing the question of racial equality into the classroom. One of the things that the school board had against the teacher was his use of an article of mine, "A Four-Letter Word That Hurts," which had appeared in the *Saturday Review* of October 2, 1965. It came as a distinct shock to a fairly shock-proof anthropologist to find that such a firing could still take place. I am rather embarrassed that I was shocked, for it indicates that I forgot my own XXIVth Law: you can't kill a bad idea.

Periodically, the United Nations Educational, Scientific, and Cultural Organization (UNESCO) tries to kill the bad idea of racism by assembling an international group of distinguished scientists from those fields, including both physical and cultural anthropology, that have most experience with the subject. Several such statements have been published through the years. What follows is the most recent.

▼△▼△▼

1. 'All men are born free and equal both in dignity and in rights.' This universally proclaimed democratic principle stands in jeopardy wherever political, economic, social and cultural inequalities affect human group relations. A particularly striking obstacle to the recognition of equal dignity for all is racism. Racism continues to haunt the world. As a major social phenomenon it requires the attention of all students of the sciences of man.

SOURCE: "Statement on Race and Racial Prejudice," *International Social Science Journal,* Vol. 20, No. 1 (1968): 93–97. Reprinted by permission of UNESCO.

2. Racism stultifies the development of those who suffer from it, perverts those who apply it, divides nations within themselves, aggravates international conflict and threatens world peace.

3. The conference of experts meeting in Paris in September 1967 agreed that racist doctrines lack any scientific basis whatsoever. It reaffirmed the propositions adopted by the international meeting held in Moscow in 1964 [1] which was called to re-examine the biological aspects of the statements on race and racial differences issued in 1950 and 1951.[2] In particular, it draws attention to the following points:

a] All men living today belong to the same species and descend from the same stock.

b] The division of the human species into 'races' is partly conventional and partly arbitrary and does not imply any hierarchy whatsoever. Many anthropologists stress the importance of human variations, but believe that 'racial' divisions have limited scientific interest and may even carry the risk of inviting abusive generalization.

c] Current biological knowledge does not permit us to impute cultural achievements to differences in genetic potential. Differences in the achievements of different peoples should be attributed solely to their cultural history. The peoples of the world today appear to possess equal biological potentialities for attaining any level of civilization.

Racism grossly falsifies the knowledge of human biology.

4. The human problems arising from so-called 'race' relations are social in origin rather than biological. A basic problem is racism, namely,

[1] See *International Social Science Journal,* Vol. XVII, No. 1, 1965, p. 157–61.

[2] See *International Social Science Bulletin,* Vol. II, No. 3, 1950 and Vol. III, No. 3, 1951.

anti-social beliefs and acts which are based on the fallacy that discriminatory intergroup relations are justifiable on biological grounds.

5. Groups commonly evaluate their characteristics in comparison with others. Racism falsely claims that there is a scientific basis for arranging groups hierarchically in terms of psychological and cultural characteristics that are immutable and innate. In this way it seeks to make existing differences appear inviolable as a means of permanently maintaining current relations between groups.

6. Faced with the exposure of the falsity of its biological doctrines, racism finds ever new stratagems for justifying the inequality of groups. It points to the fact that groups do not intermarry, a fact which follows, in part, from the divisions created by racism. It uses this fact to argue the thesis that this absence of intermarriage derives from differences of a biological order. Whenever it fails in its attempts to prove that the source of group differences lies in the biological field, it falls back upon justifications in terms of divine purpose, cultural differences, disparity of educational standards or some other doctrine which would serve to mask its continued racist beliefs. Thus, many of the problems which racism presents in the world today do not arise merely from its open manifestations, but from the activities of those who discriminate on racial grounds but are unwilling to acknowledge it.

7. Racism has historical roots. It has not been a universal phenomenon. Many contemporary societies and cultures show little trace of it. It was not evident for long periods in world history. Many forms of racism have arisen out of the conditions of conquest—as exemplified in the case of Indians in the New World—out of the justification of Negro slavery and its aftermath of racial inequality in the West, and out of the colonial relationship. Among other examples is that of anti-semitism, which has played a particular role in history, with Jews being the chosen scapegoat to take the blame for problems and crises met by many societies.

8. The anti-colonial revolution of the twentieth century has opened up new possibilities for eliminating the scourge of racism. In some formerly dependent countries, people formerly classified as inferior have for the first time obtained full political rights. Moreover, the participation of formerly dependent nations in international organizations in terms of equality has done much to undermine racism.

9. There are, however, some instances in certain societies in which groups, victims of racialistic practices, have themselves applied doctrines with racist implications in their struggle for freedom. Such an attitude is a secondary phenomenon, a reaction stemming from men's search for an identity which prior racist theory and racialistic practices denied them. None the less, the new forms of racist ideology, resulting from this prior exploitation, have no justification in biology. They are a product of a political struggle and have no scientific foundation.

10. In order to undermine racism it is not sufficient that biologists should expose its fallacies. It is also necessary that psychologists and sociologists should demonstrate its causes. The social structure is always an important factor. However, within the same social structure, there may be great individual variation in racialistic behaviour, associated with the personality of the individuals and their personal circumstances.

11. The committee of experts agreed on the following conclusions about the social causes of race prejudice:

a] Social and economic causes of racial prejudice are particularly observed in settled societies wherein are found conditions of great disparity of power and property, in certain urban areas where there have emerged ghettoes in which individuals are deprived of equal access to employment, housing, political participation, education, and the administration of justice, and in many societies where social and economic tasks which are deemed to be contrary to the ethics or beneath the dignity of its members are assigned to a group of different origins who are derided, blamed, and punished for taking on these tasks.

b] Individuals with certain personality troubles may be particularly inclined to adopt and manifest racial prejudices. Small groups, associations, and social movements of a certain kind sometimes preserve and transmit racial prejudices. The foundations of the prejudices lie, however, in the economic and social system of a society.

c] Racism tends to be cumulative. Discrimination deprives a group of equal treatment and presents that group as a problem. The group then tends to be blamed for its own condition, leading to further elaboration of racist theory.

12. The major techniques for coping with racism involve changing those social situations which give rise to prejudice, preventing the prejudiced from acting in accordance with their beliefs, and combating the false beliefs themselves.

13. It is recognized that the basically important changes in the social structure that may lead to the elimination of racial prejudice may require decisions of a political nature. It is also recognized, however, that certain agencies of enlightenment, such as education and other means of social and economic advancement, mass media, and law can be immediately and effectively mobilized for the elimination of racial prejudice.

14. The school and other instruments for social and economic progress can be one of the most effective agents for the achievement of broadened understanding and the fulfilment of the potentialities of man. They can equally much be used for the perpetuation of discrimination and inequality. It is therefore essential that the resources for education and for social and economic action of all nations be employed in two ways:

a] The schools should ensure that their curricula contain scientific understandings about race and human unity, and that invidious distinctions about peoples are not made in texts and classrooms.

b] (i) Because the skills to be gained in formal and vocational education become increasingly important with the processes of technological development, the resources of the schools and other resources should be fully available to all parts of the population with neither restriction nor discrimination.

(ii) Furthermore, in cases where, for historical reasons, certain groups have a lower average education and economic standing, it is the responsibility of the society to take corrective measures. These measures should ensure, so far as possible, that the limitations of poor environments are not passed on to the children.

In view of the importance of teachers in any educational programme, special attention should be given to their training. Teachers should be made conscious of the degree to which they reflect the prejudices which may be current in their society. They should be encouraged to avoid these prejudices.

15. Governmental units and other organizations concerned should give special attention to improving the housing situations and work opportunities available to victims of racism. This will not only counteract the effects of racism, but in itself can be a positive way of modifying racist attitudes and behaviour.

16. The media of mass communication are increasingly important in promoting knowledge and understanding, but their exact potentiality is not fully known. Continuing research into the social utilization of the media is needed in order to assess their influence in relation to formation of attitudes and behavioural patterns in the field of race prejudice and race discrimination. Because the mass media reach vast numbers of people at different educational and social levels, their role in encouraging or combating race prejudice can be crucial. Those who work in these media should maintain a positive approach to the promotion of understanding between groups and populations. Representation of peoples in stereotypes and holding them up to ridicule should be avoided. Attachment to news reports of racial designations which are not germane to the accounts should also be avoided.

17. Law is among the most important means of ensuring equality between individuals and one of the most effective means of fighting racism.

The Universal Declaration of Human Rights of 10 December 1948 and the related international agreements and conventions which have taken effect subsequently can contribute effectively, on both the national and international level, to the fight against any injustice of racist origin.

National legislation is a means of effectively outlawing racist propaganda and acts based upon racial discrimination. Moreover, the policy expressed in such legislation must bind not only the courts and judges charged with its enforcement, but also all agencies of government of whatever level or whatever character.

It is not claimed that legislation can immediately eliminate prejudice. Nevertheless, by being a means of protecting the victims of acts based upon prejudice, and by setting a moral example backed by the dignity of the courts, it can, in the long run, even change attitudes.

18. Ethnic groups which represent the object of some form of discrimination are sometimes accepted and tolerated by dominating groups at the cost of their having to abandon completely their cultural identity. It should be stressed that the effort of these ethnic groups to preserve their cultural values should be encouraged. They will thus be better able to contribute to the enrichment of the total culture of humanity.

19. Racial prejudice and discrimination in the world today arise from historical and social phenomena and falsely claim the sanction of science. It is, therefore, the responsibility of all biological and social scientists, philosophers, and others working in related disciplines, to ensure that the results of their research are not misused by those who wish to propagate racial prejudice and encourage discrimination.

This statement was unanimously adopted at the conclusion of a meeting of experts on race and racial prejudice which was held at Unesco House, Paris, from 18 to 26 September 1967. The experts attending the meeting were:

Dr. Muddathir Abdel Rahim, University of Khartoum, Sudan.
Professor Georges Balandier, University of Paris, France.
Professor Celio de Oliveira Borja, University of Guanabara, Brazil.
Professor Lloyd Braithwaite, University of the West Indies, Jamaica.
Professor Leonard Broom, University of Texas, United States of America.
Professor G. F. Debetz, Institute of Ethnography, Moscow, Union of Soviet Socialist Republics.
Professor J. Djordjevic, University of Belgrade, Yugoslavia.
Dean Clarence Clyde Ferguson, Howard University, United States of America.
Dr. Dharam P. Ghai, University College, Kenya.
Dr. Louis Guttman, Hebrew University, Israel.
Professor Jean Hiernaux, Free University of Brussels, Belgium.
Professor A. Kloskowska, University of Lodz, Poland.
Judge Kéba M'Baye, President of the Supreme Court, Senegal.
Professor John Rex, University of Durham, United Kingdom.
Professor Mariano R. Solveira, University of Havana, Cuba.
Professor Hisashi Suzuki, University of Tokyo, Japan.
Dr. Romila Thapar, University of Delhi, India.
Professor C. H. Waddington, University of Edinburgh, United Kingdom.

FOUR
CULTURE AND ANTHROPOLOGY

12

THE CONCEPT OF CULTURE AND THE SCIENCE OF MAN

MORTON H. FRIED

The split in the subject matter of anthropology, between biology and culture, has many theoretical and methodological consequences. Not the least of these is the periodic rediscovery by some bunch of anthropologists of the fact that human beings are animals and that biological factors play some role in their development and behavior. This is often followed by the rediscovery of culture and a recrudescence of fear of reductionism, the application of the explanatory devices developed for the understanding of lower levels of phenomena to higher levels, where such devices may indeed be inappropriate and lead to misunderstanding and confusion.

Although problems concerning levels of integration and reductionism appear at various points in anthropology, the classical and most important case has to do with the distinction between organic and superorganic realms. The former applies to biology and the latter to culture. Attempts to explain cultural phenomena in terms of biological generalizations are therefore reductionist. Reductionism is a scientific tool, a part of method, and by itself neither good nor bad. Indeed, to some extent reductionistic explanation is a major goal of science. When carried out properly it yields explanations of great use and elegance. New fields of investigation can take shape around such reductionistic goals, as is the case, for example, in biochemistry, or perhaps more clearly in biophysics. The existence and significance of such combined areas of research does not escape the anthropologist specializing in culture. It helps the anthropologist recognize that understanding is a product of many approaches and that synthetic approaches may help solve problems of culture too.

We keep on referring to culture and may well identify it as the single most pivotal concept in the repertoire of anthropology. It is essential to make clear exactly what we mean by it and that is the function of this brief selection from one of the editor's own works. We will encounter the culture concept at other junctures in the pages that follow, often in much more complex settings and sometimes in association with somewhat contentious theories. It is interesting to note that all anthropologists, including those specializing in human biology and other aspects of physical anthropology, concern themselves with culture and are alert to the influence emanating from it. As cultural anthropologists pay heed to underlying biological factors that condition culture, so physical anthropologists look to culture as a source of conditions changing selection pressures and other mechanisms of evolution.

A final introductory comment: the use of the phrase "the science of man" in the title of this selection can surely not pass without notice. It is quite appropriate, indeed necessary, for anthropologists to worry about the things that language sets up for a culture. For example, the use of a great number of vocabulary items that in normal communication convey a notion of maleness in contradistinction to femaleness does say something about a culture. On the other hand, there is great weight of tradition and sometimes a lack of clearly established alternatives—in other words, an active culture reinforcing and perpetuating conventional usage—so that even those who would have it otherwise are pressured into some degree of conformity. Against this background I would like once again to repeat David Hume's comment of about two centuries ago, that in using the generic term "man," I refer to "all men, both male and female."

▼△▼△▼

It is readily demonstrated that, behaviorally, man displays a level of complexity quantitatively so different from other animals that it is necessary for simple efficiency to set his behavior apart qualitatively. This has been done conventionally for about a century through the formal use of the concept of culture. Yet the use of the culture concept has been jeopardized in recent years by growth of knowledge. As ethologists have contributed more accurate

---

SOURCE: *The Study of Anthropology*, Copyright © 1972 by Thomas Y. Crowell Co., Inc. Chapter 1, pp. 7–11. Reprinted by permission.

and sophisticated observations, it has become evident that much larger portions of the behavioral repertories of many animals are composed of learned action sequences than previously were thought possible. Conversely, some anthropologists have been able to throw into doubt the degree to which formal and even informal social rules govern human behavior. Since many anthropologists tend to place such rules at the very core of their definition of culture, the logical structures they have erected now display certain weaknesses. I argue, however, that these threats to the concept of culture necessitate its refinement; they do not require us to throw it away.

The problem can be resolved, it seems to me, by distinguishing three different kinds of learning processes. The first is virtually coterminous with life. Almost all living things known to us can be shown to acquire new behavioral responses through experience; hence, the simplest and most widespread form of learning is *situational.* An organism encounters a novel situation and behaves in a novel way (although the novelty may be tiny indeed). When the novel situation recurs, so does the new behavior; the organism has learned. The analytically significant aspect of situational learning is that it is exclusive to the organism experiencing the stimulus of the new situation; furthermore, the situation-stimulus must be encountered directly. It follows that situational learning is nontransferable—it cannot be communicated. The sole contrary possibility is that the novel response is somehow recorded in the genetic matter of the organism and thus is passed on to the descendants of the initiating organism through purely biogenetic means. The degree to which such a process operates, indeed, whether such a process truly exists, is not yet known for sure but is the subject of continuing debate. There is no question of the importance of situational learning among all the more complex animals, including man. In the course of individual isolated play, human infants and children make innumerable homely discoveries leading to greater or lesser changes in their behavioral repertory. Adults continue to learn this way throughout their lives and our culture has taken formal notice of this; we often say, "Experience is the best teacher." It may not in fact be "best," but it is very important.

Simple organisms display no means of learning other than situational, but more complex animals have a second process, *social learning.* Basically, this is simply the act of imitation. One animal observes another encountering a stimulus and emitting an appropriate behavioral response and adds the new behavioral item to its own repertory. The literature of ethology is becoming richer in carefully documented sequences of this kind. Analytically, the crucial aspect of this kind of learning is that its possibility for transmission is limited and strictly controlled by the real and immediate presence of the concrete stimulus and the equally concrete response. Any variation or substitution whatsoever, and this kind of learning will not take place. Once again, it is clear that this kind of learning is of inestimable importance to human beings. A major portion of the learning of children derives from imitative actions in social settings; such learning continues throughout the lifetime of all of us. Despite its importance, however, social learning takes second place to the only type of learning process that, as far as we know, makes massive cultural activity possible, that of *symbolic learning.*

In Leslie A. White's neat culture-oriented definition, the symbol is something without implicit meaning that is made to represent something else. Within the curious concatenation of sounds there is no reason why I am represented by the phonemic formula *mɔ:tn frid.* It just so happens that my society dictated that my "last name," or "family name," should be that carried by my father; while, for reasons never made clear to me, my parents gave me Morton as a personal name. There is no more inevitable connection between a certain large carnivorous quadruped and the word *tiger*, or our most adjacent star and the designation *sun*. There is no reason why green shouldn't mean stop, and red, go. The analytical significance of this remarkable ability to make some things represent completely different other things lies in its transformation of the learning process as it is completely freed of dependence upon the key situation. As we have seen, both situational and social learning require the real, physical presence of the original stimulus, reaction to which is the essence of the learning process. But in symbolic learning, the key situation is represented by something else, usually by a string of sounds or even by visual representations of those sounds. You, of course, are at this very second looking at precisely such symbols, and you are engaged in symbolic learning.

Three correlates of symbolic learning must be mentioned, although they are implicit, perhaps even obvious, in the previous discussion. First, symbols are indefinitely cumulative. Hence the learning process based upon them is of virtually unlimited flexibility, due to the endless possibilities of combining and recombining each and every individual element in the system. Second, combinations and recombinations do not merely repeat old situations but are capable of generating new ones. Symbolic learning makes it possible for human beings to learn how to go to the moon before they can actually go there. Such a feat is absolutely impossible when learning is of only the situational or social kind. Third, and most obvious of all, symbolic learning is not only capable of communication, of transmission of information, but can exist only in the presence of communication.

What emerges from the process of symbolic learning is a behavior so rich as to make its recording a matter of despair. Primate ethologists find the behavior of animals quite complex and the job of observation extremely rigorous. The animals stop and go and move unexpectedly in unpredictable directions. They interact and break off, enter combinations, form cliques and alliances. Behavior changes with age and varies with sex and social rank. For all of this, the behavior of the most complexly acting primates in the most complexly organized primate society is of another, incomparably simpler, order compared with that of the humans living in the simplest cultures ever studied. Such a human society has a kinship terminology with concomitant behavioral distinctions. It has a technology with a variety of implements and weapons, and knowledge of their manufacture and differential use. It has an exchange system that lacks even a rudimentary precursor on the simpler primate level. Beyond the kinship system, it has a means of socially categorizing all people ever encountered, and without necessarily regarding all aliens as enemies or worse. It also has an ideology that includes notions about the meaning of life and death and the place of human beings in the world, probably also deals with the supernatural, and provides concepts of proper conduct.

As cultures have grown in complexity, so there has developed increasing elaboration of different institutional sectors. Though these continue to overlap in life, they can and must be distinguished to facilitate their analysis. So far has separation of institutional complexes gone that special fields of knowledge, disciplines, have long since appeared merely for their separate study. The kind of specialization implied in even the most partial list of disciplines dealing directly with human behavior and its products—linguistics, sociology, economics, history, political science, mathematics, engineering, literature, art, medicine, and law, merely to scratch the surface—is inconceivable in dealing with the behavior of any other known species, not because the student is so closely identified with his subject but because only human behavior has the complexity requiring such an elaborate division of labor for its proper study.

This matter of the qualitative gap between

the behavior of cultured and noncultured animals can be put another way. Cultured animals are bound by all biological laws, but no merely biological description of a cultured animal, no matter how thorough and complete, can encapsulate its range of possible behaviors. As we well know, technology is the means whereby biological incapacities of culture bearers are redressed. For example, having no biological means of flight, a cultured species can develop mechanical substitutes which rival and exceed the efficiency of biologically evolved features. Such a species can also develop and perfect life-support systems which enable it to conform to all applicable biological laws and rules under extraordinary circumstances: to breathe an artificial atmosphere where no natural one exists, to provide nutrients where none are otherwise available, to create a life-sustaining temperature in the presence of incredible cold or fantastic heat—these are some of the adaptations that can be provided by culture, enabling a bioform to exist far beyond its "natural" range.

This means that to a degree not possible with man, the behavior of other animals can, by available knowledge and techniques, be understood and accounted for on the biological level. Comparable reduction of human behavior, which is to say cultural behavior, to biological laws and rules is not possible within the framework of presently available knowledge. That it may become possible to engage in complete reductionism on such a scale is theoretically and methodologically improbable. Conversely, it must be pointed out that some reductionism is both possible and desirable. For example, analysis of culture must always be informed with knowledge of the biological setting of the cultural behavior. [A few brief and gross illustrations: no understanding of human social organization is possible without comprehension of sexual reproduction; no useful picture of economic institutions can be constructed without recognition of biological dependence on access to certain life essentials, such as food and water; no culturally structured society can be adequately comprehended without the inclusion of such biological phenomena as birth and death, growth, maturation, health and disease, although we are now deeply aware that all of these fundamentally biological processes respond to cultural factors.] Growing realization of the need for simultaneous study of biological and cultural factors in human ethology is a major factor in the recent revitalization of the field of physical anthropology, which, like some ruin-dotted desert given intensive irrigation, has begun to bloom with fascinating and important intellectual contributions. But this pious recognition of the desirability of simultaneous study of biological and cultural aspects of human ethology returns us to the dilemma we began with. The cultural aspects of that ethology are too numerous to enable anthropology to become simply an extension of biology. Anthropology, then, is placed by its fundamental nature in the difficult position of straddling a number of major disciplines pointed in different directions.

13

THE CONCEPT OF CULTURE AND THE CULTURE OF POVERTY

ELEANOR BURKE LEACOCK

The culture concept has been and remains the pivot of anthropological analysis in all its subdisciplinary variations. As a consequence, the problems of defining and analyzing culture have provided the substance of complete volumes, such as Kroeber and Kluckhohn's *Culture: A Critical Review of Concepts and Definitions* (1952).

One of the main components of most technically competent views of culture has been the careful separation of biologically set behavior from that which has a predominantly symbolic milieu. That is to say, cultural behavior is recognized as having minimal genetic coordinates, being maximally dependent upon learning, particularly on learning through symbolic means. The culture concept, therefore, seems on *a priori* grounds to be constituted in opposition to reductionistic theories of human behavior such as necessarily characterize all forms of racist thought. This is because the latter assume that certain behavioral patterns or even certain tendencies are likely to appear in greater frequency in certain races because of the biological composition of the population. As the reader must know, positions such as these have been used in the political history of our own country; the most convenient example is to justify slavery, and when that was abolished, to justify the continued systematic mistreatment, exploitation, and abuse of Black people and other ethnic minorities.

A growing number of citizens in our country, especially among the young, now seem ready to cast off some of the shackles of racist thought. This is particularly the case with regard to "mark of Cain" theories of genetic inferiority. Ironically, the same effects are now being achieved via theories of cultural inferiority.

Racism is not simply the product of erroneous thought; both are produced by something else, namely the conditions of society at particular times and in particular places. When the conditions are changed, so too will change all dependent phenomena. Meanwhile, however, it may hasten such changes to know clearly what the roots of social phenomena are. At the same time it is advantageous to expose faulty reasoning and baseless social myths. That is why we turn to the next article in which Eleanor Leacock sums up some of the main components of the theory of permanent cultural deprivation and its analogs, and with abundant evidence and sure logic exposes the shortcomings of these widespread and unfortunately influential ideas.

The Culture Concept

The special contribution that the science of anthropology has made to the study of man has been to clarify the enormous significance of "enculturation," or socialization, as the process whereby a group's characteristic attitudes, behaviors, and talents are passed on to the young. The detailed study of man and his many lifeways has led to the recognition that it is the cultural—the historically developed and traditionally accepted—attitudes and standards for behavior of a society which are transmitted to children, rather than genetic determinants of such attitudes and behaviors. The study of human infants and of animal societies has shown that man's biological inheritance, his "human nature," involves not only a high degree of intelligence, but also a strong emphasis on *sociality,* or the predisposition to learn and accept the behaviors and share the concerns that make a person an accepted part of his group.

Sociologists and social psychologists have adopted the culture concept from anthropology

SOURCE: *The Culture of Poverty: A Critique,* Eleanor Leacock (ed.). New York: Simon & Schuster, Inc. 1971. pp. 9–37. Introduction. Reprinted by permission of the publisher and the author.

as helpful in revealing the ways in which social conditions (instead of innate propensities) lead to differences in group behavior. It is a bitter irony, therefore, that the concept of culture is now being widely applied in such a form as to be almost as pernicious in its application as biological determinist and racist views have been in the past. As an extreme example, consider the use of the term "dregs-culture" in a book on *Social Issues in Public Education.* The author, John A. Bartky, refers to the Chicago ghetto as "dregs areas" where Southern urban leaders or farm hands "contribute the worst of the cultural values they have brought with them to . . . dregs cultures, and soon acquire the most vicious of their values." Bartky continues with such statements as "The dregs-culture child, if he is old enough, is probably being cared for by his second father and third mother" and "is inculcated with a race consciousness that is likely to get him into difficulties." Crime is so rampant in "dregs-culture communities" that the law must work "fast and ruthlessly," and the "policeman must often be judge, prosecutor, and punisher." The storefront church, rather than being something of a fraternal organization and community center, is to Bartky a "wild cat church," which "is more of an amusement than . . . a moral influence." Teachers in the "Negro dregs-culture schools" are frustrated in their attempts to teach by such "cultural considerations." In sum:

> In the dregs-culture community we find the Negro philosophy of life is quite different from that of the middle-class white man or Negro. He accepts, with or without resistance, the fact that he is barred from many material successes, and as a result material values are paramount for him. He refuses to encourage his children to study because the advantages to be gained from study are too remote. We call him improvident, but in reality he is merely a fatalist . . . [Bartky, 1963:135–41.]

Here the term "culture" is used as a thin veil for the expression of the most vulgar stereotypes about the experience of black Americans, the vast majority of whom are poor. (Bartky exonerates the "very few" Negroes in Chicago who are "well-to-do fugitives from the restrictions of Southern culture" from participation in "dregs-culture.") No anthropologist would countenance such views as even partially describing ghetto culture. However, some of the writings by anthropologists and other behavioral scientists, that deal with concepts as "lower-class culture," "cultural deprivation," and the popular "culture of poverty," have contributed to distorted characterizations of the poor, and especially the black poor. The fact is that, through the "culture of poverty" and similar notions, the nineteenth-century argument that the poor are poor through their own lack of ability and initiative, has reentered the scene in a new form, well decked out with scientific jargon. . . . The concern of the social scientists and educators who discuss their own research and experience in the pages that follow is to correct the misconceptions that support such a view.

The major assumption made by many "culture of poverty" theorists is that a virtually autonomous subculture exists among the poor, one which is self-perpetuating and self-defeating. This subculture, it is argued, involves a sense of resignation or fatalism and an inability to put off the satisfaction of immediate desires in order to plan for the future. These characteristics are linked with low educational motivation and inadequate preparation for an occupation—factors that perpetuate unemployment, poverty and despair. For example, Oscar Lewis makes a statement to this effect:

> The culture of poverty is not only an adaptation to a set of objective conditions of the larger society. Once it comes into existence it tends to perpetuate itself from generation to generation because of its effect on the children. By the time slum children are age six or seven they have usually absorbed the basic values and attitudes of their subculture and are not psychologically geared to take full advantage of changing conditions or increased opportunities which may occur in their lifetime. [Lewis, 1966:xlv.]

Along similar lines, the position taken by Daniel P. Moynihan in his report *The Negro Family: The Case for National Action* was that the "tangle of pathology" he described as characterizing the Negro community was "capable of perpetuating itself without assistance from the white world." Its basis was to be found in the Negro family, which, "once or twice removed, . . . will be found to be the principal source of most of the aberrant, inadequate, or antisocial behavior that did not establish, but now serves to perpetuate the cycle of poverty and deprivation" (Moynihan, 1965:30, 47).

Culturally established standards for behavior and goals for achievement—often loosely referred to as "values"—can be remarkably persistent. For example, Indian groups have for generations maintained their own attitudes about the proper and desirable way children should relate to adults. And in our cities we observe the sense of identity and cultural distinctiveness possessed by many national groups who refuse to be entirely "melted" away. Rolland Wright (1971) suggests in discussing the "stranger" mentality of the urbanized industrialized world that some of the attitudes ascribed to a so-called culture of poverty are attitudes which stem not from poverty, but from the more familial traditions of Mexican Americans, American Indians, American blacks, and rural Europeans.

On the whole, however, those cultural traditions that are valued and kept alive by precept and example are either distorted or ignored by culture of poverty theorists. Instead, there is a focus on traits that contribute to a failure to live up to presumed "middle-class" ideals. For instance, while culture-of-poverty theory stresses the "tangle of pathology" of the black ghetto and its relation to "lower-class values," black America has its own concept of its values, as connoted, for example, by the term "soul." "Soul is the essence of blackness," stated Professor C. Eric Lincoln in his address at the founding of a new Black Academy of Arts and Letters. "If black is beautiful, it is soul that makes it so." The term embodies a positive assertion of a common identity, history and tradition. It suggests, among other things, a sense of life and vitality and a feeling of distinctiveness from white society that is viewed as inhumanly cold and impersonal in its competitiveness and assertion of superiority.

Not only does poverty-culture theory focus on a negative, distorted and truncated view of a cultural whole, but it also implies an untenable view of the process whereby cultural traits are evolved and transmitted. At first glance, the passing down of a "poverty culture" along family lines may seem to involve a process similar to the preservation of somewhat separate traditions among different groups in the larger society. However, some social scientists and educators have presented quite a different view of the culture process and of the relations among individual personality, culturally patterned belief systems, and historically evolving social and economic structures. These differences pertain to assumptions in three intricately related areas: (1) child development, (2) the effect of culture on individual personality, and (3) the effect in turn that individual personalities *in toto* have on the further development of culture.

1. Developmental Stages and the Culture of Poverty. Culture-of-poverty theory assumes a person's "value-attitude system" and response pattern to be virtually set by the age of six or seven. Discussions of the ill effects of poverty culture on children generally assume that what happens prior to school entry is more important than what happens later. Few would argue that some of what we refer to as an individual's "personality" takes shape in the early years, and even in the early months. And few would argue that the particular way each individual, with some given but vaguely defined propensities, organizes his life experience and internalizes it as a network of patterns for thinking about and relating to other people, to the world around him, and to himself becomes increasingly well established over time and increasingly more difficult to change. But to say or imply that *values* and *motivations* are set by six or seven flies in the face of findings in developmental psychology. For example, Jerome Kagan enumerates the profound developments which take place in our society between the ages of six and ten, and which involve the conscious definition by children of attitudes about relations with peers, about intellectual mastery and rational thought, and about sexual identification and sex-role behavior (Kagan and Moss, 1962).

2. *The Effect of Culture on Individual Personality.* Poverty-culture theory generally implies that culture is a mold which produces a uniform set of dominant characteristics in those growing up under its influence. The match between culturally prescribed behavior and individual personality is thereby exaggerated and an unwarranted homogeneity of both is assumed. To some extent this problem stems from early writings on culture and personality, such as Ruth Benedict's *Patterns of Culture.* The central point Benedict made was that cultures do not draw equally upon the wide arc of potential human behavior, but select different aspects for particular emphasis and elaboration. Benedict made an important contribution in demonstrating the plasticity of man's nature, and the variety of cultural courses mankind has taken. However, individual behavioral styles do not simply mirror dominant cultural goals. Cultural norms do not exist outside man's living history, and they involve conflicting and contradictory goals and values, from which people choose, and which allow for change and development.

Furthermore, individuals may either passively accept their cultural environment or actively seek to develop or change some part of it, and they will exhibit a wide variety of styles in the way they do either one. C. W. M. Hart commented on the variety of personalities to be found even within a small and culturally homogeneous band of Australian aborigines. He wrote that, while an individual will follow a cultural course, he will follow it "cheerfully or sourly, silently or garrulously, in a relaxed manner or a tense manner, like a leader or like a follower, with his eye on the gallery or regardless of the world's opinion" (Hart, 1954:259). As a matter of fact, the earlier work of Oscar Lewis (1961) explicitly documented the diversity of responses to poverty that he found within a single Mexican family. In a critique of personality and culture writings, Anthony F. C. Wallace notes that the direction of much contemporary research in this area is away from a view of culture as producing motivational uniformity. Wallace proposes that a more productive approach to culture would be to view it "as a mechanism for the organization of a diversity of individual psychological differences within cultural boundaries," a diversity so great that "the analytical problem would be the elucidation of the processes of the organization of diversity rather than the mechanism of inducing a supposed uniformity" (Wallace, 1962:4).

Perhaps an even more important drawback to poverty-culture theory than the variety of responses individuals make within a given cultural setting is the lack of internal consistency within any one person. The ambivalence of conflicting desires is constantly at play in the choices and decisions a person makes, the results of which then become incorporated into his ongoing development. The powerlessness of the poor is clearly undermining, but contemporary events offer ample evidence of the new energy which can be released when steps are taken for a redress of grievance. Interviews with black high-school youths, some from extremely poor homes, who were taking part in a school boycott gave testimony of the exhilaration they experienced when doing something together toward improving the situation they had found so demoralizing (Fuchs, 1966).

3. *The Effect of Individual Personalities on Culture.* The third failing of poverty-culture theory lies in the closed-circle relationship between the individual and society that it implies.

Often implicit, rather than explicitly stated, the assumption is that childhood experiences in the family, which have become encapsulated in the personality, are somehow projected into the institutional structures that pattern adult behavior and beliefs. Thus, social-economic organization, technological developments, and unresolved conflicts within and among institutional structures with which the individual must cope if he is to live are not taken into account as exerting a constant and pervasive influence on the culture patterns that define adult behavior. Shortcomings in this static view of culture as perpetuating itself through the medium of "group personality" were not quite so obvious when the concept was applied to self-contained primitive societies in which change appeared to be relatively slow and tradition strong. Furthermore, anthropologists studied such societies after their autonomy had been destroyed by Western colonialism, and it was difficult to reconstruct the internal processes of change that were evidenced by the archeological remains of their earlier histories. However, such a nondynamic and "psychological reductionist" view of the individual in society as the above is clearly absurd, given the contemporary world of accelerated change and conflict, and virtually instantaneous worldwide communication and cross-cultural influence. . . .

In my own study of second- and fifth-grade classrooms in city schools, I observed the extent to which teacher attitudes and practices varied according to the children's home and backgrounds, black and white, middle and lower income, and I documented the active role the school plays in socializing the young for the occupational roles (including that of unemployment) they are expected to fill as adults (Leacock, 1969). This is obviously not a matter of conscious connivance. It follows from the way institutional structures in a society mesh and reinforce one another, and the way individuals learn the rationales that make sense of their behavior in given settings. It is true that all human behavior is in some sense adaptive, and when repeated over generations adaptive behaviors become institutionalized as cultural norms that may be internalized as "values." However, the process of adaptation continues actively throughout an individual's lifetime; individuals are not simply set in motion as children to respond automatically for the rest of their lives. Cultural norms and definitions of roles are constantly reinforced for an individual, or redirected, by the institutional structures within which he functions.

Urban school systems have a dual track, one for middle-income children who will for the most part go on to college and more or less professional occupations, and one for poor and minority children who will go into trades or service occupations if they do not fall into the categories of under- or unemployed. Every mother who fights to get her child into the fast class on a grade in a heterogeneous school, or who moves away from a "changing" neighborhood so that her child can go to a "good" school, knows this fact. The double-track system meshes in turn with patterns of urban demography and neighborhood segregation by race and income, and with the structure of employment, of decision-making political institutions, and so forth. The child from a poor family meets anew at each stage of his life difficulties parallel to those which he had to face when growing up. The complex intertwining of institutional structures and individual habits and expectations has been dramatically underlined by the intensity of the reaction to the recent movement for community control, which has threatened to upset existing status systems and redistribute decision-making powers.

Stereotyped Interpretation in Culture-of-Poverty Writings

When we turn from the definition of culture implied by culture-of-poverty theory to a consideration of the presumed content of poverty culture, we find an ethnocentric tendency to interpret behavioral patterns among lower-class people as isolated traits rather than in terms of their total context, and as shortcomings from some presumed "middle-class" ideal. As a comment on this, Janet Castro (1971) notes that she has yet to find in her classrooms the well-organized and motivated middle-class youngsters implied by the discussions of deprived children. However, it is not too surprising if it is difficult for researchers to avoid misinterpreting and distorting "how the other half live," given certain deeply ingrained American attitudes toward class differences that follow from the particular history of this country.

The social history of the United States is usually presented in terms of poor people coming to these shores and working their way up toward security and success. Although studies suggest that upward mobility was not as great as it is commonly assumed, many family histories include parents or grandparents who came with very little and worked their way, if not that far "up," at least definitely "in." One might think that, as a result, Americans would feel more akin to those below them on the social scale than seems to be the case.

It appears, instead, that the closer a person's experience has been to that of his poorer brethren, the more strenuously he may argue that it takes will and ability to get ahead, and that the poor are poor out of laziness, stupidity, or lack of ambition. He thereby not only vindicates his own gains, and assuages, perhaps, a lingering guilt that he does not wish to cast behind a helping hand, but he also reassures himself. It is important to him that his position should follow from an intrinsically greater worthiness; this helps protect him from the threat of social vagaries like the rise and fall of unemployment, the greater insecurity that comes with age (apart from those in assured upper-status positions), the unpredictability of technological displacements, or the occurrence of serious accident or illness. Furthermore, the fact that the vast majority of black Americans have historically been relegated to a lower-class status means that traditionally learned and deeply held attitudes of white superiority contribute to the sense of distance middle-class white people feel in relation to their lower-class compatriots. In her book *Pickets at the Gates*, Estelle Fuchs documents how some of these middle-class attitudes influence a school principal of immigrant background who is at loggerheads with the black parents of his school (Fuchs, 1966: 43ff.).

Social scientists aim to achieve an objective, detached, and truly scientific attitude toward society, free from subjective involvements in their own social position. Unfortunately, however, the findings of their own sciences constantly affirm the fact that, though they may constantly strive for the goal of objectivity, they should never assume that it can be completely attained. Social scientists are human beings, which means social and cultural beings whose needs, desires, fears and persuasions must impinge upon their work in various ways. By definition "middle-class," their scientific calling does not automatically make them immune to ethnocentrism when looking at members of the lower classes. Since the vast majority of social scientists are white, their attempts to achieve understanding across black–white lines are also subject to the chauvinism embedded in our culture. When viewing black members of the lower classes, we must examine their claim to objectivity with a particularly critical eye.

An anthropologist knows well that the faces he meets as an outsider when he first enters an American Indian, African, or Polynesian community are far different from those he comes to know after living with a people and gaining some insight into their life from their own viewpoint and within the context of the objective conditions with which they must cope. Yet he too can fall into a trap and, along with his colleagues in sociology and psychology, can project his own biases as a middle-class person on members of the lower class, interpreting the latter's behaviors in terms of unstated assumptions about what is sensible and worthy. When we examine the literature on poverty culture, we find that this misinterpretation may be made in any of three ways: (1) through assuming that the behavior observed or attitudes tapped in the limited interaction situations in which a researcher often works with members of a low-status group represent the range of lower-class behavior and attitudes; (2) by working with a partial or biased sample of situations, groups, or individuals, and overgeneralizing from these to a major segment of some undefined "lower-class" group, or even to blue collar workers as a whole; or (3) by interpreting lower-class behaviors in terms of single dimensions that are seen as the polar opposites of certain behaviors imputed to the middle class. To elaborate:

1. *The Interaction Situation of the Research as Unrepresentative.* It is axiomatic in the behavioral sciences that human behavior can be largely defined in terms of "role playing." A person does not simply "express himself," or even any considerable part of himself, in a given situation, but acts according to the patterns defined as appropriate to the situation and to his status within it. He expresses different aspects of himself as a teacher, as a husband, as a neighbor, as a warm friend, as a father, etc. Among the more restricted roles a person enacts—those in which he is most circumspect and controlled—are subordinate roles in formal situations. No matter what façade of easy informality one may adopt when meeting, say, a prospective employer, a department chairman, a supervisor, or a school principal, one is well aware that a proper reserve and deference is expected and one does not allow oneself to be unguardedly spontaneous. Obviously, behavior is the more wary the greater the distance between two people and the lower the status of the subordinate. Yet roles that are defined primarily in terms of clear superordinate and subordinate statuses are precisely those which have predominated in situations where data on lower-class behaviors are collected. Thus the social-service worker, or the social scientist, meets the unemployed worker, or welfare client, or delinquent youth under circumstances where the latter groups have to be extremely cautious and reserved. (Or, as an angry reaction, perhaps they may be assertively surly or hostile.) The "findings" resulting from such interactions have all too often been taken at face value, or the unwarranted assumption has been made that the restricted nature of the interaction between the data collector and the subject has been taken into account.

When the partial view gained from the outside is replaced by some knowledge of total community life as seen from the inside, the results are altogether different. Years ago, in his pioneering study of an Italian slum neighborhood written up as *Street Corner Society*, William Foote White reported that a level of organization existed that was not reflected in the social-science literature of the time. In order to understand this organization, White stated, "the sociologist [must] become a participant observer of the most intimate activities in the social life of the slums." He continued, "Proceeding by this route, he will find many evidences of conflict and maladjustment, but he will not find the chaotic conditions once thought to exist throughout this area" (White, 1943:39).

It seems each generation of social scientists makes and must correct the same mistakes when it comes to views of the poor. Some twenty-five years after White's work, Charles and Betty Lou Valentine write, as participant observers in a black and very poor community, that "it is proving difficult to find major community patterns that correspond to many of the subcultural traits often associated with poverty in learned writings about the poor." Instead the Valentines cite as common such practices as participation in organizations both inside and outside the community, the saving of money, and the planned acquisition of household appliances. They also note adherence to many goals and standards considered to be middle-class, that involve various aspects of style and behavior, as well as career orientations, commitment to education for children, and aspirations for community improvement. They write:

> We see much energetic activity, great aesthetic and organizational variety, quite a number of highly patterned and well displayed behavior styles. Apathetic resignation does exist [as indeed it does in American society generally—E. L.], but it is by no means the dominant tone of the community. Social disorganization can be found, but it occurs only within a highly structured context. Individual pathology is certainly present, but adaptive coping with adversity is more common. Positive strengths (often ignored in the literature) include the ability to deal with misfortune through humor, the capacity to respond to defeat with renewed effort, recourse to widely varied sacred and secular ideologies for psychological strength, and resourceful devices to manipulate existing structures for maximum individual or group benefit. Perhaps least expectable from popular models is the capacity to mobilize initiatives for large-scale change like the movement for local control. [Valentine and Valentine, 1969:412.]

. . . . .

In relation to misinterpretations of behavior based on observation of a very narrow behavioral range, Drucker (1971) discusses the distorted images yielded by techniques of testing and measurement. I.Q. tests have long been criticized for ignoring the rich diversity and range of human aptitudes and abilities. In the words of Irving Taylor, they show "how quickly people can solve relatively unimportant problems making as few errors as possible, rather than measuring how people grapple with relatively important problems, making as many productive errors as necessary with time no factor" (quoted in Frank Riessman, 1962:49). Test scores are also known to measure educational experience rather than innate ability, and to be readily influenced by such things as a few hours of previous training and various modifications in the test-taking situation. A most dramatic instance of I.Q. modification is reported by Rosenthal and Jacobson (1968). As a result of their study-design, a Mexican-American boy was thought by his teacher to show promise of a jump in achievement. Indeed he did jump, moving from a retarded 61 to 106 during the course of the study year.

The citing of group test scores persists, however, and is accepted by those who would like to prove that there are differences in innate potentials along racial lines. Furthermore, since tests measure previous learning in a given school system, they are reasonably predictive of future learning in the same system, despite the fact that they yield a very restricted view of individual or group potentials. Anthropologists, who are on the whole skeptical of such data-collection techniques and who use them (when sometimes viewed as hopelessly idealistic and naïvely biased in favor of the people with whom they work—typically low status people from they do at all) with great reservations, are "backward" nations. Indeed, anthropologists do comprise the one academic group that gives virtual consensus to the conviction that inferior "intelligence" cannot be ascribed to any racially defined group. What is noteworthy is not only that anthropologists are the only social scientists to focus on the study of lifeways other than their own, but also that *they necessarily employ as their major technique of data collection a systematic learning from the people they study.* By putting themselves, however temporarily, in the subordinate position of pupils who wish to learn and understand something they do not already know, they come to know and respect the true measure of their subjects.

2. *Sample Bias.* Most discussions of poverty culture have been oriented toward seeking solutions for urban problems. In fact, however, there is a serious paucity of sound data on lifeways of the urban poor. The primary data upon which inferences have been based have been statistics drawn from records of people who are dependent upon or in trouble with the authori-

ties in some way—welfare records, mental-hospital records, statistics on delinquency and crime, etc. The data focus on those who are demoralized, addicted, delinquent, etc., and do not concern those who manage to overcome the difficulties of poverty. Furthermore, statistics can easily be misused. Often figures are cited only in part. For example, reference may be made to the rising rate of divorce in black families, without referring to the rising rate nationally (or internationally, for that matter), or to the fact that the rate of increase happens to be higher at present among whites. Statistical materials can also give a skewed impression of what they are supposed to reveal. Moynihan cites rates of illegitimacy as an index of disorganization in the black community, but after analyzing the figures and what they indicate, the public-health psychologist William Ryan writes:

> . . . the reported rates of illegitimacy among Negroes and whites tell us nothing at all about differences in family structure, historical forces, instability, or anything else about which the authors speculate [in the "Moynihan Report"]. From the known data, we can conclude only that Negro and white girls probably engage in premarital intercourse in about the same proportions, but that the white girl more often takes Enovid or uses a diaphragm; if she gets pregnant, she more often obtains an abortion; if she has the baby, first she is more often able to conceal it and, second, she has an infinitely greater opportunity to give it up for adoption. [Ryan, 1965:381.]

Another example of how partial a view statistics can give is afforded by the figures showing a greater incidence of severe mental illness as one moves down the economic scale. An increase of mental illness is certainly not surprising, considering the stress that accompanies poverty. However, the statistics do not do justice to the strengths to be found among the poor. They reflect more than differences of occurrence of mental illness across classes, for they also include the effects of a differential access to treatment. A New Haven study of treatment for mental illness, both private and public, showed that the vast majority of the more wealthy and better-educated, 78 percent of the classes designated as I and II, were receiving psychotherapy by comparison with 53 percent of Class III, 31 percent of Class IV, and 16 percent of the lowest group, or Class V. Conversely, 51 percent at the lowest levels were receiving no treatment at all, but simply custodial care, with the proportion diminishing to 11 percent at the upper levels (Hollingshead and Redlich, 1958). A follow-up study of an outpatient clinic showed a marked bias in admission procedures, with the higher-status person standing a much better chance of being accepted for psychotherapy (Meyers and Schaffer, 1954:308–9). Thus, the lower his class status, the greater the chance for a person to become so sick as to reach the attention of the authorities through legal procedures, and to be committed to custodial care for the rest of his life. In short, statistics on the prevalence of mental illness say as much about the care available to people as about the variations of incidence across classes.

Studies which have gone beyond statistical materials and have followed up various populations have concentrated largely on "problem" groups that have been seen from the partial or "outside" viewpoint discussed above. Conclusions drawn from these studies have then been projected onto some large but ill-defined section of what may be called the "poor," or "lower class," or "working class." Thus bias in the sample, combined with bias in the situations studied, as discussed above, and bias in the interpretation of the material, to be discussed below, all reconfirm assumptions that the difficulties of the poor follow for the most part from their own failings.

3. *"Sociocentric" Interpretations of Data.* The same attitudes that underlie the reluctance of therapists to accept lower-class applicants for outpatient treatment in the study reported above have been noted with relation to diagnostic procedures generally. As pointed out by

William Haase, a number of studies show that the clinician influences "both the results that he will elicit from any given test and the significance assigned to them," and further research indicates that this influence takes the form of class bias when lower-status patients are involved (Haase, 1964:241, *passim*).

We have discussed the biased judgments about behavior across classes that follow from the nature of interclass relationships. These are so largely defined in terms of authority and control of resources, on the one hand, and dependence, servitude, or employee status, on the other, that the middle-class person experiences the lower-class person either as easygoing and not very "deep" or as hostile and guarded, or whatever the situation may dictate. The middle-class person tends not to become engaged with a lower-class person in relationships that involve such acts as a common sizing up and interpreting of situations and events or a mutual weighing of alternatives and consideration of means. The resulting assumption on the part of the middle-class person is that such behavior does not obtain in lower-status groups. Further, the researcher often forgets that his own analytic bent is not a standard "middle-class" characteristic—Babbitt has by no means suddenly disappeared from our national life—but is the concomitant of the specific training and type of occupation he has chosen. He does not recognize that the amount of introspective, contemplative, and analytic behavior indulged in varies enormously from individual to individual and that such behavior is by no means the property of any one group.

Instead the tendency in discussions of class differences in behavior is for them to become exaggerated by being stated in terms of polar opposites. Middle-class people plan; the poor do not. Middle-class people defer gratifications; the poor do not. Middle-class child-rearing modes are democratic; those of the poor are authoritarian. A middle-class person considers his life chances rationally; a poor person approaches them fatalistically. Middle-class families are patrifocal; poor families are matrifocal. Middle-class people think abstractly; the poor think concretely. And so on and on. When Lewis writes that "it would be . . . helpful to think of the subculture of poverty as the zero point on a continuum which leads to the working class and middle class," the focus is on quantitative differences along single dimensions, with the middle class as the norm (Lewis, 1969:190).

However, both the middle and working, or lower, classes, while sharing certain universals of American culture, also manifest many subcultural variations according to the specific histories and circumstances of different regions, nationalities, religious groups, occupational groups, and residence styles (rural-urban). Such variations, either within or across cultures, cannot be adequately described or understood in terms of continua. Another distortion which results when thinking in terms of continua is that differences in trends can become magnified into unfounded contrasts. For example, that 23.2 percent of nonwhite families are matrifocal by comparison with 8.6 percent of white families means that *more* matrifocality exists in the nonwhite group. But it is quite a trick to say that the nonwhite population *is* matrifocal, when 76.8 percent of the families are not.[1] As to child-rearing modes, they vary so widely and change so rapidly—and are so imperfectly studied, to boot—that broad generalizations like the above cannot be made with any accuracy. Furthermore, it is not so easy to distinguish between such categories as "demo-

[1] In a review of discussions of "class culture," Hyman Rodman writes: "One important point that underlies all discussions of class culture revolves about the distinction that must be made between statistically significant class differences and characteristics of a class. There is a danger that the statistically significant differences—which may be represented by a finding that 25 per cent of lower-class adults are 'authoritarian' in comparison to 15 per cent of middle-class adults—will be converted into an unqualified statement that authoritarianism is a lower-class characteristic." (Rodman, 1968: 335.)

cratic" and "authoritarian" behavior. The use of corporal punishment is often considered *ipso facto* authoritarian, and the authoritarian component is ignored in presumed middle-class manipulative techniques of discipline such as threatened withdrawal of affection and denial of desired activities.

The conceptualization of behavior in terms of single dimensions obscures the fact that differences in group behaviors are more generally qualitative than quantitative. It is not that middle-class people plan and the poor do not, but that they necessarily plan about different things in different ways. For example, the strike is a characteristically lower-class form of planning and delayed gratification, one which may be undertaken by the very poor even without benefit of union sanction and support.

Since the situations with which middle- and lower-class groups are dealing may differ widely, one cannot jump to the conclusion that one form of behavior is necessarily more effective than another. Hyman Rodman speaks of the "cross-eyed, middle-class view of lower-class behavior," and writes that lower-class behaviors which deviate from middle-class ideals (what middle-class *realities* may be is another question) "are frequently viewed in a gross manner as, simply, *problems* of the lower class." Rodman continues: "My own feeling is that it makes more sense to think of them as *solutions* of the lower class to problems that they face in the social, economic, and perhaps legal and political spheres of life" (Rodman, 1964:65).

Culture-of-poverty theorists all too often talk about the "orality" of the poor and their inability to delay gratification, forgetting that the more affluent take for granted as necessities a good diet, comfortable surroundings, and the constant enjoyment of many other such gratifications that the poor must defer for their lives long, with at best, perhaps, some forlorn hope for gratification in an afterlife. Furthermore, the comments often made by culture-of-poverty theorists on the fatalism and resignation of the poor are strangely out of step with middle-class complaints about the impropriety of the means the black poor are using to express their anger with their situation and their demands for redress.

Life Style and Education

It has been widely assumed that the different atmospheres to be found in middle-income and lower-income schools follow from differences in the children's out-of-school experiences. The greater disciplinary problems, and what seems to be a lesser inclination to learn, are viewed as concomitants of "cultural deprivation," reinforced by the distance between the "middle-class" goals and orientation of the schools and the "lower-class values" of the children. From the standpoint of teachers who face bored and dispirited children, and who do not know how to arouse interest and awaken abilities, the "culture of poverty" explanation seems apt. Teachers commonly feel they are in conflict with something, and that it is their "middle-class values" versus those of the "lower class" is persuasive.

A strong counterposition has developed, following the Supreme Court decision on desegregation of schools and the exposure of the double-track system along class and race lines that exists in Northern cities. That the structure of the schools mirrors an existing status system and that there is greater financial expenditure per child in middle-income areas have become clear. Children in low-income areas, and particularly black low-income areas, go to poorer schools (or, in heterogeneous neighborhoods, into "slower" classes in a grade), which lead into slow classes in junior high, or poorer junior highs, and thence into catch-all commercial and industrial high schools where standards are low and dropouts high. By contrast, children from middle-income areas go to "good" schools, or "fast" classes which feed into "special" programs in the later elementary and junior-high years, and into specialized college preparatory high schools. The structuring of this double-track system and the expectations for children's performance which it presupposes dictate that economic and racial status, rather than ability, will determine for the most part who shall ascend the educational ladder and gain positions with prestige and security. The lower expectations for poor children are self-fulfilling.

Within this structure, teachers are both the victims and the villains, a position which has caused them great stress and confusion in the recent battles fought over the education of black and Puerto Rican children. Teachers, after all, daily face the children in the classroom, and have the responsibility of teaching them. However, as cogs in a machine so structured that teaching is well-nigh impossible in low-income schools, only the most gifted and insightful among them do not fail. Hence teachers both are and are not responsible, and hence the bitterness and anger surrounding attempts to restructure the educational system. (Hence, too, the perfect setting for "divide and rule" ploys by those in positions of real decision making and responsibility.) Teachers may ultimately be frustrated by a situation in which they have not been successful at their trade, but most of them have adapted to it either by accepting outright racist rationales for their failure with the poor and the black or by grasping at the "culture of poverty" rationale. Only a few have found ways to act on the understanding of how their failure is built into the very structure of the school system and from their own restricted position within it. Jonathan Kozol, author of *Death at an Early Age*, is an example, and he was expelled from the Boston school system as a consequence of his dissidence.

I have referred above to the active role the school plays in the socialization of children for their role in society. On the basis of observing classrooms in both black and white schools, in both middle- and lower-income neighborhoods, it became apparent to me that the projection of a middle-class orientation to life in general was not the major problem for poor and black children. It was rather that *a middle class attitude toward them and their inferior status as poor and black was being foisted upon them.* Tragically, this could be observed on the part of black as well as white teachers. This was before the assertion of black demands for some power over their own lives gave black teachers the moral support necessary for transcending the status quo. Expectations for the children's future subordinate status were expressed in various ways, particularly for black children from low-income homes: through the minimal goals for them expressed by the teachers in interviews and stated in the classroom; through the failure to structure the classroom in ways which would encourage the children to handle formal responsibility (although the children's classroom behavior indicated their readiness to do so); and through the negative ways in which teachers would respond to a child's proffered discussion and would evaluate the performance of a lesson.

. . . There is a process whereby attitudes founded in racist ideology are reinforced by experiences based on superordinate–subordinate relations. The result is the inability of teachers to empathize with and respect the children, and the projection of teachers' expectations of failure upon the children. On the other hand, there are dramatic examples of what can happen when someone determined to *teach* children starts by first *listening* to them. Herbert Kohl relates an experience as an elementary-school teacher in East Harlem, when he dropped a stilted and superficial lesson plan on "How We Became Modern Americans" and encouraged the children to write of their blocks, their lives, their experiences and concerns. Once their suspicion was allayed, the children wrote and wrote. "Everything I'd been told about the children's language was irrelevant," Kohl stated, and continued:

Yes, they were hip when they spoke, inarticulate and concrete. But their writing was something else, when they felt that no white man was judging their words, threatening their confidence and pride . . . Recently I have mentioned this to teachers who have accepted the current analysis of "the language" of the "disadvantaged." They asked their children to write and have been as surprised as I was, and shocked by the obvious fact that "disadvantaged" children will not speak in class because they cannot trust their audience. [Kohl, 1966:27.]

. . . . .

The Conclusion

To sum up, differences between the poor and the nonpoor in our society stem from three sources. First, there are the different traditions of peoples with different histories; these are often reinforced by racial or religious segregation and discrimination. Second, there are realistic attempts to deal with objective conditions that vary from one class to another. There is no hard fast line between this order of behavior and the third, which are those adaptive acts and attitudes that become institutionalized, and incorporated into internalized values and norms appropriate for living in a given position in the social-economic system. It is, of course, the last—the subcultural variations along class lines—which come closest to what culture-of-poverty theory is supposedly documenting. However, as discussed above, sociocentric methods of data collection and analysis, plus a nonhistorical theory of culture and its relation to personality, have contributed to stereotypical and distorted views of these class-linked cultural variations.[2] . . .

As used by anthropologists, "culture" refers to the totality of a group's learned norms for behavior and the manifestations of this behavior. This includes the technological and economic mechanisms through which a group adapts to its environment, its related social and political institutions, and the values, goals, definitions, prescriptions, and assumptions which define and rationalize individual motivation and participation. Social anthropology as a science is concerned with describing and analyzing four aspects of man's culture: (1) the variety of cultural forms which has existed, past and present; (2) cultural changes over time and the influence different cultures have had upon each other; (3) relationships among the various components of culture in general, and of specific cultures in particular; and (4) the relationship between cultural norms and individual personality and behavior. To the non-anthropologist, however, the term "culture" is often limited to its ideological and psychological aspects. It is these that are constantly and directly experienced in our heterogeneous nation, in which many different cultural traditions have been brought together within a common social-economic system. Emphasis on these dimensions of culture without some understanding of the whole has resulted in a lack of awareness that ideological aspects of culture develop and change in complex interaction with fundamental economic and social institutions.

Anthropologists vary in how they interpret the relation between the social-economic and the more ideological or psychological sides of culture. However, even those anthropologists who place strong emphasis in their studies on the psychological dimension do not in the last analysis accept the notion that social and economic structure are secondary to psychological mechanisms. In a recent debate with Charles Valentine, Oscar Lewis contradicts the implication of his earlier statement quoted in the beginning of this chapter when he writes:

The crucial question from both the scientific and the political point of view is: How much weight is to be given to the internal, self-perpetuating factors in the subculture of poverty as compared to

[2] For a review of the literature on class culture, see Rodman, 1968: 332–37.

the external, societal factors? My own position is that in the long run the self-perpetuating factors are relatively minor and unimportant as compared to the basic structure of the larger society. [Lewis, 1969:192.]

And Lee Rainwater, who has elsewhere stressed the self-perpetuating psychological aspects of lower-class culture, states succinctly:

. . . one can hope that as a result of the social science efforts to date, "thinking people" will stop deluding themselves that the underclass is other than a product of an economic system so designed that it generates a destructive amount of income inequality, and face the fact that the only solution of the problem of underclass is to change that economic system accordingly. [Rainwater, 1969:9.]

Bibliography

BARTKY, JOHN A., *Social Issues in Public Education.* Boston: Houghton Mifflin, 1963.

CASTRO, JANET, "Untapped Verbal Fluency of Black Schoolchildren," in *The Culture of Poverty: A Critique,* ed. Eleanor Leacock (New York: Simon and Schuster, 1971).

DRUCKER, ERNEST, "Cognitive Styles and Class Stereotypes," in *The Culture of Poverty: A Critique,* ed. Eleanor Leacock (New York: Simon and Schuster, 1971).

FUCHS, ESTELLE, *Pickets at the Gates.* New York: Free Press, 1966.

GRAHAM, GRACE, *The Public School in the American Community.* New York: Harper and Row, 1963.

HAASE, WILLIAM, "The Role of Socioeconomic Class in Examiner Bias," in *Mental Health of the Poor: New Treatment Approaches for Low Income People,* ed. Frank Riessman, Jerome Cohen and Arthur Pearl (New York: Free Press, 1964).

HART, C. W. M., "The Sons of Turimpi," *American Anthropologist,* Vol. 56 (1954), No. 2.

HOLLINGSHEAD, A. B., and F. C. REDLICH, *Social Class and Mental Illness: A Community Study.* New York: Wiley and Sons, 1958.

KAGAN, JEROME, and HOWARD MOSS, *Birth to Maturity.* New York: Wiley and Sons, 1962.

KOHL, HERBERT, "Children Writing: The Story of an Experiment," *The New York Review of Books,* Nov. 17, 1966.

LEACOCK, ELEANOR, *Teaching and Learning in City Schools: A Comparative Study.* New York: Basic Books, 1969.

LEWIS, OSCAR, *The Children of Sanchez.* New York: Random House, 1961.

———, *La Vida.* New York: Random House, 1966.

———, Review of Charles A. Valentine, *Culture and Poverty: Critique and Counter-Proposals,* in *Current Anthropology,* Vol. 10 (1969), No. 2–3.

MEYERS, JEROME K., and LESLIE SCHAFFER, "Social Stratification and Psychiatric Practice," *American Sociological Review,* Vol. 19 (1954), No. 3.

MOYNIHAN, DANIEL P., *The Negro Family: The Case for National Action.* Washington: U.S. Department of Labor, 1965.

RAINWATER, LEE, "The American Underclass, Comment: Looking Back and Looking Up," *Transaction,* Vol. 6 (1969), No. 4.

RIESSMAN, FRANK, *The Culturally Deprived Child.* New York: Harper and Brothers, 1962.

RODMAN, HYMAN, "Middle-Class Misconceptions about Lower-Class Families," in *Blue-Collar World: Studies of the American Worker,* ed. Arthur B. Shostak and William Gomberg (Englewood Cliffs, N.J.: Prentice-Hall, 1964).

———, "Stratification, Social: Class Culture," in *The International Encyclopedia of the Social Sciences* (New York: Macmillan, 1968).

ROSENTHAL, ROBERT, and LENORE JACOBSON, *Pygmalion in the Classroom: Teacher Expectation and Pupils' Intellectual Development.* New York: Holt, Rinehart and Winston, 1968.

RYAN, WILLIAM, "Savage Discovery: The Moynihan Report," *The Nation,* Nov. 22, 1965.

VALENTINE, CHARLES A., and BETTY LOU VALENTINE, "Making the Scene, Digging the Action, and Telling It Like It Is: Anthropologists at Work in a Dark Ghetto," in *Afro-American Anthropology: Contemporary Perspectives,* ed. Norman Whitten and John Szwed (New York: Free Press, 1969).

WALLACE, ANTHONY F. C., "The New Culture-and-Personality," in *Anthropology and Human Behavior* (Washington: Anthropological Society of Washington, 1962).

WHITE, WILLIAM FOOTE, "Social Organization in the Slums," *American Sociological Review,* Vol. 8, February 1943.

WHORF, BENJAMIN LEE, *Language, Thought and Reality.* Cambridge: Massachusetts Institute of Technology Press, 1956.

WRIGHT, ROLLAND, "The Stranger Mentality and the Culture of Poverty," in *The Culture of Poverty: A Critique,* ed. Eleanor Leacock (New York: Simon and Schuster, 1971).

ASPECTS OF LINGUISTICS

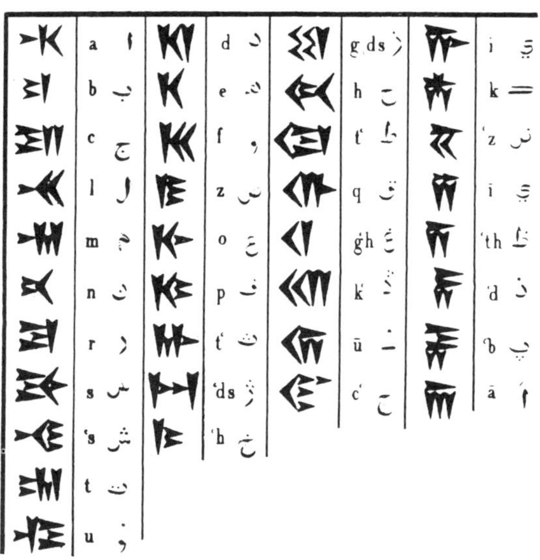

14

THE GENERAL PROPERTIES OF LANGUAGE

NOAM CHOMSKY

The anthropologist Marvin Harris speaks of the "transition from semantically finite ape to semantically infinite man." Noting the extensive experimental attempts to induce language in chimpanzees, Harris commented that one of the most remarkable of such animals seemed unlikely to live long enough to surpass the level expected of a human two-year-old. There is, then, both magic and mystery in the linguistic gap between ourselves and other animals, even those most closely related to us. One aspect of that gap seems, logically, to refer to the considerable differences between human and nonhuman brains, differences in size, weight, organization, and structure. The subject is complicated, however, by clear evidence that, within rather wide limits, differences in the size or weight of brains seem to bear no relation whatsoever to intellect. Moreover, we are aware that the gulf between hominids and pongids with respect to any particular aspect of the brain is bridged through fossil ancestors.

A few years ago the matter of the linguistic gap between man and animals was approached from the point of view of neurology at a conference devoted to the mechanisms of the brain that were thought to underlie speech and language. Present at the conference was a linguist whose book, *Syntactic Structures,* published in 1957, heralded a major event in linguistics. While some of the elements entering into the approach known as transformational or generative grammar had been proposed and utilized for some time, the synthesis associated with the work of Noam Chomsky constituted a genuine breakthrough. The selection that follows is a slightly edited version of the remarks made by Chomsky at the conference. They allude to one of the essential contributions of transformational grammer, namely, the distinction between surface (superficial) and deep (underlying) linguistic structure. But the comments that follow show Chomsky dealing with a related but somewhat different matter, the question of how language ability enables its possessor to formulate or comprehend utterances that have never been heard before.

Though concern for this problem is not new, rigorous work on it is not yet extensive. We still stand at the threshold of understanding what is involved. Perhaps as a consequence of this, Chomsky can conclude his remarks by pointing to discontinuity between human and animal communications systems. It is generally true that interpretations of evolution have, in the past, emphasized the apparently sudden appearance of a new phenomenon, seemingly without antecedents—a qualitative gap. Hypotheses have then been advanced involving a process of leaping (saltation) over such gaps. As information has grown, explanations of the miraculous-leap-type have declined. Chomsky admits elsewhere that his linguistic theories may ultimately be greatly revised in this respect. At the level of present understanding, however, we are well advised to approach Chomsky's theories with an open mind.

▼△▼△▼

I would like to make some rather informal remarks about certain aspects of language. . . . It seems to me there is no striking similarity between animal communication systems and human language. If we rise to the level of abstraction at which human language and animal communications systems fall together, then we find plenty of other things incorporated under the same generalizations which no one would have regarded as being continuous with language or particularly relevant to the mechanisms of language. This is clear, if we consider the properties which are shared by animal communication systems and human language:

SOURCE: *Brain Mechanisms Underlying Speech and Language,* Millikan and Darley (eds.). New York: Grune & Stratton. 1967. pp. 73–81. Reprinted by permission of Grune & Stratton, Inc. and the author.

This work was supported by the Joint Services Electronics Program (Contract DA 36-039-AMC-03200 [EL]), NSF Grant GK-835, NIH Grant 2PO1 MH-04737-06, U.S.A.F. Contract AF 19 (628)-2487.

specifically, the properties of purposiveness, of having syntactic organization, and of being propositional, in a sense, informative.

I think it is perfectly true in a sense that both systems are propositional, syntactic, and purposive. So are many other things. For example, consider walking. Walking certainly is purposive. It is certainly syntactic, that is, it has some global organization. It is also informative; for example, the rate of speed with which someone is walking suggests to us how interested he is in his goal. In fact, it is perfectly conceivable that one could use rate of walking to give information about precisely that.

Or, to take something which one might think is, perhaps, a little bit closer to language, consider the common gestures one uses in helping someone park a car. When you indicate to him by the distance between your two hands how far he is from the car behind, your actions are purposive, integrated, and propositional. But, it is unlikely that any significant purpose would be served by studying such gestures and human language within the same framework. In fact, if you consider how these various systems are purposive, informative, and structured, then very striking differences appear between human language, on the one hand, and all the other systems (that is, animal communication, gesturing, and walking), on the other.

Consider first the matter of informativeness. As I understand it, animal communication systems are informative in one of two ways. Either they consist of a finite number, a finite population of available signals, or else, in the case where they have an infinite number of possibilities, there is a finite number of dimensions in the "language," each of which is correlated to some physical, nonlinguistic dimension in such a way that by picking a point along the linguistic dimension, you uniquely specify a point along the correlated nonlinguistic dimension. . . . My example of walking has just this property. Rate of walking is informative about desire to get somewhere in just this sense, and the same is true of the gesture system that I mentioned. The same is true of the bee dances and other examples.

But the devices used by human language are of an entirely different kind. If I say that there is a bird in the tree outside, or that I wish I could go to New York to see a movie tonight, or anything else, it is quite senseless to ask the question: "What are the dimensions of this utterance that correlate with some dimensions in the outside world, such that picking a point along the linguistic dimension selects a correlated point along the dimension in the nonlinguistic system?" It is obvious that there is no sense in asking that question.

In short, if we rise to the level of generality at which animal communication and human language fall together, we find such other systems as, for example, walking. If we try to analyze these kinds of behavior into natural classes, we find that human language separates out as rather different in its fundamental properties from other types of behavior that fall together at this level of generality, for example, walking and animal communication.

It has been remarked that there is some similarity between human language and animal communication systems in another sense, namely, that the ordinary use of language, like the ordinary use of animal communication systems, is to change behavior, to modify thoughts, or something of this type. I rather doubt that this is true. As a matter of fact, I think there is little reason to believe that the primary use of language is to modify behavior or modify thought.

Language can be used for all kinds of other purposes. It can be used to inform or to mislead, to clarify one's thoughts or to show how clever one is; or, in fact, it can be used for play in a very general sense, that is, to utilize intellectual capacities and maintain some feeling of relationship with others, or something of this kind. I am not using language any less, if I do not care whether I convince anyone or change anyone's behavior or change his thoughts—I am not using it any less under those circumstances than if I say exactly the same things, and I do care whether I convince him or change his behavior or change his thoughts. In either case, I may be using language in a perfectly normal way.

If one wants to find out something significant about the nature of language, I think it is important to look not at its uses, which may be almost any imaginable, but, rather, at its structure—to ask what it is, not what is done with it.

Language can be used for a huge variety of purposes. On the other hand, almost any system that contains discriminable stimuli can be used to modify behavior or to provide information. It is a mistake, a bad habit, to approach the study of language by considering its "characteristic" uses. For one thing, the general assumptions about what are "characteristic uses" are highly suspect. Second, even if correct, these statistical guesses would suggest very little about the nature of language. The same kind of comment can be made about various attempts to "extrapolate" from experimental work with animals to conclusions about human language.

It has been brought out in the discussion in the last few sessions that "linguistic concepts" are rather different in important respects from concepts that are taught by so-called "associative learning," concepts specified in terms of some set of physical properties, such as the concept of round object with green spots in it, and so on. A good deal of evidence was provided concerning the failure of cross-modal transfer in the case of concepts developed in this fashion. Then it was observed that linguistic concepts do exhibit cross-modal transfer and are thus rather different from the concepts taught by associative learning. It was concluded that it is the verbal tag that mediates the cross-modal transfer.

There is another interpretation of such data, namely, that the linguistic concepts have nothing to do with "associative learning," that linguistic concepts are not characterized in terms of a network of physical properties. Then, instead of attributing cross-modal transfer to the verbal tag, we might assume simply that linguistic concepts (which, in fact, have verbal tags) differ in a fundamental way from these artificial concepts characterized in terms of some network of physical properties. Actually, I think there is good reason to accept that latter interpretation; on independent grounds, it is clear that the concepts normally assigned "verbal tags" are not, in general, characterized in terms of physical properties, as are the artificial concepts of the concept-formation experiments. Concepts such as "knife" or "house" are not characterized in terms of some set of physical properties but are, rather, defined in functional terms, as has long been known. Ordinary human concepts simply do not have the property of being characterizable in terms of some collection of physical properties. They are concepts of a different type. There is no reason to expect the very different, arbitrary, and artificial concepts taught by "associative learning" to share the properties of concepts of the normal type, which are probably not "taught," in any interesting sense of this term.

Again, to call all these things "concepts" may be as misleading as to call animal communication systems and human language "languages." That is, although at some level of abstraction the word applies to both, there may be fundamental differences between them. One has to be careful about jumping to the conclusion that because such a thing as associative learning does exist, because you can demonstrate it, it therefore has anything to do with something else that exists, namely, human concepts.

In fact, there are many specific human concepts, such as the one I want to talk about more specifically, namely, the concept of a sentence (of English or of any other language) which certainly cannot be characterized in terms of some arrangement of physical properties or association or anything else of this kind. It is totally out of range of any of these notions.

With these introductory remarks, let me try to say a few things about what seem to be general properties of human language, more specifically, what it means to have command of a language. When a person has command of a language, when a person has command of English, what kind of things does he know? What kind of information is in some fashion represented in his nervous system? We may assume that a language is a specific sound-meaning correspondence, and that when a person has command of the language, he knows, in some sense, the intrinsic meaning of a variety of signals. Command of the language involves knowing that correspondence and involves the ability to select, when one of the signals is presented, the correlated semantic content; also the ability, given some idea in mind, to find the appropriate signal to express it. This connection between sound and meaning is not a connection at the level of words but at the level of sentences. That is, command of English involves an understanding of each sentence of English, a knowledge of what that sentence of English means. The most obvious and most important and most neglected fact about language is that this knowledge of the intrinsic connection between signal and semantic interpretation, between sound and meaning, is a correlation that extends over an infinite range of objects. This is no logician's quibble, or anything of this sort. Actually, the most obvious aspect of normal use of language is that it is unbounded, that it rarely involves repetition, even repetition of items of the "same pattern" as those that have occurred before. Repetition of utterances certainly is the exception in normal linguistic behavior. There are certain clichés, or idioms, like "Good morning," which may have empirically detectable probabilities of occurrence. Characteristically these clichés do not have the ordinary structure of the sentences of the language. But normal linguistic behavior, one's normal behavior, as speaker or reader or hearer, is quite generally with novel utterances, with utterances that have no physical or formal similarity to any of the utterances that have ever been produced in the past experience of the hearer or, for that matter, in the history of the language, as far as anyone knows.

If you want to convince yourself of the truth of this remark, the easiest way to do so is to take an arbitrary sentence and wait until you hear it, or read the New York Times until you find it; or take the first sentence in the first book in the Library of Congress and keep reading until you find a repetition of it; or any other such test you wish to try. It is rather obvious, without trying the "experiment," that you are unlikely to find a repetition, or even an utterance which is similar, point by point, in category; or anything of this kind. Normal use of language has this property of unboundedness. It is not a matter of matching certain stimuli or forms of stimuli against associated meanings or kinds of meanings, or anything of this type; but, rather, there is some abstract system of rules which, in some manner, characterize an unbounded meaning-sound correspondence. The grammar of the language, which is somehow represented in the brain, must have this property of determining a sound-meaning correspondence over an infinite range. One normally encounters these absolutely new signals or produces them on the appropriate occasion without any feeling of strangeness or feeling of novelty. This is the basic, most elementary fact that has to be accounted for by anyone who is interested in dealing with the phenomenon of human language in a serious way. It might be thought that "animal language" also has this property. As I have pointed out before, however, it provides for novelty and innovation in a very different manner.

Let me turn briefly to the question of the correspondence between sound and meaning. What is the nature of the grammar that determines this relation? Instead of trying to outline the structure of grammar and the general properties of grammatical structure that seem to be universal, what I would like to do is to give a few examples which illustrate the kind of property these grammatical rules seem to have, that must somehow be accounted for. I think I can probably illustrate this with only two or three examples.

I think someone mentioned earlier that the "integrity of the sentence," what makes it "hang together," is determined by relations among successive items. It is quite clear that that cannot be the case. The fact that it cannot be the case can be seen if you look at some very simple examples of sentences. Let me give you a couple to illustrate.

Consider the sentence: "What disturbed John was being disregarded by everyone." Consider the sound-meaning correspondence. First, we must ask how the signal is determined. I won't try to argue this here, but will simply assert that the form of the signal is determined by two factors: one, by the choice of words, for example, by the choice of "John" instead of "Bill"; and second, by the phrasing, in the normal sense of grammar school. It is clearly true that this sentence can be bracketed into a subject part "What disturbed John" and the predicate "was being disregarded by everyone." Furthermore, the subject part can be identified as a category of a particular type, a nominal category. Furthermore, the phrases "John" and "everyone" are also categories of this nominal type. I won't bother with details, but it is clear that a labeled bracketing of the sentence is an appropriate description of it at some level—I will call it level of "surface structure." This is a psychologically real level of structure in the sense that the rules determining the phonetic form make explicit and essential reference to this level of structure. That is, knowing the intrinsic, ideal form of each lexical item, one can determine from this labeled bracketing the ideal physical form of the signal.

I think this fact plays a role in perception as well as in production of speech. However, let me put this question aside and turn to another point, namely, how the semantic content of the utterance is represented.

A very significant fact about semantic content is that it is not in general represented by the system of labeled bracketing that constitutes surface structure. This is quite obvious if you think about this sentence, or almost any other you pick. Look more carefully at this sentence. Notice, first, that it is ambiguous; that is, it might mean that John is disturbed by the fact that everyone disregards him. That is one sense: "What disturbed John was the fact that everyone disregards him, John." But the sentence has another interpretation, namely, that everyone is disregarding the thing which disturbs John. There is no physical difference between these two interpretations. This is easy to demonstrate. If you put this same signal in two different contexts, you force one or the other interpretation.

The basis for difference of interpretation, again, to use traditional and familiar terms, is the difference in the network of grammatical relations one finds in the sentence. For example, in the paranoid sense, in which what it means is that John is disturbed by the fact that everyone disregards him, it is clear there is a certain grammatical relation called traditionally the "verb-object relation," which holds between "disregard" and "John"; whereas in the other interpretation, where we mean that everyone disregards whatever it is that disturbs John—under that interpretation there is no grammatical relation between "disregard" and "John." Rather, this same verb-object relation holds between "disregard" and, perhaps, "what." Furthermore, the verb-object relation which holds in these two different ways also holds in other parts of the sentence between "disturbed" and "John," and so on.

Furthermore, if I add the word "our" to the sentence, giving "what disturbed John is our being disregarded by everyone," then the ambiguity disappears.

One could go on to show various other complexities in this network of relationships in a sentence. The important point to observe is that the structural properties of the sentence that determine its meaning are not represented in surface structure. So, there is some other aspect of linguistic structure—let me call it "deep structure"—which involves some rather abstract network of grammatical relations. It is this network of grammatical relations, not represented in the signal or in the organization of the signal, that determines the semantic content.

There are many other examples that illustrate the same point. Let me mention two more and say a word about each of them. I have just given an example of an ambiguous sentence. One can draw the same conclusion by looking at the opposite extreme, that is, at two sentences which are essentially synonymous. Compare the following two sentences: "I expected the doctor to examine John" and "I expected John to be examined by the doctor."

There is relationship of paraphrase between the two. That is, although the surface structure of the two sentences is clearly quite different—the signals are entirely different in labeled bracketing—nevertheless, there is something in common which determines the same interpretation.

One might be inclined to say that what makes them the same in meaning is that the embedded sentences, "The doctor examined John" or "John was examined by the doctor," have a very simple relation, namely, the active-passive relation. But matters are not that simple.

Consider the very analogous sentences formed by replacing the word "expect" by "persuade": "I persuaded the doctor to examine John" and "I persuaded John to be examined by the doctor." Although "persuade" and "expect" play the same surface role, it seems this change has made a fundamental difference in the deep structure. Though the two sentences with "expect" are paraphrases, the two sentences with "persuade" are definitely not paraphrases. It is not true if I persuaded the doctor to examine John, then I persuaded John to be examined by the doctor. But it is true that if I expected the doctor to examine John, then, in fact, I expected John to be examined by the doctor, and conversely. There is a much more abstract feature of the grammatical structure of these sentences which somehow determines their semantic content and does it in an entirely nontransparent fashion.

The two significant facts that I want to draw from this discussion are these. First, surface structure of any type, any type of labeled bracketing of the sentence, any attempt to account for the structure of the sentence in terms of contiguity of parts or association between successive parts or anything of this type is certainly going to fail, as you can see by examples of this type, by the fact that whatever it is that determines the structure of the sentence completely transcends any such representation. Whatever it is about the sentence that determines its semantic interpretation, whatever determines that aspect of the sound-meaning correspondence, is very different from the organization of the utterance into grouped parts, even if you categorize the grouped parts.

The second point is that observations of this very elementary kind illustrate the point I made before, namely, that one's knowledge of a language goes well beyond any experience and well beyond any possible teaching. It is entirely out of the question that everyone in this room was taught these facts about "persuade" and "expect"; in fact, nobody even knew them consciously, until a couple of years ago; at least, there is apparently no grammar of English which observes that "persuade" and "expect" differ in this respect. Certainly no one was taught the fact, yet everyone knows it, and knows it without having had experience with these sentences or anything like that. It is extremely unlikely that any of you has ever seen sentences like these or been presented with some kind of indication, by teachers or parents, that these sentences differ in this fashion. The same is true in the case of the first example.

So, somehow, one has represented in one's brain a set of rules which differentiate sharply between surface structure and deep structure in such a way that that aspect of the sentence structure which determines semantic content is extremely abstract and not represented in the physical form or in the arrangement. That is, I think, a crucial point.

Let me give one further example and make a final comment about it and then summarize briefly. Consider the following, again, ambiguous sentence: "Mary saw the boy walking to the railroad station." It is clearly ambiguous. It can mean either that the boy was seen walking toward the railroad station by Mary or that the boy walking toward the railroad station was seen by Mary. So there are at least those two interpretations, and, in fact, others.

Furthermore, we can resolve the ambiguity very simply by replacing "walking" by, say, "walk," giving "Mary saw the boy walk to the railroad station," which has only one interpretation; or by inserting the words "who was," giving "Mary saw the boy who was walking toward the railroad station," which resolves the ambiguity the other way. These are facts that everybody knows and that are somehow determined by the grammatical structure of the sentences. But this is not the point I want to illustrate. The point I want to illustrate relates to the information that every speaker of the language has about the kind of operations that can be performed on these sentences, to assign new interpretations to them.

Although I cannot give details, let me try to illustrate in informal fashion. Consider the problem of how to form questions and relative clauses in English. Given the sentence "John saw Bill," we can form such questions as "Who saw Bill?" and "Whom did Bill see?" We do this by two operations: first, by an operation that we may call "*wh* placement," in which we identify a certain noun phrase and assign *wh* to it, so that if I want to question "Bill" in "John saw Bill," I assign *wh* to "Bill" and I get "John saw *wh* Bill," meaning that the position filled by the word "Bill" is going to be the position questioned.

The second operation, *wh* inversion, takes that *wh* element and puts it in front. Thus, we start with "John saw Bill" and get, by *wh* placement, "John saw *wh* Bill." We then place "*wh* Bill" in front, giving "*wh* Bill did John see." By other rules, "*wh*-Bill" (or, if we were being more accurate, "*wh*-someone") becomes "who." These two operations of *wh* placement and *wh* inversion will basically account for the formation of questions. If we want to form "Who saw Bill?" then, of course, *wh* inversion is vacuous, but we may still say that it applies. The operation of *wh* placement and *wh* inversion will, in fact, with some minor, automatic changes, account for the formation of questions in English.

Precisely the same two operations will account for the formation of relative clauses. If we take the sentence "John saw Bill," we can form the relative clause "who John saw" or "whom John saw," in this case, by again taking the element "Bill," the second noun, assigning *wh*, and placing it in front; similarly, we can form "who saw Bill" by applying the same two operations (the second, vacuously) to "John." Both the question forms of sentences and the relative clause forms of sentences are formed by essentially the same two operations, namely, the operation of *wh* placement and *wh* inversion. Obviously everybody knows these rules—everybody forms questions and relatives using these operations with some elaborations that I omit.

However, notice that these two operations, namely, *wh* placement and *wh* inversion, differ from one another in the following way: *wh* placement is a free operation. I can apply it as many times as I like in a sentence. For example, if I have the sentence "John saw Bill," I can apply it twice to get "Who saw whom?";

or, I can form "Who gave what to whom?" and so on. I can apply *wh* placement as many times as I like, questioning as many aspects of the sentence as I like. On the other hand, *wh* inversion can be applied only once. That is, if I have the sentence "John saw Bill" and I apply *wh* placement twice giving "Who saw whom?" I can't apply the inversion twice to get, say, "Who whom saw?"

Similarly, if I say "John gave what to whom?" I have a possible question in English, but I cannot put both "what" and "whom" in front. I cannot say "What whom did John give to?"

The same is true of relative clauses. You can apply *wh* inversion once but you cannot apply it twice. You can have a *wh* element inside a relative clause, in which case you have a question like this one: "Mary saw the boy who was walking toward what?" Answer: "Railroad station." But I cannot put "what" at the point where the "who" was and get "what who was walking toward." A general constraint says that *wh* inversion can be applied only once.

Summarizing briefly, *wh* placement can be applied freely but *wh* inversion only once within a particular phrase. Actually, what I have shown so far is that *wh* inversion can be applied only once to form a question and only once to form a relative.

Can it be applied once to form a question and once to form a relative? Can I take a sentence with two *wh*'s and apply *wh* once to form a relative and a second time to form a question? The general constraint that restricts *wh*-inversion to a single application should exclude this. In fact, notice what happens if we take the three sentences, "Mary saw the boy walk toward the railroad station," "Mary saw the boy who was walking toward the railroad station," and "Mary saw the boy walking toward the railroad station." If we apply *wh* placement to "railroad station," this will give us the sentences "Mary saw the boy who was walking toward what?" "Mary saw the boy walking toward what?" and "Mary saw the boy walk toward what?"

In considering the sentence "Mary saw the boy who was walking toward what?" notice that in the embedded sentence "who was walking toward what?" I have already applied *wh* inversion once, vacuously, to form the relative clause. Therefore, the general principle should imply that I cannot apply *wh* inversion again, putting the word "what" at the beginning of the sentence. It should imply that I cannot form "What did Mary see the boy who was walking toward?" And this is, in fact, an impossible sentence. But now consider the sentence "Mary saw the boy walk toward what?" There has been no application of *wh* inversion in this sentence; therefore, I ought to be able to form the question by *wh* inversion, giving "What did Mary see the boy walk toward?" This is, in fact, perfectly acceptable.

Consider the third, ambiguous case, namely, "Mary saw the boy walking toward what?" And consider the associated question, namely, "What did Mary see the boy walking toward?" Observe that it is unambiguous. It can only have the interpretation of "what did Mary see the boy walk toward?" It cannot have the interpretation of "the boy who was walking toward the railroad station." So, clearly, it is true that *wh* inversion can be applied only once. If it is applied once to form a relative, it cannot be applied a second time to form a question. That is, it is true with respect to this very abstract operation which somehow we have represented in our minds, that we know how to apply it in such complex cases as this, and we know when it applies to give sentences and when it does not. The principle of this application is apparently something quite abstract. In fact, the explanation just suggested for these facts is not adequate, but this does not affect the point of the example.

These principles of *wh* placement and *wh* inversion, and so on, are what are called in the linguistic literature "grammatical transformations." The significant points about them are two. First, they relate deep structures to surface structure. Deep structures are extremely abstract objects which cannot be arrived at from data by any type of association or inductive procedure and are not represented in the data in any physical form. Second, these transformations, if you look at them as formal operations, are of an extremely special and peculiar kind, meeting very abstract conditions such as the condition of noniterability of inversion, just mentioned. When we acquire language, we acquire a system of operations of this type. We acquire the system of abstract structures that underlies them, the deep structures, and we acquire a set of abstract conditions on these operations, such as the condition of noniterability of inversion. The few examples given illustrate these facts.

It seems to be true that the underlying deep structures vary very slightly, at most, from language to language. That is quite reasonable, because it seems impossible to learn them, since they are not signaled in the sentence and are not recoverable from the signal in any nontrivial way by any inductive or analytical operation, so far as I can see. Since it is hard to imagine how anyone could learn them, it is pleasant to discover that they do not vary much from language to language. That fact enables us to postulate that they form part of the technic which a person uses for acquiring language; that is, they are part of the conceptual apparatus he uses to specify the form of the language to which he is exposed, and not something to be acquired. It is fortunate that this postulate is tenable, since it is difficult to imagine an alternative.

Second, it seems to be true that the abstract properties of transformation are also universal. This is what one would expect, again for the same reason, since it is difficult to imagine how operations of this type could be abstracted from data. There is certainly no process of generalization or association of any kind known to psychology or philosophy, or any procedure of analysis that is known in linguistics that can come close to determining structures of this kind. Again, it is to be expected that these operations and their general properties will be uniform across languages, and this seems to be the case.

From considerations of this kind, there are several basic conclusions, I think, that seem to emerge. A person who knows a language has represented in his brain some very abstract system of underlying structures along with an abstract system of rules that determine, by free iteration, an infinite range of sound-meaning correspondence. Possession of this grammar is a fact which psychology and neurophysiology must ultimately account for.

Second, investigation of the properties of such grammars seems to suggest that these systems are, to a significant extent, not learned, but rather that their basic properties constitute preconditions for learning. One is led to conclude that a grammar is no more learned than, say, ability to walk is learned. There are certain aspects of walking, certain aspects of gait, that may be culture-dependent and may be learned. It is also true there are undoubtedly some superficial aspects of language which are learned and which vary from language to language, but it seems that the deeper properties do not vary and are so abstract that it is hard to imagine how they could be learned.

This raises a second question for ultimate neurophysiological or psychological investigation, namely, what are the mechanisms responsible for the structures which seem to be preconditions for acquisition for language?

It seems to me that there is no significant evidence of continuity, in an evolutionary sense, between the grammars of human languages and animal communication systems. I have no doubt that other cognitive systems, other aspects of human behavior, other aspects of animal behavior, share many of these properties, but it is unlikely that animal communication systems are the ones that share these properties in a most striking sense.

15

THE LOGIC OF NONSTANDARD ENGLISH

WILLIAM LABOV

The editor of a volume such as this is grateful to all the scholars whose brains and expository skills he exploits in constructing an anthology. Yet, among the reproduced articles are some that elicit unusual admiration and gratitude. There are various reasons for this, including exceptional disciplinary control and competence, grace and felicity of expression, directness and the ability to convey simply rather complex scientific messages, timeliness and relevance. Articles that accomplish the latter functions manage to indicate in brief compass that the discipline of anthropology, broadly construed, is capable of making extremely serious and useful contributions to our understanding and possible solution of major social problems. So it is that the bringing of this paper by William Labov to an audience that might never have read it in its original setting is an act that by itself may justify the whole volume. The editor believes this is true of several other articles in this anthology. In any case, the Labov essay happens to throw the clearest illumination on one of the most difficult matters presently besetting American society—the handling of our racial problems.

For many people mention of the science of linguistics conjures up an image of remote and probably sterile research carried out by a bunch of ancient professors who talk to each other and have nothing to say to the world. Hopefully, in our other linguistic selections, this view is subverted as the student sees something of the range of inputs that linguists make into the social and behavioral sciences generally and anthropology specifically. In this selection by Labov, however, skilled linguistic analysis is turned to the exposure of a myth that has been used to feed one of the worst cancers threatening our society—the cancer being racism, and the myth comprising widely publicized assertions of the genetic inferiority of Black people and their alleged uneducability.

Actually, among the congeries of problems attacked here by Labov are some that can be considered old chestnuts in anthropological linguistics. One of these is the question of the relation of a "language" to a "dialect." Labov, however, is struggling with a peculiarly complex version of this question. He must first establish that NNE (Nonstandard Negro English) *is* a full-fledged system of oral communication that presents a regular apparatus of linguistic rules for achieving and altering meaning. Obviously, the full-scale proof of this assertion cannot be contained in one brief article; Labov gives us the bibliographic information necessary to find our way to such a proof in other of his contributions and in the works of additional linguists.

Then attention is directed to the viability of Black English as a mode of communication. With economy and dispatch Labov shows us how vital NNE is, how equal it is to the task of rendering logical categories and discriminations. Along the way, he showers scorn on those whose ignorance of sociolinguistics has led them to easy, and unwarranted, racist conclusions about learning and educability.

It is not Labov's job to give us a blueprint for fulfilling the dreams some of us have about educational equality. Note that he does not in this article even take sides on the question of NNE vs. SAE (Standard American English) as the preferred means of instruction. There are serious voices in Black communities that take sharply divergent views of this particular question. But Labov's contribution stands apart from that dispute. Whatever decision may be made about NNE as a medium of instruction, there can be no doubt of its linguistic integrity. Labov has helped to remove the aegis of science from those who would invoke inadequate and erroneous research in educational psychology and related fields to make the public and many working teachers, regard a portion of our population as basically unfit for learning.

▼△▼△▼

SOURCE: This paper was originally presented at the Twentieth Annual Georgetown Round Table meeting on Linguistics and Language Studies, Washington, D.C., March 14, 1969, where the theme was "Linguistics and the Teaching of Standard English to Speakers of Other Languages or Dialects." We are indebted to Prof. William Labov for permission to use this paper, which also appeared in *Language and Poverty: Perspectives on a Theme*, Frederick Williams (ed.), Chicago: Markham Publishing Company, 1970.

In the past decade, a great deal of federally sponsored research has been devoted to the educational problems of children in ghetto schools. In order to account for the poor performance of children in these schools, educational psychologists have attempted to discover what kind of disadvantage or defect they are suffering from. The viewpoint that has been widely accepted and used as the basis for large scale intervention programs is that the children show a cultural deficit as a result of an impoverished environment in their early years. Considerable attention has been given to language. In this area the deficit theory appears as the concept of verbal deprivation. Negro children from the ghetto area are said to receive little verbal stimulation, to hear very little well-formed language, and as a result are impoverished in their means of verbal expression. They cannot speak complete sentences, do not know the names of common objects, cannot form concepts or convey logical thoughts.

Unfortunately, these notions are based upon the work of educational psychologists who know very little about language and even less about Negro children. The concept of verbal deprivation has no basis in social reality. In fact, Negro children in the urban ghettos receive a great deal of verbal stimulation, hear more well-formed sentences than middle-class children, and participate fully in a highly verbal culture. They have the same basic vocabulary, possess the same capacity for conceptual learning, and use the same logic as anyone else who learns to speak and understand English.

The notion of verbal deprivation is a part of the modern mythology of educational psychology, typical of the unfounded notions which tend to expand rapidly in our educational system. In past decades linguists have been as guilty as others in promoting such intellectual fashions at the expense of both teachers and children. But the myth of verbal deprivation is particularly dangerous, because it diverts attention from real defects of our educational system to imaginary defects of the child. As we shall see, it leads its sponsors inevitably to the hypothesis of the genetic inferiority of Negro children that it was originally designed to avoid.

The most useful service which linguists can perform today is to clear away the illusion of verbal deprivation and to provide a more adequate notion of the relations between standard and nonstandard dialects. In the writings of many prominent educational psychologists, we find very poor understanding of the nature of language. Children are treated as if they have no language of their own in the preschool programs put forward by Bereiter and Engelmann (1966). The linguistic behavior of ghetto children in test situations is the principal evidence of genetic inferiority in the view of Jensen (1969). In this paper, we will examine critically both of these approaches to the language and intelligence of the populations labeled "verbally deprived" and "culturally deprived,"[1] and attempt to explain how the myth of verbal deprivation has arisen, bringing to bear the methodological findings of sociolinguistic work and some substantive facts about language which are known to all linguists. Of particular concern is the relation between concept formation on the one hand, and dialect differences on the other, since it is in this area that the most dangerous misunderstandings are to be found.

Verbality

The general setting in which the deficit theory arises consists of a number of facts which are known to all of us. One is that Negro children in the central urban ghettos do badly in all

[1] I am indebted to Rosalind Weiner of the Early Childhood Education group of Operation Head Start in New York City, and to Joan Baratz of the Education Study Center, Washington, D.C., for pointing out to me the scope and seriousness of the educational issues involved here, and the ways in which the cultural deprivation theory has affected federal intervention programs in recent years.

school subjects, including arithmetic and reading. In reading, they average more than two years behind the national norm (see *New York Times*, December 3, 1968). Furthermore, this lag is cumulative, so that they do worse comparatively in the fifth grade than in the first grade. Reports in the literature show that this poor performance is correlated most closely with socioeconomic status. Segregated ethnic groups seem to do worse than others—in particular, Indian, Mexican-American, and Negro children. Our own work in New York City confirms that most Negro children read very poorly; however, studies in the speech community show that the situation is even worse than has been reported. If one separates the isolated and peripheral individuals from members of central peer groups, the peer-group members show even worse reading records, and to all intents and purposes are not learning to read at all during the time they spend in school (see Labov et al. 1968).

In speaking of children in the urban ghetto areas, the term *lower class* frequently is used, as opposed to *middle class*. In the several sociolinguistic studies we have carried out, and in many parallel studies, it has been useful to distinguish a lower-class group from a working-class one. Lower-class families are typically female-based, or matrifocal, with no father present to provide steady economic support, whereas for the working-class there is typically an intact nuclear family with the father holding a semiskilled or skilled job. The educational problems of ghetto areas run across this important class distinction. There is no evidence, for example, that the father's presence or absence is closely correlated with educational achievement (e.g., Langer and Michaels 1963; Coleman, et al. 1966). The peer groups we have studied in south-central Harlem, representing the basic vernacular culture, include members from both family types. The attack against cultural deprivation in the ghetto is overtly directed at family structures typical of lower-class families, but the educational failure we have been discussing is characteristic of both working-class and lower-class children.

This paper, therefore, will refer to children from urban ghetto areas rather than lower-class children. The population we are concerned with comprises those who participate fully in the vernacular culture of the street and who have been alienated from the school system.[2] We are obviously dealing with the effects of the caste system of American society—essentially a color-marking system. Everyone recognizes this. The question is: By what mechanism does the color bar prevent children from learning to read? One answer is the notion of cultural deprivation put forward by Martin Deutsch and others (Deutsch and associates 1967; Deutsch, Katz, and Jensen 1968). Negro children are said to lack the favorable factors in their home environment which enable middle-class children to do well in school. These factors involve the development of various cognitive skills through verbal interaction with adults, including the ability to reason abstractly, speak fluently, and focus upon long-range goals. In their publications, these psychologists also recognize broader social factors.[3] However, the deficit theory does not focus upon the interaction of the Negro child with white society so much as on his failure to interact with his mother at home. In the literature we find very little direct observation of verbal interaction in the Negro home. Most typically, the investigators ask the

[2] The concept of nonstandard Negro English (NNE) and the vernacular culture in which it is embedded is presented in detail in Labov, et al. (1968, sections 1.2.3 and 4.1). See volume 2, section 4.3 for the linguistic traits which distinguish speakers who participate fully in the NNE culture from marginal and isolated individuals.

[3] For example, in Deutsch, Katz, and Jensen (1968) there is a section on Social and Psychological Perspectives which includes a chapter by Proshansky and Newton on "The Nature and Meaning of Negro Self-Identity," and one by Rosenthal and Jacobson on "Self-Fulfilling Prophecies in the Classroom."

child if he has dinner with his parents, if he engages in dinner-table conversation with them, if his family takes him on trips to museums and other cultural activities, and so on. This slender thread of evidence is used to explain and interpret the large body of tests carried out in the laboratory and in the school.

The most extreme view which proceeds from this orientation—and one that is now being widely accepted—is that lower-class Negro children have no language at all. The notion is first drawn from Basil Bernstein's writings that "much of lower-class language consists of a kind of incidental 'emotional' accompaniment to action here and now" (Jensen 1968, p. 118). Bernstein's views are filtered through a strong bias against all forms of working-class behavior, so that middle-class language is seen as superior in every respect—as "more abstract, and necessarily somewhat more flexible, detailed and subtle" (p. 119). One can proceed through a range of such views until he comes to the preschool programs of Bereiter and Engelmann (1966; Bereiter, et al. 1966). Bereiter's program for an academically oriented preschool is based upon the premise that Negro children must have a language with which they can learn and the empirical finding that these children come to school without such a language. In his work with four-year-old Negro children from Urbana, Bereiter (et al. 1966, pp. 113 ff.) reports that their communication was by gestures, single words, and "a series of badly connected words or phrases," such as *They mine* and *Me got juice*. He reports that Negro children could not ask questions, that "without exaggerating . . . these four-year-olds could make no statements of any kind." Furthermore, when these children were asked "Where is the book?" they did not know enough to look at the table where the book was lying in order to answer. Thus Bereiter concludes that these children's speech forms are nothing more than a series of emotional cries, and he decides to treat them "as if the children had no language at all." He identifies their speech with his interpretation of Bernstein's restricted code: "the language of culturally deprived children . . . is not merely an underdeveloped version of standard English, but is a basically non-logical mode of expressive behavior" (Bereiter, et al. 1966, pp. 112–13). The basic program of his preschool is to teach them a new language devised by Engelmann, which consists of a limited series of questions and answers such as "Where is the squirrel?" "The squirrel is in the tree." The children will not be punished if they use their vernacular speech on the playground, but they will not be allowed to use it in the schoolroom. If they should answer the question, "Where is the squirrel?" with the illogical vernacular form "In the tree" they will be reprehended by various means and made to say, "The squirrel is in the tree."

Linguists and psycholinguists who have worked with Negro children are apt to dismiss this view of their language as utter nonsense. Yet there is no reason to reject Bereiter's observations as spurious. They were certainly not made up. On the contrary, they give us a very clear view of the behavior of student and teacher which can be duplicated in any classroom. In our own work outside of adult-dominated environments of school and home, we have not observed Negro children behaving like this.[4] However, on many occasions we have been asked to help analyze the results of research into verbal deprivation conducted in such test situations.

Here, for example, is a complete interview with a Negro boy, one of hundreds carried out in a New York City school. The boy enters a

[4] The research cited here was carried out in south-central Harlem and other ghetto areas in 1965-1968 to describe the structural and functional differences between Negro nonstandard English and standard English in the classroom. It was supported by the Office of Education as Cooperative Research Projects 3091 and 3288. Detailed reports are given in Labov, et al. (1965), Labov (1967), and Labov, et al. (1968).

room where there is a large, friendly, white interviewer, who puts on the table in front of him a toy and says: "Tell me everything you can about this." (The interviewer's further remarks are in parentheses.)

> [12 seconds of silence]
> (What would you say it looks like?)
> [8 seconds of silence]
> A space ship.
> (Hmmmm.)
> [13 seconds of silence]
> Like a je-et.
> [12 seconds of silence]
> Like a plane.
> [20 seconds of silence]
> (What color is it?)
> Orange. (2 seconds) An' whi-ite. (2 seconds) An' green.
> [6 seconds of silence]
> (An' what could you use it for?)
> [8 seconds of silence]
>
> A je-et.
> [6 seconds of silence]
> (If you had two of them, what would you do with them?)
> [6 seconds of silence]
> Give one to some-body.
> (Hmmm. Who do you think would like to have it?)
> [10 seconds of silence]
> Cla-rence.
> (Mm. Where do you think we could get another one of these?)
> At the store.
> (Oh ka-ay!)

We have here the same kind of defensive, monosyllabic behavior which is reported in Bereiter's work. What is the situation that produces it? The child is in an asymmetrical situation where anything he says can literally be held against him. He has learned a number of devices to avoid saying anything in this situation, and he works very hard to achieve this end. One may observe the intonation patterns of

^{2}a ^{3}'o' ^{2}know

and

a ^{2} space ^{2} sh^{3} ip

which Negro children often use when they are asked a question to which the answer is obvious. The answer may be read as: "Will this satisfy you?"

If one takes this interview as a measure of the verbal capacity of the child, it must be as his capacity to defend himself in a hostile and threatening situation. But unfortunately, thousands of such interviews are used as evidence of the child's total verbal capacity, or more simply his verbality. It is argued that this lack of verbality explains his poor performance in school. Operation Head Start and other intervention programs have largely been based upon the deficit theory—the notions that such interviews give us a measure of the child's verbal capacity and that the verbal stimulation which he has been missing can be supplied in a preschool environment.

The verbal behavior which is shown by the child in the situation quoted above is not the result of the ineptness of the interviewer. It is rather the result of regular sociolinguistic factors operating upon adult and child in this asymmetrical situation. In our work in urban ghetto areas, we have often encountered such behavior. Ordinarily we worked with boys ten to seventeen years old, and whenever we extended our approach downward to eight- or nine-year-olds, we began to see the need for different techniques to explore the verbal capacity of the child. At one point we began a series of interviews with younger brothers of the Thunderbirds in 1390 Fifth Avenue (Ed. Note: a preadolescent group studied in this research). Clarence Robins (CR) returned after an interview with eight-year-old Leon L., who showed the following minimal response to topics which arouse intense interest in other interviews with older boys.

CR: What if you saw somebody kickin' somebody else on the ground, or was using a stick, what would you do if you saw that?
LEON: Mmmm.
CR: If it was supposed to be a fair fight—
LEON: I don' know.
CR: You don' know? Would you do anything? . . . huh? I can't hear you.
LEON: No.
CR: Did you ever see somebody got beat up real bad?
LEON: . . . Nope . . .
CR: Well—uh—did you ever get into a fight with a guy?
LEON: . . . Nope . . .
CR: That was bigger than you?
LEON: Nope . . .
CR: You never been in a fight?
LEON: Nope.
CR: Nobody ever pick on you?
LEON: Nope.
CR: Nobody ever hit you?
LEON: Nope.
CR: How come?
LEON: Ah 'on' know.
CR: Didn't you ever hit somebody?
LEON: Nope.
CR: (incredulously) You never hit nobody?
LEON: Mhm.
CR: Aww, ba-a-a-be, you ain't gonna tell me that!

It may be that Leon is here defending himself against accusations of wrongdoing, since Clarence knows that Leon has been in fights, that he has been taking pencils away from little boys, and so on. But if we turn to a more neutral subject, we find the same pattern:

CR: You watch—you like to watch television? . . . Hey, Leon . . . you like to watch television? (Leon nods) What's your favorite program?
LEON: Uhhmmmm . . . I look at cartoons.
CR: Well, what's your favorite one? What's your favorite program?
LEON: Superman . . .
CR: Yeah? Did you see Superman—ah—yesterday, or day before yesterday? When's the last time you saw Superman?
LEON: Sa-aturday . . .
CR: You rem—you saw it Saturday? What was the story all about? You remember the story?
LEON: M-m.
CR: You don't remember the story of what—that you saw of Superman?
LEON: Nope.
CR: You don't remember what happened, huh?
LEON: Hm-m.
CR: I see—ah—what other stories do you like to watch on TV?
LEON: Mmmm? . . . umm . . . (glottalization)
CR: Hmm? (four seconds)
LEON: Hh?
CR: What's th' other stories that you like to watch?
LEON: Mi-ighty Mouse . . .
CR: And what else?
LEON: Ummmm . . . ahm . . .

This nonverbal behavior occurs in a relatively favorable context for adult-child interaction. The adult is a Negro man raised in Harlem, who knows this particular neighborhood and these boys very well. He is a skilled interviewer who has obtained a very high level of verbal response with techniques developed for a different age level, and he has an extraordinary advantage over most teachers or experimenters in these respects. But even his skills and personality are ineffective in breaking down the social constraints that prevail here.

When we reviewed the record of this interview with Leon, we decided to use it as a test of our own knowledge of the sociolinguistic factors which control speech. In the next interview with Leon we made the following changes in the social situation:

1. Clarence brought along a supply of potato chips, changing the interview into something more in the nature of a party.

2. He brought along Leon's best friend, eight-year-old Gregory.
3. We reduced the height in balance by having Clarence get down on the floor of Leon's room; he dropped from six feet, two inches to three feet, six inches.
4. Clarence introduced taboo words and taboo topics, and proved, to Leon's surprise, that one can say anything into our microphone without any fear of retaliation. The result of these changes is a striking difference in the volume and style of speech. (The tape is punctuated throughout by the sound of potato chips.)

CR: Is there anybody who says *your momma drink pee?*

LEON: (rapidly and breathlessly) Yee-ah!
GREG: Yup!

LEON: And *your father eat doo-doo for breakfas'!*

CR: Ohhh! ! (laughs)

LEON: And they say your father—*your father eat doo-doo for dinner!*

GREG: When they sound on me, I say *C.B.S. C.B.M.*

CR: What that mean?

LEON: Congo booger-snatch! (laughs)
GREG: Congo booger-snatcher! (laughs)

GREG: And sometimes I'll curse with *B.B.*

CR: What that?

GREG: Black boy! (Leon crunching on potato chips) Oh that's a *M.B.B.*

CR: *M.B.B.* What's that?

GREG: 'Merican Black Boy.

CG: Ohh . . .

GREG: Anyway, 'Mericans is same like white people, right?

LEON: And they talk about Allah.

CR: Oh yeah?

GREG: Yeah.

CR: What they say about Allah?

LEON: Allah—Allah is God.
GREG: Allah—

CR: And what else?

LEON: I don' know the res'.

GREG: Allah i—Allah is God, Allah is the only God, Allah . . .

LEON: Allah is the *son* of God.

GREG: But can he make magic?

LEON: Nope.

GREG: I know who can make magic.

CR: Who can?

LEON: The God, the *real* one.

CR: Who can make magic?

GREG: The son of po'—(CR: Hm?) I'm sayin' the po'k chop God![5] He only a po'k chop God! (Leon chuckles).

(The "nonverbal" Leon is now competing actively for the floor; Gregory and Leon talk to each other as much as they do to the interviewer.)

We can make a more direct comparison of the two interviews by examining the section on fighting. Leon persists in denying that he fights, but he can no longer use monosyllabic answers, and Gregory cuts through his facade in a way that Clarence Robins alone was unable to do.

CR: Now, you said you had this fight now; but I wanted you to tell me about the fight that you had.

LEON: I ain't had no fight.

GREG: Yes you did! He said Barry . . .
CR: You said you had one! you had a fight with Butchie,

GREG: An he say Garland! . . . an' Michael!
CR: an' Barry . . .

LEON: I di'n'; you said that, Gregory!
GREG: You did!

LEON: You know you said that!
GREG: You said Garland, remember that?

GREG: You said Garland! Yes you did!
CR: You said Garland, that's right.

[5] The reference to the *pork chop God* condenses several concepts of black nationalism current in the Harlem community. A *pork chop* is a Negro who has not lost the traditional subservient ideology of the South, who has no knowledge of himself in Muslim terms, and the *pork chop God* would be the traditional God of Southern Baptists. He and His followers may be pork chops, but He still holds the power in Leon and Gregory's world.

GREG: He said Mich—an' I say Michael.
CR: Did you have a fight with Garland?
LEON: Uh-Uh.
CR: You had one, and he beat you up, too!
GREG: Yes he did!
LEON: No, I di—I never had a fight with Butch! . . .

The same pattern can be seen on other local topics, where the interviewer brings neighborhood gossip to bear on Leon, and Gregory acts as a witness.

CR: . . . Hey Gregory! I heard that around here . . . and I'm 'on' tell you who said it, too . . .
LEON: Who?
CR: about you . . .
LEON: Who?
GREG: I'd say it!
CR: They said that—they say that the only person you play with is David Gilbert.
LEON: Yee-ah! yee-ah! yee-ah! . . .
GREG: That's who you play with!
LEON: I 'on' play with him no more!
GREG: Yes you do!
LEON: I 'on' play with him no more!
GREG: But remember, about me and Robbie?
LEON: So that's not—
GREG: and you went to Petey and Gilbert's house, 'member? *Ah haaah!!*
LEON: So that's—so—but I would—I had came back out, an' I ain't go to his house no more . . .

The observer must now draw a very different conclusion about the verbal capacity of Leon. The monosyllabic speaker who had nothing to say about anything and cannot remember what he did yesterday has disappeared. Instead, we have two boys who have so much to say they keep interrupting each other, and who seem to have no difficulty in using the English language to express themselves. In turn we obtain the volume of speech and the rich array of grammatical devices which we need for analyzing the structure of nonstandard Negro English; for example: negative concord ("I 'on' play with him no more"), the pluperfect ("had came back out"), negative perfect ("I ain't had"), the negative preterite ("I ain't go"), and so on.

We can now transfer this demonstration of the sociolinguistic control of speech to other test situations, including IQ and reading tests in school. It should be immediately apparent that none of the standard tests will come anywhere near measuring Leon's verbal capacity. On these tests he will show up as very much the monosyllabic, inept, ignorant, bumbling child of our first interview. The teacher has far less ability than Clarence Robins to elicit speech from this child. Clarence knows the community, the things that Leon has been doing, and the things that Leon would like to talk about. But the power relationships in a one-to-one confrontation between adult and child are too asymmetrical. This does not mean that some Negro children will not talk a great deal when alone with an adult, or that an adult cannot get close to any child. It means that the social situation is the most powerful determinant of verbal behavior and that an adult must enter into the right social relation with a child if he wants to find out what a child can do. This is just what many teachers cannot do.

The view of the Negro speech community which we obtain from our work in the ghetto areas is precisely the opposite from that reported by Deutsch or by Bereiter and Engelmann. We see a child bathed in verbal stimulation from morning to night. We see many speech events which depend upon the competitive exhibition of verbal skills—sounding, singing, toasts, rifting, louding—a whole range of activities in which the individual gains status through his use of language (see Labov, et al. 1968, section 4.2). We see the younger child trying to acquire these skills from older children, hanging around on the outskirts of older peer groups, and imitating this behavior to the best of his ability. We see no connection between verbal skill in the speech events characteristic of the street culture and success in the schoolroom.

Verbosity

There are undoubtedly many verbal skills which children from ghetto areas must learn in order to do well in the school situation, and some of these are indeed characteristic of middle-class verbal behavior. Precision in spelling, practice in handling abstract symbols, the ability to state explicitly the meaning of words, and a richer knowledge of the Latinate vocabulary, may all be useful acquisitions. But is it true that all of the middle-class verbal habits are functional and desirable in the school situation? Before we impose middle-class verbal style upon children from other cultural groups, we should find out how much of this is useful for the main work of analyzing and generalizing, and how much is merely stylistic—or even dysfunctional. In high school and college, middle-class children spontaneously complicate their syntax to the point that instructors despair of getting them to make their language simpler and clearer. In every learned journal one can find examples of jargon and empty elaboration, as well as complaints about it. Is the elaborated code of Bernstein really so "flexible, detailed and subtle" as some psychologists (e.g., Jensen 1969, p. 119) believe? Isn't it also turgid, redundant, bombastic, and empty? Is it not simply an elaborated style, rather than a superior code or system? [6]

Our work in the speech community makes it painfully obvious that in many ways working-class speakers are more effective narrators, reasoners, and debaters than many middle-class speakers who temporize, qualify, and lose their argument in a mass of irrelevant detail. Many academic writers try to rid themselves of that part of middle-class style that is empty pretension, and keep that part that is needed for precision. But the average middle-class speaker that we encounter makes no such effort; he is enmeshed in verbiage, the victim of sociolinguistic factors beyond his control.

I will not attempt to support this argument here with systematic quantitative evidence, although it is possible to develop measures which show how far middle-class speakers can wander from the point. I would like to contrast two speakers dealing with roughly the same topic—matters of belief. The first is Larry H., a fifteen-year-old core member of the Jets, being interviewed by John Lewis. Larry is one of the loudest and roughest members of the Jets, one who gives the least recognition to the conventional rules of politeness.[7] For most readers of this paper, first contact with Larry would produce some fairly negative reactions on both sides. It is probable that you would not like him any more than his teachers do. Larry causes trouble in and out of school. He was put back from the eleventh grade to the ninth, and has been threatened with further action by the school authorities.

JL: What happens to you after you die? Do you know?

LARRY: Yeah, I know. (What?) After they put you in the ground, your body turns into—ah —bones, an' shit.

JL: What happens to your spirit?

LARRY: Your spirit—soon as you die, your spirit

[6] The term *code* is central in Bernstein's (1966) description of the differences between working-class and middle-class styles of speech. The restrictions and elaborations of speech observed are labeled as codes to indicate the principles governing selection from the range of possible English sentences. No rules or detailed description of the operation of such codes are provided as yet, so that this central concept remains to be specified.

[7] A direct view of Larry's verbal style in a hostile encounter is given in Labov, et al. (1968, volume 2, pp. 39–43). Gray's Oral Reading Test was being given to a group of Jets on the steps of a brownstone house in Harlem, and the landlord tried unsuccessfully to make the Jets move. Larry's verbal style in this encounter matches the reports he gives of himself in a number of narratives cited in section 4.8 of the foregoing report.

leaves you. (And where does the spirit go?) Well, it all depends . . . (On what?) You know, like some people say if you're good an' shit, your spirit goin' t'heaven . . . 'n' if you bad, your spirit goin' to hell. Well, bullshit! Your spirit goin' to hell anyway, good or bad.

JL: Why?

LARRY: Why? I'll tell you why. 'Cause, you see, doesn' nobody really know that it's a God, y'know, 'cause I mean I have seen black gods, pink gods, white gods, all color gods, and don't nobody know it's really a God. An' when they be sayin' if you good, you goin' t'heaven, tha's bullshit, 'cause you ain't goin' to no heaven, 'cause it ain't no heaven for you to go to.

Larry is a paradigmatic speaker of nonstandard Negro English (NNE) as opposed to standard English. His grammar shows a high concentration of such characteristic NNE forms as negative inversion ("don't nobody know . . ."), negative concord ("you ain't goin' to no heaven . . ."), invariant *be* ("when they be sayin' . . ."), dummy *it* for standard *there* ("it ain't no heaven . . ."), optional copula deletion ("if you're good . . . if you bad . . .") and full forms of auxiliaries ("I have seen . . ."). The only standard English influence in this passage is the one case of "doesn't" instead of the invariant "don't" of NNE. Larry also provides a paradigmatic example of the rhetorical style of NNE: he can sum up a complex argument in a few words, and the full force of his opinions comes through without qualification or reservation. He is eminently quotable, and his interviews give us many concise statements of the NNE point of view. One can almost say that Larry speaks the NNE culture (see Labov, et al. 1968, vol. 2, pp. 38, 71–73, 291–92).

It is the logical form of this passage which is of particular interest here. Larry presents a complex set of interdependent propositions which can be explicated by setting out the standard English equivalents in linear order. The basic argument is to deny the twin propositions:

(A) If you are good, (B) then your spirit will go to heaven.

($\sim A$) If you are bad, (C) then your spirit will go to hell.

Larry denies (B) and asserts that if (A) or ($\sim A$), then (C). His argument may be outlined as follows:

1. Everyone has a different idea of what God is like.
2. Therefore nobody really knows that God exists.
3. If there is a heaven, it was made by God.
4. If God doesn't exist, he couldn't have made heaven.
5. Therefore heaven does not exist.
6. You can't go somewhere that doesn't exist.

($\sim B$) Therefore you can't go to heaven.

(C) Therefore you are going to hell.

The argument is presented in the order: (C), because (2) because (1), therefore (2), therefore ($\sim B$) because (5) and (6). Part of the argument is implicit: the connection (2) therefore ($\sim B$) leaves unstated the connecting links (3) and (4), and in this interval Larry strengthens the propositions from the form (2) "Nobody knows if there is . . ." to (5) "There is no . . ." Otherwise, the case is presented explicitly as well as economically. The complex argument is summed up in Larry's last sentence, which shows formally the dependence of ($\sim B$) on (5) and (6):

An' when they be sayin' if you good, you goin' t'heaven, (The proposition, if A, then B)

Tha's bullshit, (is absurd)

'cause you ain't goin' to no heaven (because B)

'cause it ain't no heaven for you to go to (because (5) and (6)).

This hypothetical argument is not carried on at a high level of seriousness. It is a game played with ideas as counters, in which opponents use a wide variety of verbal devices to win. There is no personal commitment to any of these propositions, and no reluctance to strengthen one's arguments by bending the rules of logic as in the (2)-(5) sequence. But if the opponent invokes the rules of logic, they hold. In John Lewis's interviews, he often makes this move, and the force of his argument is always acknowledged and countered within the rules of logic. In this case, he pointed out the fallacy that the argument (2)-(3)-(4)-(5)-(6) leads to ($\sim C$) as well as ($\sim B$), so it cannot be used to support Larry's assertion (C):

JL: Well, if there's no heaven, how could there be a hell?

LARRY: I mean—ye-eah. Well, let me tell you, it ain't no hell, 'cause this is hell right here, y'know! (This is hell?) Yeah, this is hell right here!

Larry's answer is quick, ingenious, and decisive. The application of the (3)-(4)-(5) argument to hell is denied, since hell is here, and therefore conclusion (C) stands. These are not ready-made or preconceived opinions, but new propositions devised to win the logical argument in the game being played. The reader will note the speed and precision of Larry's mental operations. He does not wander, or insert meaningless verbiage. The only repetition is (2), placed before and after (1) in his original statement. It is often said that the nonstandard vernacular is not suited for dealing with abstract or hypothetical questions, but in fact speakers from the NNE community take great delight in exercising their wit and logic in the most improbable and problematical matters. Despite the fact that Larry H. does not believe in God, and has just denied all knowledge of him, John Lewis advances the following hypothetical question:

JL: . . . but, just say that there is a God, what color is he? White or black?

LARRY: Well, if it is a God . . . I wouldn't know what color, I couldn' say,—couldn' nobody say what color he is or really *would* be.

JL: But now, jus' suppose there was a God—

LARRY: Unless'n they say . . .

JL: No, I was jus' sayin' jus' suppose there is a God, would he be white or black?

LARRY: . . . He's be white, man.

JL: Why?

LARRY: Why? I'll tell you why. 'Cause the average whitey out here got everything, you dig? And the nigger ain't got shit, y'know? Y'unnerstan'? So—um—for—in order for *that* to happen, you know it ain't no black God that's doin' that bullshit.

No one can hear Larry's answer to this question without being convinced that they are in the presence of a skilled speaker with great "verbal presence of mind," who can use the English language expertly for many purposes. Larry's answer to John Lewis is again a complex argument. The formulation is not standard English, but it is clear and effective even for those not familiar with the vernacular. The nearest standard English equivalent might be: "So you know that God isn't black, because if he was, he wouldn't have arranged things like that."

The reader will have noted that this analysis is being carried out in standard English, and the inevitable challenge is: why not write in NNE, then, or in your own nonstandard dialect? The fundamental reason is, of course, one of firmly fixed social conventions. All communities agree that standard English is the proper medium for formal writing and public communication. Furthermore, it seems likely that standard English has an advantage over NNE in explicit analysis of surface forms, which is what we are doing here. We will return to this opposition between explicitness and logical statement in subsequent sections on grammaticality and logic. First, however, it will be helpful to examine standard English in its primary natural setting, as the medium for informal spoken communication of middle-class speakers.

Let us now turn to the second speaker, an upper-middle-class, college-educated Negro man (Charles M.) being interviewed by Clarence Robins in our survey of adults in Central Harlem.

CR: Do you know of anything that someone can do, to have someone who has passed on visit him in a dream?

CHARLES: Well, I even heard my parents say that there is such a thing as something in dreams some things like that, and sometimes dreams do come true. I have personally never had a dream come true. I've never dreamt that somebody was dying and they actually died, (Mhm) or that I was going to have ten dollars the next day and somehow I got ten dollars in my pocket. (Mhm). I don't particularly believe in that, I don't think it's true. I do feel, though, that there is such a thing as—ah—witchcraft. I do feel that in certain cultures there is such a thing as witchcraft, or some sort of *science* of witchcraft; I don't think that it's just a matter of believing hard enough that there is such a thing as witchcraft. I do believe that there is such a thing that a person can put himself in a state of *mind* (Mhm), or that—er—something could be given them to intoxicate them in a certain—to a certain frame of mind—that—that could actually be considered witchcraft.

Charles M. is obviously a good speaker who strikes the listener as well-educated, intelligent, and sincere. He is a likeable and attractive person, the kind of person that middle-class listeners rate very high on a scale of job suitability and equally high as a potential friend.[8] His language is more moderate and tempered than Larry's; he makes every effort to qualify his opinions, and seems anxious to avoid any misstatements or overstatements. From these qualities emerge the primary characteristic of this passage—its verbosity. Words multiply, some modifying and qualifying, others repeating or padding the main argument. The first half of this extract is a response to the initial question on dreams, basically:

1. Some people say that dreams sometimes come true.
2. I have never had a dream come true.
3. Therefore I don't believe (1).

Some characteristic filler phrases appear here: *such a thing as, some things like that,* and *particularly.* Two examples of dreams given after (2) are afterthoughts that might have been given after (1). Proposition (3) is stated twice for no obvious reason. Nevertheless, this much of Charles M.'s response is well-directed to the point of the question. He then volunteers a statement of his beliefs about witchcraft which shows the difficulty of middle-class speakers who (a) want to express a belief in something but (b) want to show themselves as judicious, rational, and free from superstitions. The basic proposition can be stated simply in five words:

"But I believe in witchcraft."

However, the idea is enlarged to exactly 100 words, and it is difficult to see what else is being said. In the following quotations, padding which can be removed without change in meaning is shown in parentheses.

(1) "I (do) feel, though, that there is (such a thing as) witchcraft." *Feel* seems to be a euphemism for 'believe.'

(2) "(I do feel that) in certain cultures (there is such a thing as witchcraft)." This repetition seems designed only to introduce the word *culture,* which lets us know that the speaker knows about anthropology. Does *certain cultures* mean 'not in ours' or 'not in all'?

---

[8] For a description of subjective reaction tests which utilize these evaluative dimensions see Labov, et al. (1968, section 4.6).

(3) "(or some sort of *science* of witchcraft.)" This addition seems to have no clear meaning at all. What is a "science" of witchcraft as opposed to just plain witchcraft? [9] The main function is to introduce the word *science,* though it seems to have no connection to what follows.

(4) "I don't think that it's just (a matter of) believing hard enough that (there is such a thing as) witchcraft." The speaker argues that witchcraft is not merely a belief; there is more to it.

(5) "I (do) believe that (there is such a thing that) a person can put himself in a state of mind . . . that (could actually be considered) witchcraft." Is witchcraft as a state of mind different from the state of belief, denied in (4)?

(6) "or that something could be given them to intoxicate them (to a certain frame of mind). . . ." The third learned word, *intoxicate,* is introduced by this addition. The vacuity of this passage becomes more evident if we remove repetitions, fashionable words and stylistic decorations:

But I believe in witchcraft.
I don't think witchcraft is just a belief.

A person can put himself or be put in a state of mind that is witchcraft. Without the extra verbiage and the "OK" words like *science, culture,* and *intoxicate,* Charles M. appears as something less than a first-rate thinker. The initial impression of him as a good speaker is simply our long-conditioned reaction to middle-class verbosity. We know that people who use these stylistic devices are educated people, and we are inclined to credit them with saying something intelligent. Our reactions are accurate in one sense. Charles M. is more educated than Larry. But is he more rational, more logical, more intelligent? Is he any better at thinking out a problem to its solution? Does he deal more easily with abstractions? There is no reason to think so. Charles M. succeeds in letting us know that he is educated, but in the end we do not know what he is trying to say, and neither does he.

In the previous section I have attempted to explain the origin of the myth that lower-class Negro children are nonverbal. The examples just given may help to account for the corresponding myth that middle-class language is in itself better suited for dealing with abstract, logically complex, or hypothetical questions. These examples are intended to have a certain negative force. They are not controlled experiments. On the contrary, this and the preceding section are designed to convince the reader that the controlled experiments that have been offered in evidence are misleading. The only thing that is controlled is the superficial form of the stimulus. All children are asked "What do you think of capital punishment?" or "Tell me everything you can about this." But the speaker's interpretation of these requests, and the action he believes is appropriate in response, is completely uncontrolled. One can view these test stimuli as requests for information, commands for action, threats of punishment, or meaningless sequences of words. They are probably intended as something altogether different—as requests for display,[10] but in any case the experimenter is normally unaware of the problem of interpretation. The methods of educational psychologists such as used by Deutsch, Jensen, and Bereiter follow the pattern designed for animal experiments where motivation is controlled by simple methods as withholding food until a certain weight reduction is reached. With human sub-

[9] Several middle-class readers of this passage have suggested that *science* here refers to some form of control as opposed to belief. The science of witchcraft would then be a kind of engineering of mental states. Other interpretations can of course be provided. The fact remains that no such difficulties of interpretation are needed to understand Larry's remarks.

[10] The concept of a request for verbal display is here drawn from a treatment of the therapeutic interview given by Blum (in press).

jects, it is absurd to believe that identical stimuli are obtained by asking everyone the same question.

Since the crucial intervening variables of interpretation and motivation are uncontrolled, most of the literature on verbal deprivation tells us nothing about the capacities of children. They are only the trappings of science, approaches which substitute the formal procedures of the scientific method for the activity itself. With our present limited grasp of these problems, the best we can do to understand the verbal capacities of children is to study them within the cultural context in which they were developed.

It is not only the NNE vernacular which should be studied in this way, but also the language of middle-class children. The explicitness and precision which we hope to gain from copying middle-class forms are often the product of the test situation, and limited to it. For example, it was stated in the first part of this paper that working-class children hear more well-formed sentences than middle-class children. This statement may seem extraordinary in the light of the current belief of many linguists that most people do not speak in well-formed sentences, and that their actual speech production, or performance, is ungrammatical.[11] But those who have worked with any body of natural speech know that this is not the case. Our own studies (Labov 1966) of the grammaticality of everyday speech show that the great majority of utterances in all contexts are complete sentences, and most of the rest can be reduced to grammatical form by a small set of editing rules. The proportions of grammatical sentences vary with class backgrounds and styles. The highest percentage of well-formed sentences are found in casual speech, and working-class speakers use more well-formed sentences than middle-class speakers. The widespread myth that most speech is ungrammatical is no doubt based upon tapes made at learned conferences, where we obtain the maximum number of irreducibly ungrammatical sequences.

It is true that technical and scientific books are written in a style which is markedly middle-class. But unfortunately, we often fail to achieve the explicitness and precision which we look for in such writing, and the speech of many middle-class people departs maximally from this target. All too often, standard English is represented by a style that is simultaneously overparticular and vague. The accumulating flow of words buries rather than strikes the target. It is this verbosity which is most easily taught and most easily learned, so that words take the place of thoughts, and nothing can be found behind them.

When Bernstein (e.g., 1966) describes his elaborated code in general terms, it emerges as a subtle and sophisticated mode of planning utterances, where the speaker is achieving structural variety, taking the other person's knowledge into account, and so on. But when it comes to describing the actual difference between middle-class and working-class speakers (Bernstein 1966), we are presented with a proliferation of "I think," of the passive, of modals and auxiliaries, of the first-person pronoun, of uncommon words, and so on. But these are the bench marks of hemming and hawing, backing and filling, that are used by Charles M., the devices which so often obscure whatever positive contribution education can make to our use of language. When we have discovered how much of middle-class style is a matter of fashion and how much actually helps us express ideas clearly, we will have done our-

[11] In several presentations, Chomsky has asserted that the great majority (95 percent) of the sentences which a child hears are ungrammatical. Chomsky (1965, p. 58) presents this notion as one of the arguments in his general statement of the nativist position: "A consideration of the character of the grammar that is acquired, *the degenerate quality and narrowly limited extent of the available data* [my emphasis], the striking uniformity of the resulting grammars, and their independence of intelligence, motivation, and emotional state, over wide ranges of variation, leave little hope that much of the structure of the language can be learned. . . ."

selves a great service. We will then be in a position to say what standard grammatical rules must be taught to nonstandard speakers in the early grades.

Grammaticality

Let us now examine Bereiter's own data on the verbal behavior of the children he dealt with. The expressions *They mine* and *Me got juice* are cited as examples of a language which lacks the means for expressing logical relations, in this case characterized as "a series of badly connected words" (Bereiter, et al. 1966, p. 113). In the case of *They mine*, it is apparent that Bereiter confuses the notions of logic and explicitness. We know that there are many languages of the world which do not have a present copula, and which conjoin subject and predicate complement without a verb. Russian, Hungarian, and Arabic may be foreign, but they are not by that same token illogical. In the case of NNE we are not dealing with even this superficial grammatical difference, but rather with a low-level rule which carries contraction one step farther to delete single consonants representing the verbs *is*, *have* or *will* (Labov 1969). We have yet to find any children who do not sometimes use the full forms of *is* and *will*, even though they may frequently delete them. Our recent studies with Negro children four to seven years old indicate that they use the full form of the copula more often than preadolescents ten to twelve years old, or the adolescents fourteen to seventeen years old.[12]

Furthermore, the deletion of the *is* or *are* in NNE is not the result of erratic or illogical behavior; it follows the same regular rules as standard English contraction. Wherever standard English can contract, Negro children use either the contracted form or (more commonly) the deleted zero form. Thus *They mine* corresponds to standard *They're mine*, not to the full form *They are mine*. On the other hand, no such deletion is possible in positions where standard English cannot contract. Just as one cannot say, "*That's what they're" in standard English, "*That's what they" is impossible in the vernacular we are considering. [Ed. Note: The asterisk indicates forms not permitted in the dialect.] The internal constraints upon both of these rules show that we are dealing with a phonological process like contraction—one sensitive to such phonetic conditions as whether the next word begins with a vowel or a consonant. The appropriate use of the deletion rule, like the contraction rule, requires a deep and intimate knowledge of English grammar and phonology. Such knowledge is not available for conscious inspection by native speakers. The rules we have recently worked out for standard contraction (Labov 1969) have never appeared in any grammar, and are certainly not a part of the conscious knowledge of any standard English speakers. Nevertheless, the adult or child who uses these rules must have formed at some level of psychological organization, clear concepts of tense marker, verb phrase, rule ordering, sentence embedding, pronoun, and many other grammatical categories which are essential parts of any logical system.

Bereiter's reaction to the sentence *Me got juice* is even more puzzling. If Bereiter believes that "Me got juice" is not a logical expression, it can only be that he interprets the use of the objective pronoun *me* as representing a difference in logical relationship to the verb—that the child is in fact saying that "the juice got him" rather than "he got the juice!" If, on the other hand, the child means "I got juice" then his sentence shows only that

---

[12] This is from work on the grammars and comprehension of Negro children, four to eight years old, being carried out by Prof. Jane Torrey of Connecticut College in extension of the research cited above in Labov, et al. (1968).

he has not learned the formal rules for the use of the subjective form *I* and oblique form *me*. We have in fact encountered many children who do not have these formal rules in order at the ages of four, six, or even eight. It is extremely difficult to construct a minimal pair to show that the difference between *he* and *him*, or *she* and *her* carries cognitive meaning. In almost every case, it is the context which tells us who is the agent and who is acted upon. We must then ask: What differences in cognitive, structural orientation are signaled by the child's not knowing this formal rule? In the tests carried out by Jane Torrey, it is evident that the children concerned do understand the difference in meaning between *she* and *her* when another person uses the forms. All that remains, then, is that the children themselves do not use the two forms. Our knowledge of the cognitive correlates of grammatical differences is certainly in its infancy, for this is one of very many questions which we simply cannot answer. At the moment we do not know how to construct any kind of experiment which would lead to an answer; we do not even know what type of cognitive correlate we would be looking for.

Bereiter shows even more profound ignorance of the rules of discourse and of syntax when he rejects "In the tree" as an illogical, or badly formed answer to "Where is the squirrel?" Such elliptical answers are, of course, used by everyone. They show the appropriate deletion of subject and main verb, leaving the locative which is questioned by *wh* + *there*. The reply "In the tree" demonstrates that the listener has been attentive to and apprehended the syntax of the speaker.[13] Whatever formal structure we wish to write for expressions such as *Yes* or *Home* or *In the tree*, it is obvious that they cannot be interpreted without knowing the structure of the question which preceded them, and that they presuppose an understanding of the syntax of the question. Thus if you ask me, "Where is the squirrel?" it is necessary for me to understand the processes of *wh*-attachment, *wh*-attraction to front of the sentence, and flip-flop of auxiliary and subject to produce this sentence from an underlying form which would otherwise have produced "The squirrel is there." If the child has answered "The tree," or "Squirrel the tree," or "The in tree," we would then assume that he did not understand the syntax of the full form, "The squirrel is in the tree." Given the data that Bereiter presents, we cannot conclude that the child has no grammar, but only that the investigator does not understand the rules of grammar. It does not necessarily do any harm to use the full form "The squirrel is in the tree," if one wants to make fully explicit the rules of grammar which the child has internalized. Much of logical analysis consists of making explicit just that kind of internalized rule. But it is hard to believe that any good can come from a program which begins with so many misconceptions about the input data. Bereiter and Engelmann believe that in teaching the child to say "The squirrel is in the tree" or "This is a box" and "This is not a box" they are teaching him an entirely new language, whereas in fact, they are only teaching him to produce slightly different forms of the language he already has.

Logic

For many generations, American schoolteachers have devoted themselves to correcting a small number of nonstandard English rules to their standard equivalents, under the impression that they were teaching logic. This view has been reinforced and given theoretical justification by the claim that NNE

[13] The attention to the speaker's syntax required of the listener is analyzed in detail in a series of unpublished lectures by Prof. Harvey Sacks, Department of Sociology, University of California—Irvine.

lacks the means for the expression of logical thought.

Let us consider for a moment the possibility that Negro children do not operate with the same logic that middle-class adults display. This would inevitably mean that sentences of a certain grammatical form would have different truth values for the two types of speakers. One of the most obvious places to look for such a difference is in the handling of the negative, and here we encounter one of the nonstandard items which has been stigmatized as illogical by schoolteachers—the double negative, or as we term it, *negative concord.* A child who says "He don't know nothing" is often said to be making an illogical statement without knowing it. According to the teacher, the child wants to say "He knows nothing" but puts in an extra negative without realizing it, and so he conveys the opposite meaning. "He does not know nothing," which reduces to "He knows something." I need not emphasize that this is an absurd interpretation. If a nonstandard speaker wishes to say that "He does not know *nothing,*" he does so by simply placing contrastive stress on both negatives as I have done here ("He *don't* know *nothing*") indicating that they are derived from two underlying negatives in the deep structure. But note that the middle-class speaker does exactly the same thing when he wants to signal the existence of two underlying negatives: "He *doesn't* know *nothing.*" In the standard form with one underlying negative ("He doesn't know anything"), the indefinite *anything* contains the same superficial reference to a preceding negative in the surface structure as the nonstandard *nothing* does. In the corresponding positive sentences, the indefinite *something* is used. The dialect difference, like most of the differences between the standard and nonstandard forms, is one of surface form, and has nothing to do with the underlying logic of the sentence.

We can summarize the ways in which the two dialects differ:

	STANDARD ENGLISH, SE	NONSTANDARD NEGRO ENGLISH, NNE
Positive:	He knows something.	He know something.
Negative:	He doesn't know anything.	He don't know nothing.
Double Negative:	He *doesn't* know *nothing.*	He *don't* know *nothing.*

This array makes it plain that the only difference between the two dialects is in superficial form. When a single negative is found in the deep structure, standard English converts *something* to the indefinite *anything,* NNE converts it to *nothing.* When speakers want to signal the presence of two negatives, they do it in the same way. No one would have any difficulty constructing the same table of truth values for both dialects. English is a rare language in its insistence that the negative particle be incorporated in the first indefinite only. The Anglo-Saxon authors of the Peterborough Chronicle were surely not illogical when they wrote *For ne waeren nan martyrs swa pined alse he waeron,* literally, "For never weren't no martyrs so tortured as these were." The "logical" forms of current standard English are simply the accepted conventions of our present-day formal style. Russian, Spanish, French, and Hungarian show the same negative concord as nonstandard English, and they are surely not illogical in this. What is termed "logical" in standard English is of course the conventions which are habitual. The distribution of negative concord in English dialects can be summarized in this way (Labov, et al. 1968, section 3.6; Labov 1968):

1. In all dialects of English, the negative is attracted to a lone indefinite before the verb: "Nobody knows anything," not "*Anybody doesn't know anything."
2. In some nonstandard white dialects, the negative also combines optionally with all other indefinites: "Nobody knows nothing," "He never took none of them."
3. In other white nonstandard dialects, the

negative may also appear in preverbal position in the same clause: "Nobody doesn't know nothing."

4. In nonstandard Negro English, negative concord is obligatory to all indefinites within the clause, and it may even be added to preverbal position in following clauses: "Nobody didn't know he didn't" (meaning, "Nobody knew he did").

Thus all dialects of English share a categorical rule which attracts the negative to an indefinite subject, and they merely differ in the extent to which the negative particle is also distributed to other indefinites in preverbal position. It would have been impossible for us to arrive at this analysis if we did not know that Negro speakers are using the same underlying logic as everyone else.

Negative concord is more firmly established in nonstandard Negro English than in other nonstandard dialects. The white nonstandard speaker shows variation in this rule, saying one time, "Nobody ever goes there" and the next, "Nobody never goes there." Core speakers of the NNE vernacular consistently use the latter form. In repetition tests which we conducted with adolescent Negro boys (Labov, et al. 1968, section 3.9), standard forms were repeated with negative concord. Here, for example, are three trials by two thirteen-year-old members (Boot and David) of the Thunderbirds:

MODEL BY INTERVIEWER: "Nobody ever sat at any of those desks, anyhow."

BOOT:

(1) Nobody never sa—No [whitey] never sat at any o' tho' dess, anyhow.

(2) Nobody never sat any any o' tho' dess, anyhow.

(3) Nobody as ever sat at no desses, anyhow.

DAVID:

(1) Nobody ever sat in-in-in-in- none o'— say it again?

(2) Nobody never sat in none o' tho' desses anyhow.

(3) Nobody—aww! Nobody never ex— Dawg!

It can certainly be said that Boot and David fail the test; they have not repeated the sentence correctly—that is, word for word. But have they failed because they could not grasp the meaning of the sentence? The situation is in fact just the opposite; they failed because they perceived only the meaning and not the superficial form. Boot and David are typical of many speakers who do not perceive the surface details of the utterance so much as the underlying semantic structure, which they unhesitatingly translate into the vernacular form. Thus they have an asymmetrical system:

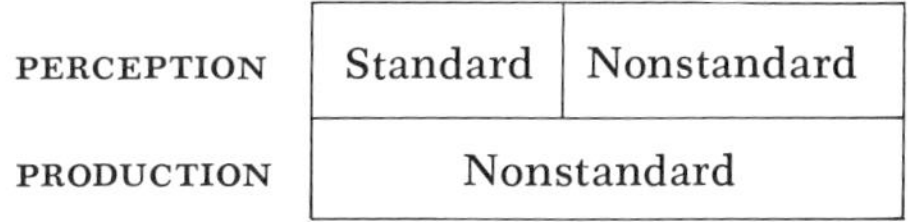

PERCEPTION	Standard	Nonstandard
PRODUCTION	Nonstandard	

This tendency to process the semantic components directly can be seen even more dramatically in responses to sentences with embedded questions; for example:

MODEL:

I asked Alvin if he knows how to play basketball.

BOOT:

I ax Alvin do he know how to play basketball.

MONEY:

I ax Alvin if—do he know how to play basketball.

MODEL:

I asked Alvin whether he knows how to play basketball.

LARRY F:

(1) I axt Alvin does he know how to play basketball.

(2) I axt Alvin does he know how to play basketball.

Here the difference between the words used in the model sentence and in the repetition is striking. Again, there is a failure to pass the test. But it is also true that these boys understand the standard sentence, and translate it with extraordinary speed into the NNE form, which is here the regular Southern colloquial form. This form retains the inverted order to signal the underlying meaning of the question, instead of the complementizer *if* or *whether* which standard English uses for this purpose. Thus Boot, Money, and Larry perceive the deep structure of the model sentence (Figure 1).

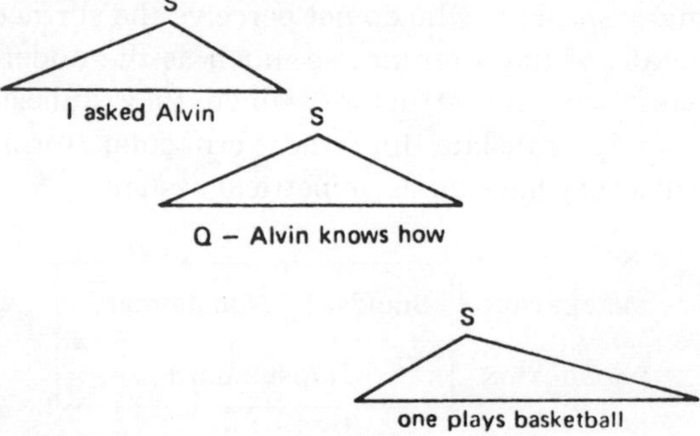

Figure 1

The complementizers *if* or *whether* are not required to express this underlying meaning. They are merely two of the formal options which one dialect selects to signal the embedded question. The colloquial Southern form utilizes a different device—preserving the order of the direct question. To say that this dialect lacks the means for logical expression is to confuse logic with surface detail.

To pass the repetition test, Boot and the others have to learn to listen to surface detail. They do not need a new logic; they need practice in paying attention to the explicit form of an utterance rather than its meaning. Careful attention to surface features is a temporary skill needed for language learning—and neglected thereafter by competent speakers. Nothing more than this is involved in the language training in the Bereiter and Engelmann program, or in most methods of teaching English. There is of course nothing wrong with learning to be explicit. As we have seen, that is one of the main advantages of standard English at its best; but it is important that we recognize what is actually taking place, and what teachers are in fact trying to do.

I doubt if we can teach people to be logical, though we can teach them to recognize the logic that they use. Piaget has shown us that in middle-class children logic develops much more slowly than grammar, and that we cannot expect four-year-olds to have mastered the conservation of quantity, let alone syllogistic reasoning. The problems working-class children may have in handling logical operations are not to be blamed on the structure of their language. There is nothing in the vernacular which will interfere with the development of logical thought, for the logic of standard English cannot be distinguished from the logic of any other dialect of English by any test that we can find.

What's Wrong with Being Wrong?

If there is a failure of logic involved here, it is surely in the approach of the verbal deprivation theorists, rather than in the mental abilities of the children concerned. We can isolate six distinct steps in the reasoning which has led to positions such as those of Deutsch, or Bereiter and Engelmann:

1. The lower-class child's verbal response to a formal and threatening situation is used to demonstrate his lack of verbal capacity, or verbal deficit.
2. This verbal deficit is declared to be a major cause of the lower-class child's poor performance in school.
3. Since middle-class children do better in school, middle-class speech habits are seen to be necessary for learning.
4. Class and ethnic differences in grammatical form are equated with differences in the capacity for logical analysis.
5. Teaching the child to mimic certain formal speech patterns used by middle-class

teachers is seen as teaching him to think logically.

6. Children who learn these formal speech patterns are then said to be thinking logically and it is predicted that they will do much better in reading and arithmetic in the years to follow.

In the preceding sections of this paper I have tried to show that the above propositions are wrong, concentrating on 1, 4, and 5. Proposition 3 is the primary logical fallacy which illicitly identifies a form of speech as the cause of middle-class achievement in school. Proposition 6 is the one which is most easily shown to be wrong in fact, as we will note below.

However, it is not too naive to ask: "What is wrong with being wrong? There is no competing educational theory which is being dismantled by this program, and there does not seem to be any great harm in having children repeat, "This is not a box" for twenty minutes a day. We have already conceded that NNE children need help in analyzing language into its surface components, and in being more explicit. But there are serious and damaging consequences of the verbal deprivation theory which may be considered under two headings: theoretical bias, and consequences of failure.

Theoretical Bias

It is widely recognized that the teacher's attitude toward the child is an important factor in his success or failure. The work of Rosenthal and Jacobson (1968) on self-fulfilling prophecies shows that the progress of children in the early grades can be dramatically affected by a single random labeling of certain children as "intellectual bloomers." When the everyday language of Negro children is stigmatized as "not a language at all" and "not possessing the means for logical thought," the effect of such a labeling is repeated many times during each day of the school year. Every time that a child uses a form of NNE without the copula or with negative concord, he will be labeling himself for the teacher's benefit as "illogical," as a "nonconceptual thinker." Bereiter and Engelmann, Deutsch, and Jensen are giving teachers a ready-made, theoretical basis for the prejudice they already feel against the lower-class Negro child and his language. When teachers hear him say "I dont want none" or "They mine," they will be hearing through the bias provided by the verbal deprivation theory—not an English dialect different from theirs, but the "primitive mentality of the savage mind."

But what if the teacher succeeds in training the child to use the new language consistently? The verbal deprivation theory holds that this will lead to a whole chain of successes in school, and that the child will be drawn away from the vernacular culture into the middle-class world. Undoubtedly this will happen with a few isolated individuals, just as it happens for a few children in every school system today. But we are concerned not with the few but the many, and for the majority of Negro children the distance between them and the school is bound to widen under this approach.

Proponents of the deficit theory have a strange view of social organization outside of the classroom. They see the attraction of the peer group as a substitute for success and gratification normally provided by the school. For example, Whiteman and Deutsch (1968, pp. 86–87) introduce their account of the deprivation hypothesis with an eyewitness account of a child who accidentally dropped his school notebook into a puddle of water and walked away without picking it up: "A policeman who had been standing nearby walked over to the puddle and stared at the notebook with some degree of disbelief." The child's alienation from school is explained as the result of his coming to school without the "verbal, conceptual, attentional, and learning skills requisite to school success." The authors see the child as "suffering from feelings of inferiority because he is failing; he withdraws or becomes hostile, finding gratification elsewhere, such as in his peer group."

To view the peer group as a mere substitute for school shows an extraordinary lack of knowledge of adolescent culture. In our studies in south-central Harlem we have seen the reverse situation—the children who are rejected by the peer group are most likely to succeed in school. Although in middle-class suburban areas, many children do fail in school because of their personal deficiencies, in ghetto areas it is the healthy, vigorous, popular child with normal intelligence who cannot read and fails all along the line. It is not necessary to document here the influence of the peer group upon the behavior of youth in our society, but we may note that somewhere between the time that children first learn to talk and puberty, their language is restructured to fit the rules used by their peer group. From a linguistic viewpoint, the peer group is certainly a more powerful influence than the family (e.g., Gans 1962). Less directly, the pressures of peer-group activity are also felt within the school. Many children, particularly those who are not doing well in school, show a sudden sharp downward turn in the fourth and fifth grades, and children in the ghetto schools are no exception. It is at the same age, at nine or ten years old, that the influence of the vernacular peer group becomes predominant (see Wilmott 1966). Instead of dealing with isolated individuals, the school is then dealing with children who are integrated into groups of their own, with rewards and value systems which oppose those of the school. Those who know the sociolinguistic situation cannot doubt that reaction against the Bereiter-Engelmann approach in later years will be even more violent on the part of the students involved, and their rejection of the school system will be even more categorical.

The essential fallacy of the verbal deprivation theory lies in tracing the educational failure of the child to his personal deficiencies. At present, these deficiencies are said to be caused by his home environment. It is traditional to explain a child's failure in school by his inadequacy. But when failure reaches such massive proportions, it seems to us necessary to look at the social and cultural obstacles to learning, and the inability of the school to adjust to the social situation. Operation Head Start is designed to repair the child, rather than the school; to the extent that it is based upon this inverted logic, it is bound to fall.

Consequences of Failure

The second area in which the verbal deprivation theory is doing serious harm to our educational system is in the consequences of this failure, and the reaction to it. As failures are reported of Operation Head Start, the interpretations which we receive will be from the same educational psychologists who designed this program. The fault will be found not in the data, the theory, nor in the methods used, but rather in the children who have failed to respond to the opportunities offered to them. When Negro children fail to show the significant advance which the deprivation theory predicts, it will be taken as further proof of the profound gulf which separates their mental processes from those of "civilized," middle-class mankind.

A sense of the failure of Head Start is already in the air. Some prominent figures in the program are reacting to this situation by saying that intervention did not take place early enough. Caldwell (1967, p. 16) notes that:

> . . . the research literature of the last decade dealing with social-class differences has made abundantly clear that all parents are not qualified to provide even the basic essentials of physical and psychological care to their children.

The deficit theory now begins to focus on the "long-standing patterns of parental deficit" which fill the literature. "There is, perhaps unfortunately," writes Caldwell (1967, p. 17), "no literacy test for motherhood." Failing such eugenic measures, she has proposed "educationally oriented day care for culturally deprived children between six months and three years of age." The children are returned home each evening to "maintain primary emotional relationships with their own families," but during the day they are removed to "hopefully prevent the deceleration in rate of development which seems to occur in many deprived children around the age of two to three years."

There are others who feel that even the best of the intervention programs, such as those of Bereiter and Engelmann, will not help the Negro child no matter when such programs are applied—that we are faced once again with the "inevitable hypothesis" of the genetic inferiority of the Negro people. Many readers of this paper are undoubtedly familiar with the paper of Arthur Jensen in the *Harvard Educational Review* (1969) which received immediate and widespread publicity. Jensen (p. 3) begins with the following quotation from the United States Commission on Civil Rights as evidence of the failure of compensatory education:

> The fact remains, however, that none of the programs appear to have raised significantly the achievement of participating pupils, as a group, within the period evaluated by the Commission. (U.S. Commission on Civil Rights 1967, p. 138)

Jensen believes that the verbal-deprivation theorists with whom he had been associated—Deutsch, Whiteman, Katz, Bereiter—have been given every opportunity to prove their case, and have failed. This opinion is part of the argument which leads him to the overall conclusion (p. 82) that "the preponderance of the evidence is . . . less consistent with a strictly environmental hypothesis than with the genetic hypothesis." In other words, racism—the belief in the genetic inferiority of Negroes—is the most correct view in the light of the present evidence.

Jensen argues that the middle-class white population is differentiated from the working-class white and Negro population in the ability for "cognitive or conceptual learning," which Jensen calls Level II intelligence as against mere "associative learning" or Level I intelligence:

> . . . certain neural structures must also be available for Level II abilities to develop, and these are conceived of as being different from the neural structures underlying Level I. The genetic factors involved in each of these types of ability are presumed to have become differentially distributed in the population as a function of social class, since Level II has been most important for scholastic performance under the traditional methods of instruction. (Jensen 1969, p. 114)

Jensen found, for example, that one group of middle-class children were helped by their concept-forming ability to recall twenty familiar objects that could be classified into four categories: animals, furniture, clothing, or foods. Lower-class Negro children did just as well as middle-class children with a miscellaneous set, but showed no improvement with objects that could be so categorized.

The research of the educational psychologists cited here is presented by them in formal and objective style, and is widely received as impartial scientific evidence. Jensen's paper has been reported by Joseph Alsop and William F. Buckley, Jr. (*New York Post*, March 20, 1969) as "massive, apparently authoritative. . . ." It is not my intention to examine these materials in detail, but it is important to realize that we are dealing with special pleading by those who have a strong personal commitment. Jensen is concerned with class differences in cognitive style and verbal learning. His earlier papers incorporated the cultural deprivation theory which he now rejects as a basic explanation.[14] Jensen (1968, p. 167) clas-

[14] In Deutsch, et al. (1968), Jensen expounds the verbal deprivation theory in considerable detail, for example (p. 119): "During this 'labeling' period . . . some very important social-class differences may exert their effects on verbal learning. Lower-class parents engage in relatively little of this naming or 'labeling' play with their children. . . . That words are discrete labels for things seems to be better known by the middle-class child entering first grade than by the lower-class child. Much of this knowledge is gained in the parent-child interaction, as when the parent looks at a picture book with the child. . . ."

sified the Negro children who fail in school as "slow learners" and "mentally retarded" and urged that we find out how much their retardation is due to environmental factors and how much is due to "more basic biological factors." His conviction that the problem must be located in the child leads him to accept and reprint some truly extraordinary data. To support the genetic hypothesis Jensen (1969, p. 83) cites the following percentage estimates by Heber (1968) of the racial distribution of mental retardation (based upon IQs below 75) in the general population: [15]

SOCIOECONOMIC STATUS	PERCENT OF WHITES	PERCENT OF NEGROES
1 (highest)	0.5	3.1
2	0.8	14.5
3	2.1	22.8
4	3.1	37.8
5 (lowest)	7.8	42.9

These estimates, that almost half of lower-class Negro children are mentally retarded, could be accepted only by someone who has no knowledge of the children or the community. If he had wished to, Jensen could easily have checked this against the records of any school in any urban ghetto area. Taking IQ tests at their face value, there is no correspondence between these figures and the communities we know. For example, among seventy-five boys we worked with in central Harlem who would fall into status categories 4 or 5 above, there were only three with IQs below 75. One spoke very little English; one could barely see; the third was emotionally disturbed. When the second was retested, he scored 91, and the third retested at 87.[16] There are of course hundreds of realistic reports available to Jensen. He simply selected one which would strengthen his case for the genetic inferiority of Negro children.

In so doing, Jensen was following a standing tradition among the psychologists who developed the deficit hypothesis. The core of Deutsch's environmental explanation of poor performance in school is the Deprivation Index, a numerical scale based on six dichotomized variables. One variable is "the educational aspirational level of the parent for the child." Most people would agree that a parent who did not care if a child finished high-school would be a disadvantageous factor in the child's educational career. In dichotomizing this variable Deutsch was faced with the fact that the educational aspiration of Negro parents is in fact very high, higher than for the white population, as he shows in other papers.[17] In order to make the Deprivation Index work, he therefore set the cutting point for the deprived group as "college or less" (see Whiteman and Deutsch 1968, p.100). Thus if a Negro child's father says that he wants his son to go all the way through college, the child will fall into the "deprived" class on this variable. In order to receive the two points given to the "less deprived" on the index, it would be necessary for the child's parent to insist on graduate school or medical school! This decision is not discussed by the author; it simply stands as a *fait accompli* in the tables. This is the type of data manipulation carried on by those who are strongly committed to a particular hypothesis.

[15] Heber's (esp. 1968) studies of eighty-eight Negro mothers in Milwaukee are cited frequently throughout Jensen's paper. The estimates in this table are not given in relation to a particular Milwaukee sample, but for the general United States population. Heber's study was specifically designed to cover an area of Milwaukee which was known to contain a large concentration of retarded children, Negro and white, and he has stated that his findings were "grossly misinterpreted" by Jensen (*Milwaukee Sentinel,* June 11, 1969).

[16] The IQ scores given here are from group rather than individual tests and must therefore not be weighed heavily; the scores are from the Pintner-Cunningham test, usually given in the first grade in New York City schools in the 1950s.

[17] In Table 15–1 in Deutsch and associates (1967, p. 312), section C shows that some degree of college training was desired by 96, 97, and 100 percent of Negro parents in class levels I, II, and III, respectively. The corresponding figures for whites were 79, 95, and 97 percent.

No one can doubt that the reported inadequacy of Operation Head Start and of the verbal deprivation hypothesis has now become a crucial issue in our society.[18] The controversy which has arisen over Jensen's article typically assumes that programs such as Bereiter and Engelmann's have tested and measured the verbal capacity of the ghetto child. The cultural sociolinguistic obstacles to this intervention program are not considered, and the argument proceeds upon the data provided by the large, friendly interviewers whom we have seen at work in the extracts given above.

The Linguistic View

Linguists are in excellent position to demonstrate the fallacies of the verbal deprivation theory. All linguists agree that nonstandard dialects are highly structured systems. They do not see these dialects as accumulations of errors caused by the failure of their speakers to master standard English. When linguists hear Negro children saying "He crazy" or "Her my friend," they do not hear a primitive language. Nor do they believe that the speech of working-class people is merely a form of emotional expression, incapable of expressing logical thought.

All linguists who work with NNE recognize that it is a separate system, closely related to standard English but set apart from the surrounding white dialects by a number of persistent and systematic differences. Differences in analysis by various linguists in recent years are the inevitable products of differing theoretical approaches and perspectives as we explore these dialect patterns by different routes—differences which are rapidly diminishing as we exchange our findings. For example, Stewart (see Chapter 17 in Williams 1970) differs with me on how deeply the invariant *be* of "She be always messin' around" is integrated into the semantics of the copula system with *am, is, are,* and so on. The position and meaning of *have . . . ed* in NNE is very unclear, and there are a variety of positions on this point. But the grammatical features involved are not the fundamental predicators of the logical system. They are optional ways of contrasting, foregrounding, emphasizing, or deleting elements of the underlying sentence. There are a few semantic features of NNE grammar which may be unique to this system. But the semantic features we are talking about here are items such as "habitual," "general," "intensive." These linguistic markers are essentially *points of view*—different ways of looking at the same events, and they do not determine the truth values of propositions upon which all speakers of English agree.

The great majority of the differences between NNE and standard English do not even represent such subtle semantic features as those, but rather extensions and restrictions of certain formal rules, and different choices of redundant elements. For example, standard English uses two signals to express the progressive, *be* and *-ing,* while NNE often drops the former. Standard English signals the third person in the present by the subject noun phrase and by a third singular *-s;* NNE does not have this second redundant feature. On the other hand, NNE uses redundant negative elements in negative concord, in possessives like *mines,* uses *or either* where standard English uses a simple *or,* and so on.

When linguists say that NNE is a system,

[18] The negative report of the Westinghouse Learning Corporation and Ohio University on Operation Head Start was published in the *New York Times* (April 13, 1969). The evidence of the failure of the program is accepted by many, and it seems likely that the report's discouraging conclusions will be used by conservative Congressmen as a weapon against any kind of expenditure for disadvantaged children, especially Negroes. The two hypotheses mentioned to account for this failure are that the impact of Head Start is lost through poor teaching later on, and more recently, that poor children have been so badly damaged in infancy by their lower-class environment that Head Start cannot make much difference. The third "inevitable" hypothesis of Jensen is not reported here.

we mean that it differs from other dialects in regular and rule-governed ways, so that it has equivalent ways of expressing the same logical content. When we say that it is a separate subsystem, we mean that there are compensating sets of rules which combine in different ways to preserve the distinctions found in other dialects. Thus as noted above NNE does not use the *if* or *whether* complementizer in embedded questions, but the meaning is preserved by the formal device of reversing the order of subject and auxiliary.

Linguists therefore speak with a single voice in condemning Bereiter's view that the vernacular can be disregarded. I exchanged views on this matter with all of the participants in the Twentieth Annual Georgetown Round Table where this paper was first presented, and their responses were in complete agreement in rejecting the verbal deprivation theory and its misapprehension of the nature of language. The other papers in the report (Alatis 1970) of that conference testified to the strength of the linguistic view in this area. It was William Stewart who first pointed out that Negro English should be studied as a coherent system, and in this all of us follow his lead. Dialectologists like Raven McDavid, Albert Marckwardt, and Roger Shuy have been working for years against the notion that vernacular dialects are inferior and illogical means of communication. Linguists now agree that teachers must know as much as possible about Negro nonstandard English as a communicative system.

The exact nature and relative importance of the structural differences between NNE and standard English are not in question here. It is agreed that the teacher must approach the teaching of the standard through a knowledge of the child's own system. The methods used in teaching English as a foreign language are recommended, not to declare that NNE is a foreign language, but to underline the importance of studying the native dialect as a coherent system for communication. This is in fact the method that should be applied in any English class.

Linguists are also in excellent position to assess Jensen's claim that the middle-class white population is superior to the working-class and Negro populations in the distribution of Level II, or conceptual, intelligence. The notion that large numbers of children have no capacity for conceptual thinking would inevitably mean that they speak a primitive language, for even the simplest linguistic rules we discussed above involve conceptual operations more complex than those used in the experiment Jensen cities. Let us consider what is involved in the use of the general English rule that incorporates the negative with the first indefinite. To learn and use this rule, one must first identify the class of indefinites involved—*any, one, ever,* which are formally quite diverse. How is this done? These indefinites share a number of common properties which can be expressed as the concepts "indefinite," "hypothetical," and "nonpartitive." One might argue that these indefinites are learned as a simple list, by association learning. But this is only one of the many syntactic rules involving indefinites—rules known to every speaker of English, which could not be learned except by an understanding of their common, abstract properties. For example, everyone knows, unconsciously, that *anyone* cannot be used with preterit verbs or progressives. One does not say, "*Anyone went to the party" or "*Anyone is going to the party." The rule which operates here is sensitive to the property [+ hypothetical] of the indefinites. Whenever the proposition is not inconsistent with this feature, *anyone* can be used. Everyone knows, therefore, that one can say "Anyone who was anyone went to the party" or "If anyone went to the party . . ." or "Before anyone went to the party . . ." There is another property of *anyone* which is grasped unconsciously by all native speakers of English; it is [+ distributive]. Thus if we need one more man for a game of bridge or basketball, and there is a crowd outside, we ask, "Do any of you want to play?" not "Do some of you want to play?" In both cases, we are considering a plurality, but with *any*, we consider them one at a time, or distributively.

What are we then to make of Jensen's contention that Level I thinkers cannot make use of the concept *animal* to group together a miscellaneous set of toy animals? It is one thing to say that someone is not in the habit of using a certain skill. But to say that his failure to use it is genetically determined implies dramatic consequences for other forms of behavior, which are not found in experience. The knowledge of what people must do in order to learn language makes Jensen's theories seem more and more distant from the realities of human behavior. Like Bereiter and Engelmann, Jensen is handicapped by his ignorance of the most basic facts about human language and the people who speak it.

There is no reason to believe that any nonstandard vernacular is in itself an obstacle to learning. The chief problem is ignorance of language on the part of all concerned. Our job as linguists is to remedy this ignorance; but Bereiter and Engelmann want to reinforce it and justify it. Teachers are now being told to ignore the language of Negro children as unworthy of attention and useless for learning. They are being taught to hear every natural utterance of the child as evidence of his mental inferiority. As linguists we are unanimous in condemning this view as bad observation, bad theory, and bad practice.

That educational psychology should be strongly influenced by a theory so false to the facts of language is unfortunate; but that children should be the victims of this ignorance is intolerable. It may seem that the fallacies of the verbal deprivation theory are so obvious that they are hardly worth exposing. I have tried to show that such exposure is an important job for us to undertake. If linguists can contribute some of their available knowledge and energy toward this end, we will have done a great deal to justify the support that society has given to basic research in our field.

References

ALATIS, J., ed. *Georgetown Monographs in Language and Linguistics, No.* 22. Washington, D.C.: Georgetown University Press, 1970.

BEREITER, C., and ENGELMANN, S. *Teaching Disadvantaged Children in the Preschool.* Englewood Cliffs, N.J.: Prentice-Hall, 1966.

BEREITER, C.; ENGELMANN, S.; OSBORN, JEAN; and REIDFORD, P. A. An academically oriented preschool for culturally deprived children. In F. Hechinger, ed., *Pre-school Education Today.* New York: Doubleday, 1966.

BERNSTEIN, B. Elaborated and restricted codes: Their social origins and some consequences. In A. G. Smith, ed., *Communication and Culture.* New York: Holt, Rinehart & Winston, 1966.

BLUM, A. The sociology of mental illness. In J. Douglas, ed., *Deviance and Respectability.* New York: Basic Books (in press).

CALDWELL, BETTYE M. What is the optimal learning environment for the young child? *American J. Orthopsychiatry* 1967, 37:8–21.

CHOMSKY, N. *Aspects of the Theory of Syntax.* Cambridge, Mass.: M.I.T. Press, 1965.

COLEMAN, J. S., et al. *Equality of Educational Opportunity.* Washington, D.C.: U.S. Office of Education, 1966.

DEUTSCH, M., and associates. *The Disadvantaged Child.* New York: Basic Books, 1967.

DEUTSCH, M.; KATZ, I.; and JENSEN, A. R., eds., *Social Class, Race, and Psychological Development.* New York: Holt, Rinehart & Winston, 1968.

GANS, H. *The Urban Villagers.* New York: Free Press, 1962.

HEBER, R. Research on education and habilitation of the mentally retarded. Paper read at Conference on Sociocultural Aspects of Mental Retardation, June 1968, Peabody College, Nashville, Tenn.

JENSEN, A. R. Social class and verbal learning. In M. Deutsch, et al., eds., *Social Class, Race, and Psychological Development.* New York: Holt, Rinehart & Winston, 1968.

———. How much can we boost IQ and scholastic achievement? *Harvard Educational Review* 1969, 39:1–123.

LABOV, W. On the grammaticality of everyday speech. Paper presented at the annual meeting of the

Linguistic Society of America, December 1966, New York.

———. Some sources of reading problems for Negro speakers of nonstandard English. In A. Frazier, ed., *New Directions in Elementary English*. Champaign, Ill.: National Council of Teachers of English, 1967. Also reprinted in J. C. Baratz and R. W. Shuy, eds., *Teaching Black Children to Read*. Washington, D.C.: Center for Applied Linguistics, 1969.

———. Negative attraction and negative concord in four English dialects. Paper presented at the annual meeting of the Linguistic Society of America, December 1968, New York.

———. Contraction, deletion, and inherent variability of the English copula. *Language* 1969, 45:715–62.

LABOV, W.; COHEN, P.; ROBINS, C. A preliminary study of the structure of English used by Negro and Puerto Rican speakers in New York City. Final report, U.S. Office of Education Cooperative Research Project No. 3091, 1965.

LABOV, W.; COHEN, P.; ROBINS, C.; and LEWIS, J. A study of the nonstandard English of Negro and Puerto Rican speakers in New York City. Final report, U.S. Office of Education Cooperative Research Project No. 3288 Vols. 1, 2. Mimeographed. Columbia University, 1968.

LABOV, W., and ROBINS, C. A note on the relation of reading failure to peer-group status in urban ghettos. *The Teachers College Record* 1969, 70: 396–405.

LANGER, T. S., and MICHAELS, S. T. *Life Stress and Mental Health*. New York: Free Press, 1963.

ROSENTHAL, R., and JACOBSON, LENORE. Self-fulfilling prophecies in the classroom: teachers' expectations as unintended determinants of pupils' intellectual competence. In M. Deutsch, et al., eds., *Social Class, Race, and Psychological Development*. New York: Holt, Rinehart & Winston, 1968.

United States Commission on Civil Rights. *Racial Isolation in the Public Schools*, Vol. 1. Washington, D.C.: U.S. Government Printing Office, 1967.

WHITEMAN, M., and DEUTSCH, M. Social disadvantage as related to intellective and language development. In M. Deutsch, et al., eds., *Social Class, Race, and Psychological Development*. New York: Holt, Rinehart & Winston, 1968.

WILLIAMS, FREDERICK, ed. *Language and Poverty: Perspectives on a Theme*. Chicago: Markham Publishing Company, 1970.

WILMOTT, P. *Adolescent Boys of East London*. London: Routledge & Kegan Paul, 1966.

16

LANGUAGE AND COMMUNICATION

JOHN J. GUMPERZ

There are ample grounds for assuming that the ideal worlds of readers and editors are rather distinct. The latter are oppressed by any limitation on the number of pages they may fill. This observation might arise at almost any juncture in this book, but it is singularly appropriate here. A great deal is going on in linguistics that is of direct consequence to anthropology, but only a small portion of this volume is devoted to it. By way of redress, the following selection looks over the field and indicates some of the main thrusts of contemporary research among anthropological linguists and in the general field of linguistics.

▼△▼△▼

Language is central to human groups and its problems to all types of social science investigation. Different disciplines, however, have different approaches to language. While linguists deal with the structure of human codes, other social scientists take these structures for granted and are concerned only with the effect of verbal messages. Although the two types of endeavor have generally been kept separate, they have always influenced each other somewhat.[1]

Recent developments have strengthened this mutual influence. Concepts and research techniques derived from the study of linguistic

SOURCE: *The Annals of the American Academy of Social and Political Science*, Vol. 373 (1967): 219–31. Reprinted by permission of The American Academy of Political and Social Science and the author.

My approach to the subject of language and communication has been considerably broadened through recent field research in India and Norway, supported by the National Science Foundation. I am grateful to Patricia Calkins for bibliographical and editorial assistance.

form have profoundly affected the anthropologist's view of the nature of human culture. They threaten to revolutionize psychological theories of learning and concept-formation and the sociologists' study of social interaction.[2] Many of the linguists' new tasks, on the other hand, are beginning to require increasing amounts of social science sophistication. This paper will review some of the most important of these developments in the light of their relevance to our understanding of social science theory and human communication.

The impetus for much of modern linguistics derives from the ethnographic investigation of speakers of unwritten, hitherto almost unknown, languages. Detailed field investigations during the first decades of this century had shown that many of the accepted generalizations about primitive thought and culture were based on inadequate factual information. In their efforts to generalize, earlier scholars had unwittingly imposed the categories of known European languages on the tribal languages that they were studying.[3] This had kept them from noticing some of the most basic features of these languages. The result was a call for more field work and a renewed search for techniques that would enable the investigator to overcome his predispositions to analyze all speech in the categories of his own language, and to concentrate upon the significant characteristics which set off the new language.

The discovery that the actual articulatory or acoustic characteristics of sounds are less important in characterizing interlanguage differences than the speakers' perception of these stimuli led to the formation of the phonemic principle: each language categorizes sound signals into a finite number of perceptually distinct and functionally related units, the phonemes. These, in turn, combine to form larger meaningful units, the morphemes. It is the set of such units, that is, the grammatical system, which distinguishes speakers of one language from another. From the point of view of perception, the phonemes constitute a yardstick by which speakers evaluate the acoustic signals that they receive. The ability to segment the stream of sound into discrete phonemes and morphemes was regarded as the hallmark of human linguistic ability.[4]

The concept of the phoneme was inherent in much of the work of European and American linguists of the 1920's and 1930's, and one of its most recent important refinements,[5] the theory of distinctive features, derives from the work of the European writings of Roman Jakobson and others.[6] Techniques for the discovery of phonemes, however, were developed primarily by Americans, following the principles laid down by Leonard Bloomfield.[7] These techniques relied on the classification of perceptually distinct articulatory segments strictly in terms of their distribution with respect to surrounding articulatory segments, without recourse to semantic information. By limiting the scope of linguistic analysis in this way, the Bloomfieldian grammars achieved a unique degree of explicitness of statement and of replicability. For the first time in any social science, any two trained investigators making independent studies of similar bodies of data could expect with fair certainty to arrive at equivalent results. These procedures earned for linguistics a reputation as the "most scientific" of the social sciences, but in view of the limited nature of the subject matter, the linguists' findings appeared in large part unimportant to other social scientists' interests.

With the recent shift in focus from sounds to syntax and with the broadening of linguists' views on the nature of language, much of this has changed. Rather than concentrating on the isolation of phonemic and morphological categories, the new writings address themselves to the more basic problem of how meanings are encoded into sounds.

As Sydney Lamb puts it, sounds and meanings are, by their very nature, patterned separately from each other.[8] While the production of sound is limited by the physiology of human articulatory organs, thought is not so limited.

It would be unreasonable, therefore, to expect that there is a one to one correspondence between meaning and sound sequences, as some of Bloomfield's early followers seemed to imply. The problem of sound-meaning relationships was discussed extensively in the writings of Saussure, Jesperson, and other early linguists.[9] Modern scholars like Louis Hjelmslev, Charles Hockett, and Zellig Harris have made fundamental contributions to its solution.[10] The new grammar accounts for it by postulating three (or more) independently patterned components of language; the semantic, the syntactic, and the phonological. The semantic component deals with the way in which ideas are strung together into meaningful sequences, while the phonological component deals with phonologically realistic sequences.

The concept of syntax as elaborated by Noam Chomsky and his followers is by far the most accepted and explicit method of accomplishing the transition between the above two components.[11] Chomsky assumes that syntax can be divided into two sections, deep structure and surface structure. Deep structure consists of the output of the semantic rules, that is, the phrase structures or kernel structures of the language, as they used to be called. By application of transformation rules which allow for processes of elision, embedding, and other complex processes, these structures are then converted into the phonologically more realistic surface structures.

Grammar in these terms is not simply a collection of categories but is also a set of rules for relating different types of categories. Because of the elusiveness of meaning, the operation of rules is not directly observable. The aim of modern grammar, like that of modern science, is not to describe reality but to construct a model capable of accounting for what goes on. Grammatical rules thus describe a speaker's linguistic competence, that is, the knowledge that he must have in order to produce grammatically correct sentences or in order to interpret others' speech.

Knowledge of a language, however, is not identified with the way in which this knowledge is used. The actual production of linguistic forms may be affected by a number of special conditions, such as error, interruption of sentences, and the like. Such errors rarely affect interpretation of messages because the speaker's linguistic competence enables him to disregard these deviations by guessing correctly what could have been said. A grammar, then, is a theory of a language rather than a classification of sound sequences. Human linguistic ability is an intricate cognitive process involving both categorization of sounds and meanings and the conversion of one into the other in accordance with syntactic rules.

Concepts such as phrase structure and transformational rule, deep and surface structure, and the notational conventions applying to them refer to human language in general. The new grammar has as its goal a theory of human linguistic ability. In the earlier Bloomfieldian linguistics, by contrast, each language was regarded as a system of its own. Hence it was possible to maintain, as Joos did,[12] that, at least in theory, there can be an infinite variety of discrete phonemic systems. Jakobson and his collaborators' concept of distinctive features,[13] which showed that all known phonemic systems could, in fact, be described as clusters of a few universal distinctive features or components, has already suggested Joos's position to be an extreme one. Recent linguistic writings go considerably farther than Jakobson in assuming that all grammars are ultimately related—that is, they share certain common features which are part of universal grammar. It is the task of particular grammars to describe particular languages within this general framework and to specify in what way they differ. This renewed concern with linguistic universals [14] shows promise of deepening our understanding of human behavior in general through comparative studies within a single and consistent conceptual framework.

The Psychological Reality of Grammatical Rules

Psycholinguistics as an area of investigation which applies some of the results of linguistic analysis to human cognition and perception had been established several years prior to the work of generative grammarians.[15] Recent writings stimulated by Chomsky's own critique of Skinner's notion of language behavior as a stimulus-response phenomenon [16] have raised new and basic problems in the study of the psychological processes involved in language behavior and developmental psycholinguistics, the study of the child's acquisition of linguistic competence.

The first area of investigation is, in part, defined in Miller's coding hypothesis: humans process language in two parts, semantic and syntactic.[17] Semantic structures are generated first, and transformations are applied to them afterwards. The hypothesis has been tested in several studies measuring the time that subjects took to learn sentences of varying syntactic complexity.[18] These studies clearly establish the important effect that syntactic structure has on the coding process, although other factors such as sentence length and memory limitations may interfere. A second line of investigation tests the strength of grammatical relationships among words within the sentence. Since it was shown that sentence subjects were more effective prompts for sentence recall than objects, it can be assumed that the speakers' performance reflects the linguists' prediction that the break between subject and verb is more fundamental than the break between object and verb.

Language Develcpment

While research on the behavioral correlates of grammatical operations is only beginning, the studies of language development have already produced some striking results. Here, as in linguistics proper, there has been a shift in interest from phonology to syntax. A number of carefully designed longitudinal studies involving several subjects have now supplemented our earlier, largely anecdotal information.[19] These studies show that the old assumptions that children learn language by mirroring (imitating) adult speech is incapable of explaining the experimental data. Ervin-Tripp,[20] for example, observes that children in learning the past tense of verbs first learn irregular strong verb forms such as *went* and *sat;* when the regular verb pasts such as *walked, learned,* and *laughed* are learned, strong verbs are modified to follow the regular pattern and words such as *sitted* and *comed* appear. Slobin [21] cites similar information from Russian language development studies, where ungrammatical forms which do not occur in any form of adult speech appear as part of the normal process of language development. Obviously, these incorrect forms cannot be the result of direct imitation.

McNeill [22] suggests that the simplest explanation of these and similar phenomena is one which, in line with transformational theory, views language-learning as a process of hypothesis-formation in which the child begins with the simplest possible grammar to accommodate his communicative needs and then changes this grammer as his communicative needs become more complex. In the same article, McNeill goes on to argue that, in view of the complexity of the language-learning task and in view of the amount of creativity it involves, the categories of universal grammar are, in fact, innate, not learned. Thus, every human being is said to be born with a knowledge of the categories of universal grammar, and language-learning requires no special training. Stimulating as this hypothesis is, the suggestion that grammatical categories are innate seems somewhat extreme. It might be more reasonable to suggest, as Slobin does,[23] that what the child brings to learning is a set of procedures and inference rules which he uses to process linguistic data and that the linguistic universals arise as a result of these processing procedures rather than the reverse. Although the question of innateness is far from being resolved, it would seem that the use of linguistic techniques can make a fundamental contribution to our understanding of human learning.

Language and Cognition

Much of the discussion in this area, commonly referred to as language and culture, has revolved around the Sapir-Whorf hypothesis,[24] that is, that language determines a speaker's perception of the universe around him. Some of the earlier studies attempting to test the relationship between culture and grammatical categories directly have brought little in the way of significant results.[25] They have, however, given rise to a whole new tradition of formal ethnographic investigation. The objects of analysis here are semantic domains, groups of words sharing some features of meaning and referring to well-defined areas of culture. Two pioneering studies by Lounsbury and Goodenough for the first time applied linguistic techniques to the semantic analysis of kinship terminologies.[26] During the last ten years, these have been followed by a great deal of additional work in kinship, color terminology, pronoun systems, terms of direction, botanical terminologies, and the like.[27] Work in ethnographic semantics goes beyond mere enumeration of terminology to establish that lexical domains are structured, and that these structures are describable in terms of abstract systems which relate to the actual terms in somewhat the same way as phonemes relate to sounds.[28] Presumably, it is these abstract patterns of relationships among terms that affect our perception of our sociocultural environment. Learning about a new culture is thus not simply a matter of adding to an already existing body of information, but one requiring a restructuring of perception akin to the learning of new grammatical patterns.

It follows from the above studies that, whenever we apply language to describe our surroundings, our very view of these surroundings is affected by our speech patterns. This is true for the isolated tribals' perception of color, disease, and botanical terminology as well as for the application of highly refined Western scientific concepts to new areas of inquiry.[29] Assuming such scientific concepts to be universally applicable and unquestioningly applying them to the study of different cultures may thus generate the same kind of inaccuracies that linguists of the Bloomfieldian tradition found in the work of their predecessors. Ethnographic semanticists hence call for new, more sophisticated field work and search for discovery procedures capable of overcoming the limitations imposed by our own conceptual structure.[30]

Important in this respect is a recent study by Roy D'Andrade [31] which points to a basic contradiction in psychological approaches to measurement. When questionnaires are administered to subjects, correlations between test items are considered to reflect the fact that these items elicit similar behavior on the part of the persons questioned, while when psychologists rate the behavior of subjects, similar correlations between items are taken as evidence of underlying unities in the psychological processes of the subjects rather than in those of the psychologists themselves. In a restudy of a well-known analysis of personality terms, he shows that correlations found between these terms which are commonly attributed to similarity of behavior on the part of the subjects can be equally explained on the basis of the linguistically determined semantic similarity among the terms employed by the testers.

The claims of ethnographic semanticists to the behavioral reality of their findings have not been uniformly accepted. Schneider [32] suggests that formal analysis of kinship terminology is unable to explain some of the socially most important aspects of kinship behavior. Berreman [33] criticizes the lack of terminological clarity and the confusion which characterize many of the formal studies, while Harris [34] suggests that formalization tends to distort empirical reality.

Few today would support the most extreme Whorfian view, that language completely inhibits the expression of certain types of ideas. With sufficient effort, it is possible to say anything in any language. However, it has been shown by Brown and Lenneberg [35] that certain things are more easy to say—to use Brown's term, more readily codable—in some languages than in others, and it is this difference in codability which tends to guide and ultimately affect our perceptive processes unless special effort is made to guard against its effect.

Although there is still considerable disagreement about techniques of semantic analysis and about its implications, most scholars agree in rejecting the notion of culture as a set of beliefs and traditions which are independent of everyday behavior. Instead, they have adopted a more modest view of culture as a set of rules or expectations which we apply to the interpretation of behavior.[36] Although considerably more restricted than the traditional notion of culture, it is at the same time considerably more powerful, since it is capable of coping with the diversity of values and background characteristic of complex societies. Two people can be said to share the same culture if they can understand each other, that is, if they can communicate effectively in a significant number of situations. However, since, in the course of their daily routines, individuals may communicate with a wide variety of others, and since different norms may apply in each case, there is no longer any reason to assume that any particular human group—even a relatively small community—is culturally uniform. Single communities may be culturally very diverse indeed. The present notion of culture accounts for this fact by assuming that persons may apply different semantic models to their interaction with different individuals.

The Social Significance of Speech Variation

Although there is a long tradition of research in intrasocietal variation in language, this work has for the most part been unaffected by structural linguistics. Dialectologists concerned with this subject have frequently doubted the structuralists' formalization, pointing to their lack of attention to the details of everyday behavior. Structural linguists, on the other hand, by the very nature of their attempts at formalization, have felt it necessary to operate with the assumption that languages are unitary homogeneous wholes. Even with the recent expansion of the scope of linguistic analysis, this attitude has not changed. The concept of linguistic competence, so far, is applied only to those rather general aspects of grammar which apply to all individuals in a society; interpersonal and intergroup variation tend to be assigned to the level of performance and, by implication, are viewed as not subject to systematic analysis.[37]

Hertzler's recent *Sociology of Language*,[38] the first general treatment of the subject to appear in some years, to some extent reflects the intellectual gap between formalists and students of speech variation. It fails almost completely to account for the recent advances in linguistic theory, cultural anthropology, and psychology. Although it presents an extensive list of literature on almost all aspects of language and society, it does not give any criteria for evaluating the significance of these writings for general social science theory.

In spite of its shortcomings, the earlier dialectological work has some important and sometimes unrealized implications for the general social scientist. Bloomfield's review of this literature, and Halliday, McIntosh and Stevens' more recent treatment,[39] show that variation within speech communities is a close reflection of internal ethnic and cultural diversity, settlement patterns, division of labor, and, above all, the intensity of interpersonal and intergroup communication. During the last ten years, research combining structural linguistic analysis with highly sophisticated sampling and interviewing techniques of modern social science has deepened our understanding of speech variation and its function in society.[40]

While earlier writings had focused on relatively simple rural groups, this latter work deals primarily with complex class and caste societies of Asia and the urban West. In all these societies, speakers, as part of their linguistic competence, control a number of speech styles, dialects, or languages and shift among these as the context demands. The most important results derive from the analysis of the linguistic correlates of such stylistic shift, the variables. As described by Labov,[41] these variables are of three types: indicators, markers, and stereotypes. The term "indicators" refers to variations such as the difference in vowel quality between the vowels in English *cot* and *caught* which although quite evident to the linguist are rarely recognized by speakers themselves. In general, indicators do not change with change of style. "Markers" are features like the presence or absence of consonantal *r* in words like *are* or *part* in New York English, which tend to shift with context, that is, degree of formality and the like. Speakers are frequently not aware of this shift. "Stereotypes," on the other hand, are commonly cited dialect characteristics which appear as the topic of overt discussion, such as the vowel-consonant cluster in the New York pronunciation of words like *work* and *bird* or in the negative *ain't*. The three types of variables function independently of each other and are thus capable of differentiating between what Lévi-Strauss[42] has called "conscious and subconscious behavior" as well as separating inter- from intra-group variation. They form a highly refined index for social differentiations of all kinds, be they the result of ethnic, socioeconomic, occupational, or role differences.

One of the most important results of recent studies in speech variation so far has been the clarification of the relationship between intensity of communication and the assimilation of linguistic forms. Bloomfield's assumption that intensity of communication leads to a decrease in speech variation is only partly justified. In highly stratified societies such as the caste societies of India, it is quite possible for people to be in constant and regular communication over long periods of time without adopting each other's speech patterns.[43] It would seem that communication leads to uniformity only when there is both the possibility and the desire for social assimilation. Where social norms put a premium on social distinctness, linguistic symbols of such distinctness tend to be maintained.

Whenever ethnically distant groups live side by side within a single community, the emphasis on cultural distinctions may conflict with the need for economic co-operation. These conflicts are frequently resolved by grammatical convergence, that is, linguistic changes resulting in the appearance of underlying similarity in grammatical and syntactic structure, while surface distinctions are preserved. Recent investigation of such problems shows that, as a result of these phenomena, even genetically different languages when in contact over long periods of time come to have almost identical grammatical structure.[44] In spite of what seem like important distinctions of language, multilingualism does not serve as a profound barrier to the transmission of information in such cases. Profound social and structural change resulting in a realignment of power relationships among individuals and groups, on the other hand, does tend to lead to linguistic uniformity.[45] Thus, individuals torn out of their environment and settling, as individuals, in a foreign country do tend to adopt the speech characteristics of the group among which they settle. Similarly, urbanization, when it results in an increase of social mobility and breakdown of traditional barriers, also leads to a disappearance of preexisting language differences.

Since language contains indicators of an individual's status and family background, speech serves as an important clue for the transmission of such social information. Several recent studies have been concerned with this problem.[46] Perhaps the most interesting of these studies are those employing the matched-guise technique developed by Wallace Lambert [47] and his associates. Here judges are asked to rate identical passages produced in two languages or two dialects by individuals who control both equally well. Ratings for performances in the two languages often differ radically, and the technique is a highly sensitive tool for the measurement of intergroup stereotypes, as well as an important aid in the pedagogy of second-language instruction.

The Place of Language in Society

Most discussions of language and society operate with the assumption that the two entities constitute different kinds of reality, subject to correlational studies. Thus, sociolinguistics, as the study of socially determined speech variation in society has begun to be called, is said by one recent author to be concerned with the systematic covariance of linguistic structure and social structure.[48] Presumably, such covariance could be studied by comparing linguistic data collected in accordance with traditional interview methods with independently collected information on social structure. Even a brief look at the field methods of modern sociolinguists however shows that this is not the case. The results of recent studies are, in large part, due to the fact that sociolinguists, like ethnographic semanticists, have developed new and bias-free data-collection techniques which emphasize the recording of speech in natural contexts,[49] attempt to simulate natural context by prolonged experimentation with culturally realistic questionnaire construction,[50] or work with group discussion.[51] In effect, then, sociolinguists have acknowledged that linguistic form is to some extent a function of social context, and that the ability to communicate effectively involves more than what is implied in Chomsky's rather narrowly defined view of linguistic competence. Hymes has suggested the term "communicative competence" for this broader, socially determined skill.[52]

The concept of the speech event suggested by Roman Jakobson and elaborated in Hymes' "Ethnography of Speaking" [53] provides the theoretical framework for the above position. Within a speech event, linguistic codes are only one of several constituent elements, along with the social characteristics of speakers and audiences, their cultural background, the environment in which they interact, and the social nature of the interaction. Ervin-Tripp's [54] examination of the interrelationship of these factors shows that they are, in fact, related, forming structures of their own separate from that of individual codes. Frake provides an analysis of one such sequence of events showing a sequential structure determining what can be said when and how.[55]

One of the most stimulating approaches to the interrelationship between speakers' linguistic competence and their communicative competence in actual speech events is Bernstein's [56] notion that social relationships act as intervening variables between linguistic structures and their realization in a particular speech event. In documenting this thesis, Bernstein points to the difference between what he calls restricted codes, characteristic of working-class speakers (and possibly of certain other socially isolated groups) and elaborated codes, characteristic of urban middle-class speakers, that is, those showing a higher number of intergroup contacts. Restricted codes, as Bernstein describes them, generally provide a narrow range of syntactic alternatives and are, in general, more formulaic and less oriented toward the introduction of new information than are more elaborated codes. The difference between the two codes is assumed to be the result of different socialization processes involving different modes of social control between the groups in question. Although Bernstein's theories have given rise to considerable discussion in the United States and elsewhere on the causes of linguistic deprivation among the lower classes in urban ghettos and its effect on social mobility,[57] the details of his findings have not yet been validated. A recent experiment, however, provides some empirical support for Bernstein's theoretical position by demonstrating that it is possible to generate different patterns of language usage by exposing discussion groups having different social characteristics to similar topical stimuli. Language usage in such cases is independent of overt attitudes to language.[58]

Further empirical evidence for the way in which language usage symbolizes social relationships derives from recent anthropological and psychological work on forms of address.[59] In surveying the use of the respectful *vous* and the familiar *tu* in French and of equivalent forms in other languages, Roger Brown and his associates distinguish between reciprocal and nonreciprocal usages. In nonreciprocal usage, one person in a dyad, that is, the socially superior or more prestigious, addresses the other with *tu* and is, in turn, addressed with *vous*. In reciprocal usage, each member of the dyad has the choice between the two forms, in which case the familiar form indicates an attitude of mutual solidarity while the formal form indicates an attitude of relative distance or hostility. While Brown is interested primarily in the psychological aspects of choice of the personal pronoun, it would seem that his distinction between reciprocal and nonreciprocal usage also refers to differences in the norms governing the enactment of social relationships. In the one case, usage is status-determined, whereas, in the other case, it is a matter of individual option. Work with language- or dialect-switching in linguistically diverse communities indicates that similar distinctions between socially prescribed and optional usage also apply here.[60] The greater the social barriers or social compartmentalization, the more the emphasis on status-determined usage. The greater the social fluidity and opportunities for social mobility, the greater the degree of reciprocal usage. Brown's studies, as well as some of the studies on language shift cited above, in fact, suggest that the transition from traditional to urbanized societies is accompanied by an equivalent change in the norms of language usage.

Social Constraints on Language Behavior

Although the recent work lists a variety of factors affecting language usage, such as the speakers, their audience, their social position, their occupation, the time and the place in which the interaction takes place, its function, and the like, our experience with the relationship between sounds and phonemes suggests that it is the participants' categorization of these factors which is significant rather than the social scientist's measure of role, class, degree of education, and the like. It seems reasonable to assume, then, that—in social interaction at least—these categories are communicative phenomena. Linguistic interaction, then, is a process in which speakers take in clues from the outside environment and, by a culturally determined process of perception similar to that which converts sounds into phonemes and meanings into words, arrive at appropriate behavioral strategies. These are, in turn, translated into verbal symbols. Stimulated by Goffman's [61] suggestion and by recent writings of Garfinkel, a group of sociologists have begun detailed investigations of this process, using techniques and principles roughly similar to those employed in linguistic analysis.[62] Although this work is still in its beginning stages, there are indications that persons behave in accordance with rules of social interaction which, like the rules of grammar, function below the level of consciousness. If this is the case, then linguistic and social categories are phenomena of the same order; and moving from statements of social constraints to grammatical rules thus represents a transformation from one level of abstraction to another within a single communicative system.[63]

Footnotes

[1] Charles F. Hockett and Robert Ascher, "The Human Revolution," *Current Anthropology*, Vol. 5, No. 3 (June 1964), a review of evidence on the evolution of language, also touches on this question.

[2] For some reactions to these developments, see Jenkins' comments in Frank Smith and George A. Miller (eds.), *The Genesis of Language* (Cambridge, Mass.: M.I.T. Press, 1966), pp. 347–360.

[3] Archibald A. Hill, "A Note on Primitive Languages," in Dell Hymes (ed.), *Language in Culture and Society* (New York: Harper and Row, 1964), pp. 86–89.

[4] See, for example, the discussion in John B. Carroll, *The Study of Language* (Cambridge, Mass.: Harvard University Press, 1953).

[5] Basic American writings on this subject are brought together in Martin Joos (ed.), *Readings in Linguistics* (Washington, D.C.: American Council of Learned Societies, 1957), also published as *Readings in Linguistics I* (4th ed.; Chicago: University of Chicago Press, 1966). Basic European writings are collected in Eric P. Hamp, Fred W. Householder, and Robert Austerlitz (eds.), *Readings in Linguistics II* (Chicago: University of Chicago Press, 1966).

[6] Roman Jakobson, C. M. Fant, and M. Halle, *Preliminaries to Speech Analysis* (Cambridge, Mass.: M.I.T. Press, 1961); N. S. Troubetzkoy, *Principes de Phonologie,* trans. J. Cantineau (Paris: Klincksieck, 1949).

[7] Leonard Bloomfield, *Language* (New York: Henry Holt, 1933) and "A Set of Postulates for the Science of Language," in Joos (ed.), *op. cit.*, pp. 26–31.

[8] Sydney M. Lamb, *Outline of Stratificational Grammar* (Washington, D.C.: Georgetown University Press, 1966).

[9] Ferdinand de Saussure, *Cours de Linguistique Generale* (Paris: Payot, 1916). There is an English translation by Wade Baskin: *Course in General Linguistics* (New York: Philosophical Library, 1958).

[10] For an evaluation of Hjelmslev's work, see Sydney Lamb, "Epilegomena to a Theory of Language," *Romance Philology,* Vol. 19, pp. 531–573. See also Charles F. Hockett, "Linguistic Elements and Their Relations," *Language,* Vol. 37 (1961), pp. 29–53; Zellig S. Harris, "Discourse Analysis," *Language,* Vol. 28 (1952), pp. 18–23, "Co-occurrence and Transformation in Linguistic Structure," *Language,* Vol. 33 (1957), pp. 283–340, and "Transformational Theory," *Language,* Vol. 41 (1965), pp. 363–401; Sydney Lamb, "The Sememic Approach to Structural Semantics," in A. Kimball Romney and Roy G. D'Andrade (eds.), "Transcultural Studies in Cognition." *American Anthropologist,* Vol. 66, No. 3, Part 2 (1964), pp. 57–78. Thomas Sebeok (ed.), *Current Trends in Linguistics,* Vol. III (The Hague: Mouton, 1966), contains articles by Hockett, Pike, Weinicich, Chomsky, and others surveying their own and other contributions to modern linguistic theory.

[11] Chomsky's ideas first appeared in *Syntactic Structures* (The Hague: Mouton, 1957). The discussion here is, however, largely based on the more mature statement of the theory in *Aspects of the Theory of Syntax* (Cambridge, Mass.: M.I.T. Press, 1965).

[12] See Joos (ed.), *op. cit.*

[13] Jakobson, Fant, and Halle, *op. cit.*

[14] Some empirical investigations of this problem are found in Joseph H. Greenberg (ed.), *Universals of Language* (Cambridge, Mass.: M.I.T. Press, 1963). For Chomsky's view of universals, see his *Aspects of the Theory of Syntax, op. cit.*

[15] See Charles E. Osgood and Thomas A. Sebeok, *Psycholinguistics: A Survey of Theory and Research Problems* (Supplement to *Journal of Abnormal and Social Psychology,* Vol. 49 [1954]); Roger Brown, *Words and Things* (Glencoe, Ill.: Free Press, 1958); Sol Saporta (ed.), *Psycholinguistics: A Book of Readings* (New York: Holt, Rinehart, and Winston, 1961).

[16] Noam Chomsky, "A Review of B. F. Skinner's *Verbal Behavior,*" in Jerry A. Fodor and Jerrold J. Katz (eds.), *The Structure of Language* (Englewood Cliffs, N.J.: Prentice-Hall, 1964), pp. 547–578.

[17] George A. Miller, "Some Psychological Studies of Grammar," *American Psychologist,* Vol. 17 (1962), pp. 748–762.

[18] George A. Miller and Kathryn O. McKean, "A Chronometric Study of Some Relations between Sentences," *Quarterly Journal of Experimental Psychology,* Vol. 16 (1964), pp. 297–308; for a review of other literature, see Elisabeth Ann Turner, "Developmental Studies of Sentence, Voice, and Reversibility" (unpublished Ph.D. Thesis, Cornell University, 1966). Much of the material in this and the following section will be covered in W. Weksel and T. G. Bever, *The Structure and Psychology of Language* (New York: Holt, Rinehart, and Winston, forthcoming, 1968).

[19] David McNeill, "Developmental Psycholinguistics,"

in Smith and Miller (eds.), *op. cit.*, pp. 15–85; Susan Ervin-Tripp, "Language Development," in Lois and Martin Hoffman (eds.), *Review of Child Development Research*, Vol. II (New York: Russell Sage Foundation, 1966), pp. 55–106; Martin Braine, "The Ontogeny of English Phrase Structure: The First Phase," *Language*, Vol. 39 (1963), pp. 1–13; Roger Brown and Ursula Bellugi (eds.), "The Acquisition of Language" ("Society for Research in Child Development Monographs," Vol. 29, No. 1; Lafayette, Ind.: Society for Research in Child Development, 1964); Wick Miller and Susan Ervin-Tripp, "The Development of Grammar in Child Language," in Brown and Bellugi (eds.), *op. cit.*, pp. 9–34.

[20] Susan Ervin-Tripp, "Imitation and Structural Change in Children's Language," in E. Lenneberg (ed.), *New Directions in the Study of Language* (Cambridge, Mass.: M.I.T. Press, 1964).

[21] Dan I. Slobin, "The Acquisition of Russian as a Native Language," in Smith and Miller (eds.), *op. cit.*, pp. 129–148.

[22] McNeill, *op. cit.*

[23] Dan I. Slobin, "Comments on 'Developmental Psycholinguistics,'" in Smith and Miller (eds.), *op. cit.*, pp. 85–92.

[24] For Whorf's writing on this topic, see John B. Carroll (ed.), *Language, Thought, and Reality* (New York: John Wiley & Sons, 1956).

[25] See Harry Hoijer (ed.), *Language in Culture* (Chicago: University of Chicago Press, 1954).

[26] Ward Goodenough, "Componential Analysis and the Study of Meaning," *Language*, Vol. 32 (1956), pp. 195–216; Floyd Lounsbury, "Semantic Analysis of the Pawnee Kinship Usage," *Language*, Vol. 32 (1956), pp. 158–194.

[27] For a review of this work, see B. N. Colby, "Ethnographic Semantics: A Preliminary Survey," *Current Anthropology*, Vol. 7, No. 1 (1966), pp. 3–32. Some of the most significant work in this field is found in the following recent publications: Ward H. Goodenough (ed.), *Explorations in Cultural Anthropology* (New York: McGraw-Hill, 1964); A. K. Romney and Roy G. D'Andrade (eds.), *Transcultural Studies in Cognition* (special issue, *American Anthropologist*, Vol. 66, No. 3, Part 2 (1964); E. A. Hammel (ed.), *Formal Semantic Analysis* (special issue, *American Anthropologist*, Vol. 67, No. 5, Part 2 (1965); Stephen Tyler (ed.), *Cognitive Anthropology* (New York: Holt, Rinehart and Winston, forthcoming, 1968).

[28] See Harold C. Conklin, "Ethnogenealogical Method," in Ward H. Goodenough (ed.), 1964, *op. cit.* For a more recent summary, see Paul Kay, "Comments on B. N. Colby," *Current Anthropology*, Vol. 7, No. 1 (1966), pp. 20–22.

[29] Harold C. Conklin, "Hanunoo Color Categories," *Southwestern Journal of Anthropology*, Vol. 11 (1955), pp. 339–344; Charles O. Frake, "The Diagnosis of Disease among the Subanum of Mindanao," in Dell Hymes, *op. cit.*, pp. 193–214.

[30] Charles O. Frake, "Notes on Queries in Ethnography," in Romney and D'Andrade (eds.), *op. cit.*, pp. 132–145; Mary Black and Duane Metzger, "Ethnographic Description and the Study of Law," in Laura Nader (ed.), *The Ethnography of Law* (special issue, *American Anthropologist*, Vol. 67, No. 6, Part 2 (1965), pp. 141–165; Duane Metzger and G. E. Williams, "A Formal Ethnographic Analysis of Tenejapa Ladino Weddings," *American Anthropologist*, Vol. 65, No. 5 (1963), pp. 1076–1101.

[31] Roy G. D'Andrade, "Trait Psychology and Componential Analysis," in Hammel (ed.), *op. cit.*, pp. 215–228.

[32] D. M. Schneider, "American Kin Terms and Terms for Kinsmen: A Critique of Goodenough's Componential Analysis of Yankee Kinship Terminology," in Hammel (ed.), *op. cit.*, pp. 288–308.

[33] Gerald D. Berreman, "Anemic and Emetic Analysis in Social Anthropology," *American Anthropologist*, Vol. 68, No. 2 (1966).

[34] Marvin Harris, *The Nature of Cultural Things* (New York: Random House, 1963).

[35] Roger Brown and Eric H. Lenneberg, "A Study in Language and Cognition," *Journal of Abnormal and Social Psychology*, Vol. 49 (1954), pp. 454–462.

[36] Ward H. Goodenough, "Cultural Anthropology and Linguistics," in Dell Hymes (ed.), *op. cit.*, pp. 36–39.

[37] Jerrold J. Katz and Jerry A. Fodor, "The Structure of a Semantic Theory," in Fodor and Katz, *op. cit.*, pp. 479–518.

[38] Joyce O. Hertzler, *A Sociology of Language* (New York: Random House, 1965).

[39] Bloomfield, *op. cit.*, pp. 42–56; M. A. K. Halliday, Angus McIntosh, and Peter Strevens, *The Linguistic Sciences and Language-Teaching* (London: Longmans, Green, 1964), pp. 75–110.

[40] For a popular review of relevant work see William Labov, "Variation in Language," in Carrol Reed (ed.), *The Learning of Language* (Washington, D.C.: National Council of Teachers of English, in preparation). Other significant contributions can be found in Charles Ferguson and John J. Gumperz, *Linguistic Diversity in South Asia* (*International Journal of American Linguistics*, Vol. 26, No. 3, Part 3 [1960]); William Bright (ed.), *Sociolinguistics* (The Hague: Mouton, 1966); Stanley Lieberson (ed.), *Explorations in Sociolinguistics* (*Sociological Inquiry*, Vol. 36, No. 2 [whole issue, 1966]); John Macnamara (ed.), *Problems of Bilingualism* (*Jour-*

nal of Social Issues, Vol. 23, No. 2 [whole issue, 1967]).

41 William Labov, *op. cit.,* and William Labov, *The Social Stratification of English in New York City* (Washington, D.C.: Center for Applied Linguistics, 1966).

42 Claude Lévi-Strauss, "Language and the Analysis of Social Laws," *American Anthropologist,* Vol. 53 (1951), pp. 155–163.

43 John J. Gumperz, "Dialect Differences and Social Stratification in a North Indian Village," *American Anthropologist,* Vol. 60 (1958), pp. 668–682; P. B. Pandit, "Sanskritic Clusters and Caste Dialects," *Indian Linguistics,* Vol. 24 (1963), pp. 70–80.

44 John J. Gumperz, "On the Linguistic Markers of Bilingual Communication," in Macnamara (ed.), *op. cit.,* pp. 48–57.

45 Fredrik Barth, "Ethnic Processes in the Pathan-Baluchi Boundary," in *Indo-Iranica: Mélanges Présente a George Morgenstierne a l'Occasion de son Soixante-Dixième Anniversaire* (Wiesbaden: Otto Harrassowitz, 1964).

46 For a discussion of this work, see L. S. Harms, "Status Cues in Speech: Extra-Race and Extra-Region Identification," *Lingua,* Vol. 12 (1963), pp. 300–306; G. N. Putnam and E. M. O'Hern, "The Status Significance of an Isolated Urban Dialect," *Language Supplement,* Language Dissertation No. 53 (1955).

47 Wallace E. Lambert, "A Social Psychology of Bilingualism," in Macnamara (ed.), *op. cit.,* pp. 91–109.

48 William Bright, "Introduction: The Dimensions of Sociolinguistics," in Bright (ed.), *op. cit.,* pp. 11–15.

49 William F. Soskin and Vera John, "The Study of Spontaneous Talk," in R. G. Barker (ed.), *The Stream of Behavior* (New York: Appleton-Century-Crofts, 1963), pp. 228–281.

50 William Labov, *op. cit.,* 1966.

51 Basil Bernstein, "Social Class, Linguistic Codes and Grammatical Elements," *Language and Speech,* Vol. 5 (1962), pp. 221–240.

52 Dell Hymes, "Models of the Interaction of Language and Social Setting," in Macnamara (ed.), *op. cit.,* pp. 8–28.

53 Dell Hymes, "The Ethnography of Speaking," in T. Gladwin and W. Sturtevant (eds.), *Anthropology and Human Behavior* (Washington, D.C.: Anthropological Society of Washington, 1962), pp. 13–53. Research embodying this approach appears in John J. Gumperz and Dell Hymes (eds.), *The Ethnography of Communication* (special issue, *American Anthropologist,* Vol. 66, No. 6, Part 2 [1964]); John J. Gumperz and Dell Hymes, *Directions in Sociolinguistics* (New York: Holt, Rinehart and Winston, in preparation).

54 Susan Ervin-Tripp, "An Analysis of the Interaction of Language, Topic and Listener," in Gumperz and Hymes (eds.), *op. cit.,* 1964, pp. 86–102.

55 Charles O. Frake, "How to Ask for a Drink in Subanun," in Gumperz and Hymes (eds.), *op. cit.,* 1964, pp. 127–132.

56 Basil Bernstein, "Social Class, Linguistic Codes, and Grammatical Elements," *Language and Speech,* Vol. 5 (1962), pp. 221–240.

57 B. J. Raph, "Language Development in Socially Disadvantaged Children," *Review of Educational Research,* Vol. 35, No. 5 (1966), pp. 389–400.

58 John J. Gumperz, "On the Ethnology of Linguistic Change," in Bright (ed.), *op. cit.,* pp. 27–49.

59 This work and its implications are discussed in Roger Brown, *Social Psychology* (Glencoe, Ill.: Free Press, 1965). For an anthropological approach to similar problems, see Paul Friedrich, "Structural Implications of Russian Pronominal Usage," in Bright, *op. cit.,* pp. 214–259. For a review of work on address in relation to sociolinguistic theory, see Richard Howell, "Linguistic Choice as an Index to Social Change" (unpublished Ph.D. dissertation, University of California, Berkeley, 1967).

60 John J. Gumperz, "Linguistic and Social Interaction in Two Communities," in Gumperz and Hymes (eds.), *op. cit.,* 1964, pp. 137–153.

61 Erving Goffman, *Behavior in Public Places* (Glencoe, Ill.: Free Press, 1963).

62 Results of this work are about to appear in two volumes: Harold Garfinkel, *Studies in Ethnomethodology* (Englewood Cliffs, N.J.: Prentice-Hall, forthcoming), and Harold Garfinkel and Harvey Sacks (eds.), *Contributions in Ethnomethodology* (Bloomington: Indiana University Press, forthcoming).

63 Jon-Petter Blom and John J. Gumperz, "Some Social Determinants of Verbal Behavior," in Gumperz and Hymes' forthcoming volume (see ftn. 53).

SIX
ASPECTS OF THE ARCHEOLOGICAL RECORD

17

THE EMERGENCE OF MAN THE TOOL-MAKER

J. DESMOND CLARK

As the archeologist delves into the origins of culture, his field of vision overlaps more and more with that of the human paleontologist. The hunter of fossil evidence of hominid evolution chances upon the crudely cracked rocks that mark the most ancient confirmed tool use by our ancestors, and the fortunate seeker of just such artifacts may uncover skeletal remains. While *a priori* assumptions of the correlation of physical type and culture must be avoided, such associations as are actually discovered, between specific fossils and specific tool types, must be analyzed and understood. It is necessary for anthropology to synthesize a consistent picture, subject only to the limitations of the empirical evidence, of the evolution of hominid biology and culture.

As we have already seen, the data currently available support the notion that it was in Africa that the hominids evolved, both biologically and culturally, to the level of *Homo.* After a period of doubt, and despite the persistence of unsettled points, the australopithecines are now widely accepted as our direct ancestors. We have already seen some very interesting speculation about the cultural proclivities of these forebears, but what do we actually know of the behavior of these creatures? What kinds of tools did they make and use? How did their technological traditions develop?

For light on these questions we turn to J. Desmond Clark, a scientist who has made original contributions to the subject, but who also has a flair for writing in general terms about it. As we follow his synthesis of what is known about the biological and cultural evolution of hominids in Africa during the Pleistocene, however, it will be well to compare his views with those put forward by Washburn Jolly, Wolpoff, and Brace (selections 5, 6, 7 and 8). Also see the editor's headnote for selection 8.

SOURCE: *The Prehistory of Africa,* New York: Praeger Publishers, Inc. 1970. Chapter 2. London: Thames & Hudson Ltd.

The Geographical Zones of Africa

The abundance of fossil remains of early man and his immediate ancestors that have been brought to light during the last thirty years —often in spectacular circumstances—amply confirms Charles Darwin's belief that it would be in the tropics—perhaps in Africa—that man would prove to have evolved from a simian ancestor. It is in Africa that man's closest relatives among the great apes are found—the chimpanzee and the gorilla—and recent studies are showing that we are appreciably closer biologically to these African apes than had at one time been thought. For this reason primate studies, especially those concerning the anatomy and behaviour of the gorilla and chimpanzee, are directly relevant to an understanding of the biological nature and behaviour of the early hominids.

Before discussing the evidence and its implications, however, we need to consider the factor of environment since this varyingly affected the way of life of the human populations occupying the five main biogeographical zones. For climatic reasons these zones are complementary north and south of an equatorial, tropical region but undergo modification on account of topography, winds and ocean currents.

In equatoria is the humid, evergreen rainforest—'that towering multitude of trees . . . all perfectly still' of which Joseph Conrad writes so graphically in *Heart of Darkness.* These forests are undergoing steady destruction at the hands of slash-and-burn cultivators and have done so for the past three thousand years. To the north and south and throughout much of the eastern area are the savanna lands—open forest, woodland and grass savanna—which support an ungulate fauna fantastically rich, both in species and in the extreme size of the populations. Here also, on the higher plateaux, ridges and mountains, are found the high altitude evergreen forest and the montane grasslands that replace it when man interferes. The African savanna is one of the richest habitats in the world and stretches from the Atlantic to the Indian Ocean and from the southern border of the Sahara to South Africa's south coast.

The third of these biogeographical zones is the dry steppe country—the Sahel areas north and south of the Sahara, and the Karroo and Kalahari regions in the south of the continent. The vegetation of the steppe country consists of short, dry grass, succulents, low bushes and thorn trees. It is often rich in food reserves and supports a mammalian fauna of medium- to small-sized animals.

Fourthly, there is the desert of which, again, there are several kinds—salt steppes, semi-desert and the dune fields and stony pavements of the desert proper. These are among the most unfavourable parts of the continent for human settlement but are, nevertheless, capable of supporting populations of economically self-sufficient hunters and herdsmen.

Fifthly, in the extreme north on the Mediterranean coast and in the southwestern parts of the Cape at the other end of the continent, there is country enjoying a winter rainfall and supporting a Mediterranean vegetation of evergreen forest and macchia. In north Africa generally this Mediterranean zone has had a profound effect upon the course of cultural development.

As was mentioned before, each of these zones has, in the past, undergone modification on several occasions, its boundaries expanding and contracting in response to fluctuations of climate which are best seen through fossil pollen evidence. In pre-Pleistocene times the vegetation pattern was markedly different from that of the present.

The Earliest Fossils: Hominoids and Hominids

Evolutionary theory shows how the hominid line derives from an arboreal ancestor; and the chimpanzee and the gorilla are both forest-dwellers so that it is to be expected that it might be in the forested or formerly forested regions of Africa that the fossil forms intermediate between ape and man will mostly be found. This is, in fact, what has now transpired in those parts of east Africa that are, or were once, covered by forest or a mosaic of forest and savanna vegetation. Very important fossil material is also known from the Fayum Depression in Egypt thus showing the former extent of the forests during the mid-Tertiary in a region that is now desert.[1]

Unfortunately, it is only in a comparatively few parts of the continent that fossils of the past twenty-five million years are preserved and there is, for example, hardly a bone from the whole of the west African forest zone or the Congo basin. Similarly, vast areas of savanna on the central plateau and in the east and south are also devoid of any fossil material because of the acid nature of the soil and the ground-water.

The main fossil-bearing regions are the Maghreb (northwest Africa), the east African region of the Western and Gregory Rifts, certain localities in South Africa, and a few isolated localities in Egypt, the Sahara and Rhodesia. Far the richest of these is the east African region. Here the formation of deep troughs, basins and volcanoes, the rapid accumulation of sediments and burial of the fossils have combined to preserve a unique record extending back to the earlier Miocene, some twenty-two million years ago.

Man is distinguished from other primates by his upright posture, bipedal locomotion, peculiarly prehensile fore-limbs, his large brain and the ability to make and use many kinds of tools. Each of the parts of the body here distinguished appears to have evolved separately and at dif-

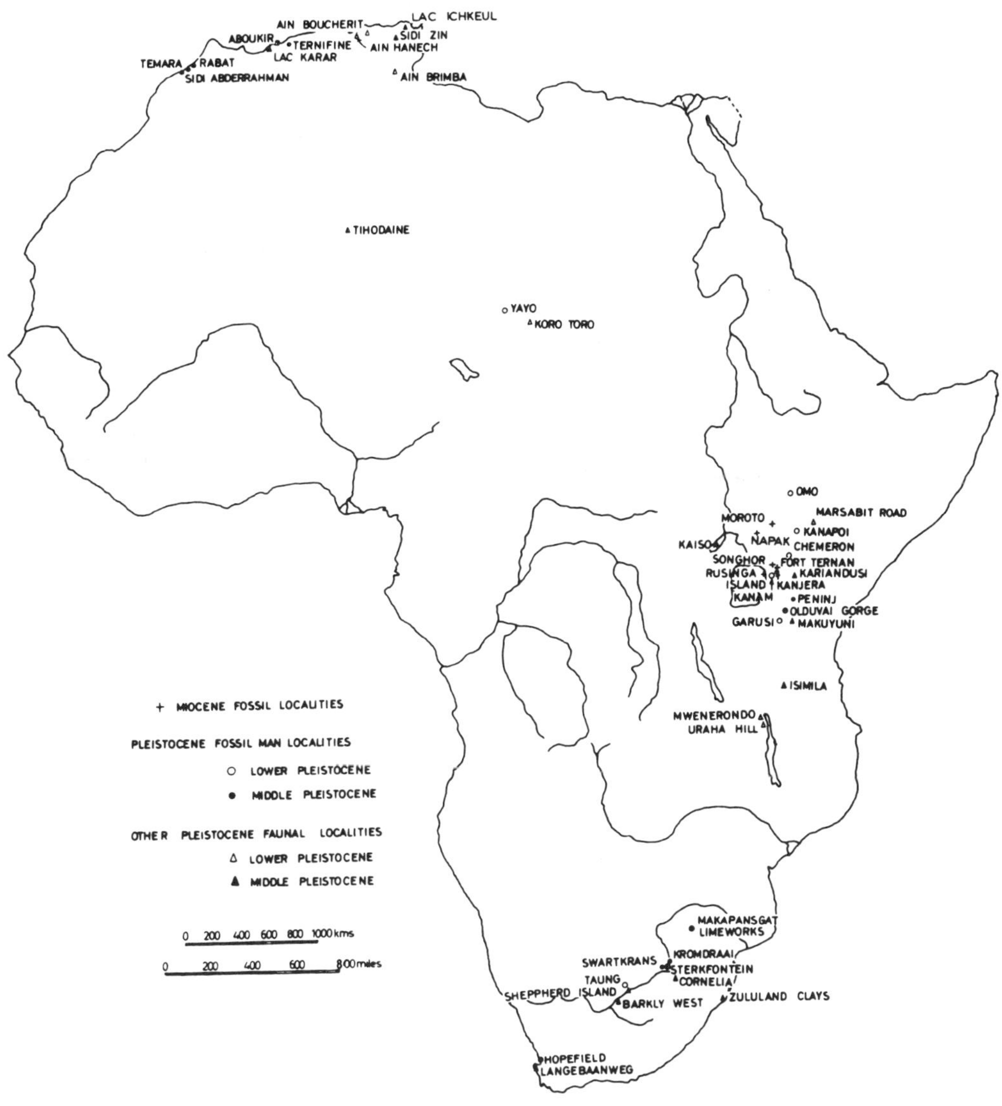

The main faunal and fossil man localities in Africa (Miocene and earlier Pleistocene). (After J. D. Clark, 1967)

ferent times: thorax and arms first, then pelvis, legs and feet and, lastly, the head and brain. Man's humanity shows itself in the many complicated social and cultural patterns that are unique to his kind. Some of the stages whereby this transformation from a quadrupedal ancestor was effected can be adduced from a study of the fossil record that is now coming to light in east Africa and Egypt.

During the early to mid Tertiary, some fifteen to twenty-five million years ago, there existed in Asia, Europe and Africa a number of *Dryopithecus* ape forms. These fossils show modification of the limb bones and face, indicating that they were adapted to living *primarily* in the trees, although *also* on the ground.[2] Judging from their wide distribution, these prebrachiators, as they have been called,[3] must have been living in a very favourable environment which was one of forest that, in Africa, constituted a mosaic with the savanna. This is well established by the finds of uniquely preserved fruits, seeds and insects of this time-period from the Miocene deposits on Rusinga Island in Lake Victoria and those on the slopes of the volcanoes.[4]

By some fourteen million years ago, however, a more evolved form was present in India and east Africa, known as *Ramapithecus*.[5] Whereas the dryopithecines were unspecialized apes, morphological features point to *Ramapithecus*' having been a hominid. Unfortunately, the remains consist mostly of fragments of the face and teeth and nothing is known of the rest of the skeleton. However, the face has undergone considerable modification and has been reduced in length, the teeth having an arrangement and pattern that are essentially human. Therefore, it has been inferred from this that *Ramapithecus* must have walked upright and must have had fore-limbs adapted to using simple tools.

The remains of the later Miocene/Pliocene hominids are known only from rather small fragments of the face and from individual teeth and it has been pointed out that the face may have become modified at a different time from the limbs. When, therefore, remains of these are found they may not be as evolved as has been suggested.[6] Such observations are also very relevant for the interpretation of fossils of this kind (*Kenyapithecus africanus*) recovered by Leakey in a Lower Miocene context at Rusinga Island and Songhor, which suggest the possibility that hominids were present some eight to ten million years earlier still.[7] Recently good reason has been shown to think that man and apes may have shared a ground-dwelling, knuckle-walking existence up to the time that the human line developed bipedalism.[8] Whether, therefore, the hominid line had become separated from the common ancestor with the Pongids as early as the mid-Tertiary must remain in doubt until more complete fossil material becomes available. Rather does the recent work on chromosomes, serum proteins and hemoglobin [9] and on the calibration of the immunological distance between man and other primates indicate that the separation of the Hominid and Pongid lines more probably took place as recently as four to five, certainly no earlier than ten million years ago—that is to say in the Pliocene.[10] (See Figure 1.)

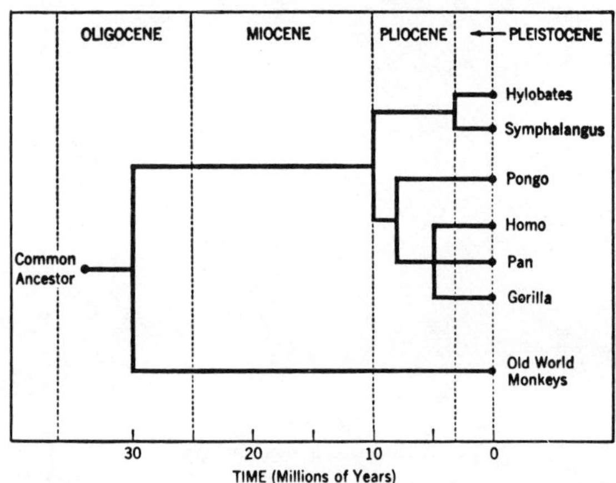

Figure 1. Times of divergence between the various hominids as estimated from immunological data. The time of divergence of hominids and Old World monkeys is assumed to be 30 million years. (Courtesy of V. M. Sarich and A. C. Wilson and *Science,* 1967.) Copyright by the American Association for the Advancement of Science.

The suggestion has been made that the late Miocene/Pliocene ancestor (*Ramapithecus*) may have been a ground-dwelling, knuckle-walker, like the modern African great apes and that, like them, he escaped the extinction that overtook the smaller Miocene apes through competition with the forest-dwelling monkeys, by reason of his greater weight and his adaptation to ground-dwelling in addition to tool manipulation.[11] Since the gorilla and chimpanzee are forest-dwellers, it is most likely that this was also the habitat of *Ramapithecus*—a habitat that then stretched from east Africa across to northern India. *Ramapithecus* is associated in India with plant and animal fossils indicating a habitat of broad water-courses bordered by forest, giving place to savanna away from the rivers. As also at Fort Ternan evidence indicates that there was considerable migration of land mammals between Africa and Eurasia in later Tertiary times, it is likely that the environment was similar in both continents. If this was, indeed, so it demonstrates to some extent the fundamental changes in climate and biome (ecological unit) that have taken place, particularly in the Arabian peninsula and southwest Asia generally since the later Tertiary.

The east African form of *Ramapithecus* (*Ramapithecus* [*Kenyapithecus*] *wickeri*) from the Fort Ternan site east of Lake Victoria [12] may have made and used simple tools. This site also provides evidence of what are believed to have been bone-bashing activities: a lump of lava with a battered and bruised edge was found associated with a long-bone with a depressed fracture.[13] Further evidence is necessary to confirm this type of activity, but existing finds certainly suggest that *Ramapithecus* [*Kenyapithecus*] *wickeri* was a meat-eater.

It is interesting also that, in the parts that are preserved, there is no very significant difference between *Ramapithecus* and the Australopithecines that characterize the next hominid stage, and continued selection for increased use of the rear-limbs for bipedal locomotion and of the fore-limbs for tool manipulation could have been responsible for the developments to be seen in the anatomy of the Australopithecines in the earlier Pleistocene some two million or more years ago.

If *Ramapithecus wickeri* is a hominid, these morphological developments took place over a period of about ten to twelve million years. On the other hand, using the chronology based on the immunological scale,[14] there are between three million and one-and-a-half million years during which the Hominidae, now separated from the Pongid (or ape) line, were evolving the lower limbs toward efficient bipedalism and the upper limbs toward more complex tool use and manufacture. If the latter estimate is correct then *Ramapithecus wickeri* would have been an aberrant ape with fortuitous dental resemblances to the hominids. Unfortunately, very few deposits of Pliocene age are known from Africa so that we possess as yet no fossils of this time other than the Mio-Pliocene ones from the Fort Ternan site. During 1968, however, a new Middle Pliocene formation together with a hominid tooth were discovered to the north of Lake Baringo in Kenya, so that other finds may now be expected which will throw light on the biological character of the Pliocene hominids.[15] It is not going to be easy to recover evidence for tool-use at this time since, as will appear later, intentional and consistent fracture of stone to make a more efficient tool is likely to have been minimal or non-existent and, in any case, only stone and bone, of any of the materials that *may* have been used, can be expected to have survived. More convincing evidence is likely to be forthcoming from the association of natural fragments, sometimes modified by use, with hominid and other bone showing artificial modification, on land surfaces to which these materials could not have been transported by geological or animal (other than hominid) agencies.

There is every reason to suppose that this mode of tool-using behaviour and omnivorous feeding habits would have made available many more resources and so provided a greatly enriched environment which encouraged experimentation and so, in turn, brought about more rapid evolutionary change than would have been possible without the use of tools.

Lower Pleistocene Fossils

During the later Miocene and Pliocene crustal movement began to disrupt the earlier Tertiary pattern of internal drainage basins, replacing it with the present hydrographic system. At the same time there was faulting, deep rifting, orographic and volcanic activity along the line of the Great Rift Valley and certain other unstable parts of the continent. The later stages of these processes and, possibly, the fragmentation of the evergreen forest vegetation coincided with a significant lowering of temperature in Europe and the onset of the Pleistocene Period. The later Tertiary also saw the accumulation of the Kalahari Sands over much of the western half of the subcontinent during a time of more arid climate, and drier conditions were generally widespread during the Pliocene. It may have been at this time also that the xerophytic Karroo vegetation spread over a large part of southern Africa at the expense of the lowland humid tropical forest.

It appears likely that these events played a not unimportant part in accelerating hominid evolution some nine to six million years ago. The fossil record from the Lower Pleistocene is very much better known than is that of the Pliocene in Africa. The now famous Australopithecines, or Man-Apes, dating from the early Lower Pleistocene are known chiefly from limestone caves in the Transvaal in South Africa and from certain sites in east Africa, in particular the Olduvai Gorge in Tanzania. An advanced Australopithecine has recently come to light in Chad and there is an enigmatic fossil —*Meganthropus*—from Java that may belong in this group also though in some respects it is further advanced.[16] The discovery of the Australopithecines we owe primarily to three men—Dr. Raymond Dart, the late Dr. Robert Broom and Dr. Louis Leakey—whose tireless and persistent researches have resulted in so much material being available today; in fact, no other fossil hominid genus is so well known as *Australopithecus*.

Without doubt, these are early tool-making hominids combining a small brain (435–562 cc.) with a large and massive jaw which was the feature that made scientists first consider them to be fossil apes, related more closely to the modern apes than they were to man. The discovery of a nearly complete foot at Olduvai and of a number of the bones of a hand, together with a reasonably complete vertebral column and pelvis from Sterkfontein in South Africa, and of complete and fragmentary limb bones from both regions, show that the Australopithecines walked erect and used their hands for manipulating tools and so foreshadowed the later hominids of the Middle Pleistocene.

Two races of Australopithecines are represented in the South African caves—a slenderly built and smaller form, *Australopithecus africanus*, and a robust, larger form, *Australopithecus robustus*, originally named *Paranthropus*.[17] The gracile form occurs at three sites—Taung, Makapan and Sterkfontein—and the robust form at two sites—Swartkrans and Kromdraai. They are found cemented in breccia filling old caves in the limestone and are associated with many animal bones.[18] Palaeontological evidence,[19,20] suggests that Taung, Sterkfontein and Makapan are the oldest, followed by Swartkrans and then Kromdraai and the rhythm of climatic fluctuations obtained from sedimentation studies done on the breccias [21] shows the consistency to be expected when based upon this sequence. *Australopithecus africanus*, the gracile form, therefore, precedes *Australopithecus robustus*.

These discoveries were mostly made in the 1930's to 1950's but in 1959 Leakey made the first discovery of a hominid fossil from Bed 1, the lower part of the long lacustrine and terrestrial sequence of beds at the Olduvai Gorge (see Figure 2). This discovery was the famous 'Nutcracker Man'—*Zinjanthropus boisei*, now called *Australopithecus boisei*.[22] The fossil was found in close association with a buried occupation site with broken animal bones and stone tools of which 'Nutcracker Man' was at first hailed as the maker.

In 1964 an almost perfect jaw, with teeth, of the robust Australopithecine was found eroding from beds of Middle Pleistocene age at Peninj, west of Lake Natron on the Kenya/Tanzania border.[23]

In 1960, remains of another hominid had been found at Olduvai from a level slightly

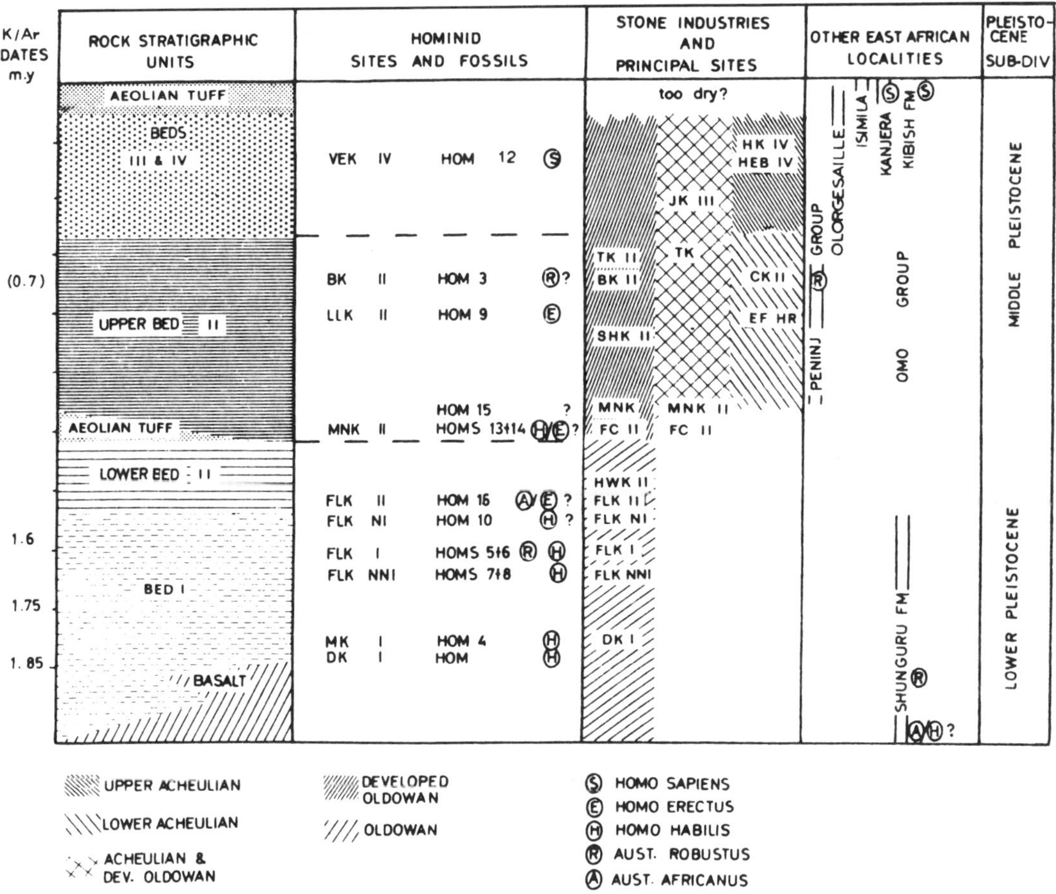

Figure 2. Stratigraphy, hominids and stone industries at Olduvai Gorge.

below that from which *Zinjanthropus* came and near the same locality. These remains comprised parts of the side and back bones of the skull of a juvenile, that had been broken prior to fossilization. With them were a collar bone and fifteen hand bones from two individuals, an adult and a juvenile, and most of the bones of the foot of an adult individual. With these remains were ten worked stone tools and evidence of carnivore activity. The cranial fragments have been shown to belong to a somewhat larger-brained hominid (680 cc.) with a dental pattern different from that of *Australopithecus boisei* (or *Zinjanthropus*), but not very different from that of *A. africanus*.[24]

The associated hand and foot bones show close comparability to those of man, though with certain primitive features suggesting, so far as the foot is concerned, that its owner was adapted to running but not, perhaps, to striding. Unfortunately, the ends of the toes had been chewed off, but a toe bone from higher up and near the top of Bed II shows that by this time striding was possible.[25] The hand falls into a position immediately between that of *Homo sapiens* and the apes and the great flexure and muscularity of the finger bones confirms the near ancestry with knuckle-walkers. The Olduvai hand was small and has been described as having an opposable thumb [26] that was not only capable of the power grip, but also probably of the 'precision grip' that made possible finer manipulation of objects in addition to the manufacture of simple tools.

Leakey and his associates who have studied these remains have described them as belonging to a new species of the genus *Homo* which they have named *Homo habilis*—meaning 'Man having the ability to manipulate tools'—and stone artifacts are found associated with these remains from the bottom of Bed I into the lower part of Bed II.[27]

In addition to the finds from the type locality (FLK NNI) there are a number of others—individual teeth from Bed I and more complete cranial and jaw material from the lower part of Bed II (from sites MNK II and FLK II)—that have been ascribed to this form. The only nearly complete limb bones are a tibia and fibula from the same site that produced *Australopithecus boisei*.[28] They are well adapted to bipedal walking though differences suggest that the manner in which these early men did so may not have been very like our own striding gait. Because teeth similar to those of *Homo habilis* were also present on this horizon, these leg bones are attributed to that form rather than to the robust Australopithecine. As yet no complete thigh bone has come to light but fragments are known from the caves in the Transvaal and they generally confirm the bipedal though clumsy gait of these early hominids.[29]

The other finds attributed to *Homo habilis* at Olduvai Gorge include a large part of the vault of a skull and the greater part of a lower jaw and parts of the upper jaw from one site (MNK II); and at another locality (FLK II: Maiko Gully) a skull, rendered fragmentary by an inconsiderate herd of Masai cattle that had passed over it as it lay exposed by erosion. Both these finds came from the lower part of Bed II and belong probably in the earlier part of the Middle Pleistocene.[30] They are considered to be morphologically more advanced than those from Bed I but no detailed descriptions have yet been published. Thus, the *Homo habilis* fossils as currently defined span a long range of time, perhaps a million years, and clearly, when comparisons are made with *Australopithecus africanus*, we must use the earlier fossils.

Fossils from two other regions confirm that there was at this time a more advanced hominid present, contemporary with the robust Australopithecine. These are the front part of a skull and face from the Chad basin [31] and a crushed jaw, palate and other fragmentary remains from the Cave of Swartkrans in the Transvaal, where they occur together with stone implements and *Australopithecus robustus*.[32] The Swartkrans remains have been attributed to a small species of *Homo erectus* though LeGros Clark and others consider they could well fall within the possible range of *Australopithecus africanus*. The remains from Chad are said to be transitional between *Australopithecus* and *Homo erectus*.

Controversy ranges mostly round whether the *Homo habilis* remains and those just referred to from Swartkrans can be included within, or whether they lie outside the range of *Australopithecus africanus*. Some, like Sir Wilfrid LeGros Clark, as has been said, maintain that they can be included within the possible range of the Man-Apes. Others, including Leakey, consider that they are too advanced and so lie outside this range and represent the oldest true *Homo*.

A look at the relative ages of these and other recent finds will help to explain better what was probably happening during this time—in the earlier part of the Pleistocene. Recent work by American and French teams shows that the gracile and the robust Australopithecines were *both* living in the Omo basin, north of Lake Rudolph, in the late Pliocene to early Pleistocene, between 3.5 million and 1.8 million years ago, on the evidence of the potassium/argon dates.[33] The Olduvai sequence overlaps slightly the upper end of the Omo Beds but, while the robust Australopithecine is present unchanged at Olduvai, the other contemporary form is now *Homo habilis*.

Although no detailed description has yet appeared, it has been suggested that the *Homo habilis* fossils from Bed II at Olduvai are more advanced than those from Bed I and nearer to *Homo erectus*—a large-brained form of which occurs at a site (LLK II) in the upper part of Bed II. On the other hand, the robust Australopithecine, *Paranthropus*, continues apparently unchanged into the upper part of Bed II and thereafter disappears from the record.

The interpretation of this evidence is complicated by the uncertainty surrounding the age of the Australopithecine cave breccias in South Africa where there are few fossil animal forms in common with those of the east African open savanna sites and for which there are no chronometric dates. Re-examination of the associated fauna suggests that the sites with *Australopithecus africanus* [34] may be older than Bed I at Olduvai and could, therefore, be contemporary in part with the Omo Beds. The sites with *Paranthropus* (Swartkrans and Kromdraai) and the enigmatic *Homo erectus* fossil, on the other hand, are later and the possible equivalent of the lower part of Bed II at Olduvai; they have also yielded stone tools. Any suggestion, moreover, that the robust form might have evolved from the gracile in the Lower Pleistocene can now be shown to be unfounded on the basis of the new finds from Omo, where the two are contemporaneous.

If the South African fossils are not later than has been indicated, all this evidence can best be explained by the view that the gracile form evolved into *Homo habilis* and so into *Homo erectus*, by reason of the fact that it early developed the ability to make more efficient and complicated tools; whilst the robust form remained a tool-*user* only and so stayed biologically unchanged, eventually succumbing to competition with the tool-maker. If, on the other hand, the older sites in South Africa (Taung, Sterkfontein and Makapan) are contemporary and later than those in Bed I at the Olduvai Gorge, then the gracile Australopithecine fossils they contain cannot lie in the direct line of descent of man and would represent late survivals of the likely ancestor of *Homo habilis*. The first hypothesis would seem the most likely but whether it will stand the test of time, only time itself will show; however, every year new discoveries make the evidence more complete and interpretation easier. If the intermediate position of the *Homo habilis* fossils between *Australopithecus africanus* and *Homo erectus* is confirmed it is not of too great significance whether they are classified as an advanced Australopithecine or a lowly form of *Homo*, though the cultural evidence seems to favour inclusion with *Homo*. (See Figure 3.)

Potassium/argon dating indicates that it would have taken about one million years or more to complete the transition (represented by the *Homo habilis* stage) from the gracile Australopithecine to *Homo erectus*. Such evolutionary developments could have been possible only through the medium of culture and the feed-back mechanism brought into play between physiological and cultural development. If this time-range is substantiated, the changes that have come about in the bony structure show how truly significant was the acquisition of culture.

With two doubtful exceptions, deposits older than Bed I at Olduvai have as yet produced no flaked stone tools, though, on the Omo evidence, the gracile Australopithecine was present at least a million-and-a-half years earlier. If further work confirms the absence of flaked stone tools from deposits older than two to two-and-a-half million years, we would be justified in associating the tools with *Homo habilis* more specifically and can, therefore, expect the rate of evolutionary change to have been appreciably slower, while the transformation occurred

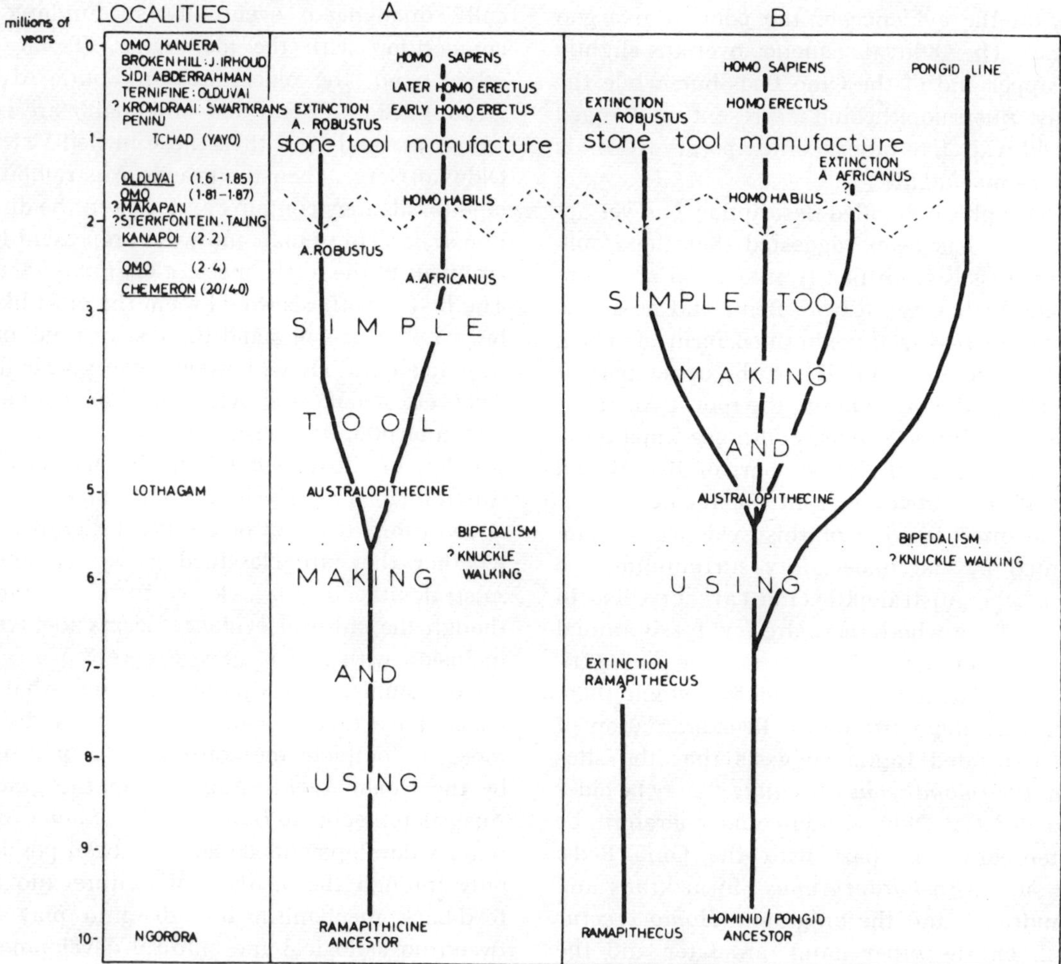

Figure 3. Two possible interpretations of hominid evolution.

that changed a knuckle-walking to a fully erect posture and effected the coincidental increase in brain size and changes in the hand which made conceptual and skilled stone working and utilization possible, in the later part of the Lower Pleistocene. The immunological time-scale suggests that it could have taken as little as from one to three million years to evolve from the ancestral form common to Man and the African apes to a fully bipedal hominid form.[35]

Of course, it should not be imagined that this was a simple process of unilinear development, since the behavioural adaptations that would have been called for in the transition from a Pliocene forest-dweller to a savanna-dweller in the Lower Pleistocene, must surely have resulted in some diversification, though only the most successful survived. Similarly, in the initial stages of tool manufacture more than one form may have made simple tools, though only one, in which developing brain size permitted increasing complexity of artifact manufacture, made the transition to *Homo erectus*.

Australopithecine Behaviour

The chief sources of evidence on which to attempt to understand and reconstruct the behaviour of the earliest tool-makers are the fossils themselves, the associated artifacts, animal remains and features of the sites on which these occur and, last but not least, chimpanzee and gorilla behaviour. To these should also be added any palaeo-climatic evidence that can be deduced from a study of the lithology of the beds in which the remains are found.

On the palaeo-climatic evidence from the Transvaal cave breccias there can be little doubt that the Australopithecines were living in a habitat somewhat drier than that of the region today but becoming wetter at the upper end of the sequence.[36] At Olduvai the habitat has been shown to be not unlike the Serengeti Plains today—open and adjacent to a brackish or saline shallow water lake—while that of Chad was savanna associated with forest galleries and occasional patches of evergreen forest.[37] This is a far cry from the forest or forest fringe environment occupied by the Later Tertiary ancestral forms, so that considerable adaptability can be postulated for successful existence in dry savanna by this time. It is probable, since the social patterns of the great apes—in particular of the African ones—do not show a great range of variation, that these did not differ very much from those of the common ancestor they shared with man. Moreover, if the separation took place as recently as the immunological approach suggests, then chimpanzee and gorilla behaviour is especially relevant to understanding that of the earliest hominids.

We know from the work of Baroness Jane van Lawick-Goodall and others [38] among the free-ranging chimpanzees in the Gombe Stream Reserve in Tanzania, that chimps are highly social animals and also make and use a number of simple tools. They select twigs for getting at termites; sticks to break open tree-ant nests and get out honey; sponges to mop up water from holes in hollow trees; and they are capable of using stones to break nuts. They have been observed throwing sticks and stones, both over- and under-arm, in several different kinds of display against predators or at times of excitement.[39] Moreover, they are reasonably adept at carrying objects and they construct sleeping platforms. Interpretation of Man-Ape behaviour must, therefore, take into account this and other aspects of chimpanzee behaviour as well as the closer anatomical relationship to ourselves shown by the Australopithecine fossils. In other words, the greater brain size and character of the post-cranial skeleton show that what the chimpanzee does the Australopithecine must have done a good deal better and much more besides that the chimpanzee cannot do.

The chimpanzees at the Gombe Stream Reserve live in open groups that vary between thirty-three individuals and nine or less; the groups are constantly changing in size and composition. Sometimes they comprise males, females and juveniles; sometimes males only or only females with young; sometimes adult males and females. The males in particular are long-ranging for purposes of foraging and when food is plentiful the groups are largest. When food is obtained the group is called together by vocalization and drumming and there is some evidence that the food is shared. The most permanent association is between mother, infant and juveniles. Adult males are attracted, however, not so much for sexual reasons as by the mother-infant relationship. The greeting ceremonies when individuals or small groups come together (both among chimpanzees and gorillas) indicate the open nature of these societies, which is greater in the case of the chimpanzees than of the gorillas. In other words a returning member of the group is welcomed and a new arrival must be 'vetted,' as it were, before the group accepts him.

A change from life in a forest to one in a savanna would necessitate an alteration in the dietary habits from a primarily vegetarian to an omnivorous diet in which meat eating acquired increasing importance. The Gombe Stream chimpanzees are, as yet, the only ones that have been observed to hunt and kill fairly large animals for food. This practice is, however, now known to be commoner than was previously thought, though whether it is a general characteristic of chimpanzee behaviour, not only in savanna/forest mosaic, as at Gombe, but also in forest [40] is not yet known, due to lack of adequate observation. It is, however, to be expected that the greatly increased source of animal protein available in the savanna and the less continuous supply of fruits would have served to encourage any hunting propensities possessed by the early hominids.

Another possible cause of the greater emphasis on animal foods now discernible, may have been the need to supplement the dwindling vegetable resources in an environment that was becoming increasingly drier. Whether or not continent-wide climatic deterioration was a factor in bringing this about cannot, however, be shown as yet since the evidence for these changes is too poorly documented. But there is no doubt that the micro-environment at the Olduvai Gorge in which the early hominids were living was essentially an arid one, though forest on the volcano slopes cannot have been far away. Whatever the process, therefore, it is certain that the possession of culture by the hominids ensured their success as predators and had by this time permitted groups of them to occupy a range of habitats outside the forest.

As our knowledge of the free-ranging behaviour of the African apes grows, it becomes increasingly apparent that the Australopithecines were not the aggressive 'armed killers' that one school of thought has so vividly represented them to be. The desire to interpret has overstretched the facts. The Transvaal caves cannot yet be shown to have been the places where the Man-Apes lived, neither can the assemblages of broken animal bone with which they are associated be proved to have resulted from the predatory and aggressive habits of the Man-Apes themselves.[41] It still remains to be shown that the differential preservation of the various skeletal parts in these caves was not due to the natural selective agencies that have recently been so effectively distinguished,[42] or that the so-called wear on certain bones was not, similarly, a naturally controlled phenomenon. Some very persuasive voices have been raised in support of the idea that 'man is a predator whose natural instinct is to kill with a weapon.' The associations of bones and hominids in the tropical caves and lake-side camps is used by these prophets of primeval violence as mute evidence of the 'courage and cunning' that was said to be already part and parcel of our heritage two million years ago.[43]

Defence of territory lies behind the aggressiveness of many animals and of modern man, but the African apes do not appear to engage in vigorous defence of their territory and, as we have seen, their groupings are essentially open ones, the composition of which is frequently changing. Territoriality in human societies is very likely, therefore, to have come about appreciably later in the Pleistocene. The stone implements at the occupation sites can, therefore, better be seen as evidence of man's reliance on artifacts of his own selection and manufacture, primarily for obtaining and preparing food and for defence. Thus, leaving aside for the moment the controversial, so called 'implements' of bone from the South African caves, we find indisputable manufactured tools of stone that relate to life at the home base and represent, not weapons, but domestic equipment. The industry to which they belong has been termed *Oldowan* from the type site at the Olduvai Gorge. If there is thus little evidence to substantiate Hobbes' thesis that the natural state of man was one of '. . . warre, as if everyman against every man,' there is just as little reason for crediting the earliest tool-makers with the compassion and humanity of Rousseau's 'gentle savage.'

The occupation sites of this time are found in Bed I and at the base of Bed II at the Olduvai Gorge and are unique in providing information on the nature of the early hominid living-places.[44] These sites are small concentrations of occupation débris. One such oval area (FLK I with which *Zinjanthropus* was associated) measured twenty-one by fifteen feet and contained a quantity of broken bone fragments, stone implements and chipping waste. At these sites are collected natural stones (manuports) and others that have been used for hammering and bashing. There are a number of flaked stone tools: choppers worked from one or both faces giving the tool an irregular chopping edge; polyhedrals, discoids, scrapers, burins and spheroids as well as a number of utilized flakes. Many unmodified flakes also occur. Three basic forms of worked stone predominate—polyhedral bashing stones, choppers and flake knives. There is nothing esoteric about their manufacture and they are all small implements with no 'formality' about them. They show, however, clear evidence of a rudimentary knowledge of working stone for the production of flakes and chopping edges. Assemblages such as these must lie very close to the beginnings of stone-working.

It is a common misconception that the Oldowan tools were made from pebbles and the term 'Pebble Culture' has been used as synonymous with Oldowan. Where pebbles and cobbles abounded, these were frequently used but the Olduvai evidence shows that angular lumps and flakes of lava and quartz were equally selected for making into tools. There are very few other sites in addition to the Olduvai Gorge where well-dated Oldowan artifacts have been found. They occur in the oldest sediments of the coastal sequence of Atlantic Morocco and in stream sediments at Ain Hanech in Tunisia where a number of polyhedral spheroids and a few choppers are associated with a late Lower Pleistocene (Upper Villafranchian) fauna. A very few artifacts have been found also in lake beds in east Africa—at Kanam in the Lake Victoria basin and at Kanyati in the Lake Albert Rift. The associated fauna dates these to the earlier part of the Lower Pleistocene—earlier, therefore, than the beginning of the Olduvai sequence. 'Pebble tools' have been reported from a number of other sites, usually from river gravels, but the evidence is insufficient or too incomplete to confirm their Lower Pleistocene age. Of course pebbles continued to be used for making tools in some regions until modern times.

Vegetable foods form about 60–80 percent of the food of hunters and gatherers today in warm and temperate climates.[45] Such foods, however, leave very little evidence in the archaeological record. It is, nevertheless, possible to regard the numerous polyhedral and other heavier stones, not only as tools for breaking animal bones and dealing with tough parts of the skin (also eaten by present-day hunters) but also for breaking open nuts and preparing the otherwise unpalatable parts of plants by the breaking-down of the fibrous portions. Experiment shows the so-called choppers to be effective for pointing a stick to use for digging out buried plant foods or small burrowing animals as well as for cutting, by means of a sawing action. Unmodified flakes form very efficient knives for skinning and cutting. Occasionally wear on a bone also suggests use, though not intentional shaping, by hominids. Two broken bones with Oldowan aggregates from Bed I (FLK NNI and FLK north) show striations and polishing similar to the kind of wear resulting from rubbing a hide or digging in the ground. A few of the 'Osteodontokeratic' bones show this kind of wear and there are others that cannot be readily explained as due to natural causes.

The Oldowan artifacts thus comprise the basic equipment necessary for obtaining a varied and unselected supply of plant and animal foods which were carried back to the home base. Ample evidence of this collecting behaviour is provided by the animal remains on the sites but as yet the full details have not been published. At one site (FLK 1) the remains have been described as coming mostly from small to medium-sized animals, though bones from larger animals are also present.[46] Usually individuals are represented by only very incomplete remains and this is particularly so in the case of the few large animals that occur. This may, perhaps, indicate the importance of scavenging as a means of supplementing the meat supply though it could also reflect the habits of the hunters in that the animals may have been butchered and partly eaten or distributed away from the home base. There are also sites (DK I and FLK NI) where the full range of large to small animals is present. Thus, while it may be postulated that the Australopithecines and early tool-makers were hunting mostly small game and scavenging larger animals, the evidence is as yet insufficient to provide the necessary confirmation.

Two butchery sites of large animals are known at the Olduvai Gorge from the top of Bed I (FLK NI, Level 6) and the base of Bed II at the same site. At the first, the nearly complete skeleton of an extinct elephant (*Elephas reckii*) was associated with one hundred and twenty-three artifacts and at the second the barely disarticulated remains of a Deinotherium had thirty-nine artifacts associated. However these creatures met their death, and they may equally have died from natural causes as have been killed, there is no doubt that by this time the makers of the Oldowan Industry had learned how to deal with the meat from large animals.

The degree to which hunting formed an essential part of Australopithecine behaviour is open to debate, but it need not have amounted to much more than the individual capturing of small mammals—young antelopes, pigs for example, or lizards—by running them down and killing them with the bare hands or the aid of a stick or stone, as is still done today by some African peoples. However, some animals can hardly have been taken except by organized group hunting skills and the recent evidence on chimpanzee hunting methods shows that group hunting must by now have formed an integral part of the behaviour pattern. Successful hunting organisation need not necessarily imply any complex communication system or the existence of language. The group hunting practised by wild dog packs, though it makes little use of vocalization, is, nonetheless, highly successful. Chimpanzees are known to make use of some twenty-three distinct calls or vocalizations, besides a number of gestures, facial expressions and bodily postures and it is a legitimate assumption that tool-making hominids would have had an even larger range of sounds and gestures at their command.

The *home base* is one of the most significant features of the early hominid sites since it represents a place of continuous, though temporary, occupation. The existence of a home base can probably be explained by the prolongation of pre-adult life and the greater dependence of the young upon the adults which emphasizes the mother/infant relationship. On the evidence of the eruption cycle of the teeth in Australopithecines, this dependence continued for much the same length of time as in modern man.[47] Primate studies show that this stretching-out of the period before full maturity is reached is closely related to the learning of skills and behaviour necessary for adult life. The young chimpanzee becomes independent at between seven and eight years of age and the transmission of the more complex learned skills of the Man-Apes must have required an even longer time. The home base can, therefore, be seen as the answer to the constraint imposed upon the mobility of the group by this longer period of learning. One particularly interesting base of this kind (DKI) from the very bottom of the Olduvai sequence contains a sharply defined area of stones with the usual stone and bone waste and Oldowan tools. This suggests an intentional piling, perhaps as some form of shelter or hide.[48]

There is no good means of estimating the size of a hominid grouping at this time, but the area covered by the home base suggests that the bands were not large, though it may be expected that the actual numbers and individuals underwent fairly continuous change. It has been calculated that the Australopithecine fossils from Swartkrans represent between fifty and seventy individuals but, of course, this has to be spaced over the time taken for the breccia to accumulate.[49] Bands probably consisted of members of two or three compatible families of mothers and juveniles and perhaps three or four adult males. All these individuals were mutually dependent and shared the results of their hunting and foraging activities; indeed, food-sharing is the basis of human society and one of the most fundamental differences between human and mammalian behaviour. That it is practised by chimpanzees (and, to a lesser extent, by wild dogs) is of great interest but this is only a minor part of a very varied pattern of behaviour; their society does not depend upon it as does human society. This is in marked contrast to the picture of the club-wielding aggressor that is usually painted.

If most of the females were concerned with looking after infants and juveniles and with foraging for plant foods in the vicinity of the base, the males and the females without young would have been directly engaged in hunting and the carrying-back of the proceeds of the chase. The variety and number of individual animals represented on the living-sites shows that these were not places of purely ephemeral occupation but must always have served as a base for at least several days. There is not much of a problem in carrying small or medium-sized animals and larger ones can be cut up and the pieces divided among the hunters. But the gathering of vegetable products—fruits, nuts, roots and seeds, for example—requires the use of some kind of receptacle if any quantity is to be gathered. It seems that one of the things that most infuriates a chimpanzee is his inability to carry away more bananas than he can hold in his arms, so that it is likely that, even at this early time, the Man-Apes will have evolved some simple form of carrying device—a piece of bark or skin, a hollow tree burl or a tortoise shell—more specifically for the collection of vegetable foods.

These early sites are all close to water and this could reflect man's inability to live far away from a permanent water supply. Certainly such localities were the most favoured by man as well as animals. Probably no adequate way existed of storing and carrying water and waterside sites provided not only the best opportunities for hunting but (since the meat was, of course, not cooked) a regular supply of water to slake the thirst that invariably follows the eating of raw meat.

Such sites may have been sought-after for these reasons but probably also their popularity may have been connected with the thicker vegetation and tree growth usual at waterside localities in the tropics. Not only would this have provided vegetable foods in greater abundance but would also have admitted of tree-climbing as one means of protection from the larger predators. Quite clearly, also, the use of sticks and stones must have been one of the ways in which the Man-Apes sought to protect themselves and the reduction in the size of the canine teeth that is a feature of Australopithecine dentition was coincident with, and a direct outcome of the increasing and more efficient use of tools. As we have seen, chimpanzees have been observed to throw sticks and to use them as clubs against leopards as well as to throw stones. Many natural stones—'manuports,' as the Leakeys call them—occur on the living-sites and the circular concentration of natural stones at the DKI site at the base of Bed I at the Olduvai Gorge could, besides any other purpose they may have served, have provided a reserve supply of ammunition with which to keep away scavengers from food stocks, especially during the hours of darkness.

One of the dangers for interpreting the stones and bones that constitute the cultural remains associated with the earliest hominids on the living sites, lies in the difficulty we experience in escaping from the preconceived notions that derive from membership in the evolved but rigid social system in which we live today. The opportunity of understanding the psychology and motive agencies that lie behind the behaviour of present-day hunting-gathering peoples like the Bushmen and the Hadza, is undoubtedly of the greatest relevance for understanding the behaviour of prehistoric groups at a similar economic level, though few such studies have yet been made. But even the most lowly of present-day hunter-gatherers are far in advance of *Homo habilis* physiologically, intellectually and culturally.

On the other hand, if we approach prehistory from the other direction, as it were, through studies of primates, in particular of man's closest living relative, the chimpanzee, we have a means of gauging the minimal intellectual and cultural achievements possessed by the early Pleistocene hominids. The truth lies between these two, though probably closer to the chimpanzee.

The close association between the development of the brain and the evolution of technical skills has been stressed [50] and as these skills advanced, more efficient adaptive behaviour resulted. In turn, this was made possible by the development of those parts of the brain connected with motor skills and the ability to communicate, so that culture and brain growth stand in a feedback relationship to one another. The comparative speed with which (it is inferred) *Australopithecus africanus* changed into *Homo habilis* while *A. robustus* remained biologically unchanged until overcome by competition, can only be due to skilful tool-making and use originated by the gracile form.

The picture that now emerges, therefore, is one of small-brained, bipedal tool-makers, spread widely across the continent and living in small but variable, highly social, open groups existing by collecting vegetable foods and by organized hunting, the proceeds of which were shared with the other members of the group. The success of this behavioral adaptation lay in the way the learned skills of tool-making were transmitted from parent to offspring and the increasing experimental use to which the tools were put that led to new parameters, new adaptive behaviour and parallel biological evolution.

Notes

1 SIMONS, E. L. 1965. New fossil apes from Egypt and the initial differentiation of the Hominoidea. *Nature*, 205, 135–9.

2 SIMONS, E. L. 1963. Some fallacies in the study of Hominid Phylogeny. *Science*, 141 (3584) 879–89.

3 WASHBURN, S. L. 1968. *The study of human evolution.* Condon Lectures, Eugene, Oregon. p. 48.

4 a. CHESTERS, K. I. M. 1957. The Miocene flora of Rusinga Island; Lake Victoria, Kenya. *Paläontographica, Stuttgart*, 101 B, 30–71. b. BISHOP, W. W. 1968. The evolution of fossil environments in East Africa. *Trans. Leicester Literary and Philosophical Society*, Vol. LXII, pp. 22–44.

5 a. SIMONS, E. L. 1961. The phyletic position of *Ramapithecus. Postilla*, New Haven, Connecticut, 57, 1–9. b. SIMONS, E. L. 1969. Late Miocene hominid from Fort Ternan, Kenya. *Nature*, 221. 448–51. c. TATTERSALL, I. 1969. Ecology of north Indian *Ramapithecus. Nature* 221, 451–2.

6 *Op. cit.* (3). pp. 14–15.

7 LEAKEY, L. S. B. 1967. An early Miocene member of the Hominidae. *Nature*, 213 (5072) 155–63.

8 WASHBURN, S. L. 1967. Behaviour and the origin of man. Huxley Memorial Lecture, 1967. *Proc. of the Royal Anthropological Institute*, 21–7.

9 a. KLINGER, H. P., J. L. HAMERTON, D. MUTTON and E. M. LANG. 1963. The chromosomes of the Hominoidea. *In:* WASHBURN, S. L. *ed. Classification and human evolution.* Wenner-Gren Foundation, Viking Fund Publications in Anthropology, No. 37, pp. 235–52. b. GOODMAN, M. 1963. Man's place in the phylogeny of the primates as reflected in serum proteins. *In:* WASHBURN, S. L. *op. cit.* (9a) pp. 204–34.

10 a. SARICH, V. M. 1968. The origin of the Hominids:

an immunological approach. *In:* WASHBURN, S. L. and P. C. JAY, *eds. Perspectives on human evolution, I.* New York, pp. 94–121. b. WILSON, A. C. and V. M. SARICH, 1969. A molecular time scale for human evolution. *Proceedings of the National Academy of Sciences* (USA) Vol. 63, No. 4, pp. 1088–93.

The recently carried out quantitative comparisons of serum albumins, transferrins, haemoglobins and DNA show that man is genetically much closer to the African apes than are the apes to Old World monkeys. The close agreement between the haemoglobin and albumin results and the indications that molecular evolution rates are the same in all mammalian lineages that have been compared, make it possible that those of man and the African apes separated as recently as four to five million years ago.

11 *Op. cit.* (8) p. 23.

12 LEAKEY, L. S. B. 1961. A new Lower Pliocene fossil primate from Kenya. *American Magazine of Natural History,* Ser. 13. iv:689–96.

13 LEAKEY, L. S. B. 1968. Bone smashing by Late Miocene Hominidae. *Nature,* 218, no. 5141, pp. 528–30.

14 *Op. cit.* (10).

15 L. S. B. LEAKEY—personal communication.

16 TOBIAS, P. V. and G. H. R. von KOENIGSWALD. 1964. A comparison between the Olduvai hominines and those of Java and some implications for hominid phylogeny. *Nature,* 204, 515–8.

17 CLARK, SIR W. E. LE GROS. 1967. *Man-apes or apemen?* New York. The literature on the Australopithecines and Lower Pleistocene Hominids is voluminous but this book provides the best overall summary of the evidence and the status of these fossils.

18 BRAIN, C. K. 1958. The Transvaal ape-man-bearing cave deposits. *Transvaal Museum Memoir No. 11,* pp. 1–131.

19 EWER, R. F. 1967. The fossil Hyaenids of Africa: A reappraisal. *In:* BISHOP, W. W. and J. D. CLARK, *eds. Background to Evolution in Africa.* Chicago. pp. 109–22.

20 COOKE, H. B. S. 1963. Pleistocene mammal faunas of Africa, with particular reference to southern Africa. *In:* HOWELL, F. C. and F. BOURLIERE, *eds. African ecology and human evolution.* Wenner-Gren Foundation, Viking Fund Publications in Anthropology No. 36. pp. 65–116.

21 *Op. cit.* (18).

22 TOBIAS, P. V. 1967. *The cranium and maxillary dentition of Australopithecus* (*Zinjanthropus*) *boisei.* Cambridge.

23 ISAAC, G. L. 1967. The stratigraphy of the Peninj Group—early Middle Pleistocene formations west of Lake Natron, Tanzania. *In:* BISHOP, W. W. and J. D. CLARK, *eds. Background to Evolution in Africa.* Chicago. pp. 229–57.

24 LEAKEY, L. S. B. 1960. Recent discoveries at Olduvai Gorge. *Nature,* 188, 1050–52.

25 DAY, M. H. and J. R. NAPIER. 1964. Hominid fossils from Bed I, Olduvai Gorge, Tanzania: fossil foot bones. *Nature,* 201, 969.

26 NAPIER, J. R. 1962. Fossil hand bones from Olduvai Gorge. *Nature,* 196, 409–11.

27 LEAKEY, L. S. B., P. V. TOBIAS and J. R. NAPIER. 1964. A new species of the genus *Homo* from Olduvai Gorge. *Nature,* 202, 7–9.

28 DAVIS, P. R. *et al.* 1964. Hominid fossils from Bed I, Olduvai Gorge, Tanganyika: A tibia and fibula. *Nature,* 201, 967.

29 *Op. cit.* (17) pp. 103–6.

30 *Op. cit.* (27) pp. 8–9.

31 COPPENS, Y. 1967. L'hominien du Tchad. *Actas del V congreso panafricano de prehistoria y de estudio del Cuaternario.* Tenerife (1963). pp. 329–30.

32 ROBINSON, J. T. 1953. Telanthropus and its phylogenetic significance. *American Journal of Physical Anthropology,* 11, pp. 445–501.

33 HOWELL, F. C. 1969. Remains of Hominidae from Pliocene/Pleistocene formations in the lower Omo basin, Ethiopia. *Nature,* 223, 1234–9.

34 H. B. S. COOKE—personal communication.

35 *Op. cit.* (10a) p. 119.

36 *Op. cit.* (18) pp. 119–22.

37 a. HAY, R. L. 1967. Revised stratigraphy of Olduvai Gorge. *In: Op. cit.* at note (15) of Chapter I, p. 221. b. COPPENS, Y. and J.-C. KOENIGUER. 1967. Sur les flores ligneuses disparues Plio-Quaternaires du Tchad et du Niger. *C.R. Acad. Sc. Paris,* vol. 265, pp. 1282–5.

38 a. VAN LAWICK-GOODALL, J. 1968. A preliminary report on expressive movements and communication in the Gombe Stream chimpanzees. *In:* JAY, P. C., *ed. Primates.* New York, pp. 313–74. b. GOODALL, J. 1964. Tool-using and aimed throwing in a community of free-living chimpanzees. *Nature,* 201, 1264–6.

39 KORTLANDT, A. 1968. Handgebrauch bei freilebenden Schimpansen. *In:* RENSCH, B. *Handgebrauch und Verständigung bei Affen und Frühmenschen.* Stuttgart. pp. 59–102.

40 REYNOLDS, V. and F. 1965. Chimpanzees of the Budongo Forest. *In:* DE VORE, I. *ed. Primate Behaviour.* New York. pp. 368–424.

41 DART, R. A. 1957. The Makapansgat Australopithecine Osteodontokeratic Culture. *In:* CLARK, J. D.

and S. COLE, *eds. Proceedings of the 3rd Pan-African Congress on Prehistory, 1955, Livingstone.* London. pp. 161–71.

42 See BRAIN, C. K. 1967. *Op. cit.* (21a and b) Chapter I.

43 ARDREY, R. 1961. *African Genesis.* London and New York. pp. 293–306.

44 *Op. cit.* at note (7) of Chapter I, Leakey, M. D. 1967.

45 a. WOODBURN, J. 1968. An introduction to Hadza ecology. *In:* LEE, R. B. and I. DE VORE, *eds. Man the hunter.* Chicago. p. 51. b. LEE, R. B. 1968. What hunters do for a living or How to make out on scarce resources. *Op. cit.* (a) above, p. 40.

46 a. LEAKEY, L. S. B. 1963. Very early East African Hominidae and their ecological setting. *In:* HOWELL, F. C. and F. BOURLIERE, *eds. African ecology and human evolution.* Wenner-Gren Foundation, Viking Fund Publications in Anthropology, No. 36, pp. 451–2. b. LEAKEY, M. D. 1967, p. 428 of *Op. cit.* at note (7) of Chapter I.

47 MANN, A. E. The *palaeodemography of* Australopithecus. Doctoral dissertation, Department of Anthropology, University of California, Berkeley. p. 64.

48 LEAKEY, M. D. 1967, p. 426 of *Op. cit.* at note (7) of Chapter I.

49 *Op. cit.* at note (47) above, p. 69.

50 *Op. cit.* (8).

18

NEANDERTHAL—WORTHY ANCESTOR

RALPH S. SOLECKI

There are many reasons for including Ralph Solecki's piece about neanderthals in this collection. Foremost is the fact that the editor disagrees with him, although valuing him as long-time associate, colleague, and friend. Let me explain.

Some time ago I gave up one fond linguistic usage still maintained by many. I decided to stop referring to hopeless political conservatives as "neanderthals." The reason for doing so was a growing conviction that the neanderthals, who might well have been the evolutionary progressives of their time, were playing a role in the reconstructed epic of human evolution that related more to the nineteenth- and twentieth-century view of the world than it did to the facts of human prehistory. I refer to the thesis, here endorsed by Solecki, that the neanderthals were not an evolutionary stage in our development but a specialized subspecies that was replaced by *sapiens.*

Shades of the two species hypothesis! (See selection 7.) Although the editor is not a physical anthropologist, he is willing to predict that in the interpretation of the place of the neanderthals in human evolution, it will be the Brace position (see selection 8), rather than the Solecki interpretation that will ultimately be accepted. To be candid, this is adduced on evidence that is primarily cultural rather than biological. To put the matter briefly, the historical context in which our understanding of our neanderthal ancestors has formed has been dominated by rather crude experiences of conflict between commercially expanding populations of European colonialists/imperialists and often eclipsed native populations victimized by that expansion. In the course of the events thus encapsulated, genocide, in the most proper sense of the term,

---

SOURCE: "Neanderthal is not an epithet but a worthy ancestor." *Smithsonian, I* (1971):20–26. *Smithsonian*,

has quite definitely occurred. Many specific populations no longer exist, having been driven to extinction by the Euro-American expansion. Part of the action entailed a retroactive interpretation of evolution and history in which figured reconstructions of prototypical events, a mythological charter as it were. The basic point is a simple one. Given the ascendancy of science and of evolutionary theory, no more powerful justification of contemporary events involving the forceful suppression of minorities can be invoked than the imagined succession of human types in the emergence of contemporary *Homo sapiens.*

But Solecki's informed essay carries within itself the data necessary to challenge such an interpretation. The editor believes that the original full title of the article comes very close to the full truth. "Neanderthal is not an epithet but a worthy ancestor," is what Solecki used to head his contribution. There is evidence, you will see, that the neanderthals cared for their sick and crippled fellows and bestowed loving tributes on the dead. This, the earliest evidence of such concern yet to appear in the archeological record, supports the assertion of direct ancestry. The confusion of variously interpreted differences in details of anatomy pales beside this critical information.

Although science can, at least for a time, be entrapped by other aspects of ideology, being turned temporarily to the service of one or another political cause, its ultimate freedom rests in the ability to constantly question whatever is declared to be true. The problem of the interpretation of neanderthal remains in scientific limbo. The reader may elect to support one position or another with regard to the question of the neanderthals, but the ultimate scientific answer remains to be determined.

▼△▼△▼

The top of a skull was perched on the edge of the yawning excavation in the huge cavern. At first it was difficult to realize that we had before us an extreme rarity in human paleontology.

Except for its heavy brow ridge, the skullcap looked like a gigantic egg, soiled and broken. When fully exposed on the narrow excavation shelf, it was an awesome sight—obviously the head of a person who had suffered a sudden, violent end. The bashed-in skull, the displaced lower jaw and the unnatural twist of the head were mute evidence of a horrible death.

As we exposed the skeleton which lay under a heavy burden of stones, we had confirmation that this individual had been killed on the spot by a rockfall. His bones were broken, sheared and crushed on the underlying stones. A large number of rocks must have fallen on him within a split second, throwing his body backward, full-length down the slight slope while at the same time a block of stone severed his head and neck from his trunk.

Among his remains there were small concentrations of mammal bones, which might have been rodent nests. But it is equally possible these bones were dropped there as part of a funeral feast for the dead.

This was "Nandy," as we called him, a member of the species *Homo neanderthalensis* who had died about 48,000 years before. In the scientific literature he is referred to as Shanidar I, because his were the first adult human remains that we identified as Neanderthal from a cave near the village of Shanidar high in the mountains of Kurdistan in northern Iraq.

Large, airy, and conveniently near a water supply, Shanidar Cave is still a seasonal home for modern Kurdish tribesmen, as it has been for various groups of men for thousands upon thousands of years. I had led our expedition to Shanidar Cave in a search for cultural artifacts from the Old Stone Age in this part of Kurdistan, Iraq. Human remains, much less Neanderthal remains, were not the goal, yet altogether in four expeditions from 1951 to 1960 we uncovered nine Neanderthal skeletons.

Laboratory studies of these remains continue to this day and the results are bringing the Neanderthals closer to us in spirit and mind than we would ever have thought likely.

The Neanderthals have been a nettling problem ever since the first find was made more than 100 years ago. This was the famous faceless skull and other skeletal parts found during quarrying operations around a cave in the Neander Valley not far from Düsseldorf in Germany. Primarily through the writings of one man, Marcellin Boule, who was a greatly respected Frenchman in the field of human paleontology, the owner of the Neander skull was soon cast in the role of a brutish figure, slow, dull and bereft of sentiment.

Although we now know much more about Neanderthal man—there have been at least 155 individuals uncovered in 68 sites in Europe, the Near East and elsewhere—he still seems to hang in space on the tree of human evolution. Some anthropologists feel that he had reached a "dead-end" branch on this tree. In any case, his time span on Earth (about 80,000 years) was more than double that of modern man who replaced him, but roughly one-tenth of the time span of *Homo erectus* who preceded him.

An Abundance of Neanderthals

The classical hypothesis, now abandoned, was that Neanderthal man was an ancestral stage through which *Homo sapiens* passed. A second theory is that Neanderthal man was a species apart from *Homo sapiens,* contemporary but reproductively isolated, as donkeys are from horses. The third is that Neanderthal man was a subspecies of early *sapiens,* forming a geographic race. On the whole, the evidence appears to indicate that the Neanderthal did not gradually change into *sapiens,* but was replaced by invading *sapiens*. The greatest difficulty for human paleontologists is that there is a real scarcity of skeletal finds to which they can point with confidence as *sapiens* of an age comparable to that of the Neanderthals.

There was, however, no scarcity of Neanderthals at Shanidar Cave. Prior to the discovery of Nandy, or Shanidar I, we had recovered the remains of an infant. It was later identified as Neanderthal by our Turkish colleague, Dr. Muzaffer Senyürek of the University of Ankara. When it was found, we had little reason to suspect that it was a Neanderthal child.

But not so with Nandy. "A Neanderthal if I ever saw one," is the comment in my field notes for the day of April 27, 1957, the day we found him. Although he was born into a savage and brutal environment, Nandy provides proof that his people were not lacking in compassion.

According to the findings of T. Dale Stewart, the Smithsonian Institution physical anthropologist who has studied all the remains of the Shanidar Neanderthals (except for the Shanidar child), Shanidar I lived for 40 years, a very old man for a Neanderthal—equivalent to a man of about 80 today. He was a prime example of rehabilitation. His right shoulder blade, collar bone and upper arm bone were undeveloped from birth. Stewart believes that his useless right arm was amputated early in life just above the elbow. Moreover, he must have been blind in his left eye since he had extensive bone scar tissue on the left side of his face. And as if this was not enough, the top right side of his head had received some damage which had healed before the time of his death.

In short, Shanidar I was at a distinct disadvantage in an environment where even men in the best condition had a hard time. That Nandy made himself useful around the hearth (two hearths were found close to him) is evidenced by his unusually worn front teeth. Presumably, in lieu of his right arm, he used his jaws for grasping. But he could barely forage and fend for himself, and we must assume that he was accepted and supported by his people up to the day he died. The stone heap we found over his skeleton and the nearby mammal food remains show that even in death he was an object of some esteem, if not respect, born of close association against a hostile environment.

The discovery of Shanidar I was for us a major, and unexpected, event. The discovery, about a month later on May 23, of Shanidar II was overwhelming.

The initial exposure was made by Phil

Smith, then a Harvard University graduate student, who laid bare the great eye sockets and broken face of a new Neanderthal. My first impression was of the horror a rockfall could do to a man's face. The lower jaw was broken, the mouth agape. The eye sockets, crushed out of shape by the stones, stared hollowly from under a warped heavy brow ridge, behind which was the characteristic slanting brow of the Neanderthal.

From later reconstruction of the event, we determined that Shanidar II was killed by a relatively minor rockfall, followed closely by a major rockfall that missed the dead man. His demise did not go unnoticed by his companions. Sometime after the tumult, thunder and subsiding dust of the crashing rocks, they returned to see what had happened to their cave mate. It looks as though a small collection of stones was placed over the body and a large fire lit above it. In the hearth we found several stone points, and several split and broken mammal bones nearby that may have been the remains of a funeral feast. It appears that, when the ceremony was at an end, the hearth was covered over with soil while the fire was still burning.

As with the first two adults, Shanidar III was found in the course of cleaning and straightening the profile of an excavation. It was as if some Near Eastern genie was testing my alertness by tucking away the skeletons on the borders of the exacavation proper.

Like the other two, Shanidar III had been accidentally caught under a rockfall and instantly killed. One of his ribs had a strange cut. X rays taken at Georgetown University Hospital revealed that he had been wounded by a rectangular-shaped implement of wood and the wound had been in the process of healing for about a week when he died. Most likely, he had been disabled in a conflict with unfriendly neighbors and was recuperating when he was killed. Clearly, the dangers of the caveman's life were by no means shut out when he crossed the portal to his airy home.

On August 3, 1960, during our fourth and last season at Shanidar, we uncovered the fragile and rotted bones of Shanidar IV. While Stewart exposed these remains, I started to explore the stones and soil near the place where three years before we had found Shanidar III. Parts of his skeleton were missing and unaccounted for in our collection.

In my first trowelings, several animal bones turned up. One did not look like an animal bone; it looked human. Later I encountered a rib bone that Stewart authenticated as human, but it was not until I uncovered a human molar tooth that we confirmed the presence of Shanidar V. This was becoming too much.

Within four days we found several other bones of this fifth Neanderthal including the scattered fragments of the skull. It appeared that he too was killed by a rockfall, perhaps the same one that killed Nandy.

There was yet another discovery to be made. Stewart was clearing around the southern side of Shanidar IV when he encountered some crushed pieces of a humerus near the skull. "It doesn't make sense," said Stewart, "not in anatomical position." His immediate reaction was that he hated to think that there was yet another Neanderthal in the cave. Furthermore, there were already two humeri for Shanidar IV, the correct number, and now a third: Here was Shanidar VI.

In the space of only five days we had discovered three Neanderthal skeletal groups. Before us were the vast problems of preserving, recording and transporting the remains safely to the Iraq Museum in Baghdad. In the course of feverishly carrying out these activities, we discovered—in some loose material associated with Shanidar VI—more bones which later proved to be from yet another Neanderthal, Shanidar VII. These two, VI and VII, were females. We also retrieved some bones of a baby.

The skeleton remains of IV (a male), VI, VII and the baby (VIII) all appeared to lie in a niche bounded on two sides by large stone blocks. The nature of the soft soil and the position of the stone blocks leads me to believe that a crypt had been scooped out among the rocks and that the four individuals had been interred and covered over with earth. The child had been laid in first; the two females next, perhaps at a later time. The remains of these three were incomplete. Shanidar IV, the adult male, received the main attention of the burial. Probably, to make room for Shanidar IV, the bones of the others were disturbed.

As part of the archaeological routine, I had taken soil samples from around and within the area of Shanidar IV and Shanidar VI, as well as some samples from outside the area of the skeletal remains. These were sent for pollen analysis to Mme. Arlette Leroi-Gourhan, a paleobotanist in Paris.

Under the microscope, several of the prepared slides showed not only the usual kinds of pollen from trees and grasses, but also pollen from flowers. Mme. Leroi-Gourhan found clusters of flower pollen from at least eight species of flowers—mainly small, brightly colored varieties. They were probably woven into the branches of a pine-like shrub, evidence of which was also found in the soil. No accident of nature could have deposited such remains so deep in the cave. Shanidar IV had been buried with flowers.

Someone in the Last Ice Age must have ranged the mountainside in the mournful task of collecting flowers for the dead. Here were the first "Flower People," a discovery unprecedented in archaeology. It seems logical to us today that pretty things like flowers should be placed with the cherished dead, but to find flowers in a Neanderthal burial that took place about 60,000 years ago is another matter and makes all the more piquant our curiosity about these people.

Regarding their livelihood, we can certainly say the Neanderthals of Shanidar were hunters/foragers/gatherers. They most likely made a seasonal round of their wilderness domain, returning to shelter in Shanidar Cave.

The animals they hunted are represented in the cave by the bones of wild goat, sheep, cattle, pig and land tortoise. More rare are bear, deer, fox, marten and gerbil. It should be noted that the most common animals represented are the more docile type, the gregarious herbivorous mammals. It is likely that the Neanderthals caught them by running them over cliffs in herds or, conceivably, by running them into blind canyons where they could be slaughtered. There are several such canyons within easy striking distance of Shanidar Cave.

Communal Life in a Cultural Backwater

The picture of the lone stalker cannot be ruled out in the case of the Neanderthal but, since these people lived in a communal setting, it would be more natural for them to have engaged in communal hunting. And the fact that their lame and disabled (Shanidar I and Shanidar III) had been cared for in the cave is excellent testimony for communal living and cooperation.

By projecting carbon 14 dates that we have received for certain portions of the cave, I estimate that its first occupation was at most about 100,000 years ago. For perhaps 2,000 generations, over a period of some 60,000 years, we think that groups of Neanderthals—probably numbering 25 members at a time—made their seasonal home in Shanidar Cave. Preliminary findings from the analysis of pollen samples show that, through the long history of their occupation of the cave, the climate vacillated from cool to warm.

Yet throughout the period, the Neanderthals changed little in their means of adapting to these climatic changes. Their tool kit remained much the same throughout: It included their flaked stone tools identified as a "typical Mousterian" industry of points, knives, scrapers, and some perforators, all struck off from locally derived flint pebbles. Only a few fragments of bone tools were found. With this meager tool kit Neanderthal man was able to survive and prosper in his own way.

Shanidar seems to have been a kind of cultural backwater, a "refuge" area bypassed by the stream of history because of the remoteness of the area—a condition still reflected in the Kurdish tribal compartmentalizations of today.

Then, around 40,000–35,000 B.C., the Neanderthals were gone from Shanidar Cave, replaced by a wave of *Homo sapiens* whom we have called Baradostians. We have no skeletal remains of these people but ample evidence that they possessed a brand new stone tool kit. Using the same raw materials available to their predecessors, the Baradostians used the Upper Paleolithic technique of flint-knapping, striking off blades which were used as blanks for tools. They had more stone tool types, a variety of bone tools and they also possessed a woodworking technology such as the Neanderthals never had. Probably they used elaborate woodcarving stone tools to fashion traps and more advanced kinds of hunting apparatus and with this equipment they pursued much the same kind of game animals (mainly goats) as their extinct Neanderthal predecessors had.

By 35,000 B.C., the Neanderthals seem to have disappeared from the world altogether and we may well ask, what did Upper Paleolithic *Homo sapiens* have that the Neanderthals did not have? To my way of thinking, there were probably two things that weighed heavily in the balance. One was language. Jacquetta Hawkes, the English student of language and prehistory, feels that although the Neanderthal was a skilled toolmaker, his tool kit shows a conspicuous lack of invention and adaptability. He was probably handicapped because he did not develop a fully articulate and precise language. This was the new weapon which we think his Upper Paleolithic replacement possessed and used to make a tool kit so diversified that in the graver category he had more working edges than master cabinetmakers are accustomed to working with today. With his greater articulateness, he was able to describe and demonstrate the details of the manufacture of these stone tools to his people, including the children who were to carry on the group's activities.

The second critical cultural achievement of Upper Paleolithic man, in my opinion, is his ability to keep track of events for the future. Alexander Marshack, a research fellow at Harvard, has provided us with this recent and powerful insight into prehistoric man. Thousands of notational sequences have been found on engraved bones and stones dating as far back as at least 30 millennia. These markings have been puzzled over or guessed about by archaeologists since the time they were first discovered more than 100 years ago. Marshack has determined that they served Upper Paleolithic man as a kind of farmer's almanac tied in with a lunar notational count. Some are illustrated with the natural history of the events, giving the possessor of the object a mnemonic device reminding him when to expect the change of seasons and the movements and dispersal of game.

An Ancestor of Sympathetic Character

In short, this was of tremendous economic advantage to Upper Paleolithic man, and it gave him a control over his environment and destiny such as was evidently denied to his predecessor, the Neanderthal.

So, men with these remarkable abilities and all that flowed from them overtook and presumably eliminated the Neanderthals. We have long thought of the Neanderthals as ultimate examples of the Hobbesian dictum that the life of a primitive man is "nasty, brutish and short." They have been characterized as having a near-bestial appearance with an ape-like face in profile, a thick neck, stooped shoulders and a shuffling gait. But now it appears that they were actually very similar to *Homo sapiens* in skeletal structure. Stewart's study of the Shanidar Neanderthals led him to the conclusion that below the head there was not too much difference between these early men and modern man. Of course, one cannot deny the bulging prominent eyebrows and the heavy coarse-featured face of the Neanderthal in general, though Anthropologist Earnest Hooton once said: "You can, with equal facility, model on a Neanderthal skull the features of a chimpanzee or the lineaments of a philosopher."

His own biological evolution is something man really does not have conscious control over. But his culture, his social and religious life, is something else. In the millions of years of evolution that began with the ape-like hominids of Africa it is among the Neanderthals that we have the first stirrings of social and religious sense and feelings: the obvious care with which the lame and crippled were treated, the burials—and the flowers. Flowers have never been found in prehistoric burials before, though this may simply be because no one has ever looked for them. And to be sure, only one of the burials in Shanidar Cave yielded such evidence. But the others buried there could have died during the wrong season for flowers, since death knows no season.

The Neanderthal has been ridiculed and rejected for a century but despite this he is still our ancestor. Of course we may still have the privilege of ridiculing him, but in the face of the growing evidence, especially in the light of the recent findings at Shanidar, we can not actually reject him. And what person will mind having as an ancestor one of such sympathetic character, one who laid his dead to rest with flowers?

19

THE ORIGINS OF AGRICULTURE: A RECONSIDERATION

E. S. HIGGS and M. R. JARMAN

Although individual scientists may be as dogmatic and closed-minded as anyone else, a major distinguishing mark of science is scepticism: everything we know in science is, at least theoretically, up for grabs, every scientific fact and concept may be challenged. Some challenges fail to make any significant impression; the evidence is too lopsided. These introductory remarks are not intended to suggest that the authors of the following article are way out; it is rather to make clear that they are acting in the finest of scientific traditions. It will be quite clear to the reader that, far from lacking control of the data, Higgs and Jarman are abreast of the very latest developments in their field. That is precisely what has led them to challenge some of its fondest conceptions.

One of the most frequently encountered notions about the advent of domestication is that it occurred relatively suddenly. There are many, including professional archeologists, who, in discussing the transition from wild to domesticated sources of food, have few qualms about using the phrase "the Neolithic revolution." Coined by the late V. Gordon Childe, the phrase expresses precisely the notion of rapid passage from one stage to the next, an evolutionary saltation or leap believed to be associated with a number of other phenomena, such as the shift from a migratory and nomadic existence to sedentary village life.

Actually, it has long been obvious to those familiar with the evidence of ethnography that sedentary settlements and food domestication are not in one-to-one relationship. The native civilization of the northwestern coast of North America, including such local variants as the Kwakiutl and Tsimshian, seem to have achieved a fair degree of sessility in the absence of a domesti-

SOURCE: "The Origins of Agriculture: A Reconsideration," *Antiquity* 43 (1969):31–41. Reprinted by permission of the publisher and the authors.

cated food supply. Conversely, many cultures that are heavily dependent upon cultivated crops are also required by virtue of their systems of land exploitation to periodically abandon villages in order to set up new ones amidst fresh soil resources, their previous locale having been rendered exhausted by several successive cultivations.

Looking at the problem of the emergence of cultivation and domestication through familiarity with botanical, zoological, and archeological data, and armed with an ecological point of view, Higgs and Jarman raise some interesting speculations that shake some too-easily-held assumptions. Though this article attracted a number of critical replies shortly after it was first published, the full implications of the Higgs and Jarman suggestions have yet to be digested by the archeologists who are most concerned. Future developments should be, as they say, very interesting.

▼△▼△▼

In recent years increasing attention has been focused on the economic aspects of the changes that took place in human groups in their evolution from 'Palaeolithic' to 'Neolithic' ways of life. Braidwood and Howe carried out valuable pioneer work in this field and it is appropriate to quote their view of the problem [1].

> How are we to understand those great changes in mankind's way of life which attended the first appearance of the settled village-farming community?
>
> The appearance of the village-farming community marked a transition, in cultural history, of great import for what was to follow. Before it were some half million years of savagery during which small wandering bands of people . . . led an essentially 'natural' catch as catch can existence.

This statement emphasizes the static nature of the original, supposed 'natural' way of life, and contrasts it with a relatively sudden development which led to sedentary village communities. It implies a number of assumptions: that before the changes took place 'natural' man lived quite a different life, a life of random nomadism, exploiting his environment haphazardly; that the changes entailed the concentration of energies within a limited area, allowing sedentary occupation and the domestication of plants and animals; that the changes were of such a nature as to warrant the separation of economies into agricultural and non-agricultural groups.

The first assumption is not supported by any evidence and a 'wandering catch as catch can existence' contrasts with the work of many authorities, from Carr-Saunders [2] to Wynne-Edwards [3], who stress an orderly territorial exploitation by both man and animals.

Similar criticisms may be made of the second assumption. Macneish [4] in the Tehuacán valley, and Flannery [5] in the Oaxaca valley, Mexico, have shown that in the New World the advent of sedentary societies took place long after the earliest occurrences of domestic plants. In fact there is little evidence for changes in human behaviour between those levels in which there is no evidence for differences in plant form, and those in which such changes can be seen to have taken place. Nor need it necessarily be assumed that the appearance of more or less permanent buildings indicates all-the-year-round occupation. The Vlachs of the Balkans afford one of the many existing examples of groups which combine permanent houses and villages with a seasonal migration, for they move to the mountains away from the dry season in the lowlands. Indeed, the hut structures of the Russian Palaeolithic cultures must not be forgotten when sedentism is considered [6, 7, 8]. Flannery [9] has rightly stressed the likelihood that transhumance was a mechanism by which human societies may have been enabled to exploit several different ecosystems, but there seems to be no logical reason to limit this model to a 'pre-agricultural' phase.

The third assumption that societies are agricultural or non-agricultural, or that animals are wild or domestic, rests on a classification of the data into two groups which it may be convenient to form, but which may not in fact have had any reality. In a similar way certain horses might be separated into two groups, white horses and black horses. It might be troublesome that there are some grey horses but for convenience those with more than 50 per cent white hair might be called white and those with less, black. It might be possible then to draw a line on a map and say those to the east of it are white and those to the west, black. If, however, the marginal area is examined it would not be surprising if there were no perceptible difference between the horses on either side of the line, for a clear cut taxonomic line does not necessarily correspond to a clear cut line in nature. When such an artificial taxonomic line is created, subsequently it may be used as if it were an absolute division, a usage which obscures the fact that in reality there is an important and steady gradation from one class to another.

Thus, before an investigation is made involving the beginnings of agriculture or of domestication, it would be as well to inquire into the meaning of these concepts to see if they are indeed usefully classifiable in presence-absence terms, or if to do so obscures the true nature of the phenomena. Was there a 'beginning' of either agriculture or domestication?

The 'Domesticated' Animal and 'Domestication'

What, for instance, is meant by a domesticated animal? The Oxford Dictionary says a domesticated animal is one which is under control. This is approximately what we mean when we use the word. We mean a close relationship between man and animal, and in general the term is adequate to convey a meaning from one person to another. But when a close analysis is required, there is need for a more precise definition. To say that a domesticated animal is one which is under control, includes in that category tame animals and zoo animals. A lion in a cage is under control, but it is not a domesticated animal; neither is a tame animal, such as a badger. Therefore, the classes 'domesticated animal' and 'domestication' are ill-defined, for wild animals merge into domesticated animals by imperceptible gradations.

An attempt has been made, however, to define a point at which domestication began. The current and widely accepted view is that it began when man began to practise controlled or selective breeding of an animal population (Herre [10] and others). It is held that wild animals tend to breed randomly so that there is little variation in free, interbreeding wild populations. This is due to the fact that there is uncontrolled breeding so that all the variables are evenly distributed, and, with a tight natural selection in operation, the result is uniformity. Man, however, practising selective breeding, may select his breeding stock for a variety of reasons and purposes and he broadens their habitat. The result is a greater variety in the animal population. It does not follow, of course, that man, at the time when he began to do this, changed his behaviour or way of life in any other way than in this particular aspect of it.

The osteological record from archaeological sites is used to show that after a certain time in prehistory, there are observable differences between the bones of sheep, goat, cattle, pig and dog, and those of their forerunners. Goats are said to have developed twisted horns, female sheep to have become hornless, the skulls of cattle to have changed and cattle and pigs to have become smaller. It is assumed that these changes are due to human interference with the gene pools with or without selective breeding. This is a hypothesis but it is not a known fact. Indeed, it is the basic hypothesis on the subject, and others follow if this one is accepted. What other reason could there be for changes such as these taking place?

Post-Glacial Changes in Animal Form

Plant and animal populations are not static. Mutations and gene re-combinations are constantly occurring, and if they meet a favourable environment they may be preserved and spread through the population. If a mutation has been successful it has met an environment which is favourable, or at least not unfavourable, to its preservation. The environment of a plant or animal includes climatic and pedological factors, and all living organisms which affect it, including man. The change in cereals from a brittle to a tough rachis may be an example of a mutation which met a favourable environment. The fact that those stems with a tough rachis are more easily harvested and stored would give them a selective advantage over those with a brittle rachis, once man started to harvest and sow them; that is, man may have constituted a factor in the plant's environment which was favourable to the spread of a mutation for a tough rachis. In this way a selection would have occurred which need not necessarily have been by human intent, but may have been due to human influence.

The observed changes in populations in the post-glacial period may have been due however to one, or a combination of any, of the following factors:

1. post-glacial climatic changes;
2. change in any other factor in the physical environment;
3. a change in the man/animal relationship, which is basically a change in the animal's environment;
4. an evolutionary mechanism set in motion at an earlier time.

Taking one observed change as an example, it is clear that in North-West Europe in post-glacial times cattle became much smaller. This change has been observed to have taken place over this area in Neolithic or later time. With the present dispersion theory the interpretation given is that agriculture flowed into Europe from east to west and the spreading techniques of domestication caused a diminution in size of the cattle. A reasonable hypothesis, perhaps, on the observed data, but it remains a hypothesis which prefers one factor in a changing biotope as the primary cause. There is, also, some danger of a circular argument here that agriculture came in from east to west because the cattle became smaller, which was because agriculture flowed in from east to west.

It has also been said that wild cattle were in glacial times larger in North-Western Europe than in Eastern Europe (Jewell [11], Leithner [12], Requate [13]). This is perhaps an example which illustrates Bergmann's rule that the colder it is the larger the animals. In the northern hemisphere the north-west was certainly more glaciated than the south-east. If we accept Bergman's rule, and it would appear to apply to cattle in the northern hemisphere, then it is reasonable to suppose that in general smaller wild cattle would have met a more favourable environment in Eastern Europe than in Western Europe in glacial times, and that in post-glacial times larger wild cattle would have been no longer selected out for survival. It is also well known, in fact, that whenever there is a drastic change in environment there is a high premium on mutations which can cope with the new circumstances, and that in hotter climates there is a premium on a smaller body size. So the decrease in size could have been due to the warmer post-glacial climate and not to human selection. It does not need to have been contemporary with the climate change itself, as the rates of change in the two phenomena may be different and in any case it would have taken some time for a definite change to have had a noticeable effect upon animal populations.* Such a tendency for a decrease in size may have been encouraged or not effectively discouraged by human selection.

The reasons often quoted for human selection for smaller animals are by no means con-

* One of us (M. J.) has noted that over a period of 1,000 years domestication caused no appreciable diminution in cattle size at Neolithic Knossos.

vincing. Zeuner's explanation that the smaller animals (especially in the case of cattle) would have been selected as less fierce and more manageable than the larger [14], is not supported by available evidence. Mason has pointed out, and it is well known, that the larger breeds of modern cattle tend to be more placid than the smaller [15], and Dr. J. Teal (pers. comm.) has noted that the larger individuals in a musk ox population tend to be easier to tame. It is possible that, as has been widely suggested (Higgs [16] and others), there may have been selection for small size in order that more individuals could survive the lean period of the year. It is difficult to see, however, a human reason, or for that matter a natural reason, for the development of twisted horns in goats, hornless female sheep or cattle with a slight difference in skull formation. It appears most likely that there is a relationship between these characteristics and some other hereditary factors as yet undetermined. Of course, as the preferred hypothesis human whim could be chosen as the causative factor, but there is no direct evidence to support such a choice.

Certainly, however, Degerbol has shown a decrease in cattle size from Neolithic times onwards in Denmark and attributed it to the introduction of domesticates [17, 18]. Unfortunately we do not know the Pleistocene situation and whether or not this was a continuation of a localized long-term process. Jewell [11, 19] has shown the same process going on in Britain but a similar criticism applies, while Flannery [20] has attempted to show a similar occurrence in the Near East. For the Near East, cattle from Star Carr and Denmark, which come from a totally different biotope, are taken as a baseline. Bökönyi [21], Herre [10, 22] and Reed [23] have pointed out the inadequacies of such comparisons.

It is true that the Ali Kosh cattle seem of comparable size to the late North-West European *Bos primigenius*. This does not necessarily mean that they are the same size as the wild cattle of the Near East, and again no information is given concerning the size of Late Pleistocene *Bos primigenius* from the area. In addition, the Ali Kosh cattle come from a long time range (7500–5600 BC) and the possibility cannot be excluded that there is a size change within this period. Furthermore, the measurements of supposed domestic cattle from Tepe Sabz represent only three bones, two of which are astragali and may thus come from immature individuals. The third bone, a distal metacarpal, comes within the size range of the cattle from Star Carr and Ali Kosh. It may also be noted that the quoted date of the measured Tepe Sabz cattle bones is 5500–3750 BC, and that even if we accepted the unproven hypothesis that they were smaller than local wild cattle, the evidence still does not justify the statement (p. 185) that 'The cattle of the Sabz Phase (5500–5000 BC) were much smaller than the wild aurochs.' In the Near East, therefore, the data is so far unsatisfactory.

That post-glacial changes in animal form are due to a closer man/animal relationship is the preferred but not the only possible hypothesis; Kurtén's work [24, 25] suggests that where such changes exist they may have been partly due to other factors. Several carnivore species show a consistent diminution in size over the last 10,000 years or more; other species increased in size at the time of the change from glacial to post-glacial conditions in North-Western Europe. While it is true that the gene pools of wild populations may be disturbed or even swamped by the proximity of domestic animals which provide a source of feral domesticates, in many of the species studied by Kurtén there is no reason to believe that this occurred or that the man/animal relationship changed over the time period involved.

Similar considerations occur in palaeobotanical studies. Thus Bottema (in Higgs et al. [26]) has shown that the colonization of the Ioannina lake basin by *Quercus ilex* precedes evidence of local agriculture. This could either be the first indication of human influence on the vegetation or part of a process of invasion by a Mediterranean flora brought about by post-glacial climatic changes.

The customary interpretation of the date is also based on the assumption that where osteological changes attributed in one area to domestication are not found in another area, then in the latter area domestication has not taken place. The artificial taxonomic line based on osteological dissimilarities has at this point taken over and need have little to do with the man/animal relationship. As Berry [27] has shown with rats: 'there is no reason to believe that domestication *per se* will alter the phenotype or even a major part of the genotype.' There need not have been a difference in the way of life of those people who had animals whose form had changed, from those whose animals had not changed. The absence of a man/animal relationship such as is implied by the use of the term domestication cannot be determined by the absence of these morphological changes.

Nor is it reasonable to guess that changes attributed to domestication, which occur in one biotope, will be repeated in different biotopes if domestication has taken place. For example, the grey steppe cattle of Siberia today are almost within the size range of the big wild *Bos primigenius* of North-West Europe and certainly as large as and larger than Neolithic cattle (Zalkin [28]).

In dealing with these changes of form we are also, in fact, looking for differences between domesticated and wild animals, indeed differences in the domesticated animals from their wild prototypes. What, however, is the form of the wild prototype? This must be established before we can perceive differences due possibly to domestication, and in this respect populations have not as yet been satisfactorily studied. With cattle we can see however that in northerly latitudes generally, through time, there are differences in bone size, based on the fossil record, and also differences in the skull and horn shape.

With sheep and goats, however, it has been inferred that the wild prototypes still exist unchanged, in the bezoar of the Near East and the argali, urial, and other wild sheep of Asia. The distribution of early agricultural settlements does coincide to some extent with the distribution of the bezoar and the wild sheep. The distribution of wild cereals coincides even more closely. What hypothetical reasons could be put forward for such a coincidence? An alternative to the usual hypothesis on the evidence of distribution above could be that the so-called present-day prototypes are not the original prototypes but feral domesticates. Sheep, according to the present hypothesis, were domesticated 11,000 years ago. Is it likely that over a period of 11,000 years no domesticated animals escaped and diluted or changed in any way the wild sheep populations of the area? Are the wild sheep and their distribution worth very much in a study of this nature, except to show that the data can be arranged logically in a way which is not contrary to an already preferred hypothesis? The distribution of so-called wild sheep today is a major criterion by which the location of the origin of agriculture is determined. The speed with which feral pigs established themselves in Australia and reverted to a phenotype somewhat similar to that of wild pigs may be a similar occurrence. It may be possible that comparable events took place with species of cereals, and that some of the presumed modern wild distribution reflects the spread of feral domesticates or of hybrids between these and wild forms.

The Slaughter of Young Animals and Domestication

The percentage of young animals as determined from the bones from a site is regarded as another criterion by which it may be decided whether or not the animals present were domesticated. The hypothesis is that if man had a close control over a flock or herd he would kill off a higher percentage of young animals than would a hunting culture which would tend to kill at random.

There is no general agreement on what percentage of young animals are required before the flock is regarded as domesticated—although one authority has named 70 per cent as being an unlikely figure to be achieved by a hunting culture—or for that matter how old a young animal may be. However, it requires little thought to realize that a hunting culture may in certain situations kill a high percentage of young animals, as, for example, at the Mousterian site of Ehringsdorf where more young rhinoceroses were killed off than old ones. Herd followers, who may or may not be regarded as hunters, may also kill for consumption with a selective bias, for it would not be difficult to learn that nearly all the young males could be killed off without reducing the breeding potential of the herd or herds within the group's territory. Further, the percentage of young animals killed off with a domesticated herd may be an indication of the economic situation of the group. Where the human pressure upon animal populations is high, it might be necessary to kill young animals; where it is still high but not quite so high, a human group may need to hold its livestock over until it reaches a maximum size and achieve maximum production; where there is a surplus over requirements many young animals may be killed as a matter of preference but a preference may be exactly the reverse and be, for example, for mature beef or, as in pre-war Britain, for two-year-old wether mutton. Other examples are two sites at which extremely low percentages of young animals had been killed off. One was at a Roman villa site during an occupation which occurred after the legionaries had departed and when the economy was presumably in an unfortunate situation, and a medieval site where the locality was heavily engaged in the wool trade and the older sheep were presumably retained to produce the maximum quantity of wool [29]. It might be said that where there is a very high percentage of young animals killed off, domestication may have taken place, but the fact that a high percentage has not been killed off does not mean that a less close man/animal relationship existed.

Where there is both a diminution in size of the animals and a high percentage of young animals present in the bone assemblage it may be tempting to conclude that domestication may have taken place, but where either or both of these phenomena are absent it still does not follow that domestication has not taken place.

The Beginning of Domestication

Returning to the proposition that there was a 'beginning' of domestication, and that its time and place of origin are worth seeking, the widely accepted present-day opinion is shown by the following quotation:

> It has long been apparent that agricultural economies did not appear to develop all over the Old World as the natural outcome of local final Mesolithic traditions, but originated in a restricted area centred on Western Asia and spreading thence by a complex process of transmission that we can only guess at. [S. PIGGOTT, *Ancient Europe*, 25]

This view has therefore a history and it may be as well to ask what that history is.

Previously the generally accepted opinion was that a revolution had taken place in the Near East where a people had arisen who invented pottery, the polished axe and domesticated animals. This broke down when radiocarbon dating showed that the first occurrences of these various artifacts and activities were widely dispersed in time. Earlier still we are back with the Garden of Eden story. Does this history in fact show the persistence of a truth or the persistence of a legend?

It can be seen that much of the interpretation of our data depends on preferred hypotheses. How many of these hypotheses, archaeological, zoological or botanical, are preferred because of the preconceived ideas arising out of a legend, rather than out of the data itself?

It is not the purpose of this article to suggest a new area for a hypothetical origin of agriculture. However, some limitations of the present position must be pointed out before a new standpoint may be established. If we accept the customary hypothesis regarding the criteria for inferring domestication, how far does the present evidence suggest an origin of domestication in the Near East or does our present interpretation of the data recall the work of Keller on lake villages?

The Dog

The general view is that the dog was domesticated from the wolf. The jackal has been suggested as an ancestor but is not now preferred [30], [31]. The pariah dog and an unknown generalized canine ancestor, perhaps similar to the dingo, have also been postulated.

The wolf was available for domestication in both Europe and Asia. At one time a dog was thought to have been domesticated in Natufian times in the Near East. This has since been re-identified as a jackal [31]. The earliest known dogs are from Star Carr in Yorkshire; and from Idaho in the United States with a C14 date of 8420 BC [32]. The Star Carr dog was originally determined as a wolf [33]. Subsequently it was decided that it was a dog, largely on the fact that it had a crowding of the teeth [31]. The crowding of the teeth is regarded by some zoologists as being a result of the foreshortening of the jaw, due, it is thought, to the process of domestication. Why is not clear. The occurrence has been observed to take place in wolves in confinement in zoos. Degerbol has suggested that dogs were first of all kept in captivity for eating [31]. This suggestion has found support in the view that hunting communities at the present time do not use hunting dogs. This, however, does not now appear to be true. Clutton-Brock has also pointed out, perceptively, that no one has so far studied the incidence of the crowding of teeth in wolves [30]. Again there is need for the study of populations before much real advance can be made. On the available evidence and accepting the customary criteria, Yorkshire, England, and Idaho in the United States have the earliest known domesticated dogs, although the Idaho C14 date is only one date and both the stratigraphy and the date need confirmation and critical assessment. The number of dogs which have been found in North Temperate Europe of possibly an early date does seem to indicate that the domestication of the dog may have been earlier there than elsewhere. But the position is by no means satisfactory. By no conceivable means, however, can it be shown to be likely on the present evidence, that the domestication of the dog began in the Near East.

Cattle

Cattle are generally thought to have had *Bos primigenius* as an ancestor and there is considerable evidence for this animal in the fossil record of the Pleistocene in Europe, Asia and North Africa. Certainly if we accept the present criteria then they would appear to have been domesticated on the grounds that the cattle became smaller as early as the 6th millennium BC in Mesopotamia but in the 7th millennium in Greece and Crete. Races of small 'wild' cattle however have been reported, for instance in the Near East (at Shanidar), in North Africa (*Bos ibericus*) and in the Tardenoisian of France. None of these has been adequately studied as yet nor has their presence been adequately explained. The record, however, judged by the criteria which are generally accepted today, points clearly to an earlier domestication of cattle in Eastern Europe or Turkey rather than in the Near East.

Sheep and Goat

It is not possible to say whether or not the so-called wild sheep are the original prototype wild stock or whether they are feral or part feral domesticates. There is one curious aspect of the fossil evidence for wild sheep. It is almost, perhaps quite, absent. Rarely do they appear to have been hunted by Palaeolithic man and such determinations as have been made of them in an early Palaeolithic context are of dubious value either stratigraphically or zoologically [34]. In contrast one of the commonest animals to be hunted was the goat, and indeed almost every available animal except the sheep was hunted by Palaeolithic man. There seems to be no process of ecological reasoning which could explain this, particularly as sheep and goat easily invade each other's preferred environments, if one of them is absent. After 11,000 BP, however, sheep became numerous in the archaeological record. A possible explanation put forward is that in late Palaeolithic times there was one interbreeding population from which the sheep and goat as we know them were ultimately derived [34]. A hypothesis as good as that, which is currently preferred, would be that the present-day wild sheep are in whole or in part feral, and indeed it could be that the sheep itself, even the American Bighorn, is a domesticate, the result of human selection upon a capra-ovine stock. As for the sheep, at a guess, it may well be that it was in a domesticated form, at an earlier stage, north of the Fertile Crescent. To place its original domestication in the Near East is not warranted by the available information.

The Pig

The pig is a difficult animal to study in the archaeological record. Certainly in the Near East it is supposed to have been domesticated in the 7th millennium. But this determination, based on a few teeth, is premature. There is now good evidence of the early domestication of pigs in the Crimea [35]. At such sites as Tash Ai'r, Zamil Koba II and Soroki, pigs occur in very high percentages (itself perhaps an indication of a close relationship with man), and seem to have been domesticated at a stage shortly after the retreat of the cold fauna prevalent in the area until about 10,000 years ago.* Again the assertion that the Near East had priority in the domestication of pigs is not warranted by the evidence.

We therefore see that even on the basis of present criteria and the accepted interpretation of the evidence there is little to suggest that the origin of much domestication was in the Near East and indeed much of the evidence at the moment is to the contrary.

The evidence of cultivated cereals is more scanty, partly because of the fragility of the remains, and partly because serious research on the subject is a comparatively recent development. Most of the relevant work has been done on Near Eastern material, and so it is not surprising that the majority of the early records of cereals lies in this area. However, there is increasing evidence that the evolution of close man/plant associations took place at an early date in Anatolia and Eastern Europe. One cannot at present even guess at the position which may be revealed when such areas as Northern Anatolia and the Crimea have been studied in detail or, for that matter, vast areas east of the Fertile Crescent. The earliest occurrence of bread wheat yet recorded is in Stratum X at Knossos, Crete, with C14 dates of 6100 ± 180 years BC, and 5980 ± 180 years. Hacilar in Anatolia has domestic emmer at a date comparable with that of its appearance at Ali Kosh. Ghediki and Argissa Magula in North Greece and Hacilar all have early cultivated barleys

* At this early stage pigs seem to have become smaller and subsequently larger. It is perhaps worth noting that the feral pigs of Australia are large compared with their ancestor—the introduced domesticated pig.

at similar periods to those of the earliest Near Eastern occurrences [36], [37]. Nevertheless the best evidence for early domestication in the Near East concerns wheat and barley. But what cereals like *Setaria* [41] were once cultivated and their cultivation subsequently dropped?

It appears that the dog, cattle and pig were probably domesticated, according to the present-day criteria, elsewhere than in the Near East. The sheep may also have been domesticated earlier elsewhere and possibly, but less likely, the goat. The best evidence for a Near Eastern source of domestication is for wheat and barley, although the domestication of these plants could have taken place over a much wider area than is at present envisaged. The location of the earliest domestication of other cultigens is even less well understood. What does appear to emerge at the moment, however, is that, on the present evidence Anatolia may have been another 'early centre' for domestication. However, as we have suggested, the term domestication and domestic animal obscure the gradation from one form to another, and draw a classificatory line which may not correspond with nature. It might prove wise to look at the problem in another way.

Domestication and Symbiosis

Zeuner and many other authors have remarked on the similarity of the man/domesticated animal, and indeed man/domesticated plant relationship, to other symbiotic relationships in the animal/plant worlds. If this is so, and there is very little dissent from the view that domestication is a symbiotic relationship, it apparently arose only towards the end of prehistory. But similar close man/animal relationships could be inferred from the data as far back at least as Middle Palaeolithic times, from such sites as Tash Ai'r and Salzgitter-Lebenstedt where there was a concentration upon one animal species [38], [39].

Cutting across this possibility, however, is the hypothetical ladder of progress, that is to say that there was a time when all men were hunter/gatherers, and that this hunter/gatherer phase was followed by an incipient agricultural phase and that by a full agricultural phase. How do we determine that the main exploitation of a human group at a particular site was in fact hunting and gathering? Little can be said from a study of the tools. The British Neolithic and Bronze Age is full of arrowheads but clear-cut 'hunting' tools are always rare in prehistory. One may quote the spear-thrower and the *bâton de commandement,* but the former is exceedingly rare and the latter is not only enigmatic as to its use but is commonly associated with reindeer, an animal which is very likely to have been domesticated at an early stage. From the bones there is some help. Where a wide variety of species has been eaten at a particular site it may be reasonable to assume that the major exploitation was hunting. Where there is a concentration, however, on one or two species a close man/animal relationship (or symbiotic relationship or domestication) is *at least as likely as a hunter/gatherer hypothesis.* The fox at Jericho, the gazelle at many Near Eastern sites, the mammoth with the hut-dwellers of the Russian steppes or the horse at Solutrean sites may all have been, on the available evidence, in the same relationship with man as the morphologically unchanged sheep at Shanidar. Indeed there may not have been a hunter/gatherer age. One might be tempted to consider that symbiotic relationships may have occurred even at an early stage of the Pleistocene, but the evidence for the economy of early sites is so little that hardly anything can at present be inferred.* Then, as now, there may have been hunters, hunter/gatherers and those practising close man/animal, man/plant symbiotic relationships according to the environ-

* Leakey on Olduvai comments on the plentiful remains of the larger *Bovidae* in the living floors of the hominid, and declares that there must therefore be some other, and at the present unexplained, reason for the scarcity of the smaller antelopes.

ment. The last two forms of economic exploitation gradually became more successful and tended to supersede other forms. It may be regarded as a long-term record of the development of a symbiotic relationship which is not available for any of the other plants or animals. The choice of which form of exploitation was to be pursued, may have been determined by which form of economy was the more successful in particular environments.

If this is so, one may expect to find a long continuity of close man/animal relationships in particular areas, partly as a continuance of a tradition highly conducive to survival of successful economies based on the herd as an existing mechanism of food storage and/or on storable seeds, and partly as an adaptation to an environment which continued to be favourable through time for close man/animal relationships.

In this connexion we may turn to southern Russia as a possible example of where such a continuity may be seen. At Molodova on the Dniestr, *c.* 9000 BC, over 90 per cent of the animals killed were reindeer. The people at this site are commonly regarded as hunters for no better reason than that they are thought to have lived at a time which was too early for 'domesticates' to have occurred and that morphological changes in the animals concerned have not been observed. The same may be said of the Hamburgian and other sites in NW Europe. Less than 1,000 miles away from Molodova, and at the same time, were the sheep herders of Shanidar. The Molodova reindeer people and Shanidar sheep people are not likely to have been the most southerly and the most northerly of their kind. It could also be, and it is not unlikely, that sheep herders were adjacent to reindeer hunters. It is also likely that the techniques of herding were known to both peoples. It is at present impossible to decide which hypothesis to choose. The evidence will not tell us which they were and the question must be left open. The close association with the reindeer in this area appears to have been terminated by the advance of post-glacial conditions, but it is noteworthy that as soon as the cold fauna begins to withdraw from the area there is a concentration by the Mesolithic communities upon pig. In the opposite direction in time for an earlier close man/animal relationship there is the evidence at Amvrosievka, and even as far back as the Middle Palaeolithic at Il'skaia, for a concentration on bison [40], [38].

A hypothesis can be made that almost throughout the Last Glaciation and at least throughout Europe and the Near East there is evidence at some sites for close man/animal relationships, wherein the animals concerned changed according to the environmental changes, but a symbiotic relationship was maintained. With such a hypothesis it would be absurd to look for a beginning of agriculture in a particular area for it does not imply an invention or a series of inventions, or 'mutations' of human behaviour at a certain time. The economies of Palaeolithic peoples remain unstudied, largely because of the unwarranted assumption that all men were then hunter/gatherers. On this assumption rests the hypothesis that the Near East was an innovating centre where the innovations necessary for a beginning of domestication first occurred. It seems more likely that it was an area where the techniques and symbioses of the inhabitants of colder regions were adjacent to temperate and sub-tropical areas in each of which different forms of symbiosis had long existed. Collected together and integrated they formed complex, powerful and expanding economies.

As for America, if the presence of early forms of symbiosis is accepted, and the widely dispersed nature of the evidence for early domestication in that continent is in accord with this hypothesis, then there is no need to postulate a separate and similar pattern of 'inventions' in the New World.

The cultural model has dominated thought and speculation in European archaeology for many decades, yet we have only to look at relatively recent events in America, Africa and

Australia and later in New Guinea to see how long-established cultures, customs and social structures topple at the first contact of a superior economy. The study of economy, the major selective force in prehistory has, until now, largely been ignored. With its development, and if a hypothesis, such as the alternative one set out above, is accepted as an approach to the problem, then the whims, fashions, and freedom of choice associated with cultures may become of less importance to archaeology than the study in man's past of natural mechanisms as the true causes of human behaviour.

Notes

1 R. J. BRAIDWOOD and B. HOWE, 'Prehistoric Investigations in Iraqi-Kurdistan', *Studies in Ancient Oriental Civilisation,* no. 31 (Chicago, 1960).

2 A. M. CARR-SAUNDERS, *The Population Problem: a Study in Human Evolution* (Oxford, 1922).

3 V. C. WYNNE-EDWARDS, *Animal Dispersion in Relation to Social Behavior* (Edinburgh, 1962).

4 R. S. MACNEISH, 'Ancient Mesoamerican Civilization', *Science,* CXLIII, 1964, no. 2606, 531–7.

5 K. V. FLANNERY, unpublished.

6 I. K. IVANOVA and A. P. CHERNYSH, 'The Paleolithic Site of Molodova V on the Middle Dnestr (USSR)', *Quaternaria,* VII, 1965, 197.

7 P. P. EFIMENKO, *Kostienki I* (Moscow, 1958).

8 A. N. ROGACHEV, 'Alexandrovskoye Poselenie Drevnekamennogo Veka y Sela Kostienki na Dony', *Materialy i Issledovanyia po Arkeologii SSSR'* 1955, no. 45.

9 K. V. FLANNERY, 'The Ecology of Early Food Production in Mesopotamia', *Science,* CXLVII, 1965, no. 3663, 1247–56.

10 W. HERRE, 'The Science and History of Domestic Animals', in (eds.), D. Brothwell and E. S. Higgs, *Science in Archaeology* (London, 1963), 235–49.

11 P. A. JEWELL, 'Cattle from British Archaeological Sites', in A. E. Mourant and F. E. Zeuner, *Man and Cattle. FRAI Occasional Paper,* no. 18, 1963, 80–101.

12 O. F. VON LEITHNER, *Der Ur. Ber. Intern. Ges. Erhaltung des Wisents,* II (1), 1927, 1–139.

13 H. REQUATE, 'Zur Naturgeschichte des Ures (*Bos primigenius* Bojanus 1827), nach Schädel-und Skelettfunden in Schleswig-Holstein', *Zeit. Tierzucht. Züchtungsbiol.,* LXX, 1957, 297.

14 F. E. ZEUNER, *A History of Domesticated Animals* (London, 1963).

15 I. L. MASON in Mourant and Zeuner [11], 18–19.

16 E. S. HIGGS in C. B. McBurney, *The Haua Fteah (Cyrenaica)* (Cambridge, 1967), 313–23.

17 M. DEGERBOL, 'Ur und Hausrind', *Zeit. Tierzucht. Züchtungsbiol.,* LXXVI (2–3), 1961, 243–51.

18 M. DEGERBOL, 'Prehistoric Cattle in Denmark and Adjacent Areas' in Mourant and Zeuner [11], 68–79.

19 P. A. JEWELL, 'Changes in the Size and Type of Cattle from Prehistoric to Medieval Times in Britain', *Zeit. Tierzucht. Zuchtungsbiol.,* LXXVII (2), 1961, 159–67.

20 K. V. FLANNERY in F. Hole and K. V. Flannery, "The Prehistory of Southwestern Iran: a Preliminary Report', *Proc. Prehist. Soc.* for 1967, XXXIII, 1968, 147–206.

21 S. BOKONYI, 'Zur Naturgeschichte des Ures in Ungarn und das Problem der Domestikations Beginn', *Palaeohistoria,* XIV, 1968, 283–5.

22 W. HERRE, 'Zoologische Betrachtungen zu Aussangen . . .', *Acta Arch. Acad. Sci. Hung.,* XXIV (3–4), 1962, 175–214.

23 C. A. REED, 'Osteological Evidences for Prehistoric Domestication in Southwestern Asia', *Zeit. Tierzucht. Zuchtungsbiol.,* LXXVI (1), 1961, 31–8.

24 B. KURTÉN, 'Rates of Evolution in Fossil Mammals', *Cold Spring Harbor Symposia on Quantitative Biology,* XXIV, 1959, 205–15.

25 B. KURTÉN, 'The Rate of Evolution' in Brothwell and Higgs [10], 217–23.

26 E. S. HIGGS, C. VITA-FINZI, D. R. HARRIS and A. E. FAGG, 'The Climate, Environment and Industries of Stone Age Greece: Part III', *Proc. Prehist. Soc.* for 1967, XXXIII, 1968, 1–29.

27 R. J. BERRY, 'The Genetical Implications of Domestication in Mammals'. Paper delivered at the Research Seminar on Domestication and Exploitation of Plants and Animals (London, 1968).

28 V. I. ZALKIN, *The Grey Steppe Cattle and* Bos primigenius (1965).

29 E. S. HIGGS in R. H. Hilton and P. Rahtz, 'Upton, Gloucestershire', *Trans. Bristol and Glos. Arch. Soc.,* 1966.

30 J. CLUTTON-BROCK, 'The Origins of the Dog' in Brothwell and Higgs [10], 269–74.

31 M. DEGERBOL, 'On the Find of a Preboreal Domestic Dog (*Canis familiaris* L.) from Star Carr, Yorkshire, with Remarks on Other Mesolithic Dogs', *Proc. Prehist. Soc.,* 1961, XXVII, 25–55.

32 B. LAWRENCE, 'Early Domestic Dogs', *Zeit. Säuge-tierkunde,* XXXII (1), 1967, 44–59.

33 F. C. FRASER and J. E. KING in J. G. D. Clark, *Star Carr* (Cambridge, 1954).

34 S. PAYNE, *PPS,* xxxiv, 1968, 368.

35 D. A. KRAINOV, 'Pestichernaya Stoyanka Tash-Ai'r I',

Materialy i Issledovaniya po Arkeologii SSSR, XLI, 1960.

36 H. HELBAEK, 'Commentary on the Phylogenesis of *Triticum* and *Hordeum*', *Econ. Botany*, XX, 1966, 350–60.

37 J. M. RENFREW, 'The Archaeological Evidence for the Domestication of Plants: Methods and Problems'. Paper delivered at the Research Seminar on Domestication and Exploitation of Plants and Animals (London, 1968).

38 H. L. MOVIUS, 'The Mousterian Cave of Teshik Tash, Southeastern Uzbekistan, Central Asia', *Amer. School of Prehist. Research Bull.* 17, 1953, 11–71.

39 A. KLEINSCHMIDT in A. Tode *et al.*, 'Die Untersuchung der Palaolithischen Freilandstation von Salzgitter-Lebenstedt', *Eiszeitalter und Gegenwart*, III, 1953, 144–220.

40 P. I. BORISKOVSKY, 'Le Paléolithique de l'Ukraine', *Ann. du Service d'Information Géologique*, 1958, no. 27, 1–368.

41 E. O. CALLEN, 'The First New World Cereal', *American Antiquity*, XXXII, 1967, 4.

20

THE DISCOVERY OF THE FIRST CIVILIZATION

GLYN DANIEL

The single most-quoted definition of culture among anthropologists is undoubtedly that of Edward Tylor, first set out in 1871. It begins, "Culture, or civilization . . . ," and with those words helps maintain the confusion that pertains to the overlap of meaning between these two terms. For some anthropologists, the distinction that is sometimes insisted upon between "culture" and "civilization" is invidious and can be used for pejorative purposes. Others find the distinction of considerable utility, marking a major watershed in the evolution of cultural complexity. Thus, the term was clarified, among others, by V. Gordon Childe, who associated it with a number of highly specific diagnostic features, including (1) a great leap in population size of communities, (2) considerable enlargement in the scale of buildings, especially those for religious or governmental use, (3) significant increase in the complexity of the division of labor with (4) a concomitant development of social stratification leading to the formation of socioeconomic classes. Childe also looked favorably on the criterion that Lewis Henry Morgan had recognized to be of great significance, namely, (5) writing. Finally, there was (6) "an artistic revolution," mainly in the naturalistic representation of the human face and form, which Childe believed associated with the political and ideological position of the king and other members of the ruling class who were the main and often the only subjects of portraiture.

While Professor Glyn Daniel does not necessarily endorse the Childe definition of civilization, he does use the concept in a very similar way. However, it is less for such material that we turn to a chapter of one

SOURCE: *The First Civilizations*, Glyn Daniel ch. 2, pp. 36–68. New York: Thomas Y. Crowell Company, 1968. Reprinted by permission of the publisher and author.

of Daniel's very interesting books, and more for something that often is completely neglected when a social science approach is taken to the content of anthropology. In brief, people who are professionally involved in the discipline sometimes forget, or seem embarrassed to recall, that theirs is a subject with more than scientific interest and appeal. But Professor Daniel, steeped in the history of his field, not only has surpassing control of the theory and substance of archeology, but a good feeling for its romantic aspects as well.

Even as we read Daniel's anecdotal account of the slow development of awareness of the civilization that occupied Mesopotamia before the Babylonians, however, we become aware of other subtleties that might otherwise elude us. We see that regions that once led the world in technological development and general complexity of culture can fall upon hard times and lapse until it becomes difficult to associate the contemporary cultures in the area with the grandeurs of the past. Simultaneously, we become aware that for all of the apparent neutrality of archeology as an ideological field, it too developed in a context of colonialism, as some of the stories recounted by Daniel unconsciously reveal. This does not mean that the data or the theories developed in that context are necessarily false or distorted, but it does alert us to the necessity of constantly looking for bias (a theme that reappears much more strongly in selection 38 by Willis).

Awarenesses such as these are essentially by-products of the piece that follows. The main reason for its appearance is to give us some idea of the slow development of scientific archeology in the particular context of one of its greatest problems—the emergence of civilization. It also gives the reader one example of archeological approaches that hover toward the historically descriptive and idiographic end of the archeological theory continuum.

▼△▼△▼

In the eleventh chapter of the *Book of Genesis* are these words: 'And it came to pass, as they journeyed from the east, that they found a plain in the land of Shinar, and they dwelt there. And they said to one another, "Go to, let us make brick and burn them thoroughly." And they had brick for stone and slime had they for mortar. And they said "Go to, let us build a city and a tower, whose top may reach unto heaven, and let us make a name, lest we be scattered abroad upon the face of the whole earth." ' These words were set down in Hebrew not earlier than 800 BC and give, in a few sentences, an account of the origins of the earliest, the oldest, the first civilization made by man—the civilization of the land of Shinar, the land of Sumer. They did make a name for themselves, and that name was the Sumerians.[1]

In this chapter our concern is with the light which archaeology throws on the origins of Sumerian civilization. I have already referred to the doubtful historicity of the Bible, and by that I meant our inability to accept all that is in the beginning of the Old Testament as a true and certain guide to the origin of the world, the genesis of man and the development of his culture from the savagery—if that is the right word—of the Garden of Eden through the peasant agriculture of Cain and the stock-raising of Abel to the city life of Babel and to the ancient civilizations of the Near East which the Old Testament people witnessed in Egypt, Babylon and elsewhere. But, hidden in that interesting congeries of myths and legends, many directly derived from Mesopotamia before Abraham set off from Ur of the Chaldees, are some historical facts, as we shall see, and indeed as it is easy to see nowadays with the hindsight of a hundred and more years of archaeological research in south-west Asia. Noah and the Flood must surely reflect some of the floods that inundated lower Mesopotamia from time to time, and did flood the known world though not of course the whole world; and the story of the conflict between Abel and Cain is a reflection of the conflict between the steppe and the sown, the desert and the irrigated river valley—a constant theme in ancient Mesopotamian history.[2]

Sumer is the territory which after 2000 BC was called Babylonia. The plain of the land of Shinar is the land between the rivers, the land between the twin rivers, the Tigris and the

Euphrates. The Greeks called this land Mesopotamia, which word means just that—the land between the rivers. Most of it today is part of the modern state of Iraq although the Euphrates rises in Syria and the Tigris in Turkey. From the Turkish border and the Armenian mountains in the north to the Persian Gulf in the south is roughly six hundred miles, about the distance from Aberdeen to Dover. From the Syrian Desert on the west to the mountains of Persia—the Zagros Mountains—on the east is some two hundred to two hundred and fifty miles. In this area, and more especially in the south, the Sumerian civilization came into existence in the second half of the fourth millennium BC.[3]

That Mesopotamia had been the homeland of ancient civilizations was of course very well known for a long time. Babylon and Assyria were part of the historical picture of man based on classical writers and the Old Testament. Herodotus visited Babylon in 450 BC and described the great temple or *ziggurat* there; he said that 'as a grain-bearing country Assyria is the richest in the world.' The figures given by Strabo and Herodotus for a yield of corn of two to three hundredfold may not have been wildly exaggerated. Jacobsen has calculated from the cuneiform texts that the yield of wheat in southern Iraq in 2400 BC could compare favourably with that of the best modern Canadian wheatfields, and this may well be one of the reasons for the growth and the flourishing of Sumerian civilization—the fertility and agricultural wealth of southern Mesopotamia—when well farmed. I should of course have said 'pre-disposing conditions' rather than 'reasons': I do not want here or at any other point in this book to appear to slip into an easy economic or geographical determinism.

The Jews had been captive in Babylon and by its waters had wept. Everyone knows the dramatic account of the Hebrew poet-prophet Daniel who was an unwilling guest at Belshazzar's feast: 'Belshazzar the king made a great feast to a thousand of his lords and drank wine before the thousand.' During the feast Cyrus's men waded across the river and broke into the city: 'In the same hour came forth fingers of a man's hand, and wrote . . . upon the plaster of the wall of the king's palace . . . and this is the writing that was written, *Mene, mene, tekel, upharsin.*' This was in 538 BC. The Babylonians and Assyrians had ruled in Mesopotamia off and on since 2000 BC. Hammurabi was the greatest of the Babylonian kings and the author of the famous Code of Law issued by him

> To cause justice to prevail in the country
> To destroy the wicked and evil.
> That the strong may not oppress the weak.

Hammurabi's dates have long been a matter for discussion: Professor Sydney Smith argued for a long chronology and his argument which gave the date of Hammurabi's accession as 1792 BC. has been much strengthened by recent evidence.

You may well ask who were the Chaldeans and what exactly was Chaldea in this study of ancient peoples and early civilizations. Most people have heard of Abraham as living in 'Ur of the Chaldees' (*Genesis*, xi, 28); the terms Chaldees, Chaldeans, Chaldea are frequent in the Old Testament where they are used as equivalents for Babylonia and the Babylonians. The old term was *mat Kaldu.* Possibly at one early stage the Chaldeans were a separate Semitic-speaking people, but soon in ancient history they were indistinguishable from the Semitic-speaking peoples of Babylon.

So, nowadays, when we speak of the ancient peoples of Mesopotamia, we speak of Assyrians and Babylonians rather than of Assyrians and Chaldeans. By the way, subsequently the word Chaldee was wrongly used for the Aramaic language itself, while in the *Book of Daniel,* in Herodotus, Strabo and Diodorus it means astrologers and astronomers: and the term lived on for a long time to mean 'wise men.'[4]

There are two special features which have for long been associated in the minds of historians and archaeologists with early Mesopotamia. The first is the presence of *tells*, and the second is cuneiform writing. Both need some brief words of explanation here. The early houses and temples of ancient Mesopotamia were built of clay, either of *pisé* (cob), which is roughly piled-up earth, or of *adobe*, shapeless lumps of clay pressed together. Later, sun-dried bricks were used and, latest of all, kiln-fired bricks which were naturally more durable especially when joined together with bitumen. These kiln-fired bricks were costly and reserved for the construction of temples and palaces: the great majority of Mesopotamian buildings were of clay or mud-brick. Rain and natural usage wore these mud-clay structures down, and it has been estimated that the average time-span of a mud house in Mesopotamia would be about seventy-five years. New houses were built on the collapsed and scattered remains of the old houses and so, over the centuries, there began to accumulate a man-made mound, a hill built accidentally out of man's own material past. These artificial and steadily accumulating mounds of successive settlements are called *tells* in Mesopotamia—this is incidentally a pre-Islamic word—and have other local names in other parts of the Near East, such as *tepe* in northern Mesopotamia and Iran, *hüyük* in Turkey. Sometimes they are very high indeed, and some of them, like Erbil (old Arbela), and Kirkuk, are still lived in—or perhaps one should say lived on; they have been more or less continuously occupied from very early times to the present day—perhaps for six to eight thousand years.[5]

These man-made settlement mounds—*tells, tepes, hüyüks*—are a feature of the archaeology of Iran, Iraq, Palestine and Turkey; they also occur in southern Russia and in Bulgaria. They are not a feature of the surviving past of barbarian western and northwestern Europe, nor indeed of Egypt, where, as we shall see, traces of early settlements are difficult to find. Indeed one American archaeologist working in Egypt, John Wilson, has called the early civilization of Egypt 'a civilization without cities.' But where *tells* do occur they are an obvious place for the antiquary and traveller interested in the past, and for the modern archaeologist with his trenches, *sondages,* and large-scale excavations. This is why accounts of excavations in the Near East are full of numbered levels like Uruk XVIII, Tepe Gawra XII (a), Ninevite III, and so on. You will not be concerned with the minutiae of excavation reports, which are the secondary form of archaeological knowledge—the past as it seems to the excavator, as distinct from the *tells* themselves—the past as it survived. Here we are concerned with the third level of archaeological scholarship—the past as it seems to us from a synthesis of excavators' reports, but if you should ever refer to these sources—the excavation reports—you must bear in mind the fact that some excavations are published with the levels numbered from the top downwards as they appeared in the work of excavation, and others numbered from the bottom upwards in historical succession. Thus at Al 'Ubaid and Nineveh period I is the oldest, but at Uruk and Tepe Gawra it is the latest.

For a very long time before they were excavated the ancient mounds of the Near East were recognized as the remains of early settlements. The two large *tells* near Hillah in Babylonia and near Mosul in Assyria were pointed to in Jewish and Arab tradition as the sites of Babylon and Nineveh; and these and other sites were visited by European travellers from the twelfth century onwards. These travellers often collected bricks and potsherds and fragments of tablets from these *tells*. An Italian noblemen, Pietro della Valle, who wrote a most entertaining account of his journey across Mesopotamia, brought back to Europe in 1625 some baked clay tablets 'on which were writing in certain unknown characters.' This was cuneiform writing—the oldest writing in the world. The Sumerians wrote on clay, with a stylus made of a reed or wood. The first signs set down were pictographic—a kind of picture writing as used by the Chinese; later the Babylonians used the stylus for setting down a syllabic script. The cut edge of the reed stylus made wedge-shaped impressions, and hence the name cuneiform for this earliest writing.[6]

But it was not only on clay tablets that this cuneiform writing occurred. There were also monumental inscriptions. Faced with the writing on monuments and tablets, the learned world of Western Europe began to realize that here was a mystery, and a new field for scientific exploration. In 1761 the King of Denmark sent out a scientific expedition to the east to gather as much information as possible in all fields, including archaeology. Its leader was Professor Karsten Niebuhr, a mathematician, but a man of very wide interests, who himself copied numerous inscriptions at Persepolis. Philologists began to work on the copies of these inscriptions. Niebuhr had himself noted that they seemed to be of three different kinds, and here he was right: they were in the three languages we now know to be Old Persian, Susian or Elamite, and Babylonian.

At the beginning of the nineteenth century, a young German by name Georg Friedrich Grotefend began working on Niebuhr's copyings of the Persepolis trilingual inscriptions. In 1802, when only twenty-seven years of age, he had managed to decipher three royal names in the simplest of the three scripts, the old Persian, and later he managed to decipher correctly about a third of the letters in this language. By an inspired guess he had found the key to the decipherment of cuneiform writing. But, alas, Grotefend was not an oriental scholar; he was not a member of the Faculty of the University of Göttingen to whose Academy of Sciences he submitted a dissertation in Latin on his epoch-making discovery. Grotefend was a little-known college teacher and the Göttingen Academy, to their eternal shame, refused to publish his dissertation: it was in fact not published until 1893, when it was of purely historical interest, and by which time others had received the credit for the decipherment.[7]

From the sad story of Grotefend's rejection by the Göttingen Academy we pass to the success story of one of the most interesting and colourful characters in the development of Near Eastern studies—Henry Creswicke Rawlinson who lived from 1810 to 1895. He was a colonel in the Indian Army who got himself posted to Baghdad as British Resident and Consul-General; he was later knighted for his varied achievements. With a knowledge of oriental languages but no knowledge of Grotefend's work, he began to study the cuneiform inscriptions. He started on two short trilingual inscriptions from near Hamadan and then worked on the famous trilingual inscription cut in 516 BC at the instruction of Darius Hystaspes (521–485 BC) on the great rock of Behistun or Bisotun, twenty-two miles east of Kermanshah. This inscription is cut four hundred feet above the ground on the face of a rock-mass which itself rises one thousand seven hundred feet from the plain. This giant inscription, 'a Mesopotamian Rosetta stone' as it has been called, measures 150 feet by 100. The difficulty lay in copying the inscription.

Rawlinson began working alone. In 1852 he wrote:

> When I was living at Kermanshah fifteen years ago, and was somewhat more active than I am at present, I used frequently to scale the rock three or four times a day without the aid of a rope or a ladder; without any assistance in fact, whatsoever. During my late visits I have found it more convenient to ascend and descend by the help of ropes where the track lies up a precipitate cleft, and to throw a plank over those chasms where a false step in leaping across would be fatal. On reaching the recess which contains the Persian text . . . ladders are indispensable . . . and even with ladders there is considerable risk, for the footledge is so narrow, about eighteen inches or at most two feet in breadth . . . the upper inscription can only be copied by standing on the topmost step of the ladder with no other support than steadying the body against the rock with the left arm, while

the left hand holds the note-book and the right arm is employed with the pencil.

'In this position,' Rawlinson adds laconically, 'I copied all the upper inscriptions, and the interest of the occupation entirely did away with any sense of danger.'

He was thus able to copy the Old Persian inscription, but had greater difficulty with the Elamite inscription, which, incidentally, he called Scythic; but the real difficulties began when he tried to make a transcript of the Babylonian version. I quote Rawlinson's words again:

> The writing can be copied by the aid of a good telescope from below, but I long despaired of obtaining a cast of the inscription; for I found it quite beyond my powers of climbing to reach the spot where it was engraved, and the cragsmen of the place, who were accustomed to track the mountain goats over the entire face of the mountain, declared the particular block inscribed with the Babylonian legend to be unapproachable. At length however, a wild Kurdish boy, who had come from a distance volunteered to make the attempt . . . the boy's first move was to squeeze himself up a cleft in the rock . . . he drove a wooden peg firmly in to the cleft, fastened a rope to this. It then remained to him to cross over to the cleft by hanging on with his toes and fingers to the slight inequalities . . . in this he succeeded, passing over a distance of twenty feet of almost smooth perpendicular rock in a manner which to a looker-on appeared quite miraculous. . . . He had brought a rope with him attached to the first peg, and now, driving in a second, he was enabled to swing himself right over the projecting mass of rock. Here, with a short ladder, he formed a swinging seat, like a painter's cradle, and, fixed upon this seat, he took down under my direction the paper cast of the Babylonian translation of the records of Darius which is now in the Royal Asiatic Society's Rooms, and which is almost of equal value for the interpretation of the Assyrian inscriptions as was the Greek translation on the Rosetta Stone for the intelligence of the hieroglyphic texts of Egypt.[8]

The wild Kurdish boy 'who had come from a distance' is one of my most favourite characters in the history of archaeology. Rawlinson himself is another. He retired to the Residency in Baghdad with his copies and worked away at the decipherment and 'in order to enable himself to continue working in the hot weather, built a little shelter at the bottom of the garden overlooking the river, and over this shelter water was continually being pumped.' He was a great character: Sir Wallis Budge tells a story that when he visited Baghdad in the nineties a Turkish official there, speaking of Rawlinson, said the following:

> He lived here for twelve years, and each year his power became stronger. And towards the end of his time, had he taken one dog, and put his English hat on his head, and sent the dog to the *Serai,* all the people in the Bazaar would have made way for him and bowed to him. And the soldiers would have stood still and presented arms to him as he passed.[9]

The adventure with the Kurdish boy was in 1847. Ten years before, Rawlinson had succeeded in translating the first two paragraphs of the cuneiform inscription in Old Persian. In 1846 the Royal Asiatic Society published in two volumes his *The Persian Cuneiform Inscription at Behistun,* which was a complete translation of the Old Perisan text, and in the same year, Dr. Edward Hincks published an independent translation in the *Transactions of the Royal Irish Academy.*

When the Babylonian inscription was available, Rawlinson, Hincks and others including Oppert, de Saulcy and Fox Talbot, worked at its decipherment; soon this was done and the key to Babylonian and Assyrian obtained. But not everyone was satisfied that this was so. When, in 1857, Rawlinson translated for the British Museum an inscription on a cylinder of Tiglath Pileser I, there was some discussion and before publication it was decided to ask Hincks, Fox Talbot and Oppert to translate the inscription independently—and this they did. Rawlinson's translation and the three others were sent in sealed envelopes to the President of the Royal Asiatic Society, who had them examined by a select Committee. The Committee reported that the translations were so alike that there could be no longer any doubt that the true key to the decipherment of cuneiform writing had been found.

This was, in the first place, the key to the cuneiform writing of the Babylonians and Assyrians: it took Mesopotamian history back to 2000 BC. But it was also a key to something else—to the Sumerians, whose existence in the land of Shinar no one at that time suspected. Except perhaps for Edward Hincks who, with great acumen, pointed out that the Semitic-speaking Babylonians could not have been the originators of the cuneiform form of writing which they themselves used. Babylonian, he argued, was a syllabic writing; and he thought that the cuneiform script was borrowed from an earlier people with syllabic writing. In this he was right, but he posed the question: Who were these people? Were they possibly earlier people who lived in the south of Mesopotamia? [10]

Serious excavation in Mesopotamia began in 1843 when P. E. Botta, the French consular agent at Mosul, started digging in the mound of Kuyunjik across the Tigris from Mosul. While excavating there late in 1842 and early in 1843 he learnt of sculptured stones found in the mound of Khorsabad, fourteen miles to the north, and at the end of March began work there; within a week he had discovered the remains of a huge Assyrian palace with large sculptured slabs and cuneiform inscriptions; at once he sent a telegram to Paris, 'Ninève est retrouvé.'

Actually Botta was mistaken: Khorsabad was not Nineveh but Dur-Sharrukin, the city of one of the greatest Assyrian kings, Sargon II (721–705 BC), and it was Sargon the Second's palace that Botta had found: Nineveh was in fact the site of Kuyunjik which he had abandoned. But this did not matter; what mattered was that the spade was being used to examine the *tells* of Mesopotamia. In 1845 Layard began work at Nimrud, and in the 1850s Botta was succeeded by Place, and Layard by his former assistant Hormuzd Rassam.

Mesopotamian excavation had begun, though admittedly it was often very badly carried out, and no more than a scramble for antiques. Layard himself described his object in excavating at Nimrud as 'to obtain the largest possible number of well-preserved objects of art at the least possible outlay of time and money,' and Rassam's work was in the words of Seton Lloyd 'an undignified scramble for archaeological loot.' [11]

Excavation in the south of Mesopotamia—homeland of the Sumerians—also began at this time. At the end of 1849 two Englishmen, W. K. Loftus and H. A. Churchill, rode across the deserts and marshes of southern Mesopotamia from the Eurphrates to the Tigris and they saw the great Sumerian *tells* and, to their great surprise, the marks of former prosperity and intensive cultivation. Let me quote briefly from what Loftus wrote of Warka:

> The desolation and solitude of Warka are even more striking than the scene presented by Babylon itself. There is no life for miles around. No river glides in grandeur at the base of its mounds, no green dates flourish near its ruins . . . A blade of grass, or an insect, finds no existence there. The shrivelled lichen alone, clinging to the weathered surface of the broken brick, seems to glory in its universal dominion over these barren walls. Of all the desolate pictures I have ever beheld, that of Warka incomparably surpasses all.[12]

Loftus visited many of the *tells* in this region of southern Mesopotamia which, he said, 'from our childhood we have been led to regard as the cradle of the human race'—a curious sentence and presumably not a percipient guess at the Sumerians as the first to create a civilization, but a reference to the Garden of Eden. 'I know nothing more exciting or impressive,' he wrote, 'than the first sight of one of those great Chaldean piles looming in solitary grandeur from the surrounding plains and marshes. A thousand thoughts and surmises concerning its past eventful history and origin—its grad-

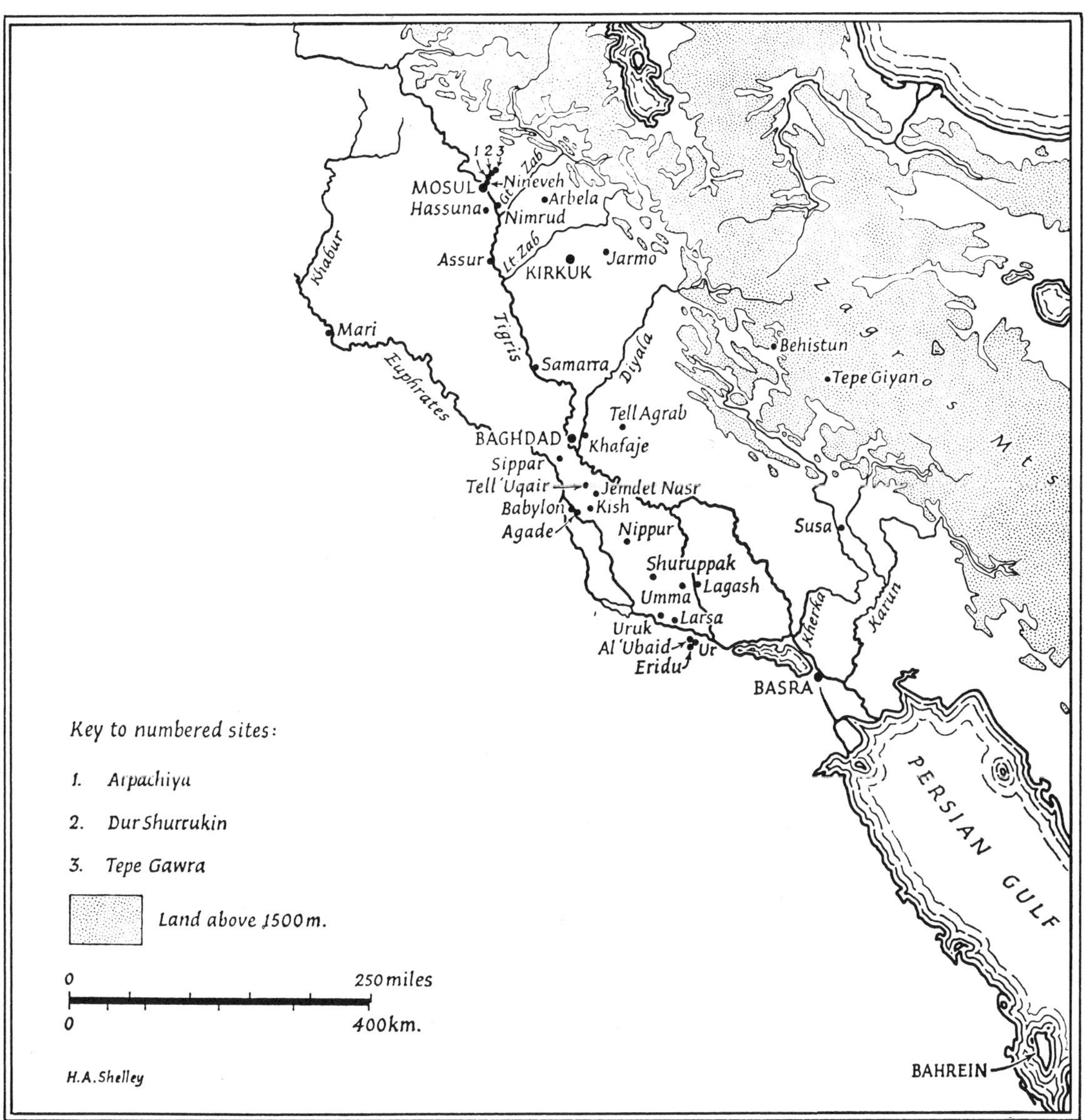

The Tigris-Euphrates region, showing sites.

ual rise and rapid fall—naturally present themselves to the mind of the spectator.' In 1850 Loftus began excavations at Warka, where he found a section of walling decorated with coloured mosaics of terracotta cones, and some cuneiform tablets. He then dug at other sites like Senkera, where he found terraces of kiln-backed brick and more clay tablets with cuneiform writing. He was not a scientific excavator—indeed who was at that time? Loftus frankly admitted that in excavating Warka he was actuated by 'a nervous desire to find important large museum pieces'; but however that may be, Rawlinson was able to work on the clay tablets. He identified Senkera as the ancient city of Larsa (the Biblical

Ellarsar), and Warka as the Biblical Erech: 'And Cush begat Nimrud. And the beginning of his kingdom was Babel, and Erech, and Accad and Calneh in the land of Shinar.' (*Genesis*, x, 10).

In 1854–5, J. E. Taylor, the British Vice-Consul at Basra, began excavating Tell Mukayyar and a group of mounds south of this at Tell-Abu-Shahrein. Rawlinson was able to identify the first site as Ur—Ur of the Chaldees, birthplace of Abraham—and the second as Eridu. The land of Shinar had been found and four of its ancient cities—Erech, Larsa, Ur and Eridu, also. We have said that Hincks, with great acumen, had argued for a pre-Babylonian people from whom the Babylonians borrowed their cuneiform writing. In 1869 Oppert boldly identified these non-Semitic pre-Babylonian people as the Sumerians. The finds of Loftus and Taylor were of these Sumerians, but Oppert's theory that the Sumerians had been in Iraq before the Babylonians and Assyrians was not widely accepted. Indeed there was nothing to show that the finds at Ur, Eridu, and elsewhere were much older, if older at all, than the palaces which Botta and Layard were digging near Mosul. The south Mesopotamian discoveries at first attracted little attention: they had yielded no great monumental sculpture. What was needed was some sensational discovery of aesthetic beauty before the world would interest itself or believe in the Sumerians.

That sensational discovery was made by Ernest de Sarzec, the French Consul in Basra. In 1874 some Arabs informed him that stone statuettes could be found in a place called Telloh, and in 1877 he dug trial trenches in this mound and found a number of fine diorite statues and many cuneiform inscriptions. He took them to Paris and sold them to the Louvre, and afterwards continued digging at the site intermittently, now under the auspices of the Louvre, until 1900. He was able to show that this was the Sumerian city of Lagash; his finds included many archaic sculptures of the late third millennium BC, including the famous portrait statues of Gudea, the seventh Governor of Lagash—his date was some time in the period 2100 to 2000 BC. The numerous statues and inscriptions of Gudea provided without any doubt the finest examples of Sumerian art and literature, and the discoveries of de Sarzec created sensations similar to those made by the discoveries of Botta at Khorsabad and Layard at Nineveh. The Louvre Catalogue of 1901 described Lagash as 'the Pompeii of early Babylonian antiquity', and De Genouillac said, 'C'est Telloh qui nous a révélé les Sumériens.' True, but they were not only revealed—they were found to be interesting and exciting. Not only were they old, and mentioned in the Bible—always a help in the nineteenth century when it seemed that those 'subterranean sciences' of geology and archaeology were undermining faith—but they were revealed as great artists practising a new art; that is to say, an art which was different from the familiar conventional ancient arts such as those of Greece and Rome and Egypt.

By 1900 the Sumerians had arrived, and by that year, too, their language was well understood. In this century we have seen the intensive and accurate revelation of the Sumerians by the spade and the skill of the translator of Sumerian. I single out two great moments in the twentieth-century excavation of this ancient people. In 1922 a joint expedition of the British Museum and the University Museum of Pennsylvania under the direction of Sir Leonard Woolley, as he later became, dug at Ur and in 1926 found the great cemetery with its Royal Tombs. The discovery of these tombs with their splendid treasures of gold and lapis lazuli and their remarkable evidence of funerary ritual caused a sensation comparable with Schliemann's discoveries at Mycenae and the discovery of Tutankhamen's tomb. If the Sumerians were 'discovered' by 1900 there were still few people who had heard of them.

By 1930 they had been added to the small collection of ancient peoples of whom nearly everyone had heard something. This was due in part to the sensational nature of the Ur excavations, but also to the clear and skilful popular writing of Woolley about his finds there.[13]

The second moment relates to the 1946–7 excavations at Eridu by the Iraq Government Directorate of Antiquities under the direction of Sayyid Fuad Safar. The site of Eridu-Tell Abu Shahrein had been, as we have said, dug by Taylor ninety years before. Taylor had been baffled by deep accumulations of sand, and, hampered in the same way as were two British expeditions of this century by dust storms, by the general insecurity of the country and by great difficulties of communication. The excavations in the forties of this century however triumphed over these difficulties and revealed in Eridu the earliest Sumerian city, and perhaps the earliest city in the world. We have quoted the sentence in *Genesis,* x, which mentioned Erech—that is, Warka—as one of the old cities in the land of Shinar. The Babylonian Legend of Creation is more specific: it says, 'All the lands were sea; then Eridu was made.' And in Sumerian literature the god Enki dwelt at Eridu, and Enki was the god of the Abyss who dwelt in his shrine on the shores of the deep, which was divided as a preliminary to creation.

It has been my intention to introduce you deliberately to the Sumerians by going back to the time when we knew nothing of what their *tells* and cuneiform writing meant, so that you can appreciate how our knowledge of man's first civilization was achieved. In the next chapter I shall outline the detail of the archaeological finds and it will be seen that by level IV at Uruk we can say that civilization had been born—the first civilization in the history of man.

The lowest building levels at Eridu—that is to say, Eridu XVIII to XV (the numbering is from the top down)—revealed small houses and shrines built of mud-brick to rectangular plans. This phase, the earliest in the known occupation of southern Mesopotamia, dates back to about five thousand years BC. The people were settled agriculturists and peasants, and at this stage the civilization of the Sumerians is far ahead. The second and next phase in the prehistory of southern Mesopotamia is called after the site of Hajji Muhammad; it began, perhaps, around 4750 BC, and at Eridu it occupies five building levels. This phase had sites all over southern Mesopotamia and was even better represented in Susiana and Luristan. It develops into the next, the third phase, named after the site of Al 'Ubaid. A C 14 date from Warka suggests that the early 'Ubaid phase was fully fledged by 4350 BC. The people of the 'Ubaid phase developed and spread over the whole of Mesopotamia.

Now, the existence of people in southern Mesopotamia in this phase without efficient irrigation is quite unthinkable. The rich and fertile plain was being tilled and it became overpopulated, so that the 'Ubaid people from the south moved up the Tigris and Euphrates in search of new land.

Twenty-five years ago the picture of the 'Ubaid people was rather that of primitive marsh-dwellers living in reed huts, hunting, fishing and practising sporadic agriculture like the Ma'dan or Marsh Arabs of today. Now all that picture is changed, and the Eridu excavations of 1946–7 were largely responsible for that change. The people of Al 'Ubaid were using copper and casting axes; gold made its appearance at the end of the period, their agriculture was efficient and they engaged in extensive trade. If we do not give them the name of civilization at least they were a proto-civilization, a civilization in the making, because they already had towns; and this is obvious from two things: first, their large cemeteries (that at Eridu contained over a thousand graves), and secondly, the monumental temples that now appeared for the first time—

the ceremonial centres which we have said by definition are one of the prerequisites of civilized society. Built of mud-brick and sometimes on stone foundations they dominated the cities from the top of the mounds. At Eridu, set on mud-brick platforms made by filling-in earlier buildings, a flight of steps gave access to a door in the long side of the building. The outside was ornamented with elaborate projections and recesses, a characteristic of all later Sumerian sacred buildings. At Eridu we find the beginning of that most characteristic feature of early Mesopotamian archaeology—the temple tower or ziggurat. We are already within sight—perhaps talking distance is the right word—of the Tower of Babel. And we are in a town or small city—Professor Max Mallowan thinks that even before 4000 BC Eridu was a place of several thousand souls.[14]

In the established archaeological sequence of southern Mesopotamia the 'Ubaid phase is succeeded by the Uruk phase which lasted from 3800 or 3700 to 3200 BC: the culture of Uruk is already in its maturity by about 3500 BC. The site of Uruk itself consists of eighteen levels observed by excavations in a deep sounding in the precincts of the ceremonial centre—the ziggurat of E-anna. This deep pit, or sondage, was about twenty metres in depth and contained in it the accumulated debris of settlements beginning with the people of 'Ubaid times. I have already said that archaeologists sometimes label their levels from top to bottom, but at other times from the bottom, the earliest level, up. Uruk is another example of the bottom-to-top method: the first and oldest level at that site is XVIII, and the full development of the site is in level Uruk IV. At this time Sumerian pottery and architecture were at a high state of development, and contemporary with the great temples of Uruk IV we find the earliest abundant evidence of writing. A civilization has been born: the first civilization in the history of man—the Sumerian civilization, and its date was perhaps 3200 BC, five thousand years ago.

References

1 *Genesis*, xi, verses 2 to 4. The wording of the Authorized Version is 'from the east'; the Revised Version says 'they journeyed east' or 'in the east'.

2 See H. PEAKE and H. J. FLEURE, *Peasants and Potters* (Oxford, the Clarendon Press, 1927), 42. This is volume III of the authors' series of which volume V is called *The Steppe and the Sown* (Oxford, the Clarendon Press, 1928). The biblical quotation is: 'And Abel was a keeper of sheep, but Cain was a tiller of the ground' (*Genesis*, iv, 2). I always feel that it should have been Abel, the pastoral nomad from the steppe and desert, who murdered the peaceful agriculturist, and not the other way round. On the Flood story (*Genesis*, vii, viii) in relation to archaeology see A. Parrot, *The Flood and Noah's Ark* (London, S.C.M. Press, 1955), and Sir Leonard Woolley in (ed. G. E. Daniel), *Myth or Legend?* (London, Bell and Sons, 1955), 39. Mesopotamia was the original home of the story in *Genesis* which is itself recorded in *The Epic of Gilgamesh*. Archbishop Ussher gave the precise date of the Flood as 2349 BC.

3 On the geographical conditions in early Mesopotamia see Lees and Falcon, 'The Geographical History of the Mesopotamia Plain', *The Geographical Journal*, 1942, 24.

4 The *Oxford English Dictionary* defines a Chaldean as 'a native of Chaldea, especially (as at Babylon) one skilled in occult learning, astrology, etc.' Rawlinson in his Bampton Lectures, V, 23 (1859) says: 'In *Daniel* the Chaldeans are a special set of persons at Babylon having a "learning" and a "tongue" of their own, and classed with the magicians, astrologers etc.' André Parrot in his *Sumer* (London, Thames and Hudson, 1960), says that Chaldea was 'a name applied in the 19th century to Mesopotamia as a whole. It should be restricted to the area near the Persian Gulf and to the period of the first millennium BC'; and the Chaldeans that this was 'a name incorrectly used in many books to designate the Sumerians. Strictly speaking it only applies to the tribes that settled Lower Mesopotamia in the 7th and 6th centuries BC.' It is clearly unwise to use the words Chaldea and the Chaldeans at the present day.

5 On *tells* see P. CARLETON, *Buried Empires* (London, Edward Arnold, 1939) and SETON LLOYD, *Mounds of the Near East* (Edinburgh, the University Press, 1963).

6 For a good general account of cuneiform writing see E. CHIERA, *They wrote on Clay: The Babylonian Tablets speak Today* (Cambridge, the University Press, 1939).

7 On Grotefend see SETON LLOYD, *Foundations in the Dust* (London, Oxford University Press, 1947), 78–9.

8 See E. A. W. BUDGE, *The Rise and Progress of Assyriology,* and GEORGE RAWLINSON, *A Memoir of Major-General Sir Henry Creswicke Rawlinson* (London, 1898), 146.

9 E. A. W. BUDGE, *By Nile and Tigris* (London, 1920), I, 232.

10 The contributions of Edward Hincks (1792–1866) to the decipherment of hieroglyphics are mainly made in articles between 1833 and 1865 in the *Transactions of the Royal Irish Academy.*

11 SETON LLOYD, *Foundations in the Dust* (London, Oxford University Press, 1947), especially chapter 10.

12 The quotation is from W. K. Loftus, *Travel and Researches in Chaldaea and Susiana* (London, 1857).

13 See especially his *Abraham* (London, 1935), *Ur of the Chaldees* (London, 1950), *Excavations at Ur* (London, 1954). The word Sumerology was being used in 1897. A. H. Sayce is in 1875 referring to Sumerians, but there were then two other spellings —namely, Sumirians and Shumerians.

14 M. E. L. MALLOWAN, *Early Mesopotamia and Iran* (London, Thames and Hudson, 1965), 15.

21

PREHISPANIC IRRIGATION AGRICULTURE IN NUCLEAR AMERICA

BARBARA J. PRICE

The word *ecology,* now so familiar, was coined as *œcology* towards the end of the nineteenth century by the biologist Ernst Haeckel who meant by it "all the various relations of animals and plants to one another and to the outer world. . . ." Long before ecological thinking was acknowledged in dealing with biological phenomena, varieties of ecological explanation thrived in what were to become the social sciences. Forms of geographical determinism, although quite distinct from modern ecological notions, have been known in explanatory theory at least since the time of the ancient Greeks. One of the most complex of the geographical theories of culture goes back two or three centuries and seeks to explain certain common characteristics

---

SOURCE: Edited and adapted from "Prehispanic Irrigation Agriculture in Nuclear America," *Latin American Research Review.* Vol. 6, No. 3 (1971): 3–60. Reprinted by permission of the publisher and author.

Given the recency of much of the field work cited in this paper, many substantive data remain unpublished. I wish to express my thanks to those who have graciously permitted me to quote often preliminary results of their recent work and recent thinking sent to me as personal communications. Thus, many investigators have contributed significantly to the preparation of this paper, although they are in no way responsible for its conclusions, with which many of them would probably more or less disagree. Special thanks go to Pedro Armillas for showing me selected areas of his chinampa survey in the southern Valley of Mexico; to Kent V. Flannery for taking me to Hierve el Agua, Oaxaca; to M. Edward Moseley, Carol J. Mackey, and Kent C. Day for my extremely productive stay with the Harvard Chanchan Project, Trujillo, Peru; to Richard S. MacNeish and Gary Vescelius for an instructive visit to Ayacucho; and to Thomas C. Patterson for reporting data from his recent research on the Central Coast of Peru and for copies of several unpublished manuscripts. This paper has benefited further from comments and suggestions from Edward Calnek, Marvin Harris, Jeremy A. Sabloff, and William T. Sanders.

that could be described in some of the most massive and enduring states the world has known. Because the earliest known examples of these states shared a common continent, they were called "Asiatic." Because they displayed powerful centralized governments which sometimes ruled ruthlessly, they were designated as "despotisms." The phrase *Asiatic despotism* was applied to ancient Persia, to India, and to China, and to other similar empires of the "Orient." Karl Marx and John Stuart Mill inherited the term from Hegel, Adam Smith, Richard Jones, Montesquieu, Turgot, and others. They and their colleagues passed it on to Max Weber and Karl August Wittfogel. The theory developed various forms and sometimes assumed different names, such as Marx's "Asiatic mode of production" or Wittfogel's "hydraulic society."

At the core of all these theories is a set of simple assumptions. All preindustrial states have economies rooted in agricultural production and therefore face varying possibilities for maintaining their agrarian systems. Some states will develop in regions blessed with general adequacy and timeliness of the water that all farming depends on. Others will face problems in that regard. In some places water is scant and irrigation is required. Elsewhere, floods are a constant threat to population and to land and crops. Sometimes it is a matter of a combination of factors. In any event, it is argued, there are many locations that have witnessed the development of complex societies in conjunction with pressing needs for the mobilization and management of large labor forces to control the water problem (hence the term "hydraulic").

The hydraulic theory, then, plays two very interesting roles in explaining the evolution of culture. On one hand, it applies to specific ecological situations and helps us to understand the historical development of particular civilizations. On the other hand, it can be generalized into a higher-level theory that tries to account for certain nomothetic regularities in the overall evolution of cultural complexity.

While acceptance of the hydraulic theory waxes and wanes, the benefits of applying the theory have been great enough to carry interest in it to various scholarly specializations. Quite obviously, archeologists will find much in such a theory to attract their critical attention whether they like the theory or wish to limit or refute it. So it has been that one of the most interested sets of scientists in recent years has included some of the most productive workers in the fields of nuclear American archeology.

The selection that follows is one of the longest in this volume. It may be read from at least two points of view. It summarizes our present understanding of some of the major comparative developments in the ancient civilizations of the New World. More than this, Barbara Price makes skillful use of her encyclopedic control of the data to investigate the explanatory weight of certain critical aspects of the irrigation thesis. Doing so, she shows us how the contemporary science of archeology functions best in a broad ecological context. Gone is single-minded concentration on potsherds, monuments, and ruined temples. Her eye is on the big picture; she has in mind the question of how the movement toward demographic and cultural complexity is supported in the basics of production. The final contribution of the article overrides the integration of diverse data from the evolution of the civilizations of nuclear America and addresses itself to global problems in the causes of the evolution of the state.

I. Introduction

Among archaeologists concerned with the study of cultural regularities in the evolution of the early civilizations, few general hypotheses have stirred such controversy as that which postulates a causal link between the phenomenon of irrigation agriculture and the origins of the state. Adumbrated initially by Karl Wittfogel in the 1920s and stated by him most completely in *Oriental Despotism* (1957), the hydraulic theory has been subject to much discussion and to varying fates in recent literature and research history. Although Wittfogel's original formulation was based chiefly on Old World data, the theory has had major impact on research and interpretation in the New. The first large-scale use of the approach in American archaeology followed World War II, when the Institute of Andean Research sponsored the Viru Valley Project in North Coastal Peru (Bennett, 1948; Willey, 1953). In recent years American archaeology has become concerned with questions of process beyond the limits of simple historical reconstruction (Binford and Binford, 1968). Concepts derived from systems theory (Flannery, 1968a; Hole and Heizer, 1969) are increasingly invoked to explain the cause-and-effect feedback mechanisms involved in the evolution of culture. Concomitantly, a virtual explosion of data has occurred concerning the chronology, size, and sociological and demographic matrix of New World irrigation systems. Thus, both investigative techniques and theoretical frameworks have undergone considerable recent modification and the body of relevant data is large and growing. While some might consider the hydraulic agriculture hypothesis a dead issue, such is not the case. Changes in the total conceptual context of any theory, and new evidence both pro and con, necessitate reevaluation of the theory.

Such a reevaluation is the aim of this paper. We will not attempt an exhaustive view of all the literature on irrigation systems, but will instead deal selectively with certain problems that have constituted foci of contemporary debate. The overall perspective of this study will be ecological and evolutionary, dealing with the changing relationships through time of populations to their physical and social environments. We view irrigation as merely one aspect of a total adaptive system, with its causal nexus and its effects varying with the nature of the environment, the size and structure of the population it serves, and the overall agricultural technology. An irrigation system is seen, therefore, not as a unique entity which wherever and whenever it occurs must have everywhere the same implications, but instead as the tangible outcome of the intersection of a number of cultural processes which operate in specifiable ways under specified conditions. Since considerations of agricultural productivity in general are thus of major importance, we cannot simply dichotomize irrigated vs. non-irrigated cultivation. Irrigation is, after all, far from the only technological means used to augment agricultural production; thus its resemblances and differences vis-à-vis other such methods are necessary considerations for its study. Given a population of cultivators, their problems will vary from one environment to another. Each environment will impose different kinds of limiting factors on population growth, factors which may differ in the degree of their severity from one case to another. Thus, the adaptive responses manifested by these populations may also differ: an adaptive response in one area may not occur in another. Single-factor explanations of cultural evolution are, accordingly, necessarily limited and simplistic. In our concern with evolutionary regularities, we will treat the interaction of various processes that may in typology seem different, yet act in specifiable ways to produce similar results.

Of what Fried (1960, 1967) has termed the pristine states—civilizations whose growth was essentially autochthonous—two are located in the New World, in Mesoamerica and the Central Andes. These constitute the principal nuclear areas of the pre-Columbian Western Hemisphere, areas within which culture-historical processes had wide and significant extra-local repercussions. At the time of the conquest these regions supported unusually large populations of high density, populations characterized by the possession of social systems generally conforming to the criteria of civilization set forth by Childe (1950). The sequence of cultural development in these areas thus constitutes evidence essential to the investigation of the causal dynamics involved in the evolution of this type of society. The observation of the fundamental similarities of all these early civilizations, in both the Old World and the New, is not recent (Steward, 1949). Attaching a classificatory label such as "early civilizations" or "pristine states" is not an end in itself, but is merely a recognition of their non-uniqueness. Mesopotamia, Egypt, China, the Indus Valley, Mesoamerica, and the Central Andes share certain basic common characteristics: all are societies of large size, based on social stratification, economic diversity and specialization, and institutionalized use and control of internal and external force. Their economic bases were also remarkably similar: all the early civilizations were founded on the intensive cultivation of a cereal staple and, specifically, on irrigation cultivation. Empirical observation suggests in turn that we are dealing with a lawful, regular process of cause and effect. If these multiple instances indicate that this kind of society constitutes what Steward (1955a) calls a cross-cultural type, it remains to ask why. The observed forms are considered the results of certain regular, nonidiosyncratic factors in stipulated interrelation with each other. Thus, the forms observed are capable of explanation. It is to these problems that this paper will be addressed.

Major emphasis in American archaeological literature on the role of irrigation in the development of complex societies is notable by 1949, with the publication of Armillas' "Notas sobre los sistemas de cultivo en Mesoamerica," and Steward's "Cultural Causality and Law." A symposium at the 1953 meetings of the American Anthropological Association was published in 1955 under Steward's editorship, as *Irrigation Civilizations: A Comparative Study.* The implications of the hypothesis for research strategy had been instrumental in determining the course of the Viru Valley Project, and this influence continued into the 1960s. Both the Teotihuacan and the Tehuacan Valley Projects were in part modeled after the Viru work, and were concerned with the total relationships of populations to environments and with the history of land use. One of the principal aims of the Teotihuacan Valley Project was, indeed, the testing of the irrigation hypothesis in a critical area where data on the antiquity of hydraulic cultivation had been lacking—quite uncomfortably so—at the time of the Irrigation Civilizations symposium.

By the middle 1960s, however, a good deal of controversy attended the theory. Adams (1966) questions its utility in explaining either the Mesopotamian or the Mesoamerican sequences, while Lanning (1967) explicitly rejects the postulated causal relations between irrigation and state formation in Peru. The association of large-scale irrigation and of large-scale complex polities is not the point at issue. But a correlation is not, speaking analytically, necessarily a cause. To define a cause, both clear establishment of chronological precedence and stipulation of the mechanisms by which that cause operates must be considered. For the present, it is observed merely that after an initial impact of substantial scope on the research direction and theoretical emphasis of American archaeology, the theory is coming increasingly under fire. It has certainly been misunderstood and consequently misapplied, and there seem indeed to be a number of phenomena it explains only with difficulty, if at all. One of the purposes of this paper might be stated as that of clarification of the circumstances in which the theory has explanatory power (and why), and those in which it does not.

In neither of the New World civilizations have we any written records except for the very latest periods of their growth. We are therefore left with only archaeological evidence in answer to any questions we ask concerning their development. Much of the evidence is fragmentary and its potential significance not readily apparent. Although considerations of agricultural productivity, for example, involve material traits, the processes themselves are no longer directly observable. We will thus employ contemporary evidence in conjunction with archaeological data in an attempt to reconstruct and interpret the productive systems of the past. This in turn creates methodological problems of operationalization, and of assessment of the reliability of inference. Still further problems are raised in that much of sociopolitical organization is nonmaterial and must be reconstructed from the material remains these organizations have left behind them. Speaking more generally, we are reconstructing causes no longer directly observable from the nature and magnitude of their effects; the development of a methodology for this sort of inference is just beginning in American archaeology.

II. The Comparative Study of Agricultural Systems in Nuclear America

Irrigation systems, small or large, ancient or modern, wherever they occur, generally comprise an aspect of what Steward (1955a) calls the culture core—i.e., features empirically determined to be closely connected to the subsistence base of the society or, more generally, to be intimately related to the adaptation of a population to its environment (Sanders and Price, 1968). The importance of irrigation may thus vary from one ecosystem to another. In an arid or semi-arid region, control of the supply and distribution of water may be essential to the survival of an agricultural population; in more naturally humid areas, artificial water control would be responsible for proportionately less of the total subsistence base. The drier environment can, of course, be exploited by some means other than agriculture; if so, the attendant demographic and sociological consequences will be radically different, and beyond the scope of the present discussion. No geographic area has a fixed carrying capacity; carrying capacity is instead a variable, dependent on geographic factors in interaction with the technology of the population. At least certain critical subzones of the areas in which all the early civilizations developed qualify as arid or semi-arid. It remains to investigate whether irrigation would have been either necessary or sufficient for substantial and dependable agricultural production in some of these subzones, and what other alternatives may have existed. Since the data on productivity to be presented below are modern, there may be some question concerning the reliability of projecting them into the past. The relevant methodological problems will be treated as they arise; under specified conditions it is regarded as fully legitimate and necessary to proceed in this fashion.

Irrigated and Nonirrigated Agriculture: Productivity Differentials

Data on food production obtained in selected areas in the contemporary Valley of Teotihuacan (Sanders, 1957) supports several generalizations. There is an obvious difference in the productive regimes of the middle and lower valleys, in that only in the lower valley is a dry-season crop possible. Within the middle valley, rainfall agriculture alone produces the lowest yields. Production is improved over 100 per cent with the use of more intensive methods—deep planting and floodwater irrigation. Floodwater irrigation, unlike the canal system, is, however, restricted to the rainy season. Since no floodwater occurs during the dry season, only one crop a year is possible.

For the lower valley, permanent springs provide irrigation water for double-cropping. Availability of water rather than of land today limits the expansion of the agricultural system (Millon, 1954; Sanders, 1957, 1965): there is more potentially irrigable land than there is water supply. Canal irrigation offers all the advantage of the floodwater system—permitting sowing prior to the onset of the rains, making available additional water during growth (often critical in the frequent years of below-average rainfall). In addition, the permanence of the water source permits a winter crop as well, particularly of a frost-resistant cultigen such as wheat. The use of artificial water sources increases yields substantially, and minimizes risk of crop loss in a bad year.

The question of the necessity of irrigation for the production of maize in Teotihuacan Valley is an old one. Gamio (1922) concludes that it is necessary, while Armillas (1948) suggests that it is not. Millon (1954) supports Gamio, particularly in view of the suggestion that the Classic period may have been significantly drier than the present. The question thus asked, however, is simplistic in ecological terms. Clearly irrigation is not "necessary" to produce a crop, in that an agricultural population inhabited the Teotihuacan Valley prior to the development of techniques of artificial water control; some farmers even today produce a maize crop through exclusive dependence on rainfall. Evaluating the efficiency of an agricultural system depends not only upon strictly climatic considerations, however, but also upon the size of the population involved. Every techno-environmental system everywhere has within it varying factors which act to limit population growth. Such factors, empirically, will not be everywhere the same ones. As a population possessing any exploitative technology approaches the carrying capacity of its environment under that regime, there will be population pressure which, over time, will act to stabilize further growth. Emigration, famine, malnutrition and disease, competition and conflict are all natural means of inhibiting growth and permitting a population to be contained at the level permitted by its food supply, whether this food is naturally occurring or artificially produced.

Technological changes are considered adaptive when they result in a *substantial increase in the numbers and densities of human beings, or in markedly increased efficiency of the individual human producer* (Sanders and Price, 1968:9; italics theirs). In an environment such as Teotihuacan Valley, irrigation would clearly represent one such adaptive change. We will discuss the question of the chronology of irrigation in a later section of this paper. For the moment, we consider the demographic situation of a population that has reached a ceiling to be of fundamental importance in technological change. If the origins of innovation are regarded as essentially random, the survival of innovation is non-random. A population at or near its limit will be most likely to adopt any technique that will increase productivity, even where such a technique involves greater labor input. As Boserup states (1965:117):

> As long as the population of a given area is very sparse, food can be produced with little input of labour per unit of output and with virtually no capital investment, since a very long fallow period helps to preserve soil fertility. As the density of population in the area increases, the fertility of the soil can no longer be preserved by means of long fallow and it becomes necessary to introduce other systems. . . .

The overall history of both Teotihuacan Valley and the Valley of Oaxaca in Mesoamerica, and of the Viru Valley in Peru tends to substantiate this relationship.

Under these circumstances, what irrigation does is to remove one of the major environmental limitations on demographic growth or, rather, to raise its ceiling significantly and permit the stabilization of population at a higher level. Phrased another way, it raises the total carrying capacity of the land. The question for Teotihuacan Valley is not one of the necessity of irrigation for the production of the staple crop, maize, in this environment. Instead, it concerns the extent to which the presence of irrigation raises, and its absence lowers, the demographic limit for a population dependent on the cultivation of this staple.

Teotihuacan Valley is actually not an extreme example for the question of the necessity of irrigation—in most years sufficient rain falls to produce at least some maize. It is not an either-or, but a more-than-vs.-less-than situation. The Nile Valley or the Mesopotamian Plain, with little or no precipitation, would be entirely dependent on artificial control of exotic water if an agricultural population is to live there at all. For Mesopotamia, Braidwood and Howe (1962:140) postulate that the occupation of the riverine plain by cultivators did not occur until Halafian times; Adams (1960:25) suggests that until then the population of the alluvial plain consisted primarily of riverine food-collectors, with the cultivators living elsewhere. We suggest that the effective agricultural utilization of this area, under natural conditions either swamp or desert, would not have been possible without the use of artificial water control. This is a kind of necessity that is lacking in Teotihuacan Valley, but would for the most part obtain for most of coastal Peru.

The foregoing considerations are clearly recognized too by Wittfogel in his concept of hydraulic density. Hydraulic density is highest in those situations where all water is exotic, where cultivation depends entirely upon the artificial creation of oases, where the difference in agricultural productivity between nonirrigated and irrigated land is the difference between zero production and any production, and where a population is thus entirely dependent on irrigated land for its subsistence. Hydraulic density lowers in proportion to the increased relative productivity of nonirrigated land, whether through the cultivation of alternative drought-resistant crops or through nonagricultural exploitation of alternative resource bases. The concept merely describes the degree of dependence of producers upon an irrigation system and, thus, the impact of such a system on a total economy. Hydraulic density would today be clearly higher for the inhabitants of coastal Peru than for the inhabitants of Teotihuacan Valley. In turn, it would be higher for Teotihuacan Valley than for the Valley of Guatemala, where rainfall agriculture is not only possible but is indeed the only system generally practiced, and where there is no lack of rainfall.

In the agricultural regime briefly summarized for Teotihuacan Valley, two principal techniques of raising the demographic ceiling imposed by low rainfall—canal irrigation and floodwater irrigation—were discussed. One major reason for the frequent misinterpretation of the hydraulic theory is that, in our view, canal irrigation is often considered as a unique entity. We prefer at this time to stress instead its functional similarity to other technological means of solving the problems of a growing population of cultivators in an arid to semi-arid environment. If, as the Teotihuacan data cited thus far suggest, the major effect of artificial water control is to increase production, then there are seen to be a number of other ways to accomplish this end. Irrigation, in sum, must be viewed in context—as part of the more general question of agricultural intensification.

Types of Agricultural Systems

The classification of agricultural systems along a continuum of relative intensiveness involves the manipulation of two major parameters, land area and labor input, in relation to each other. More extensive systems involve comparatively larger areas, combined with comparatively little labor to produce a crop; more intensive systems compensate with greater labor input for a lesser quantity of total land exploited per cultivator. This continuum has been divided in somewhat different ways by Wolf (1966:20–21), who considers hydraulic agriculture a subtype, and by Boserup (1965:15–16), who regards it as one possible variant of intensive agriculture. For both, the relative length of the fallow portion of the cycle is an important diagnostic of labor input per unit of land; in general, the shorter the fallow, the more intensive the system. The differences between Wolf's long-term, sectorial, and short-term fallowing systems represent points along the continuum; similarly does Boserup's distinction between forest-fallow and bush-fallow. The distinction of subtypes may vary, depending in part upon environmental variables; all very broadly constitute variants of what is essentially slash-and-burn, swidden, or shifting cultivation. In contemporary Mesoamerica a highland variant of comparatively long duration, called *tlacolol* by Lewis (1951), may be distinguished from the classical tropical lowland forest swidden systems. The major differences are environmentally conditioned; if lowland soils are more subject to loss of productivity through leaching and through weed competition than are highland ones, then lowland fields must also be fallowed more frequently. In comparing the extensive systems of the lowlands and highlands of Mesoamerica, the minimal fallow period possible with maintenance of productivity depends on the time minimally necessary for the growth of more easily cleared woody plants to the point where these are dominant over herbaceous plants. In the highlands, control of competing vegetation is generally easier, and the soils are less subject to fertility loss through leaching; the major problem in many parts of the highlands is rather erosion on slopes, unless technology—and thus labor—is expended to control this factor. Typical of nearly all relatively extensive systems is that productivity is dependent primarily upon the characteristics of the natural environment itself, far less upon human modification of these characteristics.

Productivity of land per hectare under extensive cultivation is thus extremely variable. Furthermore, most total habitats contain within them niches of greater or lesser productivity, given equivalent labor input. The differential utilization of such natural differences may be the first small, almost accidental step toward overall maximization of what a region as a whole will produce. In general, the first cultivators in a region will tend to select those lands which are most productive; as an area fills up, there will be competition for these lands, and only when they are all occupied will people tend to exploit other niches. In extensive cultivation, factors such as soil type and quantity of precipitation affect crop yields directly, and also indirectly as well: these would be major determinants of the speed of regeneration of natural vegetation, thus affecting the frequency of planting of any given plot and thus its productivity through time. Whatever else irrigation may or may not explain, it is a system of agriculture which, where used, increases productivity per hectare over the yields possible without its use. It is thus advisable to examine irrigation within a more general context; it is only one of a number of alternative means of increasing productivity. The variations observed in contemporary nonirrigated cultivation can provide a baseline, and can delineate the range of productivity of extensive systems in a variety of environmental settings. This is essential for comparative purposes. Even within extensive systems, certain types of intensification are possible and, under some circumstances, practiced. We have observed that differential land utilization within a habitat which, while requiring perhaps little additional labor input, nonetheless acts to maximize production, can, like many labor-intensive situations, generate competitive pressures with a growing population.

III. The Intensification of Production: Variation and Chronology *

Typologically and chronologically, extensive systems of production are simpler and in general earlier than intensive ones. This is not to imply that everywhere intensive cultivation has replaced extensive. Extensive systems similarly vary among themselves in the amount of labor involved, in their productivity, and in the extent to which additional labor input can significantly raise production. A combination of environmental and demographic factors is regarded as the most powerful determinant of the form of any productive system. Similar parameters must be invoked to explain why particular means of intensifying production were adopted in some areas at particular points in their development. The ultimate effects of technological change cannot be analyzed without reference to the antecedents of such change. While a change from a longer to a shorter fallow cycle is per se a technological intensification of production, the changes to be considered in this section will differ in that they involve human modification of the environmental parameters themselves through technological means. In this respect they differ in principle from other observed changes in land use patterns. The systems to be described below are various; canal irrigation in some

* This section heavily abridged; cf., Price, 1971.

ways resembles, in other ways differs from, other members of the class of types of intensive agriculture.

Thus far, the chronology of intensive agriculture in the New World is unclear. Current trends, the result of recent research, have been to consider such phenomena considerably earlier, in both absolute and relative terms, in comparison to the estimates of only ten years ago. The origins of domestication in some areas now go back to approximately 6,000 BC for some cultigens. Palerm (1955) could cite no specific archaeological evidence for irrigation in Central Mexico prior to the Postclassic. On the basis of sound reasoning and indirect evidence, Armillas (1951) believed that intensive systems of production in Central Mexico were at least Classic in date, associated with the florescence of Teotihuacan. Steward (1955b) concurred with Armillas that what seemed in every typological respect to constitute an Irrigation Civilization, but which yet evidently lacked irrigation agriculture, was anomalous. To Armillas, the contrasts of size and scale, and of those material remains that indicate the characteristics of sociopolitical organization—contrasts between Teotihuacan and its antecedents—indicated a fundamental economic change. Additional evidence adduced by Palerm for probable antiquity included the almost pan-Central Mexican distribution of irrigation at the time of the conquest, and the great degree of dependence of these populations on this mode of production at that period. These are still valid arguments. Furthermore, the use of certain kinds of indirect archaeological evidence must be considered legitimate, justifiable, and necessary. In a sense, the very lack of substantive data on a topic regarded as of fundamental explanatory significance in the 1950s was itself a major determinant of research strategies in Mesoamerica to the present time. The result is that at this writing, concrete data exist to demonstrate the existence of irrigation in parts of Mesoamerica well into the Formative period. It is interesting, though hardly surprising, that these data derive from the central highland area, where irrigation techniques were of known importance in the Postclassic. For Mesoamerican agriculture it is in these areas, not the lowlands or the coast, where aridity is likely to be the principal limiting factor in productivity or expansion.

Regarding the two areas Mesoamerica and the Central Andes, it should be noted that in parts of both these highly complex and internally diverse environments aridity is a fundamental challenge to cultivators. It is interesting that in Mesoamerica lack of water is a problem primarily in the highlands, while in Peru it is the Pacific coast that is nearly desert. Thus, in Mesoamerica the heartland of the origins of domestic maize became in later times the area of greatest antiquity and greatest diversity of techniques of agricultural intensification involving water control. In Peru, on the other hand, the area in which cultivation was most probably developed—the highlands—is almost unknown in terms of its history of land use; the antiquity of irrigation in the Andean highlands is as problematical now as it was in 1955. Finally, the relationship between irrigated and nonirrigated areas in Mesoamerica has been sufficiently clarified at present to permit some statement of cultural dynamics, while no such interpretative possibilities exist for Peru, where we cannot be certain that an unirrigated area is so merely as an artifact of research or its lack.

Irrigation is merely one episode in the overall evolution of agricultural systems. For Mesoamerica, two areas, the Valley of Oaxaca and Tehuacan Valley, have yielded virtually entire local sequences, from the apparent initial experimentation with domesticated foods into the beginnings of the application of labor-intensive techniques of food production, and well into the historic high civilizations. Preclassic irrigation is known from the site of Amalucan, Puebla. The Teotihuacan Valley provides somewhat later information than Oaxaca and Tehuacan, probably as the function of a somewhat different demographic history. If the succeeding discussion should seem sketchy, this fact reflects the incompleteness to date of publications of work that is still in progress.

The following data summarize the history of various water-control techniques of intensification in Nuclear American agriculture. While a much fuller statement appears in Price (1971), of which the present article is an abridgement, our object here is to demonstrate the contexts in which such techniques appear, and their impact upon local ecosystems. Two observations seem to be borne out: 1) the technology of water control may in the course of time be intensified in an area of heavy settlement in order to enhance the productivity and carrying capacity of such a niche, and 2) such technology may be employed in ways which open up additional niches not formerly usable for agriculture. In both cases, the demographic ceiling of a region as a whole is raised. If some form of water control is probably as old as agriculture itself, the techniques practiced are conditioned by the geographical environment and by the size of the population it supports at any given time. Our model for Mesoamerica assumes the early and probably rapid spread of extensive cultivation during the Early Formative (2500–1200 BC), with relative uniformity of technology and labor input, and with emphasis on those areas relatively more productive with relatively less expenditure of labor. Such an emphasis would lead to an almost serendipitous type of infield-outfield agriculture (Wolf 1966), simply through differential land use. Coe (1968) has postulated such a system as the economic base of the Olmec site of San Lorenzo during the San Lorenzo phase (1200–900 BC); a zone of annually inundated river-levee land constituted an infield that could be planted annually, with a less-favored, non-riverine outfield in which some sort of fallow cycle would have been employed. The significance of the flooding is not to provide water—this is not a problem in Southern Veracruz—but to deposit fresh soil, thus obviating the need to fallow.

For the Valley of Oaxaca, the Middle and Late Formative periods witness the transition from selective land use to the investment of increasing amounts of labor on the land to increase productivity, along with the development of various microecologically adapted differential technologies (Flannery *et al.* 1967; Flannery 1968b). Settlement during the San Jose phase (1200–900 BC) was concentrated in an alluvial zone where the water table was maximally 3m. below ground surface; by the succeeding Guadalupe phase (900–600 BC) a technique called pot-irrigation was demonstrably practiced in this zone (Orlandini 1967). Wells are dug to ground water, and individual plants are watered by hand. This technique, still in use today, is associated with labor-intensive practices of seedbedding and transplanting, and is capable of producing three harvests per year; there are no winter frosts and the land is never rested. Modern data thus indicate the productive potential of the system, without necessarily implying that it was so intensively used during the Middle Formative. By the subsequent Monte Alban I phase, early in the Late Formative, settlement has spread outside this high-water-table zone (Flannery *et al.* 1967) to upstream locations on the piedmont, where water is most easily diverted. This suggests the beginning of canal irrigation, and one spectacularly preserved site, Hierve el Agua (Neely 1967), taps local springs by a series of canals down over stone-terraced fields approximately a square kilometer in extent.

From the state of Puebla, additional data on Middle to Late Formative irrigation comes from the Tehuacan Valley (MacNeish 1964; MacNeish, pers. comm., Brunet 1967). Although as yet published in only incomplete form, the damming of barrancas to impound floodwater was practiced by the Ajalpan and Santa Maria phases. Both the Tehuacan and Oaxaca Valleys have long sequences from Archaic food-collectors, through incipient to progressively more intensive agriculture. Elsewhere in Puebla, direct evidence of canal irrigation comes from the site of Amalucan (Fowler 1966, 1969), where a pyramid of the Late Formative (500–200 BC) was built over an earlier canal feature. By the law of superposition, the pyramid date constitutes a terminus a quo for the relative dating of the canal.

These extremely early components of the sequence are lacking in Teotihuacan Valley, the immediate sustaining area for the Early Classic city of Teotihuacan. Evidence (Sanders 1965) suggests that there is little agricultural occupation until early in the Late Formative. Following the argument of Tolstoy and Paradis (1970) it may be that the entire Basin of Mexico was only sparsely populated until rather late in the Middle Formative. Lying above 2000 meters altitude, the combination of aridity and fall frosts would have made the Basin relatively unattractive to cultivators when more favorable zones nearby were still available. Yet the subvalley of Teotihuacan supported a city of at least 85,000 (Millon 1967) and perhaps as many as 125,000 (Millon, pers. comm.); it was the focus of a pan-Mesoamerican horizon style which probably owes much of its diffusion to true imperial expansion. Armillas (1951) correlates the rapid emergence of the city with a shift in productive techniques from an extensive (tlacolol) to an intensive (irrigation) system of cultivation.

Evidence for this shift, however, is nearly all indirect, but based on several different kinds of data which all support each other (Sanders 1965). The best evidence comes from diachronic settlement pattern analysis. Prior to the Tzacualli (Teotihuacan I) phase, most settlements are situated well up in the hills, with relatively little population in the valley bottom or its immediately adjacent piedmonts. For extensive, rainfall-dependent agriculture, these high slopes are most favorable. The downward shift in settlement location in Terminal Formative times suggests that lower-lying areas had become more valuable—that the technology had been developed to exploit these zones more productively. Pollen cores from springs at El Tular, analyzed by Anton Kovar, show a sudden drop at this time in the percentage of sedges from 30–37 percent to 2–10 percent of the samples. This indicates that water from the springs may have been taken elsewhere, since there seems to be no evidence of valley-wide dessication at this time. Additionally, in the area of Cerro Gordo, an anomalous pattern of drainage observed today may be the result of former floodwater canals (of unknown age) which, following their abandonment, were transformed into otherwise natural-looking barrancas. Teotihuacan's location, furthermore, is strategic with respect to the springs which today provide water to irrigate the Lower Teotihuacan Valley. Mooser (1968) suggests that these springs were formerly more extensive than they are today. Additionally, evidence from the city itself indicates that the technology existed for a sophisticated system of water control: the Rio de San Juan is canalized where it traverses the city to make it conform to the gridded streets, and the central section of the city is equipped with an elaborate drainage system. The existence of this urban evidence does not per se imply a "hydraulic state" in Wittfogel's or any other terms, in that the critical factor—augmenting productivity, and thus the size and energy content of the society—was lacking; but the existence of a city the size of Teotihuacan in this area strongly implies that this available technology was indeed applied to agricultural production.

In summary, we have, from several areas of Highland Mexico, evidence for the early development of small irrigation systems. For Teotihuacan Valley, there is indirect evidence of various kinds that such small systems ultimately grew and coalesced into larger ones. Such growth was correlated with an enormous growth in population and with evidence of considerable sociopolitical change as well. The Teotihuacan Valley probably represents what is in demographic terms the first large-scale hydraulic system in Mesoamerica. When the Classic is compared to the Postclassic, it is the differences in distribution of irrigation that become apparent. The Postclassic is a time of demographic filling-in, of overall population maximum, of the inception of Teotihuacan-like large-scale systems to other areas where environmental conditions permitted their use. Thus, in Late Postclassic times, much potentially irrigable land was actually irrigated: the Texcoco Plain and Texcotzingo systems (Palerm 1955; Wolf and Palerm 1955), Cholula, the Izucar Valley, and Cempoala (Palerm 1955:36). All were associated with dense populations and a fully developed urbanism.

Along with the expansion and intensification of canal systems in the Postclassic is the development of other labor-intensive types of agriculture. Terrace systems in the southern Valley of Mexico may be a response to large populations with limited amounts of land level enough to cultivate. Chinampa agriculture, one of the most spectacular of Mesoamerican local ecosystems, was practiced in swampy lakeshore lands, and in the shallow fresh-water Lakes Chalco and Xochimilco. This extraordinarily intensive technique involves the actual creation of agricultural land; swampy lakeshores are drained by ditching, and alternation of layers of mud and aquatic vegetation on the lake bottom can construct a long, narrow artificial island that is perpetually irrigated. West and Armillas (1950) and Sanders (1957) have described chinampa agriculture in more detail than is possible here. Although Coe (1964) believes this system to be Classic in date, this seems too early, in that associated artifacts are overwhelmingly Late Postclassic in date, and the Late Postclassic was demonstrably the period of population maximum in this area, when such labor-intensive systems would have been most needed. In Aztec times, the chinampa area was protected from flooding and salinity by a complex state-initiated system of dikes and causeways (Palerm, pers. comm.).

As previously noted in this paper, the Peruvian data are, by contrast with the Mesoamerican, grossly incomplete where paradoxically they seemed so abundant ten years ago. The major problem is the lack of information concerning highland agricultural development, particularly for the early periods of incipient cultivation and the emergence of agriculturally based communities comparable to the Purron of Tehuacan Valley. Recent work by MacNeish (pers. comm.) near Ayacucho has suggested the probability of an early focus of independent New World domestication of maize in the Peruvian highlands. Next to nothing is known of the antiquity or processes in the domestication of other Andean cultigens—potato, sweet potato, quinoa and the other chenopodia, to mention some basic staples. This is a critical problem in the study of South American agriculture; most of our Andean data come from studies on the coast, where in all probability cultivation was introduced from the highlands. Few if any of the Andean repertoire of domestic food plants appear to be natives of the coast or to have wild ancestors or relatives there; it is impossible for a population to obtain control of a species that does not exist in its environment. Like the agriculturists of the Mesopotamian Plain cited above, the first cultivators on the coast of Peru must have brought it with them.

The long preagricultural occupation of coastal Peru involved the exploitation of a number of ecological niches, of which the most consistently productive was the coast, particularly at river mouths (Lanning 1967); riverine and marine fishing resources supported relatively large and sedentary populations of collectors. Upon its initial introduction into this ecosystem, agriculture provided only a small supplement to the diet and was thus only a minor determinant of the coastal settlement pattern. Initially, immediately riverine lands, especially at the river mouths, were used to provide a single summer crop. We thus have an environmentally-conditioned variant of swidden, where, as at San Lorenzo, annual flooding restored fertility; on the Peruvian coast, however, such flooding provided the water without which no cultivation would be possible.

Settlement pattern data again provide the best evidence for the economic shift to an ever-greater reliance on agriculture rather than on marine collecting. As settlements move upriver and inland, they indicate that for those communities, agriculture rather than fishing had become the dominant economic activity (Collier 1955, Kidder *et al.* 1963, Kidder 1964)—probably at least in part one result of a demographic forcing situation where littoral niches were already occupied to capacity (Lanning 1967:106). Since the Peruvian coast is almost totally rainless, this upriver expansion must have been underwritten by irrigation cultivation, which would have been essential to production beyond the restricted natural floodplain areas. Patterson (n.d.) suggests that on the Central Coast this process was as early as the preceramic Gaviota phase (1900–1750 BC), and it is notable elsewhere at least by the Early Horizon (Kidder 1964). Patterson and Lanning (1964) observe the relationship between settlement pattern, irrigation, and warfare in the Chillon Valley during the Early Horizon.

The subsequent history of irrigation in Coastal Peru involves the gradual geographic and demographic transformation of what began as essentially local systems, first into valley-wide, ultimately into transvalley, networks. These processes occur from the Early Intermediate, Middle Horizon, and Late Intermediate periods. Early Intermediate, valley-wide, systems are known from the Chancay, Chillon, Rimac, and Lurin Valleys of the Central Coast (Patterson, pers. comm.), and from the North Coast valleys of Viru (Willey 1953), Moche (Collier 1955) and probably also Chicama (cf. Kosok 1965).

By Late Intermediate (Chimu) times, a transvalley system of canals linking the Moche and Chicama Rivers was in operation (Moseley, pers. comm.). Mapping of the canals and associated agricultural fields is still under way, by the Harvard Chanchan Project. The city of Chanchan is strategically located, between the Moche and Chicama Rivers, and is linked by clearly traceable roads to the junction point of this Grand Canal system. This Chimu capital had a population estimated by Kosok (1965) as 50,000, and by West (1970) as 68–100,000. The degree of dependence of the city upon the Moche-Chicama canal system is shown in the success of the tactics employed by the Inca in the conquest of Chanchan (Day 1970): cutting off the irrigation system at the point where the rivers were joined. The Late Intermediate seems to be the maximal development of this system, and this development facilitated an ancillary technique of intensive agriculture in the Moche Valley—a sunken-field agriculture called pukio by Willey (1953) and mahamae by Parsons (1968), which involves excavating a field down to soil layers immediately adjacent to ground water. The full operation of the canal system would, through seepage, raise the downstream water table above the levels observed today (Moseley 1969, Day 1970), and thus reduce the labor input necessary to this form of cultivation.

Little, in contrast, is as yet known of comparable agricultural intensification practices in the Andean Highlands. In many of the highland basins, shortage of arable land may have inhibited demographic and agricultural expansion more sharply than shortage of water (the highlands at least have a rainy season, which the coast lacks). Lanning (1967) suggests that some of the elaborate terrace systems of the highlands may have been begun during the Late Intermediate. By the Late Horizon, however, the significance of such terrace systems in the heartland of the Inca Empire is incontrovertible. The author's observation of Inca terracing in the Cuzco Basin and along the Urubamba Valley from Cuzco to Machu Picchu reveals several interesting associations. Terrace systems are all located below permanent or seasonal water sources. The sites of Ollantaytambo and Machu Picchu are perhaps most impressive; at the latter site, traces of the direct association of canals and terraces are still preserved.

Another intensive agricultural technique of the Andean Highlands is similarly of unknown date: the ridged field system. Discovered only recently in various parts of South America (Parsons and Denevan 1967), this technique seems to be an adaptation to marshy or seasonally inundated ground. In this, it resembles the chinampas of Mexico, although no artificial islands seem to be constructed. Ridged fields occur on both the Peruvian and Bolivian shores of Lake Titicaca, above 3800 meters altitude, where both frosts and irregularity of rainfall constitute hazards to agriculture. Given the proximity of this area to Tiahuanaco, it is tempting to speculate that they were in use by the Middle Horizon; the bulk of the directly associated artifacts, however, is Inca. The varying patterns of ridges are of unknown functional or chronological significance (Smith *et al.* 1968); no excavations or systematic settlement surveys have been carried out in this area.

Any type of differential land use would, with growing population, tend to stimulate competition and demographic pressure. Some lands, naturally more productive, would tend to fill up first, and only later would people begin to occupy less favorable zones, less productive and requiring greater labor. The result of this process of demographic expansion may in time lead to diversification of production within the region as a whole—differential crop repertoires in different niches, for example, or different technology applied to agricultural production in these varied niches. Canal irrigation in the slopes adjacent to the Valley of Oaxaca, for example, was important in that it opened up a new sector for agricultural utilization. This we interpret as at once a result and a cause of population pressure. Demographic expansion in the zone initially favored for cultivation entirely filled that niche with the existing technology. Two probable responses occurred: 1) population was forced into less productive zones and 2) in the favorable zone itself there was a probable intensification of technology to the limit of the regime. Process 2) would have begun to occur as well among the inhabitants of the marginal or fringe zones. That the empirical results—in the high-water-table zone the production of three harvests per year, in the piedmonts canal irrigation of probably a single crop—were different reflects the difference in environmental setting. Techniques applicable to one setting did not work in the other.

It could be hypothesized that the expansion of a single valley system, such as represented by the Moche culture in Peru, into a multi-valley state by military conquest could have been the result of the pressures induced by the demographic ceiling. One way in which a state can obtain new resources is by conquering an adjacent area and siphoning off its surplus. A similar process may also explain the constant warfare that obtained between the Sumerian city-states (Adams, 1966).

In both the Sumerian and coastal Peruvian examples, such warfare appears to precede the expansion of the irrigation systems themselves. As a solution to the problem of population pressure, it is a limited one in that it is necessarily temporary (Sanders and Price, 1968). Within at most a generation or two, the initial problem again reemerges. If such temporary advantage accrues to the stronger combatant at the expense of the weaker, and even where sufficient numbers on one or both sides are eliminated to reduce the pressure, the total carrying capacity of the region as a whole is not increased by competition of this kind. Any gains are thus short-term, regardless of whether the societies involved perceive them as such. The advantage of warfare at this stage of the demographic cycle lies primarily in the fact that it requires less input of labor and of capital than does the expansion of the technology. In turn, the presence of this type of chronic warfare itself alters the selective pressures upon both the technology and its attendant sociopolitical organization. Intensification of the techno-economic base, and any innovation fostering this, would under such circumstances be more likely to be adopted by the societies involved, in spite of the greater energy-input requirements.

IV. Irrigation: Sociopolitical Dynamics and the Growth of Civilization

Having previously treated first the relationship of irrigation to other types of agricultural techniques, and second, the relative chronology of various types of intensive agriculture in selected areas of Nuclear America, we may now consider the nature of the relationship between irrigation and sociopolitical structure. It is here that controversy in contemporary anthropology is most acute. One of the reasons for this fact is the general failure to take into account the parameters previously discussed, notably the interrelated factors of agricultural productivity in general, and population growth. Only in this fashion can the impact of irrigation be evaluated: if irrigation is postulated to have certain effects, then what other techniques or processes might have similar kinds of impact on local ecosystems? We shall in turn relate these considerations to general problems of the interpretation of the evolution of social organization.

Childe (1950) states several characteristics of civilization as a culture type, among them large size, social stratification into distinct classes, and economic specialization. Writers on social organization from Durkheim (1933) to Fried (1967) have used the distinguishing criterion of institutionalized force to define the state: the state exists when some body in the overall structure arrogates to itself all legitimate use of internal and external force. Put another way, the state is founded on relationships of differential power. This returns us immediately to the criterion of social stratification, defined by Fried (1960) as differential access to strategic resources. Economic power is ultimately political power as well; the two are inextricably interwoven. Some resource bases, among them hydroagriculture, are inherently more controllable in this fashion than are others. The relation between what archaeologists term "civilization" and what in political terms is called the state may be debated by some. However, for the present discussion the two terms may be considered equivalent, and will be used interchangeably (Sanders and Price, 1968). In the case of the New World pristine states which developed in Mesoamerica and the Central Andes, our analyses of social and political structure are necessarily based on the material remains these societies have left in the sequence of their development. It is a methodological requisite that we establish a degree of equivalence between archaeological remains and the kind of society that produced them. This will be the operational basis of our inferences concerning the evolution of culture (Sanders and Price, 1968: Ch. 2).

A basic archaeological criterion of civilization is that of architectural monumentality (Childe, 1950). The existence of large-scale public works of any kind tells us something about the society that built them: they are the material expression of a kind of social organization. White (1949, 1959) maintains that cultural evolution is based on the increase of the total energy content of the society. Monumental architecture is, in a real sense, the frozen, permanent indication of the amount of energy harnessed; it is thus possible to compare societies on this quantitative basis. It is further possible to consider social organization of any kind as a sort of flow diagram of the utilization of energy captured and consumed by a population. Monumental architecture, because the capital and labor (energy) investment in its construction is high, is thus a legitimate and justifiable indication, not only of total energy capacity, but of the fact that this energy was used in a particular way. It is an aspect of technology that has very clear sociological requisites and implications.

Large-scale irrigation systems, if they are functionally similar to various other kinds of agricultural methods in their effects on productivity (see preceding pages), are functionally similar in other respects to any other kind of architectural monumentality. They share with pyramids, temples, fortification walls, palaces, and burial mounds the need for large quantities of systematically amassed materiel; a large, organized and directed labor force; and a diversity of labor force, from unskilled hewers of wood and drawers of water, to professional specialists in engineering, architecture, planning, and administration. Thus, on the level of process, the existence of large-scale hydraulic works of the kind described by Wittfogel (1957) can be analyzed as resembling any monumental civic construction, in that similar kinds and organization of resources and manpower are requisite for them all. Where hydraulic works differ from these other examples is precisely where they resemble chinampas, terraces, pukios, etc. They represent energy inputs that result in augmented productivity: they are capital investments in a way that temples, palaces, and fortifications are not. Irrigation systems require investment of energy to produce more energy, where monumental pyramids and massive walls can be viewed as taking energy out of circulation. The latter category of monumentality is thus more properly considered an effect or product of a certain kind of society whose techno-environmental causal bases lie elsewhere (Sanders and Price, 1968:9). The question is the extent to which canal irrigation can be regarded as a major component of these techno-environmental causal bases, and can thus be seen as a determinant of institutional structure.

Irrigation agriculture is not, as the previous two sections of this paper demonstrate, a unitary phenomenon of unique characteristics. Irrigation in general shares many of the causes and effects common to other systems of intensive agriculture. Further, not all systems of canal irrigation are themselves strictly alike. Many of the characteristics in which irrigation systems differ among themselves are those which determine the actual or potential scale or degree of monumentality of the system. Many of these determinants are basically environmental. The conditions of construction and use of an artificially controlled water source and its impact on the size and institutions of a population are not everywhere the same.

Most obviously, environments vary in the degree to which control of water supply is necessary to the successful exploitation of the habitat by cultivators; environmental challenges largely govern the direction and degree of success of cultural responses. In some environments such as coastal Peru or parts of the American southwest the total productivity of the region is sharply and dramatically increased with irrigation; without it, very little land will produce a reliable harvest. In the Teotihuacan Valley, the difference, while highly significant, is less drastic than the situation on the Peruvian coast. Even on the Peruvian coast, however, carrying capacity does not reduce to zero without irrigation: cultivation is not the only means of possible or observed subsistence, and a sizable population can be maintained by marine food collecting. But if population is to expand beyond the limitations imposed by this mode of life, a shift in technology and economy to agriculture is necessary to open up additional niches of the habitat to occupation. And if such a shift is to provide more than merely an occasional supplement to the diet—that is, for its expansion of the demographic ceiling of the valley to be significant—in coastal Peru that shift must include the technology of water control, since there is no rainfall. A similar analysis is possible for the shift in the Mesopotamian Plain whereby cultivators assumed dominance over riverine collectors—not so much by replacing them, since the contemporary Marsh Arabs continue to practice a similar way of life, but by substantially outnumbering them. Such a change indicates a shift in the subzone of the region which is most favorable to occupation by man: more people can live by cultivation in the plain than by collecting wild foods from the river. For them to have done so would involve water control since, like the Peruvian coast, the most striking orographic characteristic of this environment is its near-total lack of precipitation.

What is, or is not, a limiting factor to demographic expansion will vary from one environment to another, depending upon physical geography and also upon the size and technological repertoire of the population. To continue our consideration of environmental parameters, the quantity, nature, and degree of permanence of the water source will induce differences among and between various empirical instances of irrigation cultivators. For cultivators, normally either land or water limitations will be the most critical inhibitor of expansion. Any population, human or animal, can expand only to the extent permitted by that resource basic to its way of life that is in the shortest supply. In the Teotihuacan Valley, there is more land irrigable with existing technology than there is available water. Thus the irrigation system observed today is at its limit and cannot in practical terms be further expanded (Millon, 1954; Millon *et al.*, 1962; Sanders, 1965). By Middle Horizon times in north coastal Peru (Willey, 1953; Moseley, 1969), the expansion of the river-fed canal systems was already supporting as many people as it could. All available water was in use; where there was no water, the rest of the presumably otherwise cultivable valleys remained desert, lacking any demographic potential. The result was a relative isolation of the valleys from each other, in a fashion parallel to the situation obtaining in the American southwest, though on a larger scale.

In the southwest, the Pueblo Sphere of Kroeber (1939:136) includes a total area estimated at 44,600 square kilometers, and a total population of 33,800, for an overall density of 0.75 per square kilometer. The southwestern population is distributed in a number of small clusters, some internally quite dense, but each separated from the others by considerable stretches of uninhabited desert. Each of these nucleated settlements has fewer than 5,000 and most under 3,000 inhabitants; densities of individual groups cited by Kroeber range from .21 to 2.71 per square kilometer. The subsistence base of many of these pueblos is irrigation agriculture, particularly floodwater and seasonal-spring irrigation. Each is surrounded by unused land for which no water is available. In some instances, however, it may be land rather than water that is the critical resource in the shortest supply. In the southern part of the Basin of Mexico, for example, the lakeshore plain is narrow, and the response to this restriction under increasing population pressure has been the terracing of the adjacent hill slopes and the creation of chinampas as artificial islands in the lakes. While the chinampas are also permanently irrigated by virtue of their location, most of the terraces observed today are dry (Sanders, 1957). The spectacular terracing of the Cuzco Basin seems to represent a similar solution to a similar problem.

The nature of the water source, particularly its seasonality or permanence, as well as its quantity, will affect the technology and sociology of its exploitation. In the Teotihuacan Valley, there is a marked difference between the floodwater canals of the middle valley and the spring-fed perennial flow into the lower valley canals. Only rainy-season agriculture is possible with a floodwater system. If the yields and the security are increased over the levels possible with rainfall alone, the total harvest per year cannot be expanded through double-cropping. Thus, the carrying capacity of lower valley land is much higher than that of the middle valley. Conversely, the absence of an appropriate permanent water source in the middle valley limits the use of any perennial irrigation there. The valleys of the south coast of Peru were similarly limited in their demographic growth; they are drier than the north coast valleys, and many of their rivers are either seasonal or are dry before they reach the Pacific.

The carrying capacity of an environment cannot therefore be assumed as given, or evaluated without reference to the total technology of the population. This is the basic methodological error in the discussion by Meggers (1954) of environmental potential; she compares environments and their relative productivity on the basis of a 1950 technology as a baseline. However, the productivity of environments in comparison with each other has notably shifted through time, as the preceding pages have indicated. Many of these shifts, inferred on the basis of settlement distribution, are directly attributed to changes in technology which modify those factors of an environment affecting production and carrying capacity. For some environments, modifiability is a function of investment of labor; success in this case is a function of the extent to which the output of the land is increased by the additional labor input. In other words, it may be uneconomic to invest labor if the return on the labor is less than the input required. For other environments, the technology for "reclamation" may simply not exist.

The technology exists today, for example (as it did not in pre-Columbian times), to pump water from the Columbia River drainage in Oregon and Washington to the Napa Valley of California. It is expensive to utilize this technology, and yet economic to do so because other soil and climate factors make it possible for this region to then produce an immense variety of truck garden crops of high market value, often either out of season or uncultivable elsewhere in the country. Concomitantly, an efficient transportation system exists to get this produce quickly to areas in which maximum demand exists. If the Napa Valley, however, used this complex and expensive irrigation technology to produce wheat or cotton, which can be grown as well and more cheaply elsewhere, the cost of irrigation would be too high, and the profits too small. Similarly, if there were no means to deliver the produce to its market, or if there were no demand, again there would be no economic basis for the heavy investment in irrigation.

For still other environments no technology yet exists that is capable of intensifying methods of agricultural production. Lowland tropical forest regions in general constitute such an example. The only way to produce maize in, say, southern Veracruz or Tabasco, is by swidden cultivation. Fallow cycles may be longer or shorter depending on population. Where land is plentiful and people few, there may be no effective cycling at all until all virgin territory has been occupied and used. But there are natural, effectively environmental, limitations (empirically variable) on how short the fallow period can be. In some of the best lands in Tabasco a 1:3 cycle is used, and yields fall off if this is reduced to 1:2. The amount of land to which so short a fallow cycle is applicable is, moreover, limited. In parts of Yucatán the cycle may range from 1:6 to 1:10 or longer. Increased weed competition and thus greater labor required, in combination with yields declining from loss of fertility through leaching, make cultivation for longer than two successive years uneconomic. Along river levees of the Gulf Coast, nearly permanent cultivation may be possible (Coe, 1968), where annual inundation and silting renew fertility; but the total quantity of such land is limited. Intensification of agricultural production by technology in practicable terms in the lowland tropics generally takes the form of production based on tree crops which do not deplete the soil to the extent of annual cultivation of cereals. Given such a specialization, in turn, the region involved necessarily depends upon importation of staples from elsewhere, and upon access to markets for its own produce.

Thus, in only a few settings will irrigation be the key to demographic expansion. Its functions in raising carrying capacity may vary. It may increase productivity in a zone already cultivated by more extensive techniques by increasing yield, security of harvest, or by permitting multi-cropping, the production of new crops, or more productive varieties of existing crops. It may open additional areas for agriculture, areas that prior to irrigation were unused or only marginally productive. In the course of the development of the early New World civilizations, hydraulic systems in parts of these nuclear areas could be expanded until at their maxima they were the economic bases of the large, complex societies discovered by the Spaniards. While many other societies were and are known to practice irrigation agriculture, these for various reasons never attained the scale or degree of complexity of the high civilizations.

Irrigation alone, therefore, is incapable of fully explaining the growth of civilizations. Irrigation cultivation, while freeing a population from some of the limitations on its growth, may itself be subject to limitations—both environmental and technological—in its expansion. We must look to some of the parameters discussed above, and to their functional implications, for an explanation of why some irrigated systems grow large, to include increasingly larger numbers of people and extents of territory, while others remain small, simple, and local.

Not all irrigation constitutes hydraulic agriculture of the kind described by Wittfogel. And if Wittfogel (1957) does include a discussion of the American southwest, he strays from his central point and to that extent dilutes his own argument. No one can consider a southwestern pueblo to be anything but an essentially egalitarian tribal group, however dependent on irrigation it may be for subsistence, however high its hydraulic density. Groups of this size and degree of complexity are clearly competent to manage this level of technology without the kinds of sociopolitical institutions described for the Irrigation Civilizations. Their reliance on irrigation has not per se transformed them into Irrigation Civilizations.

Wittfogel's Oriental Society is characterized by a centralized and highly despotic bureaucracy as the locus of power and entrepreneurship in the society, often incorporating both ecclesiastical and secular arms (understandably, since both church and state are institutions of social control). The bureaucracy is the group of full-time specialists, maintained from the surplus of the primary producers; economic, political, and military power are concentrated in the hands of these specialists. Wittfogel maintains (1955, 1957) that the power of this group derives in turn from the requisites of hydraulic agriculture and the need for centralized direction and control of the hydraulic works in order to keep them functioning efficiently. The capital and labor needs for construction and maintenance of large-scale irrigation systems are such that, first, only the central bureaucracy could undertake these projects successfully: no other segment of the society could afford them. Second, the competitive situation, within the society and between societies, is greatly exacerbated when the basic means of production are artificial; some central authority is thus necessary to control the use of force and to adjudicate disputes which could potentially disrupt the entire system. Third, the cooperative nature of the labor requisites, on a large scale, suggest the advantages of centralized control in the massing of manpower when and where needed. Fourth, the hydraulic management needs per se give to a group in control extremely effective sanctions and thus enormous power to back up its demands. As Childe (1946:90) observes,

> Rain falleth upon the just and the unjust alike, but irrigating waters reach the fields by channels the community has constructed. And what society has provided, society can also withdraw from the unjust and confine to the just alone.

The government, in other words, need not even call out the army to enforce its decisions: all it has to do is turn off the water.

If it is agreed that Wittfogel's hypothesis of the causal linkage between a particular kind of economy and a given form of government is applicable only to large-scale systems, two basic questions may then be asked. First, how large is large enough? Second, does hydroagriculture "cause" the state, or does a strong central government then "cause" hydroagriculture? We consider these two interrelated questions below.

How Large Is Large Enough?

We have alluded to the question of relative scale and expandability of irrigation systems above, in order to point out the techno-environmental parameters that may act to impede or to permit growth. The size of the system is in turn a major determinant of the labor and management needs involved. Since this, in Wittfogel's developmental scheme, is the underlying dynamic on which the argument linking production to political structure rests, it merits more detailed examination. Our best evidence is obtained through the use of the comparative method. Both ethnographic and archaeological data are relevant to what is essentially a problem of defining the situation in which a qualitative change is likely to result from the operation of essentially quantitative processes.

Millon (1962) has questioned the Wittfogel hypothesis of the relationship between centralized authority and irrigation agriculture. He has observed quite correctly that the dynamics of water management are, on the basis of comparative ethnography, far more variable than Wittfogel's theory would indicate. His example of the Sonjo (Gray, 1963) and the case of Pul Eliya (Leach, 1961) are small, single-community systems. They thus resemble both the contemporary southwest and the inferred situation for a system such as Hierve el Agua. Comparatively small population groups are involved in all these cases—in the case of Pul Eliya, only 146 people, irrigating a total of 135 acres. Under such circumstances, in spite of the reliance upon artificial water control, kinship and sodality ties are sufficient to integrate the society, and to control both water supply and distribution and the labor requisite for maintenance of the system. Where the source of water is both local and limited in quantity, the question of disputes between different communities competing for its control is less likely to arise. And where quantity limits expansion, kinship and other essentially egalitarian ties are sufficient to control intracommunity competition and conflict. Millon cites a Balinese example in which parts of several settlements are involved in irrigation cooperatives, but the numbers include only 5500–7500 people each—again, evidently below the level at which centralization of authority becomes an effective solution to the problems of management and control.

Irrigation systems in general do have requisites different from most other types of agriculture in that, no matter how small their scale, cooperative rather than individual effort is generally necessary to use and maintain them effectively: the productive unit is therefore larger than the single household. Such cooperation of course need not be amicable; indeed it is fraught with conflict. However, the need for cooperative labor means, in effect, that the amount of total output of the system per unit of labor expended will be greater if a number of workers pool their efforts than it would be if the same number of workers each operated independently, each expending the same amount of effort. Expansion of the system will be efficient and economic only when additional labor investment will add more than the value of its own input to the total output of energy, by bringing more land under cultivation or by adding to the yields from land in production. When putting additional labor into the land does not result in this kind of increased output, the agricultural situation, no matter what its technology, may, following Geertz (1963), be referred to as "involuted."

If cooperative enterprise is a virtual necessity for irrigated land at even the single-community level, this is not necessarily the case for other kinds of productive systems. In the several varieties of swidden, while farmers may cooperate in one or several of the necessary operations, the labor is essentially individual. Three farmers clearing three fields together involves the same input-output ratio as each of three farmers separately clearing each of three fields; it is merely additive rather than multiplicative. Pot-irrigation, while an intensive technique in that it maximizes production per hectare by means of labor investment (Flannery *et al.*, 1967), is similarly an individual-household enterprise; cooperation of larger groups does not result in increased output. Both the enormous yields and the enormous labor inputs of contemporary chinampa agriculture in the southern Valley of Mexico similarly involve an essentially individual rather than cooperative patterning. Terracing is, in a sense, an intermediate case. The labor investment to produce a crop in terraced agriculture not simultaneously involving floodwater or permanent irrigation is again basically individual. But terraces usually occur in groups rather larger than the isolated holding of an individual family. Terraces, like irrigation canals, require continuous upkeep to maintain them in good repair. While chinampas also require such attention, a single farmer's eroded chinampa menaces the security of no one but himself. A single disintegrating terrace, however, can threaten the productivity of all the holdings located below it. Thus, like small irrigation systems operating at the single community level, community-level cooperation is generally advantageous in terrace cultivation.

When either geographical or technological factors, or the combination of both, inhibit the expansion of an irrigation system and its demographic ceiling, the system will stabilize at that level. While the economic advantages of cooperative labor in its management will still obtain, the total labor force will remain sufficiently small so that centralized institutions of control will not be necessary. Nor could they be supported: there would not be enough work for such specialists to do to justify their upkeep. Size and elaborateness of any institution of social control will depend directly on the size of the society; the number of chiefs, so to speak, depends on the number of Indians.

It is difficult and perhaps ultimately somewhat arbitrary to attempt precise definition of the point along the continuum where quantitative changes may be analyzed as qualitative ones. We may observe that a kind of variable, critical-mass phenomenon is evidently involved, in which the absolute size and density of population must be viewed not by itself but in relationship to parameters such as the degree of environmental circumscription (Carneiro, 1961), the degree of environmental diversity, the overall technological level of the population and thus the extent to which differential utilization of different sectors of the habitat may be both possible and economically efficient. Specialization and symbiosis (Sanders, 1956) may thus themselves be viewed as adaptive developments, techno-economic and sociopolitical means of raising the demographic ceiling of a total region and thereby responding to conditions of population pressure (Sanders, 1968). However, if, as we have done, we stress the applicability of Wittfogel's hypothesis only to large-scale hydraulic and social systems, at least an attempt must be made, despite these cautions, to define the range within which a "small" system becomes for the purposes of analysis a "large" one.

Again we turn to the comparative method

for assistance. There is clearly a difference of degree that operates as a difference in kind if we compare, say, Hierve el Agua with the Chicama-Moche transvalley system. All change proceeds quantitatively just as all process is incremental; the poles of the continuum are clear, but the intermediate ground far less so. Comparative data, both ethnographic and archaeological, may perhaps help to clarify and order this middle range. If we are to speak of "large" systems, such analysis will be critical. Armillas (1948), for example, considers the hydraulic systems of Late Postclassic Central Mexico to have been essentially "cantonal." The multiplicity of individually limited water sources, and their localized distribution, effectively barred the development of a unified and centralized basinwide single system. Limitations of geography thus restricted the size and distribution both of population dependent on a single system, and the possibility of merging several smaller systems into a single larger and more highly centralized one. Adams (1966) similarly notes the late inception of a pan-Mesopotamian single, huge irrigation network—in the Iron Age. It is our view that such super-systems are far larger than either necessary or sufficient for explanation of the sociological concomitants and consequents of large-scale irrigation. Clearly, techno-environmental parameters limit the possibility or probability of this degree of expansion; in Mesoamerica it was not feasible, while in Mesopotamia this did ultimately occur, but as the end product of long, individual sequences of localized growth. While Wittfogel's formulations are clearly applicable to such super-systems, these dynamics can be regarded as operative at levels well below this point.

The contemporary Teotihuacan system, "small" in Millon's sense (1962), serves all or parts of 16 villages. Overall, the contemporary, Aztec, and Classic populations were similar in size (Sanders, 1965) though varying in composition and distribution. The settlement pattern of the Classic, described in a previous section of this paper, implies that some 85–100,000 people at least—the population of the city of Teotihuacan itself—were ultimately wholly or partly dependent on the productivity of this system. Furthermore, this same evidence of settlement patterns strongly implies the conclusion that the regulation of the system involved a high degree of centralized control. First, Teotihuacan is the largest single settlement in the entire Basin of Mexico, and very probably in all of Mesoamerica at the time; its pan-Mesoamerican repercussions were immense and far-reaching in nearly all aspects of culture (Sanders and Price, 1968; L. A. Parsons, 1969: Ch. 5; Parsons and Price, 1970). Second, Teotihuacan, while not the only Classic period settlement in Teotihuacan Valley, does seem to have virtually depopulated the lower valley—the permanently irrigated sector of its immediate sustaining area; its presence evidently inhibited significant population expansion in the Texcoco Plain area as well, though this zone, as previously indicated, more probably constituted a part of the outfield aspect of the economy of Classic primary production.

Sanders and Price have suggested (1968: 195–196) a parallel with the post-conquest Spanish policy of *congregación*, or enforced nucleation of population. As in the post-Hispanic instance, imposition of a settlement policy and its enforcement involves the wielding of considerable power. The Classic period lower valley settlement pattern seems largely uneconomic and anti-ecological. It is generally more efficient for farmers to live on or near their holdings, and particularly so when they have no access to any mode of transport more efficient than feet. Yet, as we have described, the few rural villages in the lower Valley of Teotihuacan contemporary with the height of the city seem to have exploited the upper piedmont in which they are located, and to have had no access at all to the irrigated valley floor. The explanation may lie in the inferred imposition of a congregación, which would in turn imply strong central authority. The settlement pattern looks as though access to the prized lower valley lands may have actually been contingent on city residence, where the central authority could exert considerable socioeconomic control over the population, and could in short have behaved very much like an Oriental Despotism. The sanctions involved would have been extremely potent and not difficult to apply. The overall degree of local centralization, on the basis of the settlement pattern, thus seems strikingly higher than that observed at present in Teotihuacan Valley.

For the Viru Valley, we have previously cited Willey's estimate (1953) that a population maximum of 25,000 was reached by Late Gallinazo times, and the suggestion of Moseley (1969) that the irrigation system had also reached its maximal capacity then. It is also in Late Gallinazo times that truly monumental architecture appears in Viru, particularly so at the largest site of the period. On this evidence, Willey postulates the existence of a local state based on control of a unified, valley-wide irrigation system. In the Moche Valley, the Huaca del Sol and Huaca de la Luna date from approximately this period or somewhat later, at the peak of Moche military and political expansion. That expansion, however, indicates that a parallel process to that of local state formation in Viru was probably contemporary with or somewhat earlier than the Viru developments. We shall return subsequently to the questions of militarism and conquest states, in a different but related context.

As additional comparative material in this question of scale, we cite the evidence on size of system from Mesopotamia. Braidwood and Reed (1957) estimate an average population of some 17,000 for each of the Sumerian city-states by approximately 3000 BC. Associated with each such unit is considerable monumental civic architecture, thriving long-distance commerce, and social stratification, which are among Childe's previously mentioned criteria for the archaeological recognition of civilization. Parallel to the evidence of militarism in north coastal Peru in Moche and immediately pre-Moche times (Willey, 1953; Lanning, 1967), and in Central Mexico in Teotihuacan times (Sanders and Price, 1968), the Sumerian city-states were in a constant state of warfare with each other (Adams, 1966). That the local irrigation systems of Sumer only much later coalesced into the unified pan-Mesopotamian system is for the present irrelevant. It does, however, appear to be the case that each individual local city-state system was large enough to produce the effects observed, just as with the individual Viru, Moche, or Teotihuacan systems.

Irrigation: Cause and Effect

The question of whether irrigation causes the state is of course far too simplistic, and in that form cannot be answered. As indicated in the preceding pages, the answers lie in a consideration of the dynamics of a large number of processes and their interrelationships in time and space. Every observed period of each empirical example represents merely one possible way in which these parameters may intersect and crystallize. To put the case so is by no means to deny that regularities exist; it says only that such regularities are those of process and are thus extremely complex, so much so that neither a dogmatically unilineal approach, nor any explanation based on the operation of any single factor taken in isolation will be adequate to deal with them.

In general, for any factor to be regarded as the cause of any given effect, that factor must precede the observed effect in time. Any analysis of causality is therefore necessarily diachronic. A second requisite for the attribution of causality, broadly stated, is that the process by which the presumed cause produced the presumed effect must be stated. Analysis must therefore be functional as well. Third, the concept of causality is itself a probabilistic one, rather than a model of inevitable push-pull. What "inevitably" really means, then, is the statement of a relatively high degree of probability: that "it must follow as the night the day" is a prediction (or retrodiction) of the likelihood of occurrence of the event or pattern in question (Harris, 1968).

Both synchronic and diachronic evidence strongly suggest that the use of canal irrigation precedes the state. On synchronic grounds we can observe today a large number of relatively small and typologically simple societies which practice irrigation agriculture. Although typological simplicity need not logically or necessarily imply chronological priority, worldwide archaeological evidence is conclusive that in the evolution of world culture, such societies are indeed found to antedate the later emergence, in some areas, of progressively larger and more complex polities. Archaeological evidence further suggests that the emergence of such large and complex polities is, in the instance of the pristine states, associated with an economic base of large-scale irrigation agriculture. As the larger societies developed from smaller ones, so too are the roots of large-scale hydroagriculture found in small-scale, local intensifications of the productive system. Neither arises full-blown. An association, a correlation, is, however, not a cause. This consideration underlies the immediately preceding treatment of the problem of scale.

The hypothesis that large-scale hydraulic agriculture is the cause of certain kinds of state organization is, if strictly construed, open to question as stated. At least as early as 1955, when Wolf and Palerm investigated the Acolhua irrigation system, they raised the point (1955:274) that, "If our dating of the Texcocan system is correct, we must recognize that we are dealing with a case in which the state did not grow out of irrigation, but preceded it." And they state (p. 275) that, "Once established, of course, irrigation probably operated in turn to centralize and intensify political controls." Their doubts, with the perspective of hindsight, seem to be based on lacunae in the data then available. The recent evidence of the relationship of hydraulic agriculture to the growth of Teotihuacan, evidence that was lacking in 1955, would have been more to their original point. The Acolhua state was, in Fried's terms, a secondary state, formed in response to pressures emanating from preexisting states and, indeed, a historical descendant of a good thousand years of state organization existing in its immediate vicinity. No one, furthermore, to our knowledge, has ever doubted the capacity of states once formed to undertake such projects, and thus this point is not, for us, an issue. It does, however, underlie several more recent criticisms of the hydraulic theory, of which two will be discussed in more detail below.

Adams (1966) has argued that the state precedes the development of large-scale irrigation in Mesopotamia. His argument rests on the fundamental misconception that "large-scale" necessarily implies pan-Mesopotamian; we have previously treated this question. The level of inclusiveness of only the single city-state system appears to have been ample to demonstrate the association of large-scale irrigation agriculture and this level of political organization. That the Mesopotamian states of the Iron Age were, not unexpectedly, themselves much larger than the Sumerian city states would tend to strengthen rather than vitiate the connection we propose. If Braidwood and Howe's suggestion (1962) is adopted, to the effect that significant agricultural occupation of the Mesopotamian Plain began during the Halaf phase, such occupation vindicates the assumption of the chronological priority of irrigation-based cultivation over the state in this region. Such occupation would necessarily have involved the basic techniques of irrigation and drainage in order for the area to have supported cultivators at all. Halafian culture almost certainly did not involve states; a more reasonable chronology for the emergence of the state in Mesopotamia would postulate a Late Predynastic, certainly Early Dynastic, date.

Another recent proponent of the state-precedes-irrigation hypothesis is Lanning, who asserts (1967:94) that small states existed on the Peruvian Coast by 1800 BC (the Initial Period). It is his interpretation of his evidence—the sites of La Florida and Las Haldas—that we consider highly dubious. He considers that the La Florida pyramid and the Las Haldas temple were of necessity constructed as intercommunity enterprises, and his own population estimates (1967:63–64) can in fact be invoked in support of that suggestion. A site with a population of 500–1,000—or even twice or three times that number—is, however, not construed by the present writer as the capital of a state. In actuality it far more closely resembles a village. The ceremonial functions of the structures in question are fully accepted, as is the hypothesis that they were built by and served a population from several different settlements in their respective areas. What is very strongly doubted is that intercommunity cooperation at so feeble a demographic level would either require or imply state institutions. Such an assumption is not substantiated archaeologically or ethnographically, and particularly not when the sites involved are so very small. A more reasonable dating of the emergence of the state on the Andean coast would involve an Early Intermediate Period placement.

The debate concerning the which-came-first question is, in our view, sterile when asked in so simplistic a way, in obvious expectation of a yes-or-no answer that is equally simplistic. In other words, we regard this as a pseudoproblem. It is our contention that the expansion of a productive system based on hydraulic agriculture and the attendant social complexity are related in a positive feedback system of cause and effect that is essentially self-reinforcing and self-intensifying. The rapidity of this process will be variable, depending upon a number of ecological and evolutionary parameters previously cited. Growth of productive base and of sociopolitical structures are aspects of the same adaptive and ecosystemic processes. The ultimate cause of both is population pressure, which determines the natural selective forces that govern the survival, adoption, and spread of any innovations that act to raise the demographic ceiling. Expansion so caused in turn sets off further expansion in both productive base and sociopolitical complexity. This entire cycle acts to strengthen the power of the developing or developed state institutions. Not all irrigated productive systems, moreover, will develop in the fashion summarized below. As we have suggested, growth may be aborted and stabilization occur at much lower levels.

We envision the causal complex as one involving demography, production, and social organization in the broadest sense. These parameters are all interrelated, suggesting that changes anywhere in the system including them all will bring about compensatory changes elsewhere in that system. As we have stated previously, these processes of change tend, under some circumstances, to intensify and reinforce each other. First, as the energy content of the system as a whole increases, there will be more and larger problems in coordination and administration; kinship and sodality organization and, increasingly, even simple ranked structures will, as overall size increases, become increasingly inadequate as sole means of control and direction. Second, as there is more work for an emerging bureaucracy to do, the greater is the likelihood that it will be composed of full-time professional specialists, supported from the surplus production of others. Third, as the system grows, this group will acquire increased power within the society. Growth means increasing numbers of people dependent on the expanding hydraulic agriculture and thus subject to the sanctions imposed by the group in control. The latter thereby grows more powerful and more able to exact the surpluses in both labor and kind from the rest of the society. Fourth, the services performed by this group not only enrich its members but provide some benefit for everyone in the society, although some sectors of society will profit more than others. Taxation, tribute, corvee labor, sharecrop arrangements, etc., are simply particular examples of what Wolf (1966) more generally terms a fund of rent. Last, if the processes of growth are to continue, this additionally strengthens the power of the controlling group, which has unimpeded access to the largest share of the capital and labor requisite for further expansion. It would thus have no serious potential competitor in exploiting new sources of wealth (these may be expanded hydraulic works, large-scale commerce or manufacturing, or any other potentially profitable enterprise).

Social Stratification, Competition, and Militarism

The preceding two paragraphs have followed Wittfogel's own discussion quite closely, even where the terminology used is in some respects different. They have provided a brief summary of a series of interrelated processes which underlie and generate social stratification, the differential access to strategic resources. For a fundamentally agrarian population, those resources are land and water. In the case of the emerging state described above, virtually the entire population of primary producers have only restricted access to the means of production, contingent on their payment of some form of rent or taxes. If an agricultural population lives in an environment where the major problem in the productive cycle is shortage of water (not all agricultural populations) and where the solution to that problem has been canal irrigation (not all arid-land cultivators) and where the principal challenge to expansion of such a productive system has been labor or technological input (not all irrigation cultivators), we can trace a distinctive cause-and-effect system in which social stratification is inherent. The reasons are primarily economic: a nonegalitarian social organization is required to keep the productive system going at full capacity, to compel the cleaning and repair of canals, and to allocate the water which is available only through human agency. That these structural arrangements are adaptive is seen in the observation that the societies which have them are larger in size and in energy content than those which lack them. This is in evolutionary terms the indication of an adaptive trait, defined as one which tends to increase the number of its carriers.

Other inequalities too are inherent in hydraulic agriculture as its scale increases. Some of these are, of course, paralleled in other agricultural systems as well, and are viewed therefore as merely intensified in a hydraulic regime. We have previously noted that very few habitats are so uniform that they do not contain within them some sectors that are more productive than others, given the same amount of energy input. In the first stages of agricultural occupation of an area, these lands will be occupied first; only when they have been filled to capacity will people be effectively forced into other zones in the environment. As the area fills demographically, a resource formerly abundant relative to the group dependent on it becomes a resource in comparatively short supply. There will thus be competition, within a society or between societies, for access to that resource. This process of competition (Sanders and Price, 1968), far from unique to irrigation cultivators, is probably best considered a human universal. As the society or societies in question grow larger, the scale of the competition—both internal and external—escalates correspondingly. Probably the competition situation on the Peruvian Coast developed quite rapidly, as cultivators began to exploit the narrow strip of annually flooded lands along the margins of the rivers. Such a limited area would fill up quite rapidly; the ultimate solution to the problem—the development of artificial irrigation on an initially small and progressively expanded scale—was undoubtedly preceded by considerable conflict. Patterson (pers. comm.) notes the presence of fortified sites and the practice of taking trophy heads on the central coast by the late Early Horizon. Similarly, at San Lorenzo there would have been a significant difference in productivity between the river-levee lands and areas removed from the immediate floodplain. This would have been less striking than the Peruvian coast situation, but nonetheless present. Coe (1968) postulates an effectively infield-outfield agriculture as the economic base of San Lorenzo, but there would probably have been a certain amount of competition over the choice lands. Initially in Teotihuacan Valley, choice lands were the upper hill slopes; the settlement pattern in Late Formative-Protoclassic times suggests competition, presumably over land, in this area (Sanders, 1965). Ethnographic examples of this sort of competitive pressure are numerous in various parts of the world. Competition is not unique to emerging or developed states, and competitive situations may occur both within and between societies.

The powerful exacerbation of these general competitive conditions by the introduction of irrigation into a local ecosystem is due in large measure to the controllable nature of this vital resource—the water supply. The dependence of the population on an artificial, technologically created resource—especially in environments like the Peruvian coast which are sharply circumscribed by aridity—makes that population unusually vulnerable. Relationships of true political and economic power are impossible among hunters and gatherers: these are small societies, integrated by kinship, where population growth is reflected in fissioning of bands and consequent growth of numbers of bands. The strategic resource is wild food, and people cannot "control" game, or the production of wild plants. Among shifting cultivators, and particularly those in open environments the productive resource, land, can be differentially controlled. But the need to do so comes only when the environment is completely filled in to its limits, or nearly so. With non-permanent cultivation, the impetus for control of land is rather weaker than is the case with permanent fields. There is, however, a marked difference in the possible degree of social control, and thus of internal competition, where the productive potential of the land depends wholly or in large part upon an artificial resource; it will be greatest particularly where the contrast in productivity between irrigated and nonirrigated land is sharpest (Aschmann, 1962).

Other bases of conflict are present in societies dependent on irrigation agriculture (Millon *et al.*, 1962), particularly so where these irrigation systems serve a number of separate communities economically linked through common dependence on a single resource base. What one swidden farmer does, affects his neighbors or the residents of the next village only minimally if at all. This is not true in irrigated systems where, if farmers upstream use too much water, there may be none at all available for downstream users. Riparian controversies between upstream and downstream users of the modern Teotihuacan Valley system are rife, often to the point of exploding into armed conflict between villages. Their common dependence on this resource base has acted to favor political integration on a regional level, but this need not imply that it is at all pacific. Sanders and Price (1968) have suggested that centralized control is an adaptive solution to the problems posed by this kind of conflict.

At a higher level of development, examples are numerous of the conflicts arising between entire polities that have reached a ceiling of expansion. Among the archaeologically known Irrigation Civilizations, this process seems to have been basically similar in Mesopotamia (Adams, 1966) and in coastal Peru during the Early Intermediate (Willey, 1953; Patterson and Lanning, 1964; Kosok, 1965). The relationship between intersocietal warfare or militarism and agricultural production has been alluded to above; the formation of the multivalley Moche conquest state is particularly interesting. If, like Viru, the Moche Valley ecosystem had reached its maximal expansion, the only remaining economical way of procuring additional needed resources would be by the external conquest and expropriation of those resources from someone else. The Moche conquests may, as Collier (1955) implies, have involved the initial inception of transvalley irrigation between Moche and Chicama; the Mesopotamian evidence suggests, however, that this would not have been necessary. Often, external conquest, for instance the Mesopotamian case, is more economic and involves less labor, than further intensification of the local productive base; in the case of Moche, such intensification may not have been possible. Sanders and Price (1968) suggest that the control of internal force within polities of this type effectively preadapts them for external expansion as well.

Competition, cooperation, and expansion are basic ecological processes applicable to the analysis of first the internal dynamics of individual societies, and second to the kinds of relations obtaining between and among the societies of a region (Sanders and Price, 1968). Questions such as those involving the nature of militaristic expansion of civilizations cannot be satisfactorily or intelligibly explained apart from this more inclusive context. The preadaptation of state institutions for such expansion is characteristic of societies at this level of development. But this too must be regarded as one special class or case of a more general consideration: what determines which areas are nuclear and which marginal? More colloquially, what are the determinants of the balance of power, and how do these determinants change through time?

All ecological processes are diachronic. Thus, each phase must be viewed in terms of what precedes and follows it: we are dealing not merely with a sequence of forms but with the explanation of processes of change. Palerm and Wolf (1957:9) consider a nuclear area as one of "massed power in both economic and demographic terms;" Sanders and Price define it (1968:51) as a particularly vigorous focus of culture change where "such change had strong extra-local repercussions." In general, an ecological explanation of the processes of cultural development must take into account not only particular local adaptive problems and their solutions, but also the ways in which adjacent local developments of this sort impinge on each other. The total environment of any human population necessarily includes the factor of other human populations as well. Since the adaptive processes involved are diachronic, the balance may shift through time—an area may be nuclear (an innovating center) in one period, and marginal (a receiver of influences) in another.

Mesoamerican prehistory offers an instructive illustration of the processes involved. At a time when the subsistence base involved exclusive dependence on wild foods, the demographic potential of sectors of this complex environment varied considerably with the range and quantity of naturally occurring food resources. The nuclear area in the origins of maize agriculture—an intensification of environmental productivity—was a zone that included a number of tierra templada, highland, semi-arid, mountain basins. At this time other regions, such as the Pacific Coast of Guatemala, continued to support a sedentary population of littoral and marine gatherers (Coe and Flannery, 1964, 1967). As the essentially extensive techniques of the developing agriculture became more widespread in Mesoamerica, the possession of this technology altered the carrying capacity of each area in which it was applied, and in this fashion altered the former relationship of areas to each other. The best zone for hunting and gathering in the La Victoria vicinity, for example, became almost depopulated with a change to an agricultural subsistence base.

By the Middle Formative the Gulf Coast Plain of Mexico had very clearly become nuclear with respect to Mesoamerica as a whole. For an overall population having access to basically extensive techniques of agricultural production, this is the area in which yields so obtained are highest. The highland zones that are the apparent hearth of agricultural origins will produce similarly high yields per hectare only with a labor input considerably greater than that necessary for production on the Gulf Coast. Tracts of arable land cultivable with available technology were also more limited in the highlands, while the Gulf Coast is a comparatively more open environment. Thus, differential agricultural potential can be seen as the major factor underlying the Middle Formative florescence of Olmec culture. Compared to other regions, this area of southern Veracruz-Tabasco was precocious and very definitely nuclear. From this zone the first of the Mesoamerican horizon styles spread into areas from the Valley of Mexico to Chalchuapa in El Salvador. The cultural preeminence of this Olmec area is evident in a comparison of the contemporary sites at San Lorenzo in Veracruz and San Jose Mogote in Oaxaca. San Lorenzo is clearly a larger and more internally differentiated society, as judged by both the quantity and complexity of building activity, which we are using as an indicator of the total energy content of the society. Olmec, similarly, was a nonegalitarian society not dependent on hydraulic institutions, Coe (1968) to the contrary. Flannery (1968b) and Parsons and Price (1970) have developed a nonhydraulic model based on trade that is capable of generating nonegalitarian society at this demographic level, which is considerably smaller than that of the Classic civilizations.

Olmec was surpassed as a locus of demographic and economic influence only as the highland areas not only initiated but expanded the capacity of labor-intensive means of production. As we have observed, these highland areas turned out, in the long run, to be more improvable by technological means than the lowlands. Some technological experimentation of this sort seems contemporary with the apogee of Olmec, but its initial impact on total productivity was necessarily small. The eclipse of Olmec did not occur until the Late Formative, when the nuclear area shifted to and thereafter remained in the highlands. It seems that in this particular empirical instance, the productivity based on increased reliance on an efficient irrigation agriculture in the highlands was largely responsible for the shift: an area that supports a larger and denser population will have an advantage over other competing areas, whatever the time period, whatever the specific characteristics of the economic base involved.

In Mesoamerica, given the specific characteristics of those environmental factors that affect agriculture and thus demographic potential, it was irrigation which largely determined the competitive balance among societies. That claim, however, hardly shows reliance on our part upon a single-factor explanation. There were differentials of similar sorts in the Middle Formative, based on the interrelation of completely different kinds of productive parameters; there were no hydraulic societies in Mesoamerica at that time period. The implication that irrigation was responsible for the balance of power in Classic and Postclassic Mesoamerica is based essentially on its impact on the productivity of different ecological niches relative to each other. We use these points as part of a statement of functional relationships rather than as reliance on a monistic panacea.

By the early sixteenth century the Basin of Mexico supported a number of highly differentiated ecological niches, including a great diversity of agricultural techniques, specialized crops adapted to various sectors, and both full- and part-time specialists in the production of an enormous repertoire of nonagricultural goods and services, these last supported ultimately from surpluses produced by cultivators and obtained from them by regular market exchange, taxation, and tribute. Between the Classic and the conquest the agricultural history appears to have comprised largely a process of filling in, of expanding intensive techniques to the virtual maximum permitted by the limitations of geography. In addition, a number of additional labor-intensive methods of production, notably chinampas, were added to the total agricultural technology. The Teotihuacan, Toltec, and Aztec expansions involved the formation of conquest-based supra-local and supraregional states, with the archaeological spread of horizon styles that blanketed local traditions on a virtually pan-Mesoamerican basis. We turn now to an examination of the role played by hydraulic agriculture in these developments.

Clearly not all of the Basin of Mexico was, or could ever be, irrigated. During those phases in the overall sequence when the entire area was more or less unified politically, and certainly during the maxima of empire, such unity was based on something other than the single integrated hydraulic system which never existed. Sanders and Price (1968:186–187) explain the complex dynamics as follows:

> If one considers, however, the interplay of the two processes of competition and cooperation within the geographical setting of Central Mexico, the role of hydraulic agriculture seems clear. The complex interdigiting of hydraulic and nonhydraulic zones with their consequent variations in population density, the short distances between hydraulic zones, and the dramatic contrast in productivity between hydraulic and nonhydraulic agriculture in a sharply circumscribed environment would provide an extremely competitive social environment. The combination of a system of agriculture that requires cooperation, the consequent uneven distribution of population, and a competitive social environment would all act to stimulate the development of highly organized, centralized political systems. Once the communities of a hydraulic zone were organized in this fashion the resultant state would enjoy an obvious competitive advantage over neighboring nonhydraulic zones and more distant hydraulic zones of smaller size or less efficient organization.

Therefore, even the "cantonal" nature of the individual systems could have been effective in the direction of the political development of the region as a whole. No such region was isolated, and events within these regions had considerable impact in the areas adjacent to them. These zones, if individually quite small, yet functioned as nodes in processes affecting areas at greater or lesser remove from them. Even by the sixteenth century, any single system integrated from 10,000 to a maximum of only 100,000 people. While Wittfogel—although pointing out the powerful expansive capacities of irrigation states—tends to stress the internal political dynamics of their organization, Sanders and Price emphasize instead the effects of the existence of such units in the context of larger symbiotic units, internally diverse and mutually interdependent. These "external" effects are an essential component of the processes of the formation of empire. Indeed, "internal" factors cannot be considered apart from "external" ones, since there is a feedback linkage between the two.

Yet the internal dynamics of the individual hydraulic clusters themselves are thrown into sharpest relief particularly during the periods of interregnum, when the level of sociocultural integration in Mesoamerica reverted to the smaller scale of the city state. These are exceptionally stable units which periodically are incorporated into large territorial empires; the latter, however, are less stable through time. This may well be a function of the cantonal nature of the productive system. At the city-state level there is a high degree of coincidence between the productive and the political systems. Concerning the Texcoco system, Wolf and Palerm (1955:276) state:

> The irrigation cluster discussed here lent a cohesion to the Old Acolhua domain which it might not have acquired otherwise. It is important to note that the limits of the domain coincided closely with the limits of irrigation in the area. Huexotla, marginal to the system of water distribution, was also marginal politically. The domain retained its unity even when the political structure of Texcoco reached out to include a wider area and a larger and more diverse population. Certainly, once the state expanded, the very marginal location of the domain in the narrow corridor leading from north to south along the eastern shore of the lake would have tended to reduce the area to secondary importance, had irrigation not provided a permanent backbone of political cohesion.

We have previously discussed the competitive relation of irrigated and nonirrigated zones to each other in Central Mexico. The "permanent backbone of political cohesion" of the

Texcocan state described by Wolf and Palerm represents one example, a special instance of what Sanders (1968:103) refers to as "niche dominance." The locus of political power in a region—within a state, as here, or between entire polities—will be situated in that ecological niche which is superior to adjacent ones in productivity and demographic potential. This zone will constitute a nuclear area. The niche dominance effect should be enhanced as the total population of the region as a whole increases and, more significantly, as the productive differential between the component niches is increased. The concept (Wittfogel's hydraulic density is another special case) is thus a general statement of competitive relations, and summarizes the processes by which even a cantonal hydroagriculture can lead to political centralization in an area. In a sense, any agriculturally "infield" area could produce these effects to some extent as it interacts with the "outfield" area and its population; our postulated dominance of riverine over inland niches for the Gulf Coast Olmec can be explained in this fashion. Sanders considers chinampa cultivation in sixteenth century Xochimilco to have exerted a niche dominance effect comparable to that of the Texcocan irrigation system, producing an approximately similar political and demographic centralization. He contrasts the more decentralized and perhaps inherently less stable situation of sixteenth century Chalco, which lacked both hydraulic agriculture and a single consistently dominant niche.

Extant data from Peru highlight a number of interesting similarities and differences when compared to the Mesoamerican sequence. The two areas in general exhibit remarkably parallel large-scale resemblances of development, resemblances that have long been observed. Both areas constitute what Bennett (1948) and Armillas (1948) term co-traditions: alternating phases of local cultural development periodically crosscut by horizon styles temporarily unifying entire diverse regions into virtually a single cultural province, though not always, apparently, on the basis of military conquest. The earliest of the major horizons in each region—Olmec in Mesoamerica, Chavin in the Central Andes—seem unaccompanied by any process recognizable as empire formation. The later instances—Teotihuacan, Toltec, Aztec in Mesoamerica; Tiahuanaco-Huari and Inca in the Central Andes—do seem to involve militarism, conquest, and some degree of incorporation of conquered populations into a single political system. In parts of both Mesoamerica and the Central Andes hydraulic agriculture, well prior to the conquest, constituted the principal subsistence base for large, dense, economically specialized populations.

It is these overall similarities that make one major difference that much more puzzling and paradoxical. In Mesoamerica, the development of hydraulic agriculture gave to those areas possessing it a consistent competitive advantage. Where the spread of a horizon style did involve conquest and empire formation—the Classic and Postclassic—the nuclear area for these events was the irrigation-based Meseta Central. The reasons for this phenomenon have been discussed above. The wave of conquest spread out of the irrigated highlands into the nonirrigated lowlands to the south. In Peru, current knowledge points to the coast, particularly the north and north-central coasts, as the heartland of the early development and maximal expansion of hydraulic agriculture. All the pan-Peruvian horizon styles, however, are of highland origin, and all the Central Andean empires have a highland core. It was always the highlands that conquered and incorporated the irrigated coast.

We have previously noted the near absence of data concerning the evolution of highland agricultural systems. This dearth of information makes the fact that this area was consistently the seat of empire virtually impossible to explain. The repeated conquests of the coast from the highlands presupposes a demographic advantage in the highlands—otherwise they could not have succeeded in gaining this kind of systematic access to the resources of the coast (probably the principal motivation for the cycles of conquest). But the nature of the subsistence base that evidently supported this presumed demographic superiority is totally unknown. The principal problem in most highland areas is more likely to be a shortage of arable land than a scarcity of water; this too, presumably, would vary from one basin to another. The apparent productive precocity of the coast, detailed earlier in this paper, may be merely an artifact of inadequate comparative research and thus a function of lack of data. At present, the phenomenon that the irrigated areas of Mesoamerica were nuclear, and those of Peru apparently marginal, cannot be satisfactorily explained, but only noted as one of a number of outstanding problems in the interpretation of the development of pre-Columbian civilization in the New World.

V. Conclusions

The aims of this paper have been largely explanatory. We have attempted to provide a conceptual framework for clarifying the interrelationships of agricultural productivity, demography, the internal dynamics of certain kinds of society, and the relationships between societies. Cultural evolution is seen ultimately as the result of a series of ecological processes operating in time, to intensify or to neutralize each other. No single practice or trait can be assigned as a priori causal preeminence; but some kinds of causal parameters will be more powerful determinants of development than will others. The most important characteristic of the ecological method lies in its broadly interactive approach, which includes consideration of certain kinds of sociopolitical factors as part of the total ecosystem of a people. Thus, it is not the existence of irrigation agriculture as an entity to which causation can be uncritically attributed that concerns us. We ask instead what its repercussions are throughout the ecosystem in particular cases and, thus, by relying on process and function rather than on form, we may examine other cultural phenomena which may, under specified circumstances, produce similar effects.

Irrigation, for cultivators in arid lands, has its initial impact on the productive cycle itself. So too may other technological practices. Conversely, an artifact or structure may represent some cultural means of water control but lack impact on the productive potential of the environment. Coe's (1968:64) stone drain at San Lorenzo is such an example; so is the system of drains observed at Teotihuacan. These represent energy utilization by a population in exactly the way a colossal stone head or a pyramid does: the materials used must be collected, and energy is expended to give these raw materials their final form. While there are practical advantages to removing the rainwater from one's patio, these do not increase the total energy content of the society. Thus, not all observed technology of water control can be analyzed in the same manner. Processes and functional implications as well as form must be considered; not all water control necessarily represents investment of energy that produces more energy.

Besides their impact on productivity in many instances of their occurrence, artificial water works are significant because they represent not only a critical resource on which a greater or lesser percentage of the population depends, but also a critical resource which is controllable with great ease. Irrigation is not unique in this respect. Any factor on which a population is dependent may at some level of demographic growth impose a ceiling on further expansion, but some kinds of resources are more subject to technological and sociological controls than are others. Particularly in some phases of demographic expansion, access to trade routes may function as an equally, or nearly equally, vital resource. Where populations have grown to the point where egalitarian direction of trade relations is no longer sufficient to secure regular and consistent access to goods needed but not locally produced, access to trade institutions may stimulate both a nonegalitarian social structure and some degree of economic centralization. This seems to have been the case in Middle Formative Mesoamerica, as we have previously observed. A similar interpretation is the basis of Steward's (1955b) treatment of a Teotihuacan for which, at the time, no substantive evidence existed to support its status as an Irrigation Civilization. The basis of political power may lie in the controllability of the "lifeline" of the population in the ecosystem in question, whatever that lifeline may be. The impact of irrigation in this respect is extremely powerful, but under certain conditions other parameters may operate, to a greater or lesser extent, to produce similar effects.

The relationship between irrigation and centralization is therefore not considered unique. Both centralization of authority and internal social differentiation may be responses to a number of different empirical factors. While irrigation agriculture is inefficient without cooperative effort, such cooperation may be stimulated, again in certain stated demographic and geographic contexts, by other factors. Access to markets, as cited, may be such a factor, especially in areas of close microgeographic zoning where intense specialization has been a response to population growth and a solution to the problem of maximizing overall production. The economy of each component of such a symbiotic region (Sanders, 1956) depends on regular access to the produce of all other components. Although swidden agriculture, as another example, is usually regarded as strongly centrifugal, the approach of the demographic ceiling may be accompanied by centralized control of the agricultural cycle and the allocation of farmland. There is some indication that this or a related process may have been operative in Late Classic Maya society. The point is that environmental circumscription which deters expansion may be sociological as well as strictly geographical. Under such conditions, the land itself becomes controllable, far more so than is usually characteristic of swidden systems. In circumstances where increasing numbers depend on a resource available in limited supply, that resource becomes more controllable sociologically than it would otherwise be; sanctions may be applied easily and made to stick.

The sociocultural effects of irrigation are, as we have noted, very powerful in all these respects. They will be especially powerful where the combination of geography and productive technology permit, in time, the expansion of small local systems—and small local populations—into large supralocal ones. But irrigation is not unique in this respect. The approach we advocate is an essentially multilinear one: it cannot be assumed that "the same" trait formally defined will always behave functionally in the same way in all ecosystems. "The same" trait may be a response to different challenges in different contexts. Similarly, traits that are formally quite different may, depending upon total context, produce quite similar kinds of effects. These are necessarily matters for empirical determination.

Bibliography

ADAMS, ROBERT M.

1960 "Factors Influencing the Rise of Civilization in the Alluvium: Illustrated by Mesopotamia." In: *City Invincible.* Carl H. Kraeling and Robert M. Adams, eds. Chicago.

1966 *The Evolution of Urban Society: Early Mesopotamia and Prehispanic Mexico.* Chicago.

ARMILLAS, PEDRO

1948 "A Sequence of Cultural Development in Mesoamerica," In: *A Reappraisal of Peruvian Archaeology.* Wendell C. Bennett, ed. Menasha: Society for American Archaeology, Memoir No. 4:105–111.

1951 "Tecnologia, formaciones socioeconómicas y religión en Mesoamérica." In: *The Civilizations of Ancient America* (XXIX International Congress of Americanists). Sol Tax, ed. Chicago.

ASCHMANN, HOMER

1962 "Evaluations of Dry Land Environments by Societies at Various Levels of Technical Competence." In: *Civilizations in Desert Lands.* Richard B. Woodbury, ed. University of Utah, Department of Anthropology: Anthropological Papers, No. 62:1–14.

BENNETT, WENDELL C.

1948 "The Peruvian Co-tradition." In: *A Reappraisal of Peruvian Archaeology.* Wendell C. Bennett, ed. Menasha: Society for American Archaeology, Memoir No. 4:1–7.

BINFORD, SALLY R., and LEWIS R. BINFORD, eds.

1968 *New Perspectives in Archeology.* Chicago.

BOSERUP, ESTER

1965 *The Conditions of Agricultural Growth.* Chicago.

BRAIDWOOD, ROBERT J., and BRUCE HOWE

1962 "Southwestern Asia Beyond the Lands of the Mediterranean Littoral." In: *Courses toward Urban Life.* Robert J. Braidwood and Gordon R. Willey, eds. Chicago.

BRAIDWOOD, ROBERT J., and CHARLES A. REED

1957 "The Achievement and Early Consequences of Food Production." In: *Cold Spring Harbor Symposia on Quantitative Biology.* 22:19–31.

BRUNET, JEAN

1967 "Geologic Studies." In: *The Prehistory of the Tehuacan Valley.* Douglas S. Byers, gen. ed. Austin. 1:66–90.

CARNEIRO, ROBERT

1961 "Slash and Burn Cultivation among the Kui-Kuru and its Implications for Cultural Development in the Amazon Basin." *Anthropologia.* No. 10.

CHILDE, V. GORDON

1946 *What Happened in History.* New York.

1950 "The Urban Revolution." *Town Planning Review.* 21.

COE, MICHAEL D.

1964 "The Chinampas of Mexico." *Scientific American.* 211:1:90–98.

1968 "San Lorenzo and the Olmec Civilization." In: *Dumbarton Oaks Conference on the Olmec.* Elizabeth P. Benson, ed. Washington.

COE, MICHAEL D., and KENT V. FLANNERY

1964 "Microenvironments and Mesoamerican Prehistory." *Science.* 143:3607:650–654.

1967 *Early Cultures and Human Ecology in South Coastal Guatemala.* Washington: Smithsonian Contributions to Anthropology. 3.

COLLIER, DONALD

1955 "Development of Civilization on the Coast of Peru." In: *Irrigation Civilizations: A Comparative Study.* Julian H. Steward, ed. Washington.

DAY, KENT C.

1970 *Walk-in Wells and Water Management at Chan Chan, Peru.* XXXIX Congreso Internacional de Americanistas. Lima.

DURKHEIM, EMILE

1933 *The Division of Labor in Society.* George Simpson, trans. New York.

FLANNERY, KENT V.

1968a "Archeological Systems Theory and Early Mesoamerica." In: *Anthropological Archeology in the Americas.* Washington.

1968b "The Olmec and the Valley of Oaxaca." In: *Dumbarton Oaks Conference on the Olmec.* Elizabeth P. Benson, ed. Washington.

FLANNERY, KENT V., ANNE V. T. KIRKBY, MICHAEL J. KIRKBY, and AUBREY W. WILLIAMS, JR.

1967 "Farming Systems and Political Growth in Ancient Oaxaca." *Science.* 158:3800:445–454.

FOWLER, MELVIN L.

1966 *The Temple Town Community: Cahokia and Amalucan Compared.* XXVII International Congress of Americanists, Mar del Plata, Argentina. (In press).

1969 "A Preclassic Water Distribution System in Amalucan, Mexico." *Archaeology.* 22:3:208–215.

FRIED, MORTON H.

1960 "On the Evolution of Social Stratification and the State." In: *Culture in History: Essays in Honor of Paul Radin.* Stanley Diamond, ed. New York.

1967 *The Evolution of Political Society.* New York.

GAMIO, MANUEL

1922 *La Población del Valle de Teotihuacan, México.* 3 vols. México.

GEERTZ, CLIFFORD

1963 *Agricultural Involution: The Process of Ecological Change in Indonesia.* Berkeley.

GRAY, R. F.

1963 *The Sonjo of Tanganyika.* London.

HARRIS, MARVIN

1968 *The Rise of Anthropological Theory.* New York.

HOLE, FRANK, and ROBERT F. HEIZER

1969 *An Introduction to Prehistoric Archeology.* 2nd ed. New York.

KIDDER, ALFRED V. II

1964 "South American High Cultures." In: *Prehistoric Man in the New World.* Jesse D. Jennings and Edward Norbeck, eds. Chicago.

KIDDER, ALFRED V. II, LUIS A. LUMBRERAS, and DAVID B. SMITH

1963 "Cultural Development in the Central Andes—Peru and Bolivia." In: *Aboriginal Cultural Development in Latin America: An Interpretative Review.* Betty J. Meggers and Clifford Evans, eds. Washington: Smithsonian Institution Miscellaneous Collections. 1:89–117.

KOSOK, PAUL

1965 *Life, Land and Water in Ancient Peru.* New York.

KROEBER, ALFRED L.

1939 *Cultural and Natural Areas of Native North America.* Berkeley. University of California Publications in American Archaeology and Ethnology.

LANNING, EDWARD P.

1967 *Peru before the Incas.* Englewood Cliffs, N.J.

LEACH, E. R.

1961 *Pul Eliya: A Village in Ceylon.* Cambridge.

LEWIS, OSCAR

1951 *Life in a Mexican Village: Tepoztlan Restudied.* Urbana.

MACNEISH, RICHARD S.

1964 "Ancient Mesoamerican Civilization." *Science.* 143:3606:531–537.

MEGGERS, BETTY J.

1954 "Environmental Limitation on the Development of Culture." *American Anthropologist.* 56: 5:801–824.

MILLON, RENÉ F.

1954 "Irrigation at Teotihuacan." *American Antiquity.* 20:2:177–180.

1962 "Variations in Response to the Practice of Irrigation Agriculture." In: *Civilizations in Desert Lands.* Richard B. Woodbury, ed. University of Utah, Department of Anthropology: Anthropological Papers, No. 62:56–58.

1967 "Teotihuacan." *Scientific American.* 216:6: 38–48.

MILLON, RENÉ F., CLARA HALL, and MAY DIAZ

1962 "Conflict in the Modern Teotihuacan Irrigation System," *Comparative Studies in Society and History.* 4:4.

MOOSER, FEDERICO

1968 "Geología, naturaleza y desarrollo del Valle de Teotihuacan." In: *Materiales para la Arqueología de Teotihuacan.* José L. Lorenzo, ed. México: Instituto Nacional de Antropología e Historia, Investigaciones, No. 17:29–38.

MOSELEY, M. EDWARD

1969 "Assessing the Archaeological significance of *mahamaes,*" *American Antiquity.* 34:4:485–487.

NEELY, JAMES A.

1967 *Formative, Classic and Post-Classic Water Control and Irrigation Systems in the Valley of Oaxaca.* 32nd annual meeting of the Society for American Archaeology. Ann Arbor, Mich.

ORLANDINI, RICHARD J.

1967 *A Formative Well from the Valley of Oaxaca.* 32nd annual meeting of the Society for American Archaeology. Ann Arbor, Mich.

PALERM, ANGEL

1955 "The Agricultural Basis of Urban Civilization in Mesoamerica." In: *Irrigation Civilizations: A Comparative Study.* Julian H. Steward, ed. Washington.

PALERM, ANGEL, and ERIC R. WOLF

1957 "Ecological Potential and Cultural Development in Mesoamerica." In: *Studies in Human Ecology.* Washington.

PARSONS, JAMES J., and WILLIAM M. DENEVAN

1967 "Pre-Columbian Ridged Fields." *Scientific American.* 217:1:92–100.

PARSONS, JEFFREY R.

1968 "The Archaeological Significance of *mahamaes* Cultivation on the Coast of Peru." *American Antiquity.* 33:1:80–85.

n.d. Prehispanic Settlement Patterns in the Texcoco Region, Mexico. (Mimeographed).

PARSONS, LEE A.

1969 *Bilbao, Guatemala: An Archaeological Study of the Pacific Coast Cotzumalhuapa Region.* 2. Milwaukee Public Museum, Publications in Anthropology, No. 12.

PARSONS, LEE A., and BARBARA J. PRICE

1970 *Mesoamerican Trade and its Role in the Emergence of Civilization.* Paper presented at Burg Wartenstein Symposium No. 47, Burg Wartenstein, Austria.

PATTERSON, THOMAS C.

n.d. The emergence of food production in Central Peru. (Unpublished *ms.*).

PATTERSON, THOMAS C., and EDWARD P. LANNING

1964 "Changing Settlement Patterns on the Central Peruvian Coast." *Ñawpa Pacha.* 2:113–123.

PRICE, BARBARA L.

1971 "Prehispanic Irrigation Agriculture in Nuclear America," *Latin American Research Review.* 6:3:3–60.

SANDERS, WILLIAM T.

1956 "The Central Mexican Symbiotic Region." In: *Prehistoric Settlement Patterns in the New World.* Gordon R. Willey, ed. New York.

1957 Tierra y Agua. (Ph.D. dissertation, Harvard University).

1965 Cultural Ecology of the Teotihuacan Valley. Pennsylvania State University, Department of Anthropology (multilith).

1968 "Hydraulic Agriculture, Economic Symbiosis and the Evolution of States in Central Mexico." In: *Anthropological Archeology in the Americas.* Washington.

SANDERS, WILLIAM T., and BARBARA J. PRICE

1968 *Mesoamerica: The Evolution of a Civilization.* New York.

SMITH, C. T., W. M. DENEVAN, and P. HAMILTON

1968 "Ancient Ridged Fields in the Region of Lake Titicaca." *The Geographical Journal.* 134: Part 3: 353–367.

STEWARD, JULIAN H.

1949 "Cultural Causality and Law: A Trial Formu-

lation of the Development of Early Civilizations." *American Anthropologist.* 51:1:1–27.
1955a *Theory of Culture Change.* Urbana.
1955b "Some Implications of the Symposium." In: *Irrigation Civilizations: A Comparative Study.* Julian H. Steward, ed. Washington.

TOLSTOY, PAUL, and LOUISE I. PARADIS
1970 "Early and Middle Preclassic Culture in the Basin of Mexico." *Science.* 167:3917:344–351.

WEST, ROBERT, and PEDRO ARMILLAS
1950 "Las chinampas de México." *Cuadernos Americanos.* 50.

WHITE, LESLIE A.
1949 *The Science of Culture.* New York.
1959 *The Evolution of Culture.* New York.

WILLEY, GORDON R.
1953 *Prehistoric Settlement Patterns in the Viru Valley, Peru.* Washington.

WITTFOGEL, KARL A.
1955 "Developmental Aspects of Hydraulic Societies." In: *Irrigation Civilizations: A Comparative Study.* Julian H. Steward, ed. Washington.
1957 *Oriental Despotism: A Study in Total Power.* New Haven.

WOLF, ERIC R.
1966 *Peasants.* Englewood Cliffs, N.J.

WOLF, ERIC R., and ANGEL PALERM
1955 "Irrigation in the Old Acolhua Domain, Mexico." *Southwestern Journal of Anthropology.* 11:3:265–281.

SEVEN

EXPLORATIONS IN CULTURAL ANTHROPOLOGY

22

AN ECOLOGICAL APPROACH IN CULTURAL ANTHROPOLOGY

ANDREW P. VAYDA

Ecology is one of the pet phrases of our times. It is the hula hoop of our contemporary vocabulary, and we know what happened to the hula hoop. But the question of ecology is somewhat different from other fads—if it is unheeded or if the messages delivered in its name go unheard. If it is forgotten, our species might die, our world become yet another uninhabited planet. We are familiar with the dire predictions and, even if some politicians and businessmen insist that present concern about ecology is only another communist plot to "get" America, some of us recycle our glass and paper and take additional moments of care when purchasing detergents.

Ecology is not a new concept in anthropology. It is, however, a most strategic and important one and its weight is being felt in every major field of the discipline with the possible exception of linguistics. As the following selection shows, one of the most serious consequences of ecological thinking in anthropology is its tendency to drive scholars out of narrow ruts into broad construals of their problems. Armed with an ecological point of view, a social scientist sees an economic problem in social, political, and ideological contexts, or looks upon religious rituals as the expression of underlying inputs of diverse cultural and even noncultural nature.

Although brief and succinct, Vayda's overview of the ecological approach in modern cultural anthropology serves to orient the reader to much that is discussed in greater detail in the selections that follow.

▼△▼△▼

Ecological studies are concerned with relations between living organisms and their environment. Their environment comprises not only land, water, and other components of the physical environment but also the biotic environment, that is, other living organisms. A characteristic focus in ecological studies is upon relations between organisms belonging to different species, and there has, for example, been much work describing which species eat which other species in so-called food chains or food webs.

The main relevance of ecological studies to cultural anthropology derives from the fact that the behavioral as well as the physical traits of organisms are important in their relations with their environments and that, in the case of man, much behavior involved in such relations is learned behavior that has become part of the repertoire of responses of particular human groups. It is, in other words, cultural behavior. By showing connections between such behavior and the environment of the behaving people, we help to make cultural practices intelligible and, in doing so, we are meeting basic objectives of cultural anthropology.

For convenience, two main ways of showing connections between the environment and cultural behavior may be distinguished: either showing that particular cultural practices function as parts of systems that also include environmental phenomena or else showing that the environmental phenomena are responsible in some manner for the origin or development of the practices under investigation. The first approach helps to make cultural practices intelligible by showing something about how they work, but it does not necessarily contribute to answering the questions about their evolution

SOURCE: "An Ecological Approach in Cultural Anthropology," *Bucknell Review,* 17 (1969):112–19. This article is based on a copyrighted lecture recorded for the Institute for University Studies, Inc., Fort Lee, N.J. Reprinted by permission of Institute for Universal Studies, Inc. and the author.

to which the second approach is directed.[1] In this article, my main concern will be with illustrating the first approach.

Looking at the relations between cultural and environmental phenomena is of course nothing new. The ancient Greeks wrote on the subject and made suggestions on matters as varied as the influence of seasonal changes on labor patterns [2] and the influence of a harsh environment on the development of music and dance.[3] But although the concern with the relations between cultural and environmental phenomena is old and, by now, well established, viewing these relations in what may be designated as a "systems" frame is relatively new. Such an approach marks a departure from the timeworn practice of looking for one-way cause-to-effect sequences from environmental to cultural phenomena and puts the emphasis instead on the nature and operation of systems having components that relate to one another not so much in one-way processes as in feedback ones. Much of the interest in such systems has developed since World War Two and has, no doubt, been stimulated by the advances in cybernetics, computer technology, and related fields.

The presumption is that these systems with interacting cultural and environmental components are generally the products of processes of evolutionary selection. However, as I have already suggested, it is possible to analyze the operation of the systems without having to analyze, at the same time, the events and processes that have brought the systems into being. Accordingly, in the examples I shall give, my concern will be not with the genesis of the system but rather with showing how their operation has been interpreted as involving the interaction of cultural and environmental components.

A relatively simple example concerning a North American Indian hunting people may be noted first. The Naskapi are Indians of the Labrador peninsula who use animal shoulder blades in divination. This practice has been interpreted by the sociologist Omar Khayyam Moore as a part of a system contributing to success in hunting caribou and other game.[4] Specifically, Moore notes that when the Naskapi become uncertain about where to find game and when, accordingly, their food supplies are running low, they hold a specially prepared caribou or beaver shoulder blade over hot coals. The heat produces cracks and burnt spots in the bone and these signify to the hunters the direction in which they must move to look for game. Moore sees this as contributing to success in hunting by serving to randomize the choice of hunting sites and thereby to prevent the Naskapi from regularly going to hunt where they had previously been successful and where, accordingly, the animals may have become sensitized to human beings and have learned to avoid them more effectively than in other places. In other words, the recourse to divination saves the Naskapi from success-induced failure in hunting. The main point Moore seeks to make with this interpretation is that, as he says, "some practices which have been classified as magic may well be directly efficacious as techniques for attaining the ends envisaged by their practitioners." The point of greatest interest for us, however, is that the interpretation sets forth a system in which the recourse to such cultural practices as divination is affected by and, in turn, affects such environ-

[1] Studies representative of both approaches are included in *Environment and Cultural Behavior: Ecological Studies in Cultural Anthropology*, ed. Andrew P. Vayda (Garden City, N.Y., Natural History Press, 1969). Among the articles reprinted in the volume are three that are cited in the present paper: the articles by Omar Khayyam Moore, Roy A. Rappaport, and Charles Wagley.

[2] Hippocrates, "On Airs, Waters, and Places," in *The Genuine Works of Hippocrates*, trans. Francis Adams (Baltimore, 1939), pp. 36–37.

[3] *The Histories of Polybius*, trans. Evelyn E. Shuckburgh (London, 1889), I, 297–298, Book IV, Sect. 21.

[4] "Divination—A New Perspective," *American Anthropologist*, 59 (1957), 69–74.

mental phenomena as the spatial distribution of game animals.

A possibly more complicated example concerns changes of residence as a response to witchcraft accusations or suspicions in parts of tribal Africa. This kind of response has been interpreted by at least some anthropologists as operating within a system that has environmental as well as cultural components.[5] The witchcraft accusations or suspicions are viewed as expressions of in-group tensions that result from increasing intra-group competition for resources and a diminishing per capita food supply, and these in turn are regarded as the concomitants of an increasing pressure of population upon the land. When some tribesmen move away, either because they themselves are accused of being witches or because they feel that they have to get away from other people they suspect of witchcraft, the effect is to reduce the pressure of population upon the land and this can mean that the diminution of per capita food supply and the increase of intragroup competition over resources are arrested and that in-group tensions and their expression in witchcraft accusations and suspicions are kept within tolerable limits. The system can be viewed as operating to maintain favorable man-land ratios and to prevent local overpopulation and an associated over-exploitation and deterioration of resources.

A final example concerns the ritual slaughter of pigs in New Guinea, particularly in the highlands and adjacent regions. Two important contexts in which such slaughter takes place are: (1) great festivals at which large numbers of pigs are killed and guests stuff themselves with pork; and (2) situations of misfortune or emergency which call for the sacrifice of one or a few pigs to ancestor spirits. As interpreted by some anthropologists, the slaughters in one context have a systemic relation to the slaughters in the other.[6] The great festivals are, for the festival hosts, occasions for paying off obligations and gaining prestige through presentations of pork. Accordingly, a major motivation for accumulating pigs is to have them for the great festivals. However, pigs intended for slaughter in the festivals are disposed of earlier if misfortunes or emergencies so require. That is to say, if people are suffering from certain severe illnesses or injuries or if warfare is about to be undertaken, then various spirits must be immediately placated by being presented with the souls of pigs. The flesh of the sacrificial animals is retained for consumption by the individuals suffering from illness or injury or otherwise undergoing stress and, as the anthropologist Roy A. Rappaport has pointed out, is probably important for counteracting the stress-induced increase in these individuals' catabolization of protein; the negative nitrogen balancing resulting from this increase, if not offset by the ingestion of high-quality proteins, may impair the healing of wounds and the production of antibodies and have other physically harmful consequences for people on low-protein diets.[7] From the fact that the misfortunes or emergencies call for the immediate sacrifice of pigs, it follows that if these stress situations are frequent, the festivals must be postponed because of insufficient pigs. In other words, when a festival does take place, it is, among other things, because the expansion of the pig population has not had to be curtailed through frequent ritual slaughters of pigs in connection with misfortunes or emer-

[5] See Andrew P. Vayda and Roy A. Rappaport, "Ecology, Cultural and Noncultural," in *Introduction to Cultural Anthropology: Essays in the Scope and Methods of the Science of Man,* ed. James A. Clifton (Boston, 1968), pp. 491–492.

[6] Roy A. Rappaport, *Pigs for the Ancestors: Ritual in the Ecology of a New Guinea People* (New Haven, Conn., 1967 [1968]), Chapters 3 and 5; Rappaport, "Ritual Regulation of Environmental Relations among a New Guinea People," *Ethnology,* 6 (1967), 17–30; Andrew P. Vayda, "The Pig Complex," in *Encyclopaedia of Papua and New Guinea* (Melbourne, in press).

[7] *Pigs for the Ancestors,* pp. 84–87; "Ritual Regulation of Environmental Relations," p. 22.

gencies. The festivals are held when the people have had good fortune for a number of years and when, accordingly, the pigs may have become "too much of a good thing" for them. Indeed, expanding pig populations increasingly compete with human beings for garden food and their care calls for larger and larger outlays of energy by the pig-keepers in such activities as providing food for the pigs and building fences to keep them out of gardens. Thus, the lavish festival slaughters, which may seem wasteful in the short run, serve in the long run to maintain a balance among pigs, people, and garden crops.

Although we could consider numerous other examples (including some massively complex ones from both the modern and the primitive world), these three examples of systems with interacting cultural and environmental components should suffice for purposes of illustration. At this point, some cautions must be sounded concerning the significance of the examples.

One caution is to note that the data available at present are insufficient for making a firm conclusion that the systems in the examples do in fact operate in the described manner. The available data do not disagree with the interpretations presented, but for firm conclusions we need much more extensive observation for measurement of the systemic variables than has so far been obtained. There is a task for the future here, and it may be noted that it is a task which requires scientists to move outside the traditional boundaries of their disciplines. For instance, the interpretation concerning New Guinea pig slaughters calls for quantitative data on such diverse variables as human protein levels, energy expenditure, soil fertility, rate of reforestation of farmed land, and natality, mortality, immigration, and emigration of pigs as well as people. Although there are ways of obtaining the needed data on all of these variables, it is doubtful whether any single investigator would have the capacity to obtain them. The task for the future is best seen as one for coordinated research by investigators from a variety of disciplines.

The fact that in the three examples given the cultural and environmental variables are interpreted to be interacting to the material advantage of human populations makes it necessary to sound some other cautions. One of these is a warning against assuming that the systemic interacting of cultural and environmental variables *always* works to the material advantage of human populations. There are several kinds of situations in which this need not be so. First of all, there are cases of significant change in the setting in which a system operates without concomitant change in the system itself, and the effect of this sometimes is to make an advantageous or adaptive system into a disadvantageous or maladaptive one. An example of this might be the persistence of systems involving such population-limiting devices as the cultural practice of infanticide among certain South American Indians whose early contacts with Europeans and their decimating diseases were making underpopulation rather than overpopulation a critical problem.[8]

Somewhat similar are cases where something crucial is eliminated from a system without its being replaced by something else. For example, the registration of land titles and the establishment of more or less permament land boundaries by colonial or new national administrations can have the effect of tying people to the land they have and thereby eliminating migration as a response to witchcraft accusations or suspicions in the system previously described. The system remaining may continue to operate at least for a while and may produce more and more ten-

[8] Charles Wagley, "Cultural Influences on Population: A Comparison of Two Tupí Tribes," *Revista do Museu Paulista*, n.s., 5 (1951), 95–104.

sion and accusations of witchcraft and progressively deteriorating resources and unfavorable man-land ratios.

Finally, there are cases of systems that are probably best regarded as erroneous trials in the trial-and-error process which is an essential part of cultural evolution. An example of this might be various Melanesian cult systems involving the destruction of pigs and other traditional economic goods at the behest of prophets searching for ways of obtaining the goods and other material advantages of the European foreigners.[9] The failure of particular cult systems to deliver the rewards sought leads eventually to their abandonment, and new trials in the trial-and-error process are then made.

Just as it cannot be assumed that *all* systems with interacting cultural and environmental components work to the material advantage of human populations, it also cannot be assumed that any system which *does* work to such advantage is the best possible system. One might think that no warning against this last assumption would be needed. However, since theorists or analysts concerned with showing the functions or advantages of extant systems have often been accused of adhering to just such an assumption and of thereby being opponents of change and defenders of the status quo, it becomes necessary to make explicit the rejection of the assumption.[10] The concern with showing the functions or advantages of extant systems is thoroughly consistent with subscribing to theories of change or evolution which recognize that the replacement of advantageous or adaptive systems by more advantageous or more adaptive ones is as much a feature of the evolutionary process as is the eventual elimination of plainly maladaptive systems. Such theories lead us to expect both that extant systems with interacting cultural and environmental components will sooner or later be replaced and that, at present, these systems may still confer some of the advantages that made them superior to the earlier systems which they had supplanted.[11] Far from being inimical to change, the study of systems, their operation, and their possible advantages, especially the study of systems succeeding one another, can contribute significantly to the understanding of change itself.

There is much more to be said on the subject of change and the uses of ecology in studying it, but in order not to obscure the main point in this article, I forbear from pursuing these topics further. The main point is simply that we can enhance our understanding of cultural practices by viewing them as operating within such systems as I have given examples of. Our understanding is, in other words, enhanced when we are able to regard cultural practices such as divination, witchcraft accusations, and ritual pig slaughters not as the exotic expressions of essentially inexplicable cultural values or interests but rather as systemic components in the culture-carriers' relations with the environment from which they draw the energy and materials upon which their lives and culture depend.

[9] Cf. Peter Worsley, *The Trumpet Shall Sound: A Study of "Cargo" Cults in Melanesia*, 2nd ed. (New York, 1968); Ben R. Finney, "Bigfellow Man Belong Business in New Guinea," *Ethnology*, 7 (1968), 407.

[10] See John W. Bennett, "On the Cultural Ecology of Indian Cattle," *Current Anthropology*, 8 (1967), 251–252; and the citations in Robert K. Merton, *Social Theory and Social Structure*, Rev. ed. (Glencoe, Ill., 1957), pp. 37–38.

[11] Marvin Harris has made an analysis of how the contemporary system of husbanding the religiously venerated cows of India functions to provide traction, dairy products, and dung for fuel and fertilizer ("The Cultural Ecology of India's Sacred Cattle," *Current Anthropology*, 7 [1966], 51–66). In response to a critic of the analysis, Harris says: "Low-energy agrarian cultures are undoubtedly doomed . . . because there is selection in favor of more efficient techno-environmental and techno-economic arrangements." At the same time, he notes that "in comparison with 'tribal cultures,' the ecosystem of contemporary India is a radical evolutionary advance" (*ibid.*, 8 [1967], 252–253).

23

POPULATION ANTHROPOLOGY: PROBLEMS AND PERSPECTIVES

MONI NAG

Demography is the statistical study of populations, says the dictionary, relating to births, marriages, mortality, health, and so on. It is really quite surprising that it has taken anthropologists so long to involve themselves more than superficially in demographic problems; certainly there was a generally quicker response among sociologists. For a long time anthropologists contented themselves with background applications of demographic data. Thus, ethnographers studying particular villages or residential clusters were expected to refer in their monographs to some sort of census data, thereby setting a general scene for their detailed social analyses and cultural descriptions. Yet, even here, the level of competence often fell short and only very sketchy and at times dubious population data have been recorded. A second popular demographic problem that has recurred for some time among anthropologists has to do with the attempt to estimate population sizes for civilizations and cultures no longer present, at least not in previously attained forms. For example, several anthropologists have tried to estimate the populations of North and South America prior to European contact, or Australia before such contact. The use of demographic data in theory building has already appeared in selection 21, by Barbara Price.

There are many reasons for anthropologists to develop professionally specialized interests in demography and in problems of population in even broader and less statistical senses. In the article that follows, a pioneer in the anthropological study of populations looks over his field.

▼△▼△▼

SOURCE: This selection was specially prepared for inclusion in this volume.

During the last few hundred thousand years human beings have spread themselves into almost all parts of the surface of the earth and have achieved a population size of more than three and a half billion. The rate of growth of the human population has *not* been uniform throughout history, nor have those of the societies comprising it. Some societies have become extinct, most have experienced periodic ups and downs in population size. The process of growth of the total world population is still only partially comprehended. Furthermore, reconstruction of more local population histories involves various problems of considerable magnitude.

While scholars from many fields may contribute substantially towards reconstructing the history of human population dynamics and understanding its determinants and consequences, anthropologists have their own contributions to make. These are closely related to some of the central concepts with which anthropologists are concerned, e.g., culture itself, cultural evolution, and ecological adaptation, to name but three. What follows, then, is a brief review of some important contributions which have been already made or can be made by cultural anthropologists in three critical areas of population study: 1) long-term history of population dynamics; 2) demographic processes in primitive and peasant societies; and 3) population (size, density, and pressure) and culture.

Long-Term History of Population Dynamics

Anthropologists have questioned the validity of the human population growth curve usually presented by demographers (Durand 1967:3), which shows a drastic increase in world population since about 1750 or so and a very slow but gradual increase up to that time. Anthropologists recognize that a population upsurge started with the industrial revolution but they tend to agree with Deevey (1960:198) that humanity experienced at least two other upsurges in population size at the advent of two previous technological revolutions, namely, the tool-making revolution and the agricultural revolution, and that there was an approach towards equilibrium in the two interrevolutionary periods of the past. Polgar (1972) goes further in suggesting the possibility of several other major population expansions before the advent of agriculture, but the empirical evidence of those expansions is still very meager. Several anthropologists of past generations (e.g., Kroeber 1948:389; Childe 1964:73) found it logical to assume that the agricultural revolution produced a spurt of population growth. Braidwood and Reed (1957) provided some archeological and ethnological evidence to estimate the population concentration in different developmental levels of Old World culture history. According to them, the density of population rose sequentially through the stages of "natural" food gathering, "specialized" food collecting, primary village farming, and primary urban community; the figures given were 3.0, 12.5, 2,500, and 5,000 people per 100 square miles respectively. On the basis of ethnographic sources, Kroeber (1948:389–90) estimated that the average density of population per 100 square miles was 10 in the nonfarming areas of indigenous America north of Mexico, 26 in the farming areas of the same region, and 700 among intensively settled villages in ancient nuclear Mexico. According to Carneiro and Hilse (1966:179), the average annual rate of population growth for the Near East from 8000 B.C. to 4000 B.C. (the period following the agricultural revolution) was between 0.8 and 1.2 per 1,000; according to Polgar (1972), the average rate during all of preceding human evolution was below .03 per 1,000. These estimates are, however, based on assumptions that require much further research for satisfactory validation. Even though we may recognize a general association between increases in population density and the evolution of subsistence technologies, much controversy remains concerning the causal relationships underlying this association. This issue, central to theories of cultural evolution, will be discussed in a later section.

The modern theory of "demographic transition" was developed to explain the population dynamics of western countries in the postindustrial period. From high levels of both mortality and fertility in the preindustrial period, the population of these countries settled down to low levels of mortality and fertility through a transitional stage of low mortality and high fertility levels (Thompson 1929). One of the underlying assumptions of this theory is that both the mortality and fertility levels of all preindustrial societies were generally very high. Anthropologists have questioned this assumption. For example, I have shown elsewhere that there is a great variation in the fertility levels of contemporary nonindustrial societies (Nag 1962:15–18). There is some paleopathological and ethnological evidence to suggest that the mortality level of hunting-gathering societies was not necessarily high (Polgar 1972). The high rate of population increase estimated by Birdsell (1957:52) among a few Australian tribes, out of contact with Europeans, would not be possible if they had high mortality and fertility levels (Birdsell 1957:52). These data indicate that the general assumption of a precarious balance of high birth rate and high death rate in preindustrial societies is not altogether valid.

Demographic Processes in Primitive and Peasant Societies

One of the main Malthusian propositions states that population is necessarily limited by the means of subsistence (Malthus 1914:14–19). It increases when the means of subsistence increase, unless prevented by some checks which are "resolvable into moral restraint, vice and misery." By moral restraint Malthus meant primarily voluntary postponement of marriage (sexual relations). The examples of "vice," according to Malthus, are wars and infanticide. Some checks on population, such as epidemics and famines, were categorized as "misery" by Malthus because, to him, they appeared "to arise unavoidably from the laws of nature." It is not necessary here to go into the basic truths and gross errors in his principle, except to point out that he did not foresee the tremendous burst of productivity that the following century brought forth in the western countries. He also erred in his estimate of the possibility of reducing population growth through contraceptive means (Notestein 1960: VIII–IX).

Malthus' principle refers to the relationship between population, resources, and means of subsistence, and to a few cultural and noncultural factors which may be considered as determinants of population size and density. The controversy generated by Malthus has stimulated many economists and sociologists in the last century and a half to deal seriously with population as an important variable in their respective studies; but, unfortunately, anthropologists have neglected to do so. They have traditionally conceptualized the spread of man over the surface of the earth in terms of migratory movements rather than in the framework of population growth which is a result of the balance among the three demographic processes: fertility, mortality, and migration.

It is only during recent years that anthropologists have been studying the factors which affect these processes through which, and only through which, population size and density can change. As expected, anthropological studies of population have been done mostly with reference to "primitive" and peasant societies which are generally beyond the purview of sociologically or economically oriented demographers. A few anthropologists have also taken interest in the modern family planning movements which constitute a conscious effort towards control of fertility. I shall review briefly here some of the studies done by anthropologists and other social scientists in each of these areas and also indicate a few relevant anthropological research problems. I have dealt with each demographic process separately for reasons of descriptive convenience. In reality, they affect each other, and the population dynamics of a society is a product of their constant interaction. Kunstadter's (1971) study of the populations in Northwestern Thailand provides an excellent example of such interaction.

Migration

There is no dearth of examples in human history of spontaneous migration induced by natural phenomena, such as glaciation, flood, earthquake. White (1959:286) refers to the large-scale migration of population that occurred in the Old World at the close of the last great Ice Age. He suggests that the population pressure resulting from a migration from arid areas to river valleys and oases initiated attempts to control food supply through the use of new techniques. The recognition of migration as a specific measure of population policy, is, however, not a very common phenomenon. It is interesting to note that in ancient China the schools of Confucius and a few other Chinese philosophers held the government primarily responsible for maintaining an ideal balance between land and population by moving people from overpopulated to underpopulated areas. They noted that governmental action was reinforced by spontaneous migration (United Nations 1953:21).

In Greece, Plato, while recommending 5,040 as the ideal population size of a city-state, proposed colonization elsewhere if the population grew too large in spite of restrictions on birth, and immigration if the population was diminished by wars or epidemics. Actually, the Greek city-states sent young people off to colonize the Mediterranean area and the lands around the Aegean and the Black Sea (*ibid.*:22).

Barbados, a very densely populated plantation island in the Eastern Caribbean, provides a modern example of large-scale emigration which followed the calculated policy that its government adopted in 1863 after a prolonged drought in the island (Nag 1971). For Tikopia, a Polynesian island, Firth (1963:414) records the practice of men, especially the young and unmarried, setting out on overseas voyages. Unnavigated and one-way voyages out of the islands seem to have been a common practice in Polynesia (Sharp 1963:62–74), serving the purpose of reducing population pressure in the islands.

Concern with migration through all of human history and the interminglings of peoples has been a part of the works of anthropologists for quite some time. They have tried to explain the distribution of languages and cultures in time and space in terms of the movements of peoples. According to Haddon (1912) expulsion resulting from population pressure is more important than attraction as a motivational force of migration. Kasdan (1970) summarizes the history of the continuing interest of anthropologists and sociologists in explaining migrations in terms of social, material, historical, and psychological factors. He points out that the shift from a social-psychological approach (Park 1950) to the sociological approach in the study of migration was probably initiated by anthropologists in an attempt to understand the policies of colonial administrators and the impact of western economic institutions on relatively isolated peasant and tribal societies. In addition to studying phenomena of urbanization in each context, anthropologists have been particularly interested in the changes and adjustments made in these societies when the migrants leave. The most extensive work on the subject has been carried out in Africa and the Caribbean. The concept of "networks" (social and spatial connections between individuals and groups), developed by Barnes (1954) and elaborated by Epstein (1961) and Gutkind (1965) in their studies of migration in Africa, has been utilized fruitfully in a number of migration studies presented in a recent symposium on *Migration and Anthropology* (Spencer 1970), posing a number of interesting problems about migration which require further anthropological investigation.

Mortality

It is generally agreed that the phenomenal increase in the rate of growth of population in the developing countries during recent years is mainly due to a reduction in the mortality rate caused by improvements in public health facilities, sanitation, etc. The fluctuation in the population growth of preindustrial societies is also generally accounted for by the fluctuation in mortality rate rather than the fertility rate, in situations of nil or negligible net migration. The principal factors held to be responsible for the periodic or occasional increase of mortality rate in preindustrial societies are those which have been categorized by Malthus as positive checks to population growth: famine, epidemics, and war.

Anthropologists have very rarely interested themselves in famines and epidemics. It is often assumed that there was a more secure supply of food among agriculturists and pastoralists than among hunting-gathering peoples. Yet, after closer scrutiny, it seems that there were many situations in which the risk of famine was greater among the agriculturists and pastoralists than among hunting-gathering peoples because the population units of the former were larger. Moreover, the simple agriculturists and pastoralists did not have sufficient safeguards against the failure of crops or decimation of flocks (Polgar 1964).

With regard to epidemics, it is generally accepted that these must have been less significant among hunting-gathering peoples because of the smaller size of their social groups and lesser frequency of contact between groups. The epidemic-inducing parasites that utilize man as their exclusive hosts cannot maintain themselves under these circumstances. Polgar (*ibid.*) has pointed out how the arrival of rodents and insects as permanent guests had been an unintended by-product of settled village life, how the concentration of people in preindustrial cities allowed certain microorganisms to become entirely dependent on man, and how colonialism was responsible for the transmission of these diseases to many agricultural and hunting-gathering groups in the world.

Anthropologists have shown some interest in the demographic determinants of war but have so far shown very little interest in its demographic consequences. There is general agreement (Harris 1971:226; Polgar 1972) that the conditions for bringing whole groups into total mutual hostility were probably nonexistent throughout most of the Paleolithic period and hence mortality caused by warfare is believed relatively insignificant during this period. Whatever evidence we have of armed conflicts among the contemporary hunters and gatherers tends to support this view. There is no doubt that relatively stable nucleated settlement and a few other factors associated with agriculture generated conditions favorable to armed conflicts between groups which can legitimately be called wars. Illustrations of such wars can be found in various articles written recently by Vayda (1968) and other anthropologists in a book entitled *War: The Anthropology of Armed Conflict and Aggression* (Fried *et al.* 1968). Harris (1971:228–29) argues that the principal cause of warfare among simple agriculturists is population pressure, thus viewing warfare primarily as a population regulating system. Warfare, according to him, accomplishes this in two ways: (1) by increasing the mortality rate, particularly among young males and (2) by distributing population more evenly over regions hitherto uninhabited (Vayda 1961). It is extremely difficult to prove or disprove this hypothesis. Casualties from warfare in preindustrial societies were probably quite high in some cases, but as a population regulating system, epidemics must have been more effective, at least in agricultural societies.

The practice of infanticide, a relatively well-recorded phenomenon, seems very often to have been a manifestation of population policy for the family or larger kin group. Demographers often prefer to treat infanticide as an aspect of fertility; strictly, of course, it is mortality, but its functions are more similar to fertility control (Wrigley 1969:124–25). Until fairly recent times, among the Australian aboriginals, when a mother felt that she would be unable to rear a child because she had another small child of breastfeeding age, the newborn was buried in the sand or simply allowed by the mother to die, with the approval of her husband (Spencer and Gillen 1921:39, 221). The purpose behind infanticide is very often spacing, necessitated by prolonged dependence of children on breastfeeding and by the difficulty of carrying more than one baby at a time. Among the Netsilingmuit Eskimo, girls were thought to be less economically productive than boys; female infanticide was practiced because the parents could not "afford to waste several years nursing a girl" (Balikci 1968:81). In connection with infanticide, Birdsell (1968:43) makes the following hypothesis (which is hard to test): "Difficulties of nursing and mobility in the Pleistocene may have made necessary the killing of 15–50 per cent of children born, since lactation alone would not have provided sufficient spacing of births to maintain equilibrium." In criticizing this hypothesis, Woodburn (1968:243) points out that the making of the choice of an infanticide is usually relative to the circumstances of a particular mother, not necessarily to the circumstances of the whole population, and that the female infanticide rate among the Eskimo appears to work to the disadvantage of the population in general. Montagu (1968:19) makes a very dubious generalization "that in nonliterate societies infanticide is generally not considered cruel since the newborn is believed to be not yet properly a human being." It is worthwhile to investigate cross-culturally the stage at which the fetus or newborn is considered a human being.

Infanticide is reported to have been practiced not only in hunting and gathering societies but also by many peasant societies. Pakrashi (1968) has made a survey of female infanticide in India during the eighteenth and nineteenth centuries, finding that it was practiced quite widely among certain castes of the states of Uttar Pradesh and Punjab. An investigation conducted in 1851 among the entire Chohan (Rajput) caste in the district of Mynpoorie (Uttar Pradesh) showed that there were 171 boys of six years and under per 100 girls of that age group. Female infanticide is considered to be the most likely explanation of the disparity in the sex-ratio. Pakrashi maintains that the practice of infanticide in India cannot be accepted simply as a means of elimination of surplus population, surplus, that is, in terms of available food supply; and that its root cause lies in the social structure of India characterized by institutions such as caste stratification, hypergamy, nuptial expenses, dowry, disgrace connected with the daughters remaining unmarried after attaining puberty, and others. The degree of social approval or disapproval of female infanticide in India is not well reported. Ethnographic research along with an exploration of relevant official and literary sources may yield some valuable information in this matter.

Fertility

The priority of the study of human fertility over human mortality and migration can be justified, partly, in terms of the current concern about overpopulation in many societies. Although preservation of life or reduction of mortality is not always considered a matter of supreme value in human societies, there is perhaps no human society where the members do not in general desire reduction of mortality and the prolongation of life. No society in the contemporary world will agree to check the trend towards lower mortality as a solution of the problem of overpopulation. Intersocietal or international migration is becoming more and more limited in the contemporary world for various reasons. As frontier regions are swallowed up, it appears that population control in most human societies can be achieved best by limitation of human fertility.

Carr-Saunders (1922), a British demographer, was the first to make a comprehensive study of the fertility levels of nonindustrial societies and the factors affecting them. His survey was based on the fragmentary, and hence largely unreliable, data provided by nineteenth-century anthropologists, missionaries, travelers, and others. One of his generalizations was that the fertility level of what he called "primitive races" is generally quite low. This he attributed to involuntary factors he believed widespread in the population concerned—prepubertal sexual intercourse and the prolongation of lactation. The main voluntary factors for low fertility on this level, according to him, were induced abortion and prolonged abstention from intercourse, particularly after childbirth. Ford (1945, 1952) made a cross-cultural study of reproduction in nonindustrial societies, but did not make estimates of the fertility levels of the societies in his sample. One of his important findings was that although there are customs designed to promote fertility in most of the societies in his sample, there are individual motives, such as the wish to avoid the pain, suffering, and sacrifice involved in childbearing and childrearing, that conflict with the desire for children. In his view, therefore, every society must offer rewards for bearing children sufficient to outweigh the suffering and burden involved in reproduction. In a UNESCO-sponsored study of cultural conditions affecting fertility in nonindustrial societies, Lorimer *et al.* (1954) offered the following hypotheses, among others.

1. Societies emphasizing unilineal (either patrilineal or matrilineal) descent and having corporate kinship groups tend to generate strong cultural motives for high fertility.
2. Cohesive groups, such as extended families, do not necessarily stimulate high fertility but tend to enforce conformity to societal norms.
3. Social disorganization may increase or decrease fertility, depending upon whether the disorganization favors "apathetic acceptance of circumstances" or is associated with sterility-inducing diseases.

The studies made by Lorimer *et al.* and those preceding them did not provide or use any comprehensive framework for the study of factors affecting human fertility. That is to say, without making clear the possible ways in which fertility can be affected, these studies illustrated a few specific ways by which it is affected. Davis and Blake (1956) provided a useful analytical framework for the comparative study of culture and human fertility. They identified and classified eleven "intermediate variables," such as age at marriage, fecundity, contraceptives, etc., through which, and only through which, any cultural factors influencing the level of fertility must operate. They also tried to show, in broad outline, how some types and elements of social organization, acting through these variables, appear to enhance or depress societal fertility. In my cross-cultural study of factors affecting human fertility in sixty-one selected nonindustrial societies (Nag 1962), I used the above analytical framework and found that the postpartum abstinence and sterility induced by venereal diseases were two of the important factors having significantly negative association with fertility level. My findings should be regarded as tentative since my sample of societies was not selected at random and the data provided for these societies (mostly by anthropologists), although better than those used by Carr-Saunders, were not very satisfactory. My selection of societies was limited by the fact that in addition to the data regarding many cultural factors, I needed some demographic data, especially quantitative, regarding fertility. Many ethnographies that are excellent for other purposes could not be utilized for my study. A typical example of this is Malinowski's (1929) study of the Trobriand Islanders. He discussed, in great detail, sexual behavior, adolescent sterility, contraception, and even casually suggested the hypothesis that promiscuity reduced fertility (Nag and Bedford 1969); but he failed to provide any data by which we can evaluate the fertility level of the Trobriand Islanders.

The framework provided by David and Blake was extended by Freedman (1961–62:41) to include a wider range of sociocultural and environmental influences that affect fertility through the "intermediate variables." He followed demographic tradition, beginning with variables that are or can be "hard" facts, then working out to the wider and less definite variables that influence the former. Polgar (1972) has found two major problems with this "funnel strategy": 1) the slighting of dependent variables other than birth rates and 2) the neglect of feedback effects from actual births to the "wider variables." He thinks that the implicit assumption of the existence in all societies of norms of desirable family size is an indication of the ethnocentric approach of demographers and he cites anthropological evidence that "leads" us to look for norms concerning *who should have children, when childbearing should start, what is a desirable interval between children, and at what juncture in social aging childbearing should cease.* To my understanding, the "funnel strategy" takes account of the other norms mentioned by Polgar, except that regarding the desirable interval or spacing between children. There is no doubt that adequate attention has not been given so far to the spacing of children, which is one of the main factors responsible for fertility control among the hunting-gathering and peasant societies.

Among the "intermediate variables," there are a few, such as spontaneous abortion and fecundity, that are normally beyond the regulating capacity of people, at least in primitive and peasant societies. The norms regarding some variables, such as age at marriage and abstinence, are dependent on social and cultural institutions, values, beliefs, and so on. The existing norms may affect family size or childspacing, although they may not have been intended to do so. For example, nonremarriage of widows among the high caste Hindus of India is a factor that negatively affects their fertility; but there is no belief among contemporary Hindus that the custom is intended to keep the family size low. The purpose of the same custom may be different in different societies. For example, the reason for prolonged postpartum abstinence in one society may be given as the avoidance of pregnancy until the existing baby grows up, and in another society as the danger of poisoning the mother's breast-milk. There seem to exist social institutions and practices in all known human societies that tend to keep fertility levels under biological potential. Perhaps it is also true that there are social institutions and practices in all human societies specifically intended for controlling family size and birth interval. Although these hypotheses still need further cross-cultural testing, there is some supporting historical and anthropological literature already on hand.

In their discussions of optimum population, Plato and Aristotle proposed restriction of births, if necessary (United Nations 1953:22). Aristotle mentioned abortion and child exposure as suitable means of preventing an excessive number of children. He also mentioned homosexuality as a means of population control, and homosexuality was indeed said to be practiced by the Cretans for this purpose. The ancient Romans, on the other hand, were more alert to the advantages of population growth for military and related purposes. Their writers disapproved celibacy and defended monogamous marriage. Roman legislation was aimed at raising the marriage and birth rate.

The anthropological literature shows that induced abortion is a very widespread practice in human societies. According to Carr-Saunders (1922:292) this is one of the main factors responsible for the "low" fertility level of "primitives." But it is very difficult to assess from the available literature the extent of the actual practice of abortion and how far it is or was practiced for the primary intent of limiting family size or childspacing. In a comprehensive typological and distributional analysis of abortion in 400 preindustrial societies, Devereux (1955:25–26) has remarked that "statistical data on abortion in primitive society are mostly either unavailable or else both unreliable and skimpy." There is no society in Devereux's sample that does not have some sanctions against abortion, but the degree of sanctioning varies in different societies as does the extent of the practice of abortion. Ford (1945:51) has listed a number of societies where abortion is permitted only to prevent the birth of illegitimate offspring of premarital unions. The extent of the practice of abortion seems to vary widely in both nonindustrial and industrial societies (Nag 1962:77–82). The degree of approval or disapproval of abortion may depend partly on the concept of the phase when the fetus is supposed to be imbued with life. It may also partly depend on the status and freedom enjoyed by women in a given society.

Prolonged abstinence from sexual intercourse is known to have been practiced widely in human societies. The period of postpartum abstinence has been found to be negatively associated with fertility level in nonindustrial societies (*ibid.*). Abstinence and the rhythm method are among the main methods responsible for decline of fertility in western societies. The practice of abstinence and rhythm as methods of birth control may vary according to the general attitude toward sex in various societies. It may, for example, be hypothesized that the Hindus in India are more likely to accept the rhythm method than the Muslims because the Hindus are traditionally used to ritual abstinence on various occasions throughout the year and also because of their general attitude of moderation in sexual behavior (Nag 1972).

Coitus interruptus is reported to be the most widely diffused nonappliance method of contraception in the world and "is probably nearly as old as the group life of man" (Himes 1936: 184). In the small Polynesian island of Tikopia, until recently, the heads of families were formally exhorted by the chief once a year to limit their number of children by practicing coitus interruptus (Firth 1936:492). Ryder (1959:430) suggests that it was practiced more widely in societies of preindustrial Europe than in peasant societies of Asia or in contemporary western societies. He argues that in the preindustrial European societies with conjugal familism and limited agricultural resources, marriage had to be postponed until there was sufficient guarantee for the economic viability of the union. This led unmarried couples to practice coitus interruptus in order to avoid premarital pregnancy. They continued the practice after marriage when economic difficulties arose. Their (speculated) preference for coitus interruptus over abortion and infanticide, Ryder assumes, is a reflection of their "greater respect for individual life and marriage and the more extended economic horizon" than prevalent among peoples of lower levels of science and technology. According to Petersen (1961:547), since the practice of coitus interruptus requires that the male be strongly motivated enough to frustrate his desire at the moment of highest excitation, it is expected to be less frequently practiced in societies where the economic and social responsibility for the child is borne by the broader kin group, rather than mainly by the father. It seems true that the practice is less prevalent in Asia than in Europe, but we do not have sufficient data to check whether the hypotheses suggested by Ryder and Petersen offer an adequate explanation for this difference.

The fertility regulating practices of nonindustrial societies are often ignored by demographers in their analysis of population dynamics. Population growth in these societies is considered almost exclusively as a consequence of the diminishing effect of mortality-inducing factors. Very little attention is given to the fact that at least part of the population growth may result from the lesser use of fertility regulating practices. The contact with industrial societies may mean not only the improvement of public health practices, transportation, etc., but also, at the same time, a reduction in such practices as abortion, infanticide, postpartum abstinence, and nonremarriage of widows. The reduction in the latter practices are known to have occurred in many nonindustrial societies of the world as a result of contact or indirect influence of industrial societies, but their contribution towards the growth of family size or total population is seldom recognized. The population growth in Java from the nineteenth century onward may be cited as an illustration. While Asia as a whole probably did little more than double its population during 1800 to 1961, the population of Java grew more than sixfold during this period (United Nations 1953:11; Peper 1970:84). The reasons generally given for the unusual population growth in Java point to the reduction in mortality as a result of 1) establishment of enforced peace through Dutch colonial administration, 2) elimination of famines through improved transportation of foodstuffs and 3) improvements in public health facilities (Boeke 1954:359–69; 1961:265–99; Wertheim 1950:2–4; Higgins 1958:81; Geertz 1963:81, 137). Benjamin White (*in press*), an anthropologist interested in demography, thinks it necessary to add as a factor the reduction in the practices of abortion and infanticide. Following the economic theory of population (Coontz 1957), White argues that population growth in Java was to some extent the result of an attempt on the part of the Javanese peasant to maintain his standards of living and leisure in the face of increasing Dutch demands on his land and labor. White assumes that the changes imposed by the Dutch on the Javanese economy resulted in a situation where the economic cost of producing children tended to decline, while the benefit derived from children tended to grow. Unfortunately, our knowledge about the economic and noneconomic costs of producing children and the benefits derived from them in peasant societies is extremely poor. Anthropological research on this topic will contribute towards population theories as well as towards the practical aspects of modern family planning.

Modern Family Planning

A large number of countries in the contemporary world have recently accepted family planning as a national policy, primarily for reducing their birth rates. In a number of other countries people are increasingly using birth control methods. The genetical consequences of family planning (Matsunaga 1965) are of interest to anthropologists. Perhaps more important to them is the fact that the family planning movement is a unique experiment in directed social change. Success or failure depends on various sociocultural factors and has tremendous sociocultural consequences. Yet social scientists, particularly anthropologists and psychologists, have as yet taken very little interest in family planning research. Sociologists and demographers offer a number of questionnaire surveys known as KAP studies (knowledge, attitude, and practices) related to family planning. The results obtained have been useful in removing certain misconceptions and in the initiation of national family planning programs. However, the family planning research has potential for providing wide scope to the social scientists ranging from practical needs of fertility reduction to theoretical contributions to the subject of social change. Perhaps one of the main reasons why the social scientists have not engaged seriously in family planning research is their lack of comprehension of the many aspects of this phenomenon to which they may contribute. Very few attempts have been made to propose conceptual frameworks for family planning research. I shall discuss below two such frameworks provided recently by Bogue (1966) and Marshall (1967). These are useful to anthropologists and other social scientists in identifying specific research problems in family planning.

Bogue sharply distinguishes family planning research from demographic research and defines the former as "the systematic study of the phenomenon of family planning among populations, of the processes by which the practice of family planning diffuses throughout a community or nation, and of the forces that retard or facilitate such diffusion and adoption." He identifies four subfields that family planning research is concerned with: 1) study of motives favoring and opposing family planning, 2) study of attitudes with respect to family planning, 3) study of popular knowledge about family planning, and 4) study of actual behavior with respect to family planning. Each of these subfields may be meaningfully studied in three research contexts: 1) inventory (making baseline studies), 2) explanation (testing hypotheses), and 3) evaluation (measuring change). It is clear that anthropologists living in a small community for a length of time are in a better position than other social scientists who depend only on the questionnaire type of survey to deal with the research problems falling under at least some of the twelve categories outlined above.

Analogous with the concept of stages in the acceptance or rejection process of agricultural and other innovations (Rogers 1962), Marshall (1967) has conceptualized three phases—naive, learning, and experimental—through which individuals pass as they confront family planning action programs. Each poses research problems for anthropologists and social psychologists. As an example of a research problem in the naive phase, which consists of the period of time preceding the individual's awareness and knowledge of modern contraception, Marshall cites the investigation of cultural and psychological factors predisposing attitudes towards family planning. The cultural parameters may include religious beliefs, kinship system, status structure, norms regarding marriage and sex. The psychological factors include both cognitive and affective components. The cognitive components (individual's definition of the situation in terms of his own beliefs, meaning, rules, and problem-solving strategies) reveal a "folk model" of the attitudes. The affective components (fear, desire, symbolic association, etc.) represent the emotional and evaluative aspects associated with the cognitive factor, and are probably more important ultimately in influencing the decision to accept or reject a family planning method.

The areas of research in the third or experimental phase include the differential acceptability of various techniques of family planning and factors responsible for the continuance of their use. Various hypotheses have been suggested in this field now and then, but systematic comparative research to test them has not yet been done. Some of these hypotheses and the relevant research problems are mentioned below.

COITUS-CONNECTED AND COITUS-INDEPENDENT TECHNIQUES The coitus-independent techniques are more popular than coitus-connected techniques in all human societies (Polgar 1968). The examples of coitus-independent techniques are the intrauterine device, oral contraceptives, sterilization, and abortion. Their use does not require any action at the time of sexual intercourse. Examples of coitus-connected methods are condoms, spermicidal jellies, and coitus interruptus. The coitus-connected techniques came to be widely used in nineteenth-century Western Europe and subsequently in other Western countries, but they have been far surpassed in popularity by the oral contraceptives, IUD, and sterilization since the 1960's.

STERILIZATION Differential acceptance of male and female sterilization poses a very interesting problem of research to anthropologists. India and Puerto Rico present contrasting case studies in this respect. Why is it that in India male sterilization has been so popular in the last decade and in Puerto Rico female sterilization? Indian males' anxiousness to preserve physical and spiritual strength through the conservation of semen (Nag 1972) and the existence of a culturally defined personality trait called "machismo" among Puerto Rican males (Hill, Stycos, and Back 1959:100–6) do not seem to explain the difference. It is quite possible that the acceptance or rejection of male or female sterilization is not based on any deep-rooted cultural factor but on the amount of correct knowledge regarding the nature and aftereffects of the operation and on its availability, or on the attitude of physicians.

ABORTION Various localities in the United States have recently joined Japan and a few eastern European countries in providing examples of legalization and large-scale acceptance of abortion. It is also reported to be widely practiced in a few Latin American countries in spite of legal and religious prohibitions. Are there any cultural factors that make it easier for the people of these countries to accept abortion than those of other countries?

IUD AND ORAL CONTRACEPTIVES It is reported that the continuation of vaginal bleeding beyond the usual period of menstruation is likely to be most distressing in cultures that seriously observe menstrual taboos, such as the Muslim and orthodox Jewish. Various cultural differences affecting particular side effects of the IUD or oral contraceptives have been suggested by some investigators but no systematic study has yet been undertaken to show that these are greater than the individual differences within the groups.

The failure to achieve the expected rate of birth or use of family planning methods in nonindustrial societies is often ascribed by administrators and demographers to cultural resistance of the people to the idea of family planning or to any specific method. This is usually done on the basis of some untested assumptions, and it may very well be an excuse for covering up the administrative deficiency in making the family planning services easily available to all people as well as the inadequacies of the methods in relation to a local situation. Undoubtedly there is intercultural variation in religious beliefs, values, and social structure that is associated with the variation in the motivation for using family planning. There may also be intracultural variation in this respect. For example, the bureaucratic subculture of a nation may have a different value system than that of the common people, and moreover, it may have serious misconceptions about the value system of the people. Intensive anthropological studies of small communities with a focus on the motivation for family planning have been very rare so far. The relationship between social structure and the motivation for planning poses many interesting research problems. The studies done so far on the relationship between the motivation for having children and the kinship structure, namely, descent groups and family types, are very inconclusive (Lorimer *et al.* 1954; Nag 1967, 1970; Burch and Gendell 1970). Further field investigations in various cultures are needed to have a better understanding of these relationships.

Anthropologists have so far shown more interest in the sociocultural determinants of fertility than in the sociocultural consequences of fertility change. One area of research in the consequences of fertility change, which would be of particular interest to cultural anthropologists, is the effect of reduced family size on consanguineous marriages. The temporary rise in the proportion of consanguineous marriages in two French localities at the end of the nineteenth century is ascribed to the reduction in family size (Sutter 1968). We do not know whether or not this relationship can be generalized for other societies. Lévi-Strauss (1963: 293) cites a demographic study that estimates the average size of French population "isolates" (groups of intermarrying people) as varying "from less than 1,000 to over 2,800 individuals." This seems to be too small a range compared to that existing in other industrial societies. A reduction in family size among some particular groups in a society or in the society as a whole is expected to have its impact on many aspects of its culture, such as kinship, economics, social stratification, political organization, ideology. The studies of social change in the modern world cannot afford to overlook or ignore these impacts.

Population (Size, Density, Pressure) and Culture

Most of the anthropological studies on fertility, mortality, and migration, either as distinct or as interacting processes, have been conducted in quite recent years. The interest of cultural anthropologists, along with other social scientists, in the relationship betweeen population size and density on the one hand and various aspects of culture, such as means of subsistence and social organization on the other, goes back much earlier. However, until recently this interest manifested itself generally in a superficial or casual recognition of population growth as a factor in social and cultural evolution. During the last few years, a number of anthropological studies of greater depth have come out. Those dealing with the sociocultural consequences of population growth refer mainly to four specific aspects of culture: 1) means of subsistence, 2) kinship, 3) social complexity, and 4) social stratification and political organization. A serious difficulty common to all these studies arises from the fact that the general consensus about the conceptualization and measurement of population characteristics (except population pressure) is not matched by similar agreement concerning cultural characteristics. Remarks made by Hawley (1969:190) regarding the difficulty of studying the relationship between population and society apply equally, if not more, to the study of the relationship between population and culture.

> The main difficulty lies in the great disparity between the two terms of the relationship. While population is a relatively specific variable, society, social system or social organization, however we characterize it, is a highly involuted one. There is a great deal of consensus about how to conceptualize and measure the one, but very little agreement on how to treat the other.

The studies reviewed in the following will show how cultural anthropologists have attempted to conceptualize and measure some characteristics of culture and relate them to population.

Means of Subsistence

As stated earlier, there is some ethnological and archeological evidence to suggest that population size and density increase with the evolutionary sequence of the means of subsistence. In conformity with the principles of Malthus, this relationship has been interpreted by some anthropologists to imply that population size and density are determined by improvement or innovations in the means of subsistence. According to Harris (1971:223), "the correlation between increases in techno-environmental efficiency and increases in the rate of population growth suggests that in the long run, production has determined reproduction." A few others think that the growth of population has been not determined but permitted by the improvement of learned adaptations to the environment. In these anthropological formulations, although the technological knowledge of dealing with other environmental factors is also implied, the usual emphasis is on the acquisition of foodstuffs, perhaps expressed as the harnessing of energy. From an analysis of population growth in preindustrial Europe, China, and Japan, Dumond (1965:310) suggests that the size and the growth of a population are dependent on four elements: 1) fecundity, as culturally modified; 2) incidence of disease; 3) degree of peace obtaining; and 4) subsistence possibilities. According to him, the frequent tendency is to consider the first three elements as approximately constant with variations in the size of preindustrial population resulting mainly from the variation in the fourth factor. I would like to make two comments here: 1) the four elements mentioned above are not independent of each other; 2) granted that population growth may be affected by an increase in technoenvironmental efficiency related to the acquisition of food, it is not less important to investigate the relative influences of the processes of fertility, mortality, and migration through which any population change occurs.

Some anthropologists and economists maintain that the growth of population is actually a cause of improvement in the means of subsistence rather than its effect. Leslie White (1959:286) ascribes the beginning of agriculture in the Old World, that is, the initiation of the attempts to control the growth and reproduction of food-producing plants, to increased pressure upon food supply caused by population growth. Some anthropologists have argued that specific societies they have studied have changed from shifting to permanent cultivation when faced by population pressure generated by a lack of sufficient land for adequate rotation (Dumond 1961; Carneiro 1961;

Geertz 1963:36). However, significant changes in the technology of food acquisition as well as in population size and density occur gradually over long periods. So it is extremely difficult or impossible to determine through empirical study of most historical sequences whether the change in population size and density is the cause or the effect of the changes in the technology of food acquisition. Boserup (1965: 117–18), an economist, approaches the question from a different angle. Comparing the labor costs per unit of output in various systems of nonmechanized agriculture, she concludes that "it is more sensible to record the process of agricultural change in primitive communities as an adaptation to gradually increasing population densities, brought about by changes in the ratio of natural population growth or by immigration." One important corollary of her conclusion is that the primitive and peasant societies with sustained population growth may have a better chance to get into a process of genuine economic development than those with stagnant or declining population, "provided, of course, that the necessary agricultural investments are undertaken." In some densely populated societies this condition may not be fulfilled, if their rate of population growth is high. The evidence from the relatively well-documented Javanese peasant society suggests that a sustained population growth along with a change from shifting cultivation to permanent cultivation of rice does not necessarily lead toward economic development. Geertz (1963:80–82) thinks that the introduction of large-scale sugar cultivation by the Dutch in Java during the eighteenth century had two effects: 1) sustained growth of population, mainly through transportation improvements which reduced the frequency of famine; 2) development of a process called "agricultural involution" which implies, on the one hand, a progressive intensification of wet-rice cultivation through the labor of an increasing number of persons, and, on the other hand, a gradual growth of intricacies in the tenure system, complications in the tenancy relationships, and complexities of cooperative labor arrangements. According to Geertz, the Javanese economy failed to make the transition to modernism because of the development of "agricultural involution." Keyfitz (1957), a demographer, describes the Javanese experience as an instance of technological retrogression. They substituted spade for plow and made other similar changes in agricultural technology in order to spread the agricultural work and products among an increasing number of people. There seems to be little doubt that the lack of adequate economic growth in Java was, at least in part, a consequence of the restraining hands of Dutch colonialism.

Kinship

We have already noted that kinship organization is considered an important determinant of fertility. Some anthropologists have recently begun to view it as an effect of population size, density, or pressure. Eggan (1950:288, 300) observed among the western Pueblos that the multilineage clans were more stable and better capable of organizing a larger population than the single lineages. It led him to think that multilineage clans and phratries were devices adopted by societies as a response to population growth. A search for the cultural ecological explanation of the existence of patrilineal "bands" among a number of tribes led Steward (1955:123–35) to conclude that sparse population density is one of four factors that produce this type of multifamily groups. Fox (1968:153) thinks that the societies with cognatic descent groups can adapt more easily to population pressure than those with unilineal descent groups because the greater flexibility in a cognatic group allows its members to redistribute themselves if it becomes far too large for its land. He finds support for his hypothesis in the popularity of the cognatic principle in small island communities with limited amounts of land. Harner (1970), however, contradicts Fox and postulates that the principle of cognatic kinship results from conditions of lowest population pressure while that of unilineal descent results in response to growing competition under conditions of higher population pressure. He thinks that the island societies with high population pressure (referred to by Fox) have cognatic descent groups because either they have their own class stratification or they operate under colonial administrations. Both of these conditions undermine the competitive advantages of the unilinear principle. Harner finds support for his hypothesis in a statistical test of correlation between the principle of descent and the degree of dependence on hunting and gathering, calculated on the basis of the data provided by Murdock *et al.* (1962–67) in the *Ethnographic Atlas*. In order to relate the principle of descent to population pressure he makes an assumption that is not easily testable. It is that an inverse correlation exists between the degree of dependence on hunting and gathering and the degree of population pressure in societies having any agriculture; and hence, the total degree of dependence on hunting and gathering in such societies provides a scale for measuring population pressure.

Vayda and Rappaport (1963:137–39) suggest that the nonunilineal kinship system and the widespread practice of adoption in some Polynesian island cultures developed as adjustments to the population pressure under insular conditions. These institutions, according to them, made it relatively easy for any particular social unit to maintain itself and to get specific jobs done even if particular men or women belonging to it were the biological parents of few or no children. They cite the prevalence of various fertility-controlling devices, such as abortion, infanticide, celibacy, and coitus interruptus, in a few Polynesian islands as an indication of the low motivation for having children among their inhabitants.

The decline in population size of a small society may seriously affect the traditional functions of its kin-based groupings. I cite below two such illustrations from the anthropological literature. Wagley (1951) shows how the rapid depopulation after Luso-Brazilian contact among the Tapirapé Indians of central Brazil seriously affected the normal functioning of their patrilineal ceremonial moieties (divided into three age-grades of men) and their nonexogamous "Feast Groups" (patrilineal for men and matrilineal for women). The depopulation caused a lack of necessary representation of these groups in Tapirapé villages, thus making their social structure more vulnerable to disorganization. My second illustration comes from a study of the demographic and ecological influences on aboriginal Australian marriage sections (Yengoyan: 1968) which shows that the population size of an Australian tribe sets definite limitations on the operation of its section system, and that intertribal marital exchanges, theft unions, and alternative marriages may occur (sometimes with destructive consequences) when ideal marriage partners are infrequent through decreasing tribal size. The relationship between population size and the proportion of marriages considered as ideal or preferred by a society is also corroborated in a computer simulation study of a human population. Kunstadter *et al.* (1963) found that the proportion of matrilateral cross-cousin marriage, which is the ideal in the model population, is positively related to population growth and to marriage rates, and that variability in the proportion of ideal marriages is inversely related to population size.

Social Complexity

Herbert Spencer (1885:449–50) was perhaps the first social scientist to formulate a principle regarding the relationship between population size and social complexity. He stated that the increase of mass is the causal force in social as well as organic evolution and that, as the population size of a society increases, its divisions and subdivisions "become more numerous and more decided." Durkheim (1933:256–63) pointed out that the increase in population size is a necessary but not a sufficient condition for the development of division of labor in a society. Integration of a society on the basis of progressive functional differentiation occurs, according to him, when, in addition to the increase in population size, there is also an increase in "dynamic or moral density," which may be interpreted as the degree of communication among its members. Durkheim suggested the use of readily apprehended population density as a measure of the more illusive concept of "moral density."

The formulations of Spencer and Durkheim may be regarded as nothing more than insightful speculations. In any case, they were not immediately followed by adequate empirical investigations. There seem to be two main reasons for this: 1) the relative lack of interest in the study of sociocultural evolution during the first half of this century, 2) the difficulty of devising quantitative measures of sociocultural complexity. Naroll (1956) takes a lead in devising such measures and applying them to thirty well-documented ethnic units. He finds a correlation between size of the largest community in a society and the following two measures of social complexity: 1) number of craft specialties; 2) number of "team types," where a "team" is a group of at least three people with clearly defined membership and formal leadership in regular use. Examples of "team types" based on kinship, territory, and association are extended family, village, and village council respectively.

Carneiro (1967) uses a different measure of social complexity and investigates its relationship with total population size in a sample of forty-six single-community societies. His measure is the number of traits in a society that are primarily organizational, that is, involving the coordinated activity of two or more persons. The graphic representation of the number of organizational traits of the sample societies plotted against their population shows a close relationship between the two variables. Carneiro excludes multicommunity societies from his sample and justifies this procedure on the basis of his finding that they appear to elaborate their social structure more slowly than the single-community societies as their populations grow. Carneiro has found with regard to the latter that their structural complexity increases with population growth but more slowly than the rate of population growth. This is, however, what should be expected since an increment of at least several persons is needed to bring about one structural change. In accounting for the demonstrated relationship, Carneiro makes two important qualifications: 1) more complex social structure does not arise *solely* as a response to population growth, 2) elaborating its structure is not the *only* way in which a society may respond to its population growth. The relationship indicates that if a society does increase significantly in size while it remains unified, it must elaborate its organization.

Social Stratification and Political Organization

The role of population pressure in the evolution of social stratification and political complexity has been a subject of empirical investigation by some anthropologists during recent years. Carneiro (1961, 1970) suggests that population pressure in simple farming societies living in circumscribed areas with restricted arable land acts as a stimulus to war and ultimately leads to the development of social stratification and state. He elaborates the process of this development in the coastal valleys of Peru and thinks that such developments in the areas of circumscribed agricultural land elsewhere in the world, such as the Valley of Mexico, Mesopotamia, the Nile Valley, and the Indus Valley, also occurred in much the same way. Carneiro seems to recognize population pressure not only as a necessary but also as a sufficient condition for the development of social stratification and state in societies under specific ecological and cultural conditions.

In some contrast with the foregoing, Fried (1967:196–204) considers population pressure as one of the necessary conditions for the development of social stratification and "pristine" states, but explicitly rejects warfare and slavery as essential intervening steps in the process. He cites a number of studies of aboriginal societies that indicate that an increasing population density gives rise to an increasing narrowness in granting access to basic resources, which in turn leads the society towards social stratification.

British anthropologists Fortes and Evans-Pritchard (1940:7) claimed, in their classic introduction to *African Political Systems,* that no demonstrable relationship exists between population density in a society and the complexity of its political system. They supported this assertion with empirical data from six African societies. In a recent study of the relationship between population and political systems in tropical Africa, however, Stevenson (1968) departs from the strictly synchronic functionalist approach which, he feels, was largely responsible for the conclusions of Fortes and Evans-Pritchard. His reanalysis of each of the same six African societies from a historical and evolutionary perspective shows that population density and political complexity are positively related over time and that states are more often associated with denser population. Stevenson does not attempt to develop a theoretical model concerning the relationship between population density and state formation. Nor does he propose any unicausal model for this relationship. He thinks that it is complex and mediated by a number of important factors such as productivity in the subsistence sector and the development of both regional and long-distance trade.

In his investigation of the relationship between population pressure and social evolution, Harner (1970:76–82) uses the degree of complexity in class stratification and political organization as indices of social evolution. He demonstrates by scatterplot representations and statistical correlation tests that the complexities in class stratification and political organization increase along with the decreasing dependence on hunting and gathering. As stated earlier, his assumption that the degree of dependence on hunting and gathering provides a scale for measuring population pressure is not easily testable.

Concluding Remarks

In a classic inventory and appraisal of the study of population, Hauser and Duncan (1959:2–3) make a distinction between "demographic analysis" and "population studies." The latter, according to them, are concerned not only with population variables but also with relationships between population changes and other variables—social, economic, political, biological, genetic, geographical, and the like. Their volume includes articles relating demography to the followng disciplines: ecology, human ecology, geography, physical anthropology, genetics, economics, and sociology. The omission of some other disciplines, particularly cultural anthropology and psychology, probably reflects the fact that at that time the amount of work done with respect to population in these disciplines was not really significant. By contrast, the subsequently increasing interest of psychologists in population, particularly in the area of fertility and family planning, is reflected in the book entitled *Psychology and Population* (Fawcett 1970).

The present paper reflects the increasing interest of cultural anthropologists in population and has identified some significant research issues in population studies that are relevant to their discipline. It has not been possible to include all the areas of population studies that anthropologists have contributed to (cf. the 349-item comprehensive bibliography on culture and population prepared by Marshall, Morris, and Polgar, 1972). Examples of important areas that have not been dealt with in this paper are 1) paleodemography (e.g., Angel 1947, 1968; Howells 1960; Kobayashi 1967; Vallois 1960) and 2) estimation of population size and other characteristics through genealogical, historical, and other non-conventional methods (e.g., Dobyns 1966; Hackenberg 1967, in press; Thompson 1966). The reader will not perhaps fail to notice in the paper my own special interest in fertility. My purpose, however, will be served if this brief overview stimulates more anthropologists to apply their disciplinary perspectives, concepts, and techniques in population studies, and, at the same time, if it familiarizes population specialists in other disciplines with the contribution (existing and prospective) of anthropologists in this particular field.

References Cited

ANGEL, J. LAWRENCE (1947) The Length of Life in Ancient Greece. Journal of Gerontology 2:18–24.

——— (1968) Early Man's Adaptation to Disease. Paper Presented at the Annual Meeting, American Anthropological Association, Seattle, Washington.

BALIKCI, ASEN (1968) The Netsilik Eskimos: Adaptive Processes. *In* Man the Hunter. Richard B. Lee and Irven DeVore, eds. Chicago: Aldine.

BARNES, J. A. (1954) Class and Committees in a Norwegian Island Parish. Human Relations 7:39–58.

BIRDSELL, JOSEPH B. (1957) Some Population Problems Involving Pleistocene Man. *In* Population Studies: Animal Ecology and Demography. Cold Spring Harbor Symposia on Quantitative Biology 22:47–69.

——— (1968) Population Control Factors: Infanticide, Disease, Nutrition and Food Supply. Discussion *in* Man the Hunter. Richard B. Lee and Irven DeVore, eds. Chicago: Aldine.

BOEKE, J. H. (1954) Western Influence on the Growth of Eastern Population. Economia Internazionale 7:359–369.

——— (1961) Objective and Personal Elements in Colonial Welfare Policy. *In* Indonesian Economica: The Concept of Dualism in Theory and Policy. W. F. Wertheim, ed. The Hague: van Hoeve, 265–299.

BOGUE, DONALD J. (1966) Family Planning Research: An Outline of the Field. *In* Family Planning and Population Programs. B. Berelson, *et al.* eds. Chicago: University of Chicago Press, 721–736.

BOSERUP, ESTER (1965) The Conditions of Agricultural Growth: The Economics of Agrarian Change under Population Pressure. Chicago: Aldine.

BRAIDWOOD, ROBERT J., and CHARLES A. REED (1957) The Achievement and Early Consequences of Food Production: A Consideration of the Archeological and Natural-Historical Evidence. *In* Population Studies: Animal Ecology and Demography. Cold Spring Harbor Symposia on Quantitative Biology 22:19–31.

BURCH, THOMAS, and MURRAY GENDELL (1970) Extended Family Structure and Fertility: Some Conceptual and Methodological Issues. Journal of Marriage and the Family 32:227–236.

CARNEIRO, ROBERT L. (1961) Slash-and-Burn Culivation Among the Kuikuru and Its Implications for Cultural Development in the Amazon Basin. *In* The Evolution of Horticultural Systems in Native South America. J. Wilbert, ed. Caracas: Sociedad de Ciencias Naturales La Salle.

——— (1967) On the Relationship Between Size of Population and Complexity of Social Organization. Southwestern Journal of Anthropology 23: 234–243.

——— (1970) A Theory of the Origin of the State. Science 169:733–738.

CARNEIRO, ROBERT L., and DAISY F. HILSE (1966) On Determining the Probable Rate of Population Growth During the Neolithic. American Anthropologist 68:171–181.

CARR-SAUNDERS, A. M. (1922) The Population Problem. Oxford: Clarendon Press.

CHILDE, V. GORDON (1964) What Happened in History. Baltimore: Penguin Books. (originally published in London, 1942)

COONTZ, S. H. (1957) Population Theories and the Economic Interpretation. London: Routledge and Kegan Paul.

DAVIS, K., and J. BLAKE (1956) Social Structure and Fertility: An Analytic Framework. Economic Development and Culture Change 4:211–235.

DEEVEY, EDWARD S. (1960) The Human Population. Scientific American 203:195–204.

DEVEREUX, GEORGE (1955) A Study of Abortion in Primitive Societies. New York: Julian Press.

DOBYNS, HENRY F. (1966) Estimating Aboriginal American Population. Current Anthropology 7:395–449.

DUMOND, D. E. (1961) Swidden Agriculture and the Rise of Maya Civilization. Southwestern Journal of Anthropology 17:301–316.

——— (1965) Population Growth and Culture Change.

Southwestern Journal of Anthropology 21:302–324.

DURAND, JOHN D. (1967) A Long-Range View of World Population Growth. The Annals of the American Academy of Political and Social Science 369:1–8.

DURKHEIM, EMILE (1933) The Division of Labor in Society. Translated by George Simpson. New York: The Macmillan Co. (originally published in Paris, 1893)

EGGAN, FRED (1950) Social Organization of the Western Pueblos. Chicago: University of Chicago Press.

EPSTEIN, A. L. (1961) Network and Urban Social Organization. Rhodes-Livingstone Journal 29:21.

FAWCETT, JAMES T. (1970) Psychology and Population. New York: The Population Council.

FIRTH, RAYMOND (1936) We the Tikopia. London: George Allen and Unwin, Ltd.

FORD, CLELLAN S. (1945) A Comparative Study of Human Reproduction. Yale University Publications in Anthropology, No. 32. New Haven: Department of Anthropology, Yale University.

——— (1952) Control of Conception in Cross-Cultural Perspective. Annals of the New York Academy of Sciences 54:763–768.

FORTES, MEYER, and E. E. EVANS-PRITCHARD, eds. (1940) African Political Systems. London: Oxford University Press.

FOX, ROBIN (1968) Kinship and Marriage. Baltimore: Penguin Books.

FREEDMAN, RONALD (1961–62) The Sociology of Human Fertility. Current Sociology 10–11:35–121.

FRIED, MORTON H. (1967) The Evolution of Political Society. New York: Random House.

FRIED, MORTON H., MARVIN HARRIS, and ROBERT MURPHY, eds. (1968) War: The Anthropology of Armed Conflict and Aggression. Garden City, New York: Natural History Press for the American Museum of Natural History.

GEERTZ, CLIFFORD (1963) Agricultural Involution: The Processes of Ecological Change in Indonesia. Berkeley: University of California Press.

GUTKIND, PETER (1965) African Urbanism, Mobility and Social Network. International Journal of Comparative Sociology 6:48–60.

HACKENBERG, ROBERT A. (1967) The Parameters of an Ethnic Group: A Method for Studying the Total Tribe. American Anthropologist 69:478–492.

——— (In press) Genealogical Method in Social Anthropology: The Foundations of Structural Demography. *In* Handbook of Social and Cultural Anthropology. John Honigman, ed. Chicago: Rand McNally.

HADDON, A. C. (1912) The Wanderings of Peoples. Cambridge: Cambridge University Press.

HARNER, MICHAEL J. (1970) Population Pressure and the Social Evolution of Agriculturists. Southwestern Journal of Anthropology 26:67–86.

HARRIS, MARVIN (1971) Culture, Man, and Nature. New York: Thomas Y. Crowell Co.

HAUSER, PHILIP M., and OTIS DUDLEY DUNCAN, eds. (1959) The Study of Population. Chicago: University of Chicago Press.

HAWLEY, AMOS H. (1969) Population and Society: An Essay on Growth. *In* Fertility and Family Planning: A World View. S. J. Behrman *et al.*, eds. Ann Arbor: University of Michigan Press.

HIGGINS, BENJAMIN (1958) Western Enterprise and the Economic Development of S.E. Asia. Pacific Affairs, March:74–87.

HILL, REUBEN, J. M. STYCOS, and K. W. BACK (1959) The Family and Population Control. Chapel Hill: University of North Carolina Press.

HIMES, NORMAN E. (1936) Medical History of Contraception. New York: Gamut Press.

HOWELLS, WILLIAM (1960) Estimating Population Numbers Through Archaeological and Skeletal Remains. *In* The Application of Quantitative Methods in Archaeology. R. F. Heizer and S. F. Cook, eds. Viking Fund Publications in Anthropology, No. 28.

KASDAN, LEONARD (1970) Introduction *in* Migration and Anthropology. Robert Spencer, ed. Proceedings of the 1970 Annual Spring Meeting of the American Ethnological Society. Seattle: University of Washington Press.

KEYFITZ, NATHAN (1957) The Growth of Village Populations and Economic Development in South Asia. Population Review 1:39–43.

KOBAYASHI, KAZUMASA (1967) Trend in the Length of Life Based on Human Skeletons from Prehistoric to Modern Times in Japan. Journal of the Faculty of Science, University of Tokyo, Section 5, 3:107–162.

KROEBER, A. L. (1948) Anthropology. New York: Harcourt, Brace and Co.

KUNSTADTER, PETER (1971) Natality, Mortality, and Migration in Upland and Lowland Populations in Northwestern Thailand. *In* Culture and Population. Steven Polgar, ed. Cambridge: Schenkman.

KUNSTADTER, PETER, RONALD BUHLER, FREDERICK STEPHAN, and CHARLES F. WESTOFF (1963) Demographic Variability and Preferential Marriage Patterns. American Journal of Physical Anthropology 22:511–519.

LEVI-STRAUSS, CLAUDE (1963) Structural Anthropology. Translated by C. Jacobson and B. Schoepf. New York: Basic Books. (originally published in Paris, 1958)

LORIMER, FRANK, *et al.* (1954) Culture and Human Fertility. Paris: UNESCO.

MALINOWSKI, BRONISLAW (1929) The Sexual Life of Savages. London: George Routledge and Sons.

MALTHUS, T. R. (1914) An Essay on the Principle of Population. Vol. 1. New York: E. P. Dutton and Co. (originally published in London, 1803)

MARSHALL, JOHN F. (1967) A Neglected Area of Family Planning Research. Population Review 2:30–37.

MARSHALL, JOHN F., SUSAN MORRIS, and STEVEN POLGAR (1972) Culture and Natality: A Preliminary Classified Bibliography. Current Anthropology 13, No. 2.

MATSUNAGA, Ie (1965) Measures Affecting Population Trends and Possible Genetic Consequences. *In* Proceedings of the World Population Conference, II:481–485. New York: United Nations.

MONTAGU, M. F. ASHLEY (1968) Man Observed. New York: G. P. Putnam and Sons.

MURDOCK, GEORGE P. *et al.*, eds. (1962–1967) Ethnographic Atlas. Ethnology 1(1)–6(1).

NAG, MONI (1962) Factors Affecting Human Fertility in Nonindustrial Societies: A Cross-Cultural Study. Yale University Publications in Anthropology, No. 66. New Haven: Department of Anthropology, Yale University. (Reprinted in 1968, New Haven: Human Relations Area Files.)

——— (1967) Family Type and Fertility. *In* Proceedings of the World Population Conference, 1965. New York: United Nations.

——— (1970) The Influence of Conjugal Behavior, Migration and Contraception on Natality in Barbados. *In* Culture and Population: A Collection of Current Studies. Monograph No. 9. Steven Polgar, ed. Chapel Hill: Carolina Population Center.

——— (1972) Sex, Culture and Human Fertility: India and U.S. Current Anthropology 13:231–237.

NAG, MONI, and J. M. BEDFORD (1969) Promiscuity and Fertility: Comments on Greenfield's "The Bruce Effect and Malinowski's Hypothesis on Mating and Fertility." American Anthropologist 71:1119–1122.

NAROLL, RAOUL (1956) A Preliminary Index of Social Development. American Anthropologist 58:687–713.

NOTESTEIN, FRANK W. (1960) Introduction. *In* Three Essays on Population. Thomas Malthus, Julian Huxley, and Frederick Osborn. New York: Mentor Books.

PAKRASHI, KANTI (1968) On Female Infanticide in India. Bulletin of the Cultural Research Institute 7:33–47.

PARK, ROBERT E. (1950) Human Migration and the Marginal Man. *In* Race and Culture. Robert E. Park, ed. Glencoe: The Free Press.

PEPER, BRAM (1970) Population Growth in Java in the 19th Century: A New Interpretation. Population Studies March: 71–84.

PETERSEN, WILLIAM (1961) Population. New York: Macmillan Company.

POLGAR, STEVEN (1964) Evolution and the Ills of Mankind. *In* Horizons of Anthropology. Sol Tax, ed. Chicago: Aldine.

——— (1968) Cultural Aspects of Natality Regulation Techniques. *In* Proceedings, 8th International Congress of Anthropological and Ethnological Sciences, Tokyo and Kyoto 3:232–234. Tokyo: Science Council of Japan.

——— (1972) Population Histories and Population Policies from an Anthropological Perspective. Current Anthropology 13, No. 2.

ROGERS, E. M. (1962) Diffusion of Innovations. New York: Glencoe, The Free Press.

RYDER, N. B. (1959) Fertility. *In* The Study of Population. P. M. Hauser and O. D. Duncan, eds. Chicago: University of Chicago Press.

SHARP, ANDREW (1963) Ancient Voyagers in Polynesia. Auckland: Paul's Book Arcade.

SPENCER, BALDWIN, and F. F. GILLEN (1921) The Arunta. London: Macmillan.

SPENCER, HERBERT (1885) The Principles of Sociology, vol. 1, third ed. New York: D. Appleton and Co.

SPENCER, ROBERT F., ed. (1970) Migration and Anthropology. Proceedings of the 1970 Annual Spring Meeting of the American Ethnological Society. Seattle: University of Washington Press.

STEVENSON, ROBERT F. (1968) Population and Political Systems in Tropical Africa. New York: Columbia University Press.

STEWARD, JULIAN (1955) Theory of Culture Change: The Methods of Multilinear Evolution. Urbana: University of Illinois Press.

SUTTER, JEAN (1968) Fréquence de l'endogamie et ses Facteurs au xixe Siècle. Population 23:303–324.

THOMPSON, H. PAUL (1966) Estimating Aboriginal American Population: A Technique Using Anthropological and Biological Data. Current Anthropology 7:417–424.

THOMPSON, WARREN (1929) Recent Trends in World Population. American Journal of Sociology 34: 959–975.

UNITED NATIONS (1953) Determinants and Consequences of Population Trends. Population Studies No. 17, Population Division of Department of Social Affairs. New York: United Nations.

VALLOIS, HENRY V. (1960) Vital Statistics in Prehistoric Populations as Determined from Archaeological Data. *In* The Application of Quantitative Methods in Archaeology. R. F. Heizer and S. F.

Cook, eds. Viking Fund Publications in Anthropology, No. 28.

VAYDA, A. P. (1961) Expansion and Warfare Among Swidden Agriculturalists. American Anthropologist 63:346–358.

——— (1968) Hypotheses About the Functions of War. *In* War: The Anthropology of Armed Conflict and Aggression. M. Fried, M. Harris, and R. Murphy, eds. New York: Natural History Press.

VAYDA, ANDREW P., and ROY A. RAPPAPORT (1963) Island Cultures. *In* Man's Place in the Island Ecosystem: A Symposium. F. R. Fosberg, ed. Honolulu: Bishop Museum Press.

WAGLEY, CHARLES (1951) Cultural Influences on Population: A Comparison of Two Tupi Tribes. Revista Do Museu Paulista (Nova série) 5:95–104.

WERTHEIM, W. F. (1950) Effects of Western Civilization on Indonesian Society. New York: Institute of Pacific Relations.

WHITE, BENJAMIN (In press) Demand for Labor and Population Growth in Java, 1800–1961.

WHITE, LESLIE A. (1959) The Evolution of Culture. New York: McGraw-Hill.

WOODBURN, JAMES (1968) Population Control Factors: Infanticide, Disease, Nutrition, and Food Supply. Discussion. *In* Man the Hunter. Richard B. Lee and Irven DeVore, eds. Chicago: Aldine Publishing Co.

WRIGLEY, E. A. (1969) Population and History. New York: McGraw-Hill.

YENGOYAN, ARAM A. (1968) Demographic and Ecological Influences on Aboriginal Australian Marriage Sections. *In* Man the Hunter. Richard B. Lee and Irven DeVore, eds. Chicago: Aldine Publishing Co.

24

ECONOMIC ANTHROPOLOGY AND ANTHROPOLOGICAL ECONOMICS

MARSHALL SAHLINS

The selection that follows is one of the more difficult in this collection. Why is it included? Before turning to that question, a few suggestions may make the task of mastery somewhat easier.

As conveyed by Sahlins, there is a profound debate within the discipline of anthropology concerning the nature of economic phenomena and their study. Cutting to the heart of the matter, let us begin with the work of Karl Polanyi (1886–1964), an economist with somewhat aberrant interests who ended his career by working much more happily in conjunction with anthropologists than with his own co-professionals. Polanyi maintained that the study of economics comprised two separate modes. First there is what he called *formal economics*. This is the study we are most familiar with and which we identify as the academic discipline of economics. Basically it may be described as a special form of logical analysis devoted to the determination of maximization of value in the presence of scarcity. Whatever complexities may be added, the central concept of such an economics is that value may be found at the intersection of two variables—supply and demand. Polanyi argued that emphasis on the centrality of this equation was not universal but culture-specific. Those societies using the institution of the price-making market were indeed responsive to this value-setting mechanism and hence could be studied through the medium of formal economic analysis. But, said Polanyi, other forms of economic integration existed that lacked such price-setting institutions and he suggested that a major portion, if not all, of the economic life of such societies

SOURCE: "Economic Anthropology and Anthropological Economics," *Social Science Information*, Vol. 8, No. 5, pp. 13–33, International Social Science Council, UNESCO. Slightly edited by the author, and reprinted by permission of Mouton Publishers.

could not be understood through formal economic analysis. Instead, he argued, such systems should be approached through what he termed *substantive economics*. This approach tended to ignore such things as supply-and-demand curves, concentrating instead upon intensive analysis of the larger social system in which the economic relations were seen to be "embedded." That is to say, transactions that can be isolated as "economic" in a price-market society are viewed in non-price-market societies as segments of larger, not so clearly economic, webs of relationships and activities.

Reaction to Polanyi's suggestions tended to be strong—some pro, a good many con. The literature has swelled through the years. As Sahlins points out, the formalists capped their attacks by pronouncing the substantivist approach dead.

Formalists may think that they have killed off substantivist theory; however, it is quite obvious that substantivist theorists perdure. This brings us back to the question raised at the outset. The Sahlins essay is included because it provides a sensitive response to the formalist attacks. But there is more. It is not merely a matter of learning where anthropological economics is at by surveying its major controversy. Instead, the Sahlins essay reveals how the questions being debated relate to deeply underlying problems of cultural anthropology. Along the way we see something of the present philosophical and epistemological condition of the discipline. Some old and recurrent problems reappear in new guise—individual "versus" culture, free will and determinism, cultural rules as opposed to personal actions.

Like many other contributions to this anthology, the Sahlins essay is not to be taken as a simple declaration of fact. It is a complex statement of position in an on-going argument.

▼△▼△▼

It is a precious fact that an institutionalist kind of economics first appears in anthropology in direct relation to field research among exotic societies, that is to say, as a Western experience of these societies. One need only cite Bronislaw Malinowski's pityless confrontation —already nearly half a century ago—of the primitive "economic man" known to classical doctrine with the Trobriand islanders he knew at first hand (Malinowski, 1922, pp. 60–62). But the battle was not as early won; it was only then engaged. It continues right to the present moment, and more fiercely than ever since World War II under the impetus of new field studies, a new interest in economic development and the recent theoretical writings of Karl Polanyi and George Dalton.[1] That the latter were economists who chose to enter the lists on the side of "substantive" anthropological economics and against the orthodoxies of their own science should not astonish. The same controversy had been raging on and off within economics for nearly a century; in the longer view this penetration into anthropology was only the opening of a new front in an old war. Here, however, the intellectual contours of the terrain would dictate certain tactical innovations, especially nominal. Battle was joined in anthropology under the name of "formalist" vs. "substantivist" interpretations of the primitive economies, bringing with these terms the following theoretical option: between the ready-made models of Western economic science, especially the "microeconomics", taken as universally valid and therefore applicable *grosso modo* to the primitive societies, and the necessity—supposing the formalist position unfounded—of developing a new analysis more appropriate to the historical societies in question and to the intellectual history of anthropology. Broadly speaking, it is a choice between the perspective of "business", for the formalist method must think the primitive economies as underdeveloped versions of our own, and a culturological study that as a matter of course does honor to different societies for what they are.

No resolution is in sight, no serious justification for the happy academic conclusion that "the answer lies somewhat in between". The present essay, and the collection of more concrete studies for which it was designed to serve

---

[1] For the latest salvo and a general bibliography of the controversy, see Dalton, 1969.

as preface,[2] are substantivist in outlook. The aim, given the conjuncture, is modest: merely to perpetuate the controversy, continue the dialogue. For even to insist that the controversy lives is to take exception. In a recent number of the international journal *Current Anthropology* a spokesman of the opposed position announced with no apparent regret the untimely demise of substantivist economics:

> The wordage squandered in this debate does not add up to its intellectual weight. From the beginning the substantivists (as exemplified in the justly famous works of Polanyi and others) were heroically muddled and in error. It is a tribute to the maturity of economic anthropology that we have been able to find in what the error consisted in the short space of six years. The paper [. . .] written by Cook (1966) when he was a graduate student neatly disposes of the controversy [. . .] Social science being the sort of enterprise [!] it is, however, it is virtually impossible to down a poor, useless or obfuscating hypothesis, and I expect the next generation of creators of high-level confusion will resurrect, in one guise or another, the substantive view of the economy (Nash, 1967).

But if substantive economics is dead, how then to describe the present work, which is neither the second coming nor otherwise bears the slightest traces of immortality? Perhaps best to say it shares the embarrassment once inflicted upon Mark Twain by widespread rumours of his decease; whereupon, he took the opportunity of his earliest public appearance to declare that the reports of his death had been grossly exaggerated.

Thus God and nature linked the general frame,
And bade self-love and social be the same

Competent reviewers in professional journals have understandably expressed their exasperation with the eternal reiteration by Karl Polanyi's followers of the semantic confusion concealed in the word "economic"—and also, of course, in the nominal, "economy", form in which the ambiguity will be discussed here. Obviously "economy" means two things at once, and not the same in a phrase such as "an economy of production", as in "the Zuni economy", or "the economy of nineteenth century Europe". But beyond the insinuation that orthodox economics, in taking the simultaneity as a proposition, and so rendering the economy a public outcome of private prudence, represents thus a vast logical sequitur to a fundamental ambiguity—beyond this, what further polemic profits do the critics seek by dunning epigonally on the master's insight? Too much has been written about the famous two meanings.

And not enough has been said. It is not enough to proclaim the confusion; it is necessary to analyze the distinction. The two meanings of "economy" summarize two directly opposed strategies of understanding, contrasting on every theoretical issue from the identity of the economic subject to the historic status of the economic process. In confrontation are two very different ways of practicing economic theory, which faithfully followed through must lead to very different conclusions about the same primitive facts. Regrettably then, I must ask the reader's indulgence to speak once on the two meanings, but this time with a view fixed to their systematic implications for the study of exotic economies. This without pretence of partiality, yet neither really with the purpose of debate. Arguments at this level, abstract, methodological, even if reasonable are rarely convincing—unless one is already inclined. The objective for the moment is merely to describe the main dimensions of controversy, to juxtapose the contrasting principles of formal and substantivist economics, in the ultimate hope that this effort will help situate the more concrete work being done in the anthropological field.

The two meanings of "economy" disagree from the beginning on the identity of the economic subject. At issue, besides the specific form, is the ontological locus of economy. The

[2] Sahlins, 1972.

disagreement is thereby decisive: all other differences of method and conception follow logically from it. Speaking the one of economizing, the other of production and distribution, the two definitions immediately place themselves on different levels of reality. "Economy" in the formal sense is an activity of people as such, in the substantive sense of culture as such. Consider as example of the first this proposition of Sir Lionel Robbins', generally accepted as an authentic expression of formalism: Economics is "the science which studies human behaviour as a relation between ends and scarce means that have alternate uses" (1935, p. 16). In brief, the economic subject is people: "economy" is something individuals do, how they go about their business. But "the Arunta economy" invokes a culture, not the individuals. In this substantive sense, "economy" is a subdivision of the social-cultural order. The word has been transposed to another plane whose elements are not persons but techniques and social relations goods and ideas—seized in their own terms.

It follows that "economy" in its formal signification is a category of behavior, whereas in substantive terms it is a category of culture. In the same way as the economic subject differs, the action of that subject unfolds on different levels. As Robbins writes, formal economic science is a study of "human behavior". Its object is comportment of a certain kind: economizing. How this economizing is further understood depends on the definition of ends and means. Where these are determined tangibly or monetarily, as was once the average opinion, then economy is another word for enterprise.[3] Current wisdom, however, rather refuses to attribute any particular nature to the ends and means. Defined then as the application of scarce means against graded ends to obtain the maximum benefit, content left indeterminate, economy becomes a modality of rationality. Economy, that is to say, is a subgroup within the general class of human behavior, coordinate to the logical, the practical, etc., and opposed to the improvident, the illogical—in short, the irrational.

But "the Arunta economy" says nothing in particular about how people act, only that culture is organized in a certain way. More precisely, and this is the substantive definition proper, it speaks of "the process by which materials (goods) are appropriated from nature and distributed in society to sustain the latter as constituted". Not the need-satisfying behavior of people, but the material life-process of society. Not either the way means are applied to ends to achieve the greatest possible utility, but the way techniques, goods, ideas and social relations, as qualities in their own right, interact to produce the observed material result. If economy is formally a kind of behavior, substantively it belongs in a class with politics, religion, education and comparable processes of culture.

The selection of the economic subject is therefore fateful: for the mode of interpretation, obviously, but for the practice of description equally. The initial identification entrains a whole "approach to the study of society" as the economist F. W. Walker recognized, and by it separated the workers in his own field from the anthropologists:[4]

> It would appear [. . .] that rather than ignorance being the reason why economists and anthropologists do not co-operate as well as is desirable, the cause is deeper, being a fundamentally different approach to the study of society [. . .] No one can study society without some initial assumptions, implicit or explicit, concerning the nature of society. Anthropologists are focussed on the community rather than the individual; they view society as a system of mutually dependent elements, and emphasize the influence of social forces

[3] One reason why the formal view is sometimes qualified as "business" or "bourgeois" economics.

[4] Walker was writing effectively before the development of "economic anthropology". Probably the majority of present anthropologists interested in primitive or peasant economies have formalist leanings. For that matter, substantivism has long been a minor style within the discipline of economics (*cf.* Kaplan, 1968).

on behavior. The economist, on the other hand, derives the forms of economic behavior from assumptions concerning man's original nature. He begins by considering how an isolated individual would dispose his resources and then assumes that the individual members of a social group behave in the same way (Walker, 1942–1943), p. 135).[5]

Phrased as it is in Walker's text, "individual" vs. "society", the debate between the business and substantive perspectives engages the world's oldest social science controversy. But I would not revive fond undergraduate memories —culture vs. psychology, superorganic against organic, Marat/Sade. Within the broader issue, which threatens to be eternally important even as it is already banal, is another more directly pertinent to the economic argument. Business and cultural economics do not merely part company on the proper starting-point of analysis, on the individual as opposed to the society; they harbor strictly opposed understandings of *the relation between the individual fact and the social fact.* This is the second major dimension of controversy between them, and like that concerning the economic subject it develops into a series of specific disagreements. From their respective vantages on the relation individual/society the two perspectives arrive immediately at conflicting historical perceptions, that is, differences on the temporal and cultural relativity of economic action. Moreover, this discord is at the same time another, proceeding also imperatively from the same base by the kind of logic perfectly compressed in the Walker text, where the opposition nature/culture appears as a kind of discrete transposition of individual/society. I shall attempt to explain these complex issues.

[5] For a parallel appreciation, also by an economist, see Ayres, 1952; but Ayres, an institutionalist, is highly critical of the individualist perspective, and argues vigorously for the adoption of the culturalist position in economics. "There is a universe of discourse, he writes, to which the concept 'individual' is simply irrelevant" (*ibid.*, p. 41). Elsewhere he attacks as erroneous just the procedure described by Walker, "that of defining the problem on the individual level and then raising it to the cultural level by a sort of algebraic multiplication, the way a variable is raised to the nth power" (Ayres, 1944, pp. 97–98).

In the theoretical practice of formalism, individual and society are counterposed in a relation of exteriority, outside one another, and when brought into interaction the individual assumes the instigating, dominant and autonomous role. Busied ever in the satisfaction of his best interests, the individual is actor and the society scene, a theatre of cultural elements disposable to the individual protagonist as the ends and means of his economical performance. Inasmuch as the prudent allocation of means logically supposes deliberate choice, the individual appears as autonomous in relation to society; and as the latter is construed to be so many opportunities for personal manipulation, the individual must also be dominant. It is a tale told by an economist . . . but fairly exemplified in a recent version produced by the anthropologist R. Burling (1962).

What, in Burling's view, is the crucial economic question? "If we now focus upon the individual who is caught in the web of his society, and who is trying to maximize his satisfactions, we are led to the investigation of his actual behavior in situations of choice. This is the crucial economic question" (p. 818). I pass over the contradictions of the individual "caught in the web of his society" all the same maximizing his satisfactions by choice, to ask what is the place of the social order in this analytic structure? The analytic model of economy, Burling writes, is one "which sees the individuals of a society busily engaged in maximizing their own satisfactions—desire for power, prestige, sex, food, independence, or whatever else they may be, in the context of the opportunities around them, including those offered by their own culture" (pp. 817–818). Here I pass over the mystery of what opportunities are not "offered by their own culture" to the determination of the position, within this *problématique*, of the social fact. That position is clear: it is contextual. The social order is milieu, background to that "crucial economic question" which is the individual activity of choice. This is also to say that the social order is already given to the analysis, existing beforehand as so many "opportunities" people take up to accomplish whatever desires they may have. The analysis is not designed to know how the sociocultural system works, but how people put it to work. The society is passive, contextual and external to the individual, who is active, autonomous, prevailing and enterprising.

But then who is this "individual"? Figured conceptually apart from society, what can be his provenance? To answer, consider that the individual, equipped also with a characteristic behavior of prudent economizing, has been disengaged and privileged by the theoretical structure as distinct from society. The social context is given, the human action also given and other. The existential status of the latter therefore follows with all the force of an anthropological truism. If the given human action is not social, social being its indirect object, then it must be *natural*. This individual of the formalist apparatus is a creature of nature; likewise for his inclination to gainful manipulation—it is human nature. We are face to face with *homo economicus*, but more, with a reason for his persistence in economic thought. The bourgeois economists are constantly reproached for locating the axiom and mainspring of their theory beyond culture, in the nature of man. But it is not mere ideological bad faith. The supposition of an inherent "propensity to truck and barter" is a theoretical inevitability, bound to be repeated so long as the individual *projet* is in principle detached and valued apart from the social.[6] Furthermore, insofar as this economic man is natural, he is eternal and universal. The individual constructed by formal thought is a permanent fact: outside of history, development or diversity. In respect of economizing he represents the human condition, from all times and from the Ashanti to the Zuni. This is also to say that scarcity is the human lot, that calculated choice with an eye to the greatest gains is the cross-cultural economic practice and, therefore, that the economic institutions incarnating these procedures are marked by the same generality and immortality. The formal mode of economics is in principle unhistorical . . .

> The economists have a singular way of proceeding. For them there are only two sorts of institutions, those of art and those of nature. The feudal institutions are artificial, the bourgeois institutions natural. In this they resemble the theologians, who likewise establish two sorts of religion [*i.e.*, true and false] [. . .] In saying that the existing relations—the relations of bourgeois production—are natural, the economists would have it understood that these are the relations in which wealth is created and the productive forces developed, in conformity with the laws of nature. Hence these relations are themselves natural laws, independent of the influence of time. They are eternal laws that must always govern society. Thus there has been history, but there is no more (Marx, 1968, p. 129. Author's translation from the French edition).

Fairly implicit in the foregoing discussion, as it is in every counterpart the opposite of the formal view, the substantivist conception of the relation between individual and society can be resumed more succinctly. In general it is a relation of interiority. The individual is not thought of independently of the society but as a member, inscribed in the society and "enculturated" in its practices. The individual fact is thus contingent, in the aggregate expressive of the social forces; while these, developing in virtue of their cultural properties, appear as autonomous, dominant and in themselves "the crucial economic question." [7] The question is the relation between aspects of the social order,

[6] Nor will anthropology escape this supposition so long as it builds on the same analytic basis. Herskovits launched his major work on—and by this the whole discipline of—*Economic anthropology* with the following sentence: "The elements of scarcity and choice, which are the outstanding factors in human experience that give economic science its reason for being, rest psychologically on firm ground" (1952, p. 3).

[7] "The idea that economic life has ever been a process mainly dependent on individual action—an idea based on the impression that it is concerned mainly with methods of satisfying individual needs, is mistaken with regard to all stages of human civilization, and in some respects it is more mistaken the further back we go" (Schmoller, 1910, pp. 3–4; *cf.* Godelier, 1966, pp. 46, 95, 269; Marx, 1967, I, p. 12).

say matrilineages coupled to avunculocal residence, and the distribution and production of yams in a determinate environment (say, of the Trobriand Islands).[8] But this *problématique* is patently anonymous. Now it is the individual who is given to the analysis—in something of the same way the society is assumed by formal theory. That is, if in the formal optique the social-cultural system is everywhere organized to allow the disposition of its elements by human choice, in the substantive view man is everywhere organized to allow the cultural formation of his disposition. Not then that man is endowed always with the same behavior of appropriation, but only with the same capacity to behave appropriately (principle of psychic unity). This means on one hand that human behavior is seized conceptually in its variety as culture rather than in its resemblance as nature; and, on the other hand, human capacities being the same society to society, any explanation of economic diversity must privilege the differences in the institutional order. But then, the idea of *an* economy in the cultural sense was born out of the awareness of econom*ies*, of cultural diversity. By this process differentiated historically from classic economic science, substantive economics has remained uniquely respectful of the historical differentiation. It is incurably relativist:

> The conditions under which men produce and exchange vary from country to country and within each country again from generation to generation. Political economy, therefore, cannot be the same for all countries and all historical epochs [. . .] Anyone who attempted to bring Patagonia's political economy under the same laws as are operative in present-day England would obviously produce only the most banal commonplaces (Engels, 1966, p. 163; see, for such commonplaces, Goodfellow, 1939).

We come then to a final difference in theoretical practice developing from the disagreement over the relation individual/society. When put to the work of historical comparisons, formal and substantive economics each manifest weaknesses characteristic of their strengths. In search of "regularities" over culture, substantivism would progressively impoverish reality by generality—a slightly different banality than Engels envisaged, but all the same a flattening of institutional differences more or less severe according to the scope of the comparison.[9] The power of substantive economics lies in the explanation of diversity (within a control of similarity, obviously); its strongest comparative propositions, therefore, are phrased in terms of co-variation. But a comparative formalism would negate the empirical variation in another and a more unconditional manner. Where substantivism by granting validity to all societies risks permutating their variety into an abstract common resemblance, formal practice, beginning from the universality of the enterprising individual, finishes by reducing the differences between societies to the specific principles of one among them. The comparative common denominator of formal economics is 1: there is one *kind* of economy, all apparent variations being of degree—fractional approximations of that one.[10]

This round trip of formalism between unity and diversity—with the epicycles described en route—is imposed by logical barriers encountered along the way. Fundamentally nonhistorical, when nevertheless committed to cultural comparisons formal practice translates the variety of economies into a diversity of economizing: if here the people maximize material gains, there it is the esteem of lineage kinsmen or the cumulation of personal prestige.

[8] See below, p. 285.

[9] The difficulty mentioned of course haunts much of anthropology (as well as the discipline of history); it is not the private misfortune of anthropological economics.

[10] "Practically every economic mechanism and institution known to us is found somewhere in the primitive world [. . .] The distinctions to be drawn between literate and non-literate economies are consequently of degree rather than kind" (Herskovits, 1952, pp. 487–488).

In different societies, people are bent on different "values":

> It is not so much then, by the presence of an economic organization or a rational control of their environment that primitive peoples differ from civilized, but by the different types of ends towards which this organization and control are aimed, resulting in the creation of a very different scale of values (Firth, 1950, p. 5).

This resolution of the cultural variation, in appearance a spiritualization of the economy, amounts more profoundly to a commercialization of the society. Social relations, ideas, political conditions, etc., are divested of their own qualities (as social facts) and assigned instead pecuniary qualities: they are now "values", and as such fitted to people's businesslike manipulations, which are thereby extended from the economic to all behavior and to culture in general. A category of the market, "value" is a behavioral science way of thinking culture as business on the scale of society. Insofar as the pecuniary attribution is external to the social facts so conceived, the procedure is often criticized as tautology: the valuation of kinsmen's esteem, for instance, is just another name for the activity it is designed to explain (giving gifts to kinsmen). But there is a deeper tautology, one that brings into question the entire analytical edifice. The explanation by values cannot move beyond "tradition would have it so",[11] without denying all significance to the individual fact; hence, the position is theoretically unstable, however frequently it is advanced. By the comparative juxtaposition of economizing, the dominance of the individual fact has been radicalized to the point of its own negation: not merely is the individual autonomous in relation to society, society has been presumed in the individual. For satisfaction, as C. Ayres writes, "is not a natural phenomenon like the 'five senses' of the physical organism. For every man it is determined by the social medium in which he lives; and consequently when it is adopted as a tool of analysis or a term of explanation of that social order, its adoption means the assumption in advance of all that social fabric of which an explanation is being sought" (1944, p. 75). Briefly, it is patent that the content of people's satisfactions, the hierarchy of ends determining the allocation of means, as well as the means themselves, are stipulations of society. The individual is thus rendered superfluous except as the vehicle by which the interplay of social forces is realized —indeed, he could only become an independent factor if he were not rational, incapable of responding appropriately to these forces. The formalist procedure is at an impasse: it must retreat back to nature, or else pass over to culture, camp of the substantivist adversary.

We arrive at a third dimension of contrast, the last to be discussed. The first two were concerned with identification of the economic subject and with the relation thus posed between the individual and social facts; this final difference is over the nature of economic action. More exactly, it is a disagreement about the character of economic "rationality". Again the general difference entrains a series of particular contrasts between the two perspectives, climaxed by another difference of functioning in the sphere of historical comparisons—where each "approach" once more manages to create special difficulties for itself.[12]

Economic science, to repeat Lord Robbins' characterization, "studies human behavior as a relationship between ends and scarce means which have alternate uses". Thus defined, the object of this science has no content; it is only a method. Economy is the logic of effective action toward a goal; it is getting the most for the least of whatever it may concern. Form

[11] A common substitution, as C. Meillassoux remarks, of the unexplained for the inexplicable (1960).

[12] The following discussion of economic rationality draws so heavily on M. Godelier's *Rationalité et irrationalité en économie* (1966) that it would be impossible to annotate all the specific moments of debt.

without substance and a kind of formal logic, this understanding of economy so doubly merits its usual appellation. But the "economy" of formalism, if without content ontologically, has very strict criteria as praxeology. It is faultless rationality, the "one best way" of achieving the goals in mind with the means on hand. The procedure supposes, as well as a scarcity of means relative to their possible employ, an economic subject free to choose between these means in pursuit of his given ends. That action, then, is "economic" in which the subject uses those means in the particular way that maximizes his returns in desired ends; and more specifically for a series of ends hierarchically ordered, "economic" is the successive application of the most efficacious means to the end of greatest marginal utility, thus maximizing the total gains. For every such problem there is only one solution dignified of the name economic: gain *optimus maximus*. In this the formalist's version of economy is like Rousseau's idea of the Sovereign: simply in being, it is everything it should be. Hence that chronic oscillation in economic writing between the statement of what is, and how to correct it.[13] Once again the moral overtone is not fully comprehended as an original ideological sin, a conspiracy of long date to promote a certain state of economic affairs. Constructed into the premises, the confusion between reality and morality is bound to be thought out every time and however innocently these premises are elaborated. In bourgeois economics, as Joan Robinson remarked, "goods sound good".

Too good to be true; or perhaps it is that the rational formula is too true to be good. When applied to inter-cultural comparisons, presented with the task of explaining economic variations, it suffers for its constancy. If people everywhere and at all times behave rationally, still the Trobriand gardener gives half his harvest to his brother-in-law in return for an ornament he cannot keep, while the American farmer is content not to plant half his in return for a subsidy he does not earn. Invariant and unerring, formal rationality as such does not account for these variations in its material outcome. But then, and this is another price of its verity, the rational calculus is not directly addressed to the material. The "prudent allocation of resources" applies to any behavior—or as Burling indicates it is an aspect of all behavior (1962, p. 817). In effect, the procedure is largely synonymous with living, since we all have a limited time "and miles to go before we sleep", and so constantly face decisions as between night baseball and other pastimes which presumably are resolved for the main in what we take to be our best interests. Nor would "economy" so understood preclude the textbook adoption of Che Guevara's manual on guerilla warfare, from beginning to end a discourse on the deployment of limited means to maximum effect. Without specification of content, the formal notion of the economic is unacceptable in practice: "explaining everything, it succeeds in explaining nothing". The problem is not settled, as we have seen, by the relativization of "values". In any event that is not the question directly posed by a tactical definition innocent of material content. The question, logically anterior, is whether by giving the means-ends relation that materialist content conventional to formal economics it is rendered unsuitable for comparative purposes—which could explain the retreat to pure rationalist form, equally if not as obviously unsuitable.

What then are the theoretical consequences

---

[13] For example: "But sometimes [. . .] the market does not behave in the way that micro-theory describes as the normal case [. . .] Yet even in these special cases micro-economics has a special relevance. For then it tells us what behavior would restore normality [. . .] When used in this way, price theory is goal-oriented rather than predictive; that is, it tells us how to achieve a desired state of affairs, rather than what would be the outcome of the present state, left to itself. Both uses are important, one for understanding how the market system is ordinarily capable of producing an orderly solution to the tasks it performs [. . .] the other for giving us the necessary knowledge to reintroduce order into the system, when [. . .] it threatens to break down" (Heilbroner, 1968, p. 46).

of variously assigning the elements of the rationalist calculus either material (goods, money, etc.) or nonmaterial content? Apologies; but logic-chopping becomes unavoidable, more perhaps than expected because there are more permutations of the oppositions means/ends, material/non-material than are usually made explicit. In the paradigm, scarce means among alternate uses for maximum benefits, the material status of *three* terms has to be determined: the means (resources); the uses, that is to say, their objective realizations (returns); and the satisfactions of the economic subject (utilities). The first two terms refer to things external to the subject, brought into relation by his enterprise, the last to *his own final relation* to the process. Unhappily, in much discussion the *de facto* returns and the benefits appreciated by the individual are both known and confounded as "ends", an identification tolerable perhaps in reference to consumption but which in contexts of production and distribution unpardonably confuses the objective yields of economic manipulation with the subjective satisfactions—or, in retrospective view, the motivations of the subject with the nature of his activity. Such would imply that if a productive process yields monetary profits, for example, this too, and simply, is the subject's finality, which is manifestly grotesque. Hence one reason for the popular disposition among modern economists to deny that theirs is merely a science of material welfare, or necessarily supposes a *homo economicus*, for it is evident that the good bourgeois generously devoting his profits to charity or improving himself by a trip to Europe has higher interests in the business process than love of lucre. This ennoblement of the materialist bourgeois can then join forces with the symmetrical and inverse tendency arising now in economic anthropology to "embourgeoise" the noble savage. For the latter, it is clear, though he often engages in reciprocal gift exchanges to no net material increment, may nevertheless be looking to a tangible utility, inasmuch as a gift given when it can be afforded may well be reciprocated when it is most needed.[14]

The happy common conclusion of these complementary discoveries is that people everywhere are moved by mixed "economic" and "non-economic" considerations, so that the economizing procedure is everywhere the same in principle and universally applicable in analysis. The best that can be said for this conclusion is that it is irrelevant, since the similarities in the subject's "ends" do not account for the material differences in the way they are achieved. People who live by reciprocity must find in it all their happiness, however defined, and likewise those who live by business find several and various pleasures in profits. But the fact remains, and still unexplained, that in one instance resource allocations had been oriented by net material gain and not so in the other. The spiritualization of the individual *projet* is no remedy to the difficulties faced by the formal calculus in the sphere of historical comparison. Besides, it is not really taken seriously in its home province of market analysis. It is merely a generous concession on a matter of principle, without significance for the scientific propositions—which hold only to the extent the individual actually does dispose his resources toward net financial profit:

> The propositions of the theory of [supply-demand-price] variations do not involve the assumptions that men are actuated only by considerations of money gains and losses. They only involve the assumption that money plays some part in the valuation of given alternatives. And they suggest that if from any position of equilibrium the money incentive is varied this must tend to alter the equilibrium valuations. Money may not be regarded as playing a predominant part in the situation contemplated. *So long as it plays some part*

[14] *Cf.* Cook, 1966. Cook's argument in this essay, like the complementary propositions in Robbins' book, are fatally permeated by the confusion between the objective net result of an economic activity and the subjective utility, allowing both authors to neglect the differences in the former in favor of the similarities in the latter.

then the propositions are applicable (Robbins, 1935, p. 98; e.o.).[15]

The confusion once eliminated between the real returns to resources and the subject's finality, the remaining permutations of the economizing paradigm, which concern only the relation between means and their *de facto* product, offer little interest and less hope of a comparative usefulness. Were the product of the means assumed to be material, whether or not the means are so themselves, cross-cultural extension of the rational formula would imply that everywhere and singularly people dispose their resources toward the maximum material benefit, proposition untenable empirically.[16] Otherwise, if the returns are supposed intangible and the means likewise, the rational paradigm excludes from the "economic" all maximization of goods; or, with the means (only) tangible, it includes all uses of goods not normally "economic"—such as the handling of paraphernalia in religious ceremonies, reading books, etc.

In sum, however, the economistic paradigm is declined—without content; indifferent as to content ("values"); with means, products and utilities tangible or intangible—it would not seem to merit from a comparative economics the analytic esteem it is given by formalism.

In one respect, the substantive determination of economy as the process by which society is materially provisioned is as much as the formal view lacking in content. Insisting advisedly on *process*, it coyly avoids any reference to structures. The reason is a certain deference to the empirical organization of primitive societies, where kinship relations as father-son, maternal uncle-nephew and the like, are main relations of production and exchange; or, otherwise put, where the same generalized groups and relations order economic and political as well as religious and other activities. In these societies there is no "*the* economy"—*i.e.*, as an institutionally specialized sub-system. "Economy" here is a category distinguished by certain functions rather than certain structures, that is, by the appropriation of materials from nature and their distribution as goods in society. But then, the definition submitted this way to the material, there is little possibility of dispute over the economic content of the empirical—even though the existence of a specific kind of group such as a lineage, duly remarked as critical to the economy of one society, may be, in another, where it has little material function, largely ignored (*cf.* Evans-Pritchard, 1940, p. 74; Godelier, 1966; Sahlins, 1968).

By so taking refuge in the cultural order and *its* problems of existence, substantive economics does not escape from, but merely rephrases the issue of rationality. As we shall see, it is even tempted to carry "maximization"

---

[15] Robbins goes on to provide the illustration of a small bounty granted in respect of the production of a certain good under free enterprise. That the production of this item will increase, he writes, is not dependent on the presumption that producers are motivated by financial gain. They may be motivated by all sorts of considerations. "But, if we assume that before the bounty was granted there was equilibrium, we must assume that its institution must disturb the equilibrium. The granting of the bounty implies a lowering of the terms on which real income is obtained [. . .] It is a very elementary proposition that if a price is lowered, the demand tends to increase" (pp. 98–99). Yes, so long as the price makes a difference. All this in defence of the principle that "there are no limitations on the subject matter of economic science save this": that the behavior is imposed by scarcity (pp. 16–17).

[16] Included here would be the expenditure of time or labor in production, or for the payments due for services rendered: both nonmaterial means against materials "ends". It is, incidentally, fruitless to define "services" apart from a material compensation, that is, simply as any act in another's favor. No such act is in itself an economic service, and what is properly a service in one context or society need not be so in another, for depending on context or society material reward may or may not be necessary for the realization of a given task. If services are defined apart from this relation to goods, ignoring the kind of compensation, then the term is practically synonymous with social interaction. A lot of confusion seems to exist on this point, which, along with the classic definition of economics as the production and distribution of goods and services, entails either the denial that economy is necessarily concerned with the material (as "services" are not material) or else a labyrinthine argument that it is, the intangibility of services notwithstanding. All this is avoided by the understanding that a "service" is not just doing something for someone.

to an extreme hardly distinguishable from the formal calculus. But the substantive rationality is different in origin, in the same way as the economic subject differs from the enterprising individual posed by formalism. The rationality of substantivism lies in the construction of culture—which is not so much a premise as it is a hope, for its *discovery* constitutes part of the explanation.

I hazard a long but dramatic illustration of this nuance: the Trobriand custom of *urigubu*, mentioned before in passing, custom obliging a man to pass half his yam harvest to his sister's husband—or in default of such a brother-in-law, to the husband of another close matrilineal kinswoman—in return for which the donor receives a valued ornament. Concentrating on the yams, as the ornaments would involve us in a complex exegesis of intertribal trade, harvest time in the Trobriands presents then the following picturesque scene: the entire population of gardeners carrying their crops all over the countryside to deposit them in someone else's storehouse—busy deplacement having the net material effect of a redistribution to the initial state, inasmuch as the depletion of each man's production in favor of his sister's husband is (more or less) compensated by the yams he receives from his wife's brother. In the perspective of the prudent individual, a waste of time and effort: roughly 50 percent of the annual staple output has been placed in distribution without intending, and effectively without providing, anyone a clear tangible gain.[17] But the matter appears differently in the light of Trobriand socio-political organization. That organization is matrilineal, but highly politicized, the adult men of a (matri)lineage domiciled in the village homeland of the group and there subordinated to their senior mother's brother. In this politicization of matriliny, comparatively uncommon, is also a rare contradiction. The lineage is exogamous; hence its wedded daughters, by whom the group is replenished, are widely dispersed with their offspring in their husbands' villages—which is to say that the young men marked to control the lineage's affairs and succeed their mothers' brothers are growing up somewhere else. The contradiction is morphologically resolved by "avunculocal marital residence": upon marriage a man goes off with his wife to the place of his mother's brother. The custom thus effectively regroups the adult males of the matrilineage, and it is this integration that the *urigubu* gift effectively prepares. Giving half his harvest to his sister's husband, a man all along provides for his sister's sons, so prefiguring their subordination to his command, or more generally, their attachment to a rightful lineage destiny. The *urigubu* establishes the key claim of rights upon which turns Trobriand society and polity. In this it is not a waste of time and effort, but rationality itself.

Substantive and relative, such rationality is specifically of "the system". It is the way the system is materially sustained, finality of which the well-being of people is only one aspect. Goods must also be brought to bear in support of institutions and relations, and then in ways not always to the tangible benefit of the individual. (Many relations, such as chieftainship and close kinship, are best consolidated by presentations of goods at a loss; see Sahlins, 1965.) Moreover, the substantive conception of rationality will differ accordingly from the formal in its supposition of wilfulness or intentionality. Project of the culture rather than of the individual, the substantive rationality is constituted rather than willed, unintentional (in Godelier's terms) rather than intentional. It thus no more logically supposes choice than it does acquiescence. For the person it may just as well be realized as constraint, as the moral and customary thing to do, behind it such

[17] Exception made for the paramount chief, who by virtue of many wives stands as the "glorified brother-in-law" of the community and receives enormous gifts of *urigubu* which he later redistributes. Exception also for the chance unbalance in product between a man and his wife's brother, which may result in a gain for one or the other at the cost of his disesteem as a poor gardener.

forces of cultural transmission as to render other "options" at the least improbable and in the main inconceivable. But the true aim of the substantivist argument from intentionality is neither to contest freewill nor to insist that for man in society the choices are limited and the alternatives loaded.[18] It is to avoid at all cost mystifying the causes as the rules; that is, to demarcate itself from a theoretical design which by starting from the decisions of the individual cannot envisage explication of the systematic relations between social facts—because that rationality is already presumed in, and as, the rationality of individual choice.[19]

Still, if economy is the material means of social preservation, and especially as it is mediator of culture in relation to nature, it does not by this conception deny all absolute finality or determinate rationality. Placing itself in the context of cultural adaptation, the substantive economics may ignore the calculus of personal maximization, but only to substitute the very similar rationality of ecological selection. In the end, the two varieties of rationality seem formally identical, the same praxeology; moreover, the substantive appears to arrive at the very rule of individual economizing with which the formal began—by this route merely menacing itself with the neglect reserved for unnecessary theoretical distractions. For cultural adaptation surely has definite criteria of material advantage. A society cannot expend in the process of exploiting nature more energy and material than it extracts, nor waste in distribution more than it has gained in production—or else it succumbs, sooner or later. And this constraint, set on the plane of society, must be expressed also in the behavior of the individual. In general and on balance, and especially in production, the people will have to handle their resources with a view toward utilitarian advantage.[20] Natural selection is scarcely indifferent to imprudence and purposelessness in economic activity. Therefore, even if the propensity to economize is not human nature, it is in the nature of the human condition, and substantivism can say nothing about it significantly different from formalism.

The kind of rationality difficult to defend under the name of orthodox economy tends thus to reappear in the guise of ecological anthropology. Granted of the Trobriands for example, that *urigubu* does not circulate to anyone's personal gain, nevertheless the social cachet accorded those presenting large gifts of yams stimulates gardeners to extend themselves; in the event, the custom is adaptive and advantageous, at once intensifying production and generally disseminating the benefits. Even closer to the orthodox formula—for the flirtation with private prudence—are those analyses decided upon revealing the "materialist" sense of indigenous practices long enshrined by ethnology as classic examples of irrationality and waste: the ceremonial massacres of pigs in Melanesia, the sacredness of cattle in India, the potlatch of the Northwest Coast Indians—customs which a more subtle interpretation congratulates for an unsuspected efficiency of resource management.[21]

[18] *Cf.* the discussion of the issue following Dalton's article (1969).

[19] Insofar as the willful decisions of individuals (or what are taken as such by the observer) do faithfully encapsulate the general social rationality, this point has an ethnographic implication of theoretical importance. It means that even if it be argued that the formalist apparatus is inapplicable to the explanation of exotic economies it does not follow that ethnographic description in such terms simply cannot be done. It can be, and systematically has been (*e.g.*, Salisbury, 1962). Moreover, outside the context of comparison, the explanatory deficiencies of this procedure will not be apparent.

[20] A normal thermodynamic advantage of at least 10 to 1 in energy capture, by one recent estimate (Rappoport, 1968, p. 63).

[21] "I have written this paper because I believe the irrational, non-economic, and exotic aspects of the Indian cattle complex are greatly over-emphasized at the expense of the rational, economic and mundane interpretations" (Harris, 1966, p. 51). So, for example, "insofar as the beef-eating taboo helps to discourage growth of beef-producing it is part of an ecological adjustment which maximizes rather than minimizes on the calorie and protein output of the productive process" (p. 57; *cf.* Vayda, Leeds and Smith, 1961; Rappaport, 1968).

The apparent identity between the formal rationality as economizing and the substantive rationality as adaptation is nevertheless misleading. Economizing is a strategy of the maximum, whereas adaptation is the achievement of a minimum: difference is "the name of the game" that at once rescues the logical coherence of the substantive argument—while disclosing the logical insufficiency of certain explanations from "adaptive value".

On the one side, as between the formal calculus and the positive relation to nature envisioned by substantivism, the former stipulates criteria of effective performance unknown to the latter. Procedure of maximization, economizing admits only one solution to any problem of resource allocation: "the one best way". But survival is any way that works. Success is ecologically established from a minimum point —the minimum required of a cultural system to meet the selective pressures that would decompose it.[22] And between this threshold of what the system must do (in the environment as presented) and what it could do (with the techniques available), any number of intermediate solutions differing in cultural quality and productive quantity are positively adaptive. Therefore, substantive theory, unlike the formal, demands neither a social project of maximum resource use nor an individual behavior oriented singularly to the main chance. Various degrees of resource exploitation falling short of the optimum, thus not predictable from the formal praxeology, are nonetheless functional for the cultural praxis. Besides, even dispositions of resources at a loss are tolerable, so long as they are elsewhere compensated by net gains in the productive process. The adaptation to nature is not necessarily economical; neither is economy merely the adaptation to nature.

On the other side, then, and without calling into question the whole adaptational perspective, this practice of explaining a given custom by its economic virtues does invite a certain critique of the ecological reasoning. First, the adaptive viewpoint does not theoretically require a panglossian reinterpretation of every seeming folly. Inasmuch as adaptation knows only a lower limit, "irrational" and "wasteful" customs are ecologically valid, provided they do not reduce the overall material balance below that limit. Secondly, proof that a certain trait or cultural arrangement has positive economic value is not an adequate explanation of its existence or even of its presence. The *problématique* of adaptive advantage does not specify a uniquely correct answer. As principle of causality in general and economic performance in particular, "adaptive advantage" is indeterminate: stipulating grossly what is impossible but rendering suitable anything that is possible. To say that a certain cultural trait is "adaptive" in the light of its economic virtues is only a weak kind of functionalism, accounting not for its existence but merely for its feasibility—and then not necessarily, as materially disadvantageous traits may also be feasible. Finally, the ecological reasoning might come to a new and valuable understanding if it turned itself upside down, realizing that in selecting for a certain cultural arrangement however much it is functioning above the economic minimum—but not necessarily for its functioning above the minimum—adaptation is normally a principle of non-optimal resource use. The remarkable and world-wide feature of primitive economic performance, demonstrable besides from certain studies devoted to the unsuspected efficiencies of unlikely customs, is not how well societies do, but how poorly in relation to what they could do (see Sahlins, 1972). The "new materialism" seems analytically innocent of any concern for contradiction[23]—although it sometimes figures itself a client of marxism (minus the dialectical materialism). So it is unmindful of the barriers opposed to the productive forces by established cultural organizations, each con-

[22] Or, in the particular case of competition (internal or external), selection favors *relative* advantage, which is to say, the minimum significant difference between competitors.

[23] That is to say, except in the form of "negative feedback", which is not the negation of the negation but its elimination.

gealed by its adaptive advantages in some state of fractional effectiveness.[24]

As I said, this brief survey of the disagreements between formalism and substantivism, if written without disguise of my preference for the latter, was also without the intent of polemicizing in its favor. In fact—and it may be the sole claim to dispassion—the burning polemic issues were deliberately left aside. Much could have been said about the reciprocal complicity of bourgeois society and formal economics, and thus about the status of this economics as ideology at home and ethnocentrism abroad. And it may very well be that the greater struggle on the political and ideological levels will decide, at least in this or that part of the earth, which intellectual doctrine too shall carry the day. In any event it is clear than nothing will be decided by arguments of the kind debated here. Besides most of the parties to the dispute seem weary of the interminable methodological discussion and anxious rather to get to work. And that, after all, in its ability to render the concrete intelligible, is the only honest hope either side can entertain for itself.

[24] The lack of concern for internal cultural contradictions is logically and intimately connected with another (although minority) theoretical disposition of the "new materialism": the dismissal of culture as the subject and system under scrutiny. The fetters upon the productive forces ignored, direct relations of interdependence may be presumed between elements of culture and of nature, these interacting harmoniously in the adaptive interests of given human populations. The systematics, hence "the system", cross-cuts ontological levels, cannot be merely cultural. Clearly this position is sustained only so long as the contradictions within the cultural order, resulting in a less-than-optimum relation to nature, remain unrecognized.

References

AYRES, C. (1944) *The theory of economic progress.* Chapel Hill, N.C., University of North Carolina Press.

——— (1952) *The industrial economy.* Boston, Mass., Houghton Mifflin.

BURLING, R. (1962) "Maximization theories and the study of economic anthropology", *American anthropologist* 64:802–821.

COOK, S. (1966) "The obsolete 'anti-market' mentality: A critique of the substantive approach to economic anthropology", *American anthropologist* 63:1–25.

DALTON, G. (1969) "Theoretical issues in economic anthropology", *Current anthropology* 10:63–102.

EVANS-PRITCHARD, E. E. (1940). *The Nuer.* London, Oxford University Press.

ENGELS, F. (1966) *Anti-Dühring.* New York, International Publishers (New World Paperbacks; republication of 3rd ed., 1894).

FIRTH, R. (1950) *Primitive Polynesian economy.* New York, Humanities Press (first published in 1939).

GODELIER, M. (1966) *Rationalité et irrationalité en économie.* Paris, Maspero.

GOODFELLOW, D. M. (1939) *Principles of economic sociology.* London, Routledge.

HARRIS, M. (1966) "The cultural ecology of India's sacred cattle", *Current anthropology* 7:51–66.

HEILBRONER, R. L. (1968) *Understanding microeconomics.* Englewood Cliffs, N.J., Prentice-Hall.

HERSKOVITS, M. (1952) *Economic anthropology.* New York, Knopf (revised ed.).

KAPLAN, D. (1968) "The formal-substantive controversy in economic anthropology: Some reflections on its wider implications", *Southwestern journal of anthropology* 24:228–251.

MALINOWSKI, B. (1922) *Argonauts of the Western Pacific.* London, Routledge and Kegan Paul (3rd ed. 1950).

MARX, K. (1967) *Fondements de la critique de l'économie politique.* Paris, Anthropos (2 vols.).

——— (1968). *Misère de la philosophie.* Paris, Éd. Sociales (first published 1847).

MEILLASSOUX, C. (1960) "Essai d'une interprétation du phénomène économique dans les sociétés traditionnelles d'auto-subsistance", *Cahiers d'études africaines* 4:38–67.

NASH, M. (1967) " 'Reply' to reviews of *Primitive and peasant economic systems*", *Current anthropology* 8:249–250.

RAPPAPORT, R. (1968) *Pigs for the ancestors.* New Haven, Conn., Yale University Press.

ROBBINS, L. (1935) *An essay on the nature and significance of economic science.* London, Macmillan (2nd ed. reprinted 1952).

SCHMOLLER, G. (1910) *The mercantile system and its historical significance*. London, Macmillan.

SAHLINS, M. (1965) "On the sociology of primitive exchange", in: Banton, M. (ed.). *The relevance of models for social anthropology*. London, Tavistock (ASA monographs, 1).

——— (1968) *Tribesmen*. Englewood Cliffs, N.J., Prentice-Hall.

——— (1972) *Stone age economics*. Chicago-New York, Aldine.

SALISBURY, R. F. (1962) *From stone to steel*. London-New York, Cambridge University Press.

VAYDA, A.; LEEDS, A.; SMITH, D. (1961) "The place of pigs in Melanesian subsistence", in: Garfield, V. (ed.), *Proceedings of the American Ethnological Society*. Seattle, Wash., University of Washington Press.

WALKER, K. F. (1942–1943). "The study of primitive economics", *Oceania* 13:131–142.

25

THE ORIGIN OF THE FAMILY

KATHLEEN GOUGH

Shortly after the end of World War II, Ralph Linton, a well-known cultural anthropologist, concluded an article on the family with the portentous comment that "in the Gotterdämmerung which over-wise science and over-foolish statesmanship are preparing for us, the last man will spend his last hours searching for his wife and child." Linton intended by this remark to project his view that of all human groupings the most durable and enduring was the nuclear family.

Linton was quite sophisticated with respect to the ethnology of the family. In books and lectures he helped spread the notion that "family" structure was quite culturally variable, that the nuclear family was not a necessary structural component of human society. Although, unlike Kathleen Gough, he never did field-work among the Nayar of Southwest India, he was fascinated by descriptions of their *taravad,* the family unit which was comprised of a core of women—mothers and daughters and sisters—and their brothers and children; no husbands. Yet, sophisticated as he was, Linton concluded his article with the remark quoted above which, if not altogether clearly sexist, was clearly culture-bound, mired in the society he lived in and knew well. Yet this society was shortly to begin showing radical change.

Note that in the remark quoted, it is the man who plays the active role of seeking the wife and child. (Note it is a *man* and not a husband that seeks the *wife.*) A plausible scenario for this scene is very easy to construct: disaster strikes while the man is away, at work, while the woman is at home with the children, after all, she is a housewife. I doubt that I need go

SOURCE: "The Origin of the Family," *Journal of Marriage and the Family,* Vol. 33, No. 4 (November 1971):760–71. Reprinted by permission of National Council on Family Relations and author. A shorter version also appeared in *Up from Under,* Vol. 1 (3); 1971:47–52.

any further in analyzing the complex bag of assumptions implicit in Linton's sentence. Just as a generation and more of anthropology students read and accepted such assumptions without question, so many present readers, now sensitized on such points, will have their own strong reactions. Others, of course, will continue to wonder what all the fuss is about and only more time will tell if present trends will continue until all see more clearly what has been going on in social relations between the sexes.

Among the most sensitive are those, mostly women, with some more or less direct involvement in the political movement known as Women's Liberation. In recent years there has been a healthy outpouring of criticism and commentary on behalf of that movement in various shades and phases. Statements range in validity and reliability. This is certainly the case with regard to attempts to portray the status of women in other cultures and in other times. Some statements, for example, seem to portray the structural inferiority of women as a social invention of capitalism. Others glorify the role of women in primitive society, or assert the former existence of matriarchies, societies in which predominant political control was vested in females.

It is precisely into these questions that Professor Kathleen Gough ventures. I will not interfere with her telling by summarizing her findings. Let me say instead that she is known as a skilled field worker and as one of our leading authorities on the analysis of matrilineal kinship systems. She is a self-proclaimed radical anthropologist, known for her low tolerance of nonsense.

▼△▼△▼

The trouble with the origin of the family is that no one really knows. Since Engels wrote *The Origin of the Family, Private Property and the State* in 1884, a great deal of new evidence has come in. Yet the gaps are still enormous. It is not known *when* the family originated, although it was probably between two million and 100,000 years ago. It is not known whether it developed once or in separate times and places. It is not known whether some kind of embryonic family came before, with, or after the origin of language. Since language is the accepted criterion of humanness, this means that we do not even know whether our ancestors acquired the basics of family life before or after they were human. The chances are that language and the family developed together over a long period, but the evidence is sketchy.

Although the origin of the family is speculative, it is better to speculate with than without evidence. The evidence comes from three sources. One is the social and physical lives of non-human primates—especially the New and Old World monkeys and, still more, the great apes, humanity's closest relatives. The second source is the tools and home sites of prehistoric humans and proto-humans. The third is the family lives of hunters and gatherers of wild provender who have been studied in modern times.

Each of these sources is imperfect: monkeys and apes, because they are *not* pre-human ancestors, although they are our cousins; fossil hominids, because they left so little vestige of their social life; hunters and gatherers, because none of them has, in historic times, possessed a technology and society as primitive as those of early humans. All show the results of long endeavor in specialized, marginal environments. But together, these sources give valuable clues.

Defining the Family

To discuss the origin of something we must first decide what it is. I shall define the family as "a married couple or other group of adult kinsfolk who cooperate economically and in the upbringing of children, and all or most of whom share a common dwelling."

This includes all forms of kin-based household. Some are extended families containing three generations of married brothers or sisters. Some are "grandfamilies" descended from a single pair of grandparents. Some are matrilineage households, in which brothers and sisters share a house with the sisters' children, and men merely visit their wives in other homes. Some are compound families, in which one man has several wives, or one woman, several husbands. Others are nuclear families composed of a father, mother and children.

Some kind of family exists in all known human societies, although it is not found in every segment or class of all stratified, state societies. Greek and American slaves, for example, were prevented from forming legal families, and their social families were often disrupted by sale, forced labor, or sexual exploitation. Even so, the family was an ideal which all classes and most people attained when they could.

The family implies several other universals. (1) Rules forbid sexual relations and marriage between close relatives. Which relatives are forbidden varies, but all societies forbid mother-son mating, and most, father-daughter and brother-sister. Some societies allow sex relations, but forbid marriage, between certain degrees of kin. (2) The men and women of a family cooperate through a division of labor based on gender. Again, the sexual division of labor varies in rigidity and in the tasks performed. But in no human society to date is it wholly absent. Child-care, household tasks and crafts closely connected with the household, tend to be done by women; war, hunting, and government, by men. (3) Marriage exists as a socially recognized, durable, although not necessarily lifelong relationship between individual men and women. From it springs social fatherhood, some kind of special bond between a man and the child of his wife, whether or not they are his own children physiologically. Even in polyandrous societies, where women have several husbands, or in matrilineal societies, where group membership and property pass through women, each child has one or more designated "fathers" with whom he has a special social, and often religious, relationship. This bond of *social* fatherhood is recognized among people who do not know about the male role in procreation, or where, for various reasons, it is not clear who the physiological father of a particular infant is. Social fatherhood seems to come from the division and interdependence of male and female tasks, especially in relation to children, rather than directly from physiological fatherhood, although in most societies, the social father of a child is usually presumed to be its physiological father as well. Contrary to the beliefs of some feminists, however, I think that in no human society do men, as a whole category, have *only* the role of insemination, and *no* other social or economic role, in relation to women and children. (4) Men in general have higher status and authority over the women of their families, although older women may have influence, even some authority, over junior men. The omnipresence of male authority, too, goes contrary to the belief of some feminists that in "matriarchal" societies, women were either completely equal to, or had paramount authority over, men, either in the home or in society at large.

It is true that in some matrilineal societies, such as the Hopi of Arizona or the Ashanti of Ghana, men exert little authority over their wives. In some, such as the Nayars of South India or the Minangkabau of Sumatra, men may even live separately from their wives and children, that is, in different families. In such societies, however, the fact is that women and children fall under greater or lesser authority from the women's kinsmen—their eldest brothers, mothers' brothers, or even their grown up sons.

In matrilineal societies, where property, rank, office and group membership are inherited through the female line, it is true that women tend to have greater independence than in patrilineal societies. This is especially so in matrilineal tribal societies where the state has not yet developed, and especially in those tribal societies where residence is matrilocal—that is, men come to live in the homes or villages of their wives. Even so, in all matrilineal societies for which adequate descriptions are available, the ultimate headship of households, lineages and local groups is usually with men.[1]

There is in fact no true "matriarchal," as distinct from "matrilineal," society in existence or known from literature, and the chances are that there never has been.[2] This does not mean that women and men have never had relations that were dignified and creative for both sexes, appropriate to the knowledge, skills and technology of their times. Nor does it mean that the sexes cannot be equal in the future, or that the sexual division of labor cannot be abolished. I believe that it can and must be. But it is not necessary to believe myths of a feminist Golden Age in order to plan for parity in the future.

Primate Societies

Within the primate order, humans are most closely related to the anthropoid apes (the African chimpanzee and gorilla and the Southeast Asian orang-utan and gibbon), and of these, to the chimpanzee and the gorilla. More distantly related are the Old, and then the New World, monkeys, and finally, the lemurs, tarsiers and tree-shrews.

All primates share characteristics without which the family could not have developed. The young are born relatively helpless. They suckle for several months or years and need prolonged care afterwards. Childhood is longer, the closer the species is to humans. Most monkeys reach puberty at about four to five and mature socially between about five and ten. Chimpanzees, by contrast, suckle for up to three years. Females reach puberty at seven to ten; males enter mature social and sexual relations as late as thirteen. The long childhood and maternal care produce close relations between children of the same mother, who play together and help tend their juniors until they grow up.

Monkeys and apes, like humans, mate in all months of the year instead of in a rutting season. Unlike humans, however, female apes experience unusually strong sexual desire for a few days shortly before and during ovulation (the oestrus period), and have intensive sexual relations at that time. The males are attracted to the females by their scent or by brightly colored swellings in the sexual region. Oestrus-mating appears to be especially pronounced in primate species more remote from humans. The apes and some monkeys carry on less intensive, month-round sexuality in addition to oestrus-mating, approaching human patterns more closely. In humans, sexual desires and relations are regulated less by hormonal changes and more by mental images, emotions, cultural rules and individual preferences.

Year-round (if not always month-round) sexuality means that males and females socialize more continuously among primates than among most other mammals. All primates form bands or troops composed of both sexes plus children. The numbers and proportions of the sexes vary, and in some species an individual, a mother with her young, or a subsidiary troop of male juveniles may travel temporarily alone. But in general, males and females socialize continually through mutual grooming[3] and playing as well as through frequent sex relations. Keeping close to the females, primate males play with their children and tend to protect both females and young from predators. A

---

[1] See David M. Schneider and Kathleen Gough, eds., *Matrilineal Kinship,* Berkeley, 1961, for common and variant features of matrilineal systems.

[2] The Iroquois are often quoted as a "matriarchal" society, but in fact Morgan himself refers to "the absence of equality between the sexes" and notes that women were subordinate to men, ate after men, and that women (not men) were publicly whipped as punishment for adultery. Warleaders, tribal chiefs, and *sachems* (heads of matrilineal lineages) were men. Women did, however, have a large say in the government of the long-house or home of the matrilocal extended family, and women figured as tribal counsellors and religious officials, as well as arranging marriages. (Lewis H. Morgan: The League of the *Ho-de-ne Saunee or Iroquois,* Human Relations Area Files, 1954.)

[3] Combing the hair and removing parasites with hands or teeth.

"division of labor" based on gender is thus already found in primate society between a female role of prolonged child care and a male role of defense. Males may also carry or take care of children briefly, and non-nursing females may fight. But a kind of generalized "fatherliness" appears in the protective role of adult males towards young, even in species where the sexes do not form long-term individual attachments.

Sexual Bonds Among Primates

Some non-human primates do have enduring sexual bonds and restrictions, superficially similar to those in some human societies. Among gibbons a single male and female live together with their young. The male drives off other males and the female, other females. When a juvenile reaches puberty it is thought to leave or be expelled by the parent of the same sex, and he eventually finds a mate elsewhere. Similar *de facto*, rudimentary "incest prohibitions" may have been passed on to humans from their prehuman ancestors and later codified and elaborated through language, moral custom and law. Whether this is so may become clearer when we know more about the mating patterns of the other great apes, especially of our closest relatives, the chimpanzees. Present evidence suggests that male chimpanzees do not mate with their mothers.

Orang-utans live in small, tree-dwelling groups like gibbons, but their forms are less regular. One or two mothers may wander alone with their young, mating at intervals with a male; or a male-female pair, or several juvenile males, may travel together.

Among mountain gorillas of Uganda, South Indian langurs, and hamadryas baboons of Ethiopia, a single, fully mature male mates with several females, especially in their oestrus periods. If younger adult males are present, the females may have occasional relations with them if the leader is tired or not looking.

Among East and South African baboons, rhesus macaques, and South American woolly monkeys, the troop is bigger, numbering up to two hundred. It contains a number of adult males and a much larger number of females. The males are strictly ranked in terms of dominance based on both physical strength and intelligence. The more dominant males copulate intensively with the females during the latters' oestrus periods. Toward the end of oestrus a female may briefly attach herself to a single dominant male. At other times she may have relations with any male of higher or lower rank provided that those of higher rank permit it.

Among some baboons and macaques the young males travel on the outskirts of the group and have little access to females. Some macaques expel from the troop a proportion of the young males, who then form "bachelor troops." Bachelors may later form new troops with young females.

Other primates are more thoroughly promiscuous, or rather indiscriminate, in mating. Chimpanzees, and also South American howler monkeys, live in loosely structured groups, again (as in most monkey and ape societies) with a preponderance of females. The mother-child unit is the only stable group. The sexes copulate almost at random, and most intensively and indiscriminately during oestrus.

A number of well known anthropologists have argued that various attitudes and customs often found in human societies are instinctual rather than culturally learned, and come from our primate heritage. They include hierarchies of ranking among men, male political power over women, and the greater tendency of men to form friendships with one another, as opposed to women's tendencies to cling to a man.[4]

I cannot accept these conclusions and think

[4] See, for example, Desmond Morris, *The Naked Ape*, Jonathan Cape, 1967; Robin Fox, *Kinship and Marriage*, Pelican Books, 1967.

that they stem from the male chauvinism of our own society. A "scientific" argument which states that all such features of female inferiority are instinctive is obviously a powerful weapon in maintaining the traditional family with male dominance. But in fact, these features are *not* universal among non-human primates, including some of those most closely related to humans. Chimpanzees have a low degree of male dominance and male hierarchy and are sexually virtually indiscriminate. Gibbons have a kind of fidelity for both sexes and almost no male dominance or hierarchy. Howler monkeys are sexually indiscriminate and lack male hierarchies or dominance.

The fact is that among non-human primates male dominance and male hierarchies seem to be adaptations to particular environments, some of which did become genetically established through natural selection. Among humans, however, these features are present in variable degrees and are almost certainly learned, not inherited at all. Among non-human primates there are fairly general differences between those that live mainly in trees and those that live largely on the ground. The tree dwellers (for example, gibbons, orangutans, South American howler and woolly monkeys) tend to have to defend themselves less against predators than do the ground-dwellers (such as baboons, macaques or gorillas). Where defense is important, males are much larger and stronger than females, exert dominance over females, and are strictly hierarchized and organized in relation to one another. Where defense is less important there is much less sexual dimorphism (difference in size between male and female), less or no male dominance, a less pronounced male hierarchy, and greater sexual indiscriminacy.

Comparatively speaking, humans have a rather small degree of sexual dimorphism, similar to chimpanzees. Chimpanzees live much in trees but also partly on the ground, in forest or semi-forest habitats. They build individual nests to sleep in, sometimes on the ground but usually in trees. They flee into trees from danger. Chimpanzees go mainly on all fours, but sometimes on two feet, and can use and make simple tools. Males are dominant, but not very dominant, over females. The rank hierarchy among males is unstable, and males often move between groups, which vary in size from two to fifty individuals. Food is vegetarian, supplemented with worms, grubs or occasional small animals. A mother and her young form the only stable unit. Sexual relations are largely indiscriminate, but nearby males defend young animals from danger. The chances are that our pre-human ancestors had a similar social life. Morgan and Engels were probably right in concluding that we came from a state of "original promiscuity" before we were fully human.

Judging from the fossil record, apes ancestral to humans, gorillas and chimpanzees roamed widely in Asia, Europe and Africa some twelve to twenty-eight million years ago. Toward the end of that period (the Miocene) one appears in North India and East Africa, Ramapithecus, who may be ancestral both to later hominids and to modern humans. His species were small like gibbons, walked upright on two feet, had human rather than ape corner-teeth, and therefore probably used hands rather than teeth to tear their food. From that time evolution toward humanness must have proceeded through various phases until the emergence of modern *homo sapiens*, about 70,000 years ago.

In the Miocene period before Ramapithecus appeared, there were several time-spans in which, over large areas, the climate became dryer and sub-tropical forests dwindled or disappeared. A standard reconstruction of events, which I accept, is that groups of apes, probably in Africa, had to come down from the trees and adapt to terrestrial life. Through natural selection, probably over millions of years, they developed specialized feet for walking. Thus freed, the hands came to be used not only (as among apes) for grasping and tearing, but for regular carrying of objects such as weapons (which had hitherto been sporadic) or of infants (which had hitherto clung to their mothers' body hair).

The spread of indigestible grasses on the open savannahs may have encouraged, if it did not compel, the early ground dwellers to become active hunters rather than simply to forage for small, sick or dead animals that came their way. Collective hunting and tool use involved group cooperation and helped foster the growth of language out of the call-systems of apes. Language meant the use of symbols to refer to events not present. It allowed greatly increased foresight, memory, planning and division of tasks—in short, the capacity for human thought.

With the change to hunting, group territories became much larger. Apes range only a few thousand feet daily; hunters, several miles. But because their infants were helpless, nursing women could hunt only small game close to home. This then produced the sexual division of labor on which the human family has since been founded. Women elaborated upon ape methods of child care, and greatly expanded foraging, which in most areas remained the primary and most stable source of food. Men improved upon ape methods of fighting off other animals, and of group protection in general. They adapted these methods to hunting, using weapons which for millennia remained the same for the chase as for human warfare.

Out of the sexual division of labor came, for the first time, home life as well as group cooperation. Female apes nest with and provide foraged food for their infants. But adult apes do not cooperate in food getting or nest building. They build new nests each night wherever they may happen to be. With the development of a hunting-gathering complex, it became necessary to have a G.H.Q., or home. Men could bring meat to this place for several days' supply. Women and children could meet men there after the day's hunting, and could bring their vegetable produce for general consumption. Men, women and children could build joint shelters, butcher meat, and treat skins for clothing.

Later, fire came into use for protection against wild animals, for lighting, and eventually for cooking. The hearth then provided the focus and symbol of home. With the development of cookery, some humans—chiefly women, and perhaps some children and old men—came to spend more time preparing nutrition so that all people need spend less time in chewing and tearing their food. Meals—already less frequent because of the change to a carnivorous diet—now became brief, periodic events instead of the long feeding sessions of apes.

The change to humanness brought two bodily changes that affected birth and child care. These were head-size and width of the pelvis. Walking upright produced a narrower pelvis to hold the guts in position. Yet as language developed, brains and hence heads grew much bigger relative to body size. To compensate, humans are born at an earlier stage of growth than apes. They are helpless longer and require longer and more total care. This in turn caused early women to concentrate more on child care and less on defense than do female apes.

Language made possible not only a division and cooperation in labor but also all forms of tradition, rules, morality and cultural learning. Rules banning sex relations among close kinfolk must have come very early. Precisely how or why they developed is unknown, but they had at least two useful functions. They helped to preserve order in the family as a cooperative unit, by outlawing competition for mates. They also created bonds *between* families, or even between separate bands, and so provided a basis for wider cooperation in the struggle for livelihood and the expansion of knowledge.

It is not clear when all these changes took place. Climatic change with increased drought began regionally up to 28 million years ago. The divergence between pre-human and gorilla-chimpanzee stems had occurred in both Africa and India at least 12 million years ago. The pre-human stem led to the Australopithecines of East and South Africa, about 3,000,000 years ago. These were pygmy-like, two footed, upright hominids with larger than ape brains, who made tools and probably hunted in savannah regions. It is unlikely that they knew the use of fire.

The first known use of fire is that of cave-dwelling hominids (Sinanthropus, a branch of the Pithecanthropines) at Choukoutien near Peking, some half a million years ago during the second ice age. Fire was used regularly in hearths, suggesting cookery, by the time of the Acheulean and Mousterian cultures of Neanderthal man in Europe, Africa and Asia before, during and after the third ice age, some 150,000 to 100,000 years ago. These people, too, were often cave dwellers, and buried their dead ceremonially in caves. Cave dwelling by night as well as by day was probably, in fact, not safe for humans until fire came into use to drive away predators.

Most anthropologists conclude that home life, the family and language had developed by the time of Neanderthal man, who was closely similar and may have been ancestral to modern *Homo sapiens*. At least two anthropologists, however, believe that the Australopithecenes already had language nearly two million years ago, while another thinks that language and incest prohibitions did not evolve until the time of *Homo sapiens* some 70,000 to 50,000 years ago.[5] I am myself inclined to think that family life built around tool use, the use of language, cookery, and a sexual division of labor, must have been established sometime between about 500,000 and 200,000 years ago.

[5] For the former view, see Charles F. Hockett and Robert Ascher, "The Human Revolution," in *Man in Adaptation: The Biosocial Background,* edited by Yehudi A. Cohen, Aldine, 1968; for the latter, Frank B. Livingstone, "Genetics, Ecology and the Origin of Incest and Exogamy," *Current Anthropology,* February 1969.

Hunters and Gatherers

Most of the hunting and gathering societies studied in the eighteenth to twentieth centuries had technologies similar to those that were wide-spread in the Mesolithic period, which occurred about 15,000 to 10,000 years ago, after the ice ages ended but before cultivation was invented and animals domesticated.

Modern hunters live in marginal forest, mountain, arctic or desert environments where cultivation is impracticable. Although by no means "primeval," the hunters of recent times do offer clues to the types of family found during that 99 percent of human history before the agricultural revolution. They include the Eskimo, many Canadian and South American Indian groups, the forest BaMbuti (pygmies) and the desert Bushmen of Southern Africa, the Kadar of South India, the Veddah of Ceylon, and the Andaman Islanders of the Indian Ocean. About 175 hunting and gathering cultures in Oceania, Asia, Africa and America have been described in fair detail.

In spite of their varied environments, hunters share certain features of social life. They live in bands of about 20 to 200 people, the majority of bands having fewer than 50. Bands are divided into families, which may forage alone in some seasons. Hunters have simple but ingenious technologies. Bows and arrows, spears, needles, skin clothing, and temporary leaf or wood shelters are common. Most hunters do some fishing. The band forages and hunts in a large territory and usually moves camp often.

Social life is egalitarian. There is of course no state, no organized government. Apart from religious shamans or magicians, the division of labor is based only on sex and age. Resources are owned communally; tools and personal possessions are freely exchanged. Everyone works who can. Band leadership goes to whichever man has the intelligence, courage and foresight to command the respect of his fellows. Intelligent older women are also looked up to.

The household is the main unit of economic cooperation, with the men, women and children dividing the labor and pooling their produce. In 97 percent of the 175 societies classified by G. P. Murdock, hunting is confined to men; in the other three percent it is chiefly a male pursuit. Gathering of wild plants, fruits and nuts is women's work. In 60 percent of societies, only women gather, while in another 32 percent gathering is mainly feminine. Fishing is solely or mainly men's work in 93 percent of the hunting societies where it occurs.

For the rest, men monopolize fighting, although interband warfare is rare. Women tend children and shelters and usually do most of the cooking, processing, and storage of food. Women tend, also, to be foremost in the early household crafts such as basketry, leather work, the making of skin or bark clothing, and in the more advanced hunting societies, pottery. (Considering that women probably *invented* all of these crafts, in addition to cookery, food storage and preservation, agriculture, spinning, weaving, and perhaps even house construction, it is clear that women played quite as important roles as men in early cultural development.) Building dwellings and making tools and ornaments are variously divided between the sexes, while boat-building is largely done by men. Girls help the women, and boys play at hunting or hunt small game until they reach puberty, when both take on the roles of adults. Where the environment makes it desirable, the men of a whole band or of some smaller cluster of households cooperate in hunting or fishing and divide their spoils. Women of nearby families often go gathering together.

Family composition varies among hunters as it does in other kinds of societies. About half or more of known hunting societies have nuclear families (father, mother and children), with polygynous households (a man, two or more wives, and children) as occasional variants. Clearly, nuclear families are the most common among hunters, although hunters have a slightly higher proportion of polygynous families than do non-hunting societies.

About a third of hunting societies contain some "stem-family" households—that is, older parents live together with one married child and grandchildren, while the other married children live in independent dwellings. A still smaller proportion live in large extended families containing several married brothers (or several married sisters), their spouses, and children.[6] Hunters have fewer extended and stem families than do non-hunting societies. These larger households become common with the rise of agriculture. They are especially found in large, pre-industrial agrarian states such as ancient Greece, Rome, India, the Islamic empires, China, etc.

Hunting societies also have few households composed of a widow or divorcee and her children. This is understandable, for neither men nor women can survive long without the work and produce of the other sex, and marriage is the way to obtain them. That is why so often young men must show proof of hunting prowess, and girls of cooking, before they are allowed to marry.

The family, together with territorial grouping, provides the framework of society among hunters. Indeed, as Morgan and Engels clearly saw, kinship and territory are the foundations of all societies before the rise of the state. Not only hunting and gathering bands, but the larger and more complex tribes and chiefdoms of primitive cultivators and herders organize people through descent from common ancestors or through marriage ties between

[6] For exact figures, see G. P. Murdock, World Ethnographic Sample, *American Anthropologist*, 1957; Allan D. Coult, *Cross Tabulations of Murdock's World Ethnographic Sample*, University of Missouri, 1965; and G. P. Murdock, *Ethnographic Atlas*, University of Pittsburgh, 1967. In the last-named survey, out of 175 hunting societies, 47 percent had nuclear family households, 38 percent had stem-families, and 14 percent had extended families.

groups. Among hunters, things are simple. There is only the family, and beyond it the band. With the domestication of plants and animals, the economy becomes more productive. More people can live together. Tribes form, containing several thousand people loosely organized into large kin-groups such as clans and lineages, each composed of a number of related families. With still further development of the productive forces the society throws up a central political leadership, together with craft specialization and trade, and so the chiefdom emerges. But this, too, is structured through ranked allegiances and marriage ties between kin groups.

Only with the rise of the state does class, independently of kinship, provide the basis for relations of production, distribution and power. Even then, kin groups remain large in the agrarian state and kinship persists as the prime organizing principle within each class until the rise of capitalism. The reduction in significance of the family that we see today is the outgrowth of a decline in the importance of "familism" relative to other institutions, that began with the rise of the state, but became speeded up with the development of capitalism and machine industry. In most modern socialist societies, the family is even less significant as an organizing principle. It is reasonable to suppose that in the future it will become minimal or may disappear at least as a legally constituted unit for exclusive forms of sexual and economic cooperation and of child-care.

Morgan and Engels (1942) thought that from a state of original promiscuity, early humans at first banned sex relations between the generations of parents and children, but continued to allow them indiscriminately between brothers, sisters and all kinds of cousins within the band. They called this the "consanguineal family." They thought that later, all mating within the family or some larger kin group became forbidden, but that there was a stage (the "punaluan") in which a group of sisters or other close kinswomen from one band were married jointly to a group of brothers or other close kinsmen from another. They thought that only later still, and especially with the domestication of plants and animals, did the "pairing family" develop in which each man was married to one or two women individually.

These writers drew their conclusions not from evidence of actual group-marriage among primitive peoples but from the kinship terms found today in certain tribal and chiefly societies. Some of these equate all kin of the same sex in the parents' generation, suggesting brother-sister marriage. Others equate the father's brothers with the father, and the mother's sisters with the mother, suggesting the marriage of a group of brothers with a group of sisters.

Modern evidence does not bear out these conclusions about early society. All known hunters and gatherers live in families, not in communal sexual arrangements. Most hunters even live in nuclear families rather than in large extended kin groups. Mating is individualized, although one man may occasionally have two wives, or (very rarely) a woman may have two husbands. Economic life is built primarily around the division of labor and partnership between individual men and women. The hearths, caves and other remains of Upper Palaeolithic hunters suggest that this was probably an early arrangement. We cannot say that Engels' sequences are completely ruled out for very early hominids—the evidence is simply not available. But it is hard to see what economic arrangements among hunters would give rise to group, rather than individual or "pairing" marriage arrangements, and this Engels does not explain.

Soviet anthropologists continued to believe in Morgan and Engels' early "stages" longer than did anthropologists in the West. Today, most Russian anthropologists admit the lack of evidence for "consanguineal" and "punaluan" arrangements, but some still believe that a different kind of group marriage intervened between indiscriminate mating and the pairing family. Semyonov, for example, argues that in the stage of group marriage, mating was forbidden within the hunting band, but that the men of two neighboring bands had multiple, visiting sex relations with women of the opposite band.[7]

While such an arrangement cannot be ruled out, it seems unlikely because many of the customs which Semyonov regards as "survivals" of such group marriage (for example, visiting husbands, matrilineage dwelling groups, wide-spread clans, multiple spouses for both sexes, men's and women's communal houses, and prohibitions of sexual intercourse inside the huts of the village) are actually found not so much among hunters as among horticultural tribes, and even, quite complex agricultural states. Whether or not such a stage of group-marriage occurred in the earliest societies, there seems little doubt that pairing marriage (involving family households) came about with the development of elaborate methods of hunting, cooking, and the preparation of clothing and shelters—that is, with a fully-fledged division of labor.

Even so, there *are* some senses in which mating among hunters has more of a group character than in archaic agrarian states or in capitalist society. Murdock's sample shows that sex relations before marriage are strictly prohibited in only 26 percent of hunting societies. In the rest, marriage is either arranged so early that pre-marital sex is unlikely, or (more usually) sex relations are permitted more or less freely before marriage.

With marriage, monogamy is the normal *practice* at any given time for most hunters, but it is not the normal *rule*. Only 19 percent in Murdock's survey prohibit plural unions. Where polygyny is found (79 percent) the most common type is for a man to marry two sisters or other closely related women of the same kin group—for example, the daughters of two sisters or of two brothers. When a woman dies it is common for a sister to replace her in the marriage, and when a man dies, for a brother to replace him.

Similarly, many hunting societies hold that the wives of brothers or other close kinsmen are in some senses wives of the group. They can be called on in emergencies or if one of them is ill. Again, many hunting societies have special times for sexual license between men and women of a local group who are not married to each other, such as the "lights out" games of Eskimo sharing a communal snowhouse. In other situations, an Eskimo wife will spend the night with a chance guest of her husband's. All parties expect this as normal hospitality. Finally, adultery, although often punished, tends to be common in hunting societies, and few if any of them forbid divorce or the remarriage of divorcees and widows.

The reason for all this seems to be that marriage and sexual restrictions are practical arrangements among hunters designed mainly to serve economic and survival needs. In these societies, some kind of rather stable pairing best accomplishes the division of labor and cooperation of men and women and the care of children. Beyond the immediate family, either a larger family group or the whole band has other, less intensive but important, kinds of cooperative activities. Therefore, the husbands and wives of individuals within that group can be summoned to stand in for each other if need arises. In the case of Eskimo wife-lending, the extreme climate and the need for lone wandering in search of game dictate high standards of hospitality. This evidently becomes extended to sexual sharing.

In the case of sororal polygyny or marriage to the dead wife's sister, it is natural that when two women fill the same role—either together or in sequence—they should be sisters, for sisters are more alike than other women. They

[7] Y. I. Semyonov, "Group Marriage, its Nature and Role in the Evolution of Marriage and Family Relations," *Seventh International Congress of Anthropological and Ethnological Sciences,* Volume IV, Moscow 1967.

are likely to care more for each other's children. The replacement of a dead spouse by a sister or a brother also preserves existing intergroup relations. For the rest, where the economic and survival bonds of marriage are not at stake, people can afford to be freely companionate and tolerant. Hence pre-marital sexual freedom, seasonal group-license, and a pragmatic approach to adultery.

Marriages among hunters are usually arranged by elders when a young couple are ready for adult responsibilities. But the couple know each other and usually have some choice. If the first marriage does not work, the second mate will almost certainly be self selected. Both sexual and companionate love between individual men and women are known and are deeply experienced. With comparative freedom of mating, love is less often separated from or opposed to marriage than in archaic states or even than in some modern nations.

The Position of Women

Even in hunting societies it seems that women are always in some sense the "second sex," with greater or less subordination to men. This varies. Eskimo and Australian aboriginal women are far more subordinate than women among the Kadar, the Andamanese or the Congo Pygmies—all forest people.

I suggest that women have greater power and independence among hunters when they are important food-obtainers than when they are mainly processors of meat or other supplies provided by men. The former situation is likelier to exist in societies where hunting is small-scale and intensive than where it is extensive over a large terrain, and in societies where gathering is important by comparison with hunting.

In general in hunting societies, however, women are less subordinated in certain crucial respects than they are in most, if not all, of the archaic states, or even in some capitalist nations. These respects include men's ability to deny women sexuality or to force it upon them; to command or exploit their labor or to control their produce; to control or rob them of their children; to confine them physically and prevent their movement; to use them as objects in male transactions; to cramp their creativeness; or to withhold from them large areas of the society's knowledge and cultural attainments.

Especially lacking in hunting societies is the kind of male possessiveness and exclusiveness regarding women that leads to such institutions as savage punishments or death for female adultery, the jealous guarding of female chastity and virginity, the denial of divorce to women, or the ban on a woman's remarriage after her husband's death.

For these reasons, I do not think we can speak, as some writers do, of a class-division between men and women in hunting societies. True, men are more mobile than women and they lead in public affairs. But class society requires that one class control the means of production, dictate its use by the other classes, and expropriate the surplus. These conditions do not exist among hunters. Land and other resources are held communally, although women may monopolize certain gathering areas, and men, their hunting grounds. There is rank difference, role difference, and some difference respecting degrees of authority, between the sexes, but there is reciprocity rather than domination or exploitation.

As Engels saw, the power of men to exploit women systematically springs from the existence of surplus wealth, and more directly, from the state, social stratification, and the control of property by men. With the rise of the state, because of their monopoly over weapons, and because freedom from child care allows them to enter specialized economic and political roles, some men—especially ruling class men—acquire power over other men and over women. Almost all men acquire it over women of their own or lower classes, especially within their own kinship groups. These kinds of male power are shadowy among hunters.

To the extent that men *have* power over women in hunting societies, this seems to spring from the male monopoly of heavy weapons, from the particular division of labor between the sexes, or from both. Although men seldom use weapons against women, they *possess* them (or possess superior weapons) in addition to their physical strength. This does give men an ultimate control of force. When old people or babies must be killed to ensure band or family survival, it is usually men who kill them. Infanticide—rather common among hunters, who must limit the mouths to feed—is more often female infanticide than male.

The hunting of men seems more often to require them to organize in groups than does the work of women. Perhaps because of this, about 60 percent of hunting societies have predominantly virilocal residence. That is, men choose which band to live in (often, their fathers'), and women move with their husbands. This gives a man advantages over his wife in terms of familiarity and loyalties, for the wife is often a stranger. Sixteen to 17 percent of hunting societies are, however, uxorilocal, with men moving to the households of their wives, while 15 to 17 percent are bilocal—that is, either sex may move in with the other on marriage.

Probably because of male cooperation in defense and hunting, men are more prominent in band councils and leadership, in medicine and magic, and in public rituals designed to increase game, to ward off sickness, or to initiate boys into manhood. Women do, however, often take part in band councils; they are not excluded from law and government as in many agrarian states. Some women are respected as wise leaders, story tellers, doctors, or magicians, or are feared as witches. Women have their own ceremonies of fertility, birth and healing, from which men are often excluded.

In some societies, although men control the most sacred objects, women are believed to have discovered them. Among the Congo Pygmies, religion centers about a beneficent spirit, the Animal of the Forest. It is represented by wooden trumpets that are owned and played by men. Their possession and use are hidden from the women and they are played at night when hunting is bad, someone falls ill, or death occurs. During the playing men dance in the public campfire, which is sacred and is associated with the forest. Yet the men believe that women originally owned the trumpet and that it was a woman who stole fire from the chimpanzees or from the forest spirit. When a woman has failed to bear children for several years, a special ceremony is held. Women lead in the songs that usually accompany the trumpets, and an old woman kicks apart the campfire. Temporary female dominance seems to be thought necessary to restore fertility.

In some hunting societies women are exchanged between local groups, which are thus knit together through marriages. Sometimes, men of different bands directly exchange their sisters. More often there is a generalized exchange of women between two or more groups, or a one-way movement of women within a circle of groups. Sometimes the husband's family pays weapons, tools or ornaments to the wife's in return for the wife's services and later, her children.

In such societies, although they may be well treated and their consent sought, women are clearly the moveable partners in an arrangement controlled by men. Male anthropologists have seized on this as evidence of original male dominance and patrilocal residence. Fox and others, for example, have argued that until recently, *all* hunting societies formed outmarrying patrilocal bands, linked together politically by the exchange of women. The fact that fewer than two-thirds of hunting societies are patrilocal today, and only 41 percent have band-exogamy, is explained in terms of modern conquest, economic change and depopulation.

I cannot accept this formula. It is true that modern hunting societies have been severely changed, de-culturated, and often depopulated, by capitalist imperialism. I can see little evidence, however, that the ones that are patrilocal today have undergone less change than those that are not. It is hard to believe that in spite of enormous environmental diversity and the passage of thousands, perhaps millions, of years, hunting societies all had band exogamy with patrilocal residence until they were disturbed by western imperialism. It is more likely that early band societies, like later agricultural tribes, developed variety in family life and the status of women as they spread over the earth.

There is also some likelihood that the earliest hunters had matrilocal rather than patrilocal families. Among apes and monkeys, it is almost always males who leave the troop or are driven out. Females stay closer to their mothers and their original site; males move about, attaching themselves to females where availability and competition permit. Removal of the wife to the husband's home or band may have been a relatively late development in societies where male cooperation in hunting assumed overwhelming importance.[8] Conversely, after the development of horticulture (which was probably invented and is mainly carried out by women), those tribes in which horticulture predominated over stock raising were most likely to be or to remain matrilocal and to develop matrilineal descent groups with a relatively high status of women. But where extensive hunting of large animals, or later, the herding of large domesticates, predominated, patrilocal residence flourished and women were used to form alliances between male-centered groups. With the invention of metallurgy and of agriculture as distinct from horticulture after 4000 B.C., men came to control agriculture and many crafts, and most of the great agrarian states had patrilocal residence with patriarchal, male-dominant families.

[8] Upper Palaeolithic hunters produced female figurines that were obvious emblems of fertility. The cult continued through the Mesolithic and into the Neolithic period. Goddesses and spirits of fertility are found in some patrilineal as well as matrilineal societies, but they tend to be more prominent in the latter. It is thus possible that in many areas even late Stone Age hunters had matrilocal residence and perhaps matrilineal descent, and that in some regions this pattern continued through the age of horticulture and even—as in the case of the Nayars of Kerala and the Minangkabau of Sumatra—into the age of plow agriculture, of writing, and of the small-scale state.

Conclusions

The family is a human institution, not found in its totality in any pre-human species. It required language, planning, cooperation, self-control, foresight and cultural learning, and probably developed along with these.

The family was made desirable by the early human combination of prolonged child care with the need for hunting with weapons over large terrains. The sexual division of labor on which it was based grew out of a rudimentary pre-human division between male defense and female child care. But among humans this sexual division of functions for the first time became crucial for food production and so laid the basis for future economic specialization and cooperation.

Morgan and Engels were probably right in thinking that the human family was preceded by sexual indiscriminacy. They were also right in seeing an egalitarian group-quality about early economic and marriage arrangements. They were without evidence, however, in believing that the earliest mating and economic patterns were entirely group relations.

Together with tool use and language, the family was no doubt the most significant invention of the human revolution. All three required reflective thought, which above all accounts for the vast superiority in consciousness that separates humans from apes.

The family provided the framework for all pre-state society and the fount of its creativeness. In groping for survival and for knowledge, human beings learned to control their sexual desires and to suppress their individual selfishness, aggression and competition. The other side of this self-control was an increased capacity for love—not only the love of a mother for her child, which is seen among apes, but of male for female in enduring relationships, and of each sex for ever widening groups of humans. Civilization would have been impossible without this initial self-control, seen in incest prohibitions and in the generosity and moral orderliness of primitive family life.

From the start, women have been subordinate to men in certain key areas of status, mobility and public leadership. But before the agricultural revolution, and even for several thousands of years thereafter, the inequality was based chiefly on the unalterable fact of long child care combined with the exigencies of primitive technology. The extent of inequality varied according to the ecology and the resulting sexual division of tasks. But in any case it was largely a matter of survival rather than of man-made cultural impositions. Hence the impressions we receive of dignity, freedom and mutual respect between men and women in primitive hunting and horticultural societies. This is true whether these societies are patrilocal, bilocal or matrilocal, although matrilocal societies, with matrilineal inheritance, offer greater freedom to women than do patrilocal and patrilineal societies of the same level of productivity and political development.

A distinct change occurred with the growth of individual and family property in herds, in durable craft objects and trade objects, and in stable, irrigated farm-sites or other forms of heritable wealth. This crystallized in the rise of the state, about 4000 B.C. With the growth of class society and of male dominance in the ruling class of the state, women's subordination increased, and eventually reached its depths in the patriarchal families of the great agrarian states.

Knowledge of how the family arose is interesting to women because it tells us how we differ from pre-humans, what our past has been, and what have been the biological and cultural limitations from which we are emerging. It shows us how generations of male scholars have distorted or over-interpreted the evidence to bolster beliefs in the inferiority of women's mental processes—for which there is no foundation in fact. Knowing about early families is also important to correct a reverse bias among some feminist writers, who hold that in "matriarchal" societies women were completely equal with or were even dominant over men. For this, too, there seems to be no basis in evidence.

The past of the family does not limit its future. Although the family probably emerged with humanity, neither the family itself nor particular family forms are genetically determined. The sexual division of labor—until recently, universal—need not, and in my opinion should not, survive in industrial society. Prolonged child care ceases to be a basis for female subordination when artificial birth control, spaced births, small families, patent feeding and communal nurseries allow it to be shared by men. Automation and cybernation remove most of the heavy work for which women are less well equipped than men. The exploitation of women that came with the rise of the state and of class society will presumably disappear in post-state, classless society—for which the technological and scientific basis already exists.

The family was essential to the dawn of civilization, allowing a vast qualitative leap forward in cooperation, purposive knowledge, love, and creativeness. But today, rather than enhancing them, the confinement of women in homes and small families—like their subordination in work—artificially limits these human capacities. It may be that the human gift for personal love will make some form of voluntary, long-term mating and of individual devotion between parents and children continue indefinitely, side by side with public responsibility for domestic tasks and for the care and upbringing of children. There is no need to legislate personal relations out of existence. But neither need we fear a social life in which the family is no more.

References

COULT, ALLAN D. (1965) Cross Tabulations of Murdock's World Ethnographic Sample. University of Missouri.

FOX, ROBIN (1967) Kinship and Marriage. London: Pelican Books.

HOCKETT, CHARLES F., and ROBERT ASCHER (1968) The Human Revolution. In Man in Adaptation: The Biosocial Background, Yehudi A. Cohen (ed.). Chicago: Aldine.

LIVINGSTONE, FRANK B. (1969) "Genetics, ecology and the origin of incest and exogamy." Current Anthropology (February).

MORRIS, DESMOND (1967) The Naked Ape. Jonathon Cape.

MURDOCK, G. P. (1957) World Ethnographic Sample, American Anthropologist.

——— (1967) Ethnographic Atlas. University of Pittsburgh.

SCHNEIDER, DAVID M., and KATHLEEN GOUGH (1961) Matrilineal Kinship. Berkeley: University of California Press.

SEMYONOV, Y. I. (1967) "Group marriage, its nature and role in the evolution of marriage and family relations." In Seventh International Congress of Anthropological and Ethnological Sciences. Vol. IV. Moscow.

26

KINSHIP CONCEPTS

HOPE JENSEN LEICHTER and WILLIAM E. MITCHELL

Kinship is usually confused with biology. Even professionals sometimes think of kinship as a cultural means of recognizing the reality of biological descent and the geneticist's genealogies. Of course there are some societies in which the facts of biological descent are regarded as of great importance, but even among these can be found examples of the counterfeiting of biological relationships or their premeditated obliteration and neglect. In brief, kinship in human society is a cultural category, inextricably bound up with the process of symbolization, hence open to massive "falsification" (see Rappaport, selection 32). What then is kinship? Most basically it comprises perhaps the most ancient and yet enduring of all myths, the belief that in a world populated by what seems always to be an indefinite number of generally similar human beings there are some who stand closer than others and therefore are entitled to help and support or obligated to give help or support.

What makes this a myth is the bitter knowledge that even the closest of kin can fall upon and destroy one another. In our daily lives we know of cases of the most woeful treatment of elderly parents, and child abuse itself has claimed increasing attention as a major crime. Our own mythology, the Bible for instance, dwells on brutal acts perpetrated by one close relative upon another, the case of Cain and Abel being merely the first. Yet, despite our knowledge of the violation of kinship, we tend to regard it as a safe haven and, indeed, for many it functions in just that way, particularly if one is willing to ignore the psychological conflicts that often mar even the kindliest of kin relations.

SOURCE: *Kinship and Casework*, Hope J. Leichter and William E. Mitchell. Chapter 1.

It has long been known that kinship furnishes a major axis of social relations in most simpler societies; indeed, some such societies, like those of aboriginal Australia, conceived of all social relations within the ambience of kinship and had explicit mechanisms for reckoning the kinship of total strangers. On the other hand, another of the myths of kinship, albeit one of somewhat limited distribution, holds that kinship becomes weak in complex societies, losing all functions and tending to disappear as a significant basis of social aggregation and action.

Actually, the evidence does not support that view. True, certain types of kin relations become attenuated and other bonds become restructured as their functions alter. But kinship itself does not seem to be on the way out in any society that we know of. For example, propaganda to the contrary and despite the efforts of Chinese Red Guards, the People's Republic of China continues to see major emphasis placed by the people on using kinship relations in ways reminiscent of pre-Communist society. Meanwhile, sociological studies in the United States have indicated that the technological development of telephone communications has brought about a new surge in kinship relations among even relatively distant kin. Cousin Harry, who moved from Dubuque to Cape Kennedy and has something to do with rocket ships, is, probably through his wife, in contact with "the family" he thought he was leaving behind.

Because kinship provides the first and sometimes the most intimate and enduring framework of a society, it is often a beginning place for anthropological studies. Those studies can also lead to practical advantages for other specialists who somehow in the course of their work must cope with family and kinship practices. This is particularly evident for social workers, although many others could as easily exemplify the point. In any case, the present selection is taken from a volume written primarily to bring academic anthropology and sociology to bear on problems of social casework.

▼△▼△▼

Those who are concerned with family problems ultimately deal with specific individuals and families who are the product of complex psychological, physiological, and environmental factors. Each individual is unique in so many respects that the more general features of human life everywhere can easily be taken for granted or overlooked, precisely because they are so universal.

Except for relatively few, unusual cases, each individual is born into a family; that family is bound to other families in a complex structure of interlocking ties that shifts in composition through birth, marriage, and death. Kinship is an involuntary relationship; every individual has kin and is a kin. Some of a child's earliest experiences are with kin. The forms of this interlocking structure of kinship may vary; but everywhere some such structure exists. The forms may have become so familiar that a specific effort is required to see them as forms of a universal, not as the universal itself.

The family is founded on biological facts of sex and reproduction common to all men. The nuclear family of husband, wife, and children may be distinguished from, or integrated with, other groupings in a variety of ways. The purpose of this chapter, then, is to point out some of the ways all kinship systems are structured and some of the ways in which they may differ significantly.

Kinship Systems

In all societies an individual typically marries someone other than his father, mother, brother, or sister; that is, someone outside his family of origin. Thus every individual who marries is a member of two nuclear families. After he marries and establishes a new family, the ties to his family of childhood do not disappear but are altered. Each individual in the family has "boundary roles" with his other family, of which he remains in some sense a member. As a result each person links the members of his family of childhood with those of his family of marriage; each individual in a nuclear family has ties to those in another nuclear family; and these individuals, in turn, have similar ties to others. Thus the basic links of kinship rest on common membership in a nuclear family.

Two basic types of kinship links are by blood and marriage. These ties create two types of kin: *cognatic relatives,* or those linked by blood or common ancestry; and *affinal relatives,* or those linked by marriage.

The links of kinship extend outward in geometrically increasing numbers. Therefore, a distinctive pattern of behavior cannot be associated with each possible category of relationship. Instead, all societies solve the problem of the infinite number of biological links of kinship by grouping them. Many of the principal differences among kinship systems stem from the varying ways in which kin are grouped.

Marriage

Marriage is fundamental to all systems of kinship. Every group has definitions of who may marry. The definitions may be phrased in terms of broad social groupings. For example, it may be considered preferable to marry someone who is "educated" or someone of a given ethnic group. They may be phrased in terms of specific genealogical relationships; for example, the belief that one should marry a particular cousin. Certain categories of individuals are always prohibited as marriage partners, since all societies have some form of incest taboo. In the broad sense, incest means sexual relations between participants who are related by a bond of kinship, which is culturally regarded as a bar. Marriage within the nuclear family, between parents and children or between siblings, is almost universally prohibited. Beyond this, the kin who are defined as eligible to marry vary radically from one society to another.

Social definitions of marriage also cover the number of spouses permissible at a given time, and the procedures for selecting a marriage partner, ranging from "romantic love" and individual choice to arranged marriages.

Cultural expectations defining who may have a legitimate concern with the success of a marriage also vary. In our society marriage is considered to concern primarily a man and woman and the state, which legalizes the union, and in some cases, a religious institution which sanctions it. But in many societies marriage is a compact between the kin of the man and the kin of the woman who share common interests, often economic, in the marriage and in its continuance.

Forms of the Family

Two basic questions have been asked about forms of the family: First, is the nuclear family universally recognized as a social unit? Second, is marriage a socially recognized relationship in all societies? While conclusions have hinged to a large degree on issues of definition, cross-cultural data, for example, on the Israeli kibbutz [1] and the Nayar of India,[2] have revealed exceptions to the universality of both marriage and the nuclear family. Neither marriage nor the nuclear family is universally the basis of a household unit. If a socially recognized unit is defined broadly, both may be universal; but the variations are great. Marriage in some form may be socially recognized in all societies, but the nuclear family is by no means a universal unit of residence, or even of long-term cooperation of spouses, or a universal unit of child rearing.

A related question concerns what groupings form a recognized household unit. In many societies various composite forms of the family, that is, *extended families,* made up of two, three, or more nuclear families, living together as an economic unit, are standard. This form is related both to the marriage system and to the physical characteristics of the household and the environment. A number of kinds of extended or composite families have been observed in different societies. Several brothers and their wives may establish a common household. Another type may include a man, his married sons, his sons' sons, and their wives. Similarly, a family may consist of a woman, her daughters, her daughters' daughters, and their husbands. Another variation includes a married couple, some of their married sons and daughters, and some of their grandchildren. Further variations are possible, giving rise to a great many types of household composition, which vary greatly under different circumstances.[3]

Not only are the biological nuclear family and the household often different, but in many societies the nuclear family is not the most common household unit. A sample of societies on which anthropologists have made ethnographic reports indicates that in the majority some form of extended household exists.[4] Extended families have been the most important household unit not only in primitive societies but also in highly civilized societies.

Determining the boundaries of the household is complex. Eating a regular meal in another household may not make a person a member of that household. But it is also misleading to assume that the household is necessarily bounded by four walls. The physical characteristics of households vary greatly in different societies, depending on the climate, the ecological characteristics of the terrain, building materials, and the type of house structure. It is therefore difficult to find comparable household boundaries—even physical boundaries—under different conditions. Internal divisions of the household may have highly distinct quarters for some purposes such as sleeping, but common quarters for other purposes such as cooking. Within a household, space may be divided in terms of religious and ritual functions rather than in terms of physical partitions. Definitions of households in terms of functions—whether a family has a common budget, common cooking facilities, or common property—are therefore often more useful than those related to the physical boundaries of the household.

In all societies household composition varies with the life cycle of the individual and the domestic group. But the kinds of change made by an individual from one point in his life cycle to another are not always the same.

Residence

The idea that place of residence is systematically patterned and related to social values and expectations is one of the most basic concepts about kinship systems. In connection with kinship, *residence* refers to the place where individuals live in relation to kin at different stages of the life cycle. Anthropological classifications of types of residence have frequently been based on postmarital residence, or where the newly married couple goes to live. The major types are: *virilocal* residence, when the new couple lives in or near the husband's parental home; *uxorilocal* residence, when the couple lives in or near the parental home of the wife; and *neolocal* residence, when choice of residence is not based on proximity to kin.

Residence patterns vary greatly from one society to another. But definitions of residence exist in all societies, even when it is expected that the newly married couple will not reside near any kin.

Residence is related to the incest taboo. Generally, although not always, married couples live together. Since individuals cannot marry within their family of orientation, in founding a new family husband and wife both cannot remain with their own families of origin. There must be a dislocation of residence for one or both.

The problem of defining the boundaries of the place of residence is comparable to the problem of defining the boundaries of a household. In attempting to define place of residence, anthropologists have, for example, spoken of moving "*to* or *near* the parental home,"[5] but the meaning of living near the parental home of either spouse may vary greatly with the ecological conditions of the society, just as the boundaries of the household vary. However complex it may be to describe residence patterns, it is seldom a neutral issue; great emotional investment attaches to where one lives in relation to kin.

Extended Kin Groups

In some societies extended kin groups—that is, kin groups more extensive than the nuclear family—are the basis of organization for many of the society's activities. Extended kin groups may own land and other strategic resources. Although social groups may be based on a number of criteria other than kinship, such as age, sex, social status, and locality, in some cases almost all the groups of a society are based on kinship. In some groups membership and rights are transmitted through the female line (matrilineal), in others through the male line (patrilineal). Extended kin groups vary with marriage systems and the ways in which rights are reckoned for other purposes.

Kin Networks

The term "kin network" or kindred refers to the kin of a nuclear family or individual.[6] Regardless of other features of kinship organization, the individual and nuclear family always has a kin network although its structure and function may vary.[7]

One basic feature of a network as distinct from a group is that the boundaries are different from the perspective of each individual; the individuals that are considered kin by one person are not necessarily the same as those considered kin by a close relative of this person, even though they have certain kin in common. Kin within a network do not necessarily have any significant relationship to each other except that they are both related to the specific individual who is the reference point. No two individuals in the society, except unmarried siblings, have the same network of kin. Husbands and wives may come to be incorporated in each other's kin network but they bring to the family different perspectives on the issue of who is kin.

The boundaries of the network also shift with the criteria employed, and are different for different activities: the network may include all those the individual is able to name as kin or all those living within a given geographic area, but these may be different from the kin with whom the family exchanges economic services. For every kinship event the boundaries of kinship may be redefined; decisions must constantly be made about who is and who is not to be included as a kin for particular occasions.

In almost all societies more individuals are related by blood and marriage than are actually recognized as kin. The definition of an individual as a kin is social, not purely biological. Paternity, for example, is often a social rather than a biological fact, as in adoption within our own society.

Because of the multitude of biological ties to kin, all societies have developed procedures for defining who the individual's kin are for specific social purposes, such as mutual assistance, the regulation of marriage, and membership in kin groups. The ways in which an individual's kin are defined vary greatly.[8]

Kinship Bonds

In all societies kinship statuses are used as criteria for social interaction. Three characteristics of social statuses that are basic for kinship are generation, sex, and laterality, or the side of the family to which a kin status belongs.

Kinship *bonds* are ties of obligation and sentiment between those in specific reciprocal statuses. The concept of bond implies that certain relationships within a network are accorded a *priority*, and that this patterns the organization of the network; that is, stronger bonds serve as links for other relationships. Even among genealogically close kin, real choices exist in the allocation of time and resources; for certain purposes some kinship ties are given priority.

Examination of regularities in relationships among kin may be observed and analyzed from a variety of types of data, among them kinship values, legal norms, and legal sanctions. Regularities in relationships with kin may also be analyzed through examining the frequency with which interaction occurs with kin in particular kinship statuses. From observations of the frequency of interaction, it is possible to impute rights and obligations that probably underlie the interaction. This behavioral information can be compared with perceptions of norms. An analysis of actual behavioral choices made in relationships among kin in a given area of activity thus reveals the relative priority accorded to various bonds among kin.[9] In examining kinship bonds we are dealing with the *relative* strength of a tie between one set of reciprocal statuses as compared with another. In some societies, for example, the marital bond is accorded greater importance for most social purposes than the tie between an adult son and his mother, but in other societies the reverse is true.

The notion of bond specifically implies relative priority. On the other hand, the concept of *role* covers the general content of the rights, obligations, and expectations of the individual in a particular position and is broader than the concept of bond. Each role, moreover, has a number of reciprocal statuses related to it; the role of mother may include mother-son, mother-daughter relationships. Thus a bond is the relationship between a person in a role and one in a reciprocal status with respect to that role.

Both the role expectations that are characteristic of particular kinship statuses and the specific kinship bonds that are accorded priority vary greatly in the kinship systems of different societies.

We have considered some of the most important dimensions of a kinship system as it has been studied in anthropology and sociology. Other areas, such as kinship terminology, or the terms individuals use to address and refer to each other, have also been studied and are patterned differently from one society to another.

Relationships Among Features of the Kinship System

The wide variety found in kinship systems is not completely random and unlimited. Pressures toward consistency exist within kinship systems so that, for example, certain types of marriage systems tend to go with particular types of residence. But such regularities are not uniform; the dimensions of the kinship system are not so tightly associated that they can be combined in only one way. Yet observations indicate that a closer relationship exists within dimensions of the kinship system than between the kinship system and other features of the society.[10]

Many observations and hypotheses have been made of how the various dimensions of kinship systems tend to cluster. They are important here only to illustrate the general proposition that kinship systems are sufficiently connected so that the existence of one feature places certain limitations on the range within which other dimensions may vary.

The procedure of mate selection depends on how kin groups are incorporated into the nuclear family. If the new couple will reside with or near kin, members of the kin group have a stake in the marriage; since they will live in the same household with the new spouse, they have a reason for a voice in the selection.

Strict hierarchical distinctions based on age and birth order and a continuing authority of elder kin are frequently associated with incorporation of the nuclear family in extended kin households and a high degree of social involvement with kin, and also kinship as a major organizing principle for the society.[11]

The system of reckoning descent tends to be associated with the kinship bonds that are strongest, as well as with residence patterns. Among the North-Lapp nomads it was found that rigid generational differentiation went together with solidarity among siblings as the fundamental kinship bond.[12] It has also been noted that sibling solidarity is a characteristic of American kinship, which, too, is "bilateral." [13] It has been argued that matrilineal reckoning of descent tends to go with matrilocal residence, although the correlation is not absolute.[14]

Differences in the quality of the marital bond, particularly the stability of marriage, have been noted when matrilineal rather than patrilineal descent groups are present. It has been found that men hold the primary authority roles in both matrilineal and patrilineal descent groups. In a matrilineal system the husband is incorporated into his wife's kin group for certain purposes but exercises his primary authority within his own maternal kin group and therefore must maintain ties with it. Thus the husband is caught between competing ties, those to his wife's kin and those to his maternal kin.

In a patrilineal system the wife is incorporated into her husband's kin group, but because she does not have a significant authority role within her own paternal kin group she does not have comparable obligations to maintain strong ties with it, and is thus not confronted with the same degree of conflicting loyalties. A related phenomenon is the difference in the position of the husband and wife with respect to the authority of the household into which they marry in matrilineal and patrilineal systems. The degree of authority of a father-in-law over a son-in-law in a matrilineal system is not as great as that of a mother-in-law over a daughter-in-law in patrilineal descent groups.[15]

The focal points of conflict and strain in various kinship systems show certain associations with other features of the system. In either a virilocal or a uxorilocal residence system, the spouse who must move away from his or her home and enter the home of strangers is often placed in a position of stress, stemming in part from subjugation to the authority of elder kin in contrast to the problems that typify systems where the nuclear family resides as an independent unit. Here transitions to a new household exist for both spouses, and typical problems include "parental possessiveness," "childish overdependence," and the loss of status of the aged.

Interrelationships among the dimensions of kinship systems are complex and all the possible combinations are unknown. But it is clear that elements of the kinship system do not combine at random. Rather, certain clusterings tend to occur; roles within the family are associated with the organization of relationships among kin. Because of these connections, a change in one area may have implications that extend to other areas. A change in relations with kin may, for example, have consequences for the quality of the marital relationship.

Kinship and Society

Kinship systems are interesting because of their enormous complexity and variety. In our society concern with the intricacies of reckoning descent is likely to appear either hollow and meaningless or a form of social snobbery. However, anthropologists and sociologists have studied kinship not because of an interest in complexity for its own sake, but rather because in many societies kinship ties are basic for the entire social organization.

Although we have only touched on the extensive variety of kinship systems, we have reviewed many of the major dimensions along which kinship may vary and the types of associations that have been found among these dimensions. We will now consider some of the functions that kinship may have for social organization, and the kinds of societies in which varying kinship systems have been found.

The Functions of Kinship for Social Organization

The organization of some entire societies is built on extended kin groupings; in other societies kinship plays a limited role. Where most of the social relations of the society are carried out through kin ties, kinship regulates behavior and allows individuals to know what to expect of each other in many activities.

KINSHIP AND ECONOMY. In our society kinship plays a relatively small part in structuring most work groups. In other societies kinship is a major, if not the exclusive, basis on which economic production is organized. Authority and decision-making within work groups, for example, may be assigned on the basis of kinship status, those in senior kinship statuses having authority over the work group. Distribution and exchange may also be organized on the basis of kinship. Exchange of basic economic resources may often be part of the ritual during ceremonies such as marriage. In all societies some kinds of property are held and transmitted on the basis of kinship; for example, fields, houses, and personal possessions. In some cases strategic resources, that is, the means of production, are held primarily by kin groups and are transmitted on the basis of kinship.

KINSHIP AND ASSISTANCE. Societies organize in varying ways to assist their members in times of crisis or special need. In some societies many highly specialized institutions exist for assisting the individual, such as welfare institutions and social agencies, medical institutions, insurance organizations, and banks. But in societies where few specialized institutions exist, kin may constitute the most important source of assistance for the individual. Where kinship is an important basis for economic activity, assistance among kin is often tied up with their joint economic endeavors. In traditional Chinese society, for example, the family and the extended kin group were expected to care for ill members, and hospital care was suspect. Assistance in educational pursuits was also provided by kin; schools and special tutoring facilities were often provided by a clan to enable the brightest members of an extended kin group to pass the imperial examinations.

In a society where the only mode of obtaining assistance is through kin, a person without kin may be unable to manage. Kinship ties may be so essential that those lacking real kin may resort to fictitious kinship ties.

KINSHIP AND SOCIAL CONTROL. In all societies the household group plays a significant part in social control through socializing children and motivating the individual to conform to society's norms. Elaborate institutions of legal and political control may also exist apart from the family. In other cases, legal and political control is exercised mainly through the family and extended kin groups. The political and legal controls of kinship may be very powerful, particularly when the individual's social placement in many spheres is bound up with the same groups; for example, when the kin group is also the economic and religious group. Where the individual's social network is closely interlocked, gossip, public opinion, and other forms of primary group social control have particular importance.

KINSHIP AND SOCIAL STATUS. All societies have procedures for the assignment of social positions. Some social statuses are always assigned on the basis of kinship criteria such as birth order and sex. In traditional Chinese society the eldest son of the eldest son occupied a special position of power and authority within the extended kin group. In societies where most economic activities are carried out by kin groups, the individual's position in these activities will depend on his kinship status. For example, occupations are sometimes inherited. Political positions such as those of chieftain may also be transmitted on the basis of kinship.

The process of social mobility may also be related to kinship. In our society we tend to think of mobility primarily in terms of an individual, although a man who raises his social status carries his wife and children with him. In other societies mobility is regarded more as collective than as individual; by achievement the individual raises not only himself and his immediate family, but many of his kin as well.

KINSHIP AND RELIGIOUS ACTIVITY. In many societies kinship is an important basis for organizing religious activities. The selection of individuals who participate in a religious ceremonial and their ceremonial duties are often defined in terms of kinship ties. Funerals, for example, are almost always organized, at least in part, on the basis of kinship with the expression of grief being related to kinship connections with the deceased.

Associations Between Kinship Systems and Societal Conditions

A number of studies have tried to establish relationships between certain societal conditions and different forms of kinship. One type of analysis takes a particular kinship form and traces the range of societal conditions under which it is found. Studies have been made of the kinds of societies in which the independent nuclear family is found. Another approach examines specific kinds of societies and determines the kinship systems that occur in them. For example, urban industrial societies have been studied to determine what kinds of family organization and kin groups exist in them.

An analysis of the relation between societal conditions and kinship systems must cope with a fundamental logical problem: the conditions that cause or *give rise* to a particular form of kinship may not be the same as those that *perpetuate* it. For example, it has been noted that matriliny "survives under conditions other than those which gave rise to it, that we cannot outlaw the possibility that it can spread to groups where it would not originate, and that we cannot deduce theoretically the conditions likely to terminate it." [16] From an observed correlation between kinship and society it is not possible to conclude whether kinship is the determinant of the particular societal condition or the reverse. Nor is it possible to predict that kinship and societal conditions will necessarily change together.

Moreover, relating dimensions of a kinship system to those of the society is complicated because a great many societal conditions may be related to the many dimensions of kinship. Even in examining one aspect of societal conditions, such as the economy, complex classifications have been used. Economic variables that have been related to forms of the family include: (1) size of food supply; (2) degree of spatial mobility required in subsistence activities; and (3) kind and amount of family property. Some theorists have referred to urban industrial society, or western urban industrial society, as a category in which special types of kinship are likely to arise. But within this category many dimensions of relevance for kinship have been distinguished, including the difference between early and late stages of industrialization,[17] between those societies with indigenous industrialization and those with borrowed industrial patterns, between preindustrial and industrial cities,[18] between various types of labor and market economy,[19] and between different types of political ideology and political control.[20]

As yet no general theory of the association between kinship and society that covers all of these numerous dimensions has been substantiated. Nevertheless, a number of partial theories, observations, and hypotheses are worth examining.

KINSHIP IN URBAN INDUSTRIALIZED SOCIETY. Efforts to trace the types of societies in which the independent nuclear family exists reveal no simple correlation. An independent nuclear family is found under very different economic conditions, in modern industrial societies and also in simpler hunting and gathering societies. However, a similar factor exists in both types of society, namely, the need for physical mobility. "The hunter is mobile because he pursues the game: the industrial worker, the job." [21] By contrast, in a sedentary agricultural economy where the place of work is geographically fixed by the location of land, larger kin groups can remain in the same location and yet be available for their economic tasks.

A number of hypotheses have been developed about the kinds of kinship systems that are compatible with urban industrial societies. Some theorists have assumed that the existence of corporate kin groups and an extended family will interfere with the requirements of an urban society with an industrial economy.[22] This assumption is based on several features that are presumed to characterize an urban industrial society. Industry requires geographic mobility so that workers will be available at different times and places. Thus ties of kinship should not be so extensive that individuals would be unwilling to live geographically separated from their kin. An industrial economy also requires the assignment of occupations on the basis of objective criteria of technical competence. Extensive obligations of kinship would presumably interfere with the application of these objective criteria. It has also been assumed that the activities of an industrial economy require larger, more centralized units of production than can be organized on a relatively small family or kin group basis. It should be noted that these hypotheses pertain specifically to the urban segments of industrial societies. They do not apply to preindustrial urban centers. In the past it has been assumed that these hypotheses were supported by the prevalence of an independent nuclear family in urban industrial societies.

These hypotheses have also received support from the observed breakdown of corporate kin groups in societies undergoing industrialization.[23] In societies coming in contact with previously industrialized nations through their markets, the economic power of descent groups is often undermined.[24] In a study of kinship and industrialization in Lagos, Nigeria, it was noted that the opportunities for individual profit that accompanied industrialization undermined the economic base of kinship ties. Then social differences between the more and less successful reduced the feelings of obligations among kin, which otherwise ensured that wealth was redistributed within the kin network. In turn, differences in income and status among kin were further widened and ties of kinship were further reduced.[25]

Despite the evidence that traditional kinship systems tend, under some circumstances, to be disrupted and radically changed by industrialization, there are indications that urbanization as such, and industrialization under some conditions, do not necessarily break down all kinds of kinship ties. Although the claims of the family group may exert an outworn authority and inhibit ambition, "they also represent a system of social welfare," a challenge to self-seeking and class interest, a widespreading and secure emotional attachment. To abandon them would destroy the informal social justice and emotional security which maintain the balance of a rapidly changing society.[26] Thus a conflict may exist between the development of a modern economy and traditional loyalties of kinship, but the ties of kinship by no means disappear in the process of change.

There is evidence that kin groups may sometimes remain significant as units of economic production even in industrialized nations. After reviewing instances in which kinship serves as a basis of organizing industrial activities, it was concluded that, depending on the nature and size of the industrial organization, as well as the size of the family, kinship is not necessarily incompatible with efficient organization of industrial activities. This position is supported by a study of economic activity among French-Canadians in New England,[27] and also by studies of industrial organization among overseas Chinese[28] and familistic type of industrial organization in Japan.[29]

A number of recent studies of kinship in western industrial urban societies have contributed additional data on the conditions under which various types of kinship may exist.[30] Several of these have analyzed the relationship between the nuclear family and its kin, and the extent and forms of interaction with kin outside the nuclear family. One study claims that a modified, as compared with a classical, extended family can, and does, exist in an urban industrial society, and may foster rather than inhibit both occupational and geographic mobility.[31] On the basis of a general review of a number of studies of kinship in urban industrial societies, it was concluded that kinship remains an important basis for social contact, performing many important functions for the family.[32] Thus involvement with kin, as distinct from corporate kin groups, does not disappear or become insignificant with industrialization. Moreover, even the most general theories have noted the possible variation of kinship structures with a large-scale society from one ethnic or class subgroup to another.

We have not attempted a complete review of studies in kinship and society, or even of studies of urban industrial kinship. Our purpose has been to illustrate the complexity of the connections between kinship and society and the consequent need for caution in making assumptions about the forms of kinship possible in a particular kind of society. While the data in this book imply certain modifications and refinements in hypotheses about kinship in urban industrial society, these theoretical modifications will not be spelled out in detail here.

Where extensive ties with kin exist, they have implications for the family and for the personalities of family members. Since, as will be seen, we have found ties with kin to be more extensive than might have been presumed on the basis of some previous hypotheses, we will now review some of the functions that kinship has been found to have for family and personality in societies where involvement with kin is extensive.

Kinship, Family, and Personality

Because the family is in itself part of the kinship system, a special distinction must be made when speaking of the influence of the kinship system upon the family. But dimensions of kinship such as the modes of residence and marriage have a profound effect upon the family as they determine household composition, activities that are carried out by various kin units, and relationships within the family.

Social Identity

The degree of interconnection within the family's network of kin relationship has important consequences for relationships among kin, as well as those within the family. If an individual's various memberships overlap and similar behavior is expected in various situations, he is likely to have a more coherent self-image than if radically different behavior is expected of him in a series of relationships with others who have little in common. Similarly, if many social relationships are common to the entire family, and there is considerable overlap of the groups in which different activities are carried out, such as occupation and recreation, the family's identity is likely to be more unified than that of a family whose members participate relatively little in the same social relationships. The selection of marriage partners and the role of kin in the selection help to define the marital pair as a social unit, that is, their social identity. When marriage is considered a tie not merely between two individuals but also between two extended kin groups, many kin in addition to the husband and wife are involved in the marriage economically and ceremonially; all have a stake in its success.

Patterns of residence affect the composition of the household and thus exert an influence on the family. The social position of a newly married husband and wife is particularly influenced by the system of residence.

The sharp break in the life of one spouse that is likely when residence is with the kin of the other spouse has been noted. Since the spouse who shifts residence must move into a new set of social ties, the relative position of the spouses in their most immediate social groupings is affected by residence. Moreover, the conflicts that are likely to inhere in the position of each spouse are affected by whether a sharp transition to a new kin group is necessary.

The individual may be incorporated into a nuclear family and kin group in a variety of ways. Also, the lines that distinguish the individual, the nuclear family, and the other kin units may be drawn very differently; neither the individual nor the family is conceived in the same way in all societies. In some cases the family rather than the individual is defined as the unit for most purposes. In traditional Japanese society, for example, the peasant family was the unit of most social activity and the individual was not defined as independent for most purposes; he had little sense of private identity and few private choices.[33]

Thus kinship organization exerts a significant effect upon the position of the marital pair in their new household, as well as upon the family boundaries and the units of social action. This, in turn, influences other relationships within the family.

Authority and Control

In many societies extended kin exert control over members of the nuclear family. Although this authority is not solely the product of the family's incorporation in its network of kin, it is clearly influenced by the kinship structure. Residence patterns and household composition are significant for family authority in several respects: (1) some residence patterns introduce an asymmetrical element in authority relations between husbands and wives by placing one spouse in a position of continuing membership in his family of childhood, while the other spouse must go to live with comparative strangers; (2) when one spouse remains with his own group, that spouse may have authority through control over property and economic resources of the larger kin group; (3) an individual who remains within his own kin group after marriage may have limitations placed on his authority to his own kin in senior positions; (4) kin outside the nuclear family may be defined as having direct authority over family members in some spheres; (5) activities in the larger kin group that are based on kinship organization may support authority within the household.

Economic Relations

Kinship organization also influences the role of the nuclear family or household unit in economic activities. In our own society, although the family is generally not a major unit of economic production, it is a unit of consumption; as such, ties with kin affect its consumption activities. For instance, a Jewish family may keep a kosher household for the sake of parents. Kinship may also be the basic source of available welfare and assistance, thus affecting how the family seeks and obtains aid. Sometimes ceremonial activities among kin constitute a significant economic contribution to the family. Some basic economic activities of the family, such as house building, may be carried out through the help of kin.

Socialization

Composition of the household and the proximity of kin help to determine the adults who are significant in child rearing, which, in turn, has consequences for personality development.

When many kin live in or near the same household, they can easily exchange child-rearing tasks. Individuals other than the parents may feed the child, play with him, and discipline him. As suggested by a study of Truk culture in the South Pacific, the capacity for "deep" emotional attachment to one individual may be reduced by socialization in a kinship system that has many parental surrogates. On the other hand, the personality characteristics fostered under such circumstances may be compatible with that kind of society, for example, with the marriage system and the necessity of coping with complex role organization within the family.[34]

When the nuclear family is incorporated into a larger household group or lives close to kin, the child must learn a complex set of role relationships: he must learn to relate to grandparents, to uncles, to aunts, to cousins, as well as to members of the nuclear family. In addition, the child can observe the multiple relationships among others; for instance, his own parents are children to his grandparents as well as parents to him. In many societies the child is confronted with this extended network almost at birth, not at a later stage.

Kinship structure also influences the form and resolution of the Oedipus complex. The universality of the Oedipus complex is controversial. But whether some special attachment to the parent of the opposite sex is universal, evidence indicates that its form varies with the kinship structure. For instance, in a society with matrilocal residence, the mother's brother is in some respects in a position similar to that of the father in other systems. Then, is the resentment of the son toward the father directed instead toward the mother's brother, who in this case is in a position of authority? Evidence from the Hopi Indians in southwestern United States indicates that the role of the mother's brother is not quite comparable to that of the father in other societies in terms of the Oedipus complex, because the mother's brother does not combine his authority position with being the sexual partner of the child's mother. Moreover, the relationship of the child to the mother's brother is tempered when the mother has more than one brother. However, the Oedipal conflict between father and child is reduced by diffusion of some of the father's authority to the mother's brother.[35]

Kinship structure also affects the kinds of intimacy that the child observes. Sleeping arrangements have been considered particularly important in some psychological theory. Sleeping arrangements vary greatly from one culture to another in relation to household composition, as well as to general definitions of space and concepts of privacy. Among the Hopi, the child sleeps close to many of the kin in his matrilocal extended family, has a chance to observe sexual relations from an early age, and to develop a sense of intimacy with the group that sleeps close together.

From an examination of relationships between kinship structure and child-rearing practices and personality development, it was hypothesized that insofar as kinship determines who acts as parents and parental surrogates it influences superego development. This hypothesis, based in part on psychoanalytic theory, was that "where the parents play a less important role in the socialization of their children, the children will tend to develop weaker superegos than where the parents play a more important role."[36] However, since parents play the dominant socializing role in most societies, the effects of secondary agents of socialization on superego formation were studied. It was assumed that relatives resemble parents more closely than nonrelatives, so that if relatives rather than nonrelatives are the more important secondary agents of socialization, a stronger superego formation should result. This hypothesis was supported by a significant correlation between residence patterns, the index of the importance of relatives as secondary socializers, and beliefs about the patients' responsibility for being ill—the index of guilt and superego formation. Here a specific relationship has been posited between one aspect of kinship structure and a dimension of personality.

Thus not only broad cultural patterns but social structure and, in particular, kinship structure affect socialization and personality. The relationships are complex, but kinship structure is clearly important.

Socialization occurs not only in early childhood but throughout life; entry into each new role entails socialization. Since kinship often is a basis for organizing religious and ceremonial activities, kin play an important part in rites accompanying life-cycle transitions. The ceremonial support of kin may assist those involved in accepting the idea of status transitions, for example, at marriage. Similarly the participation of kin in funeral ceremonies helps family members accept the alteration in their social status created by the loss.

Kinship structure therefore influences the way in which the family carries out its socialization functions in a variety of ways. Kin may be involved both in early training of children and in later socialization of adults, especially in connection with life-cycle transitions. Kinship structure exerts its major influence upon socialization as a determinant of who become the socializers. In some situations parental surrogates may play an active role in child rearing. The exact consequences for personality development of multiple parent figures and various ways of dividing aspects of the parental role are difficult to determine because so many factors enter into the socialization process. But it is clear that the socialization process proceeds in varied ways in different types of kinship systems.

Roles and Emotions

The composition of the household and definitions of bonds of kinship help to define the rights and duties of roles; for instance, whether the father will be the ultimate authority or merely a subordinate of his own father. In addition, the emotions that are likely to be felt by those in particular family positions are affected by the way in which the family's roles are organized with respect to kin.

The quality of the emotional relationship that is most typical between husbands and wives depends in part on how their roles fit into the kinship structure. "Romantic love as it occurs in our civilization, inextricably bound up with ideas of monogamy, exclusiveness, jealousy and undeviating fidelity," is unknown in many cultures. "The Samoans," for example, "laugh at stories of romantic love, scoff at fidelity to a long-absent wife or mistress, believe explicitly that one love will quickly cure another." [37] The notion of romantic love has a long history in western civilization, but it is also undoubtedly connected with certain features of present-day western urban kinship. In our culture romantic love serves as a basis for mate choice. However, in societies where marriages are arranged, this rationale is unnecessary. Thus the emotion of love is conditioned by the marriage system.

In any kinship system a large number of role relationships exist between different pairs of individuals, that is, between different paired statuses such as mother-son, grandson-grandmother, brother-sister. The definition of the quality of emotional relationships between those within the nuclear family is related to the definition of relationships between nuclear family members and kin. The relationship that is regarded as the individual's main source of emotional support varies from one kinship system to another. In our society the marital tie is normally considered to be the primary bond of an adult. In other systems, however, parent-child or sibling bonds may be more important and even take precedence over the marital tie as a source of emotional support.

In the traditional, and to some extent present-day, Japanese society, the kinship system is one in which the primary bond of obligation and emotional attachment is to someone other than the spouse. Even today the eldest son in the family frequently resides with his parents and his obligations to his parents are considered to be greater than those to his wife. In one recent study, respondents were asked whether an eldest son should divorce his wife if she does not get along with his mother.[38] Most of them said that the husband should not divorce his wife, but those who held "traditionalist views" felt emphatically that he should divorce her. In this point of view the parent-child bond is far stronger than the husband-wife bond.

In some instances elaborate cultural definitions prescribe the emotions that may be expressed between particular kin. This applies even to what might be considered "deeper" emotions of love and attachment. Anthropologists have used specific terms, "avoidance relationships" and "joking relationships," to refer to certain kinds of expressive behavior.[39] Such relationships have been considered to form a continuum from complete avoidance of speech and physical contact to extreme license or obligatory joking and horseplay. Joking and avoidance relationships, which are institutionalized between specific kin in many societies, exemplify one way in which an individual's emotional expression is conditioned by the definitions of kinship roles. Norms of this sort generally apply more directly to expressing an emotion than to feeling it, but the etiquette of expression undoubtedly tempers which emotions are felt.

The emotional expressions regarded as appropriate within the household are also conditioned by its composition. The traditional Chinese family, for instance, followed elaborate expressive etiquette for particular situations. Feelings were expressed by covert and indirect means to avoid embarrassment from acting openly toward a person in a way that might not be appropriate in front of someone of another status who was present within the household.[40] The young wife, for instance, was not only constrained by expressive etiquette; she had especially limited possibilities of emotional expression because she was under the authority of her mother-in-law and was not even supposed to express her feelings to her husband. The composition of the household and the relationships within it vary greatly with other features of the kinship system such as residence patterns. The social organization of the family in relation to kin therefore has significant consequences for the definition of roles and appropriate emotions of those within it.

The research, then, was guided by the concepts that have been outlined briefly in this chapter—that different kinship systems can exist under different social conditions, and that the dimensions of a kinship system are related to each other. The kin relationships of client families have both common and distinguishing features compared with other structures of kinship ties. Thus it was important to investigate kinship values and experiences for both clients and caseworkers to find similarities and divergent patterns to understand the ways in which kinship is dealt with in casework treatment. Moreover, the kinship environment of a client family has significant functions both for social organization outside the family and for relationships within the family. To diagnose and treat families most effectively it is essential, therefore, to have some knowledge about this aspect of its environment.

Some of the questions that these guiding concepts pose are: How are the boundaries of the kin network defined? What are the experiences concerning proximity to kin? Are extended kin groups present in an urban industrial setting? What are the consistent patterns of interaction and conflict? What is the strength of the marital as compared with the parent-child bond? How do kinship ties influence economic relations among kin? What kinds of emotional support and assistance do kin offer the family? In what ways do kin exert a controlling influence on the behavior of family members?

These questions and others are of theoretical interest when applied to any kinship system but they become particularly meaningful when applied to this group because it has the special characteristic of also being a group of casework clients. For it is the purpose of this book to describe kin relationships in order to assess their significance for casework.

Notes

1 SPIRO, MELFORD E., "Is the Family Universal?—The Israeli Case" in *A Modern Introduction to the Family,* edited by Norman W. Bell and Ezra F. Vogel. The Free Press, Glencoe, Ill., 1960, p. 74.

2 GOUGH, KATHLEEN, "Is the Family Universal?—The Nayar Case," *ibid.,* p. 80.

3 MURDOCK, GEORGE PETER, *Social Structure.* Macmillan Co., New York, 1949, p. 33.

4 *Ibid.,* pp. 34–35.

5 *Ibid.,* p. 16.

6 BOTT, ELIZABETH, *Family and Social Network.* Tavistock Publications, Ltd., London, 1957.

7 MITCHELL, WILLIAM E., "Theoretical Problems in the Concept of Kindred," *American Anthropologist,* vol. 65, April, 1963, pp. 343–354.

8 PARSONS, TALCOTT, "The Kinship System of the Contemporary United States" in *Essays in Sociological Theory,* edited by Talcott Parons. Rev. ed. The Free Press, Glencoe, Ill., 1954, p. 178.

9 For discussions of this point, see *Two Studies of Kinship in London,* edited by Raymond W. Firth, The Athlone Press, London, 1956; and Leach, E. R., "The Sinhalese of the Dry Zone of Northern Ceylon" in *Social Structure in Southeast Asia,* edited by George Peter Murdock, Quadrangle Books, Chicago, 1960.

10 ABERLE, DAVID, "Matrilineal Descent in Cross-Cultural Perspective" in *Matrilineal Kinship,* edited by David M. Schneider and Kathleen Gough. University of California Press, Berkeley and Los Angeles, 1961, pp. 655–727.

11 WILLIAMS, ROBIN M., JR., *American Society: A Sociological Interpretation.* Alfred A. Knopf, Inc., New York, 1951, pp. 492–510.

12 PEHRSON, ROBERT N., "Bilateral Kin Groupings as a Structural Type: A Preliminary Statement," University of Manila *Journal of East Asiatic Studies,* vol. 3, January, 1954, pp. 199–202.

13 CUMMING, ELAINE, and DAVID M. SCHNEIDER, "Sibling Solidarity: A Property of American Kinship," *American Anthropologist,* vol. 63, June, 1961, pp. 498–507.

14 GOUGH, KATHLEEN, "The Modern Disintegration of Matrilineal Descent Groups" in Schneider and Gough, editors, *op. cit.,* pp. 631–652.

15 SCHNEIDER, DAVID M., "The Distinctive Features of Matrilineal Descent Groups," *ibid.,* p. 16.

16 ABERLE, DAVID F., "Matrilineal Descent in Cross-Cultural Perspective," *op. cit.,* p. 659.

17 LITWAK, EUGENE, "Occupational Mobility and Extended Family Cohesion," *American Sociological Review,* vol. 25, February, 1960, pp. 9–21; and "Geographic Mobility and Family Cohesion," *American Sociological Review,* vol. 25, June, 1960, pp. 385–394.

18 SJOBERG, GIDEON, "Familial Organization in the Preindustrial City," *Marriage and Family Living,* vol. 18, February, 1956, p. 32.

19 GOUGH, KATHLEEN, "The Modern Disintegration of Matrilineal Descent Groups" in Schneider and Gough, editors, *op. cit.,* pp. 631–652.

20 YANG, C. K., *The Chinese Family in the Communist Revolution.* The Technology Press, Massachusetts Institute of Technology, Cambridge, Mass., 1959.

21 NIMKOFF, M. F., and RUSSELL MIDDLETON, "Types of Family and Types of Economy," *American Journal of Sociology,* vol. 66, November, 1960, pp. 215–225.

22 PARSONS, TALCOTT, "The Social Structure of the Family in *The Family: Its Function and Destiny,* edited by Ruth N. Anshen, Harper and Bros., New York, 1949, pp. 173–201; and "Revised Analytical Approach to the Theory of Social Stratification" in *Class, Status and Power: A Reader in Social Stratification,* edited by Reinhard Bendix and Seymour M. Lipset, The Free Press, Glencoe, Ill., 1953, pp. 92–128. Also see Williams, Robin M., Jr., *op. cit.* For another classic statement of the hypothesis that kinship ties tend to break down in urban industrial societies, see Wirth, Louis, "Urbanism as

a Way of Life," *American Journal of Sociology,* vol. 44, July, 1938, pp. 1–24.

23 GOODE, WILLIAM J., *World Revolution and Family Patterns.* The Free Press of Glencoe, New York, 1963, p. 369.

24 GOUGH, KATHLEEN, "The Modern Disintegration of Matrilineal Descent Groups" in Schneider and Gough, editors, *op. cit.*, p. 640.

25 MARRIS, PETER, *Family and Social Change in an African City: A Study of Rehousing in Lagos.* Routledge and Kegan Paul, London, 1961, pp. 136–137.

26 *Ibid.*, p. 141.

27 BENNETT, JOHN W., and LEO A. DESPRES, "Kinship and Instrumental Activities: A Theoretical Inquiry," *American Anthropologist,* vol. 62, April, 1960, p. 254; Despres, Leo A., "A Function of Bilateral Kinship Patterns in a New England Industry," *Human Organization,* vol. 17, Summer, 1958, pp. 15–22.

28 BARNETT, MILTON L., "Kinship as a Factor Affecting Cantonese Economic Adaptation in the United States, "*Human Organization,* vol. 19, Spring, 1960, p. 41.

29 WILKINSON, THOMAS O., "Family Structure and Industrialization in Japan," *American Sociological Review,* vol. 27, October, 1962, pp. 678–682.

30 See Bibliography to this volume for listing of relevant books and articles.

31 LITWAK, EUGENE, "Occupational Mobility and Extended Family Cohesion," and "Geographic Mobility and Family Cohesion," *op. cit.*

32 SUSSMAN, MARVIN B., and LEE BURCHINAL, "Kin Family Network: Unheralded Structure in Current Conceptualizations of Family Functioning," *Marriage and Family Living,* vol. 24, August, 1962, pp. 231–240. Another review of studies of kinship in industrial society can be found in Wilensky, Harold L., and Charles N. Lebeaux, *Industrial Society and Social Welfare,* Russell Sage Foundation, New York, 1958.

33 DORE, RONALD P., *City Life in Japan: A Study of a Tokyo Ward.* University of California Press, Berkeley and Los Angeles, 1958, p. 376.

34 GLADWIN, THOMAS, and SEYMOUR B. SARASON, "Culture and Individual Personality Integration on Truk" in *Culture and Mental Health: Cross Cultural Studies,* edited by Marvin K. Opler. Macmillan Co., New York, 1959, pp. 173–210.

35 EGGAN, DOROTHY, "The General Problem of Hopi Adjustment" in *Personality in Nature, Society, and Culture,* edited by Clyde Kluckhohn and Henry A. Murray. 2d ed. Alfred A. Knopf, Inc., New York, 1953, pp. 280–281.

36 WHITING, JOHN W. M., and IRVIN L. CHILD, "Origins of Guilt" in *Child Training and Personality: A Cross-Cultural Study.* Yale University Press, New Haven, 1953, p. 246. For another discussion that relates kinship structure and personality, see Winch, Robert F., *Identification and its Familial Determinants,* Bobbs-Merrill Co., Indianapolis, Ind., 1962.

37 MEAD, MARGARET, *Coming of Age in Samoa.* William Morrow and Co., New York, 1928, pp. 104–105.

38 DORE, RONALD P., *op. cit.*, p. 126.

39 MURDOCK, GEORGE PETER, *op. cit.*, pp. 260–283.

40 HSU, FRANCIS L. K., *Americans and Chinese: Two Ways of Life,* Abelard-Schuman, Ltd., New York, 1953; and "Suppression versus Repression: A Limited Psychological Interpretation of Four Cultures," *Psychiatry,* vol. 12, August, 1949, pp. 223–242.

27

ANTHROPOLOGY AND POLITICAL SCIENCE: COURTSHIP OR MARRIAGE?

RONALD COHEN

Possibly more than any other discipline, anthropology stands at the crossroads of intellectual pursuit. Almost any subject can become grist for an anthropologist's mill, either for itself, because it is a product of human labor, because it affects human development and behavior, or because, like the use of techniques derived from nuclear physics to date ancient biological and cultural remains, it can be utilized as a tool of inquiry. The problem of the overlap of anthropology with other fields of knowledge, other modes of inquiry, is constantly manifested in the social and cultural aspects of the discipline. I do not suppose there is an anthropologist who has not, at one time or another, been approached with a request to explain how anthropology differs from sociology. While the same query is less likely to arise about anthropology and history, anthropology and geography, and so forth, there is no question that in developing its approaches to various kinds of problems, anthropology tends to rely very heavily on the techniques of, and the information already available in other fields.

Turning to political anthropology, we note that politics, as an outstanding political scientist has written, is "who gets what, when, and how." Every time I think about Lasswell's remarkably pithy definition, I get to wondering how politics differs from economics. I have concluded that it doesn't, very much, and that the main point of contrast is in the way things are looked at: when we are primarily interested in the things that are gotten and in the systems whereby they are evaluated and exchanged, we may be said to be doing "economics." But when our concern is with the power that defines possession or structures accumulation, then we are looking at very much the same phenomena from the perspective of "politics."

What do anthropologists do when they look at something politically? In reality, there is a range of anthropological behaviors depending on the sophistication of the society being studied and the goals and theoretical awareness of the investigator. The overlap of political and other activities is greater in simpler societies than in more complex societies. Or, to put it slightly differently, there is less functional specificity of different cultural aspects. Or, in simpler societies activities that we would regard as clearly and predominantly political are usually embedded in other kinds of activities. For example, in some societies it is difficult to extricate political actions from the normal and constant round of kinship obligations and interactions.

Now, back to the relations between anthropology and political science. Clearly, what is happening in those portions of anthropology that lie close to political science is some developing degree of interdependence. Because of a heavy two-way flow between anthropologists and political scientists, one anthropologically trained specialist in the investigation of political systems asks about the assignation going on between these fields. Is it really a marriage, or just an affair of the moment? What does the relationship entail, and what can it contribute to knowledge? Here is one informed view.

▼△▼△▼

Introduction: The Courtship

When disciplines begin exchanging materials one may say that they are attracted to one another. If this behavior continues the situation may well develop into a full courtship. In this latter case, consistent references to one another become quite common and concepts from the one discipline may be widely accepted by the other. However, such proto-unions are, in my view, not fully consummated until an area of overlap between the two fields begins to emerge as a new sub-field of the two that were originally attracted. Thus physical chemistry, social psychology, even political sociology, are

SOURCE: "Anthropology and Political Science: Courtship or Marriage?" by Ronald Cohen, in *The American Behavioral Scientist,* Vol. XI, No. 2 (Nov.–Dec. 1967) pp. 1–7. Reprinted by permission of the Publisher, Sage Publications, Inc., and the author.

today accepted areas of research and teaching that overlap into neighboring disciplines. In general the stimulus for such development comes from some theory, some research and some faith that utilizing a mixture of the two disciplines can provide insights and explanations that were hitherto unavailable. The question then becomes where in this process of marital and premarital relations can we place anthropology and political science, and what are the prospects for the union . . . if such is to take place.

Although my own knowledge is severely limited to African research and my experiences as a member of one department of political science, I will try to assess the situation and make some prognostications about whether there is a blossoming love affair developing that has any real contributions to make to both of the disciplines concerned.

In a recent article on New Nations and their contributions to the development of political theory, Lucien Pye (1964) borrows a number of terms that have a familiar ring to the anthropologist—cultural relativism, social evolution, cultural diffusion and acculturation—all seem to be concepts that Pye is able to use in order to focus on processes of nation building. As he says, theories developed from western nation states cannot do the job of describing something as different as the new national entities of the non-western world. On the anthropologist's side, terms such as "regime," inputs and outputs (as these have been used in recent political theory), are now becoming quite common . . . especially among American anthropologists interested in political phenomena. The fact that Pye does not feel it is necessary to define his terms, and that a number of terms from political theory are now commonly used in anthropology, indicates that a readership has developed that is becoming familiar enough with these terms so that definitions are unnecessary.

In terms of contact indicated by citations it is becoming, again, ordinary to see political scientists quoting anthropologists and vice versa. However the emphasis is still strongly rooted in one discipline or the other. Thus Glickman (1965) in his review article of political science in Africa refers to a hundred and seventy-three separate works by political scientists and twenty-nine by anthropologists, while a recent book on political anthropology does exactly the reverse and only authors trained in anthropology were invited to contribute to this volume.

Furthermore, unlike physical chemistry, social psychology, or political sociology, I know of only one (my own) appointment at the university level which allows either an anthropologist or a political scientist to actively join in the work of both departments and have formal access to graduate students in both fields. In some ways, then, it would be difficult to assess the present situation as one of marriage. However, there does seem to be enough mutual attraction going on so that a number of people in both disciplines can now honestly say of each other: "Some of my best friends are . . . !"

The Role of the Interdisciplinarian

Because there is as yet no established sub-field unifying political science and anthropology, the role of the person who attempts to create such linkages is a particularly difficult one. Training is thoroughly rooted in one or the other of the disciplines and a great deal of this training may, at least in the short run, seem inapplicable. Depending upon the types of problems, the background of the colleagues and students with whom interaction is taking place, the time of day, and several other factors having to do with the personalities involved, the interdisciplinarian is either a pioneer or a fraud. As a pioneer he sees complexities and opportunities in an original and often stimulating way usually because very few students have actually viewed things from this vantage point. As a fraud he is a person who may refer to competence beyond that of his critics in each of his "fields"—thus having an extra defense against criticism, and an extra set of barbs among his own critical arrows. In other words it is not unthinkable that a person of fairly weak talents in several disciplines could survive by straddling all of them.

Nonetheless, as I shall try to show, the need for interdisciplinary work between anthropology and political science does exist. The danger exists as well, however, that in pioneering such interstitial positions we can create areas of refuge for the incompetent, or at least until recognizable demands of training and background become more standardized. This leads to the conclusion that for the persons involved in interdisciplinary work there is a commitment to gain some definite measures of competence in all of the fields he is attempting to fuse or straddle. The ideal in this regard is well-nigh impossible, so that in practice the would-be interdisciplinarian generally hovers between the poles of pioneering and fraud hoping somehow that the goals of the game are, in the end, worth the strain. Whether such goals are in fact worthwhile depends upon the issues that have stimulated the courtship and whether a combined effort using the energies and resources of both disciplines has anything creative and worthwhile to contribute to problems being raised within each discipline.

The Issues

(1) Political Science

As political science has expanded its field of interests beyond that of the formally instituted governmental system it has come more and more to appreciate and study the socio-cultural milieu of political life. Pressure groups, voting behavior, social movements, and political socialization are just a few of the directions that have given political scientists a more general social science orientation. In doing so political science has turned to sister disciplines—especially sociology and psychology. These disciplines were already equipped with a body of theory and techniques directed at the new variables that came more and more to be included within the purview of political science research. Thus, in terms of actual empirical research, political scientists have in the past two decades widened their conception of what is politically relevant to include a large number of factors related to the formal structure of government and how the activities of the political system are related to both internal and environmental conditions. This move into society and culture using empirical research has created a mood of receptivity and openness among political scientists that serves as a background within which other developments have taken place.

Along with this development has come an increase in variance occasioned primarily by the rise of new nations during the last ten to fifteen years. With a plethora of new states to be studied the variance in political phenomena has increased in a sudden spurt and stimulated interest in the functional approach to political systems such that particular and novel societal structures can be viewed as adaptations to universal requirements of political life. However such claims to universality require broad testing. Many of the new nations are made up of traditional non-western societies whose local political organization is often not that of the nation state. Do the so-called universal categories of political activity apply to these societies as entities in and of themselves, or only as sub-units of the larger nation state whose political life is the main focus of the political scientists? Theoretically, if such an entity as *the* political system exists, political theory should be applicable to all societies no matter how simple or complex they happen to be. If, for example, political activity is an aspect of all human social action, and "interest articulation" is a universal function of all systems—then how is this function performed among a small isolated hunting band in the high Arctic? In other words the gamit of societies known to the anthropologists represents a highly various set of polities for whom political theory should be applicable if such ideas lay claim to universality. The data of the anthropologists, basic descriptions of non-western societies around the world, provide a wide spectrum of behavior against which political theory should be tested.

It is naive, however, to think such testing is easy. I have tried with students to apply Almond and Coleman's ideas as well as those of Easton concerning the political system to a variety of non-western politics. In general I think that such work has taught us that applying a complex set of categories to a very simple political system constantly involves the danger that one behavior or set of role activities can easily become an indicator for several variables in the political theory model. Thus if an Eskimo band articulates interest at the time a decision is to be made, the activity of decision making and interest articulation is fused into one behavior which if counted for each variable means measuring the same behavior twice in order to make a correlation. On the other hand the application of theory from political science to anthropological data can point out weaknesses in the anthropological materials. Thus one student, in trying to apply some of Riker's ideas on coalitions to a very simple island society in the Pacific, found that the requisite data were unavailable. There were wide areas of relevant political activities simply not reported by the ethnographer.

For the political scientist the presence of the anthropological literature is not only a stimulus to theory testing but forms a basis for understanding local political situations as well. Coleman (1960) realized this when he said "traditional political systems have largely shaped the political perspectives, orientation to politics and attitudes towards authority of all but a small fraction . . . of Africans involved in modern political activity" (1960:258). Certainly a number of individual case studies have taken this approach to heart. Thus Young and Fosbrooke (1960) have looked at local political organizations in analyzing the effect of a modernizing program in Tanzania, and Apter (1961) utilized such materials in attempting to understand the Buganda contribution to Uganda political development. However, systematic work along these lines is still quite rare (cf. Zolberg 1966:153). In this regard John Paden and his colleagues at Northwestern have begun a study of internal stability and national integration in Africa. Through the use of aggregate data they hope to outline some of the major variables which are related to stability and instability among modern African states. Their approach involves taking into account the major traditional political systems within each country, so that the characteristics of these traditional societies will be able to compete with each other as variables in assessing what is related to the differences between more and less stable systems. In order to carry out the study, of course, the researchers have had to utilize the ethnographic materials on major tribal societies in each country.

At both the substantive and theoretical levels the most important reason why there is a coming together of anthropological and political science research interest stems, I believe, from the relative weakness of the so-called country study among the new nations. By country study, I mean that many of the earlier field investigations by political scientists in places like Africa focused on national elites, colonialism, the growth of nationalism and independence, central government policies and other national data such as constitutional history, national elections and party politics. When local politics are mentioned they are generally summarized quickly or typed as to indigenous political features that might have an effect on the national scene. In some cases we are left in doubt as to what the traditional system is and only the most meagre data is presented for quite abstract generalizations about local populations.

Thus Kilson (1966) in his work on Sierra Leone characterizes peasant disturbances from the 1930s to the mid 1950s as a political awakening of this group. We are not told, except through colonial reports and comparative interpretations by researchers from elsewhere in Africa, why in fact the peasants were causing disturbances—except that it seemed to be related to taxation. Was taxation felt to be excessive? Was it never accepted in its Western form? Were the peasants attempting to destroy the traditional authority as Kilson (1966:61) claims? Or were they trying to restore an older precolonial situation of relationship between themselves and their leaders? Unfortunately the research emphasis is from the point of view of the central government, not the peasants; therefore there are no data from peasants themselves to substantiate one of several possible interpretations of their rioting. However, since the general trend of change in the country as a whole (especially in the cities) has been away from tradition, the researcher feels justified in assuming that a peasant riot must be in the same direction as well—that is to say, away from tradition. But given the method of argument, the generalization still remains an assumption rather than a validated conclusion.

Country studies are nevertheless important as first steps, since they have helped us to map out and describe the variety of national units that make up the new nations. However, the very nature of such studies has tended to reinforce theoretical developments in political science that embody the weaknesses of such a research approach.

Let me explain. If the political scientist working in a new nation has to comprehend the entire national entity and its sub-parts, it is simpler to classify the entire nation as being of a particular type. This classification is then assumed to have causal power which determines the way that social change and political developments are taking place. Supporting data for such a position then comes from an analysis of the elite—who are assumed to have ultimate power and authority in the new nation. Thus Pye claims that "in these systems [the new countries] the source of dynamic change often resides largely with the small governing elite who control the formal structures of government which in turn do not represent the institutionalization of indigenous cultural patterns but rather foreign importations" (1964:7).

A concrete example of such theorizing is given by David Apter, who has recently attempted to characterize modernizing nations. Out of his experience with various approaches in political theory and his rich understanding of new nations, he sets up ideal categories for the modernizing countries. The implied assumption here is that the characterization of a whole unit—the new nation and its government—will allow us to predict to, and understand, its parts and their development: the institutional infrastructure and the attitudes of the people. Thus a "mobilizing" state is doing one set of things having some effect throughout the entire nation, while a "reconciliation" state is doing something quite different.

Although characterizing whole nations this way may be in fact quite an accurate account of a national policy through the efforts and activities of central government agencies—is it an accurate picture of what is really going on inside the nation? And how deterministic is such a characterization? Is a "mobilizing" state that much different from a "reconciliation" one over time? Or are there sets of internal determinants such as traditional political systems and their interrelationships, the natural resource base, population pressures, etc., that predict to developmental paths more accurately than the apparent structural and ideological characterization of the whole nation (cf. Zolberg 1966)? Put in other terms, can we say Russia and the United States (which are both modern industrial nations) have reached similar or different societal results because they have different political structures and ideological features? (See Galbraith 1967.) Can we trace out the similarities and differences and explain them by simply analyzing each society as a whole? [1] Obviously research on the internal features of such societies is required before we answer such questions—and research on the local areas and institutions of the new nations brings the political scientist and the anthropologist into the same area treating with the same populations and many of the same behaviors.

In many parts of the non-western world, local political systems are heavily dependent on forms of socio-political structures that are still strongly influenced by their traditional cultures. To say that these are "traditional" or "primitive," hides the fact that there is a bewildering array of such systems. Furthermore, the means by which they are articulated and are becoming incorporated into larger systems are as yet poorly known and many of the results we have are often contradictory. Thus we have hypotheses to suggest that traditional state-like societies adapt more easily to incorporation within a larger modern state than do acephalous tribal societies in east Africa (Fallers 1955)—while others working close by in central Africa claim just the reverse (Apthorpe 1959). Each different variety of traditional political systems has its own means of recruitment to office, its own structures for making decisions, and there are, probably, different varieties of political culture and attitudes toward authority that go along with such systems (cf. Levine 1966).

Besides the type of traditional political system that is being incorporated, there are different effects of modernization itself on the population at large. Terms like "development," "modernization," "national immigration," mean that processes of change are operating at both the institutional and the individual behavioral level. We can describe and analyze changes in national and local institutions often by using documents alone. However the effects of these changes on the people and their behavior in both political and non-political roles can only be achieved through field work. Urbanization, labor unions, western education, agricultural developments, new industry, and new forms of political participation must be studied among local segments of the population to gauge their effects. In such studies ethnicity is a variable, as is the traditional socio-political structure. Thus Southall (1965) points out that in Kampala urbanites from acephalous ethnic groups have many more voluntary associations and more official office holders per organization than those from ethnic groups organized traditionally into centralized polities. In my own work, secondary school students from non-centralized tribes in Northern Nigeria report that their future marriage and family relations will be more independent of those around them than people from traditional state societies who see themselves as having a marriage and family unit embedded into larger groupings to which they will defer for many of their decisions. The research strategy here is a well developed one in anthropology. Each of these studies focuses on a modern situation and then asks what effect traditional cultural variables have in determining the paths of change. Thus, to be precise about the actual direction of development, research at the local level is essential—and only when such work is carried out can we assess whether or not national policies or local contingencies (or what combination of both) decided the direction of national development.

In the sphere of methodology and techniques, political science has moved very quickly in recent times towards a hard science approach—so that research design and quantitative measurement have become heavily emphasized. Anthropology has been much slower to adapt such techniques, although changes are evident. However, research at a local level in developing areas presents the political scientists with field work conditions not unlike those the anthropologist has been facing for years. It is these conditions, and not the conservatism of anthropologists, that have slowed down the growth of more rigorous research techniques in anthropology—and because that is so, the political scientist must face up to many of the same problems.

The problems are complex but can be summarized. First, the language of almost all but a few of the local people is not English and meaningful research must be carried on through an interpreter or by learning the language or a combination of both. Secondly, there is often a vast difference between the standard of living of the researcher and that of his informants. Thirdly, the cultural milieu of his informants is to an unknown degree different.

To solve such problems many anthropologists try to learn the language and they are all trained within a mystique from their own disciplinary past which preaches that endurance of physical hardship in field work is somehow ennobling and fruitful with respect to the goals of science. The assumed (but not yet rigorously tested) rationale here is that being able to cope with, and appreciate, differences in living standards enables the field worker to interact on a daily basis with members of another culture—while remaining within his own western living standard produces a shield between the researcher and those whom he seeks to understand. Thus differences in standard of living are often not only expected but welcomed—by the doctoral candidate as part of the initiation into full professional status, and by the experienced field worker as a validation of his professional abilities.

For data collection in a strange culture, anthropology has developed participant observation using both directive and non-directed interviews, as well as living in and observing on a full day to day basis the behavior of people acting out their local roles in their local institutions. The essence, or fundamental assumption, of this anthropological field technique is easily stated but not so easily learned. In any non-western situation an anthropologist assumes that all behavior, all representations, and manifestations by other people are not fully understandable unless placed in their own context. Thus a spoon may not be just a spoon as we know it; or a leader and his follower may conceive of their relationship in terms that are totally unfamiliar, but which make sense given the full understanding of the local ideology of leader-follower relationships. For such work the personality of the investigator, his patience, continual curiosity, and ability to systematize everyday life into some set of meaningful categories for data analysis become the essentials for what has become a highly sensitive technique. Certainly it is not only the method available for studying local political activity in non-western areas. Both anthropology and political science will use many techniques in these local areas in the coming years. However, some use of this traditional anthropological approach is probably essential for any social scientist who wishes to obtain an intelligent basis for more restrictive and focused data collection having to do with a well developed research design in a non-western area.

At the level of theory construction, it has been suggested that anthropology (along with sociology and general systems theory) has stimulated an emphasis on functionalism in political science (Glickman 1965:149). This is probably true, although I suspect it would have happened anyway with or without anthropology. I say this because requisite functional theory is one of the few ways (and perhaps the most efficient) of handling a sudden burst in variance, which is what happened to political phenomena once the plethora of new nations arrived on the scene. However, just as in anthropology such "theory" has contributed to the description of variety, so too in political science requisite functions such as "rule making" or "political demands" are no more than descriptive categories which allow for unknown amounts of variety in the structures that express such theoretically universal functions.

Much still remains to be done within the new nations. But once the variety has been mapped there is still the much more essential job of explaining why such variety exists. Thus in anthropology knowing about widely varying forms of kinship, marriage, religion, and politics has been only an initial step in "explaining" why such variety has occurred and what factors condition its change over time. The reason requisite functional models seem appropriate at the present time in political science, is that older typologies in comparative politics simply have not been applicable to the wide variety now available for study. Using a structural approach to theory construction is, in effect, complementary to functionalism. As political anthropologists have recently tried to show (Cohen 1965, 1967; Smith 1966) such an approach still provides a fruitful way of building theories and designing research once the range of variance has been dealt with. Thus functionalism can answer the question: "How is a certain purpose performed?" Structuralism then takes over and directs our attention towards explaining why certain forms differ from one another and how they change through time.[2]

Another theoretical contribution that anthropology is making to political science, related to functionalism, is the evolutionary point of view (cf. Barringer, Blanksten, and Mack 1965). Explicitly or implicitly, anthropologists have almost always ordered the societies they study into an evolutionary framework. Theories that discuss how societies change from simple to complex, and from one type to another, are viewed as evolutionary although they may not always meet the conditions that such studies demand (see Cohen 1962). However by attempting to see a large gamut of societies with the same point of view as that of biology, the anthropologist assumes that developmental direction is a natural quality of his comparative material. As a theorist he arranges material in order to ask what creates the changes or differences as one set of systems develops into another. In large scale comparative work, evolution involves as a constituent property differentiation. This approaches to a Guttman scale, since each "higher" or more evolved system contains, theoretically, many of the same elements as the "lower" or less evolved ones, plus new aspects not present in the earlier, less differentiated systems. Such evolutionary analyses can help us to develop typological characterizations of new nations based on empirical data. Structural analysis can proceed from there to guide research towards an understanding of why societies differ at higher and lower ends of the scale. In effect, this is what Adelman and her colleagues (1967) have been doing by dividing a large sample of underdeveloped countries into low, middle and high groupings based on GNP per capita and then attempting to analyze them through factor analysis and discriminant function analysis in order to see just what social, political, and economic, variables are associated with these different levels of development.

Another possible realm of theoretical and empirical interchange between anthropology and political science is in the area of international relations. If we assume that theoretical work in international relations is intended to create generalizations about the way in which independent polities interact across political boundaries, then such theories (to be truly general) should help to explain interaction between preindustrial polities as well. In turn, such comparative data can help stimulate new insights into the nature of international interaction. However such work must, if it is to be seriously approached, use the full gamut of interpolity relations found among non-western peoples. To create a comparative model of international relations by examining one type of system, such as the segmentary lineage societies (which vary among themselves), is to avoid the very quality that anthropological data has to offer—i.e. its ability to extend and increase variance such that we are in fact talking of the political life of mankind. Here anthropology has been somewhat remiss in developing comparative analyses and theoretical schemas. However there is available in the literature a respectable amount of material on inter-tribal relations. How such phenomena as blood brotherhood, joking relations between tribes, intercommunity alliances through marriage and trade, clan alliance, cooperative economic activities, hostages, and warfare, all fit together is still virtually an unworked area of comparative analysis within anthropology. What is needed here are functional categories that systematize the nature of interpolity relations, which can then be directed at pre-industrial societies. Only when such work has been done will we have a fully comparative basis for the study of international relations.

(2) Anthropology

In my view, anthropology has experienced two major stimuli in the last half century, each of which has seriously changed the direction of its development. The first was a field work revolution that had its roots in natural history prior to the twentieth century, but which (as a method) provided a new thrust away from the somewhat simplistic evolutionism of the latter nineteenth century. How the field work tradition played itself out as "normal" research in England, United States, France, and elsewhere was a function of local academic conditions and the particular areas of the world where each national group did most of its field work. Out of this research came the holistic approach, social structural studies, psychological anthropology, acculturation studies, and above all, a unit—the tribe or ethnic group. Anthropologists became identifiable as those chaps who knew about the Bongo Bongo. In so doing they achieved an academic niche in the universities, as well as an identifiable role in the overseas colonies of the imperial powers. As long as the groups studied by anthropologists remained isolated or semi-isolated, field work rested on something mildly real, i.e. these groups had some meaningful integrity as wholes. Thus, the interrelationships of their parts, and the comparisons of these relationships across a number of such ethnic units, was methodologically appropriate, defensible, and enriching to the general social science community.

The second major change in anthropology began with the end of World War II. During the last two and a half decades, with ever quickening pace, the tribal societies have come more and more to play a role in modern nation states—whose leaders envisage rapid social change as a basic assumption in any ideology they expound for their country as a unit. Thus in a flash, as it were, the older unit of anthropology—the ethnic group—has lost much of its wholeness because one of its most significant features is the fact that it is now part of a larger nation state. In some instances (i.e. Fallers 1955; Cohen 1963; and others)—where the ethnic group maintains its corporate identity, politically and economically—we have been able to study how the national and local systems intermesh, what the effect of role conflict is in the intermediate role, and how each system affects the other. But many local community activities are new and emergent. Trade unions, neighborhood and ward organizations in cities, political party organizations at the local ward level, student organizations, attitudes to modern versus traditional ways of doing things—all of these are interesting and vital features of contemporary social life in the new nations. However there is one major difference to the traditional field situation of the anthropologist. In these modern situations ethnicity is only one among many properties of local community life and thus it becomes one variable in the new research situation.

This is the stimulus to change that has provided the anthropologist with a new research orientation; indeed it forces these orientations upon the field worker. By looking at the field situation in these ways, new kinds of data emerge which are derived from different sources and the use of different techniques. Furthermore, whereas twenty years ago the anthropologist was almost alone in his interest in the social, cultural, economic, and psychological behavior of non-western man, today he has been joined by many others—all of whom, from their various disciplinary orientations as well as their interest in new nations, are studying specific aspects of behavior among non-western peoples. The anthropologist then has to choose which particular problem he wishes to study; he is no longer an expert on everything. As one of my African colleagues suggested, commenting on this point, he could see no reason whatsoever for any anthropologist trying, under contemporary conditions, to write a book that attempted to describe all of Yoruba culture or all of Buganda culture; to do so, he claims, would be to remain superficial in a scholarly sense and probably condescending in a normative one.

Rapid change is taking place all over the underdeveloped world. Urbanization, western education, nationalism, and other forces are producing wide variations in attitudes and behavior. To simply gather data using participant observation techniques means that one must attempt to assess a pattern that is some kind of central tendency, or give some estimate of the ranges of variation using several independent variables as a means of grouping the population. Thus, in speaking of political participation, the writer may note what overall differences there are according to sex, age, class, rural-urban residence, in terms of the observations he has made on each of these categories of people through using participant observation techniques. Obviously, to be precise such generalizations require some quantitative measures of the variances involved, and this requirement again forces the anthropological researcher to limit the scope of his problem. In turn, this means that, in the future, general ethnographic techniques will probably be used to understand the local context, while more precise social science techniques will become common in order to gather data on specific problems.

In overall terms, what these developments mean for social and cultural anthropology as a discipline is that the foundation of its unity—the study of a whole ethnic group (often through intensive work in only a few settlements)—is proving to be a less durable study than anyone twenty years ago would have believed. It also means that some specialties within anthropology—such as economic anthropology and political anthropology, psychological anthropology—are developing and moving out towards other social sciences. In fact a regrouping of interests across disciplinary boundaries is taking place. This can be seen at Northwestern University—where the Anthropology Department, out of nine faculty members, has six with joint appointments in other social science departments. Although this situation is probably extreme, I suspect that it represents a trend not just towards the breaking down of disciplinary boundaries in the social sciences, but towards a reshaping of these boundaries based on the common interests of the people concerned.

In the realm of theory, anthropologists have traditionally had an over-simplified view of what the political system is, and what kinds of categories of behavior must be observed in order to fully report on the political life of the people. Through the work of contemporary theorists much more adequate conceptualization of politics is being diffused into anthropology (cf. Easton 1959, 1966; Almond and Powell 1966).

Perhaps the best example of such interchange is in the area of conflict theory. Many anthropologists, with their traditional interests in understanding how exotic systems work, have tended to ask functional questions and create interpretations of data, including conflict, in terms of the contributions such activities make to the ongoing system. Political scientists have more often used conflict as a causal engine to explain adjustments, social and political movements, and change in general. Although it is always important to assume that conflict may have positive as well as negative effect given a rapidly changing social milieu, I suspect that anthropologists will become progressively interested in conflict as a stimulus to change—not only in terms of role conflict, and class conflict, but also in terms of social or inter-ethnic rivalries and interregional ones and so on. Here hypotheses and theories abound in political science which could be meaningfully tested by anthropologists working at the local level in the new nations. For example, Karl Deutsch has developed a theory (1953: 179–180) that a policy which includes sharply differentiated living standards should also have an intensity of nationalistic feelings: (a) inversely proportional to mobility between classes and regions, (b) directly proportional to the barriers against cultural assimilation, and (c) directly proportional to the extent of economic and prestige differences between culture, classes and regions.

What Deutsch is suggesting here is that inequalities produce tensions and frustrations while nationalism provides a social and political catharsis or channel through which collective aggressions may be expressed. This may be true, at least for the modernizing world, but it needs testing in local areas; and I suspect it needs refinement in terms of types of the traditional systems to which it is applied. Thus, I would suspect the hypothesis to produce very different sets of results for India, as compared with Eastern Nigeria. In the latter case, people have practically no sharp class distinction traditionally and N-achievement has been described as relatively high—at least in relation to other Nigerian groups (Levine 1966). The hypothesis might be strongly validated in Eastern Nigeria where economic and prestige differentiation can be theorized to be a new and frustrating characteristic of the modernizing situation. However India, with its ancient and locally developed inequities of class status and economic positions, must have already developed in its traditional life non-nationalistic modes of adaptation to these same conflicts . . . and these could be utilized, at least partially, in the modern situation as well.

In terms of method, the behavioral techniques being developed in both political science and sociology are also diffusing over into anthropology—although this movement can be seen most clearly among those doing cross-cultural surgevys of large samples of societies. Nevertheless, within the next ten years, I expect that training in research design, questionnaire construction, statistical techniques and computer analysis will become much more common in social anthropology than it is at the moment; on the other hand the relativism of anthropology will be expressed in a strong emphasis on the use of culturally specific indicators for theoretically derived variables. This means that the traditional emphasis on understanding the local cultural context will not be given up, but rather used as a building block or stepping stone to the more restrictive problems derived from comparative research and theory.

Conclusion: The Result of Courtship and the Promise of Consummation

As I have already pointed out, the relations between anthropology and political science have gone beyond the point of dalliance to a stiuation of courtship. However marriage is not yet, indeed may never be, because social science itself is moving towards group marriage. However a number of things are clear:

1. For the political scientist, anthropological data provides an increase in variance such that theory may be tested on wider samples of political systems. In order to accomplish this political scientists should have courses and texts available to them in political anthropology and such materials should introduce the student to the range of political variety known to the anthropologist. A start has been made in this direction and it will expand in the future (see Schapera 1956; Mair 1962; Gluckman 1965; Swartz, Turner and Tuden 1966; Almond and Powell 1966; Cohen and Middleton 1967; also *Rural*

Africana: Research Notes on Local Politics and Political Anthropology, edited by Norman Miller, Michigan State University).

2. For research purposes, political scientists should be made aware of aggregate data sources in anthropology—such as the HRAF files—and research must be designed at the local level in the new nations (cf. Zolberg 1966). This latter feature is well advanced already and seems to be a growing trend in political science research in foreign areas.
3. Anthropology can aid political science in the analysis of ethnicity and in preparing researchers for the use of participant observation techniques in the field.
4. Anthropology on its side has a great deal to gain from political science, in terms of theory and more precise behavioral methods —which at this point in its development the discipline sorely needs.

Discussion

The overall conclusion toward which all of these statements point, is that outside the milieu of the industrialized western nations in particular, and for comparative purposes in general, anthropology and political science are both facing issues and specific research problems that must eventually bring them closer together. However such convergence is not simply a matter of each discipline reaching over into the other's bailiwick and grabbing for a solution. The issues raised in this article call for new and different kinds of work in both disciplines in order that something constructive come out of their mutual attraction. Unfortunately, work already completed can only partially solve new problems for which such research was not intended.

Let me illustrate this point with a problem that is plaguing some of us at Northwestern—that of local unit definition. To say, as many do these days, that research must move to the local or micro-political level in new nation research is one thing; but it begs a number of difficult operational and research design problems. As of now, there are a number of studies going on at the local level among the African nations. But in order to coordinate and systematize such research we need to know what are the significant units of study at the local level; are they the ethnic groups? the towns? local institutions such as trade unions, local government or combinations of these? Unfortunately much of the best traditional ethnography in Africa is concerned with small (often isolated) groups, while larger more complex and variegated "tribes" are usually less well studied. Furthermore, such ethnographic accounts are often time-bound, in that they describe conditions at the time the research was carried out. How then can a researcher use this literature to characterize the ethnic properties of a new African nation.

In addition, ethnicity may not be a stable entity. So-called ethnic groups can coalesce and subdivide over time and in the face of different situations. Indeed one anthropologist (Fried 1966) has suggested that the sense of ethnic identification is a reaction formation that results from the nature of a wider political unit of which the ethnic group is a part. Thus "easterner" and "northerner" may be emergent ethnic groups in Nigeria, but if these areas were to become separate political entities, then subdivisions within them such as Hausa, Fulani, Ibo, Ijaw, etc., would become more important politically. Thus choosing local ethnic units may be somewhat arbitrary. Zolberg (1964) has tried to work out "culture centers" for the Ivory Coast and my colleague John Paden is working with the idea of constructing local ethnic entities that are politically relevant in the modern era.

The question can then be posed as to whether these units have any significant effect on national developments. If so, we must ask what is it about these groupings that produces such results. Another way of solving the same problem may be to devise some means for isolating "natural" developmental units or regions within or even across the new nations. Such units could be isolated, hopefully, through the objective measurement and analysis of various kinds of transaction flows such as telephone calls, trade, use of natural resources, road use, migration patterns, etc. Then, traditional ethnicity, local political structures, traditional authority patterns, attitudes, national policy goals, and other socio-cultural and political variables could be studied in relation to these units.

Whether or not these solutions are the "right" ones is not as important as the fact that the problem exists. Neither political science nor anthropology has a simple, pat answer already worked out. And this is only one example. As already noted above, comparative work in international relations involving non-western polities requires that data in anthropology be organized with this purpose in mind. Thus a convergence of goals in anthropology and political science means that some significant restructuring of both field research and their comparative foci must be accomplished before common interests can be pursued. Marriage often results from courtship but unless it results from complete self-deception it creates as many new problems as it solves.

Notes

1. I wrote this before reading Professor Zolberg's interesting and useful account of the West African party states. He too questions the usefulness of such characterizations as "reconciliation" and "mobilization" because they do not take account of changes in such states over time in which reconciliation and mobilization are simply aspects of state politics. He then builds up an alternate configuration (*viz.* the party state). My criticism can, however, also be leveled at his typological analysis (as he readily admits), since we still know very little, if anything, about the micro-politics of these new nations and much of these characterizations are based on analyses of national elites and nationally-based ideological developments.
2. Functionalism is concerned with the contribution a partial activity makes to the total activity of which it is a part. Structuralism is concerned with the relations of parts to one another and the conditions which are correlated with such relations to effect their change and/or stability.

References

ADELMAN, IRMA. *Society, Politics, and Economic Development: A Quantitative Approach.* Baltimore: Johns Hopkins Press, 1967.

ALMOND, GABRIEL A., and G. B. POWELL, JR. *Comparative Politics: A Developmental Approach.* Boston: Little, Brown, 1966.

APTER, DAVID E. *The Political Kingdom in Uganda.* Princeton: Princeton University Press, 1961.

APTHORPE, RAYMOND (ed.), *From Tribal Rule to Modern Government.* Lusaka: Rhodes Livingstone Institute, 1959.

BARRINGER, H. R., G. I. BLANKSTEN, and R. W. MACK. *Social Change in Developing Areas.* Boston: Schenkman, 1965.

COHEN, R. "The Strategy of Social Evolution," *Anthropologica,* 1962.

———. "Conflict and Change in a Northern Nigerian Emirate." In G. K. Zollschan and W. Hirsch (eds.), *Explorations in Social Change.* Boston: Houghton Mifflin, 1963. Pp. 495–521.

———. "Political Anthropology: The Future of a Pioneer," *Anthropological Quarterly,* XXXVIII (1965), pp. 117–131.

——— and J. MIDDLETON (eds.). *Comparative Political Systems: Studies in the Politics of Pre-Industrial Societies.* New York: Natural History Press, 1967.

COLEMAN, JAMES S. "The Politics of Sub-Saharan Africa." In Gabriel A. Almond and James S. Coleman (eds.), *The Politics of the Developing Areas.* Princeton: Princeton University Press, 1960, pp. 247–368.

DEUTSCH, KARL. "The Growth of Nations: Some Recurrent Patterns of Political and Cultural Integration," *World Politics,* 1953, pp. 179–180.

EASTON, DAVID. "Political Anthropology." In B. Siegel (ed.), *Biennial Review of Anthropology.* Stanford: Stanford University Press, 1959, pp. 210–263.

——— (ed.). *Varieties of Political Theory.* Englewood Cliffs, N.J.: Prentice-Hall, 1966.

FALLERS, LLOYD A. *Bantu Bureaucracy.* London: Routledge and Kegan Paul, 1955.

FRIED, M. H. "On the Concept of 'Tribe' and 'Tribal Society,'" *Transactions of the New York Academy of Sciences*, ser. 2, XXVIII (1966), 4, pp. 527–540.

GALBRAITH, JOHN KENNETH. *The New Industrial State*. Boston: Houghton Mifflin, 1967.

GLICKMAN, H. "Political Science." In R. A. Lystad (ed.), *The African World: A Survey of Social Research*. New York: Praeger, 1965. Pp. 131–165.

GLUCKMAN, MAX. *Politics, Law, and Ritual in Tribal Society*. Chicago: Aldine, 1965.

KILSON, MARTIN. *Political Change in a West African State: A Study of the Modernization Process in Sierra Leone*. Cambridge: Harvard University Press, 1966.

LEVINE, R. A. *Dreams and Deeds: Achievement Motivation in Nigeria*. Chicago: University of Chicago Press, 1966.

MAIR, L. *Primitive Government*. Baltimore: Penguin, 1962.

PYE, LUCIEN. "Democracy, Modernization, and Nation Building." In J. R. Pennock (ed.), *Self-Government in Modernizing Nations*. Englewood Cliffs, N.J.: Prentice-Hall, 1964. Pp. 6–25.

SCHAPERA, ISAAC. *Government and Politics in Tribal Societies*. New York: Humanities Press, 1956.

SMITH, M. G. "A Structural Approach to Comparative Politics." In D. Easton (ed.), *Varieties of Political Theory*. Englewood Cliffs, N.J.: Prentice-Hall, 1966. Pp. 113–129.

SOUTHALL, A. "Voluntary Societies in Pampala." Paper delivered at African Studies Association meeting, 1965.

SWARTZ, M., A. TURNER, and A. TUDEN (eds.). *Political Anthropology*. Chicago: Aldine, 1966.

YOUNG, R., and H. A. FOSBROOKE. *Smoke in the Hills: Political Tension in the Morogogo District of Tanganyika*. Evanston: Northwestern University Press, 1960.

ZOLBERG, ARISTIDE R. *One Party Government in the Ivory Coast*. Princeton: Princeton University Press, 1964.

——— *Creating Political Order: The Party States of West Africa*. New York: Rand McNally, 1966.

28

YANOMAMÖ SOCIAL ORGANIZATION AND WARFARE

NAPOLEON A. CHAGNON

The placement of Napoleon Chagnon's fine paper at this juncture accomplishes several ends. To begin with, there is the recurrent problem addressed to anthropologists concerning the possibility of doing field work in simple cultures in these days of rapid travel, electronic communications, and the seeming ubiquity of modern technology. The threatening reality of the modern technological world notwithstanding, it is still possible to do ethnographic work in quite tiny, politically autonomous villages. But the main reason for including this essay by Chagnon here is to deal with the phenomenon of war, which may be deplored but nonetheless remains one of the most important of cultural practices. While the editor does not accept Chagnon's easy assertion of "the ethnographic universality of warfare" (p. 337), he does not quibble that warfare is and has been remarkably widespread and that, ironically, it is a thoroughly human activity, having only rare analogs in nonhuman society, mainly among certain social insects.

Indeed, Chagnon takes pains to show us that Yanomamö warfare is only peripherally, or indirectly, tied to material want satisfaction. For instance, it is not a means of territorial aggrandizement. Instead, Chagnon takes us through some minutiae of Yanomamö kinship and social organization to seek the functional and structural causes of war in that culture. In the final analysis, Chagnon's careful explication of Yanomamö warfare shows striking resemblances to Roy Rappaport's views on the cultural-ecological significance of

SOURCE: *War: The Anthropology of Armed Conflict and Aggression*, Morton Fried, Marvin Harris, and Robert Murphy (eds.) Pp. 109–59. Garden City: The Natural History Press, 1968. Reprinted by permission of the author.

religion and the concept of the sacred. (See selection 32.)

▼△▼△▼

Introduction [1]

"Assertions with respect to war have emanated from philosophers, clergymen, journalists, publicists, sentimentalists, peace advocates, apologists of war, and a host of others. Their views as to the causes of war, the history of conflict, and the outlook for the future are usually dogmatically stated. When placed side by side they appear inconsistent and contradictory. They have one thing in common: they lack the basis of fact. It is so much easier and more alluring to speculate as to the how and why of war than to grub for the facts." [MAURICE R. DAVIE, *The Evolution of War*]

Probably no single academic discipline has more facts bearing on the nature and social effects of war than anthropology. Yet it is true that anthropologists have devoted relatively little effort in attempts to make these facts intelligible, a state of affairs somewhat out of proportion to the profound effects this phenomenon has had in the evolution of culture. There have been a number of important exceptions; still, our comparative silence up to this point has resulted in a state of affairs of such incredible dimensions that playwrights, ethologists, generals, and politicians are presently among the leading spokesmen on the causes, nature, and effects of warfare.

This paper, to paraphrase Davie, grubs for the relevant facts of one important kind of primitive warfare. While it specifically deals with the social effects of warfare in one tribe of South American Indians, the Yanomamö of southern Venezuela, this paper purports to have a more general significance. Yanomamö warfare represents a type commonly found in the pristine primitive world, the essential features of which were outlined by Vayda (1960: 1-2). These features include: smallness of scale in military operations, short duration of active hostilities, poor development of command and discipline, great reliance on stealth and surprise attacks, and the great significance of village community or local group in organizing and conducting war parties. In short, Yanomamö warfare is a particular expression of a more general type.

But Yanomamö warfare also represents an important subvariety within this general category: *the conflicts are not initiated or perpetuated with territorial gain as an objective or consequence.* It therefore has an important bearing on theories of aggression based on territoriality, specifically, those developed in the recently published books by Ardrey (1966) and Lorenz (1966). One objective of this paper, then, is to present ethnographic data that contests explanations of warfare based exclusively on genetically determined behavioral patterns.

Another reason non-territorial warfare is significant is that adaptive explanations of it require a broader definition of cultural ecology. The Yanomamö practice swidden agriculture and are expanding geographically and numerically (Chagnon ms.; Neel and Chagnon 1968); they should therefore be easily explained with one of the two models developed by Vayda in a more recent publication (1961). But they do not fit either model because their warfare cannot be shown to be a consequence of competition for land. For the Iban and Maori, the critical feature of the environment within which they operate and to which they

[1] The field research on which this section is based was supported by a USPHS Fellowship F1 MH-25, 052 and attached grant MH 10575-01 BEH RO4, and an AEC Area Grant AT (11-1)-1552. I am also indebted to the Instituto Venezolano de Investigaciones Científicas (IVIC) for its support. I should also like to express my thanks to the following people for criticizing an earlier version of the chapter: Robert L. Carneiro, Gertrude Dole, William Irons, Rodney Needham, David Schneider and Terence Turner. I apologize to them for not having included many of the suggestions they made with respect to some aspects of social structure but hope to incorporate them in a separate treatment of the topic.

must adapt is the shortage of land, warfare being the means by which adaptation is effected through acquisition of either occupied territory or access to trade routes. The Yanomamö, by contrast, are obliged to adapt to a socio-political milieu in which the members of independent villages attempt to steal each other's women. A militant ideology in this situation is adaptive in the sense that each group enhances its position in the alliance networks by convincing others that it will defend its sovereignty with force and constantly threatens to do so.

The position adopted here is that the social relationships between Yanomamö villages are as important as the relationships of societies to land in so far as adaptive explanations of warfare are concerned. The model I propose combines the definition of cultural ecology given by Harding (1960) with the specific theory of cultural evolution in Carneiro's analysis of South American cultures (1961). The model makes use of Harding's argument that in specific historical and environmental circumstances, socio-political systems must adjust to both nature and other, neighboring socio-political systems:

> The character of its habitat will influence a culture's technology, and through technology its social and ideological components. But nearby cultures and the relations effected with them also affect a culture's sociopolitical and ideological subsystems. Moreover, the latter may in turn, in the attempt to cope with the outside world, channel the direction of technological development (1960: 47)

Carneiro's analysis of cultural evolution in South America makes use of the relationship between demography, ecological zones that are circumscribed by geographical barriers, and the relationship between level of cultural development and the practice of intensive, as opposed to extensive, agriculture. Carneiro argues that cultural developments consistently took place in areas that were geographically circumscribed because increases in population density led to a shift from extensive to intensive cultivation as the available land was used up. Political developments, based on conquest, led to confederacies, alliances and, ultimately, political empires. In the Tropical Forest, where extensive, unbroken agricultural land was abundant, local population increases resulted in migration. Consequently, there was no pressure on the carrying capacity of the land and no impetus existed to change extensive cultivation into intensive agriculture.

The facts of ethnology relating to the Tropical Forest cultures support Carneiro's analysis: contests over land were notably absent, although warfare was common and intense; population density appears to have been very low, even at the time of Conquest (Steward 1946–48); and village fission followed by migration was a common phenomenon; finally, the tribes of the Tropical Forest had uniformly underdeveloped political institutions when compared with the Circum-Caribbean or Andean peoples.

The hypothesis I put forward here is that a militant ideology and the warfare it entails function to preserve the sovereignty of independent villages in a milieu of chronic warfare. The origin of such a political milieu seems to be the result of the failure of Yanomamö political institutions to govern effectively the conflicts arising within villages, conflicts that give rise to internal fighting and village fission with the ultimate establishment of mutually hostile, independent villages. Contributing to the generally hostile relationships between villages is the suspicion that unexpected deaths are the result of harmful magic practiced by members of other groups. To maximize their chances for independent political existence in this milieu, members of sovereign villages protect their autonomy by adopting an agonistic stance toward neighboring groups. I submit that such an ideology, with its attendant expressions of violence, is adaptive. That is, I agree with Professor Vayda that wherever it exists, warfare serves a cultural-adaptive purpose in that it results in a more advantageous relationship between people and their cultural ecology. Where I think I disagree is in his implied argument that an *expanding* group of slash-and-burn horticulturists inevitably conducts warfare over territory. The facts of South American ethnology do not lend themselves to this argument. In this connection it is noteworthy that Professor Vayda developed his models in response to statements made by Julian Steward and Robert Murphy concerning the nature of warfare among the Tupinambá and Mundurucú, two South American Tropical Forest tribes whose warfare does not appear to have been stimulated by motives of territorial acquisition (Vayda 1961:346).

Perhaps the tendency to dismiss non-territorial warfare with psychological explanations such as "release from pent-up emotions" or "expressing anger on outsiders to contribute to internal solidarity" have resulted from too few accurate descriptions of aboriginal patterns of warfare, as well as to inadequate theoretical premises. While it is true that a military engagement may have the salubrious effect of releasing the pent-up emotions of the contestants and therefore results in emotional tranquility, one cannot account for the engagement itself by citing psychological variables such as anxiety or in terms of innate aggression. To do so is to confuse effects with functions and reduce cultural phenomena to bio-psychological variables.

If warfare does have the psychological effect of releasing the pent-up emotions of the combatants, how do we account for their frustrations in the first place? Why were the tribes of the Tropical Forest more frustrated and warlike than the shellfish gatherers of Tierra del Fuego? Psychology and ethology offer us no meaningful answers to these questions. At best, they draw attention to certain behavioral facts and phrase them in the special language of their respective disciplines. While it is true that human beings have the capacity for rage and aggression and that a strong case can be made for the ethnographic universality of warfare, it is equally true that cultural systems define and regulate the circumstances under which expressions of aggression are permitted, what form they take, against what or whom they are directed and the legitimate means of such expressions. In some cultures overt expressions of aggression are regarded as detrimental to the social order and are suppressed and contained, while in others, such behavior is applauded and encouraged. The stimuli evoking these responses are culturally determined and extremely varied, defense of territory being only one such stimulus and not a universal one at that.

The Yanomamö exemplify a type of society in which aggressiveness and warfare are admired, but their commitment to this way of life cannot be explained in terms of land shortages. The critical aspect of the cultural ecology is neighboring, hostile villages. It is the adaptation to this, rather than to the availability of land, that gives Yanomamö society its aggressive character. However, there are many variations in the intensity of warfare as one moves from the tribal periphery to the tribal center. Simply stated, warfare is more intense and frequent at the center, resulting in a different kind of cultural adaptation there.

Briefly, villages at the center, because of the relative proximity of neighbors, are not free to migrate into new areas at will. Instead, they must confront each other politically and militarily. Villages at the center are larger, palisaded, nucleated, and enmeshed in alliances with neighbors. Population density is higher and warfare more intense. Distances between villages at the center are much smaller than at the periphery, although they are well spaced. The adaptation here takes the form of extreme militancy and hostility toward neighbors.

Villages at the periphery, on the other hand, are more widely spaced and isolated. Conflicts with neighbors are less frequent and are easily resolved by migration. Inter-village alliances are not so common and the intensity of warfare is greatly reduced, compared to the situation at the center. Villages are much smaller and are not nucleated: sixty people in a village at the tribal center would occupy a single, palisaded dwelling, whereas the same group at the periphery would probably occupy three or four well-spaced, unpalisaded structures. Displays of aggression and violence are greatly reduced in frequency and limited in form,[2] and the entire complex of alliances based on formal, reciprocal trading, and feasting is either greatly diminished in scale or, in some areas, non-existent. One conspicuous way in which this diminished emphasis on feasting and alliance is evidenced is in the size of both the gardens and the village structure itself. As we shall see, feasting and alliance call forth a considerable amount of agricultural over-production, and village structure reflects the importance of the feast in the life of the people. A structure that sixty people would build in an area where feasting is an important component in alliance would be significantly larger than that required where feasting is not important in maintaining inter-village ties. In other words, villages at the tribal center are larger *physically* than those at the periphery, the difference in size reflecting the importance of regularized visiting, feasting, and dancing.

The description that follows is based on field work conducted among the Yanomamö at both the center of the tribal territory and at the periphery. It specifically refers, however, to the nature of the warfare pattern and social organization at the tribal center.[3]

[2] Club fights, for example, do not occur in this area of the tribe.

[3] Thirteen of my sixteen months with the Yanomamö were spent in villages at the tribal center and three months in villages at the periphery. The field work was initiated in November 1964, and is presently continuing in conjunction with a medical-anthropological project sponsored by the Department of Human Genetics at the University of Michigan and Instituto Venezolano de Investigaciones Científicas in Caracas. A considerable amount of additional field work is scheduled in conjunction with this project.

The Yanomamö Population[4]

There are about 10,000 Yanomamö occupying the area shown in Map A.[5] This zone comprises roughly 110,000 square kilometers, giving an overall population density of ten people per 100 square kilometers,[6] putting them at the lower end of the range of densities characteristic of Tropical Forest tribes (Steward 1949: 675 gives the population densities for the various culture types in South America).

The population is distributed in about a hundred widely scattered villages of sizes ranging from 40 to 250 inhabitants at the center, those at the periphery being smaller. The median population size at the center is of the order of 70 to 85 inhabitants.

At the present time about a dozen villages are in direct contact with missionaries on the Orinoco, Mucajai, Uraricoera, Demeni, Cauaburi, and Marauia rivers. The first sustained contact with the Yanomamö began in 1950 when James P. Barker of the New Tribes Mission ascended the Orinoco and took up residence in the village of Mahe-kodo-teri. In 1954, a Silesian priest, Antonion Goiaz, contacted a Yanomamö village in Brazil on the Cauaburi River and initiated sustained contact on that side of the border. The remainder of the contacts, many of them by the Unevangelized Fields Mission, were made more recently, most of them in 1957–58. The greater number of Yanomamö villages have not had direct contact with outsiders even yet, although a few steel tools and aluminum cooking pots have probably reached even the most remote village by now.

The Yanomamö are divided into five major dialect areas, the two largest of which are the

[4] The Yanomamö are also described in the literature as Waika, Sanema, Xiriana, and Guaharibo.

[5] The center of the tribe is the area circled in Map A.

[6] Converted to miles, this gives an area of 35,000 square miles and 28 people per 100 square miles.

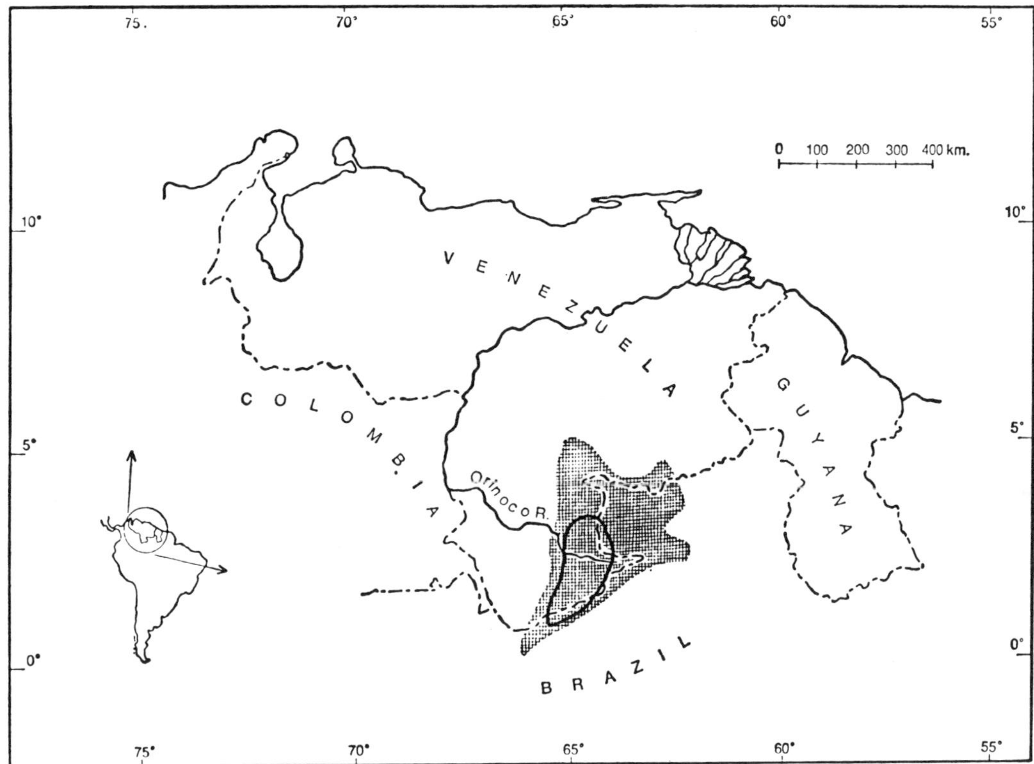

Map A. Location of Yanomamö in South America.

Central and Western, comprising roughly 75 percent of the population. With the exception of a few individuals who have learned Carib (Makiritare), the Yanomamö are monolingual. The presence of missionaries, however, will no doubt change this situation in the immediate future.

Economic Geography, Technology, and Settlement Pattern

The terrain in Yanomamö country is relatively low, humid, covered with jungle, crisscrossed by rivers and streams and subject to inundations during the peak of the wet season (June–July). Most of the land lies at an elevation of 500–700′, although it varies from 450′ to 3000′. Yanomamö villages are usually found at the lower elevations, although in the Parima "mountains" a few are found as high as 2500′.

The major rivers may vary as much as 15 feet from season to season, and inundate the low-lying jungle along their courses in full flood. During the wet season inter-village travel is difficult, if not impossible, since the Yanomamö travel only by foot.[7] Under normal circumstances, the Yanomamö occupy themselves with gardening at this time of the year, but the military situation may alter their seasonal cycle.

The rivers begin falling in September and inter-village travel again increases. By February the rivers have reached their lowest levels;

[7] They do, however, make bark canoes when they must cross a large river. The canoes are usually abandoned after one use.

inter-village visiting, trading and feasting are at their peaks at this time, as is raiding. Swamps that were impassable during the months of May, June, and July are usually no more than soggy potholes and pose no hindrance to travel. Anxiety increases in the dry season, for everyone must be on the alert for raiders.

The Yanomamö take advantage of geographical barriers such as swamps, rivers, and rugged hills when they establish new villages. A new site is established so that enemy villages will be separated by these barriers; once the military considerations of the site have been weighed, the specific location is then fixed by soil factors, amount of jungle cover, drainage of the terrain, and availability of a constant supply of drinking water.

The Yanomamö attempt to establish their villages at least a day's walk from any neighbor. Inter-village friendships are so tenuous under even the best of circumstances that an individual never trusts his neighbors and allies. Most villages are therefore at a considerable distance from their closest neighbors, but in some circumstances villages will be found just a few hours apart. In many of these cases the size of the village has more to do with the proximity of location than lack of suitable terrain: small, militarily vulnerable villages tend to be located close to their stanchest ally, to which they turn for refuge in case of war.

Mutually hostile villages are separated by at least two or three days' march: if they are separated by a distance of less than two days and intensify their hostilities, one of the two will move to a new, more distant location, abandoning its old garden.

Nearly every major village move [8] is the result of intensified hostilities; raiding becomes so intense and exacts such a heavy toll that the members of a beleaguered village are forced to abandon their gardens and establish a new one elsewhere. A study of two clusters of villages, Namowei-Tedi and Paruritawa-Tedi, showed that all but two of the numerous moves between 1875 and 1966 had been stimulated by warfare.[9] Clearly village mobility is marked, a reflection of the intensity of warfare in this area. A brief account of the historical factors relating to the moves will also be given to show the relationship between settlement pattern and warfare. Some of the villages moved subsequent to the study, an indication of the continuing nature of warfare.

Despite the frequency of village movements brought about by warfare, the Yanomamö have a relatively stable, sedentary village life characteristic of most slash-and-burn cultivators. Were it not for their wars, the Yanomamö could remain almost indefinitely in the same general area. By way of illustration, the Patanowä-teri has occupied its site more or less continuously for over forty years.[10] But regardless of the frequency of village movement, the Yanomamö must have access to cultivated foods in order to maintain coresidential groups of 40–250 people: the jungle is simply not sufficiently productive to support groups of that size for more than brief periods. Their dependence on cultivated foods therefore makes their whereabouts predictable by enemies. A group that is forced from its garden by intensive raids cannot remain away from it for very long without returning for fresh supplies of food unless, of course, it takes refuge in the village of an ally and subsists on the latter's produce. Thus raiders, knowing the current political relationships

[8] By major move I mean abandoning a given area and migrating to a new area. This is distinct from the minor garden movements associated with swidden agriculture.

[9] The two moves not stimulated by warfare resulted, in one case, from undesirable soil conditions, and in the other the arrival of foreigners: the group in question moved closer to the foreigners (a government malaria control team) in order to gain access to a source of steel tools.

[10] Although warfare has forced the Patanowä-teri to temporarily abandon its garden on a number of occasions, it continues to return when the intensity of raiding diminishes.

between all the villages, can usually find their enemies: if they are not in their village, they have either taken refuge with a friendly group or are hiding in a temporary camp nearby. An examination of the trails around the garden will usually decide the issue: if they are still in use, the group is hiding out in a temporary camp and returns for food as it is needed; if the trails show no indication of recent use, then the group has taken refuge with an ally.

The Yanomamö attempt to avoid situations that oblige them to take refuge with a neighbor, for such aid is never tendered without gain in mind. The protecting hosts inevitably demand access to their visitors' women, by either temporary rights or permanent acquisition by marriage. A group expecting a period of intensive raiding will therefore begin clearing a new garden in a more remote area. One group with which I lived initiated a war with a larger village in 1965; in anticipation of this war, they began clearing a new garden across a large river and broad swamp from their old one, putting two additional geographical obstacles in the path of their enemies. However, they miscalculated the rate at which the raiding would intensify and the fury of their opponents at having lost a kinsman; they were forced to abandon their garden before the new one began producing and had no alternative but to seek refuge in the villages of their allies. For the better part of a year they moved from one ally to another, leaving each one when demands for women became outrageous. They would carry food from their allies' gardens and camp at their new location to work in the garden, moving to another ally's village when they ran out of food. Fortunately, they had several allies, but they nevertheless had to give away several young women whom they might not otherwise have relinquished. When the wet season came and travel became difficult, they could return at last to their producing garden and transplant cuttings to the new location. If the water level dropped conspicuously, they repaired to their new garden with provisions from the old one and waited for new rains to raise the river. They spent most of 1965 moving from one ally to another, then to their producing garden, and back to their unproductive new site to work. All during this time they remained intact as a group and continued to subsist on cultivated foods, most of which were provided by allies. Their new garden began producing at the end of this year, but since most of the crops were planted simultaneously, they matured more or less at the same time, resulting in windfalls that were interrupted by periods of little. They still had to rely on allies for food, but to a much lesser extent. They had achieved self-sufficiency in 1967 when I returned to continue my field work; by that time they had planted cuttings in such a way that the garden produced a continuous supply of food.

Trading, Feasting, and Alliances

The example just given shows one of the major implications of alliance: allied villages are expected to give refuge to each other in times of need, extending the resources of gardens to the members of a beleaguered group. A second obligation in inter-village alliance is the offer of military aid during periods of active raiding. While this cannot prevent one village from raiding another, it appears to reduce the possibility of raiding: if village A plans to raid village B, its ultimate decision may be based on the relationships B has with groups C, D, E, etc. In the case of revenge, such considerations are negligible: A will raid B regardless of B's alliances. But should group A consider initiating war with group B for any other reason, B's political commitments become of great significance to A.

The members of every village, therefore, attempt to cultivate friendly ties with neighbors, but mutual suspicion is so intense and village sovereignty so crucial that the alliances are never established with the obligations spelled out by the principals involved. For example, the village in which I began my field work in 1964 had friendly ties with several neighboring villages. All the men left on a raid and were gone nearly two weeks; their women appeared every day at my hut and refused to leave it until nightfall. They incessantly asked me to show them my shotgun, a demand that began to annoy me after a number of repetitions. I finally discovered that they stayed in or around my hut because, in effect, I was protecting them from raiders! I also discovered that the few remaining men stood guard all night long, watching the trails most likely to be taken by raiders from the allied villages! As a matter of fact, a raiding party from one of these villages did set out with the apparent intention of abducting some of the poorly defended women, but the men returned before this group of raiders arrived.[11]

Hence allies confront each other somewhat boastfully and attempt to demonstrate that they do not require assistance and probably never will, for the obverse implication is that they are weak and can be exploited by a stronger group. Were it not for the fact, recognized by all Yanomamö but rarely discussed, that no village can exist indefinitely without friendly allies, the Yanomamö would probably have very little inter-village contact. This paradoxical set of attitudes—allies need each other but refuse to acknowledge it overtly—has given rise to a peculiar relationship between economic specialization, trade, and alliance.

Each group seems to create shortages of particular items, such as bows, clay pots, arrows, baskets, arrow points, hammocks, cotton, dogs, drugs, arrow point cases, and other manufactured articles, and relies on one or more of its allies for these goods. In turn, the group provides its allies with the goods the latter request. These shortages cannot be explained in terms of the distribution of resources or a specialization in production due to esoteric knowledge. Rather, a sociological explanation is required. For example, village A may be a hammock-taker from village B but a hammock-giver to village C. A more dramatic example is the production of clay pots. In one case village A gave pots to village B but obtained them from village C. The middlemen claimed to be ignorant of the art of pottery, reinforcing their story with the assertion that the clay in their area was not the proper kind for pot-making. They acknowledged, however, that they used to know how to make pots, but had long since forgotten. When they entered unexpectedly into a war with the group that provided them with pots, they promptly "remembered" how pots were made and "discovered" that the clay in their area was indeed suitable. They therefore managed to provide their partners with an uninterrupted supply of pots.

Inter-village friendship and solidarity depends to a large extent on the frequency of visiting that takes place, and the trading techniques themselves, in addition to the specialized production, stimulate visiting. An individual will give a particular item, a dog, for example, to a friend in an allied village saying: "I give you this dog *no mraiha*." Superficially, the *no mraiha* looks like a "free" gift, since the recipient does not give anything in return at that time. But *no mraiha* "gifts" are not free presentations: each object given must be repaid at a later time with a different kind of article, i.e., it is reciprocating trade of the kind described by Mauss in *The Gift* (1954). Thus, each trade calls forth another, a type of deficit spending that insures peaceful, frequent inter-village visiting. (See Chagnon, 1968b, for further discussion of trading practices.)

Trade reduces the possibility that one group will attack the other without serious, overt provocation. In effect, it reduces the chance that one group will attribute otherwise unaccountable deaths to the harmful magic of a trading partner. But trade does not eliminate the possibility of limited fighting or diminish suspicion: members of villages that stand in

---

[11] I describe this particular event in some detail in Chapter 4 of *Yanomamö: The Fierce People* (1968a).

trading relationship with each other occasionally have duels with either fists or clubs, and suspect the other group of plotting to abduct women.

Trade is important in another way; it is the first step in a possibly more intimate social relationship: inter-village feasting. While trading itself constitutes a kind of inter-village alliance, it is an unstable, tenuous alliance and easily broken. When reciprocal feasting eventually results from a long period of trading relations, trade still functions to keep the two groups bound to each other and provides, in many cases, the stimulus to feast. That is, village A may owe village B a number of woven hammocks; when these are manufactured, group A will inform group B that its hammocks are completed and a feast will be arranged to provide the social matrix within which the exchange takes place.

A feasting alliance carries with it more obligations and therefore implies a greater degree of solidarity. Enormous quantities of food must be harvested and prepared; dances and chants are invented, practiced, and recited; and the trade goods promised to the visitors must be finished. The work for a feast is considerable, promotes a good deal of cooperation within the host group itself, and generates a high level of enthusiasm and excitement that is carried over to the feast.

The visitors at a feast are presented with large quantities of food, are given a chance to display their decorations, dances, and songs, chat intimately with men from the host group, and exchange trade goods. Particularly close allies will occasionally participate in a joint endo-cannibalistic rite and consume the charred, pulverized bones of a recently deceased friend or kinsman, an act that is the supreme form of intimacy to the Yanomamö.

The obligations implied in feasting alliances involve the offering of refuge in times of need, as, for example, when one of the groups is driven from its garden by a powerful enemy. This form of alliance also carries with it an informal but weak obligation to aid the partner in his raids against an enemy.

Finally, autonomous villages may ultimately exchange women with each other and add yet another bond to their friendship. Once this phase has been reached, the two groups have achieved the greatest possible degree of solidarity. But, and this must be emphasized, even alliances based on reciprocity of women are fickle, tenuous, and easily broken. Still, compared to the two less stable forms of alliance, trading and feasting, marital exchange obligations are relatively firm and carry more binding mutual commitments.

The reasons that the marriage alliances fall apart have to do with the reluctance that each group displays in ceding women to others and the aggressiveness with which the demands for women are made. Should one of the principals in the alliance be stronger than the other, he will press his demands for women from a position of strength and hope to derive an advantage in the women exchanges that follow. Over a long term the exchanges are usually balanced, but a stronger group, especially in the initial stages of exchange, will have an advantage. One commonly employed method used to secure an early advantage is to demand nubile women and promise immature, juvenile ones in return, or even an unborn female. Another way of taking advantage of a weaker group is to press the men from that group into prolonged bride service, say three or four years, and demand exceptionally short periods of bride service for their young men, less than a year. In rare cases they may even have the bride service waived, especially in the case of headmen.

A group that is pressured by enemies will find this situation distasteful, but preferable to migrating to a new area, establishing a new garden and taking a chance on confronting neighbors that are even more exorbitant in their demands. But since the political situation is always changing, villages having a temporary advantage at one point in time will find the tables reversed at a latter point. In the long run, marriage exchanges tend to balance out.

One economic consequence resulting from the obligation to entertain allies in feasts is that gardens tend to be significantly larger at the tribal center than at the periphery. Thus, if sixty people in a village at the periphery require a garden of size X, the same sixty people at the tribal center, because of the relatively greater feasting activity brought about by alliance commitments, will require a garden of size X plus b, the additional production having been stimulated by the requirements of feasts. The surplus "b" it should be said, appears to originate because of the feast, but it is the primary reason villages are in an economic position to offer refuge to the entire group of an allied village at almost any point in time. The surplus is there, but if the village takes in refugees, it must curtail its feasting schedule.

One further effect of the enlarged gardens is that they necessitate a greater commitment to alliances rather than migration as a means for coping with chronic warfare. Since any garden entails a considerable amount of labor in clearing and planting the site, a powerful incentive is provided to attempt to cope with neighbors rather than flee and begin a new garden elsewhere. Thus it appears that by adapting to the cultural ecology by means of alliance and feasting, a stronger commitment to that adaptation leads to greater specialization. At the very least, it reduces the probability that the alternative, migration, will occur. Nevertheless, the entire adaptation is such that migration is always a last resort, thereby making a militant stance toward outsiders more possible.

The Waiteri Complex

The motif of Yanomamö ideology is contained in their notion of *waiteri* (ferocity). Members of autonomous villages gain certain advantages by presenting an agonistic stance to their neighbors in the interest of preserving their sovereignty. The primary advantage lies in the more exclusive control a village thereby maintains over its own women in a milieu where acquisition of females is a major preoccupation.

The advantages derived by adopting an agonistic stance can best be seen in the context of political behavior. Given that acquisition of females is a major goal in inter-village politics and that differences in military potential are translated into advantage in the woman-exchange practices, a good reaction for a political group is to display and imply its military potential, i.e., its ferocity: *waiteri*. In this way a village can maintain its sovereignty to a much greater extent. The closest approximation to absolute sovereignty would be when a group (a) disposed of 100 percent of its females in marriages within the village, (b) never had to take refuge in the village of an ally, and (c) never had to rely on support from allies in its raids on enemies. No village is ever completely sovereign in these respects, nor can it afford to be: remaining aloof from allies or potential allies in peaceful times is a hazardous course, for political relationships change.

Lack of sovereignty, on the other hand, reaches the extreme when a faction of a large village leaves the group and must take refuge with a friendly group. This occasionally takes place when a violent fight erupts within a village and results in the killing of one or more people, usually in a club fight. Tempers will be so hot that one of the factions must leave, usually the smaller one, before more killing takes place. If the faction is smaller than forty people, it cannot exist as a vulnerable village and must seek refuge with a larger group (a point which will be further discussed below). One of the consequences for the small faction is that it will inevitably lose women to the protectors and cease to exist as a residential, autonomous entity.

A less extreme form of dependency is found when a larger village fissions to produce two semi-viable populations of about forty people each. They may elect to fission before in-fighting becomes so intense that bloodshed cannot be avoided; by fissioning and locating their respective villages close to each other, they therefore reduce the probability of further internal fighting while at the same time are on friendly enough terms to reunite if raids threaten either's security. As their populations grow, they become increasingly independent and may eventually separate completely and lead independent political lives.

Generally, however, differences in military potential are not so obvious. When groups of roughly the same size become allies, each attempts to convince the other that it is superior and expects to gain the upper hand in the exchange of women. A difference in size, and therefore in capacity for sovereignty, results in a more conspicuous attempt on the part of the smaller group to display ferocity. In practical terms, a field worker notices that the members of smaller villages are much more aggressive, pushy, intimidating, and unpleasant to work with.[12] By behaving in this way they imply to their ambitious, larger neighbors that any attempt to coerce them will result in immediate violence. To the extent that a very small village can inflict numerous casualties on a very large village should war between them erupt, the behavior of the smaller group is adaptive in so far as it sets limits on the demands a larger group will make on it.

An ideological syndrome of this order deserves to have a name; I suggest that *waiteri complex* is suitable in that it is descriptive and emphasizes the most important single element: ferocity. Other notions and beliefs held by the Yanomamö complement and reinforce their attitudes on political behavior, and I will describe and enumerate a few of them at this point. In as much as I have asserted that their ideology is the basis of their adaptation to a milieu of chronic warfare, this complex is necessary.

The *waiteri complex* is not universal in the Yanomamö tribe, although aspects of it occur everywhere in various degrees of intensity. It exists in its most extreme, purest form within the area of the tribe where warfare is most intense, i.e., that area bounded by the circle shown on Map A (p. 339). And even within this area some variations and nuances occur.

The Yanomamö recognize that some groups are more aggressive and fierce than others. Their explanation for this variation is mythological, but fits the facts of the ethnographic distribution very accurately. According to the myth, the first creatures on earth were the *no badabö* (literally, "those who are no longer with us, our dead ancestors), part spirit and part Yanomamö. The origin of the *no badabö* is unaccounted for, but most of them functioned in the creation of specific plants, animals, and other useful things presently possessed by the Yanomamö. One of the first beings was Peribo (Periboriwä in some dialects), Moon. He habitually descended to earth and ate the soul portions (*noreshi*) of children between pieces of cassava bread.[13] Two of the first beings took offense at this despicable action and decided to shoot Peribo with their arrows. The first was a poor shot and missed, although he made many attempts as Peribo ascended to his zenith. The second, his brother, was a good shot and hit Peribo in the abdomen on the first shot. The blood that flowed from the wound fell to earth in the vicinity of Maiyo Käkö, a mountain near the headwaters of the Orinoco River, approximately at the center of the tribe. The blood changed into Yanomamö, all of whom were males. The people born in blood had one distinctive feature: they were all exceedingly

[12] A number of missionaries working with the Yanomamö have also noticed this and, like me, were a little uneasy and reluctant to spend much time with these groups. In a number of villages in Brazil, on the other hand, the Yanomamö were very pleasant and charming and do not show many of the attributes found where the warfare pattern is more intense.

[13] The fact that cassava bread is mentioned in the myth suggests that the Yanomamö may have relied more heavily on this cultivated food in the past. Now, however, plantains are the major staple in most areas, a post-Columbian introduction.

fierce and waged constant war on each other. Warfare was most intense in the area where Peribo's blood fell directly on earth; as it thinned out and mixed with water, it created Yanomamö at the periphery who were not so fierce as those generated from pure blood. The groups around the periphery did not fight as much as those at the center. Thus, the myth explains why it is the nature of man (Yanomamö) to wage war and why some groups are more warlike than others.[14]

The hostility that obtains between men is also reflected in the nature of man's relationship to the spirit world. The cosmos is thought to be comprised of four parallel layers as shown in Figure 1. According to one myth, a piece of layer 2, *hedu kä misi,* fell through layer 3, *hei kä misi* (i.e., earth), carrying a village of Yanomamö with it to *hei tä bebi,* the bottommost layer. The people of this village, the Amahiri-teri, ascend to the earth layer as spirits, or send their evil demons in their stead, to eat the souls of children, the loss of soul ultimately leading to death. The reason they do so is that their neighborhood (*urihi*) was not carried down to the bottom layer and they therefore have no game and must satisfy their hunger for meat (*naiki*) by eating the souls of children. To combat the *Amahiri-teri* spirits, men on earth send their own spirits (*hekura*) to fight and ward off the evils threatening them. This same spiritual contention, moreover, is constantly waged by village shamans, who combat the evil *hekura* sent against them by other Yanomamö on this layer of the cosmos. Thus, every day in every village the shamans gather, take hallucinogenic drugs, become intoxicated, contact their *hekura* and wage spiritual war with the spirits sent by their human enemies. Some shamans also assert that they actually leave their bodies while under the influence of the drug and travel to enemy villages to kill people by eating their souls.

Shamans also practice other forms of malevolent magic and cause deaths in enemy villages. One common practice in some areas is to blow charms through hollow tubes at the enemy and thereby cause sickness and death. In this connection, many groups cultivate numerous species of magical plants that are employed to this end, but the use of these involves physical contact with the individual against whom the evil intent is directed. A common tactic is to touch someone with the leaves of a special kind of plant. The net effect of these practices and notions is that unexplained deaths and sickness are usually attributed to the practice of harmful magic by shamans in other villages, a phenomenon that can and does lead to war. As we shall see below, the military history of one cluster of villages has been the result of an accusation of magic that led to the death of a number of people.

Hunting is also invested with magic and associated with notions of inflicting harm on enemy groups. The Yanomamö believe that each individual has an animal counterpart, an alter-ego, whose life is coexistent and coterminous with that person. When one dies, so does the other. The person and his *nọreshi* are always in complementary distribution, so that the two never meet; should they see each other, both would die instantly. When a hunter kills certain kinds of animals, he in effect causes the death of the human being, an enemy, to whom that animal corresponds.

Ethnocentrism at both the tribal and village level contribute to the *waiteri complex.* The Yanomamö believe that they were the first, finest, and most refined form of man to inhabit the earth. All other peoples are inferior because they developed later by a process of degeneration from a pure Yanomamö stock, explaining

[14] This myth is from informants who lived in the center of the tribal area and I have not found it elsewhere. A complementary myth explains the origin of women and cowards (Chagnon, 1968a) from the pregnant legs of a mythological figure. The current population resulted from miscegenation of the groups created in these two origins. My informants asserted that most of the men of pure blood origin died in the intensive fighting that developed after the blood of Moon spilled to earth.

their strange customs and peculiar languages. Yanomamö, in fact, means "humanity," or at least the most important segment of humanity. All other peoples are known by the term *nabä*,[15] a concept that implies an invidious distinction between "true" man and "sub-human" man. This distinction is reinforced linguistically in some dialects by the use of honorific pronouns.[16] Common pronouns are good enough for foreigners. The term *nabä*, moreover, seems to be related to the notion of enemy: the word for enemy is *wano nabä*, and the verb for becoming an enemy is *nowä nabä*.

The Yanomamö have a low opinion of *nabäs* and discriminate against them. A foreigner is usually tolerated if he is able to provide the Yanomamö with useful items such as steel tools, but apart from this he is usually held in some contempt. I have been invited to leave some villages, as have missionaries, because I did not bring enough presents to go around, and since that was the only possible use I could serve, I was therefore unwelcome and urged not to return until I had more gifts.

Where the Yanomamö have bordered the territory of other peoples they have fought with them and consistently pushed them out. They are presently forcing the Carib-speaking Makiritare Indians farther north and have virtually exterminated the Makú Indians.[17] Farther south, some groups of Yanomamö have expanded into areas occupied by Brazilians, who quickly withdrew and abandoned the area in fear of Yanomamö raids (Biocca 1965; Seitz 1963; Zerries 1964).

Most Yanomamö warfare, however, is confined to the tribe itself. Even here ethnocentrism is conspicuous; any difference between adjacent groups is exaggerated and ridiculed. Language differences in particular are promptly noted and criticized by the Yanomamö, and taken as evidence of degeneration. The characteristic reaction of any group to a tape recording made in another area was this: "They speak crooked; we speak straight, the right way!" And the differences need not be great to evoke this response. One young man had married into the group I lived with, and spoke almost the identical dialect, but with a few differences in pronunciation. He confidentially told me that I ought to be more careful about my language—I was picking up poor pronunciation habits and ought to go live in his village to learn the proper way to speak Yanomamö.

Although ethnocentrism cannot be cited as a primary reason for the intensity of hostilities, it nevertheless adds to or justifies them and therefore is a component in the *waiteri complex*.[18]

The socialization process selects for and encourages ferocity. Masculinity and aggressiveness are instilled in small children from an early age. It is common to see parents tease a small boy to strike at his tormentors, rewarding his anger with approving laughter. Girls, on the other hand, are taught to acquiesce timidly to the punishment they receive from their brothers, so that by the time children are six or seven years old, the boys have already learned that it is appropriate to bully the girls and spend a great deal of time at mischievous pranks calculated to intimidate them.

Boys are pampered and indulged to a much greater extent than girls and are given more freedom to play. By the time a girl is ten years

[15] In some areas of Brazil a third term, *Kreiwä*, is used to distinguish nationals from the Carib-speaking Makiritare.

[16] These pronouns are reserved for important spirits, in reference to headmen and for Yanomamö.

[17] Migliazza 1965. I am also indebted to Sue Albright of the Unevangelized Fields Mission for a detailed communication regarding the life history of the last Makú woman in the Yanomamö area and a description of the warfare between these two tribes. Albright and I interviewed this woman in 1967 and obtained only a sketchy account of the intertribal hostilities.

[18] Some sentiment between groups of common origin does appear to exist despite the fact that they may be at war with each other. It is not likely that treacherous feasts would be held for a group having a common origin, although in one case this did take place.

old, she spends much of her time babysitting, hauling water and firewood, and helping her mother cook. Boys of the same age have no domestic responsibilities whatever, and spend their time playing at club-fights, archery, or whatever they want. Girls are usually given in marriage as soon as they go through their puberty rites, and assume the onerous tasks of keeping their own house shortly thereafter. Boys are permitted to extend their childhood into their late teens, but are encouraged to be fierce fighters. They have numerous opportunities to participate in fights, as there are always a few chest-pounding or club-fighting duels every year. They are pressed into the fighting by their adult superiors, but are given privileged positions in raiding parties until they acquire the necessary skills and experience. The youngest raider I saw was only twelve years old, but he was an exception, as he was recruited into a raiding party because the man being avenged was his father. Usually a boy does not take an active role in raiding until he is seventeen years old, and even then he may be so frightened that he will fake illness and return home before the enemy village has been reached.

Yanomamö boys, like all boys, fear pain and personal danger. They must be forced to tolerate it and learn to accept ferocity as a way of life. During one feast the adult men of two allied villages agreed to satisfy their grievances in a chest-pounding duel. They also took this opportunity to educate their small sons in the art of fighting and forced all the young boys from eight to fifteen years old to duck-waddle around the village periphery and fight each other. The boys were reluctant and tried to run away, afraid they would be hurt. Their parents dragged them back by force and insisted that they hit each other. The first few blows brought tears to their eyes, but as the fight progressed, fears turned to anger and rage, and they ended up enthusiastically pounding each other as hard as they could, bawling, screaming, and rolling in the dirt while their fathers cheered them on and admired their ferocity.

Young men are competitive and attempt to show their capacity for rage, usually by temper tantrums that are ostentatious and faked. A commonly used excuse for outbursts of anger is the mention of their name in public, for when people no longer use a young man's name, it is assumed that he commands respect and is to be feared. As they grow older and acquire wives, they vent their anger on the hapless women by beating them, burning them with glowing firebrands, or even shooting them in the buttocks with a barbed arrow. One of the implications of this behavior is that the men will be equally fierce with male opponents, and so they acquire a reputation for ferocity without much potential harm to their own persons. The amount of punishment a man can mete out to his wife depends on the seriousness of the provocation and on the number of brothers the wife has in the village who will protect her from a brutal husband. Men constantly attempt to seduce the wives of their village mates and take extreme offense when their own wives, in turn, are seduced. Agnatically related males in particular are competitors in this regard, since they all are constrained by incest prohibitions to focus their amorous intentions on the same category of women. Thus a considerable amount of fighting takes place between them. One young man was given a wife who had been captured in a raid. His older brother, the headman of the village, began having an affair with the woman. The older brother was a particularly aggressive and fierce man, and his brother feared him. He therefore satisfied his rage by shooting and killing his wife, an action that was considered appropriate under the circumstances.

But the social effects of this agnatic competition are as significant as the hostility existing between men related in this fashion. Such men display their personal autonomy by refusing to comply with suggestions and requests made by their agnates, for complicity implies that the command is given from a superior to an inferior. This decreases cooperation among agnates and increases the solidarity between affines, a phenomenon dramatically illustrated in the structure of village fissioning, to which we will turn shortly.

Another example of the degree to which warfare and aggression are influential in the socialization process is the practice of memorizing "death speeches." Young men invent and commit to memory the words they will say in the event that they are mortally wounded. The speeches extol the courage of the warrior and heap contempt on his assassins. Some young men even practice the noises they will make when they are struck with arrows, a different groan being associated with wounds to different parts of the body! They seem to fear that they will say or do something unbecoming when they are wounded. Several young men described to me in contemptuous terms how one of their enemies wept and cried out for his mother when they mortally wounded him. This was considered bad form.

Expressions of ferocity can take various forms. There is a graded series of contests ranging from innocuous chest-pounding duels to treacherous feasts in which the male guests are murdered and their women abducted. From an analytic standpoint, both individuals and groups seem to attempt to establish a threshold at which their bluffs and challenges dissolve into action. Inter-personal and inter-group behavior reflects the attempt each potential opponent makes to discover precisely where this threshold lies, and to adjust behavior accordingly. Ostentation and bluff are largely attempts to convince others that the flashpoint is easily reached, although men who have deserved reputations for ferocity are less compelled to behave in this fashion. Sooner or later individuals and groups must make their boasts credible and take action, the particular form of violence being determined largely by the seriousness of the grievance. Apart from wife-beating, the most common form of violence, contests can be in the form of chest-pounding duels, club fights, spear fights, raids, or treacherous feasts, the last not being a contest (Chagnon 1967). The form that a fight takes can be escalated to the next, more serious, level: the causes of a fight are soon forgotten once it starts, and it is perpetuated largely by reasons of its own being.

Chest-pounding duels are always conducted between members of different villages and arise over accusations of cowardice or in response to excessive demands for trade goods, food, or women. The implications of the demands are that if they result in the desired articles and goods, the giver is thought to be lower in status as a political group than the receiver, i.e., one group has coerced the other.

Duels of this kind are frequently associated with feasts and are prearranged. Village A entertains village B and makes ostentatious displays and presentations of food in a general spirit of solidarity and friendship. The day after the feast, both groups go to the center of the village, take hallucinogenic drugs to put themselves in a fighting mood, and begin to fight. One man represents each village. The first to enter the fight stands with his legs spread, head in the air and arms held back to expose his chest. This challenges someone from the opposite group, who enters the ring, seizes his immobile opponent, adjusts his stance so as to give himself maximum advantage, and then delivers a tremendous, close-fisted blow to the man's chest. The blow occasionally knocks the man down, but more frequently, he merely shakes his head to recover his senses, and sticks his chest out again for another wallop. Fierce fighters will take as many as four blows before demanding to hit the opponent. The recipient of the blows then has a chance to hit the first man as many times as he was hit, unless he knocks him unconscious before delivering all the blows. One can only retire from the fight after receiving blows or because of injury. As the fight develops, tempers grow hot and everyone is in a state of frenzy. The fight ends if one of the contestants is seriously injured, although it may continue as a side-slapping duel after everybody's chests are too sore to take more punishment.

The same rules and stance are employed in the side-slapping duel except that the blow is delivered with an open hand across the flank just above the pelvic bone. Side-slapping never lasts very long, as it is quite easy to knock someone's wind out, which either ends the fight or escalates it to a club fight. Some chest-pounding duels last three hours.

The losers always insist on escalating the fight to a more violent level, while the winners are content to stop. This usually ends in a stalemate, the winners being smugly aware of their victory and the losers proud of the fact that they were so fierce that the opponents were afraid to fight them in a more manly contest.

If the duel was prearranged in conjunction with a feast, the fighters chant to each other after the duel ends. One man will sit on the ground with his legs spread out and his opponent will sit facing him, spreading his own legs over the man's thighs. They hug each other intimately around the neck and chant melodically to each other, face to face, vowing to remain life-long friends and to give trade goods and women to each other.

Club fights are more serious, and can take place within as well as between villages. These usually result from adultery or suspicion of adultery, although food theft can precipitate a club fight under some circumstances.

The offended party walks to the village clearing with a sharpened 10-foot long club and challenges his opponent by hurling insults at him. Although clubs are not intended to be used as thrusting instruments, some men sharpen them to indicate that they will escalate the club fight to a mortal contest if need be, thereby hoping to intimidate the opponent into admitting his cowardice by refusing to fight.

If the challenge is accepted, the opponent comes forward with his own club, usually a pole ripped from the house frame. The first man jams his club into the ground in a near vertical position and leans on it with his head prominently exposed. In many cases the two men just dance up and down in a frenzy, waving their clubs menacingly at each other. If the fight does take place, the opponent will strike the first man on the head with a tremendous blow. He must then expose his own head in the same fashion and let the first man hit him. Club fights rarely remain confined to the two principal fighters, for at the first sight of blood, all the able-bodied men pick sides and enter the fight with their own clubs. Thus, club fights usually end in a free-for-all, each group clubbing the other wildly, hitting whoever can be reached on whatever spot available. They are so disruptive that the village headman arms himself with his bow and arrows and threatens to shoot anybody who appears to be deliberately trying to kill his opponent or who attempts to escalate the fight to bows and arrows. In one club fight in 1966, one of the two principal contestants stabbed his opponent with the sharpened end of the club and wounded him seriously. The headman then took a sharpened club and ran the assailant completely through, killing him. The wounded man then took his deviant wife home, cut her ears off with a machete, and discarded her. The faction of the man who was killed fled to villages of their *enemies*, vowing to get revenge.[19]

Club fights are potentially mortal contests. Should someone die in the fight, a war will follow. If the death takes place in an internal village dispute, one of the groups in the fight will flee to a different village for refuge. If the

---

[19] Small factions, even from enemy groups, are allowed to join the village when it is likely they will aid in the war against that village's enemies.

death occurs in an inter-village fight, war will follow after the two groups separate.

Spear fights are very rare. Only one took place during my field work, and informants rarely mention them when discussing past hostilities. This spear fight was precipitated when the headman of a large village took his sister away from her husband in a neighboring, small village. The husband had been too brutal in his treatment of the woman. The incident resulted in an immediate club fight between the two groups, but the smaller one was thoroughly beaten. It then announced that it was going to recruit help from its allies and would return with spears. The grievance was important enough to demand a contest more serious than a club fight, but not of sufficient moment to call for an outright war. The woman over whom the fight started ran away from her brother and rejoined her husband, but the die had been cast and it was now a matter of honor and sovereignty that the fight should take place. Within a week the smaller group, its ranks swelled with men from allied villages, attacked the larger one and drove it from the village in a hail of spears. Several people were seriously wounded, and one later died of his wounds. The large group reformed and chased its assailants until it caught them, several miles from the village. Another brief skirmish with spears took place, but the two groups retired after nearly losing their tempers. One of them wanted to escalate the fight; they subsequently raided each other (see Chagnon, ms. for further details).

The next and penultimate form of violence is the raid. With this we arrive at the level of warfare proper, the previous kinds of fighting being different kinds of contests. In fact, they might even be considered as alternatives to war.

Raiding takes place between villages whose members are: (a) unrelated and unknown to each other, a situation arising when a group moves into a new but occupied area, (b) unrelated but known to each other, an outcome of a situation like the above, but after the groups have developed alliances with each other, and (c) kinsmen and have a common history. The last type of warfare is relatively common in the center of the Yanomamö tribe: it results when large villages divide into mutually hostile new groups. Hence, kinship ties are not used to define the units which are permitted to conduct war, a commonly used criterion in other parts of the world.

Warfare between related groups is peculiar and deserves further discussion, for it throws light on the relationship between the size of village at the time it fissions, the possibility of warfare developing between the resulting groups, and the general intensity of warfare in a given area.

Villages usually fission after the population reaches 80–90 people, but intensive raiding may inhibit this. If, however, it does fission and produce two groups of forty-five people, the relationship between these groups will tend to be amicable. The authority mechanisms in Yanomamö society are confined to kinship obligations, age differential, and the abilities of the headman to gain compliance with his wishes. The ability of the headman to enforce his wishes increases during times of intensive warfare, resulting in the additional authority required to govern the internal affairs of a group that exceeds a hundred people in size, the apparent limit of village growth in periods of peace. But as villages grow, internal fighting increases sharply, so that when the fission ultimately does take place, the relationships between the resulting groups tend to be hostile. Thus, feedback to the causes in inter-village hostilities results: new villages are created with a pre-existing conflict and enter into immediate hostilities. Some of the bitterest wars are waged between groups of closely related kinsmen due to the nature of the circumstances leading to their separation.

The raid has a structure, ceremony, and specific set of tactics. It is normally organized to coincide with a feast, but if the group mounting the raid does not plan to have members of allied villages participate, the feast is not held. The day before the raid a mock war is conducted: a dummy made of grass or a log is set up and decorated to represent the enemy. The raiders circle the village with their weapons and approach the target with great stealth. At the signal of the raid leader, they shoot the dummy full of arrows and retreat quickly, their hammocks dangling from their backs. Others in the village pretend they are the enemy, examine the footprints, and give chase. Occasionally the raiders will "abduct" a female as they make their escape, the entire ceremony being conducted in a spirit of merriment and horseplay. It is as much a spectacle for the non-combatants who remain at home as it is a method of training for war.

If the raiders are avenging the death of a kinsman, they will consume his calcined, powdered bones mixed with a soup of boiled, ripe plantains. They mourn for him on the eve of the raid by weeping and sobbing aloud, chanting their sorrow in a formal mournful song.

In the early evening on the day before the raid the participants sing their war song, "I Am a Meat-Hungry Buzzard." Each raider marches to the village clearing mimicking the noise of some carnivorous animal, bird, or insect, clacking his arrows against his bow as he slowly takes his place facing the enemy's village. The line-up is dramatic and full of suspense, often taking as long as twenty minutes. When the last man takes his place, the song is sung by one of the fierce men and repeated in unison by the others. Several stanzas are repeated, after which the line breaks and the men group together to shout in the direction of the enemy village. After each shout they listen for the echo to return, a good omen and reassurance that the enemy is indeed where they think he is. Then the raiders run back to their respective houses and simulate vomiting, passing out of their bodies the rotten flesh they have symbolically eaten during the line-up and singing.

At dawn the warriors line up shoulder to shoulder again, facing the direction of the enemy. Each man has painted himself with masticated charcoal, a common design being the legs and upper torso completely blackened with the intervening space undecorated. Their wives have prepared quantities of food for them, which is stored outside the village with their hammocks. This allows the raiders to leave with dignity, unencumbered with unwarlike bundles of bananas on their backs. They shout in the direction of the enemy again, and when the echo returns, they leave the village in single file, marching quickly and with great determination.

If there are novices on the raid, the older men conduct additional mock raids en route to the enemy. The most inexperienced raiders are positioned near the center of the line of marching men, the fierce ones leading the column and bringing up the rear.

Raiders travel slowly at first, since they are burdened with their provisions. They pace themselves to arrive at the enemy's village at dawn, sleeping the night before the attack without the benefit of fire for warmth. By this time they have formulated a strategy, as well as contingency plans in case they are detected and must retreat individually. Some distant spot is decided on for a meeting place should this happen. They usually split into two groups and approach the village under cover of darkness. Ideally, they hope to catch someone alone outside the village, kill him and retreat before being detected. Most raid victims are shot while bathing, fetching drinking water, or relieving themselves.

If the enemy expects a raid, the headman forbids anyone to leave the village without his permission. Nobody is allowed to leave the village alone in these circumstances, for the headman must go out and find him, a dangerous and frightening task. The raiders may lie in wait for hours before they catch someone alone. If this does not appear to be possible, they may shoot several volleys of arrows over the palisade and make a hasty retreat.

As soon as they shoot someone, or are detected, they retreat rapidly, frequently traveling all night. The retreat is well planned: two men lie in ambush while the others retreat a specified distance. The first two men then retreat past them, their flight covered by a new pair of men, etc. Thus, a raiding party separated into two groups involves the participation of at least eight or ten men; I have not seen a raiding party of fewer than ten men. The tactics of raiding, therefore, require a minimum village size of about 40–45 people, for the population must be at least that large to field a raiding party of ten men and still permit a few men to remain at home to protect the women.[20]

If their victim is some distance from the village and has a woman with him, they may abduct her and any small children with her. The decision is determined by the probability of being overtaken by pursuers, for women and children hinder the speed at which the raiders can travel, and therefore jeopardize their safety. Women are rarely killed in warfare, but in a few circumstances the animosity between enemy groups will be so great that no holds are barred and both women and children are considered fair game.

The ultimate form of violence is the *nomohoni*, or "trick." It involves the collaboration of two or more allied villages, one of which invites a different group to a feast. The unsuspecting guests are treacherously murdered and their women abducted and distributed among the confederates in the incident. For example, if village A and B are at war, one of the groups may persuade the members of a third village to hold a feast and invite the other to it. The third village must be on visiting terms with the victims. The feast is conducted, the guests fallen upon at some point during the festivities and brutally killed with clubs and staves. Those who manage to escape the slaughter inside the village are shot from ambush by the other principal in the treachery.

The *nomohoni* is a drastic and somewhat rare form of violence, but it occurs with sufficient regularity that allies can never completely trust each other. When it does occur, the victims are usually from a group having no kinship ties to their treacherous hosts, so that in one respect kinship does define the community within which at least one form of violence is not likely to occur (although another treacherous feast, described below, did involve groups that had a common origin and kinship ties between them).

Warfare and Demography

One expression of the emphasis on masculinity is the preference of the Yanomamö to have a son as the oldest child. In many cases a woman will kill a newborn female in order to keep her husband pleased. Males are desired because they will grow up to become warriors and will contribute to the group's defense and sovereignty. Females, by contrast, are not considered to be as useful and often are lost to the group because of marriages with men in other villages.

Male babies are also killed, but only when the mother has a nursing child whose health would be jeopardized if it had to compete with a younger sibling for milk and maternal attention. They are aware that infancy is the most critical period in life because of children's susceptibility to diseases, and if a child has survived the first two or three years, his

[20] Yanomamö sex and age distribution is such that about ⅓ of the population is comprised by males of the warrior age. Thus, if a few men must always remain at home to protect the women, the demographic parameters, coupled with tactics of warfare, require a village of approximately 45 people. If a village fissions in such a way that one of the factions is smaller than this, it must take refuge in other villages and is not likely to continue to exist as a sovereign, political entity.

chances for further survival should not be compromised by permitting a new baby to compete for milk.[21]

But despite the practice of killing both males and females, the bias in selecting for males as the eldest child in the family has resulted in a sex-ratio favoring males. In some villages there may be as many as 30 percent more males than females,[22] the discrepancy being most pronounced in younger age categories. As middle age is approached the high male mortality due to warfare evens out the sex-ratio, and among the older people there are more women than men.

The component of mortality due to warfare is surprisingly high by comparison to our own demographic standards (Livingstone 1967). The following table summarizes the causes of death, diagnosed by my informants, of 240 adult ancestors. As is apparent, violent death in warfare (including club fights) is second in importance only to epidemics (mostly malarial), and accounts for 24 percent of all male mortality (cf. Table 1).[23]

Another measure of the significance of warfare in shaping the demographic pattern is the fact that one village of two hundred people was raided approximately twenty-five times during a period of fifteen months (November 1964–February 1966) and lost 10 people, i.e., 5 percent of its population in slightly over a year. A more dramatic example is the outcome of a treacherous feast to which the groups I studied fell victim in 1950: fifteen people out of a population of roughly 115 were killed in a single day!

TABLE 1: CAUSES OF DEATH AMONG 240 (ADULT) ANCESTORS OF THREE RELATED GROUPS

STATED CAUSE OF DEATH [1]	MALES	FEMALES	TOTAL	PERCENTAGE
Malaria & Epidemics	58	72	130	54.2
Dysentery, Diarrhea	16	5	21	8.8
Warfare	31	6	37	15.4
Club fights	2	0	2	0.8
Snakebite	2	3	5	2.1
Sorcery [2]	15	10	25	10.4
Tigers	1	0	1	0.4
Chest infections	3	1	4	1.7
Hayaheri [3]	1	2	3	1.2
"Old age"	4	0	4	1.7
Pains in groin	3	0	3	1.2
Childbirth	0	3	3	1.2
Other	2	0	2	0.8
TOTALS:	138	102	240	99.9

[1] These diagnoses were made by the Yanomamö.

[2] These deaths were probably due to such pathological causes as malaria. When malaria first reached epidemic proportions in some of the Yanomamö villages in the middle 1950's most of the deaths were attributed to the practice of harmful magic on the part of enemies.

[3] This is a peculiar sickness associated with intense pains in the upper abdominal region; the pains may last several days. In most cases the Indians recover.

The shortage of women, indirectly a consequence of an attitude that admires masculinity, ultimately leads to keener competition for the available females and thus reinforces the entire *waiteri complex* by resulting in more fighting and aggression. In practical terms, nearly every village fissioning I investigated resulted from chronic internal feuding over women, and in many cases the groups ultimately entered into hostilities after they separated.

Yanomamö Social Organization

The Yanomamö kinship terminology is of the bifurcate merging type with Iroquois cousin terms. A number of interesting features of

[21] Babies are nursed until they are three years old. A fascinating demographic consequence of this is that the Yanomamö space their children and show unexpected similarities to industrialized populations. See Neel and Chagnon, 1968, for the demographic data bearing on this.

[22] Chagnon, ms.; Neel and Chagnon, 1968. I hope to present more demographic data after the completion of the projected 1968 field work.

[23] This is probably an underestimate. The Yanomamö have very strong proscriptions on discussing the dead by name, and statistically adequate data requires complete genealogical information which is particularly difficult to obtain with respect to individuals killed in warfare. Their anguish at the mention of killed kinsmen precludes intensive questioning on this topic.

Yanomamö kinship include a paucity of terms in general, a lack of terms that specifically differentiate affinal from consanguineal kin,[24] the merging of some lineal kinsmen with collaterals of a different generation, and the equation of wife's mother's mother with wife. Perhaps the most important single feature of the terminology is the fact that a male ego's female bilateral cross-cousins are referred to as "wife" whether or not he is married to them, reflecting the prescriptive marriage rule. Men are obliged to marry women whom they address by the term *suaböya*, two genealogical specifications of which are MoBrDa and FaSiDa, i.e., their bilateral cross-cousins. Corroborating this prescriptive rule is the fact that of the six primary kinship categories into which men classify all their female relatives, five are prohibited marriage categories because of incest regulations.

The kinship system is extended to all Yanomamö with whom one is personally acquainted and/or demonstrably related. Kinship terms are extended to members of unrelated groups and are therefore not isomorphic with biological relationship. Within the village, however, there is a good correlation between kinship usage and biological relationships, but enough incestuous marriages take place to cause genealogical manipulations and changes in kinship usage that the kinship system cannot be relied upon as an invariable, faithful reflection of genealogy. Nevertheless, the important point is that all interpersonal relationships, even between members of autonomous villages, are defined by the kinship system, and regulated to a great degree by the obligations implied in the terms used.

Extension of kinship terms to outsiders follows a pattern that reflects the Yanomamö preoccupation with marriage exchanges and the obligations deriving from them. Village headmen call each other *shoriwä*,[25] a term that at once implies friendship and mutual obligations. In brief, it relates the two men as brothers-in-law and they stand in wife-giver/wife-receiver relationship to each other. Moreover, their children stand in the same relationship and, in turn, theirs, etc. *ad infinitum*. Thus, by adopting this specific kinship usage, the headmen maximize their own and their children's advantages in terms of woman exchange possibilities and confront each other on a friendly basis: mutual obligations are structured into their interpersonal relationships. Since headmen usually represent significant factions of the villages they lead, the widest possible network of kinsmen, by a simple adoption of one kinship usage by the village headmen, confront each other as affines and friends.

Descent is patrilineal, although the agnatic ideology is very weak by comparison to, for example, the Nuer (Evans-Pritchard 1951). Genealogical relationships are always demonstrated, i.e., the Yanomamö have lineages rather than clans. Members of the same lineage have a feeling of oneness that is frequently expressed in such sayings as "We are of the same species" [26] or "We are truly one and the same." While this feeling is acknowledged wherever a demonstrable kinship link through males exists, the degree of solidarity between agnates varies tremendously, the principal axes being closeness of genealogical tie, coresidence, and age difference (Chagnon ms.: 106 ff).

Yanomamö lineages have a genealogical depth of only three or four generations, an indication of the weakness of the agnatic ideology and a measure of the lack of corporateness of the lineage members. Village fission and

[24] There is one exception: men who marry into the village from other groups are called by a term that does not embrace consanguines, although they are frequently incorporated into the kinship system by using the appropriate primary term interchangeably.

[25] Unless there is a demonstrable actual relationship of a different kind. Evans-Pritchard 1951.

[26] The word used for "species" in a kinship context, *mashi*, defines the lineage.

population growth are such that third or fourth generation descendants of a man are scattered in several widely separated villages that frequently have no contacts with each other. Unless direct contacts are maintained, members of the same lineage forget their agnatic links and pursue independent political lives. Again, village politics are such that notions of agnatic solidarity count for very little compared to the opportunism characterizing inter-village relationships, particularly with regard to obligations arising when neighboring groups enter into alliance with each other. Thus two groups linked by agnatic ties may be on neutral terms with each other, and one of the groups may be actively conducting a war against a group allied with the other. Yet the one group will not be compelled to side with its agnates in the struggle, and might even take sides with the strangers, especiallly if marriage obligations exist between them. In brief, one cannot predict hostilities exclusively on the basis of kin-non-kin data.

At the local village level, segments of the lineages are corporate groups. Their estate consists of women and the rights to dispose of these women in marriage. In large villages, there may be two or three local descent groups of the same lineage, each making its own marriage arrangements with other lineages in the village. These agnatic groups are, in effect, the corporate lineal descent groups described by Leach (1951). Their functions consist mainly of making marriage arrangements for the female members; they are corporate in the sense that membership hinges on agnatic descent and co-residence and have an existence independent of the lives of particular members.

Yanomamö villages are usually dominated in composition by two lineages. But while dual organization exists in a *de facto* sense, there is no overt ideology of dual organization. That is, the village does not have named halves, rules stipulating that half of the village should be the domain of one lineage and the other half the domain of the second, etc. One might argue that this dualism is implied in the bifurcate merging kinship system, lineal descent with lineage exogamy and a symmetrical marriage prescription, but this is not commonly taken to be the form of ideology to which we apply the definition dual organization.[27] This situation parallels the Melanesian and Polynesian cases analyzed by Sahlins (1963, 1965) and illustrates again the argument that group composition need not be enforced by the existing ideology, nor can the ideology be predicted only from a knowledge of the group composition.

The fact that villages have marked dual composition seems best explained in terms of the marriage arrangements that the local descent groups establish. Members of local descent groups enter into protracted marriage exchanges with other groups of a different lineage and exchange women back and forth over several generations. The advantage derived from this is that males stand a better chance of obtaining a wife if they give their sisters consistently to the same group, for by giving women one can therefore demand them in return. The reciprocal obligations emerging from this are strong enough to keep the two local descent groups bound to each other when a larger village fissions, and the result will be a new village containing a pair of local descent groups representing two different lineages.

Figure 1 represents a model of Yanomamö social structure based on the kinship system, marriage rules, and method of incorporating new lineages into the village. The sibships might be taken to be portions of local descent groups, the entire group being represented by three generations of sibships. In generation 1, the village is comprised of two lineages (actu-

[27] Chagnon, ms., Appendix A, contains the group composition data on which this statement is made. Field work conducted after the thesis was written indicates that the dualism is even more striking in other villages.

ally, two corporate local descent groups of lineages X and Y). Members of lineage X seek their spouses in Y and vice versa. There are still only two lineages in generation 2, and re-

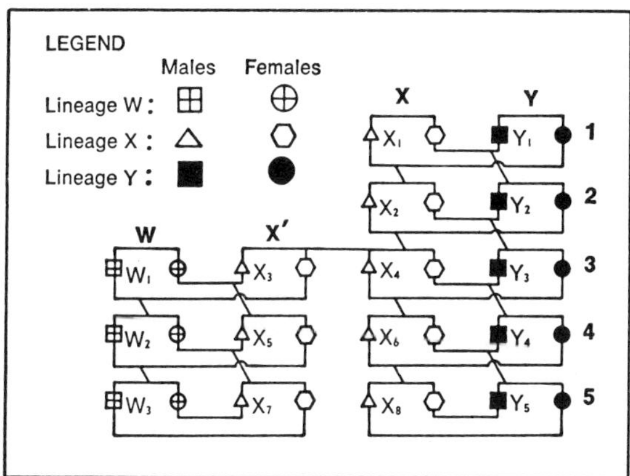

Figure 1. Yanomamö social structure.

ciprocal marriage exchange also continues as in the previous generation. But the marriages here are examples of the prescriptive marriage rule: each male has married his MoBrDa or FaSiDa. A new lineage, W, appears in generation 3 and is incorporated into the village by marriage exchanges with members of lineage X. It is at this point that two local descent groups of the same lineage begin to emerge, distinguishable only on the basis of the marriage exchange obligations they have created. Generation 4 shows more clearly the structural implications of reciprocal exchanges contracted by the respective descent groups. At this point the individuality of the two descent groups in lineage X begins to show itself in the attitudes and behavior of the agnatically related men of lineage X: individual X_5 would feel more closely related to his actual brothers than to X_6, although nominally all males of this generation and lineage would be brothers. If the village were to fission in generation 5, the paired local descent groups would comprise the newly-formed villages: W and X′ would separate from X and Y. The new groups would again show the dual composition, and lineage X would be represented in both groups (as X′ in one of them). Hence, affinal obligations are strong enough to overcome agnatic ties, and the latter break when new villages emerge from a larger one in the fissioning process.

Figure 2 represents the same phenomenon in another way. Each circle represents a village. Village A has four paired local descent groups of lineages X and Y. Members of lineage X live together on one side of the village while those of Y occupy the other. When village A fissions, the agnatic links break as shown, resulting in villages B and C, each having two paired descent groups. If the fission resulted from a club fight over a woman and someone died in the fighting, members of village B would raid village C and vice versa. The genealogical connections between members of the same lineage are sufficiently remote that the agnates, although they would call each other "brother," would have no qualms about shooting each other. If village B fissioned to produce villages D and E and the circumstances were not extremely hostile, the members of the two new villages would remain on good terms with each other. Depending on their size, they might even reunite in the face of raids from village C′. It should be noted that lineages X and Y are still represented in all three villages and that all three maintain a dual organization. Villages D and E, assuming that they represent militarily viable groups, are more constrained to enter into alliances with neighbors; compared with village C′, they are numerically inferior and more vulnerable.

One thing that cannot be specified in a diagram such as this is the role of the headman. Each of the local descent groups will have one spokesman, so that in village A there would be eight men with some authority (the oldest men, those in the second generation). In a village as large as A in Figure 2 there may be several men who are very prominent, and in fact there might be two acknowledged headmen, one rep-

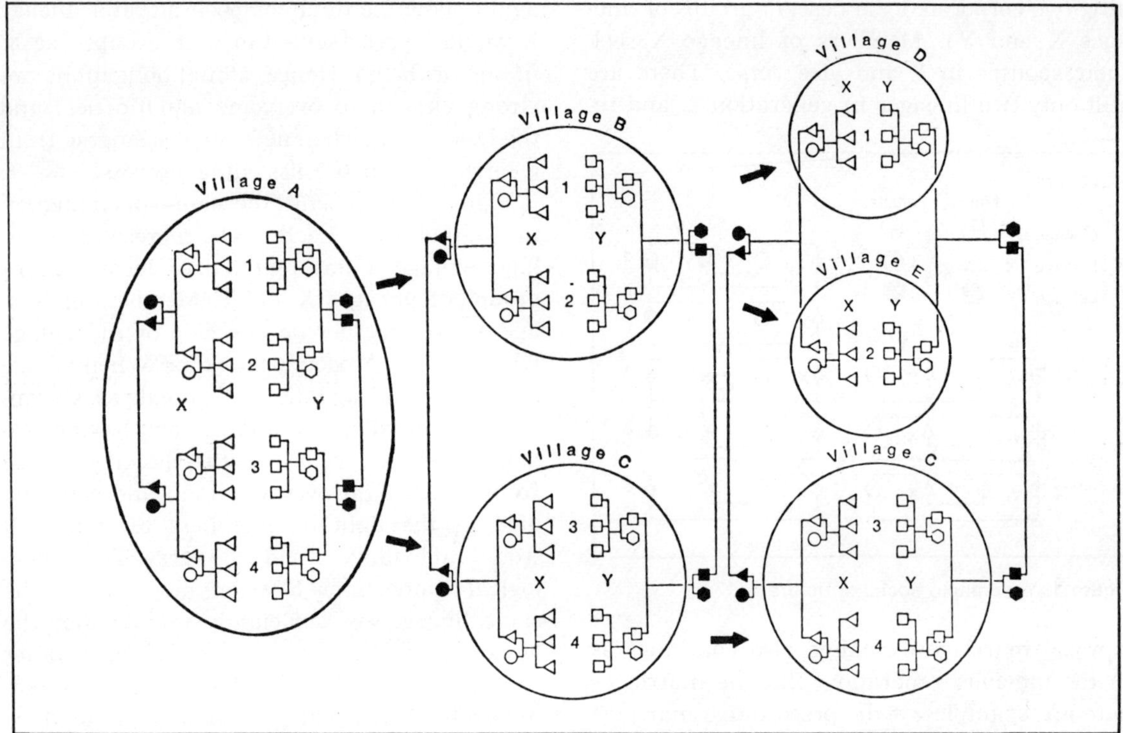

Figure 2. Distribution of paired local descent groups in village fissioning.

resenting lineage X and one lineage Y; they would be related to each other as brothers-in-law. In times of peace, it would be difficult for the headmen to control the feuding that would develop in the village, since many agnates are related so remotely that they would succumb to the temptation of conducting affairs with each other's wives. A comparison of the structures of village A and village D in Figure 2 shows that many kinds of potential problems are eliminated in the smaller village: incest prohibitions are sufficiently strong to reduce one category of sexual affair, and agnatic solidarity sufficiently great that men would not be tempted to provoke a brother's ire by trysting with his wife. The same degree of internal harmony can only be achieved in village A if the headman has increased authority, but the limits on authority in Yanomamö society are such that a considerable amount of in-fighting would take place in village A. If village A was being raided frequently, the authority of the headman would increase but still would not be sufficient to control all the fighting. Once the war diminishes in intensity, his authority likewise diminishes and he becomes largely *primus inter pares*.

The similarity of the ideal pattern represented in Figure 2 to the actual pattern is illustrated in Figure 3 and Map B. Figure 3 gives the genealogical relationships of the adult males of three related groups and shows how the lineages extend into the fourth related village. Map B shows the historical moves of these same villages, representing graphically how they fissioned. The history of these moves will be discussed below to show how the warfare pattern fits into the picture and how it specifically resulted in the pattern shown in Map B and Figure 3 (for complete genealogies see

Chagnon ms. Appendix A). The three villages given in Figure 3 are related to each other in the same way as the hypothetical villages D, E, and C′ of Figure 2, and originated by a fission process like that given for the hypothetical villages.

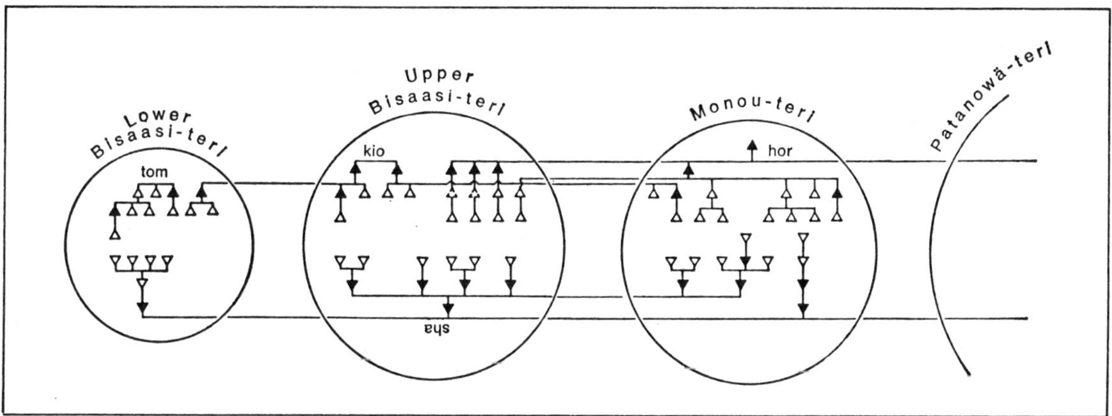

Figure 3. Actual village fissioning.

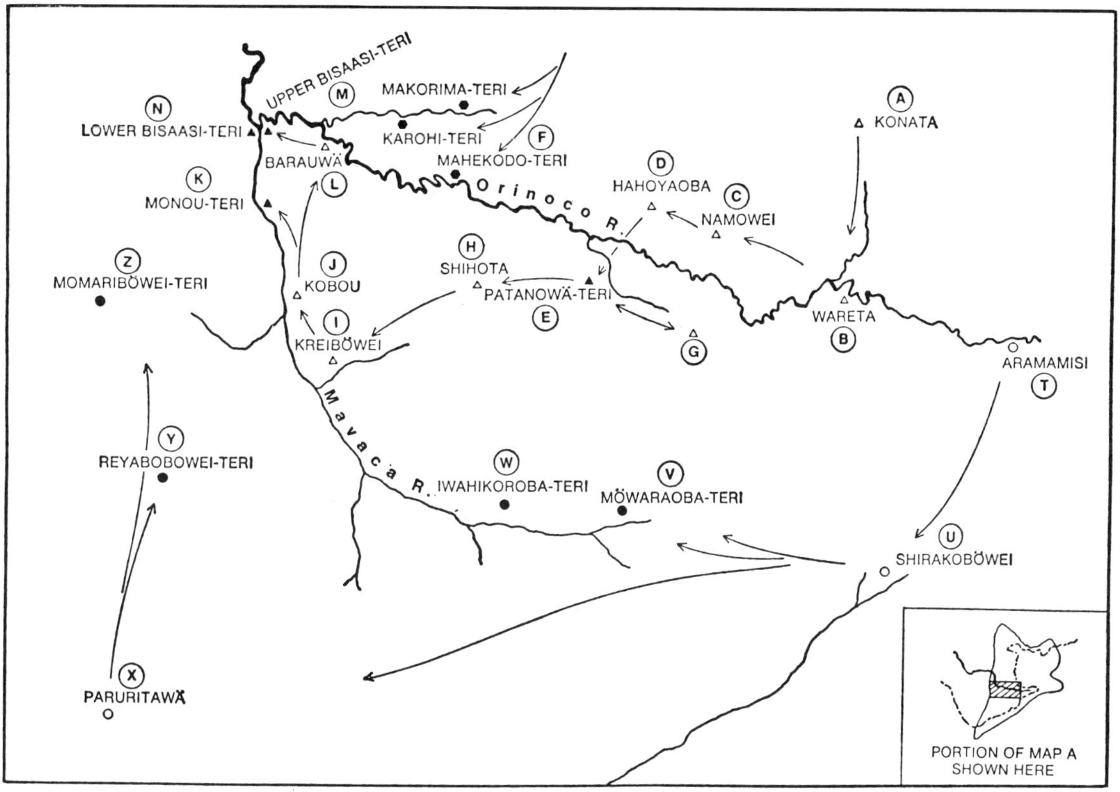

Map B. Historical Movements of Bisaasi-teri Village.

Village History, Settlement Pattern, Alliance, and Warfare

Perhaps the best way to illustrate the functional relationships between warfare, settlement pattern, marriage rules, and inter-village alliances is to present a résumé of the history of one cluster of villages and the nature of its current political relationships with other groups.

Map B shows the movements of Bisaasi-teri village (M and N on the map) from about 1875 to 1966.[28] The history begins at a site called Konata, indicated as "A" on Map B[29] The people of this village, the ancestors of the present Bisaasi-teri, were driven from their garden by a war with neighbors to their north (not shown on the map). They were forced to take refuge with their allies at location B, with whom they remained for a number of years. Their hosts kept demanding women from them and entered into hostilities with a group of villages to the east (not indicated), so the Bisaasi-teri ancestors established their own garden at C. They occupied site C for about ten years, but were driven from it by a new war with their old enemies to the north. They abandoned C and established themselves at D in about 1920, but because the soil was poor here they abandoned it after only a few years[30] and established a new garden at E, crossing the Orinoco River.[31] By this time their numbers had increased to the point where internal friction was intense, particularly over sexual liaisons. The group fissioned at this site about 1940 and two gardens were established.

Before they became fissioned, village E had entered into trading relationships with village V to their south. An epidemic broke out shortly after the two groups began visiting, and a number of deaths in village E were attributed to sorcery on the part of members of village V. An unsuspecting visitor from village V arrived to visit and trade and was summarily murdered, initiating a war between groups E and V.

The two groups at E gradually became independent of each other and ultimately entered into hostilities. The group at E abandoned its garden and established a new one at H. The war continued between H and G, and about 1949 H was abandoned and site I established.

The group at site I then entered into friendly relationships with village W, a group related to their old enemies, V. The people of W were persuaded by those of V to invite the group from I to a feast. The plan was to massacre the men and abduct the women, thereby permitting the members of V to get revenge. The feast was held early in 1950[32] at a site then occupied by the members of W, and resulted in the killing of approximately fifteen men from village I. The treacherous hosts descended on them while they reclined in their hammocks and killed them with sharpened staves and axes.[33] Those who escaped the slaughter inside the village were shot at from ambush by the members of village V, who were secluded out-

[28] This map is out of date, since some of the villages have moved and/or fissioned since it was prepared in 1966.

[29] Hereafter just letters will be used to avoid confusing native terms. Villages are named after garden sites, and the people take the name of their gardens. Thus, the present Bisaasi-teri were known as the Konata-teri when they lived at Konata, etc.

[30] This may have been an excuse to rationalize their move; the true cause of the move may have been their fear of the groups to the north.

[31] The groups north of the Orinoco call most of the people south of the Orinoco "Shamatari." See Chagnon, ms.:27 ff for a discussion of this term.

[32] This data is based on the arrival of James P. Barker, the first non-Indian to make sustained contact with the Yanomamö, at the village of Mahekodo-teri in 1950.

[33] The source of the axes was ultimately the Makiritare according to my informants; the trading network linking the villages appears to have distributed steel tools throughout Yanomamö territory at an early date. The Makiritare are known to have traveled as far east as Georgetown to acquire steel tools, and at the present, glass beads from Guyana still reach the Makiritare via a long trading network involving several tribes.

side the village. A more complete slaughter was averted when the hosts began fighting over the victims' women,[34] a number of whom were captured.

The survivors fled to site J, a garden they had begun clearing before the fateful treacherous feast, in anticipation of hostilities from that area. But the new garden had not yet begun producing, so the people were obliged to return to I for food. They remained at J long enough to recover from their wounds, subsisting on food obtained from the garden at I. Shortly after they returned to I they were visited by the headman of village F (on the Orinoco River), who had heard of the massacre. He invited them to take refuge in his village, an offer that was accepted with some reluctance. The men raided their treacherous hosts once before taking refuge in village F, managing to kill the headman and recapture some of their own women. They also took the headman's son, a boy of about 8 years, but later killed him.[35] They raided their enemies persistently from village F, being aided by their hosts. The return raids took no toll on their own population, but two men from village F were killed.

The refugees continued to work on their garden at J, hauling food from the gardens of their hosts. They also began clearing sites K and L, as they had agreed to split into two groups because of internal fighting. They also suspected their hosts of plotting a second massacre against them in order to capture their women, a fear that was later substantiated.[36] They worked assiduously at finishing their site at J, remaining with their hosts for brief periods to rest from their gardening activities. They managed to take permanent leave of their hosts within a year and moved into site J, from which they finished their gardens at K and L. As soon as they finished these new gardens, they fissioned and abandoned J. The group that occupied site L subsequently moved to M, fissioned again to produce N, two inter-dependent groups now known as Upper and Lower Bisaasi-teri. Their last move took place about 1959.

In 1960 the Bisaasi-teri, along with their congeners of site K, began visiting the group X to their south. The people of site X had fissioned from W and V many years earlier, but were still on visiting terms with them. The people of X were persuaded to invite group V to a treacherous feast. Village X was in the process of fissioning, again a result of feuds over women, so they established two new gardens at Y and Z in anticipation of the raids that they knew would follow the treacherous feast. The feast was held in 1960, but only a few people from village V actually came: a malaria epidemic was raging in this area, so most of the people were too sick to travel and remained at home. Three of the four men who came to the feast were summarily killed and their women captured. Village X then fissioned and occupied sites Y and Z. They sustained the entire brunt of the revenge raids mounted by the members of V, and had to rely on support from the Bisaasi-teri and the members of K.

But the Bisaasi-teri were not satisfied with the degree to which their revenge desires were alleviated. Village Y had, in the meantime, established peaceful contacts with V and intermittent visiting took place between the two groups. The Bisaasi-teri pressured the members of Y into staging a second treacherous feast in February 1965. The invitation was accepted by the members of group V, who began traveling toward village Y. They had gotten nearly halfway to the village before being warned by a

[34] My informants also said that a few people among the hosts did not participate in the killing and actually aided the victims in their escape.

[35] The man who killed the boy explained to me that the children were tormenting the boy, so he shot him with an arrow while he played in the river to put him out of his misery.

[36] After village F fissioned in the mid-'50s, one man in the disgruntled faction exposed the details of the plot long after it had failed to materialize. Group F had gotten into two new wars and required the aid of their visitors in the raiding.

friend in group Y of the disaster that awaited them.

The current alliance pattern of the several groups can now be interpreted against the background of this historical data. Villages Y and Z are the westernmost groups in this area; the land to their west is uninhabited, to their south are several villages with which they have hostile relationships, and to their east lie the groups they have been inviting to the treacherous feasts. Hence their only allies are the Bisaasi-teri and the group at K. When I began my field work in 1964 the relationship between the two clusters of villages was such that the Bisaasi-teri and group K had a conspicuous hegemony over villages Y and Z and were systematically stealing their women. The political relationships were so much to the advantage of the northern group that a Bisaasi-teri man forcibly took a woman who was promised to him away from her family in village Y and nobody attempted to stop him. This incident in a different set of circumstances would have resulted in a bloody club fight, or even a shooting war; but the members of group Y were so dependent on the Bisaasi-teri that they had to tolerate this behavior—if they had taken extreme offense at this they might have lost their most important ally.

The political relationships altered appreciably during the course of my field work. Group G, old enemies to the Bisaasi-teri and the members of K—but kinsmen, had gotten into a war with several villages to their north and east. They had fissioned into three distinct groups prior to the war but reunited to form a large village of over two hundred people. They had just one ally, a large village to their south (not shown), and were interested in patching up their differences with their kinsmen. They indicated their desire to make peace and were eventually invited to Bisaasi-teri for a feast in November 1964.[37] Both Lower and Upper Bisaasi-teri participated in the preparations; the members of K refrained from any involvement, but did send a delegation of men to Bisaasi-teri on the day of the feast: these men discovered a group of seven unprotected women outside the village and abducted them. Five of the women were recovered in a bloody club fight the following day, but the two groups parted on hostile terms and vowed to raid each other.

The members of village K raided first, about a month after the club fight, and killed one man. Before they raided, however, they began clearing a new garden west of their village in anticipation of the war they knew would follow. The Bisaasi-teri had elected to remain neutral in any hostilities that might develop, but when a raiding party from group G killed the headman of village K to avenge the death of one of their kinsmen, the Bisaasi-teri were infuriated and decided to aid the members of K.

Thus the Bisaasi-teri and the members of village K became actively hostile to village G, and their alliance with villages Y and Z suddenly took on a different significance: they needed the support of these two groups and lost their authority over them in the marriage exchange practice at that point. Six raids against village G were initiated by the Bisaasi-teri, members of group K, and their allies in Y and Z, and they participated in a number of raids against group G initiated by other villages.

The members of village G were harassed by no fewer than ten villages, but they confined their revenge raids to just two of their enemies, one of which was village K. The members of this village had to abandon their gardens and take refuge with allies in Y and Z and with the Bisaasi-teri.

An important consequence was that the members of village K had to cede women to men in village Z; although these women had initially been promised to village Z, village K, in a superior position until this time, had withheld payment.

[37] The feast was in progress when I initiated my field work; see Chagnon 1968b, for a brief account of the details.

Comparison of Marriage Behavior in Two Villages

A comparison of the marriage practices in Lower Bisaasi-teri and village G, Patanowä-teri, reveals that the smaller of the two villages has deviated from the ideal marriage pattern because it has been obliged to enter into alliances with its neighbors. The Patanowä-teri, a much larger group, has managed to confine most of its marriages to within the group and has not had to rely on support from allies in maintaining its autonomy; its population numbers over two hundred, compared to fifty-one in Lower Bisaasi-teri.

Table 2 gives the distribution of marriage types in the two villages. (The sample consists of all married males under 35 years of age.) The "prescriptive" marriages are those taking place between men and females standing in the proper kinship category, i.e., the women were *suaböya* to their husbands. Incestuous marriages involve individuals standing in any other kind of categorical relationship to each other when they are married, although their respective kinship categories were afterwards adjusted to fit the facts. Alliance marriages refer to those between members of different villages to establish political ties between the groups and cement their mutual friendship.[38] Finally, the unexplained marriages are those between individuals whose descent groups have only recently begun exchanging women and who therefore stand in ambiguous relationships to each other: the marriages between their descent groups have not been consistently between individuals of the same generation, a phenomenon that takes place when a new lineage is being incorporated into the village.

TABLE 2: MARRIAGE TYPES IN TWO RELATED VILLAGES

	PATANOWÄ-TERI	LOWER BISAASI-TERI
Prescriptive	37	7
Incestuous	4	1
Alliance/Abduction	8	9
Unexplained	3	0

One interesting theoretical conclusion is implied by the marriage data in Table 2; it hinges on the interpretation of the term "prescriptive" marriage. One school of thought maintains that a marriage alliance system can be called prescriptive only if men are obliged to marry women of a specific, single kinship category (Needham 1962; Leach 1965; Maybury-Lewis 1965). I have adopted this point of view in presenting the data. One of the arguments marshalled by proponents of this view is that there would be no systematic entailments to a marriage rule that were non-prescriptive (Maybury-Lewis 1965:225) and therefore the analysis of such systems would presumably require different concepts and procedures. Another, less defensible, argument would be that a model of the social structure of the type shown in Figure 1 could not properly be used to represent the marriage system. However, the model rests largely on precise genealogical specifications of the prescribed category and therefore weakens the argument made by proponents of the prescriptive definition given here: that a sharp distinction between genealogy and category is essential in an analysis of systems of this kind.

Applying the definition of prescriptive marriage just given, the data in Table 2 does not reveal any difference in kind of social structure between the two groups. Both villages are identical in their kinship and marriage rules, and the discrepancy between them in marriage behavior represents no more than the outcome of the functional interrelationships between alliance formation, economic dependence on cultivated foods, intensity of warfare, demographic parameters, and attitudes about sovereignty and ferocity.

An alternate school of thought (Coult and

[38] These include a few abductions in each village. Their removal would not alter the point of the argument.

Hammel 1963; Ackerman 1964; Mark 1967) maintains that a marriage system can be described as "prescriptive" only if a high percentage of the marriages, close to 100 percent, actually follow the rule (Coult and Hammel 1963). If the marriage behavior of the Patanowä-teri is sufficiently like their stated rules to characterize them as having a prescriptive marriage system, then we are led to the logical, but perhaps absurd, conclusion that this village has a social structure [39] different from that of their closely related congeners in Bisaasi-teri, whose frequency of prescriptive marriage behavior is significantly less than 100 percent.

But these are academic arguments; the important point is that the effects of warfare on inter-village alliance patterns, village size and composition, ideology and attitudes about neighbors, demography, and the overall social organization are clear and understandable. Perhaps a more basic issue is the utility of identifying social organization or structure with the kinship terminology, descent rule, and marriage rules. As I have attempted to show, the intensity of warfare in Yanomamö culture has important direct and indirect effects on many features of their social system. While it is possible to isolate the effects of warfare on marriage behavior for purposes of refuting or defending particular notions relating to the analysis of marriage systems, a general understanding of the relationship of warfare to social organization and adaptation can be gained only by considering many other aspects of culture in the analysis of the whole adaptive system. In an analysis of Yanomamö adaptation, one must emphasize the immense significance of the belligerent ideology in accounting for the nature of the adaptation.

The political milieu within which marriages take place emphasizes the immense significance of marriage *as alliance*. It would be my guess that labile political conditions such as those found among the Yanomamö are probably more representative of the kinds of conditions under which primitive kinship systems and marriage practices were evolved than the more stable political situations under which most field work is conducted. Tylor's dictum on exogamy, "marry out or die out," has a somewhat hollow ring to it when applied to tribal peoples for whom warfare is no longer a dominant influence in their marriage practices. I hope I have amply demonstrated that Tylor's dictum applies very convincingly to the Yanomamö; it has a universal application because these situations probably obtained to a much greater extent in the past than most of us are willing to concede.

In this connection the work of Rose (1960) among the Groote Eylandt aborigines takes on a different kind of significance than that which he intended it to have. Apart from playing down the significance of kinship as a system of categories and overemphasizing the close genealogical specifications characterizing these categories, his work raises an important question: why are some kinds of marriage rules maintained in social systems that make use of them either infrequently or not at all? I believe that we must seek the answer to this question in ecological situations such as that to which the Yanomamö must adapt—political environments that call upon the full potential of all aspects of the marriage rules—for it is largely by marriage alliances that tribal peoples of this general cultural level come to grips with the world about them. And, in the case of the Yanomamö, the major threat to security and survival is represented by the social aspects of the cultural ecology—their neighbors.

Studies of marriage as systems of alliance have paid relatively little attention to the implications alliance has for survival. While we have learned a great deal from the analyses of social systems that emphasize exchange obligations (the communication of ideas, women, and goods, as Professor Lévi-Strauss puts it),

[39] This assumes that social structure is largely the consequence of the kinship terminology, descent rule, and marriage rule, a contestable point of view, to say the least.

the ethnographic frequency of warfare would seem to suggest that the origin and perpetuation of these systems took place under conditions that gave alliance a more profound meaning, one that might have been measured in terms of positive selection. The ethnographic distribution of the bifurcate merging kinship system in general, the Iroquois sub-type in particular, and the bilateral cross-cousin marriage systems might be investigated from this perspective. It would seem that a social system that coupled these features would have an adaptive advantage in situations where it is important to relate whole groups to each other in terms of alliance, a process that is more readily accomplished in a short period of time by symmetrical marriage practices.

A final point can be made regarding Yanomamö warfare. Sovereignty and autonomy, rather than acquisition of land, are the goals in the alliance system. A model that could analyze these alliances might also be applicable in the analysis of the political behavior of modern nation states: the basic parameters of the phenomena appear to be the same. Some of these are:

1. non-territorial motives for warfare;
2. enforcement of sovereignty by displays of force and aggressiveness;
3. alliance commitments that are reluctantly honored after the political conditions under which they originated alter;
4. shifts and flux in the alliance system;
5. a greater compulsion for smaller groups to enter alliances and to suffer most of the disadvantages; and
6. attempts to maximize or improve chances of political survival as sovereign groups by entering alliances or emphasizing military capacity, or both.

References

ACKERMAN, CHARLES (1964) Structure and Statistics: the Purum case. *Amer. Anthrop.* 66:53–63.

ARDREY, ROBERT (1966) *The Territorial Imperative.* New York: Atheneum.

BIOCCA, ETTORE (1965) *Yanomamö.* Bari: Leonardo da Vinci.

CARNEIRO, ROBERT L. (1961) Slash-and-burn cultivation among the Kuikuru and its implications for cultural development in the Amazon Basin. *Anthropologica Supp.* No. 2:47–67, Caracas.

CHAGNON, NAPOLEON A. [ms.] *Yanomamö Warfare, Social Organization and Marriage Alliances.* Ann Arbor: University of Michigan. Doctoral Thesis, 1966.

——— (1967) Yanomamö—the fierce people. *Natural History.* Vol. 76:22–31.

——— (1968a) *Yanomamö: The Fierce People.* Case Studies in Cultural Anthropology. New York: Holt, Rinehart and Winston.

——— (1968b) The feast. *Natural History,* 77:4, 34–46.

COULT, A. D., and A. E. HAMMEL (1963) A corrected model for patrilateral cross-cousin marriage. *S.W. J. Anthrop.,* 19:287–296.

EVANS-PRITCHARD, E. E. (1951) *Kinship and Marriage Among the Nuer.* London: Oxford University Press.

HARDING, THOMAS (1960) Adaptation and stability. In: Marshall D. Sahlins and Elman R. Service (eds.), *Evolution and Culture.* Ann Arbor: University of Michigan Press, pp. 45–68.

LEACH, E. R. (1951) The structural implications of matrilateral cross-cousin marriage. *J. Roy. Anthrop. Inst.* 81:23–55.

——— (1965) Letter to the Editor, *Man,* 12:25.

LIVINGSTONE, FRANK B. (1967) The effects of warfare on the biology of the human species. In: Morton Fried, Marvin Harris, and Robert Murphy (eds.), *War: The Anthropology of Armed Conflict and Aggression.* Garden City, N.Y.: The Natural History Press, pp. 3–15.

LORENZ, KONRAD (1966) *On Aggression.* New York: Harcourt, Brace and World.

MARK, L. L. (1967) Patrilateral cross-cousin marriage among the Magpie Miao: Preferential or prescriptive. *Amer. Anthrop.* 69:55–62.

MAUSS, MARCEL (1954) *The Gift.* Glencoe: The Free Press. (Originally published 1925.)

MAYBURY-LEWIS, DAVID H. P. (1965) Prescriptive marriage systems. *S.W. J. Anthrop.* 21:207–230.

MIGLIAZZA, ERNESTO (1965) Fonologia Máku. *Bol. Mus. Paraense Emilio Goeldi, Anthropologia* 25:1–19.

NEEDHAM, RODNEY (1962) *Structure and Sentiment.* Chicago: University of Chicago Press.

NEEL, JAMES V., and NAPOLEON A. CHAGNON (1968) The demography of two tribes of primitive, relatively unacculturated American Indians. *Proc. Nat'l Acad. Sci.*, 59:680–689.

ROSE, F. G. G. (1960) Classification of kin, age structure and marriage amongst the Groote Eylandt aborigines: a study in method and a theory of Australian kinship. Berlin: Academie-Verlag.

SAHLINS, MARSHALL D. (1963) Poor man, rich man, big man, chief: political types in Melanesia and Polynesia. *Comp. Studies Soc. Hist.* 5:285–303.

——— (1965) On the ideology and composition of descent groups. *Man.* 12:104–107.

SEITZ, GEORG (1963) *People of the Rain Forests.* A. J. Pomerans (transl.). London: Heinemann.

STEWARD, JULIAN H. (1946–48) South American cultures: an interpretative summary. In: Julian H. Steward (ed.), The Comparative Ethnology of South American Indians, Vol. 5 of *Handbook of South American Indians, Bur. Amer. Ethnol. Bull.* No. 143.

VAYDA, ANDREW P. (1960) Maori warfare. *Polynesian Soc. Maori Mono.*, No. 2. Wellington: Polynesian Society.

——— (1961) Expansion and warfare among swidden agriculturalists. *Amer. Anthrop.* 63:346–358.

ZERRIES, OTTO (1964) Waika: Die Kulturgeschichtlich Stellung der Waika-Indianer des oberen Orinoco im Rahmen der Völkerkunde Südamerikas. *Ergebnisse der Frobenius-Expedition 1954/55 nach Südost-Venezuela.* Munich.

29

ON PEASANT REBELLIONS

ERIC R. WOLF

Some readers of the previous selection (28) may have been disconcerted to learn that some killing still goes on in the world outside the monopoly usually held by the organized political state. What may be worse, it exists outside of our usual value frameworks, so that the Yanomamö penchant for clubbing, stabbing, or shooting each other with bows and arrows seems mysterious and requires explanation. Of course, we don't have to travel very far to find killing in our own society not to mention our involvement in wholesale murder halfway across the globe in Indochina.

Hopefully, by the time this book is being read, fellow United States citizens will not still be destroying the people and land of Southeast Asia. Even if the war is brought to an end in Vietnam, and in Laos and Cambodia too, there is reason to be pessimistic about the chances of the United States staying out of further wars in the Third World as well as a third world war. Clearly it should be a critical task of anthropology to seek enlightenment on ways of averting wars of various kinds.

The anthropologist's work is particularly apt with regard to wars that basically are more revolutions and rebellions of the downtrodden than international state conflicts. This has certainly been the case in Vietnam, although to the bitter end some influential power holders in the United States and elsewhere have refused to countenance it. It was that war, some of its predecessors, and the possibility of further such wars that stimulated Eric Wolf to try to place the matter in an anthropological perspective. The piece that follows conveys only some of his ideas on the subject. Wolf is an anthropologist who has spent much of his professional life studying peasant societies. For a more extensive look at his views the reader should consult

SOURCE: "On Peasant Rebellions," *International Social Science Journal*, Vol. 21, No. 2 (1969):286–94. Reprinted by permission of UNESCO and the author.

his *Peasant Wars of the Twentieth Century* (New York, Harper & Row, 1969).

▼△▼△▼

Six major social and political upheavals, fought with peasant support, have shaken the world of the twentieth century: the Mexican revolution of 1910, the Russian revolutions of 1905 and 1917, the Chinese revolution which metamorphosed through various phases from 1921 onwards, the Vietnamese revolution which has its roots in the Second World War, the Algerian rebellion of 1954 and the Cuban revolution of 1958. All of these were to some extent based on the participation of rural populations. It is to the analysis of this participation that the present article directs its attention.

Romantics to the contrary, it is not easy for a peasantry to engage in sustained rebellion. Peasants are especially handicapped in passing from passive recognition of wrongs to political participation as a means for setting them right. First, a peasant's work is more often done alone, on his own land, than in conjunction with his fellows. Moreover, all peasants are to some extent competitors, for available resources within the community as for sources of credit from without. Secondly, the tyranny of work weighs heavily upon peasants: their life is geared to an annual routine and to planning for the year to come. Momentary alterations of routine threaten their ability to take up the routine later. Thirdly, control of land enables them, more often than not, to retreat into subsistence production should adverse conditions affect their market crop. Fourthly, ties of extended kinship and mutual aid within the community may cushion the shocks of dislocation. Fifthly, peasants' interests—especially among poor peasants—often cross-cut class alignments. Rich and poor peasant may be kinfolk, or a peasant may be at one and the same time owner, renter, share-cropper, labourer for his neighbours and seasonal hand on a near-by plantation. Each different involvement aligns him differently with his fellows and with the outside world. Finally, past exclusion of the peasant from participation in decision-making beyond the bamboo hedge of his village deprives him all too often of the knowledge needed to articulate his interests with appropriate forms of action. Hence peasants are often merely passive spectators of political struggles or long for the sudden advent of a millennium, without specifying for themselves and their neighbours the many rungs on the staircase to heaven.

If it is true that peasants are slow to rise, then peasant participation in the great rebellions of the twentieth century must obey some special factors which exacerbated the peasant condition. We will not understand that condition unless we keep in mind constantly that it has suffered greatly under the impact of three great crises: the demographic crisis, the ecological crisis and the crisis in power and authority. The demographic crisis is most easily depicted in bare figures, though its root causes remain ill understood. It may well be that its ultimate causes lie less in the reduction of mortality through spreading medical care, than in the diffusion of American food crops throughout the world which provided an existential minimum for numerous agricultural populations. Yet the bare numbers suffice to indicate the seriousness of the demographic problem. Mexico had a population of 5.8 million at the beginning of the nineteenth century; in 1910—at the outbreak of the revolution—it had 16.5 million. European Russia had a population of 20 million in 1725; at the turn of the twentieth century it had 87 million. China numbered 265 million in 1775, 430 million in 1850 and close to 600 million at the time of the revolution. Viet-Nam is estimated to have sustained a population of between 6 and 14 million in 1820; it had 30.5 million inhabitants in 1962. Algeria had an indigenous population of 10.5 million in 1963, representing a fourfold increase since the beginnings of French occupation in the first part of the nineteenth century. Cuba had 550,000 inhabitants in 1800; by 1953 it had 5.8 million. Population increases alone and by themselves would have placed a serious strain on inherited cultural arrangements.

The ecological crisis is in part related to the sheer increase in numbers; yet it is also an important measure independent of it. Population increases of the magnitude just mentioned coincided with a period in history in which land and other resources were increasingly converted into commodities—in the capitalist sense of that word. As commodities they were subjected to the demands of a market which bore only a very indirect relation to the needs of the rural populations subjected to it. Where, in the past, market behaviour had been largely subsidiary to the existential problems of subsistence, now existence and its problems became subsidiary to the market. The alienation of peasant resources proceeded directly through outright seizure or through coercive purchase, as in Mexico, Algeria and Cuba; or it took the form—especially in China and Viet-Nam—of stepped-up capitalization of rent which resulted in the transfer of resources from those unable to keep up to those able to pay. In addition, capitalist mobilization of resources was reinforced through the pressure of taxation, of demands for redemption payments and through the increased needs for industrially produced commodities on the part of the peasantry itself. All together, however, these various pressures disrupted the precarious ecological balance of peasant society. Where the peasant had required a certain combination of resources to effect an adequate living, the separate and differential mobilization of these resources broke that ecological nexus. This is perhaps best seen in Russia where successive land reforms threatened continued peasant access to pasture, forest and ploughland. Yet it is equally evident in cases where commercialization threatened peasant access to communal lands (Algeria, Mexico, Viet-Nam), to unclaimed land (Cuba, Mexico), to public granaries (Algeria, China), or where it threatened the balance between pastoral and settled populations (Algeria). At the same time as commercialization disrupted rural life, moreover, it also created new and unsettled ecological niches in industry. Disruptive change in the rural area went hand in hand with the opening up of incipient but uncertain opportunities for numerous ex-industrial peasants. Many of these retained formal ties with their home villages (Algeria, China, Russia); others migrated between country and industry in continuous turnover (especially Viet-Nam). Increased instability in the rural area was thus accompanied by a still unstable commitment to industrial work.

Finally, both the demographic and the ecological crisis converged in the crisis of authority. The development of the market produced a rapid circulation of the *élite,* in which the manipulators of the new 'free-floating resources' —labour bosses, merchants, industrial *entrepreneurs*—challenged the inherited power of the controllers of fixed social resources, the tribal chief, the mandarin, the landed nobleman.[1] Undisputed and stable claims thus yielded to unstable and disputed claims. This rivalry between primarily political and primarily economic power-holders contained its own dialectic. The imposition of the market mechanism entailed a diminution of social responsibilities for the affected population: the economic *entrepreneur* did not concern himself with the social cost of his activities; the traditional power-holder was often too limited in his power to offer assistance or subject to co-optation by his successful rivals. The advent of the market thus not merely produced a crisis in peasant ecology; it deranged the numerous middle-level ties between centre and hinterland, between the urban and the rural sectors. Commercialization disrupted the hinterland; at the very same time it also lessened the ability of power-holders to perceive and predict

[1] S. N. Eisenstadt, *Modernization: Protest and Change,* Englewood Cliffs, Prentice-Hall, 1966.

changes in the rural area. The result was an ever-widening gap between the rulers and the ruled. That such a course is not inevitable is perhaps demonstrated by Barrington Moore,[2] who showed how traditional feudal forms were utilized in both Germany and Japan to prevent the formation of such a gap in power and communication during the crucial period of transition to a commercial and industrial order. Where this was not accomplished—precisely where an administrative militarized feudalism was absent—the continued widening of the power gap invited the formation of a counter-*élite* which could challenge both a disruptive leadership based on the operation of the market and the impotent heirs of traditional power, while forging a new consensus through communication with the peasantry. Such a counter-*élite* is most frequently made up of members of provincial *élites*, relegated to the margins of commercial mobilization and political office; of officials or professionals who stand midway between the rural area and the centre and are caught in the contradictions between the two; and of intellectuals who have access to a system of symbols which can guide the interaction between leadership and rural area.

Sustained mobilization of the peasantry is, however, no easy task. Such an effort will not find its allies in a rural mass which is completely subject to the imperious demands of necessity. Peasants cannot rebel successfully in a situation of complete impotence; the powerless are easy victims. Therefore only a peasantry in possession of some tactical control over its own resources can provide a secure basis for on-going political leverage. Power, as Richard Adams [3] has said, refers ultimately 'to an actual physical control that one party may have with respect to another. The reason that most relationships are not reduced to physical struggles is that parties to them can make rational decisions based on their estimates of tactical power and other factors. Power is usually exercised, therefore, through the common recognition by two parties of the tactical control each has, and through rational decision by one to do what the other wants. Each estimates his own tactical control, compares it to the other, and decides he may or may not be superior'.

The poor peasant or the landless labourer who depends on a landlord for the largest part of his livelihood, or the totality of it, has no tactical power: he is completely within the power domain of his employer, without sufficient resources of his own to serve him usefully in the power struggle. Poor peasants, and landless labourers, therefore, are unlikely to pursue the course of rebellion, unless they are able to rely on some external power to challenge the power which constrains them. Such external power is represented in the Mexican case by the action of the Constitutionalist army in Yucatan, which liberated the peons from debt bondage 'from above'; by the collapse of the Russian army in 1917 and the reflux of the peasant soldiery, arms in hand, into the villages; by the creation of the Chinese Red Army as an instrument designed to break up landlord power in the villages. Where such external power is present the poor peasant and landless labourer have latitude of movement; where it is absent, they are under near-complete constraint. The rich peasant, in turn, is unlikely to embark on the course of rebellion. As employer of the labour of others, as money-lender, as notable co-opted by the State machine, he exercises local power in alliance with external power-holders. His power domain with the village is derivative; it depends on the maintenance of the domains of these power-holders outside the village. Only when an external force, such as the Chinese Red Army, proves capable of destroying these other superior power domains, will the rich peasant lend his support to an uprising.

[2] Barrington Moore, Jr., *Social Origin of Dictatorship and Democracy,* Boston, Beacon Press, 1966.

[3] Richard N. Adams, 'Power and Power Domains', *Americana Latina,* Year 9, 1966, p. 3–21.

There are only two components of the peasantry which possess sufficient internal leverage to enter into sustained rebellion. These are (a) a landowning 'middle peasantry' or (b) a peasantry located in a peripheral area outside the domains of landlord control. Middle peasantry refers to a peasant population which has secure access to land of its own and cultivates it with family labour. Where these middle-peasant holdings lie within the power domain of a superior, possession of their own resources provides their holders with the minimal tactical freedom required to challenge their overlord. The same, however, holds for a peasantry, poor or 'middle', whose settlements are only under marginal control from the outside. Here landholdings may be insufficient for the support of the peasant household; but subsidiary activities such as casual labour, smuggling, live-stock raising—not under the direct constraint of an external power domain—supplement land in sufficient quantity to grant the peasantry some latitude of movement. We mark the existence of such a tactically mobile peasantry: in the villages of Morelos in Mexico; in the communes of the central agricultural regions of Russia; in the northern bastion established by the Chinese Communists after the Long March; as a basis for rebellion in Vietnam; among the *fellaheen* of Algeria; and among the squatters of Oriente Province in Cuba.

Yet this recruitment of a 'tactically mobile peasantry' among the middle peasants and the 'free' peasants of peripheral areas poses a curious paradox. This is also the peasantry in whom anthropologists and rural sociologists have tended to see the main bearers of peasant tradition. If our account is correct, then—strange to say—it is precisely this culturally conservative stratum which is the most instrumental in dynamiting the peasant social order. This paradox dissolves, however, when we consider that it is also the middle peasant who is relatively the most vulnerable to economic changes wrought by commercialism, while his social relations remain encased within the traditional design. His is a balancing act in which his equilibrium is continuously threatened by population growth; by the encroachment of rival landlords; by the loss of rights to grazing, forest and water; by falling prices and unfavourable conditions of the market; by interest payments and foreclosures. Moreover, it is precisely this stratum which most depends on traditional social relations of kin and mutual aid between neighbours; middle peasants suffer most when these are abrogated, just as they are least able to withstand the depredations of tax collectors or landlords.

Finally—and this is again paradoxical—middle peasants are also the most exposed to influences from the developing proletariat. The poor peasant or landless labourer, in going to the city or the factory, also usually cuts his tie with the land. The middle peasant, however, stays on the land and sends his children to work in town; he is caught in a situation in which one part of the family retains a footing in agriculture, while the other undergoes 'the training of the cities'.[4] This makes the middle peasant a transmitter also of urban unrest and political ideas. The point bears elaboration. It is probably not so much the growth of an industrial proletariat as such which produces revolutionary activity, as the development of an industrial work force still closely geared to life in the villages.

Thus it is the very attempt of the middle and free peasant to remain traditional which makes him revolutionary.

If we now follow through the hypothesis that it is middle peasants and poor but 'free' peasants, not constrained by any power domain, who constitute the pivotal groupings for peasant uprisings, then it follows that any factor which serves to increase the latitude granted by that tactical mobility reinforces their revolutionary potential. One of these factors is peripheral location with regard to the centre of

[4] Germaine Tillion, *France and Algeria: Complementary Enemies*, p. 120–1, New York, Knopf, 1961.

State control. In fact, frontier areas quite often show a tendency to rebel against the central authorities, regardless of whether they are inhabited by peasants or not. South China has constituted a hearth of rebellion within the Chinese State, partly because it was first a frontier area in the southward march of the Han people, and later because it provided the main zone of contact between Western and Chinese civilization. The Mexican north has similarly been a zone of dissidence from the centre in Mexico City, partly because its economy was based on mining and cattle-raising rather than maize agriculture, partly because it was open to influences from the United States to the north. In the Chinese south it was dissident gentry with a peasant following which frequently made trouble for the centre; in the Mexican north it was provincial business men, ranchers and cowboys. Yet where there exists a poor peasantry located in such a peripheral area beyond the normal control of the central power, the tactical mobility of such a peasantry is 'doubled' by its location. This has been the case with Morelos, in Mexico; Nghe An province in Viet-Nam; Kabylia in Algeria; and Oriente in Cuba. The tactical effectiveness of such areas is 'tripled' if they also contain defensible mountainous redoubts: this has been true of Morelos, Kabylia and Oriente. The effect is 'quadrupled' where the population of these redoubts differs ethnically or linguistically from the surrounding population. Thus we find that the villagers of Morelos were Nahuatl-speakers, the inhabitants of Kabylia Berber-speakers. Oriente province showed no linguistic differences from the Spanish spoken in Cuba, but it did contain a significant Afro-Cuban element. Ethnic distinctions enhance the solidarity of the rebels; possession of a special linguistic code provides for an autonomous system of communication.

It is important, however, to recognize that separation from the State or the surrounding populace need not only be physical or cultural. The Russian and the Mexican cases both demonstrate that it is possible to develop a solid enclave population of peasantry through State reliance on a combination of communal autonomy with the provision of community services to the State. The organization of the peasantry into self-administering communes with stipulated responsibilities to State and landlords created in both cases veritable fortresses of peasant tradition within the body of the country itself. Held fast by the surrounding structure, they acted as sizzling pressure-cookers of unrest which, at the moment of explosion, vented their force outward to secure more living-space for their customary corporate way of life. Thus we can add a further multiplier effect to the others just cited. The presence of any one of these will raise the peasant potential for rebellion.

But what of the transition from peasant rebellion to revolution, from a movement aimed at the redress of wrongs, to the attempted overthrow of society itself? Marxists in general have long argued that peasants without outside leadership cannot make a revolution; and our case material would bear them out. Where the peasantry has successfully rebelled against the established order—under its own banner and with its own leaders—it was sometimes able to reshape the social structure of the countryside closer to its heart's desires; but it did not lay hold of the State, of the cities which house the centres of control, of the strategic non-agricultural resources of the society. Zapata stayed in his Morelos; the 'folk migration' of Pancho Villa simply receded after the defeat at Torreon; the Ukrainian rebel Nestor Makhno stopped short of the cities; and the Russian peasants of the Central Agricultural Region simply burrowed more deeply into their local communes. Thus a peasant rebellion which takes place in a complex society already caught up in commercialization and industrialization tends to be self-limiting, and hence anachronistic.

The peasant Utopia is the free village, untrammelled by tax collectors, labour recruiters, large landowners, officials. Ruled over, but never ruling, peasants also lack any acquaintance with the operation of the State as a complex machinery, experiencing it only as a 'cold monster'. Against this hostile force, they had learned, even their traditional power-holders provided but a weak shield, though they were on occasion willing to defend them if it proved to their own interest. Thus, for peasants, the State is a negative quantity, an evil, to be replaced in short shrift by their own 'home-made' social order. That order, they believe, can run without the State; hence peasants in rebellion are natural anarchists.

Often this political perspective is reinforced still further by a wider ideological vision. The peasant's experience tends to be dualistic, in that he is caught between his understanding of how the world ought properly to be ordered and the realities of a mundane existence, beset by disorder. Against this disorder, the peasant has always set his dreams of deliverance, the vision of a *mahdi* who would deliver the world from tyranny, of a Son of Heaven who would truly embody the mandate of Heaven, of a 'white' Tsar as against the 'black' Tsar of the disordered present.[5] Under conditions of modern dislocation, the disordered present is all too frequently experienced as world order reversed, and hence evil. The dualism of the past easily fuses with the dualism of the present. The true order is yet to come, whether through miraculous intervention, through rebellion, or both. Peasant anarchism and an apocalyptic vision of the world, together, provide the ideological fuel that drives the rebellious peasantry.

The peasant rebellions of the twentieth century are no longer simple responses to local problems, if indeed they ever were. They are but the parochial reactions to major social dislocations, set in motion by overwhelming societal change. The spread of the market has torn men up by their roots, and shaken them loose from the social relationships into which they were born. Industrialization and expanded communication have given rise to new social clusters, as yet unsure of their own social positions and interests, but forced by the very imbalance of their lives to seek a new adjustment. Traditional political authority has eroded or collapsed; new contenders for power are seeking new constituencies for entry into the vacant political arena. Thus when the peasant protagonist lights the torch of rebellion, the edifice of society is already smouldering and ready to take fire. When the battle is over, the structure will not be the same.

No cultural system—no complex of economy, society, polity and ideology—is ever static; all of its component parts are in constant change. Yet as long as these changes remain within tolerable limits, the over-all system persists. If they begin to exceed these limits, however, or if other components are suddenly introduced from outside, the system will be thrown out of kilter. The parts of the system are rendered inconsistent with each other; the system grows incoherent. Men in such a situation are caught painfully between various old solutions to problems which have suddenly shifted shape and meaning, and new solutions to problems they often cannot comprehend. Since incoherence rarely appears all at once, in all parts of the system, they may for some time follow now one alternative, now another and contradictory one; but in the end a breach, a major disjuncture will make its appearance somewhere in the system.[6] A peasant uprising under such circumstances, for any of the reasons we have sketched, can—without conscious intent—bring the entire society to the state of collapse.

[5] Emanuel Sarkisyanz, *Russland und der Messianismus des Orients: Sendungsbewusstsein und politischer Chiliasmus des Ostens,* Tubingen, J. C. B. Mohr, 1955.

[6] Godfrey and Monica Wilson, *The Analysis of Social Change,* Cambridge, Cambridge University Press, 1945.

30

CULTURE AND PERSONALITY

ANTHONY F. C. WALLACE

Anthropology's pivotal concern for the concept of culture ensures that its major focus will usually be on larger phenomena than the single individual. Yet there are substantial reasons, theoretical, methodological, and practical, why most anthropologists at some time concern themselves with individual behavior and why some anthropologists concentrate upon it. Most of the reasons for doing so are to be found in this overview of the theoretical placement of the field of psychological anthropology by one of its outstanding scholars.

Actually, the range of topics covered under the rubric of cultural anthropology is so broad, that no summary discussion can do justice to it. Various spokesmen have divided the field in different ways. A simple, nonexhaustive listing of major divisions would include at least five. To begin with, there are the various studies that may be loosely grouped under the heading of modal personality and national character, including the anthropological use and application of the now considerable number of personality tests and inventories. A second division might include cross-cultural studies of what may loosely be termed normal and abnormal behavior and these blend imperceptibly into medical anthropology, traversing the area of psychiatric anthropology. This area, too, may be characterized by use of tests, including those that attempt to get at what is called aptitude and intelligence. A third area is occupied by studies of enculturation in all its multiple phases. It is here that contributions are made to our understanding of child-rearing, cultural variations in expectations of childhood and adolescence, and similar social psychological phenomena. A fourth area comprises a major cluster of theoretical problems having to do with the ontological character of such concepts as "individual human being," "personality," and "culture," as well as their relationships. Finally, a fifth category of psychological anthropology can be comprised of a miscellaneous set of problems that might fall under one or more of the previous categories, but have sufficient weight or interest to attract considerable attention on their own. Thus in this portion of the field one may encounter the study of drug use and related transcendental mental states, the problems of the very old, or problems of thanatology, the new "science of death."

What the Wallace essay does for us falls mainly within the fourth of the categories just enumerated. Locating culture and personality studies in the broader field of anthropology, Wallace takes us through an orientation concerning problems of reductionism and reality into the consideration of a number of concepts that will be found basic to any further consideration of psychological anthropology.

SOURCE: *Culture and Personality,* 2nd edition, by Anthony F. C. Wallace. Chapter 1, "Introduction," pp. 3–38.

▼△▼△▼

In this short study of culture-and-personality, we shall be guided by two assumptions about the field of anthropology itself: first, it is the business of anthropology to develop a scientific theory of culture; and second, any theory that pretends to explain or to predict cultural phenomena must include noncultural phenomena in its formulations. Many of these noncultural phenomena can be subsumed under the general rubric of "personality."

The Purpose of This Study

In order to form a critical synopsis of any special branch of knowledge, the student must summarize certain major laws, principles, theories, or substantive discoveries that have current significance in that field of knowledge and must evaluate the internal logical and methodological structure of the field of knowledge itself. In the former task, the locus of reference is the "real world," the primary reality "out there," of observable phenomena that the scientist is attempting to describe, predict, and understand. In the latter task, the locus of reference is the scientific process itself by which these primary phenomena are being studied. It is one of the conspicuous features of modern science that major advances in substantive knowledge depend upon major advances in the self-awareness of the scientist. Only as the scientist comes to recognize the limitations imposed on his vision by the concepts he chooses to consider important and by the assumptions he makes about the logic of inference and the technique of observation, can he achieve the flexibility of approach required to solve new problems.

In anthropology, more than in any of the other social sciences, the need for self-evaluation is now especially acute. Anthropologists have only lately begun to realize that new ethnographic description, like daily weather reporting, is an endless task. There is not a finite number of cultures, which, once described, will stay fixed forever on some *scala culturae*. Culture change is constant, ubiquitous, and only moderately predictable; the ethnographic inventory will never be complete and will always have to be supplemented by ethnographic monitoring. Thus the problem for the theoretical anthropologist has shifted from the Linnaean classification of cultures and their aspects on a temporal or geographic continuum to the discovery and analysis of the laws of cultural process. These laws, furthermore, are recognized by most investigators to involve the dynamics not merely of cultural entities, but of ecological, demographic, physiological, and psychological entities as well. It is about as meaningful to claim that "culture must be explained in terms of culture," leaving out biological and psychological levels of explanation, as to assert that "life must be explained in terms of life," without reference to chemistry and physics.

Culture-and-personality is thus significant in the field of cultural anthropology because it is concerned with certain aspects of the theory of culture process, including the intergenerational transfer of culture ("enculturation" or socialization), culture change, and the institutionalization of modes of coping with individual diversity. Culture-and-personality is least significant in the monitoring of specific cultures, since a good ethnography permits far more accurate prediction of specific behavior than does any national character study. Its raison d'etre resides in the fact that it systematically takes account of noncultural data in explaining and predicting cultural phenomena.

But while the strategic importance of culture-and-personality is great, it has not inspired universal confidence among anthropologists. To many people (including the writer), it has often seemed "soft" in logical structure and in research method. This failure to gain acceptance commensurate with its pretensions is partly owing to the insularity of the brand of psychology that it has chiefly used: namely, psychoanalytic theory. Despite the claim of Sigmund Freud, its creator, that psychoanalysis is based on biological knowledge, his disciples have so heavily emphasized the autonomy of psychological process that two-way bridges between dynamic psychology and physiology have been few. This has tended to reduce the natural affinity between culture-and-personality and the relatively "hard" sciences of neurology, general physiology, biochemistry, and experimental psychology. Personality theory, which emphasizes the emotions, has been somewhat insulated from the academic psychological core-tradition and its concern with perceptual, cognitive, and learning processes. A complementary difficulty has been the slowness with which physical anthropology itself (to which anthropologists in search of physiological knowledge might reasonably turn) has taken up the vast resources of the modern sciences of neurology, general physiology, biochemistry, psychopharmacology, and so on. A final obstacle has been the fact that most of those who have worked in culture-and-personality were trained, as graduate students, to be descriptive ethnographers, with only peripheral acquaintance with the other substantive fields to which we have referred, or with formal logic, mathematics, descriptive statistics, and the like. Thus, even with the best will in the world, culture-and-personality workers have been hampered in their efforts to advance the theoretical understanding of cultural processes because of a relative unfamiliarity with some of the necessary tools.

There is evidence that this unsatisfactory situation is now improving. The continuing popularity of interdisciplinary research, despite the common disillusionment that afflicts some of its overly enthusiastic practitioners, attests to the awareness of the need to approach theoretical problems on many levels simultaneously. Much of such research has become institutionalized beyond the project level in various institutes, research centers, seminars, and combined departmental programs. Participation in such activities has led many anthropologists to extend their training and interest to other fields and to incorporate into their own thinking the data and concepts of other disciplines. Eventually this process of ideological expansion hopefully will result in culture-and-personality training programs that require the student to take formal instruction in subjects such as physiology, symbolic logic and mathematics, and cognitive theory, as well as in descriptive statistics, dynamic psychology, and projective testing.

The present chapter is concerned with evaluating certain features of culture-and-personality as an intellectual system; the other five chapters of this study will present and appraise some of the salient themes of the descriptive and theoretical literature. Our evaluation of the field will not merely list major interests and then invoke the pious ideal of scientific rigor; we shall attempt to expose specific contradictions, inadequacies, and flaws, and to point out promising new avenues of attack, in the hope of arousing discussion and, ultimately, progress by interested students. The treatment may seem harsh in some cases, but the intention of criticism is not to destroy but to stimulate further growth.

Operational Discriminations Among Concepts

The most celebrated definition of culture is Edward Tylor's.

> Culture . . . is that complex whole which includes knowledge, belief, art, morals, law, custom, and any other capabilities and habits acquired by man as a member of society.[1]

If the word "personality" is substituted for "culture" in the above sentence and the phrase "the individual" for "man," it will serve as a passable definition of personality as well. But there are, of course, other definitions of varying levels of abstractness, each one emphasizing those dimensions of observation that are most appealing to its author. For instance, in a probabilistic mood, I suggested that culture be defined as:

> those ways of behavior or techniques of solving problems which, being more frequently and more closely approximated than other ways, can be said to have a high probability of use by individual members of society.

Personality, in this context, would be simply:

> those ways of behavior or techniques of solving problems which have a high probability of use by one individual.[2]

In a more idealistic mood, the writer has further suggested that culture can be thought of as the asymptote of individual behavior much as a formal system of thought like Euclidean geometry is approached but never realized by the sum of individual geometers' actual reckoning.[3] Usually the author of any such a definition has in mind some kind of observation by

[1] *Primitive Culture,* Vol. I, p. 1.

[2] "Individual Differences and Cultural Uniformities," p. 750.

[3] "Culture and Cognition."

which individual cultures or personalities are recognized, bounded, and properly described. The ethnographer may think, when he gives a definition of culture, of a long sequence of operations beginning with learning the language, taking photographs, talking to people, and watching what goes on and trying it himself, and fifteen years later ending up with intricate comparative analysis of recorded data by the use of some specific schema, based on a particular theoretical position. An archeologist has in mind ecological parameters, digging, certain types of durable material remains, classification, labeling, and analysis by an equally specific but different schema. A psychoanalyst, when he thinks of "personality," has in mind the characteristic individual shape of psychodynamic structures whose elements are oedipal conflicts, castration anxieties, imagos, mechanisms of defense, and so forth. The clinical psychologist, describing personality structure from Rorschach test data, is visualizing a bar graph, based on frequencies of such phenomena as allusions to color, line, texture, perspective, and movement, and is inferring such characteristics as introversion, sterotypy, imaginativeness, and self-control. Thus there is no one concept of culture, or of personality, that is universally agreed upon and is universally useful.

We do not propose to list a set of definitions of the words "culture" and "personality" and then, by some suitable criteria, to select the best. Nor shall we offer new definitions. The student should realize that dozens, if not hundreds, of respectable definitions exist. Most of them, unfortunately, are ontological: that is, they assert that culture or personality *is* such and such. And ontological definitions are the bane of science. They postulate Platonic essences, states of being in a realm of absolutes, about which argument may rage endlessly without any resolution but that of authority. Discussion of such definitions is sterile, as David Hume pointed out long ago in his famous assertion:

> If we take in our hand any volume . . . let us ask, Does it contain any abstract reasoning concerning quantity or number? No. Does it contain any experimental reasoning concerning matter of fact and existence? No. Commit it then to the flames: for it can contain nothing but sophistry and illusion.[4]

The more profitable procedure is to regard the words "culture" and "personality" as the names for indefinitely large numbers of different empirical operations. All of the operations under the rubric "culture" have in common certain broad and general features, as do those under the rubric "personality." An examination of textbooks and symposia concerning human personality will reveal, for instance, that a number of theories of personality dynamics and a bewildering variety of observational techniques are employed by dozens of authorities: projective tests, depth interviews, questionnaires, life histories, laboratory experiments, verbalized introspection, and so forth, and an infinitude of subject matters. And on these data various distinctive and stylized abstractive manipulations are performed, the results of which are treated as descriptive of various traits, forces, factors, vectors, structures, and so on, in many different arrangements. Similarly with materials on culture: informant interviews, participant observation, film strips and photographs, tape-recorded texts, published literature, censuses, maps, material objects, and so on, are collected and then subjected to various abstractive and analytical procedures, the products of which are regarded as constituting an ethnographic description. Obviously, whatever culture "is" and whatever personality "is," the empirical operations by which they are described vary, depending on both the observer and the situation of his observations.

It is possible, however, to discriminate between the words "personality" and "culture"

[4] *Enquiry Concerning Human Understanding,* Sect. XII, Pt. 3.

and others relevant to this area of inquiry and to describe their relationship in terms of certain operational characteristics. Three dimensions are particularly relevant: the number of persons observed directly or indirectly, the number of kinds of behavior observed, and the level of abstraction achieved by various analytic and synthetic operations. All three dimensions of variation, furthermore, are to be considered under a constant condition: namely, that the observations are made of individuals within the boundaries of a specified population at a given time. The semantic relationships can best be represented in tabular form. First, we shall consider only the first two dimensions, of number of individuals and number of behavioral categories observed, allowing level of abstraction to vary. Table I [5] represents the operational differentiation of several terms by number of individuals and by number of behavioral categories.

The contents of Table I (and the meaning of the expression "equivalence structure") can perhaps best be illuminated by a series of nine illustrations, corresponding to the nine cells of Table I on page 378.

CELL 1. We observe that an old American Indian man, who lives alone in a small house on a reservation where we are staying, whenever he leaves the house (to walk to the general store or to visit relatives or for whatever reason), props a stick of wood against the lockless door. On being asked why he does this, he says, "It is a sign to people that I am away and that they should not enter." Without any further information about this type of behavior, we temporarily regard it as a personal *habit.*

[5] This table is an amplification of a smaller schema devised in manuscript by Theodore Graves to illustrate the meaning of several sociopsychological terms by reference to the concepts of behavior potential, expectancy, and reinforcement value. It is derived from his work with Dr. Julian Rotter on social learning. See Julian B. Rotter, *Social Learning and Clinical Psychology* (Englewood Cliffs, N.J.: Prentice-Hall, 1954).

CELL 2. On further inquiry, we find that a dozen of our acquaintances on this reservation follow the same practice when they leave the house empty: they prop a stick of wood, or a broom, against the door. They all say, on inquiry, that it is a sign of the occupant's temporary absence and of his wish that no one enter. Some aver that almost everyone on the reservation does this. We conclude that putting a stick against the door is a *custom* in this community, regularly followed by many persons when they leave a dwelling temporarily empty. Comparing notes later with another anthropologist, we learn that the same custom is practiced on a number of reservations in the area, and we begin to refer to it as a *culture trait* with an unknown distribution.

CELL 3. Although we are unable to make inquiry in every household in the community, we are told by some of our informants that almost everyone on the reservation props a stick against the door when leaving the house. We consider that it is likely that this custom is also a cultural *universal* on this reservation, but hesitate to make the claim categorically because of the difficulty and expense of even the attempt to demonstrate universality in the field.

CELL 4. Our curiosity is now piqued. We come from a city in which the custom is to lock all doors and windows when the house is empty and, if the absence is to be lengthy, to leave some sign (such as a burning light or the absence of accumulated mail) that the house is occupied. The rationale usually given for doing this is the prevention of theft and vandalism. We note that the Indian custom draws attention to the owner's absence, rather than conceals it, and that the leaning stick of wood constitutes no barrier to entry, since the door is not locked. Several speculations occur to us: First of all, we feel sure that the absent owner is confident that his neighbors will not enter his house when a stick is propped against

TABLE I: CULTURE-AND-PERSONALITY TERMINOLOGY DIFFERENTIATED BY NUMBERS OF INDIVIDUALS AND OF BEHAVIOR CATEGORIES OBSERVED

1. *When one has observed:*
   one individual in a group,
   many individuals in a group,
   all individuals in a group,
2. *And the behavior observed is, in the language of this investigation, of:*
   one category (that is, a particular class of act, or sequence of acts, consistently performed in a class of situations),
   many categories, arranged in an equivalence structure,
   all those categories which exist in some equivalence structure,
3. *Then, depending on the abstractive operations, the statement of the observations will be a description of a:*

NUMBER OF INDIVIDUALS	NUMBER OF BEHAVIOR CATEGORIES: *One Category*	*Two or More Categories*	*All Categories*
One	habit, response, behavior potential, etc. 1	character trait, motive, complex, value, syndrome, etc. 4	mazeway, personality, psychobiological system, etc. 7
Two or More	culture trait, custom, role, alternative, specialty, etc. 2	relationship, institution, ritual, theme, etc. 5	subculture, status-personality, etc. 8
All	culture trait, custom, role, theme, universal, etc. 3	relationship, institution, ritual, theme, focus, etc. 6	pattern, configuration, culture, national character, modal personality, etc. 9

the door; in other words, that he conceives of the two types of behavior as being equivalent and therefore expects that his house will be left alone if he plays the stick-propping role. Second, we suspect that any Indian who "stick-props" will probably display certain other behaviors as well, which have in common a quality of confidence that explicit requests will be honored. Our interest in this possibility leads us back to our earlier informant, whose habit of stick-propping had first led us to the subject. We interview him at some length, not only on stick-propping, but on matters related to confidence in the granting of wishes. We learn that he does indeed expect personal requests, both to him and from him, to be fulfilled. He makes requests of us, once we get to know him, for transportation, for errands, for legal advice, and for gifts of food, tobacco, and even money. On the other hand, he freely accedes to our wishes that he spend time as an informant without pay, accompanies us in order to introduce us to others, shares his own limited resources without stint. We feel that, at least in contrast to most whites we know, he has a characterological *trait* of expectation of wish-granting, whether he be the wisher or the granter.

CELL 5. Indeed, as we come to know many people on the reservation, we find that this wish-granting expectancy trait is so common that we can call it a *theme* in the culture. We now observe that on several occasions, when we have gone with one or another of our informants to visit a house where someone can give us certain information, our guide will not bother to knock on a door against which a stick is propped, nor will he enter in order to look for or await the occupants. We are told several times, "You don't go into a house when a stick is propped against the door." We conclude that stick-propping and house-avoidance behaviors constitute complementary roles for many pairs of persons; the two behaviors are equivalent in the logician's sense that whenever, but only when, person A plays role a, person B will play role b. We begin to refer to this equivalence structure as an *institution*.

CELL 6. Inasmuch as we suspect, although we cannot demonstrate, that the complementary stick-propping and house-avoidance behaviors are universals, and inasmuch as this institution is only one expression of a more general theme of expectancy of wish-granting, we feel that we may now be dealing with an area of cultural *focus*. This hypothesized focus would fall on the development and maintenance of institutions that express the theme of expectancy of wish-granting. The pursuit of this hypothesis leads us to consider that wishes expressed in dreams are, indeed, historically known to have been the source of a number of cultural innovations, as for instance the cultural reforms sponsored by a religious prophet in the previous century. We observe also that many religio-medical secret societies, and even major political institutions, are said to have originated in dreams or dreamlike wishes.

CELL 7. Because we are now on good terms with the old man, we ask him whether he will tell us the story of his life, recount some of his dreams, and be a subject for several tests including the Rorschach and the TAT. Although he displays some discomfort, particularly about recounting dreams (which we expected), he feels that he must grant our wish. He excuses the indelicacy of asking for dreams on the grounds that we are whites, and white people have different customs; hence telling us his dreams is not the same thing as telling a neighbor. We thus obtain a large body of psychological materials. We regard the product of the analysis of this data as a description of the structure of his *personality*, since the statements made in this description are abstractions that we consider relevant to virtually all areas of his behavior.

CELL 8. One probable source of error in any general attribution of the modal personality description, derived by the procedures outlined for Cell 9, is the existence of sex, age, and other social differentials in the sample. Wishing to avoid the possibility of an unwary reader's attributing the modal personality type to subgroups where personality norms actually differ significantly from the modal type, we construct separate modal types for males and females, for children, active adults, and inactive ("old") adults, and for the two major ethnic groups that compose the population (approximately one-third of the tribe are sixth-generation immigrant refugees from another culture area). This refinement of the analysis reveals that there are indeed significant differences among the modal types constructed for age, sex, and ethnic subgroups within the population, and between some of these subtypes and the general type. This discovery of distinctive *status personalities,* which correspond roughly with the *subcultures* of distinctive social subgroups, does not invalidate the modal personality type characteristic of the population as a whole, of course, since its definition involved specification of its relative frequency within the population. But it makes possible much more exact understanding of the interpersonal dynamics of the society than dependence on knowledge of the general modal type would permit.

CELL 9. In addition to working with the old man, we have been obtaining similar, if less extensive, projective test data from a large number of persons on the reservation. Furthermore, with the help of several excellent informants and of our own day-by-day observation, we have been filling in the content categories of the *Outline of Cultural Materials.* We do not analyze these large bodies of data carefully in the field, but on our return to the University we work with them and produce from the projective test data a description of the *modal personality structure* of the population and, from the ethnographic data, a sketch of the *culture.*

The careful student will note, in the foregoing illustrations and in the table, that there is a certain arbitrariness in the decision to regard the product of some observation as belonging to the first, second, or third column. This arbitrariness results because, although the same category of overt behavior may be described in terms of either culture or personality, what constitutes a single category (or class) of behavior will depend on the concern of the investigator. In one study, a number of things that a mother does in relation to her offspring may be construed as a large number of more particular behaviors—such as feeding, cleaning, fondling, and so on—each of which is assignable to column 1. In this case, "the mother role" will operationally fall within column 2. This should not concern the student, however, since the important thing is not to construct an absolute classification of constructs but to specify their operational relationship within any given investigation.

Another source of ambiguity is the fact that each cell beyond 1 can contain constructs at varying levels of abstraction from the same body of primary observations. For example, in Cell 7, *mazeway* refers to the entire set of cognitive maps of positive and negative goals that an individual maintains at a given time. This set includes goals of self, others, and material objects, and of their possible dynamic interrelations. *Personality* covers the same territory, but on a higher level of abstraction, in which mazeway particulars are classified and grouped under various rubrics, such as the wish-fulfillment trait that we used in our illustration, a hysterical syndrome, or whatever. The relations among the constructs in the third column of Table I may be represented by an expansion, as in Table II on page 383.

Some further discussion of the concept of mazeway may be appropriate here. Mazeway is to the individual what culture is to the group. Just as every group's history is unique, so every human individual's course of experience is unique. As a product of this experience, every human brain contains, at a given point of time, a unique mental image of a complex system of dynamically interrelated objects. This mental image—the mazeway—includes the body in which the brain is housed, various other surrounding things, and sometimes even the brain itself. It consists of an extremely large number of assemblages or cognitive residues of perception and is used by its holder as a true and more or less complete representation of the operating characteristics of a "real" world.

The mazeway may be compared to a map of a gigantic maze with an elaborate key or legend and many insets. On this map are represented three types of assemblage: (1) goals and pitfalls (values, or desirable and undesirable end-states); (2) the "self" and other objects (people and things); and (3) ways (plans, processes, or techniques) that may be circumvented or used, according to their characteristics, to facilitate the self's attainment or avoidance of values. For heuristic purposes, let us crudely categorize the content of the mazeway, recognizing that these categories (like the categories represented by different colors, shading, shapes, or thicknesses of line on a map) do not represent the only possible analytical divisions and relationships. The normal human mazeway, then, may contain representation of at least the following phenomena:

- I. Values (images of situations associated with pleasant or unpleasant feeling-tone)
  - A. Positive organic values
    - 1. Eating and drinking
    - 2. Sleeping, rest, relaxation, absence of discomfort or bodily tension
    - 3. Sexual satisfaction
    - 4. Optimal temperature maintenance
    - 5. Elimination of wastes
    - 6. Breathing
  - B. Positive symbolic values
    - 1. Testimonials of love, admiration, and respect from human objects
    - 2. Enactment of behavior-sequences satisfying "in themselves" (for example, a game or sport, conversation, meditation), or satisfying because they are instrumental to other values
    - 3. Presence of objects associated with organic and symbolic consummations (including human and nonhuman objects)
  - C. Altruistic values (images of situations in which the primary and secondary values of others are satisfied)
  - D. Negative values (associated with pain, discomfort, anxiety): the reverse of consummations outlined above
- II. Objects (images, with associations, of animate and inanimate objects)
  - A. Self
    - 1. Body image
      - a. surface of body
      - b. bodily adornment (clothing, cosmetics, perfume, and so forth)
      - c. organs and organ systems
      - d. prostheses (for example, false teeth, wooden leg)
      - e. defects or injuries (for example, "weak back," "shortness of breath")
    - 2. Self image
      - a. physiological processes (for example, digestion, sexual desire)
      - b. psychological process (nature of thoughts, dreams, emotions, and so forth)
      - c. personality (characteristic impulse and action patterns recognized in self)
      - d. evaluation (for example, good-bad, strong-weak) of parts or whole
      - e. conception of the soul
  - B. Human environment
    - 1. Particular persons
      - a. values of others
      - b. characteristics of behavior of others (in relation to self and to others)
    - 2. Classes of persons
      - a. particular classes defined (for example, on basis of residence, kinship, race, political affiliation, wealth, and so forth)
      - b. values and characteristics of classes (in relation to self and others)
    - 3. Sociocultural system as a whole
  - C. Nonhuman environment
    - 1. Animals
    - 2. Plants
    - 3. Tools and equipment ("material culture")
    - 4. Natural phenomena (for example, fire, weather, topography, and terrain)
    - 5. Natural system as a whole
  - D. Supernatural environment
    - 1. Particular supernaturals (for example, ancestors' spirits, deities, ghosts, demons, and so forth)
    - 2. Classes of supernaturals
    - 3. Supernatural processes (for ex-

ample, mana and taboo, witchcraft, and magic)

E. Statements of how entire sociocultural, self, natural, and supernatural system works

III. Techniques (images of ways of manipulating objects in order to experience desired end-states or values)

A. Techniques themselves (an extremely large number of interlocking and alternative statements of "what to do when . . .")

B. Priority systems among values (statements of which to enjoy first, or which to do to the exclusion of something else)

C. Priority systems among techniques (statements of which technique to use in order not to obstruct use of another, or the attainment of some other value)

These elements can be combined in an almost infinite variety of "imagined" action sequences.

The concept of mazeway thus embraces, in an organized fashion, several phenomena already generally recognized as common to human awareness: the "body image" [6]; "role," "self," "the other," "the generalized other" [7]; "behavioral environment" [8]; the "world view." [9] It is reminiscent of E. D. Tolman's "cognitive maps" [10] and of the topological concept of "life-space," and closely resembles certain concepts in cognitive theory: the "image" [11] and "plan." [12] And the mazeway concept borrows from traditional psychological notions of perception, association, "integration," and patterning of experience. Evidently, the mazeway includes in one field images of phenomena that, to many an outside "absolute" observer, would fall into conceptually distinct and sometimes incommensurable categories: personality, culture, society, natural environment, values, and so on. From the standpoint of the individual mazeway-holder, however, all these phenomena normally constitute one integrated dynamic system of perceptual assemblages. Within this system, self and nonself interact according to predictable (if more or less idiosyncratic) "laws," the description of which in generalized form is the business particularly of personality psychology and of dynamic psychiatry.

Reductionism and the Relation of Personality and Cultural Systems

Anthropologists sometimes like to think of culture as a closed system and regard most efforts to consider the relation between cultural and noncultural (for example, psychological and physiological) data as "reductionism." Leslie White has been the most systematic and eloquent exponent of this tendency, and consequently a discussion of White's position on this matter offers a direct way of coming to grips with the issue. We cannot help but agree with White's essential position—that culture is "real," that cultural evolution is a major subject matter of anthropology, and that the anthropologist should be interested in culture. But some of White's arguments in justification of this position seem to be not only unnecessary, but fallacious. There are, first of all, certain questionable ontological claims: on occasion he insists upon settling the question of what culture *is* by philosophical arguments ("A thing is what it is . . .") and dogmatic assertions that he *knows* what culture is and is not. Second, he explicitly regards the human organism and indeed all the physical universe as constant parameters without which culture could not exist, but which, once given, have no

[6] Schilder, *The Image and Appearance of the Human Body.*

[7] Mead, *Mind, Self, and Society.*

[8] Hallowell, *Culture and Experience.*

[9] Redfield, *The Primitive World and Its Transformations.*

[10] "Cognitive Maps in Rats and Men."

[11] Boulding, *The Image.*

[12] Miller, Galanter, and Pribram, *Plans and the Structure of Behavior.*

TABLE II: ROUTES AND LEVELS OF ABSTRACTION IN CULTURE-AND-PERSONALITY TERMINOLOGY

1. *If one has derived an approximation to a complete description of*
   one mazeway, or z
   one culture,
2. *Abstractive operations, involving classification of content into fewer, broader categories, will yield descriptions of, respectively,*
   personality, or
   national character.
3. *If one has derived an approximation to a complete description of*
   one mazeway, or
   one personality,
4. *Operations, involving addition of all individual cases to the pool of data, without altering the level of abstraction, will yield descriptions of, respectively,*
   culture, or
   modal personality structure.

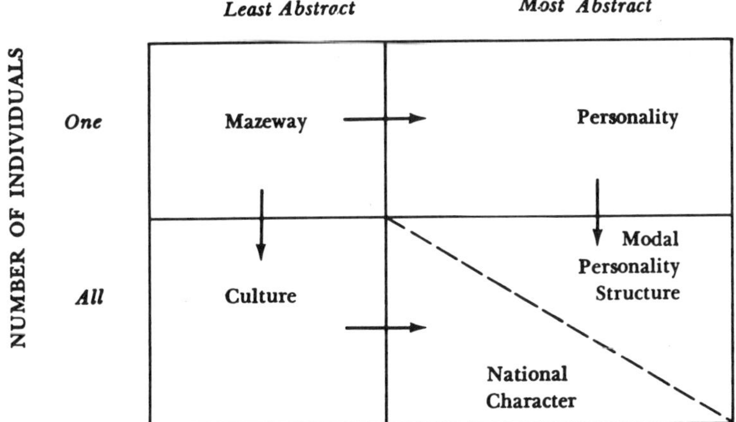

bearing on the variables involved in cultural process. "A consideration of the human organism, individually or collectively, is irrelevant to an explanation of the processes of culture change." [13] This position could only be successfully maintained if it were the case that "the human organism, individually or collectively," which White has already admitted is a parameter (albeit, in his view, a single-valued one) of cultural process, were indeed a changeless, uniform, absolute, univalued parameter. But the human organism, individually and collectively, is not uniform. It has been grossly variable, in physical evolution, synchronically in any population in response to genetic, ecological, and cultural circumstances, and in the individual in response to growth, accident, and disease. Indeed, the anthropologist must take the position that the processes of culture change (including the process by which human culture emerged) cannot be explained adequately without a consideration of the human organism, individually and collectively, and of that organism's physical environment, as well as of culture, per se. Any other position will inevitably yield a science of culture that is no science at all, but rather a sterile catalogue of cultural forms.

What sort of consideration of "the human organism" does culture-and-personality undertake in the interest of extending our knowledge of cultural process? First of all, the physiology

[13] "The Concept of Culture," p. 240.

of the organism is considered, insofar as it is relevant. The areas of relevance, however, are broad: endocrinology; neurophysiology, particularly of the limbic system; diet and nutrition; sickness and health; physical evolution; the general adaptation syndrome (of Selye); maturation, sexual differentiation, and aging; psychopharmacology (particularly in relation to narcotics and hallucinogenic agents like peyote). All of these, and more, are intimately related to both psychological and cultural processes. In regard to specifically psychological subjects a number of traditional areas are relevant: learning, perception, cognitive process, group dynamics, the structure of affect distribution (a conventional sense of "personality"), and existential phenomenology (the attempt to describe what another person perceives in categories isomorphic with those in which he perceives it). And, most importantly, the human organism is creative: it selects, rejects, seeks information, thinks, makes decisions, and ultimately modifies the systems of which it is a part. In addition to "interacting" externally with other components of social and other systems, the human organism does systematic internal work, the magnitude of which, even in a grossly physical sense, is measured by metabolic assays.

In culture-and-personality analysis, as was implied in the discussion of operational definitions, a society is usually considered to be a system on a higher level of organization than are the individual organisms, or even the social groups, that are the components of that society. There are available to the student of culture-and-personality two major, and to a degree antithetical, conceptions of the nature of the relation between cultural and personality systems; and at this point, perhaps, the dialectic should be presented, for it will sooner or later be translated into the student's research operations. These conceptions may be construed, respectively, as emphasizing the *replication of uniformity* and the *organization of diversity*. We shall discuss them at greater length later; for the moment, it will suffice to contrast the world view behind each.

The Replication of Uniformity

In many investigations, the anthropologist tacitly, and sometimes even explicitly, is primarily interested in the extent to which members of a social group, by virtue of their common group identification, behave in the same way under the same circumstances. For the sake of convenience in discourse, they may even be considered to have learned the "same things" in the "same cultural environment." Under such circumstances, the society may be regarded as culturally homogeneous and the individuals will be expected to share a uniform nuclear character. If a near-perfect correspondence between culture and individual nuclear character is assumed, the structural relation between the two becomes nonproblematical, and the interest of processual research lies rather in the mechanisms of socialization by which each generation becomes, culturally and characterologically, a replica of its predecessors. This viewpoint is particularly congenial to the world view associated with dynamic psychology, ultimately based on Freud's psychoanalytic theories but modified by conceiving the personality to reflect faithfully the culture in which it was formed and not merely universal constants, such as the Oedipus conflict and the stages of psychosexual maturation. The sense of tragedy implicit in this world view is, as everyone knows, very different from that which preceded it. From the days of the Greeks to the Industrial Revolution, Western man had, most commonly, conceived of the essence of tragedy as lying in the inevitability of sin, that is, of sacred crime, the intentional or unintentional violation of "the Law." Different as the Greek plays are from the Christian gospels, they agree on one theme: sin is unavoidable. Beginning with Freud, and increasingly with his successors, the inevitable tragedy of man's situation was seen not as sin, but as the conflict of wishes, in themselves neither evil nor good, and often growing from contradictions inherent in the person's culture. Thus, to the student who emphasizes the replication of uniformity, the point of tragic concern is the fate of those whose cultures, internally rent with contradictions, unavoidably instill painful conflict.

The Organization of Diversity

In other investigations, it is sometimes more interesting to consider the actual diversity of habits, of motives, of personalities, of customs that do, in fact, coexist within the boundaries of any culturally organized society. When the fact of diversity is emphasized, the obvious question must immediately be asked: how do such various individuals organize themselves culturally into orderly, expanding, changing societies? When the process of socialization is examined closely, it becomes apparent that, within the limits of practical human control and observation, it is not a perfectly reliable mechanism for replication. And culture, far from being, with the one exception of recent Western civilization, a slowly changing, sluggish, conservative beast, appears to be a turbulent species, constantly oscillating between the ecstasies of revitalization and the agonies of decline. Culture shifts in policy from generation to generation with kaleidoscopic variety and is characterized internally not by uniformity, but by diversity of both individuals and groups, many of whom are in continuous and overt conflict in one subsystem and in active cooperation in another. Culture, as seen from this viewpoint, becomes not so much a superorganic entity, but policy, tacitly and gradually concocted by groups of people for the furtherance of their interests, and contract, established by practice, between and among individuals to organize their strivings into mutually facilitating equivalence structures. Nor can the phenomenological world of an individual, or of a people, be assumed to be understood by the anthropologist, once he can predict the movements of their bodies; rather, he must recognize the possibility of a radical diversity of mazeways that have their orderly relationship guaranteed not by the sharing of uniformity, but by their capacities for mutual prediction.

From this organization-of-diversity viewpoint grows a different sense of tragedy. The unwanted inevitability is not sin, nor conflict, but loneliness: the only partly bridgeable chasms of mutual ignorance between whole peoples and the failures of understanding between individuals. A modicum of this loneliness would appear to be as irreducible in interpersonal relations (including the relation of the anthropologist to his subjects) as is the complementarity of perceptions in physical observation.

The Psychic Unity of Human Groups

One of the most hoary assumptions of the uniformitarian viewpoint is the belief that a society will fall apart and its members scatter if they are not threaded like beads on a string of common motives. Numerous sources may be quoted that attest to the "common thread" belief. Thus Aberle, Cohen, Davis, Levy, and Sutton [14] in an essay on the functional prerequisites of a human society, include as prerequisites a "shared, articulated set of goals." Erich Fromm asserts that a nuclear character structure must be shared by "most members of the same culture" in order for the culture to continue; socialization must make people "want to act as they have to act." [15] Emile Durkheim's thesis that society depends for integration upon the "common sentiments" of its members is a similar view.[16] John Honigmann expresses the position in the plaintive assertion, "In any community, there must be some congruence between what

[14] "The Functional Prerequisites of a Society."

[15] In Sargant and Smith (eds.), *Personality*, p. 5.

[16] *The Elementary Forms of the Religious Life.*

different people do, believe, and feel, otherwise social order would be impossible."[17] Margaret Mead has carried the argument to the point where cultural heterogeneity is conceived as almost ipso facto pathogenic:

> in a heterogeneous culture, individual life experiences differ so markedly from one another that almost every individual may find the existing cultural forms of expression inadequate to express his peculiar bent, and so be driven into more and more special forms of psychosomatic expression.[18]

Social philosophers, less humane than the scientists quoted above, but equally disturbed by the problems of their societies, at times have found the "common motive" theme a congenial one and have used the threat of social disintegration and individual degeneration to justify draconian measures for the standardization of sentiments.

It is, however, impossible to demonstrate empirically that any social system is operated by individuals all driven by the same motives; indeed, the data of personality-and-culture studies, as well as clinical observation, show conclusively that a sharing of motives is not necessary to a sharing of institutions. But is cognitive sharing a functional prerequisite of society? Here we enter the domain of the ethnographer who may not wish to tread the spongy ground of motive-analysis, but who finds it both necessary and painless to make inferences from overt behavior about cognitive matters, such as the criteria for discrimination of kinsmen by terminological category, the substantive beliefs about the order of the cosmos, and the rules of procedure by which a shaman arrives at his differential diagnosis over a sick child. The minimum task of the ethnographer, of course, is simply to describe overt human behavior. "Description," in this minimum sense, is the formulation of a set of statements that will predict, for the ethnographer, what a class of subjects will do and say under various circumstances. Accordingly, any complete ethnographic statement will include a specification of both a configuration of circumstances and of a behavior sequence that a class of subjects produces (presumptively as a result of learning) whenever that configuration presents itself. Usually, the "circumstances" that elicit a certain behavior sequence on the part of one class of subjects will include the acts and utterances of another class. Therefore, most ethnographic descriptions primarily concern repetitive patterns of reciprocal interaction in which the behaviors of each class are the circumstance for the behaviors of the other class.

It has been sometimes assumed that such systems of reciprocal interaction, in which different classes of subjects play specialized roles, as well as general norms describing constant act-and-circumstance relations for a single class of subjects, require not merely a set of cognitive maps, but a uniformity of cognitive maps among the participants for their continued successful operation. For example, in their previously quoted essay on the functional prerequisites of a human society, Aberle, Cohen, Davis, Levy, and Sutton postulate the necessity of "shared cognitive orientations," as well as a "shared, articulated set of goals."[19] Yet what few formal attempts have been made, by techniques such as componential analysis, to define the cognitive maps necessary to culturally correct behaviors have demonstrated unambiguously that it is often possible for the ethnographer to construct several different maps, each of which will predict adequately the overt behavior of subjects. Let us therefore now ask the question directly: is it necessary that all participants in a stable sociocultural system have the same "map" of the system in order that they may select the correct overt behaviors under the various relevant circumstances?

[17] *Culture and Personality,* p. 220.

[18] "The Concept of Culture and the Psychosomatic Approach," p. 72.

[19] "The Functional Prerequisites of a Society."

1. Minimal Sociocultural Systems

A system may be defined as a set of variable entities (persons, objects, customs, atoms, or whatever) so related that, first, some variation in any one is followed by a predictable (that is, nonrandom) variation in at least one other; second, that there is at least one sequence of variations which involves all of the entities.

Let us define the properties of the least complex system that an ethnographer might describe. Such a system must satisfy the following minimum requirements: first, that two parties, *A* and *B*, the initiator and respondent, respectively, interact; second, that each completion of one sequence of interactions be followed, sooner or later, by a repetition of the same sequence. Representing the acts of *A* by the symbols a_i, those of *B* by the symbols b_j, and temporal relationship by the symbol →, to be read "is followed by," we assert that the simplest such system has the following structure:

$$a_1 \longleftrightarrow b_1$$

Since it is legitimate to regard the sense of the symbol →, "is followed by," as a reasonable interpretation of the logical relationship of material implication (whenever *x*, then *y*), we may refer to the structure $a_1 \leftrightarrow b_1$ as a *primary equivalence structure* (ES_1). In such a structure, whenever *A* does a_1, then (sooner or later) *B* does b_1; and whenever *B* does b_1, then (sooner or later) *A* does a_1.

Interaction structures of ES_1 type seem too simple to serve as useful models of the components of sociocultural systems. The *secondary equivalence structure* (ES_2), however, looks more interesting:

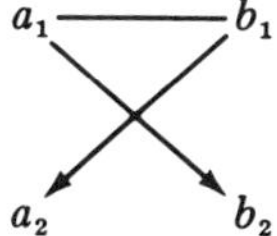

Here we may interpret acts a_1 and b_1 as instrumental acts and acts a_2 and b_2 as consummatory acts. The distinguishing feature of ES_2 is that the consummatory act of each party is released by (but is not necessarily exclusively conditional upon) the instrumental act of the other. The equivalence between a_1 and b_1 describes the repetitive nature of the interaction. A little ritual commonly found among the present inhabitants of the eastern coast of the United States (its wider distribution, in time and space, is unknown to me) provides a whimsical but culturally valid example of a secondary equivalence structure. When a child loses one of his baby teeth, he places the tooth under his pillow at night when he goes to bed; the parent, after the child has fallen asleep, comes and replaces the tooth with a coin ($a_1 \to b_1$). The child, on awakening, takes the coin and buys candy with it ($b_1 \to a_2$). (Possibly, he thereby loosens another tooth, if it is caramel candy!) The parent, meanwhile, after replacing the tooth with a coin, delightedly reports the transaction to his spouse ($a_1 \to b_1 \to b_2$). And with the next tooth he sheds, the child, who has observed that tooth-placing is followed by candy and who likes candy, repeats a_1 and thus continues the process ($b_1 \to a_1$). This simple custom is (for reasons that I shall mention later) not unlike the silent trade, so widely reported among primitive peoples. It may be diagrammed as follows:

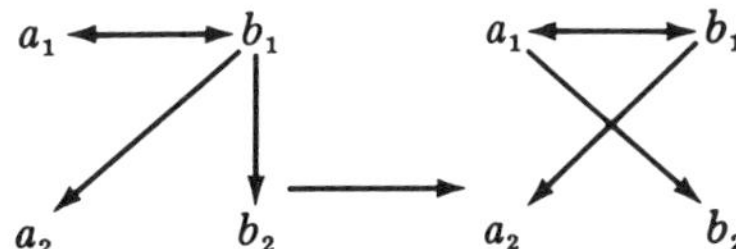

More complex structures, involving two parties, can obviously be constructed out of the same relationships. Thus a tertiary equivalence structure (ES_3) has the form:

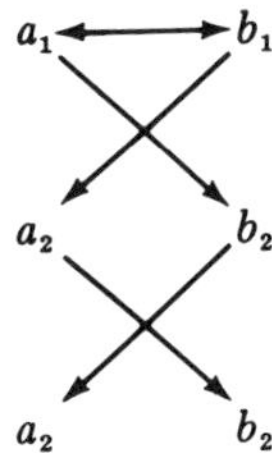

Structures of quaternary and still higher degree evidently can be made by a simple process of extension. Structures involving more than two persons also can be designed, although they are more difficult to represent on a plane surface. In general, we can consider that the two-party secondary equivalence structure, which we have suggested as the smallest practical model of a stable sociocultural system, is only one of a class of equivalence structures ${}^mES_n$, where $m > 1$ denotes the number of parties to the system, and $n \geq 1$ denotes the number of levels of equivalences $a_i \leftrightarrow b_j$ incorporated. It would be interesting to investigate in detail the logical properties of these systems and to speculate that, in principle, *any* sociosystem, involving m parties in repetitive interaction, can be described by some equivalence structure of the class ${}^mES_n$. However, these exercises would carry us beyond the purposes of this discussion.

We now conclude that the simplest possible social-interaction system that an ethnographer might describe has the form of a two-person secondary equivalence structure. This structure is, however, a model of what the ethnographer perceives; it is the ethnographer's cognitive map. We wish now to discover with what combination of maps, α_i and β_j, held by the two parties A and B, the ethnographer's model is compatible.

2. Minimal Cognitive Maps of Participants in Sociocultural Systems

At this point, we must make explicit two conventions that have been employed in the foregoing analysis. These are: first, that the ethnographer's map is valid ("true"); second, that the systems are "perfect," in the sense that there are no exceptions to the regularity of the relationships indicated by the symbols →. We know, of course, that in "real life" ethnographers make errors and that human behavior is not perfectly predictable. Although it would not invalidate the reasoning to introduce these qualifications (since a probabilistic logic would do just as well as the strict two-valued logic we are using), it would make the demonstrations more tedious. These conventions are now also applied to the cognitive maps maintained by the participants: we assume that the relationships are two-valued ("yes" or "no" rather than a probabilistic "maybe").

We have suggested already that a_1 and b_1 be regarded as "instrumental" acts and a_2 and b_2 as "consummatory." It is important to recognize that this classification is only a relative one; that is, a_1 is instrumental with respect to a_2, and b_1 with respect to b_2. In teleological terms, A does a_1 "in order to be able" to do a_2, and B does b_1 "in order to be able" to do b_2. But we do not actually need to invoke any panel of needs, drives, tensions, instincts, or whatever, the satisfaction of which makes an act ultimately consummatory, since we assume that the maps validly describe real events. It is therefore true by definition that neither A nor B will continue to participate in the system unless, first, each perceives that, *within the limits of the system*, his ability to perform his own consummatory act depends upon his partner performing his instrumental act; second, that when he performs his own instrumental act, its function is to elicit his partner's instrumental act; third, that he repeatedly performs his own instrumental act.

The simplest (but not the only) possible cognitive maps for A and B, respectively, which satisfy the foregoing requirements, are the following:

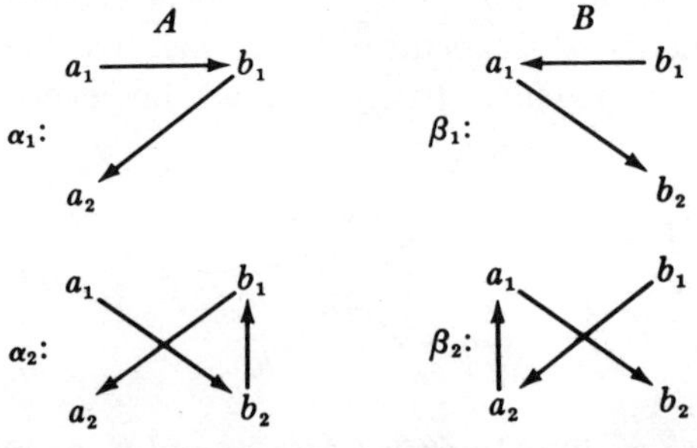

These maps are to be interpreted as follows:

α_1: A knows that whenever he does a_1, B will respond with b_1, and A will then perform a_2.

α_2: A knows that whenever he does a_1, B will respond with b_2 and then b_1, and A will then perform a_2.

β_1: B knows that whenever he does b_1, A will respond with a_1, and B will then perform b_2.

β_2: B knows that whenever he does b_1, A will respond with a_2 and then a_1, and B will then perform b_2.

Each possible combination of these cognitive maps will yield a structure that is identical with, or logically implies, ${}^2ES_2$. Thus:

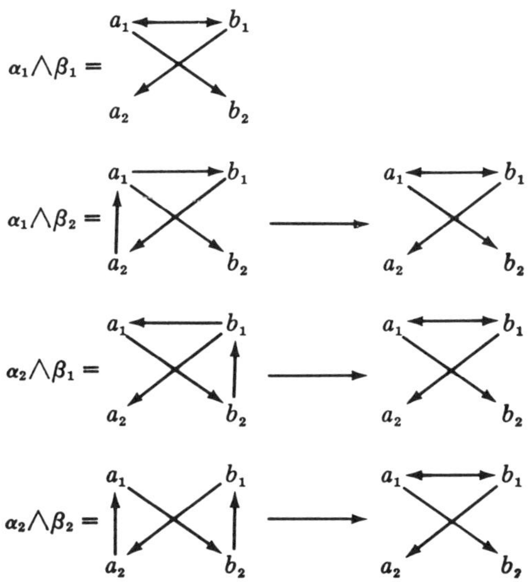

$\alpha_1 \wedge \beta_1 =$

$\alpha_1 \wedge \beta_2 =$

$\alpha_2 \wedge \beta_1 =$

$\alpha_2 \wedge \beta_2 =$

We have now demonstrated that at least four cognitive maps, in addition to the ethnographer's, are compatible with the continued existence of a simple system of social interaction. The four maps of the participant parties can exist in four possible combinations, each of which sums to ${}^2ES_2$ or to a form that implies ${}^2ES_2$. Evidently, it is not *necessary* that both participants share the same map; and we have answered our original question: is cognitive sharing a functional prerequisite of society?

3. How Many Combinations of Cognitive Maps Will Yield the Secondary Equivalence Structure?

Even a casual comparison of the ethnographer's model with the four participants' models will suggest that a number of unique cognitive maps are possible which are different from, but contain, either or both of the A structures and/or either or both of the B structures. The basic model of ${}^2ES_2$ itself, for instance, contains both α_1 and β_1; ${}^2ES_2$ added to itself will yield ${}^2ES_2$; ${}^2ES_2$ added to α_1 will yield ${}^2ES_2$; ${}^2ES_2$ added to β_1 will yield ${}^2ES_2$, and so on. Let us therefore inquire, out of curiosity, just how many unique combinations of α-maps and β-maps there are where the sum equals, contains, or implies ${}^2ES_2$, with the proviso that each component α-map include either or both α_1 and α_2, and each component β-map include either or both β_1 and β_2. The number is well over a million. The number of unique α-maps is over a thousand and the number of unique β-maps is also over a thousand. Thus it is apparent that even when one considers extremely simple systems, a very large number of different cognitive maps of such systems are, for all practical purposes, interchangeable as system components.

What are the implications of these considerations? Evidently cognitive sharing is not *necessary* for stable social interaction. The two parties to systems of form ${}^2ES_2$ do not need to know what the "motives" of their partners in the interchange are. Indeed, they need not even correctly know *who* their partners are. In the tooth exchange ritual alluded to earlier, the child at first believes that a good fairy, whom he never sees, takes the tooth, for motives unexplained, and leaves the coin. This relationship is not unlike the silent trade. Later, the child may know that the parents are responsible, but he does not "let on" from a benevolent wish not to spoil his parents' fantasies about *his* fantasies. One or the other or both of the parties may be able to perform his consummatory act *only* after the partner performs his instrumental act; or other circumstances may also permit it.

But, the advocate of togetherness may argue, whether or not it is necessary that *all* members of society share all cognitive maps, they must share at least *one*. Such an argument, however, is not convincing. I know of no criteria that would specify the one map all members of a given society should share. One cannot argue empirically that all members of all societies are *known* to share at least one map, for the data to support such an argument do not exist. And merely demonstrating that some defined group of human individuals, or even all the members of some one society, share a particular map, is irrelevant to the discussion. (Such a society would have to be peculiarly simple and at the same time clairvoyant.) Two or more parties may indeed share a common cognitive map, but such a circumstance is, in a sense, wasteful, since at least two, and therefore all, of these maps must be larger than the minimally necessary ones. And only when each actor is cognizant of the other's "motive" (consummatory act), can the actors' cognitive maps be identical and still contribute to system maintenance.

It may appear to be a bleak prospect to consider that human beings characteristically engage in a kind of silent trade with all their fellow men, rarely or never actually achieving cognitive communality. Indeed, one may suspect that the social sciences have nourished the idea of cognitive sharing for so long, just because the world may seem rather a lonely place if the wistful dream of mutual identification is abandoned. Still another anxiety may now arise: for an implication of our researches is that individuals can produce a sociocultural system that is beyond their own comprehension. If, for instance, α_k is as complex a map as *A* can maintain, and β_l is as complex as *B* can maintain, their sum (*unless* they are identical) will be a structure *containing* $^2ES_2$, but in its totality *more* complex than one or both of them can grasp. If one of these parties is an anthropologist, who is attempting to construct a general *ES* that he will call "culture," then, alas, he may be a participant-observer in a sociocultural system that is more complex than he can describe ethnographically! Even if he cannot describe the system fully, he must be able to construct a cognitive map that is more complex than that of any of his subject's.

But perhaps the most significant point to be made is a relatively practical one, growing out of concerns with the application of anthropological knowledge to psychiatric research. A principal problem for the research anthropologist, in a mental hospital setting, is to explain how a person comes to be extruded from his sociocultural system. Is it because he is a "deviant," one whose cognitive maps are not shared by other members of the community? Or is it because he has been unable to maintain stable cognitive maps sufficiently complex for them to sum to an equivalence structure with those of his fellows? From the viewpoint of the organization of diversity, it would appear that the most generally adequate explanation is the latter: particularly in a large and complex society, equivalence structures normally will be the articulation of uniquely private cognitive worlds. The measure of individual value will not be conformity, but complementarity.

4. Is Cognitive Nonsharing a Functional Prerequisite of Society?

Finally, we ask whether the fact that cognitive sharing is not a *necessary* condition of society does not mask an even more general point. Not only *can* societies contain subsystems, the cognitive maps of which are not uniform among participants, but they *do*, in fact, invariably contain such systems. Ritual, for instance, is often differently conceptualized by viewers and performers; public entertainment similarly is variously perceived by professional and audience; the doctor (or shaman) and patient relationship demands a mutual misunderstanding. Even in class and political relationships, complementary roles (as, for instance, between the holders of "Great" and "Little" Traditions) are notoriously difficult to exchange. Administrative personnel and leaders generally must understand the system on a "higher" level of synthesis than their subordinates, a level that demands a different, because more abstract, cognitive map. Indeed, we now suggest that human societies may characteristically *require* the nonsharing of certain cognitive maps among participants in a variety of institutional arrangements. Many a social subsystem simply will not "work" if all participants share common knowledge of the system. It would seem therefore that cognitive *non*-uniformity may be a functional desideratum of society (although, by the criteria we have used above, it is certainly not a formal prerequisite any more than is uniformity). For cognitive nonuniformity subserves two important functions: (1) it permits a more complex system to arise than most, or any, of its participants can comprehend; (2) it liberates the participants in a system from the heavy burden of learning and knowing each other's motivations and cognitions.

If sociocultural organization is not necessarily dependent upon a community of motives or cognitions, then by what psychological mechanism is it achieved and maintained? This mechanism is evidently the perception of partial equivalence structures. By this is implied the recognition—as the result of learning—that the behavior of other people under various circumstances is predictable, irrespective of knowledge of their motivation, and thus is capable of being predictably related to one's own actions. Evidently, groups, as well as individuals, can integrate their behaviors into reliable systems by means of equivalence structures, without extensive motivational or cognitive sharing. The equivalence structure model should be congenial to that tradition in social anthropology which interests itself in the relations between organized groups. Thus reciprocal interactions between the representatives of geographically separate groups as alien as American Indian tribes and colonial or state governments have proceeded for centuries, with only minimal sharing of motives or understanding, on a basis of carefully patterned equivalences. Similar observation might be made of the relations between castes, social classes, professional groups, kin groups, factions, parties, and so forth. In no case is it necessary that a basic personality or a basic cognitive framework be shared, but it is necessary that behaviors be mutually predictable and equivalent.

We may say that as any set of persons establish a system of equivalent behavioral expectancies, an organized relationship comes into existence. Such a system of equivalent mutual expectancies may be termed an *implicit contract*, in the general sense of the word "contract." In this sense, and not in the sense of any formal document, society is, as Rousseau intuited, built upon a set of continually changing social contracts that are possible only because human beings have cognitive equipment adequate to their maintenance and renewal. Culture can be conceived as a set of standardized models of such contractual relationships, in which the equivalent roles are specified and available for implementation to any two parties whose motives make their adoption promising. The relationship is based not on a sharing, but on a complementarity of cognitions and motives. Marital relationship, entry into an age grade, the giving of a feast—in all such contracts the motives may be diverse, but the cognitive expectations are standardized. Thus the relationship between the driver of a bus and the riders is a contractual one, involving specific and detailed mutual expectancies. The motives of drivers and riders may be as diverse as one wishes; the contract establishes the system. From this standpoint, then, it is culture that is shared (in the special sense of institutional contract) rather than personality, and culture may be conceived as an invention that makes possible the maximal organization of motivational and cognitive diversity. This it is able to accomplish because of the human (not uniquely human, but preeminently so) cognitive capacity for the perception of systems of behavioral equivalence.

Fallacies, Fads, and Specializations

The progress of research in culture-and-personality is, at times, hampered by the common use of fallacious metaphors and by faddish enthusiasms for particular jargons and techniques. But it is important to distinguish between fad and fallacy, on the one hand, and legitimate specialization, on the other.

Conspicuous examples of the fallacious metaphor are the frequently mishandled words "internalization," "impact," and "mold." It is sometimes said that personality *is* (ontologically) culture "internalized" in the individual; that culture change has an "impact" on the individual; that culture "molds" the individual. Such expressions, and theoretical formulations based on them, are meaningless in any literal sense. As Alfred Radcliffe-Brown once remarked, "To say of culture patterns that they act upon an individual . . . is as absurd as to hold a quadratic equation capable of committing a murder." As we observed in connection with systems analysis, culture and personality are constructs of different "logical type," in Bertrand Russell's sense; that is, the concept of a culture is a set of propositions about some of the same propositions which are included within the concept of one or more of the personalities within the society. Thus to use transitive metaphors like "internalize," "impact," "mold," and so on, to describe the relation between culture and personality, is precisely comparable to claiming that a circle has an "impact on," "molds," the points that constitute it, or that the points are "internalizations" (or "expressions," or "phrasings," or "transforms") of the equation describing the circle.

The obverse of the "internalization" fallacy is the "statistical" fallacy, which offers an enumeration of the properties of individual persons as if it were a description of a social or cultural system, without any demonstration that a nonrandom relationship obtains among the dimensions considered. Such statistical "structures" are mere archival material unless a systematic relationship among the dimensions can be demonstrated.

Fads in culture-and-personality, as in other fields of endeavor, are sometimes difficult to distinguish from new specializations. To some, the projective techniques have been a fad, now happily passing; to others, they appear as legitimate, highly specialized tools that will be continuously refined and employed by a few individuals concerned with particular kinds of problems for a very long time. The fad for projective techniques saw them being used for a time uncritically, as novelties, by dozens of field workers, often in inappropriate situations. Now that the fad stage has worn off and sober reflection has begun, the projective techniques and other test and measurement devices are being used by fewer but better-trained persons for the special tasks to which they are suited, or to which they may be adapted; and we may expect continuous improvement of the tools themselves and of their interpretation as this specialization continues.

A similar observation may be made with respect to a number of conceptual schemes and research procedures "borrowed" from other disciplines. Psychoanalysis, for instance, is a highly specialized branch of psychiatry, particularly successful in dealing with the character disorders and symptomatic neuroses of upper- and middle-class people who can afford and will accept protracted verbal treatment. Much of psychoanalytic theory has been, in one form or another, used by culture-and-personality workers. For a time, it was something of a fad to sprinkle psychoanalytic jargon over the pages of ethnographic reports, like the water of baptism, in order to make them read like personality descriptions. This faddish misuse of psychoanalytic theory, by both psychiatrists and anthropologists, is waning; what remains is a specialized body of concepts and research techniques that will continue to be used wherever profitable by properly trained men. Comparable remarks may be made about the utility of communication theory, reinforcement learning theory, the life history, and other special techniques and bodies of knowledge. Their incorporation into anthropological thought is regularly accompanied by inflated claims that they are universal theoretical or methodological solvents, and students flock to try them out. Enthusiasm wanes when they are recognized as being useful only in solving particular kinds of problems, and they assume the humbler but more enduring role of specializations.

References

ABERLE, DAVID F., A. COHEN, A. DAVIS, M. LEVY, and F. SUTTON, "The Functional Prerequisities of a Society," *Ethics*, 60 (1950), 100–111.

BOULDING, KENNETH E. *The Image*. Ann Arbor: University of Michigan Press, 1956.

DURKHEIM, EMILE. *The Elementary Forms of the Religious Life*. London: Allen & Unwin, n.d.

HALLOWELL, A. IRVING. *Culture and Experience*. Philadelphia: University of Pennsylvania Press, 1955.

HONIGMANN, JOHN J. *Culture and Personality*. New York: Harper & Row, 1954.

MEAD, GEORGE H. *Mind, Self, and Society*. Chicago: University of Chicago Press, 1934.

MEAD, MARGARET. "The Concept of Culture and the Psychosomatic Approach," *Psychiatry*, 10 (1947), 57–76.

MILLER, GEORGE, E. GALANTER, and K. PRIBRAM. *Plans and the Structure of Behavior*. New York: Holt, Rinehart and Winston, 1960.

REDFIELD, ROBERT. *The Primitive World and Its Transformations*. Ithaca, N.Y.: Cornell University Press, 1953.

SARGANT, S. STANSFELD, and MARIAN W. SMITH (eds.). *Culture and Personality*. New York: Viking Fund, 1949.

SCHILDER, PAUL. *The Image and Appearance of the Human Body*. London: Kegan Paul and Trench, Trubner, 1935.

TOLMAN, E. D. "Cognitive Maps in Rats and Men," *Psychological Review*, 55 (1948), 189–208.

TYLOR, EDWARD B. *Primitive Culture: Researches into the Development of Mythology, Philosophy, Religion, Language, Art and Custom*. 2 vols. New York, 1874.

WALLACE, ANTHONY F. C. "Culture and Cognition," *Science*, 135 (1962), 351–357.

———. "Individual Differences and Cultural Uniformities," *American Sociological Review*, 17 (1952), 747–750.

WHITE, LESLIE. "The Concept of Culture," *American Anthropologist*, 61 (1959), 227–251.

31

URBAN ANTHROPOLOGY

PETER C. W. GUTKIND

Anthropologists have always taken an interest in modern industrial society as, for example, scrutiny of the earliest issues of the *American Anthropologist,* published almost a century ago, will prove. Nevertheless, it is pointless to deny that the focus of anthropological studies has generally been elsewhere—on primitive or folk societies. Indeed, the orientation of cultural anthropology toward certain subjects and away from others is probably the result of certain political and economic forces in western culture, and more is said of this by William S. Willis, Jr., in selection 38.

In the article below, Peter Gutkind does not go deeply into the reasons for previous concentrations of interest in anthropology, but he sounds a clear warning about the likely effects of maintaining such foci. He is distressed that continuation of past emphases will produce increasingly sterile anthropology, until, as he foresees, the discipline itself may be discarded from even academic use on the grounds of irrelevance, if not worse. His vision, however, sees salvation for the field in a turn to more and more studies of the critical phenomena of modern life, none being more essential than those that come to grips with the processes and problems of urban life and urbanization. Making this suggestion, Gutkind reviews some of the accomplishments already made in this field, while also sketching some theoretical and methodological pitfalls.

I think it fair to indicate that Gutkind's view of the state of development of the broad field of urban anthropology seems unnecessarily severe. Without in any way diminishing the contribution of those British social anthropologists so favorably mentioned in his essay, it should be possible to note that others have also helped clear the way. For example, several scholars have made contributions to our understanding of urban life and processes in various Asian locations, while in recent years increasing attention has been paid to United States cities, particularly the so-called inner-city areas. Furthermore, although little of the work has yet reached print, there is a substantial body of studies of squatting in Latin America and elsewhere.

Gutkind is right to try to shake us up. More than this, however, he indicates some of the present problems faced by anthropologists who seek to do field work in urban areas. Gutkind also presents some of the more promising leads that make the field of urban anthropology so interesting and such a magnet for younger anthropologists.

▼△▼△▼

Despite the fact that one of the major social transformations since the end of the second world war has been the movement of people from the rural to urban areas, social anthropologists working in Africa have, until recently, found themselves professionally encapsulated in the rural areas. The reason for their continued interest in the "tribal" community is partly historical—as Gluckman has put it—we were "reared on the rural tradition of the tribe," and partly that in a demographic sense Africa remains the least urbanized of the continents with less than 11 percent of the population resident, in varying degrees of permanence, in urban areas of 20,000 and over. Furthermore, the interests of the traditional social anthropologist are geared to the documentation and analysis of the basic principles which regulate social structure, social organization and the institutional arrangements which govern small-scale and, generally, preliterate or semi-literate groups. Information about these basic principles, it is argued, is vital to social science theory, which feeds on comparative data, and to our ultimate goal of being able to formulate general laws (although this might be too strong a term) about the

SOURCE: "Urban Anthropology: Creative Pioneer of Comparative Modern Social Anthropology—The African Case," *Proceedings of the Eighth International Congress of Anthropological and Ethnological Sciences,* Tokyo and Kyoto, Vol. 2 (1970):77–81. Reprinted by permission of the Science Council of Japan and author.

structure and organization of society. From the perspective of methodology, the social anthropologist is best equipped to work in small-scale societies. Research in larger scale societies has been left to sociologists although they have shown exceedingly little interest in contemporary Africa.

However, in more recent years some social anthropologists have begun to put down their roots in the complex societies of Asia, Europe and North America and, more so since early in the 1950's, in urban studies in Africa. Their reasons for doing so have ranged from recognition that all types of societies are intrinsically important to social anthropologists, to an awareness of the strong objections on the part of the new leaders of independent African nations to the traditional interests of social anthropologists. In at least one parliament in a newly independent African country social anthropologists have been strongly criticized. Where such objections have been expressed, social anthropologists have had no choice but to change their focus of interest, unless they were prepared to withdraw from active research in Africa. It is possible that a change of interest, either forced or by conviction, will salvage anthropology from the scrap heap of professional sterility to which it has been consigned not merely by African leaders but also by some students in training who insist that anthropologists should concern themselves more with what is called "the structure of social reality."

In this paper I hope to positively meet objections expressed by our critics, partly by wholeheartedly agreeing with certain new ideological and professional trends now evident in social anthropology, and partly by suggesting that urban anthropology can become the creative new core of modern comparative social anthropology (or comparative sociology if this conceptualization defuses the strong antagonism which the word anthropology generates in some people), while at the same time offering much scope to those whose interests continue to rest in rural society *provided* they are willing to test new propositions which would, I believe, lead to a reformulation and a redefinition of the concept of tradition in the context of incipient modernity—the hallmark of contemporary African society. I would also like to suggest, perhaps too dogmatically, that we accept the premise, at least experimentally, that traditional societies are nowhere to be found in Africa, at least not now. We are now dealing with various conditions and expressions of incipient "modernity." Thus urban anthropology begins with a new conceptual base line, designed to break the linkage between (pure) tradition and modernity, which is drawn from the specificity of modernity. I am saying no more than this: tradition operates only in a traditional context, if ever there was such a context in the Africa which clashed with the colonial powers, and that the context of personal, group and national life of contemporary Africa makes it meaningless to portray romantically an alleged condition which passed away long before the social anthropologist set foot on African soil.

If, as Daniel Lerner has suggested, the low-income world has opted for modernization, social anthropologists, along with other social scientists must first isolate and then concentrate on the relevance of those variables which are most closely linked to modernization. In my view the main variable is urbanization which is a new style of life based on a firm rejection, often ambiguously expressed, of rural ways. While it might be considered premature to suggest that urbanism as a way of life has become the sought after goal of a large number of Africans (or for that matter of the still rural-anchored people of Asia and Latin America), it would seem correct to suggest that the structure of African society, i.e. the modifications which have taken place particularly over the last thirty years, progressively reflect an urban-industrial-secular way of life. This assertion is given more precision when we remember that the percentage of Africans who are born in the towns, and the percentage of Africans who stay for ever longer periods in the urban areas, is steadily increasing. It is true that Ibadan, a city of over one million people, is described as a "city-village", but the fact remains that despite the agricultural base of many of the residents of Ibadan, they live in a city with a style of life which contrasts in many ways with village life. Oluwasanmi, writing about "The Agricultural Environment" of Ibadan, notes that:

> . . . the transition to urban industrialism has been more rapid in Ibadan than in any other area of Western Nigeria. Only a third of the male population is occupied in farming as compared with two-thirds of Western Nigeria as a whole. Even then, a significant proportion as [sic] the city farmers derive part of their cash incomes from working as part-time carpenters, bricklayers, traders, tailors, weavers and contractors. The increasing importance of non-agricultural occupations as sources of income for farmers is a measure of the economic transformation taking place in the large Yoruba urban centers.[1]

In South Africa, where over thirty percent of the African population live in towns, we can now describe and analyze the way of life of what Pauw has called "The Second Generation"—the urban born African.

While these trends are clearly documented, and some of the most theoretically relevant literature of urban anthropology has been produced by Africanists, the urban anthropologist need not and should not turn his back on what is taking place in the rural areas which are ever more closely linked to the towns through regional and national transformation. Inasmuch as the urban areas of Africa, and those of Asia and Latin America, are filled primarily by means of migration and translocation from the countryside, the urban anthropologist must, obviously, incorporate in his conceptualization the rural dimension which continues to be influential in the organization, behavior and outlook of a large number of African urban migrants. At the same time, the contemporary social anthropologist must avoid being trapped in the straight jacket of typological constructs which draw an abstract and sharp distinction between the rural and the urban world. Rather than being distinct entities, urbanite and ruralite have merged into a symbolic relationship of demonstrable closeness as each needs the other for individual and collective economic, social and political well-being. While a symbiosis of social equality has not been achieved between rural and urban segments, the rapid growth of towns in Africa, unequally weighed in favor of the primate city, is perhaps the most far reaching transformation taking place.

If this last statement is correct, then urban anthropology is likely to assume far greater importance than it does presently. It is important that we set out, as clearly as possible at this early stage, the areas of our interest, the kind of questions we might ask, and the conceptual and methodological approaches we might, experimentally, utilize. At the same time we should keep open every option to allow us to stray into fields not yet clearly charted by the urban anthropologist. This is particularly important as the urban anthropologist is likely to stray into other social science disciplines which approach urban studies with a greater degree of intellectual sophistication born of a longer interest in the history, development, structure and purpose of western towns and cities.

I believe that one of the most important "justifications" for the rapid development of urban anthropology is the opportunity which is provided to test and re-test a large number of theoretical propositions which anthropologists have developed over the years. Most of these propositions have reflected the anthropologist's interest in traditional society which, as I pointed out earlier, were only traditional to the social anthropologist. The facts of social change have not always found their rightful

[1] Mabogunje, A., et al. (eds.), *The City of Ibadan*, Cambridge University Press, 1967.

and significant place in these propositions. For example, the recent publications of a set of papers on the peoples of Africa, edited by Professor James Gibbs, makes virtually no mention in any chapter of the thrust of social transformation. The student of Africa is left with the clear impression of essentially static societies—of an enumeration of traits and social forms—although contemporary social theory does compel the writers to indicate the dynamic interaction of social institutions, behavior and ideas. Each one of the writers indicates how consensus and order are achieved, and goes on to suggest that social change and modernization unbalance the social order which, until social change became a force no longer to be ignored, had generally been viewed as in a state of a self-adjusting equilibrium. Social change, it is often argued, leads to stresses and strains and to a state of normlessness and breakdown which replaces the alleged coherence and homogeneity of a rurally-anchored group. The urban anthropologist has very successfully challenged this view as a result of recent fieldwork in urban Africa which explicitly indicates that urban systems are not amorphous and anomic entities; rather coherence, structure, purpose and rationality coalesce around variables which social anthropologists have not always associated with this potential. Of course, social anthropologists have long accepted the function of conflict in (traditional) African society. They have found it far more difficult, however, to accept the view that urban social organization provides the same institutional matrix which gives rise to a structured social order and provides for both individual and collective needs and objectives. Unlike those who have concentrated on exposing and interpreting the fabric of rural life, the urban anthropologist has no difficulty in fitting together those features of individual and collective behavior labeled as "exceptions" by an earlier generation of social anthropologists. Indeed had these researchers followed up these "exceptions" they might have arrived at a very different interpretation of what they conceived to be traditional societies. But, as we now realize, a good many social anthropologists were caught conceptualizing a narrow structuralism which left little room for in-depth analysis of that large body of behavior which reveals how eclectic and pragmatic much of it is, despite the alleged constriction imposed by participation in formally constituted corporate groupings. There was even less opportunity to pay attention to the diverse motivational basis of action which is a constant feature of any society. An insightful critique of the limitations which social anthropologists imposed on their observations, and which the student of urban Africa rejects, has recently been published by Van Velsen.

There are also other propositions which the urban anthropologist will be able to test in the course of research lying before him. For example, those social anthropologists who have worked in Africa have concentrated on documenting and analyzing in detail certain "core" institutions such as marriage and the family. It has not infrequently been asserted, and more often been strongly implied, that these core institutions are of such importance that they could not operate effectively outside of the context of relative homogeneity and isolation which is said to be characteristic of rural and small-scale societies. Urban life is clearly not of this nature and a large number of social anthropologists have found themselves trapped in moralistic arguments and thinly disguised romanticism which attributed some very remarkable positive qualities to marriage and family life in tribal societies. The implication has been that in the urban context these vital institutions had lost their function and meaning and were replaced by highly fluid and unpredictable arrangements. Yet the evidence is very different. Not only have past institutional arrangements been brought forward into the future, when the situational context called for this, but the importance of marriage and family have even, in some cases, assumed greater importance. The point therefore is not that these important societal institutions have declined in importance as they had to cope with external pressures, but rather they changed in purpose and function. While this is hardly a new formulation, social anthropologists have been slow to accept it in the context of urban studies. What modifications have taken place are expressed in terms of a proliferation of diverse marital and familial arrangements which are more suitable in the urban context. The evidence before us suggests that thus far the allegedly negative features of urban social relations, of marriage and family life, are no greater and no more destructive than the common discontinuities, contradictions and upheavals which are characteristically part of these vital institutions, although negative features are, perhaps, more easily detected in the urban context.

Somewhat more complex and controversial propositions for social anthropologists rotate around the flexibility and elasticity of African social systems as a whole, their ability to withstand, modify and selectively accept (or their inability to resist) both external intrusion and internally generated pressures. Yet in the context of rural studies, a comparative perspective has been seriously restricted as fieldworkers have concentrated on one ethnic community at a time—and within that community on one or two villages or dispersed homesteads. As such the theoretical formulations, many of great and lasting significance, are based on the extrapolations from a large number of individual studies. This is a procedure which gravely limits our understanding resulting, as it does, in little more than a cataloguing of system-structures, in terms of an exposure of the dynamics of social change and modernization which invariably has drawn rural people into a more complex societal context. This has been a feature of all but a selected few rural people, but social anthropologists have paid only limited systematic attention to this. This, it seems to me, exposes our formulations to a certain degree of doubt. At best we should say: perhaps this is the way the system worked. But we should also recognize that whatever body of theory we have built up may not always usefully be used as the base line which structures and guides the research in which we are now engaged. I am not suggesting that we should overlook the brilliance of the contributions by the great men of African social anthropology who have given us perhaps the richest harvest of social anthropology. But I do suggest that first, we keep our options open as to the relevance of this literature and, secondly, that we experiment, as I indicated earlier, with different premises. This is tantamount to saying that we need a new social anthropology which reflects both new interests, new approaches and new research techniques. There is nothing unprofessional in suggesting that the profession as a whole is not ready for this next stage in its development. Nor do I think that it overdramatizes the situation when I suggest that we are faced with a major challenge which, if we do not accept it, will totally eliminate social anthropology from our universities—and in particular from the new universities in Africa. It must be asked if urban anthropology can save us from this fate.

Urban anthropology has as yet diverse interests. It is not yet bounded by an severe limitations in interests, orientations and methodology. It is not beset with a narrow and exclusive interest in only those social forms which are defined (sometimes perhaps incorrectly) as urban, to the exclusion of an interest in rural life, rural structures, habits and ideas. Indeed many urban anthropologists have yet to give precision to the concepts of urbanism and urbanization, not to mention the use of the concepts of social change and modernization which are badly in need of greater clarification. But in proposing urban anthropology as a new core subject for social anthropology I am suggesting that its broadly based interests reflect more realistically and directly the compelling and inevitable influences which are weighing heavily on contemporary African, Asian and

Latin American societies—indeed on all those societies, and new nation states, which we have come to call the underdeveloped societies. Urban anthropology combines an interest in both historical data, i.e. the roots of urban growth and urbanism seen as particular ecological and settlement patterns, with an interest in development processes and the dialectic and strategy of social change and modernization. For the sake of a definition the former, social change, is a constant condition of society whereby the parts which comprise the societal whole are constantly rearranged, sometimes slowly and sometimes drastically, and modernization is the "will to be modern", to reject the past as a guide to the future, to bring rationality to the understanding, the analysis and the function and purpose of contemporary society. Urban anthropology, in short, is concerned with the study of a multitude of different forms and expressions of incipient modernity—as we can detect these in the urban context. This incipient modernity is now the hallmark of African society. We may put it another way: modernity is the model and the goal for millions of Africans, and change and "progress", which may mean no more than seeking an alternative economic base, are not identified with older social forms, with agriculture in particular. The constrictions these older forms imposed on Africans, including those limitations imposed during the colonial era, are not generally compatible with urban life which is based on a new class model. Where older social forms are adaptable and found suitable in the search for modern (urban) ends, they might be preserved in "pure" or modified form, although the latter rather than the former is generally the case.

What is the evidence which suggests that modernity is indeed the model and the goal of Africans? There are a large variety of new social forms, of economic and political structures which could be cited in support. Each research worker seeks to expose a different set of variables and analyzes their relationship at different levels of significance. But I believe that two or three variables stand out as of exclusive importance. They are rural-urban migration, which has dramatically increased in magnitude everywhere, the rejection of agriculture as a way of life (even when cash-cropping can bring reasonable returns), and the multiplicity of choices and alternatives which have been created, as a result of prolonged and varied cultural contacts. Individuals and groups respond variously as they sample the choices eclectically and pragmatically in a context of trials and experimentation in personal and group relations. These choices and alternatives, most marked in urban areas, appear to impose a fluid quality on new urban societies—at least this appears the case until we take a closer look and discover that "order" prevails, the kind of order which serves the specific ends of modernization, and that new circumstances and conditions have produced a clearly identifiable corporate structure, clearly defined institutional arrangements and, even, a large measure of predictability in social, economic and political behavior. Thus, urbanization and modernity may not be, yet, of a specific type but they represent a functional adaptation to a common continuing process.

African urban studies have progressively moved away from the social survey stage which characterized earlier efforts in the 1950's. Restricted as work was during this period, it nevertheless revealed the broad outlines and complexity of Africa's urban areas. We soon discovered that there were significant differences between the towns of East and Southern Africa, which developed largely as the result of European colonization, and the much older towns of West Africa in which African and non-African mingled more closely. The still older and wholly African towns of the Yoruba are, of course, unique, and if proof were needed of my assertion that social anthropologists showed lamentably little interest in urban life in Africa, we need merely point to the appearance just last year of the first attempt at a systematic study of Ibadan. If social anthropologists were solely interested in indigenous African cultures and societies, they certainly overlooked Ibadan, or Ife or Oyo or any number of towns in West Africa which have considerable age. Their presence has always been influential on people in the rural areas particularly as important chiefs generally lived in these (kingdom state) towns.

Starting in the late 1950's urban anthropologists in Africa developed a far more analytical perspective, spearheaded by students of the Manchester School of Social Anthropology. Most of this work is theoretically far ahead of urban studies elsewhere, although Latin American scholars have also produced much interesting material, mostly in Spanish, while urban studies in Asia are still highly descriptive and our knowledge of Pacific towns is very limited. African urban studies of distinction have been published by Banton, Epstein, Mayer, Mitchell, Southall, Pauw, Frankel and Lloyd. More recently African scholars have also turned to the study of urban life, such as Mabogunje, a Nigerian geographer. *African Urban Notes*, a newsletter started three years ago, is currently received by over 400 subscribers. The editors of this newsletter have estimated that upward of 100 junior and senior scholars are presently working on African urban material. No other continent can boast of such a concentration of scholars clustered around a common field of interest. But therein lies both a creative future and dangers of which we must become aware. I do not know what percentage of these scholars are social anthropologists but it is not likely to be large because political scientists, sociologists, geographers and historians are all taking an increasing interest in urban studies.

What kind of interests and topics have urban anthropologists tackled? And what conceptual approaches have they adopted? Essentially, most studies have sought to document and then analyze a number of basic structures and processes which have built up the fabric of the urban system in all its dimensions, i.e. social, economic, political and ideational. In doing so, urban anthropologists have been mindful of the important conceptualization advanced by Gluckman that an African who leaves the rural area crosses irrevocably into an urban system which completely engulfs him. Gluckman's formulation has been clear and direct: "an African townsman is a townsman and an African miner is a miner." The importance of this view is that urban systems exist in their own right and not as extensions of rural systems. Leo Kuper and Eric Wood have recently pointed to the dangers when this fact is ignored. This is not to suggest that rural-urban interdependence is ignored; when Africans move back and forth we must take account of this fact and fit the reasons for and the consequences of this into our analysis. Not only does it help us to understand how individuals and groups adjust to urban life, but also what they find satisfying, important, and why, in rural life.

A great deal of research has been concerned with the structures and function of ethnicity in urban areas, its relevance in specific contexts, and its relation to other variables such as occupation, education and economic and social mobility. The development and functions of ethnic associations have received particularly full treatment, but interest in these groups has declined in favor of in-depth studies of the urban elite, youth groups and such quasi-political groups as the large number of unemployed whose presence is of considerable concern to African governments. Concern with the growing importance of specific urban-based interest groups links the field of urban anthropology to the much larger and more complex questions of objectives and policies of national development.

Another question, perhaps of particular interest to the social anthropologist, is to determine why some Africans succeed in establishing themselves in a competitive urban system, and others fail. Do the determinants rotate around the characteristics of migrants *as* migrants, or is their cultural background of greater relevance? The former has been suggested by Henderson and the latter by Morrill. Aronson has shown that indigeneity and/or migrant status may strongly determine social patterns, success or failure, depending on specific local factors. The interrelations between rural and urban areas provide another set of questions. Does rural involvement vary with urban success? Plotnicov's recent work in Jos, Nigeria, strongly indicates this to be so. Yet Elkan has shown that for the Baganda, in Uganda, rural success may determine urban participation.

A number of observers have suggested that urban areas are the pace-setters of modernization in Africa no less than they were in Europe. If this is so then the towns are the prototype of African societies of the future, and urban anthropologists will soon be working in situations which have few of the organizational features with which they have become acquainted via their experience of rural societies. In short, urban anthropologists will be working in vastly different societies which are far less homogeneous, far less isolated and internally far more complex. They will concentrate on the circumstances, conditions and processes which generate new institutional arrangements, many of which having their first beginnings in the urban areas. In doing so they will find it difficult to define the limits of their interests and the limits of their competence. It is more than likely, therefore, that the urban anthropologists will be able to make their most effective contribution as a member of an inter-disciplinary team—a recipe which is paved with many pitfalls. However, for some time yet, I suspect, the urban anthropologist will be able to carve out for himself a specific set of interests. One of these might be to concentrate on the smaller urban area about which very little is known. Thus far most urban studies have concentrated on the large, perhaps atypical, city. This has often prevented us from effectively isolating those processes which led to rapid urban growth as the internal structure of most of the larger towns has crystallized to a point which makes reconstruction a very speculative affair.

Urban anthropologists might also turn their attention to the question of whether a distinctive urban culture has developed. This clearly involves a matter of definition. Professor Mabogunje, discussing the morphology of Ibadan, notes:

> The fundamental point to remember in order to understand the physical structure and morphology of Ibadan [and perhaps other African towns] is that it represents a convergence of two traditions of urbanism—a non-mechanistic, pre-industrial African tradition more akin to the mediaeval urbanism in Europe, and a technologically orientated European tradition.[2]

One task for the urban anthropologist is to sort out the impact of each of these traditions on urban life as a whole, and on particular groups.

Many urban local government officials in Africa complain that there is very little civic sense and responsibility. Yet West African novelists, in writing about the life of the urbanite, convey a picture of values, habits and ideas which are deeply rooted in urbanism as a way of life. As yet we know very little about the departing rural migrant's image of the city, or the perception the long-term resident has about his future in an urban area. Inasmuch as urban institutions reflect this perception, it would be wise for us not to ignore this approach. It is also vital that we concentrate on a time perspective. Urban anthropologists should return to the same urban area over a period of several years.

Perhaps the greatest difficulty the urban anthropologist is likely to face is methodological. Anthropologists are not used to working among large and diverse populations concentrated in one area. The concept of the urban neighborhood does not easily replace that of the village. Life is often a lot more hectic compared with the alleged tranquillity of rural life.

What, the urban anthropologist will ask, should be the basic unit for observation? It is

---

[2] *Ibid.*

clearly impossible to study the total urban area even from a limited perspective. This is in strong contrast to a small village or a set of scattered homesteads, units over which the anthropologist feels he has some observational control. African urban studies have indicated that all the towns about which we have some information, be they new or old, large or small, are a composite of frequently very distinct units most often ordered according to ethnicity, education, occupation, class or race. Of course, each of these units should not be abstracted from the whole of which they are a part, but small-scale neighborhood studies, utilizing the techniques of microanalysis, do provide the urban anthropologist with the kind of locale in which standard anthropological field methods can be used. It is of course possible to break down each of these units into yet smaller parts such as a courtyard in an urban slum (a technique pioneered by Ellen Hellman in Johannesburg over twenty years ago), a particular street or section on a housing estate, a group of shopkeepers, a beer bar area or a marketplace. By penetrating each of these units in depth, and concentrating on more than one, we can be reasonably certain that it is possible to detect in microcosm the most vital characteristics, and the nature of their interrelationship, of the total urban area. By this means we can gradually obtain a picture of the larger macrosystem—the total urban area. But it is clear that we need to refine our techniques. Whether these should be more quantitative or whether we should refine standard anthropological methods is a subject which needs special considerations.

Another methodological *and* conceptual approach is that of "situational" and "network" analysis which has been pioneered by Gluckman, Mitchell, Epstein and Van Velsen. The approach here is to concentrate on any event which takes place, such as a meeting of a tenants' association, an urban marriage, a fight, a meeting of elders, the visit of an important person or any variety of everyday events which can be creatively used as a starting point. The assumption which underlies this approach is that a situational context reveals in broad outline the total institutional network of the community. It has been used with remarkable effect in complex situations such as those on the Copperbelt where Mitchell analyzed the history and the significance of the Kalela Dance.

Another methodological and conceptual approach which shows promise is that of network analysis. Epstein, in the Copperbelt, traced the activities of a single urban African over a period of several days, showing how and why urban Africans become involved in certain relationships, and how they manipulate economic, political and kinship networks. Mabogunje, writing about the old market in central Ibadan, indicates in what varied contexts urban Africans are involved:

> Oja Iba, however, has other, and perhaps more compelling attractions for the majority of the people in the older part of the city. It is not only a forum of economic transactions, it is also the centre of social intercourse. On an evening, a young man may attend the market in the hope of meeting a young lady who may appeal to him. He may also attend it to hear the latest in the politics of the city or even of the country, to share comradeship with his friends or even just to feel a sense of belonging. Besides, the market is the terminal point for many festivities in the older part of the city and one often notices a number of happy, dancing groups making their way to the market.[3]

Here, in microcosm, economic, social, political, ceremonial and recreational activities take place, each of which involves the individual in a different network of relationships.

Furthermore, network analysis reveals how urban Africans gradually move from a kin-based to an association-based set of relations. As these networks overlap with each other and extend into the rural areas, as well as into a regional and national domain, the urban an-

---

[3] *Ibid.*

thropologist soon becomes aware of the complex set of contacts and relations which the urban African manipulates. But more important, network analysis also indicates how Africans from various socio-economic and political backgrounds adapt themselves to urban life. Virtually every urban study has shown that there are those Africans who continue to rely heavily on ethnic and kin networks (the "encapsulated" as Mayer has called them), and those who have moved over, you might say, and have become active participants in urban life.

In this paper I have tried to indicate why urban anthropology is likely to be the new creative pioneer of comparative modern social anthropology, and some of the questions, approaches and conceptualizations which might be usefully pursued. In suggesting this new development I am mindful of the need for greater refinement, but I am more certain that the new societies of Africa are so intimately part of an incipient modernity, the key variables of which are migration and urbanization, that failure to recognize this could mean the end of our discipline. However, fear that we might lose our bread and butter is one view, the need to understand contemporary Africa is even more compelling.

32

THE SACRED IN HUMAN EVOLUTION

ROY A. RAPPAPORT

For at least as long as anthropology has existed as a recognizable field of knowledge, it has displayed deep interest in the phenomenon known as religion. As Roy Rappaport points out in the following article, one of the earliest scientific anthropologists, Edward Tylor, attempted to explain the universality of religious beliefs. Tylor began his approach to that problem by setting forth what he considered to be a minimum definition of religion. For Tylor the irreducible core of religion was a belief in spirit(s), which is to say in souls or ghosts or gods. Other nineteenth-century rationalists attempted to get beyond even this, suggesting as a minimum the belief in a power pervading the universe (animatism), or the belief that inanimate objects possess sentience and the ability to move under certain circumstances (vitalism). Others, like psychologist William James, sought the minimal conception of religion within the believer and fixed on the notion of awe in approaching the object of veneration. For a variety of reasons whose consideration would take us far beyond the small space of this introduction none of these minimal approaches is fully satisfying. We can note, however, Rappaport's highlighting of the contribution of Emile Durkheim in this respect: problems in the sociology of religion are not to be answered by simple psychological generalizations.

Precisely on the heels of that understanding, Rappaport develops one of his main contributions. Substantively, religious propositions are nonsense. In his writings Rappaport has made this assertion quite clear. The essence of religious belief, he insists, is ineffability. The core statements of any religious system exist in the context of intuitive acceptance and belief—it is meaningless to

SOURCE: *Annual Review of Ecology and Systematics.* 2 (1971):23–42. Reprinted by permission of the publisher and author.

submit them to the sorts of logical questioning and empirical validation to which scientific propositions are subjected. This is not to say that religious propositions are immune to the decay of slowly or rapidly growing disbelief. Quite to the contrary, it is evident that such a system responds to its own set of conditioning criteria, shifts in which may lead to collapse of belief.

The Rappaport essay makes other contributions, several in precisely the spirit of this volume of assorted papers. Let me point out just three, not necessarily in the order that Rappaport discusses them. First, there is the inescapable tie between the symbol, which lies under all cultural activity, and religious concepts. But the tie between religious concept and symbol is anything but self-evident. It is not only ineffable, but may well be a lie. Only the ritual circumstances and the reality of the communicant's belief can determine that. Simple as Rappaport's point may be, it clarifies and illuminates religious beliefs and practices where other more complex theories have left only doubt and dissatisfaction.

A second virtue of Rappaport's approach is its easy use of examples both from societies with complex technologies and polities and from those much more simply arranged. This is done without a trace of patronage or condescension, for in this functional area of ideology differences are not very significant—that is one necessary concomitant of ineffability. We are grateful, however, for anthropological insight into our own current behavior, particularly noting the overlaps between religious and political systems.

Finally, not to abuse the privilege of making the introductory statement, we come to Rappaport's sophisticated ecological view which incorporates religious beliefs and ceremonies as easily as it does the environment, which all aspects of culture must interact with. We have been prepared for this view of the ecological system by the briefer introductory piece by A. P. Vayda (selection 22); if there are similarities it should not occasion surprise, the two anthropologists have worked together for years.

Possibly some readers will be offended by Rappaport's approach to the sacred. Science and religion are cotenants in the realm of ideology, sharing the space with such things as world views, political philosophies, and values. At times all these coresidents manage to coexist peacefully. At other times, one begins to move at the expense of one or more of the others and conflict breaks out. This can occur when passionate attachment to a set of religious beliefs overrides the empirical demonstrations of science, or when political orthodoxy is pushed at the price of free scientific inquiry, or when the scepticism at the heart of science infiltrates received religious or political beliefs and begins to threaten them. This area of conflict, too, may be viewed as yet another problem for the anthropological imagination.

I

Neither history nor anthropology knows of societies from which religion has been totally absent, and even those modern states that have attempted to abolish religion have replaced it with beliefs and practices which themselves seem religious. A century ago E. B. Tylor (1871), whom some consider "the father" of modern anthropology, attempted to account for the universality of religion by reference to the psychic unity of mankind. It is the experience of dreaming, common to all men, that has suggested to all men the existence of the soul, he argued, and it is from a primordial belief in the soul that religion in its manifold forms has evolved. But, as Durkheim (1961) asked at the beginning of this century, "How could a vain fantasy have been able to fashion the human consciousness so strongly and so durably?" He argued that it cannot be accepted that "systems of ideas like religions, which have held so considerable a place in history, and from which, in all times, men have come to receive the energy which they must have to live, should be made up of a tissue of illusions."

We must agree with Durkheim, for it is both plausible and prudent to assume, at least initially, that anything which is universal to human culture is likely to contribute to human survival. Phenomena that are merely incidental, or peripheral, or epiphenomenal to the mechanisms of survival are hardly likely to become universal, nor to remain so if they do. When we consider further that religious beliefs and practices have frequently been central to human concerns and when we reflect upon the amount of time, energy, emotion, and treasure that men have expended in building religious monuments, supporting priestly hierarchies, fighting holy wars, and in sacrifices to assure their well-being in the next world, we find it hard to imagine that religion, as bizarre and irrational as it may seem or even be, has not contributed positively to human evolution and adaptation. Surely so expensive an enterprise would have been defeated by selective pressures if it were merely frivolous or illusory. Indeed, it would have succumbed to selection if its importance were not comparable to its cost, and our thesis here is that religion has not merely been important but crucial to human adaptation.

I take the term *adaptation* to refer to the processes by which organisms or groups of organisms maintain homeostasis in and among themselves in the face of both short-term environmental fluctuations and long-term changes in the composition and structure of their environments. Homeostasis may be given a more or less specific, if not always precise, systemic meaning if it is conceived as a set of goal ranges on a corresponding set of variables abstracted from what, for empirical or theoretical reasons, we take to be vital or indispensable conditions of the systems under consideration. Adaptation is, thus, cybernetic. In response to system-endangering changes in the states of its components or in some aspect of the environment, an adaptive system initiates corrective programs. These corrective programs may return the deviating component to a safer state, make compensating changes elsewhere in the system, or initiate changes in organization.

In this view, adaptation subsumes both the self-regulatory processes through which living systems maintain themselves in fluctuating environments and the self-organizing processes by which living systems transform themselves in response to directional environmental changes. But this distinction between self-regulation and self-organization should not be overdrawn, because in a changing universe the maintenance of organization is likely to require continual modification of organization. What Hockett & Ascher (1964:137) have called "Romer's Rule" is the connecting generalization here. As they phrase it, Romer's Rule states that "The initial survival value of a favorable innovation is conservative, in that it renders possible the maintenance of a traditional way of life in the face of changed circumstances." To put this in other terms, self-organizing change (i.e. organizational change in response to environmental changes) is a function of the self-regulatory processes of a more inclusive system. For example, in the passage that inspired Hockett and Ascher, Romer (1954) long ago argued that through the enlargement of their limbs and other relatively minor organizational modifications of various of their subsystems, the early amphibians became able to migrate from one drying-up body of water to another and thus could maintain their general riverine and lacustrine organization in the face of environmental desiccation during the Devonian period.

Romer's discussion of the amphibian also calls our attention to another aspect of living systems: their hierarchical organization. As living systems increase in complexity, there is increasing differentiation of special purpose subsystems within them. Concomitant with this "progressive segregation" of subsystems is also likely to be increasing centralization of control functions, or "progressive centralization" (Hall & Fagen 1956, Miller 1965a, 1965b, Von Bertalanffy 1969).

Thus, although it is possible to entertain a cybernetic concept of adaptation, it would be a mistake to represent adaptations as simply collections of more or less distinct corrective feedback loops. When we refer to the adaptation of any living system, in a general sense, we imply much more than the sum of its homeostatic devices (some of which may be, in part, contradictory), for these special adaptations must be adapted to each other in structured ways. Adaptation, human or otherwise, must take the form of enormously complex sets of interlocking corrective loops arranged hierarchically (Kalmus 1966) and including not only mechanisms regulating material variables, but regulators regulating these regulators, others regulating them, and so on.

Cybernetic processes, like all other processes, require energy, but they are primarily informational. In response to the receipt of information concerning the states of systemic components, messages—directives or the like—specifying corrective programs are transmitted. Similarly, although they require energy and may and frequently do have important effects upon the material environment, religious activities are primarily part of the informational processes of human societies. It is the informational aspects of religion and their place in the cybernetic processes of adaptation that will receive most of our attention here. But it is even less possible to propose a generally acceptable definition of religion than of adaptation. I mean by the term simply to refer to the sets of sacred beliefs held in common by groups of people and to the more or less standard actions (rituals) that are undertaken with respect to these beliefs. It is convenient to take up rituals and beliefs separately, and after a brief discussion of ritual we shall proceed to the sacred nature of religious beliefs and to the nature of the sacred.

II

The term *ritual* has not been restricted to religious phenomena in its application. Psychiatrists use the term, or the closely related if not synonymous term *ceremony,* to refer to the compulsive behavior of some neurotics (Freud 1907), and Webster's International tells us that a ritual is "any practice . . . regularly repeated in a set precise manner so as to satisfy one's sense of fitness. . . ." Nor has the term been restricted in its application to human activities, for ethologists have used it virtually interchangeably with *display* to refer to a class of activities observed among many species in several phyla (Cullen 1966, Etkin 1964, Hinde 1966, Huxley 1914, 1966, Lorenz 1966, Tinbergen 1964, Wynne-Edwards 1962).

Whereas scientists concerned with the behavior and social organization of humans have sometimes tended to regard ritual as pathological or as having at best anxiety-reducing functions, students of animal behavior have taken animal rituals to be communication events, and a similar view of human rituals has been adopted by Goffman (1956), Leach (1954), Wallace (1966), and other social scientists. Accordingly, for our purposes here we shall define ritual—both human and animal, religious and secular—as conventional acts of display through which one or more participants transmit information concerning their physiological, psychological, or sociological states either to themselves or to one or more of their participants.

Both the content and the occurrence of rituals may be of importance in communication. As far as content is concerned, information concerning social arrangements may be communicated in the course of public rituals, as may quantitative information. For instance, among the Maring of New Guinea information concerning the amount of military support that may be expected from a friendly group in future warlike endeavors is transmitted in rituals. Among these people there are no chiefs or other leaders who can command obedience, and individual men signify their willingness to come to the aid of another group by dancing in the latter's ritual festival. Accordingly, the hosts estimate the amount of military support they may receive by the number of visitors who participate in these entertainments (Rappaport 1968). In the potlatches of the Northwest Coast Indians rather precise information concerning the social status of individuals is communicated by the number of valuables they give away. The relative political influence of Melanesian big men can be compared by counting the number of valuables each throws into the struggle when they are engaged in competitive feasting. Some human rituals, it would seem, may be regarded as public counting devices. [Similar claims have been made by Wynne-Edwards (1962) for some animal rituals.] As such, they may play an important role in regulation by revealing the states, not otherwise apparent, of important systemic variables. On the basis of such information, corrective action may be taken if necessary or possible.

The role of ritual occurrence in communication is more subtle than that of content. The mere occurrence of a noncalendrical ritual may be a signal. Since any ritual included in the repertoire of a people can, at any particular time, be in only one of two possible states—occurring or not occurring—occurrence can transmit a binary, or *yes–no*, signal. But although the occurrence of the ritual may transmit *yes–no* information, it may have been triggered by the achievement or violation of a particular state or range of states of a continuous or *more–less* variable, or even of a complex state or range of states involving the relationship among a number of such variables. As such, the occurrence of a ritual may be a simple quantitative representation of complex quantitative information, or to put it differently, the occurrence of a ritual might summarize complex analogic information and translate it into a simple digital signal. The importance of this operation may be illustrated by reference to male puberty rites. The social, psychological, and physiological development of males is continuous and gradual, unmarked by any definite and dramatic biological event such as menarche. Therefore, considerable ambiguity inheres in the role of the adolescent male in many societies. His physiological development is insufficient to structure his behavior and consequently he is uncertain as to whether to act as a boy or a man. Conversely, others are uncertain of what to expect from him. In a few societies the youth himself ameliorates this ambiguity by deciding to undergo a *rite de passage*. In the Society Islands, for instance, a boy has his penis superincised without necessarily consulting the adult males (Robert Levy, personal communication). This act signals to the community that certain unobservable but complicated biological and psychological development processes have reached the point that the boy is prepared to assume a new status. More frequently, the signal is transmitted in the other direction, and it is the adult men who decide that the time has come to initiate one or more of the community's youths. The initiation signals to the boys that certain complex sociological processes, involving attitude change and consensus formation among the adult men and concerning which the boys can have only vague or ambiguous information, have reached such a state that a new status with its attendant responsibilities is either granted to or forced upon them.

Whether initiated by the adult men or the boy, the virtue of the ritual is that it reduces the ambiguity inherent in continuous, analogic, or *more–less* information. The *yes–no* statement of ritual occurrence, other things being equal, is free of ambiguity. Cullen (1966) has also emphasized the role of ritual in the reduction of ambiguity in animal communication.

The reduction of ambiguity clearly enhances the operation of communication systems, and it is unnecessary to argue this point. It is worth noting, however, that in this light we may regard some rituals or their occurrence as "context markers" (Bateson 1968: 19 ff), signals specifying a change in context in situations in which this would otherwise be unclear. An obvious example, to be observed among both men and animals, is stereotyped sequences of behavior indicating peaceful intentions.

There is yet another way in which the binary aspect of ritual occurrence is important in communication: it aids in transduction of information between unlike systems. In the case of male initiation, for instance, rituals articulate a psychophysiological system (an individual) on the one hand and a social system on the other. Each of these systems is characterized, of course, by continuous quantitative processes and continuous change in such variables as emotional and cognitive states, status and role behavior, affiliation, etc. Although they are related to each other and affect each other, the psychophysiological processes and the social processes are both quasi-autonomous. Neither is a direct function or outcome of the other, and information concerning the two sets of processes is not altogether commensurable. Since this is the case, continuously fluctuating quantitative information concerning the process of either of these systems is not directly meaningful in the other. By "not directly meaningful" I mean that it cannot effect systematic nonrandom proportional changes in the other. But the ritual, as binary transducer, summarizes this quantitative information into a simple statement which not only is nonambiguous but is meaningful in the system into which it is transmitted: "the boy is prepared to become, or has become, a man," or "the men are ready to transform the boy into a man." Control transduction between unlike components of physiological systems also seems to rely heavily upon binary mechanisms because of the difficulty of translating quantitative information directly between incommensurable systems (Goldman 1960), and we may further note that ritual transduction is not restricted to the relations of individuals to social systems. Elsewhere, I (1968, 1971) have discussed the role of ritual in articulating a local ecological system to a regional political system in the Highlands of New Guinea.

Both ritual occurrence and ritual content, then, have played an important part in human as well as in animal communication. Indeed, ritual remains, even in industrialized societies, a mode of communication of some importance. For instance, the march on Washington of November 15, 1969, could be regarded as a ritual. Its *occurrence* was supposed to indicate that antiwar sentiments of sufficient strength to impel people to travel considerable distances at considerable expense now gripped a significant portion of the American population. Its *contents* were meant to convey information concerning the size, composition, fervor, militancy, and orderliness of that portion of the population to the public, to the government, and to itself.

This example suggests another aspect of ritual communication that requires comment: it is extremely expensive. It should be kept in mind that the *occurrence* of a ritual can, in itself, transmit only one bit of information. And although a great deal of quantitative information may be transmitted by the *contents* of a ritual, this form of transmission requires much more energy than do other means available to men. Animals have little or no choice, but men have other modalities available to them, and we may ask why, with the development of language and writing (not to mention electronic information processing and transmitting equipment), ritual persists as a mode of communication.

For one thing humans do not communicate all manner of messages through ritual. Messages may be low in information, but highly meaningful—that is to say important—and it is probable that only important messages which are low in information content are likely to be transmitted in expensive rituals. It is further implied here that not all modalities—smoke signals, speech, letters, telegrams, books, radio, and rituals—carry all kinds of messages equally well and that ritual may have special virtues as well as limitations.

Although human ritual may, and usually does, include discourse (language), it is also likely to include music, special postures, gestures, or body movements, special uses of the voice, and assemblages of people at special places and times. Whereas other modes of communication are more or less strictly discursive, ritual is, in part, nondiscursive. The nondiscursive aspects of a ritual are likely to evoke in the participants and the observers strong emotional states—reverence, ecstasy, commitment, or whatever. Since this is so, to transmit a message in ritual is not only to transmit the information contained in that message but also to transmit a nondiscursive, or emotional, message about that information. The medium is not the message. It is a metamessage.

III

We have been speaking so far of public rituals in general. Religious rituals are yet more special. They are sacred, and the sanctity of the ritual also constitutes a metamessage concerning social information transmitted in the ritual. It is necessary now to discuss what we mean by the sacred.

Religious rituals may be formally distinguished from secular rituals. Whereas the semantic content of the secular ritual is exhausted by the psychological, physiological, or social information transmitted in the ritual, this is not so in religious rituals. Religious rituals always include, in addition to messages of social import, implicit or explicit reference to some idea, doctrine, or supernatural entity. Sentences of the latter type are generally associated with the ostensible purposes of the ritual; "Hear, oh Israel, the Lord our God, the Lord is One" and "Jesus Christ is the Son of God" are examples of such sacred sentences. The explicit purposes of the rituals in which such propositions are enunciated is to worship the deities they name, or to affirm the doctrine enunciated, or something of the sort.

Propositions such as these sacred sentences are peculiar. Since their terms have no material referents, they are not amenable to verification, but neither are they vulnerable to falsification. They are, in a strict logical positivist sense, nonsense. Yet, they are taken to be unquestionably true. This characteristic, I believe, is the *sine qua non* of sanctity. I take the term *sacred* to refer to the quality of unquestionable truthfulness imputed by the faithful to unverifiable propositions (for a more detailed discussion see Rappaport, 1971).

Although sanctity inheres ultimately in propositions which do not have material referents, it is socially important as a metastatement about sentences that do have material referents, sentences containing information upon which societies operate, sentences such as—to use the Maring example cited earlier—"We will lend you support in warfare." To sanctify sentences like these is to associate them with the unquestionable truthfulness of the ultimate sacred propositions. To put it a little differently, to sanctify sentences is to certify them.

While sentences may be sanctified through association with ultimate sacred propositions in rituals, they may also be sanctified by connection to such propositions in discursive structures like theology. Indeed, the latter is probably more usual, with the function of religious ritual more often being simply to affirm the sacred propositions themselves. To put this differently, in the liturgical aspect of religious rituals ultimate sacred propositions are periodically reaffirmed and may, outside of the rituals, sanctify sentences directly important in the regulation of society. The sacred thus escapes from strictly religious contexts, and sentences concerning economic arrangements, political authorities, and other social conventions may, in fact very likely will, be sanctified.

Our argument implies that the sacred plays an important role in human organization, but it is perhaps possible to make a stronger assertion: human organization could not have come into existence, or persisted, in the absence of ultimate sacred propositions and the sanctification of discourse.

Human organization is based upon language, that is, symbolic communication. In symbolic communication signals are only conventionally related, and not intrinsic, to their referents. The advantages of symbolic communication—that it frees signals from the constraints of what is present at present and permits discourse upon the past, future, distant, imaginary, and hoped for—have been justly celebrated by many writers. But a problem that is concomitant to these very advantages has generally been overlooked. If signals are only conventionally related to their referents, they can occur in the absence of their referents, and their referents may occur without a signal being transmitted. Therefore lying becomes possible. Lies are the bastard offspring of symbols. Since the operation of any society is dependent upon the transmission of information among its members, the ability to lie, to knowingly transmit false information, poses a serious problem to societies relying largely upon symbolic communication. How can the recipients of messages be assured that the information which they receive is sufficiently reliable for them to act upon? If they are unwilling or unable to give credence to the information they receive, their responses in any context (assuming that contexts could even be specified) may be expected to tend toward randomness, eliciting yet further random responses. Needless to say, the operation of any society depends upon some degree of orderliness and predictability.

Some messages, those containing logically necessary truths or those that can be assumed to be true from experience, present no problems. But the preponderance of messages upon which social actions rely are neither logically necessary nor can they be validated from experience, and even should means of validation exist, the recipient of important information is seldom in a position to employ them. The sanctification of such sentences, however, assures the recipient that they are sufficiently reliable to act upon. This is not to claim, of course, that sanctification insures truth, although it may help. It is to say that people are more willing to accept sanctified than unsanctified messages as true; to the extent that they do, their responses to sanctified messages will tend to be predictable and the operation of the society orderly. The acceptance of messages as true, whether they are true or not, contributes to orderliness and may, in fact, make it possible. Following Bateson's lead (1951), we suggest that the creation of such orderliness may in fact create truth, for the validity of many of the sentences upon which social orderliness depends is a function of belief in them. In short, the concept of the sacred has not only been made possible by symbolic communication, but it has made symbolic communication (upon which human adaptation rests) possible. This implies that the idea of the sacred is as old as language and that the evolution of language and of the idea of the sacred were closely related, if not indeed bound together in a single mutual causal process. It may be suggested, further, that the emergence of the sacred was perhaps an instance of the operation of Romer's Rule, for it possibly helped to maintain the general features of some previously existing social organization in the face of new threats posed by an ever-increasing capacity for lying.

IV

Sanctity, thus, serves as a foundation for symbolic discourse. But although sanctity may escape from the constrictions of ritual, it in turn is rooted in ritual. At the least, sacred propositions are affirmed in rituals, and the nature of such affirmation has both epistemological and evolutionary significance.

In the course of a religious ritual the communicant is likely to have, at least sometimes, a "religious experience." The particulars of these experiences and their intensity vary from religion to religion, from communicant to communicant, and from time to time. What seems common to these experiences is that they are not discursive. They are emotional. Since they are not in discourse, they cannot be discredited by reason. The truth of such an experience seems to the communicant to be sufficiently demonstrated by its mere occurrence, and since a sacred proposition or its symbol (e.g. the cross) is taken to be intrinsic to the experience, the sacred proposition partakes of this often powerful and compelling sense of truth.

Thus, sacred propositions, which are unfalsifiable because their terms are nonmaterial, are supported by emotions, which are material (they reflect actual psychological-physiological states) but, because nondiscursive, also unfalsifiable.

As we noted earlier, it is not only religious ritual that affects the emotional states of the participants. Just as participation in ritual, religious or secular, stimulates emotion in humans, changes in the affective states of animals also occur during rituals. Cullen (1966) has suggested that this heightening of emotion among animals in rituals may enhance the likelihood of appropriate response to the messages being transmitted. Be this as it may, it is not implausible to suggest that the emotions experienced by men and animals in some rituals may be somewhat similar. Men and the higher mammals seem to resemble each other emotionally more closely than in their rational or secondary processes, and as long ago as 1928 Kohler suggested that those emotions which we associate with the religious seem to occur among the great apes. Erikson's recent discussion (1968) of the ritualization of ontogeny in humans lends plausibility to Kohler's impression. Erikson places the ontogenetic basis of the numinous emotions—the feelings of dependence, surrender, and love that Rudolph Otto (1926) claimed to be characteristic of the religious experience—in the earliest ritualized (stereotyped, repetitive, periodic) interactions of a mother with her infant. The relationship between mothers and helpless neonates is perhaps sufficiently similar among apes and humans to generate more or less similar emotions. The implication here is that emotions called "religious" or "numinous" when they came to be associated with the concept of the sacred may not only be present in infants before they acquire language, but may have been present among the ancestors of men before language or a concept of the sacred evolved.

The development of the numinous in earliest infancy seems to have important implications for the subsequent development of the child's communicative capacity. What he learns in these earliest interactions is that she upon whom he depends utterly, and whom he experiences as a numinous presence, is reliable. That is, he learns to trust before he learns, or perhaps can learn, language. It may be argued that it is the development of this trust that enables him to accept symbolic messages, first from the mother and then from others. At any rate, it seems clear that failure in these earliest ritualized contacts has severe effects upon the development of the communicative ability of the child (Erikson 1968:714, Frank 1966).

Ontogeny is, of course, not a recapitulation of phylogeny, but it had a phylogeny itself, and we are concerned here with the evolution of the socialization of the young. Perhaps gradually, as symbolic communication became increasingly complex, the idea of the sacred arose out of the trust which, developed before all else in the numinous experience of mother by the dependent infant, is a necessary precondition for the acceptance of messages that the recipient himself cannot verify. To put this a little differently, the numinous emotions, which we suggest appeared in the hominid line before language, may have served as a nondiscursive foundation for the concept of the sacred, itself discursive, which evolved along with language and made language possible.

The affective aspects of ritual, the place of ritual in animal communication, the continuing affirmation of the sacred in ritual, and the possibility that children are socialized for the numinous in very early and highly ritualized interactions, make it reasonable to believe that the concept of the sacred first emerged in the context of rituals.

V

Although sanctity may have emerged as a response to the possibility of lying, it seems after emergence to have taken on other important social functions. The ability to use language demands a high order of intelligence, and as Bergson long ago (1935) suggested, such an order of intelligence may itself pose problems for society. For one thing, human intelligence was probably an evolutionary product of intraspecific competition and, thus, perhaps evolved in such a way as to serve the interests or needs of the individual at the possible expense of society. In a word, human intelligence perhaps evolved toward selfishness. For another thing, increasing intelligence increasingly displaced genetic specification as a basis for human social life. Human social organization is genetically underspecified, if not unspecified. Social conventions are arbitrary and humans are born with a capacity to learn any of a virtually unlimited number of sets of social conventions. This has provided humans with an adaptiveness unparalleled in the rest of the animal world, but the very intelligence that makes it possible for men to learn and behave according to *any* set of conventions makes them understand that the *particular* set of conventions by which they do live, and which often inconveniences them or even subjects them to hardship, is arbitrary. Since this is the case, they may be aware that there are, at least logically, alternatives. But no society, if it is to avoid chaos, can allow all alternatives to be practiced. For each context or situation, all but one or a few must be proscribed and the proscriptions must somehow be made effective. Thus, in addition to the possible innate selfishness of their members, human societies are faced with containing what Bergson called the "dissolving power" of their intelligence.

In the course of human evolution further problems seem to have emerged with social differentiation and craft and subsistence specialization. When discrete social groups become closely identified with particular special-purpose subsystems of a society—such as business firms, professional or trade associations, or bureaucratic agencies—they tend or attempt to elevate the more or less narrowly defined interests of their group to positions of predominance in the larger system of which they are merely parts. This process and the attitude justifying it are nicely summed up in the famous statement "What is good for General Motors is good for America." Needless to say, no matter how benign General Motors may be, this assertion cannot in the long run be true, because to elevate the interests or goals of a lower-order system to a position of predominance in a higher-order system is to increase the specificity, and therefore decrease the adaptiveness of the higher-order system.

Sanctity has quite clearly had an important, even predominant, role to play in containing the self-interested pursuits of individuals and social groups and in supporting the conventions regulating society. These are problems inherent in hierarchical relations, and we earlier characterized adaptation as a hierarchically organized regulatory structure. We may now return to a discussion of the characteristics of such control hierarchies and the functions of sanctity within them.

There may be some ambiguity in the notion of control hierarchies. I am referring explicitly to controls at various levels of inclusiveness—that is, to hierarchies of systems, subsystems, sub-subsystems, and so on. For example, if a primitive horticultural community together with its territory were taken to be a system, we might be able to discriminate within it, by virtue of partial discontinuities in systemic coherence and the existence of discrete regulatory mechanisms, a number of major subsystems (such as an enculturation subsystem, a military subsystem, a subsistence subsystem, and so on) and within these perhaps subsystems of lower order. For instance, the subsistence subsystem might include production, distribution, and consumption subsystems, each composed of variables in more coherent relations with each other than with those in other subsystems and each possessed of a more or less discrete regulatory mechanism.

Each of these regulatory mechanisms consists of an image of the regulated domain—which elsewhere I (1963, 1968) have called a "cognized model"—as well as corrective programs, reference or ideal values for the regulated variables, and mechanisms sensitive to changes in the states of these variables. The domains of the lowest-order controls include the concrete variables of the general physical, biological, and social environment. The domains of higher-order controls include the outputs of the controls of next-lower order, for which they set output reference values. For instance, a production quota (an output reference value) is not likely to be set within a production system but to emanate from the controls of a more inclusive system (here labeled a subsistence system) which regulates relations among the outputs and demands of its several subsystems.

Let us turn to the place of sanctity in such hierarchies. Sanctity flows from ultimate sacred propositions containing no material terms, but it can suffuse sentences consisting entirely of material terms, and it can and does suffuse the sentences composing cognized models and their corrective programs.

In this regard it may be suggested—though no studies, so far as I know, have been made in just these terms—that cognized models in higher-order controls are likely to contain more abstract and fewer concrete terms than do those of lower-order controls. While this feature of control hierarchies is probably more evident in primitive societies, it is to be noted in modern societies as well. For instance, the terms of economics, which may include such notions as "free enterprise" and "corporate ownership," are less concrete and carry a stronger moral connotation than those of agronomy, and the contents of the cognized models which maintain community coherence within viable limits are likely to include yet more abstract terms, such as honor, prestige, and freedom, and gods, ghosts, and demons. In other words, the higher the level of control, the greater the importance of moral and mythic terms in its cognized model. Such a progression from the concrete to the abstract is expectable on several grounds. It could be argued simply that the relations among such concrete things as soils, plants, and agricultural techniques constrain their conceptualization more than coherence among systems constrains its conceptualization. But more important, and more germane to our present discussion, is a matter that we raised earlier. The range of differences possible in the regulation of the components of a low-order system, such as a production system, is probably narrower than in higher-order systems. The physiological requirements of cultigens, for instance, probably put greater restraints upon agricultural practices and the cognized models associated with them than the necessity to maintain coherence between production and consumption systems places upon procedures of distribution, etc., and the cognized models associated with them. Thus, to use an example from modern societies, Soviet wheat agriculture probably resembles American wheat agriculture more closely than the Soviet economic system resembles the American economic system. Since there is greater latitude or freedom in the maintenance of coherence *between* systems than in regulation *within* systems, it may be suggested that the higher its level, the more arbitrary the particular control mechanism. That is, the particular control mechanism that does operate is only one of a number of possible mechanisms which could maintain the proper degree of systemic coherence. However, as we have already observed, any society must choose only one or a limited number out of the possible range if chaos is to be avoided. But the arbitrariness of the selection is possibly understood by the actors; i.e., they can conceive of other ways to maintain comparable levels of systemic coherence, and those subject to a control are not likely always to feel that it is operating in their immediate interests. Arbitrariness invites criticism and recalcitrance. However, to phrase regulation in moral or mythic terms—that is, to sanctify it—is to place it beyond criticism and to define recalcitrance as sacrilege. Sanctification transforms the arbitrary into the necessary, and regulatory mechanisms which are arbitrary are likely to be sanctified.

A related point may be made about another sense in which we may speak of sanctity and abstractness in control hierarchies. The systems with which we are dealing are "hybrid systems" in Pask's (1968) terms, for they consist of (*a*) bodies of discourse, which we have labeled cognized models, (*b*) material objects, and (*c*) the activities undertaken with reference to the cognized models but affecting the material objects. It thus seems that the structure of control hierarchies is "heterarchical," to use another of Pask's terms. The implication is that the level of discourse embodied in cognized models is likely to correspond to the level of control.

This possible feature of control hierarchies is of considerable significance with respect to a point already mentioned: the establishment of the output reference values of a regulatory mechanism is not a function of that regulatory mechanism but of one of higher order. It suggests that these reference values cannot be derived from the function or logic of the systems in which they operate. But since the reference value of a lower-order control is an output of higher-order control, it presumably may be deduced from the cognized model and input of the higher-order control. In other words, reference values either are or are something like theorems in the higher-order systems from which they emanate, but they also are or are something like axioms in the lower-order system in which they operate. Thus, the higher-order controls, which we have discriminated in terms of the greater inclusiveness of the domains subject to them, may also be what Bateson (1968), following Whitehead and Russell, has termed "of higher logical type," and Gödel's theorem [which specifies that any formal system of propositions must be incomplete, since not all of its components can be proved as theorems—M.H.F.], or something like it, may operate between controls on different levels. (I have used the phrase "something like" because the logic of the discourse with which we are concerned may not be amenable to rigorous formalization.)

This obviously can result in problems when the lower-order system, into which the reference value enters from above, is coextensive with an individual or social group with purposes of its own. Whereas most men are willing to accept such axioms as "the shortest distance between two points is a straight line" as the basis for some of their behavior, they are likely to be more dubious about accepting calls to fight in distant wars or production quotas whose rationale they do not understand or believe to be in their own interest.

Sanctification again plays an important role. On the one hand, as we have already noted, recalcitrance may become sacrilegious, and sacrilege implies punishment. But no society thrives on punishment, and sanctification also operates positively here in a way which I believe to be both more interesting and more important and which may be illustrated by reference to the Maring of New Guinea. Among these people relations between hostile local groups are mediated by sanctified truces, and even when they are more powerful than their enemies, Maring groups rarely launch attacks in violation of these truces. Although their material advantages might be well served if they did so, they do not take this to be the case because they believe that if they were guilty of such sacrilege, their deceased ancestors would not assist them in their bellicose undertaking and they would therefore fail.

This peace-keeping operation depends upon the nonmaterial nature of such components of higher-order cognized models as spirits of deceased ancestors. Through the invocation of unquestionable propositions concerning spirits whose very existence cannot be verified, or falsified, the purpose of a higher-level system, the entire Maring population, is made to appear to one of its subsystems, a local territorial group, to be its own purpose. The societies of ancient Mesopotamia, organized economically around the temples of gods whose well-being was conceived by their servants—the entire community—to be a necessary precondition for their own prosperity, could serve as another example, as could those archaic societies in which there was conceived to be a correlation between the health and prosperity of the king and the state of the crops. In more modern societies such morally laden and sanctified terms as honor may function in a similar way. In general terms, then, through sanctification the purposes of higher-order systems may be injected into lower-order systems. As such, sanctification operates as a counterthrust to attempts by individuals or social groups to promote their own purposes to positions of dominance in higher-level systems. In slightly different terms, sanctity helps to keep subsystems in their places.

In summary, to invest social conventions with sanctity is to hide their arbitrariness in a cloak of seeming necessity. Conventions, to the extent that they are sanctified, are likely to be taken by those subject to them to be as "natural" as if they were genetically determined. Indeed, they seem not to be mere conventions, but reflections of human nature, and those who flout them seem less than human. Further, to sanctify conventions is also to ameliorate, at least partially, the conflict between the individual and the society. The interests and needs of the society are presented to the individual as his own ultimate interests and needs, and his inconveniences and sacrifices on behalf of the society are rewarded symbolically. Recalcitrance, selfishness, and resentment thus are replaced by docility, compliance, cooperation, altruism, commitment, and enthusiasm. Thus, in further accordance with Romer's Rule, while the initial survival value of the concept of the sacred was conservative, it subsequently made possible the great range of new organizational forms based upon symbolic rather than genetic specification and transmission.

VI

In the last section we attempted to describe the place of the sacred in social control hierarchies generally. However, it must be recognized that the role of sanctity in the regulation of society changes in the course of sociocultural evolution. In many technologically simple societies there are no authorities with sufficient power to coerce compliance with the norms of proper social behavior. (Following Bierstedt 1950, I take power to be the product, in a mathematical sense, of men × resources × organization.) In such societies, as we argued in the last section, the sanctification of norms goes far to insure that they are honored. Sanctity, thus, is a functional equivalent of political power among some of the world's peoples. We can distinguish among past and present human societies a continuum from those governed largely by sacred conventions in the absence or near absence of human authorities [e.g. Australian Aborigines (Meggitt 1962), no date, Spencer & Gillen 1899,

Warner 1937), New Guinea Highlanders (Brookfield & Brown 1963, Rappaport 1968)], through societies in which authorities have little power but claim great sanctity [Polynesia (Sahlins 1958)], to those of the contemporary west, in which authorities stand much more heavily upon power than they do upon sanctity. This continuum seems to be correlated with technological development, which is expectable, for technological development places increasingly powerful means of coercion in the hands of authorities, and very powerful authorities consequently have less need for sanctity than weaker ones.

Although this continuum may be observed among various contemporary or new contemporary people it has evolutionary implications. The compelling nature of the sacred and of religious emotions and the possible importance of rituals in the regulation of animal societies may reasonably cause us to speculate that religious rituals were important in the regulation of primordial human societies. The ethnographic literature, moreover, provides us with numerous instances of societies still functioning—or functioning until recently—in which religious ritual regulates social, economic, and in some instances even ecological relations. It has been argued by Piddocke (1965), Suttles (1960), and Vayda (1961) that the potlatches of the Indians of the Northwest Coast of the United States served to correct disparities between the fishing success of local groups, and Ford (1971) has proposed that the calendrical ceremonies of various Indians of the American Southwest, which usually involve large-scale redistribution of foodstuffs, ameliorate differences in the harvests of the various households making up local communities. In some New Guinea Highlands societies rituals seem to regulate pig husbandry and, through pig husbandry, other aspects of social and political life and ecological relations (Brookfield & Brown 1963, Rappaport 1968, Vayda, Leeds & Smith 1961).

Pigs are important to the subsistence of Highlands societies as occasional sources of high-quality protein in a diet otherwise consisting largely of tuberous vegetables; as converters of garbage, feces, and substandard tubers; and in some instances in tillage (the beasts' rooting softens ground to be gardened). Further they are important as wealth objects. Bridal payments, homicide compensations, and other such transactions usually include pigs, either alive or cooked. But although pigs are crucial to the operation of these societies, they can become too much of a good thing (Vayda, Leeds & Smith 1961), requiring additional labor for support, invading gardens, and possibly even pressing upon the ecological capacity of local group territories. The large, spectacular, noncalendrical ritualized festivals, which have been observed in virtually all of the Highlands societies, seem to be held in response to system-endangering increases in the size of local pig populations. In these rituals large numbers of pigs are sacrificed to spirits. The resulting pork is widely distributed, providing the donors with prestige and temporary surcease from the labor and tribulations of pig husbandry, the recipients with high-quality protein, and the environment with protection from possible despoliation by a plethora of pigs. Among the Maring, Narok, and perhaps other Highlands societies these ritual cycles, whose timing is based upon the demographic processes of local pig populations, also regulate the frequency of warfare and include conventions for redistributing people over land and land among people (Rappaport 1968).

Although we earlier discussed the informational aspects of ritual, our brief references indicate that rituals may do more than communicate information. They may themselves constitute corrective programs (i.e. sets of actions, such as distributions of foodstuffs or sacrifices of pigs) which return deviating variables to desired states. In some cases, for instance in the calendrical rituals of Southwestern Indians, ritual regulation is *time-dependent*, that is, it is undertaken at fixed intervals. In others, as in the noncalendrical pig festivals of Melanesia, it is *variable-dependent*. The occurrence of the ritual is a response to changes in the state of a regulated variable.

The virtue of regulation through religious ritual is that the activities of large numbers of people may be governed in accordance with sanctified conventions in the absence of powerful authorities or even of discrete human authorities of any sort. As such, it is plausible to argue that religious ritual played an important role in social and ecological regulation during a time in human history when the arbitrariness of social conventions was increasing but it was not yet possible for authorities, if they existed at all, to enforce compliance.

But ritual regulation has its shortcomings. It is rather inflexible, it may be slow to act, and its corrective actions are likely to be imprecise. Discrete authorities, who can respond immediately, proportionally, and perhaps in innovative ways to systemic disturbance, are much finer regulating mechanisms than Melanesian ritual cycles, and the emergence of such authorities surely constituted an important evolutionary advance in which sanctification also played a part. Sentences such as "The chief has great mana," "Henry is by Grace of God King," and "Pharaoh is the living Horus" imply, to say the least, that the directives of the authorities named are to be obeyed. These sentences further indicate that the regulatory prerogatives of these authorities stood at least partially on sanctity rather than on power. Sanctity, it may be suggested, has permitted the progressive centralization of regulatory hierarchies in circumstances in which the ability of authorities to aggregate power is limited [The chiefdoms of Polynesia (Sahlins 1958) may be cited in this regard.] Since the conditions enabling authorities to aggregate power seem to have emerged rather recently, it would appear that sanctity, before power, provided a foundation for the regulatory prerogatives of discrete authorities. It is important to remember that the archaic states were, at least at the outset, theocratic. Furthermore, it can be argued that it was their sanctity that made it possible for early authorities to begin to command the men and control the resources that eventually provided them or their successors with actual power.

With increasing power, authorities have come to rely less upon sanctification, but few authorities or social systems have dispensed with it entirely. The United States is "One nation under God," and its officers take oaths when they assume their duties. Sanctity is much less expensive than police, and no society can stand only upon the threat of force. Our observation, that sanctification presents to the individual as his own goals those of the society and thus replaces possible recalcitrance with compliance, remains true in contemporary societies.

VII

I have argued elsewhere (1971) that in technologically simple societies—whose authorities, in the complete or relative absence of power, stand upon their sanctity—the sacred and the numinous form part of an encompassing cybernetic loop which maintains homeostasis among variables critical to the groups' survival.

It has already been suggested that in such societies the prerogatives of the authority derive from his association with ultimate sacred propositions, but the unquestionable status of the ultimate sacred propositions depends upon the sense of the numinous, the affective religious experiences of the faithful. Inasmuch as the religious experience is an intrinsic part of the more inclusive emotional dynamics of the organism, which are closely related to its physical state, it is at least plausible to assume that religious experiences are affected by material conditions. But in technologically undeveloped societies the latter are at least partially a function of the control hierarchy that the religious experience itself supports. It may be suggested that the willingness, indeed the ability, of the members of the congregation to affirm through religious experience the propositions that sanctify the control hierarchy may be in some degree a function of the hierarchy in maintaining homeostasis in and among those variables crucial to the congregation's survival. This is to say that should the authority be ineffective or repressive for a more or less protracted period, it may be faced with a millennial or revitalistic movement (Wallace 1966, Worsley 1957). In such movements, which have occurred countless times in human history, men sometimes withdraw the emotional support generated in their religious experiences from the sacred propositions ratifying existing authorities or regulatory institutions and bestow it upon new sacred propositions—enunciated by prophets, mystics, or messiahs—legitimizing new authorities or institutions. More frequently, such movements do not challenge ultimate sacred propositions, but the connection of existing authorities or institutions to them. In either case, needless to say, these movements may be revolutionary.

Correction or change may, of course, occur in the absence of such revolutionary events. Ultimate sacred propositions, such as "the Lord our God, the Lord is One," are in fact propositions and they contain no material terms. Earlier we noted that it was necessary that these propositions contain no material terms, for this places them beyond the reach of falsification. There is another reason. If they are *propositions* containing *no material terms,* they cannot be irrevocably bound to *particular* social forms. What is sanctified by any such ultimate sacred proposition is not specified by that proposition. Therefore, the association of particular propositions with particular directives or institutions is not intrinsic to the propositions themselves, but is rather the product of interpretive acts. Now, any product of interpretation allows reinterpretation, but reinterpretation does not challenge ultimate sacred propositions. It merely modifies, challenges, or replaces previous interpretations. Furthermore, continuing reinterpretation is likely to be assured by the cryptic nature of sacred discourse. It is not their weakness but their strength that myth and revelation are obscure. It is important, if evolution is to take place, that what is accepted as unquestionably true be clearly and definitively understood by *no one*. Thus, the concept of the sacred not only may allow but may even encourage organizational change in response to changed circumstances and at the same time provide continuity through such changes. Since we described adaptation as, in part, the process by which homeostasis is maintained through organizational change, sanctity is important or even crucial in the adaptive processes of human groups.

A possible malfunction of sanctity may have become apparent in the course of this discussion. Sentences directly involved in regulation (thus including material terms and perhaps expressed as directives) are sometimes taken not merely to be sanctified by ultimate sacred propositions but virtually to be ultimate sacred propositions themselves. This results in a loss of adaptiveness, for oversanctified regulatory mechanisms are highly resistant to modification through reinterpretation. A possible instance of such confusion in the level of sanctity to which a regulatory sentence is to be assigned is the prohibition of mechanical and chemical means of birth control to its communicants by the Catholic Church. Modification or abrogation of this prohibition could be achieved through reinterpretation without any challenge to dogma.

In the last paragraph the term *level of sanc-*

tity was employed. If adaptiveness is to be preserved, the degree of sanctity accorded to a sentence should correspond to its position in a control hierarchy. This, in turn, should correspond to its logical type, which is also to say to its specificity. The higher their position in the control hierarchy, the higher the logical type of the sentences associated with regulation, and the greater the degree of sanctity they may be accorded. Ultimate sacred propositions cannot adaptively be irrevocably associated with anything more specific than the extremely underspecified goal of the social aggregate: survival. To bind them irrevocably to particular social forms (as, by implication, to private enterprise in its opposition to "Godless" communism) is to overspecify the terms under which the society may survive, i.e., to reduce its adaptiveness.

It also must be recognized that sanctity is degraded by power. When, because of technological development, it became possible for authorities to stand upon power rather than upon sanctity, they did not dispense entirely with sanctity. Rather the relationship between sanctity and authority changed. Whereas the unquestionable status of ultimate sacred propositions previously rested upon affirmation through the religious experiences of the faithful, it now came to rest, overtly or covertly, upon force. Whereas previously authority was contingent upon its sanctification, sanctity now became the instrument of authority. Coercion is expensive and difficult, and compliance and docility are achieved more easily and inexpensively through first the encouragement of religious experiences inspired by hopes of salvation in another life and, second, inculcation of the belief that the world's evils are a result of the worshipper's own sinfulness rather than a matter of external exploitation or oppression which the worshipper could possibly resist.

But although the sacred and the numinous may be degraded in the churches of technologically developed states, they may retain a positive role in the adaptation of contemporary societies. As we have already observed, revitalistic movements have arisen throughout history among men sensing and often suffering from the malfunction of control hierarchies that, perhaps because of overspecification and the oversanctification of particular social arrangements or institutions, seem to have become unable to reform themselves. We are witnessing the emergence of such a movement now in the fervor investing ecological issues and the organizations being formed in response to these issues. It seems apparent that at least some of those participating in this movement are already according, out of emotional experiences that we may call religious, sacred status to general ecological principles at the same time that they are withdrawing sanctification from such previously sanctified notions as progress, industrialization, and free enterprise. There seems to be a new ecological religion developing around us, and it should be taken seriously by scientific ecologists concerned with ameliorating the environmental problems currently besetting life on earth. Revitalistic movements have frequently been as maladaptive as that to which they are a response, but nevertheless they may be regarded as a means, as old as religion (which is possibly to say as old as man), by which social systems that have become too rigid to correct themselves by other procedures are ultimately corrected. We may suggest that there remains for the sacred, which played an indispensable part in the emergence of man, a crucial role in his continuing survival.

Literature cited

BATESON, G. 1951. Conventions of Communication: Where Validity Depends upon Belief. In Ruesch, J., Bateson, G. *Communication: The Social Matrix of Society,* 212–27. New York: W. W. Norton.

BATESON, G. 1968. *The Logical Categories of Learning and Communication and the Acquisition of World Views.* Paper prepared for Wenner-Gren Symp. World Views: Their Nature and Their Role in Culture. Mimeo.

BERGSON, H. 1935. *The Two Sources of Morality and Religion.* Transl. R. A. Andra, C. Brerton, with assistance of W. H. Carter. New York: Holt.

BIERSTEDT, R. 1950. An Analysis of Social Power. *Am. Sociol. Rev.* 15:730–38.

BROOKFIELD, H., BROWN, P. 1963. *Struggle for Land.* Melbourne: Oxford Univ. Press.

CULLEN, J. 1966. Reduction of Ambiguity through Ritualization. In Huxley, J. S. (Convener.) *A Discussion of Ritualization of Behavior in Animals and Man. Phil. Proc. Roy. Soc. B* 271: No. 772.

DURKHEIM, E. 1961. *The Elementary Forms of the Religious Life,* 87. Transl. J. W. Swain. New York: Collier. (First printed 1915. London: George Allen & Unwin)

ERIKSON, E. 1968. The Development of Ritualization. In *The Religious Situation: 1968,* ed. D. Cutler. Boston: Beacon.

ETKIN, W. 1964. Theories of Animal Socialization and Communication. In *Social Behavior and Organization among the Vertebrates,* ed. W. Etkin. Chicago: Univ. Chicago Press.

FORD, R. I. 1971. An Ecological Perspective of the Eastern Pueblos. In *New Perspectives on the Eastern Pueblos,* ed. A. Ortiz. Albuquerque: Univ. New Mexico Press.

FRANK, L. K. 1966. Tactile Communication. In *Culture and Communication,* ed. A. G. Smith. Reprinted from *Genet. Psychol. Monogr.* 56:209–55.

FREUD, S. 1907. Obsessive Actions and Religious Practices. *Religionspsychol.* 1:4–12. (Trans. 1959 in *The Standard Edition of the Complete Psychological Works of Sigmund Freud,* ed. J. Strachey, Vol. 9. London: Hogarth)

GOFFMAN, E. 1956. The Nature of Deference and Demeanor. *Am. Anthropol.* 58:473–503.

GOLDMAN, S. 1960. Further Considerations of Cybernetic Aspects of Homeostasis. In *Self Organizing Systems,* ed. M. C. Yovitz, S. Cameron. New York: Pergamon.

HALL, A. D., FAGEN, R. E. 1956. Definition of System. *Gen. Syst. Yearb.* 1:18–28.

HINDE, R. A. 1966. *Animal Behavior, A Synthesis of Ethology and Comparative Psychology.* New York: McGraw-Hill.

HOCKETT, C. F., ASCHER, R. 1964. The Human Revolution. *Curr. Anthropol.* 5:135–68.

HUXLEY, J. 1914. The Courtship Habits of the Great Crested Grebe. *Proc. Zool. Soc. London* 35:492–562.

HUXLEY, J. 1966. Introduction. Huxley, J. (Convener.) *A Discussion of Ritualization of Behavior in Animals and Man. Phil. Trans. Roy. Soc. Ser. B* 251: No. 772, 249–72.

KALMUS, H. 1966. Control Hierarchies. In *Regulation and Control of Living Systems,* ed. H. Kalmus. New York: Wiley.

KOHLER, W. 1928. *The Mentality of Apes.*

LEACH, E. R. 1954. *Political Systems of Highland Burma.* Boston: Beacon.

LORENZ, K. 1966. *On Aggression.* Bantam.

MEGGITT, M. J. 1962. *The Desert People.* Sydney: Angus & Robertson.

MEGGITT, M. J. No date. Gadjari among the Walbiri Aborigines of Central Australia. *Oceania Monogr. 14.* Sydney.

MILLER, J. G. 1965a. Living Systems: Basic Concepts. *Behav. Sci.* 10: No. 3, 193–257.

Ibid. 1965b. Living Systems: Structure and Process. 10: No. 4, 337–79.

OTTO, R. 1926. *The Idea of the Holy.* Transl. J. W. Harvey. London: Oxford Univ. Press.

PASK, G. 1968. Some Mechanical Concepts of Goals, Individuals, Consciousness and Symbolic Evolution. Prepared for Wenner-Gren Symp. Effects of Conscious Purpose on Human Adaptation.

PIDDOCKE, S. 1965. The Potlatch System of the Southern Kwakiutl: A New Perspective. *Southwest. J. Anthropol.* 21:244–64.

RAPPAPORT, R. A. 1963. Aspects of Man's Influence on Island Ecosystems. In *Man's Place in the Island Ecosystem,* ed. F. D. Fosberg. Honolulu: Bishop Museum Press.

RAPPAPORT, R. A. 1968. *Pigs for the Ancestors.* New Haven: Yale Univ. Press.

RAPPAPORT, R. A. 1971. Ritual, Sanctity and Cybernetics. *Am. Anthropol.* 73.

ROMER, A. S. 1954. *Man and the Vertebrates,* 1:43 ff. Penguin. (First published 1933)

SAHLINS, M. 1958. *Social Stratification in Polynesia.* Seattle: Univ. Washington Press for Am. Ethnol. Soc.

SPENCER, B., GILLEN, F. J. 1899. *The Native Tribes of Central Australia.* London: Macmillan.

SUTTLES, W. 1960. Affinal Ties, Subsistence, and Prestige among the Coast Salish. *Am. Anthropol.* 62:296–305.

TINBERGEN, N. 1964. The Evolution of Signaling Devices. In *Social Behavior and Organization among the Vertebrates,* ed. W. Etkin. Chicago: Univ. Chicago Press.

TYLOR, E. B. 1871. *Religion in Primitive Culture.* (*Primitive Culture,* Vol. 2.) London: John Murray. (Reprinted 1958. New York: Harper Torchbooks)

VAYDA, A. P. 1961. A Re-examination of Northwest Coast Economic Systems. *Trans. N. Y. Acad. Sci. Ser.* 2 23:No. 7, 618–24.

VAYDA, A. P., LEEDS, A., SMITH, D. 1961. The Place of Pigs in Melanesian Subsistence. *Proc. Am. Ethol. Soc.,* ed. Viola Garfield.

VON BERTALANFFY, L. 1969. *General System Theory.* Brazilier.

WALLACE, A. F. C. 1966. *Religion: An Anthropological View.* New York: Random House.

WARNER, W. L. 1937. *A Black Civilization. A Study of an Australian Tribe.* New York & London: Harper.

WORSLEY, P. 1957. *The Trumpet Shall Sound: A Study of "Cargo Cults" in Melanesia.* London: MacGibbon & Kee.

WYNNE-EDWARDS, V. C. 1962. *Animal Dispersion in Relation to Social Behavior.* Edinburgh & London: Oliver & Boyd.

33

MYTH CHARTER IN THE MINORITY-MAJORITY CONTEXT

JOHN L. GWALTNEY

If a myth is a story of obscure origin and very uncertain reliability, what is a myth charter? In fact, folklorists of various schools distinguish several types of myths, three being a usual number and including folktales (Märchen), heroic stories or legends (such as the sagas), and myths proper. The last are usually characterized as an explanation of something, usually the origin of something of great significance, such as the universe or the earth or sex or the animals in the forest and the fish in the waters. A proper, working myth has the quality of ineffability, hence is related to the concept of the sacred. It is accepted at face value and its truth not questioned; other truths are derived from it. Mythic charters, then, tell socially significant stories about who gets what, when, and how. They tell that such-and-such a group of people own the land and are entitled to its fruits, or that power descends from last born to last born in a certain distinguished line, or that people of a certain hue of skin are forever exalted or perpetually doomed. By now it should be evident that myths are not the simple creations of simple cultures, though simple cultures too enjoy their myths. All societies based on symbols, all human societies that is, know myth, and though they may inherit some of their stock from an obscure past, they continually revitalize and refurbish their myths to support the substance and the principles of their social, economic, and political order. These are the myth charters that pass before Professor Gwaltney's sharp vision.

SOURCE: "Myth Charter in the Minority-Majority Context, *NEWSTATEments,* Vol. 1 (1971):34–40. Reprinted by permission of publisher and author.

A Tentative Formulation

"If you white, you all right.
If you black, get back.
If you brown, you can hang aroun'."

This piece of North American black folk doggerel reflects the salient realities of social and political life in the North American caste-like commonwealth. Since its inception, black and white have always represented polar positions on the power and privilege access continuum.[1]

Here as everywhere else, the ethnic pecking order was conceived in power and perpetuated by force and fraud. Social inequality is a lie agreed upon, established by powerful fathers and sanctified by their chosen heirs.

The lie and its supporting sophistry is what I should like to call, with due deference to Malinowski, myth charter.[2]

In the communal pecking order that is the minority-majority context, there are three kinds of enabling myth charters; those invented and venerated by powerful majority ethnic communities, those of the most depressed minority communities, and those of aspiring intermediate ethnicities.

The myth charters of majority cultures are designed to justify freezing the social order at the point where power monopolies yield the greatest exploitative return. Culture history teems with apical ancestors and a formidable company of this myriad has had the pyrrhic good fortune to become progenitors of unjust and exploitative caste or caste-like societies. Men like Joshua, Ieyasu Tokugawa, George Washington, Mari Djata, Hugh Capet, and Osai Tutu employed power to impose parochial qualifications upon the channels of privileged access. In the general minority-majority cultural context, the *sine qua non* of power invariably implies the imperative of legitimacy, as founding fathers who cannot take it with them are prone to herculean exertions to at least keep it in their temporally extended ethnic families. Much of the energy and resources of the master castes is devoted to the erection of a monumental structure of legitimacy, rectitude, and even divinity for the super ancestor and his extended ethnic family. Kept and aspiring artists, scholars, and artisans maintain a steady flow of accolades, commissioned and gratuitous. The conspicuous silence from the intermediate and lower depth is, when regarded at all in majority circles, taken for affirmation. Such caste and caste-like systems are transgenerational cultural conspiracies which commonly have recourse to a number of recurrent, necessary exploitative themes. Founding fathers and, by extension, their ethnic families, are transformed from the Machiavellian to the Platonic with unfailing regularity. Public ref-

---

[1] Morton H. Fried discusses differential access in the general exploitative context in "On the Evolution of Social Stratification and the State" in his *Readings in Anthropology*, 2nd. edition, Vol. II (New York: Crowell Co. 1968).

[2] Bronislaw Malinowski's ethnographic and sociological analysis of myth as "the legal charter of the community" refers to non-machine cultures. However, I believe this concept to be equally applicable to exploitative societies with machine technologies. As he put it in *Argonauts of the Western Pacific* (New York: E. P. Dutton & Co., 1961, p. 328): "Thus, through the operation of what might be called the elementary law of sociology, myth possesses the normative power of fixing custom, of sanctioning modes of behavior, of giving dignity and importance to an institution." And again in *Magic, Science and Religion* (Boston: Beacon Press, 1948, pp. 102–3) Malinowski demonstrates the general applicability of the concept of myth charter beyond his Trobriand model. "The historical consideration of myth is interesting, therefore, in that it shows that myth, taken as a whole, cannot be sober history, since it is always made *ad hoc* to fulfil a certain sociological function, to glorify a certain group, or to justify an anomalous status . . . And this brings us once more to our original contention that the really important thing about the myth is its character of a retrospective, ever-present, live actuality. It is to a native neither a fictitious story, nor an account of a dead past; it is a statement of a bigger reality still partially alive. It is alive in that its precedent, its law, its moral, still rule the social life of the natives. It is clear that myth functions especially where there is a sociological strain, such as in matters of great difference in rank and power, matters of precedence and subordination, and unquestionably where profound historical changes have taken place."

erence to the fact that such transformations rest ultimately upon pomp, repression, and highly circumstantial evidence, is from the majority point of view, treason and/or bad taste.

There is a most direct correlation between the degree of fictive genetic proximity to the founders and the quality of access. Some real or imagined physical trait roster which may or may not actually be relatively characteristic of the powerful collectivity is venerated. This may be dark skin, as in traditional Nyoro society, or paler skin, as in traditional Ruanda society.[3] But powerful ethnicities can and do generate social races even in the absence of some marked physical difference; as witness the Japanese and Latin American minority-majority contexts.[4]

Relatively untrammeled access is forcibly reserved to those who can support their claims of most direct affinity to the founder. Thus, old family, white North European Protestants in North America, or *'Arab al' Araba* (original Arabs of Saudi Arabia), the Dlamini, or truest Swazi of traditional Swazi culture, and the *imajaren,* or truest blood Tuareg of the Sahara are the most privileged groups in their respective societies.[5] Qualified privileged access is also the right of true blood populations who, although not sharing the most immediate social genetic affinity to the founder and his exalted physical type, are still not outside his extended ethnic family. Southern and Eastern Europeans in the North American minority-majority context are true blood groups with qualified privileged access because they are reckoned as white.

In addition to original Arab Bedouin populations, there are *'Arab al-Musta'riba,* or Arabs who gradually got to be Arabs. The *imrad,* or vassal true blood Tuareg tribes are descended not from Tin Hinan as are *imajaren* truest blood Tuareg. *Imrad* are descended from Takamat the "white" personal maid of Tin Hinan. The truest and true blood are privileged members of caste and caste-like exploitative societies.

Beyond the truest and true blood branches of the temporally extended ethnic family of the founder are the vast group of them that serve; the "wretched of the earth" who are, in fact, circulating as inherited goods in the truest and true blood-dominated redistributive channels. These most severely power-disadvantaged groups are slave ethnicities. Slave ethnicities are those which are the victims of rigorous, temporary power imbalances with all the attendant adverse consequences. Thus, slave populations often reckoned as black tend the stock and produce the vegetable food of truest and true blood Tuareg. Both Tuareg and Bedouin fictive genealogies remove slave ethnicities the maximum possible social and genetic distance from the founders. The gulf decreed between truest and true blood segments of the caste or caste-like society and their slave segments facilitates more material exploitation.

Some slave ethnicities opt, through their myth charters, for a complete reversal of truest and true blood hegemony, while other inter-

[3] On the Nyoro, see *Bunyoro: An African Kingdom* by John Beattie (New York: Holt, Rinehart & Winston, 1960). On the Ruanda see "The Problem of Tutsi Domination" by J. J. Maquet in *Cultures and Societies of Africa,* edited by Simon and Phoebe Ottenberg (New York: Random House, 1960).

[4] For a comprehensive review of the Japanese minority-majority context see *Japan's Invisible Race* edited by George DeVos and Hiroshi Wagatsuma (Berkeley: Univ. of California Press, 1967). For the well known Latin American phenomenon of racial categorization based on behavior, not biology see Miles Richardson's *San Pedro, Colombia: Small Town in a Developing Society* (New York: Holt, Rinehart & Winston, 1970), Eric Wolf's *Sons of the Shaking Earth* (Chicago: Univ. of Chicago Press, 1959), and Charles Wagley's "On the Concept of Social Race in the Americas" in *Actas Del 33 Congreso Internacional de Americanistas* (San Jose: Lehmann, 1959, Vol. I, pp. 403–17).

[5] For truest and true blood genealogical fabrication see Carleton Coon's *Caravan: The Story of the Middle East* (New York: Holt, Rinehart & Winston, rev. ed., 1966), *The Swazi: A South African Kingdom* by Hilda Kuper (New York: Holt, Rinehart & Winston, 1963), and Robert F. Murphy's "Social Distance and the Veil" in *Peoples and Cultures of the Middle East,* Vol. I, edited by Louise E. Sweet (Garden City, L.I.: Natural History Press, 1970).

mediate slave ethnicities elect to "pass" as a community.

If the company of man can be arbitrarily restricted to only the truest and true blood temporally extended ethnic family of the powerful founders, then the highly ramified life's work of extraction can proceed with a clear, or at least a pleasantly benumbed, conscience. The Euro-American communal conscience, for example, is only vaguely aware of the monstrous inconsistency in the spectacle of a slaveholder demanding liberty or death and the criminal inappropriateness of the phrase "Indian giver."

The subordination of women is indispensable to the proper functioning of all unjust societies. Some women are inherited directly as spoil, while others must be subject to crypto-subordination as true and truest blood women are required to breed the next generation of heirs in the temporally extended ethnic family of the founders. Thus, among the Rwala (Saudi Bedouins), true blood males may exchange genes with true blood and slave females, but true blood females are forbidden on pain of death from sexual relations with any but true blood mates.[6]

This tendency of exploitative systems to reserve true and truest blood women for the express purpose of breeding legitimate heirs and to exact a tribute of sexual gain from slave ethnicities is common to caste and caste-like systems. It is no accident that exploitative societies have given legal, customary, and proverbial expression to this mechanism whereby a distinction between inheriting and inherited segments may be maintained. The Tuareg proverb "the belly holds the child," and the *lex ventris* are both expressions of the subordination of women for the purpose of maintaining hereditary lines.

Colonial United States slave codes often condemned free white women who bore black children to slavery. Many of the choice and master spirits of American independence, including the author of the Declaration of Independence, fathered families by slave women. Such offspring invariably were reduced to the wretched legal status of their slave mothers.[7]

Although women of the truest and true blood may receive ample tribute in the debased currency of double standard deference, they are, essentially, bound. This is a necessary consequence of their surrender of rights over their bodies to truest and true blood males who use these females as vehicles for the transgenerational transmission of stolen goods to heirs of their own choosing. It is through the use of women's bodies, via procreation, that men most closely approximate the illusion of personal immortality. The apotheosis of apical ancestors, social narcissism, social race fabrication, the elevation by decree of selfish parochial powerful interests to the level of multi-communal good, the suppression of women, and the reservation of privileged access to truest and true blood divisions of the extended ethnic family of the founders are salient aspects in dominant myth constitutions. The powerful collectivity marshals the poetic, scholarly, esthetic, and proverbial resources of the total collectivity to the justification of its monopoly of power.

The myth charters of the most depressed minority societies seek to challenge institutionalized inequality. The most severely power-disadvantaged groups generate anti-establishment myth charters. Majority culture extraction exacts from these power-disadvantaged ethnicities a burdensome tax in daughters, defer-

[6] See Alois Musil, *Manners and Customs of the Rwala Bedouins,* New York: Monograph of the American Geographical Society, No. 6, 1928.

[7] For discussions of colonial United States slave codes see *The Negro in Colonial New England* (New York: Atheneum, 1968) by Lorenzo Johnston Greene, *Slave and Citizen, the Negro in the Americas* (New York: Knopf, 1947) by Frank Tannenbaum, *Slavery in the Americas: A Comparative Study of Cuba and Virginia* (Chicago: Univ. of Chicago, 1967) by Herbert S. Klein, and Kenneth M. Stampp's *The Peculiar Institution* (New York: Random House, 1956). On founding father sexual exploitation of slave women see J. A. Rogers' *Sex and Race,* Vol. I (New York: Helga Rogers, 1942), and his *100 Amazing Facts About the Negro* (New York: Helga Rogers, 1957).

ence, drudgery, and treasure. The myth charters of power-disadvantaged ethnicities impugn the legitimacy of the powerful founder and his chosen heirs. The pseudo-scientific sophistry of master social race theory and lore is countered by the generally adhered to myth of the genetic and moral one-upness of the one-down. Some migratory gypsy groups regard theft *in extremis* as divinely authorized activity.

Contrary to the teachings of that ex-slave, Plato, slave status is cultural, not natural. The powerlessness of slave ethnicities is instrumental in the proliferation of ritual elements in their myth charters. The salient societal cult requirement of slave ethnicities is for an intractable omnipotence capable of moving wicked races and exalting obedient nations. Ung 'Thaniel (Elder Nathaniel Turner), secure in the knowledge that he had observed the canons of generative black slave theology for as long as Christ had observed them, challenged truest and true blood power with every expectation of victory because he was the instrument of a God whom no man could hinder. Wovoka, the Paiute prophet, called the desperate western Indians to other worldly social dancing and dastardly massacre in the equally vain expectation of a supernatural reversal of the ecological and power realities. Many slave ethnicities of Oceania, Africa, and Asia have rung changes upon the ubiquitous one-down theme of ritual militancy. Slave ethnicities forcibly suspended midway between their imperially disrupted traditional cultures and integration in managerial metropolitan machine cultures have created conditions of ritual obligation. On the eve of the American Civil War, the Xhosa, in response to the prophetic dreams of the maiden, Nongqawuse, and other reputable ladies, began to destroy the cattle and grain which were the staves of their lives. They persisted in the creation of a situation in which it would be unthinkable that their ancestors would not act to save them from famine and the Europeans. Many Melanesian peoples have been caught up in Pentecostal millenarian fervor in which they too destroyed their gardens, threw away their money, and constructed a climate of such holy desperation that the ancestors would be compelled to satisfy the longing of the people for the material products of machine culture and deliverance from truest and true blood caste arrogance.[8]

---

[8] Contrary to the "confessions" of William Styron *The Confessions of Nat Turner* (New York: Random House, 1966), Ung 'Thaniel was not a perverted lay preacher but a member in excellent standing of the class of elders who staffed the generative institution of black slave theology. His rising was an act of holy desperation for which he had prepared himself in proper millenarian fashion, a process which he himself described, in part, as follows. "After this revelation in the year 1825, and the knowledge of the elements being made known to me, I sought more than ever to obtain true holiness before the great day of judgment should appear, and then I began to receive the true knowledge of faith. And from the first steps of righteousness until the last, was I made perfect; and the Holy Ghost was with me, and said, 'Behold me as I stand in the heavens.' . . . . And on the 12th of May, 1828, I heard a loud noise in the heavens, and the Spirit instantly appeared to me and said the Serpent was loosened, and Christ had laid down the yoke he had borne for the sins of men, and that I should take it on and fight against the Serpent, for the time was fast approaching when the first should be last and the last should be first. *Ques.* Do you not find yourself mistaken now? *Ans.* Was not Christ crucified?" From *The Confessions of Nat Turner, The Leader of the Late Insurrection in Southampton (County), Va.,* edited by Thomas R. Gray (Baltimore: 1831) reprinted as an appendix in Harriet Beecher Stowe's *Dred: A Tale of the Great Dismal Swamp* (Cambridge, Mass.: The Riverside Press, 1895, p. 583, 4). Peter Worsley's *The Trumpet Shall Sound* (New York: Schocken Books, 2nd ed., 1968), Douglas L. Oliver's *The Pacific Islands* (Cambridge: Harvard University Press, 1962), and Cyril S. Belshaw's "The Significance of Modern Cults in Melanesian Development" in *Australian Outlook,* Vol. IV, No. 2, 1950 describe the range of millenarian cults in Oceania. Marna Foster Fisher discusses gypsy enabling philosophy in Arnold M. and Caroline Rose, eds. *Minority Problems* (New York: Harper & Row, 1965). In 1923 the National Leveler's Society issued a statement, published in *Japan's Invisible Race,* p. 46, of Burakumin moral superiority. They are the "chosen" people. Monica Hunter in *Reaction to Conquest* (London: Oxford Univ. Press, 1936) discusses Xhosa reaction to contact and conquest. For discussions of Jack Wilson (Wovoka) and the Ghost Dance see Robert F. Spencer and Jesse D. Jennings et al., *The Native Americans* (New York: Harper & Row, 1965), Ruth Underhill's *Red Man's America* (Chicago: Univ. of Chicago Press, 1953), and John Collier's *Indians of the Americas* (New York: Mentor Books, 1947).

Slave ethnicities are inclined to attribute the failure of ritual militancy to some flaw in the performance of the ritual rather than to the non-existence of the supernatural. It is often erroneously supposed that slave ethnicities are less ethnocentric than the truest and true blood architects of their power disadvantage. The core black American stereotype of white people as mechanically precocious, naive, arrogant, physically weak, sexually perverted spoiled children is common to many slave ethnicities. The engineering of the mechanics of extraction justifies much of this ill opinion of truest and true blood communal character deficiency. The principal error in slave ethnicity stereotyping is the firmly held misconception that these truest and true blood negative traits are genetic. One aspect of the myth charter of the Nation of Islam, derivative from the general context of North American black slave generative theology, denies not only the alleged superiority, but the very humanity of Euro-Americans.[9]

The myth charters of intermediate ethnicities are charters of communal social climbing. The mythic constitutions of intermediate ethnicities are charters of limited mobility and escape. They derive from the desire of subordinate fathers to free their heirs from the full weight of full minority status and to secure to their posterity some of the blessings and privileges of majority status. Subsequent generations of mythcraft embellish the charters. These charters are deed, social register, and holy writ for numerous intermediate ethnicities all claiming an "others" or "half-Aryan" status. It is these intermediate myth charters of "others" communities which have sustained the persistent tribe of "greasy Indians" and "brown-skinned white men" who hold those social badlands between slave and truest and true blood ethnicities.

Truest and true blood exploitative management is essentially parasitic; feeding upon the rigorous exaction levied upon power-disadvantaged slave ethnicities. Wherever power has sustained the institutionalization of inequality, some individuals and communities have striven for a place on the upper millstone. All these groups—Anglo-Indians, Jamaican Browns, Latin American *criollos* and the considerable aggregation of intermediate North American slave ethnicities which are responding with accelerated sullenness to the roster of pejoratives such as "Brass Ankles", "Red Bones", "Guineas", "Jackson Whites", "Melungeons", and "Issues" seek a more exalted place in their respective exploitative systems by advancing claims of distant affinity with true or truest blood ethnic families and deferentially petitioning for a poor relations status in the temporally extended ethnic family of the powerful founders. This very limited mobility is generally effected by exploiting the galactic gaps in pseudo-scientific social race hierarchies of the truest and true blood. Aspiring intermediate slave ethnicities frequently bolster their often tenuous claims for "half-Aryan" status by attempting to surpass the truest and true blood in their anti-slave defensive arrogance.[10] Yuzuru Sasaki and George DeVos in *Japan's Invisible Race* report that the aspiring transitional Japanese community of Iwamoto-cho, although 70 percent outcaste itself, tends to treat the neighboring outcaste community of Uchihama with defensive disdain, even resorting to the use of the most hated pejoratives.

[9] Elijah Muhammad's *Message to the Black Man in America* (Chicago: Muhammad's Mosque No. 2, 1965) sets forth black American data concerning the one-downness of the one-up. A personal communication from Professor Nancy Bowers of the Anthropology Department at Duke University, North Carolina, reveals amazing congruity between core North American black stereotyping of whites with indigenous New Guinea anti-European stereotyping. An analogous variant of this slave ethnicity anti-true and truest blood stereotypic syndrome is also reported for the New Zealand minority-majority context in David P. Ausubel's *The Fern and the Tiki* (New York: Holt, Rinehart & Winston, 1960).

[10] For a survey of United States intermediate aspiring slave ethnicities see Brewton Berry's *Almost White* (Toronto: Collier-Macmillan, 1963).

This intermediate mobility has generated the ubiquitous tribe of "anti-Maori Maoris", "white folks' niggers," feminine anti-feminists, and "Uncle Tomahawks," to mention but a few.

Intermediate myth charter is perhaps nowhere better illustrated than in the case of the aspiring transitional Shinnecock community of Long Island, New York. That indefatigable Thucydides and Suetonius of Black Studies, Joel A. Rogers, numbers the Shinnecocks among North American "mixed blood groups who are known as other than Negroes." [11] In both the environing white and black communities of Suffolk, the Long Island county in which the Shinnecock community is located, this group's claim to Indian status is highly suspect. This ambivalent ambiguity is a permanent part of the Shinnecock political and psycho-social environment. The Federal Bureau of Indian Affairs does not recognize the Indian status of the Shinnecock community. The New York State Interdepartmental Committee on Indian Affairs, however, does recognize the Shinnecock community as one of the nine Indian reservations of that state. The same New York State agency surmises that they are "presumably of Algonkin stock." [12] No Amerindian language, Algonkin or otherwise, is spoken in the Shinnecock community, but then, Beowulf would have some rather severe communication problems in 99 and 44/100ths percent of the white Anglo-Saxon Protestant homes in North America.[13]

It is certain that the Shinnecock community is highly hybridized. Whether it is more highly hybridized than the North American Afro-American and Euro-American communities is a matter for conjecture. It is an incontrovertible fact that the Shinnecock gene pool has drawn heavily upon the genetic reservoirs of black, red, and white populations.

A small group of Shinnecock families have fabricated communal polity and myth charter which emphasizes the Amerindian genetic component, protests too much about Euro-American biological connections, and denies, or grossly minimizes the formidable genetic and cultural black component in Shinnecock heritage.

By electing to stress the Amerindian genetic component and rejecting their black genetic and cultural heritage, the Shinnecocks are seeking intra-systemic mobility through the identification with Indians, a more prestigious slave ethnicity according to the canons of North American truest and true blood social race ranking. Shinnecock pretensions to Amerindian genetic and cultural status have never been fully credited in truest and true blood eyes. The amused, sometimes condescending tolerance of the black community and the exertions of some white patrons have kept these claims from being entirely dismissed. But whenever the hard realities of caste circulation have asserted themselves, truest and true blood formal juridical qualifications of the Shinnecock claims to Amerindian status has been made. The current reservation is only a fraction of the large territory exploited by the aboriginal Shinnecock band or tribe. The present community has been reduced to less than a square mile in area by a steady campaign of alienation in which Shinnecock claims to their "tribal" patrimony have generally been rejected.[14]

[11] For a view of aspiring intermediate slave ethnicities as seen from the core black cultural point of view, see J. A. Rogers, *Sex and Race,* Vol. II, Chap. 35 (New York: Helga Rogers, 1942).

[12] The New York State Interdepartmental Committee on Indian Affairs pamphlet *The Indian Today in New York State* (Albany: 1967) has included a very brief description of the Shinnecock community on page 6.

[13] The field phase of the author's Shinnecock research was conducted during the summer of 1969 under a grant from the Faculty Research Fellowship and Grant-In-Aid, Joint Awards Council/University Awards Committee of the State University of New York.

[14] For discussions of the on-going land disputes between the Shinnecocks and their neighbors see Peter Ross' *A History of Long Island* (New York: The Lewis Publishing Co., Vol. I, pp. 41–2, 1902), Harriet Brown's *We Hang in the Balance,* a privately printed pamphlet published in the mid-1950's, and Henry S. Manley's *No Man's Land, Long Island,* reprinted from *The Long Island Forum* (Amityville, New York, 1953).

Shinnecock myth charter maintains that they are the remnant of a once proud dynasty. There is in actual fact scant literature on the band or tribelet called Shinnecock who, upon contact in the early 17th century, were exploiting a territory of several hundred square miles. True blood Yankee colonists from Lynn, Massachusetts who first invaded Shinnecock territory in force to found the present town of Southampton describe the aborigines as a clan. Toward the end of the 18th century the Shinnecock were described as one of the "thirteen aboriginal tribes" of Long Island. A more recent description of Long Island aboriginal culture characterizes it as band organized. Before the 19th century had run half its course the Shinnecock language had perished and the process of black genetic and cultural admixture had advanced so far as to render Shinnecock claims to Amerindian status tenuous in the extreme.[15]

The core element of Shinnecock myth charter is a fictive genealogy agreed upon by a small caste-like segment of the community. "Blood members" are those members of the community who claim hereditary shares in a "tribal" patrimony said to have been bequeathed them by the aboriginal Eastern Woodland Shinnecock band. Communal records are said to document "blood member" status, but there is no documentation for the claim of unbroken lineal descent from Nowedonah, the tribal patriarch or band head man who treated with those Yankee colonists in 1640, to present day Shinnecock people.

The "tribal" historian who claims descent from Nowedonah has given formal recognition to the ambiguity about Shinnecock status by describing her people as "not White, nor Black, nor Red, but true Americans."[16] A number of Shinnecock informants expressed chagrin, doubt, and resignation about their Indian status. Expressions like "we're all mixed up here," "it's a half-assed way to be an Indian" and "I don't really know what we are" are representative of a considerable segment of Shinnecock public opinion.

As is often the case with aspiring slave ethnicities, the geniuses of Shinnecock myth charter have reinforced their claims to Indian status by the inauguration of a validating festival. The "Ceremonial Chief" said that he and a relative, the "tribal" historian, initiated this tradition in 1937. He also indicated that the inauguration of this lucrative Pow Wow had occasioned a spectacular increase in general acceptance of the Shinnecock claims to Indian status.[17] A number of Shinnecocks obviously maintain a black and an Amerindian identity

[15] *Thoughts on the State of the American Indians* by Silas Wood (New York? Collector's Item, out of print, 1794), and John H. Morice, "The Indians of Long Island," in *The Long Island Forum* (Jan.–April, 1944). In 1845 the historian, Nathaniel Prime, in his *A History of Long Island* (New York: Robert Carter, 1845, p. 118) stated that the remnants of the Shinnecock "in their present mingled state" consisted of 30 families of 140 individuals. He further stated that "by mingling with the African race, whose condition in this country is even more depressed than their own, they have degraded instead of elevating their condition, in the eyes of the community and stamped an infrangible seal upon their condition. In the course of a few more more generations, if they shall have any survivors, all the characteristics of their aboriginal ancestry will be swallowed up and lost in the predominant features of a less noble, but equally injured and despised race." The 1889 *Report of the Special Committee to Investigate the Indian Problem of the State of New York* (Albany, No. 51, p. 54) described the few remaining Shinnecocks as follows: "Their social condition is not enviable, during the time the Negroes were held as slaves in this State, these Indians largely intermarried with them and their descendants have more of the Negro than of the Indian in their veins and in fact are only Indian in name."

[16] Lois Marie Hunter, *The Shinnecock Indians* (New York: Buys Brothers, 1950, p. 90).

[17] Berry in *Almost White* reports the same validating festival for a number of aspiring intermediate slave ethnicities. Ethel Boissevain in "Narragansett Survival: A Study of Group Persistence Through Adapted Traits" (Ethnohistory: Vol. 6, No. 4, Fall, 1959, p. 358), commenting on the "identity-giving" institution of the Pow Wow of the Rhode Island Narragansetts, a similarly hybridized aspiring intermediate slave ethnicity, observes that "Participation in the Pow Wow and other events that call for wearing an Indian costume makes it clear to the outside community that the individual is of Indian descent. In the community at large, to be known as a person of Indian descent is an advantage in status over the Negro minority in the community with no Indian ancestry."

and appear on the reservation only once a year at the time of the big Labor Day weekend Pow Wow to, as one informant put it, "do our Indian thing." However, a minority of enterprising Shinnecock families have maintained in the face of a steady drumfire of incredulity a tenacious insistence upon Indian status and the shrinking patrimony and privileges to which these claims give access.

Euro-Americans have employed their power monopoly to impose upon the whole of American society an iron law of descent. This social race convention assigns maximum access to wealth and privileged status to persons possessing the mythical quality of pure white descent. The minimum of privilege and access is assigned to those possessing the equally fictive biological quality of pure black descent. By the canons of Euro-American social race, the discovery of the mythical drop of mythical "black" blood in the veins of any ancestor, from the mythical flood up to the present, would be incontrovertible proof of the blackness of the contemporary descendant. The discovery of an equal quantity of the equally non-existent "white" blood in the veins of some diluvian ancestor of an individual currently called black would not qualify his blackness, as that nebulous attribute is defined by the non-objective conventions of Euro-American social race.

Pure whiteness, even if it did exist in the real world as it does in the pseudo-scientific fancy, would not be the emblem of excellence most Euro-Americans imagine it. The plain truth is that a skin reckoned as white by most whites is the passport to privilege and a skin reckoned as black by most whites is, given the current monopoly of power by white people, the emblem of exclusion from wealth and privileged status.

All components of the great American castelike commonwealth are hybridized. In the North American caste-like context then, that fragment of Afro-American folk doggerel which equates proximity to privilege with the degree of melanin in the skin does prove out. But the degree of relative de-pigmentation is only significant if supported by the attendant lie agreed upon which couches the formal denial of black descent and the communal claim of "half-Aryan" descent in a formalized, intermediate myth charter which does not challenge the validity of the castelike hierarchy, but argues for a superior, subdominant place in the system.

The chief defect in the Shinnecock "tribal" historian's true-blue American ploy is that in the existing minority-majority context, it is myth calling unto myth. The true-blue American syndrome is a cultural convention which bolsters true and truest blood legitimation mythology. Shinnecock identity would be an academic issue if the United States were not a caste organized empire. In the global negative minority-majority context then, the fact is that the melting pot is, for slave ethnicities everywhere, a crucible.

34

CONTEMPORARY ARTS IN NON-WESTERN SOCIETIES

JACQUELINE DELANGE FRY

The study of art has been an integral aspect of anthropology since the latter took shape as a recognizable discipline. Partly this has to do with the collecting activities of the field, often associated with studies and public displays at museums. As anthropology matured, interest in art expanded to include more than its tangible products. Consideration was given to the role of art and artistic objects in other, enlarged, cultural contexts. The attempt to penetrate "paleolithic religion," for example, included efforts to understand cave paintings and the most ancient sculptures. Beyond this, anthropologists and other social scientists have attempted to deal with the artist and the artist's audience in sociological and psychological interaction. Others have tried delving into problems of creativity and style or have made efforts to penetrate inner realms of cultural values through the analysis of artistic products.

In much of this there tends to be a marked degree of patronization and this is what Jacqueline Fry wishes us to see and confront. A central concept is that of "the primitive," which comes to life through contrast. "We," the moderns, the developed ones, and what "we" do are placed in opposition to "them." What "they" do is "primitive." Formerly taken for granted, the defense of this distinction has become increasingly more difficult and problematic. Moral and political problems are quickly encountered, but other difficulties also spawn. Few if any cultures exist in blessed isolation from the metropolitan powers of America, Europe, and Asia.

One product of accelerating penetrations of market/industrial societies into every inhabited region of the world is change in the realm of art. Colonialism and imperialism bring the arts of everywhere back to the metropolitan marketplace, but they also facilitate the export of new media, new techniques, new artistic ideas, new motivations and messages, new social conditions of artistic creation and production. In such situations, what is "primitive"? What is "art"? What is "primitive art"? Jacqueline Fry helps lead the way into our consideration of these problems.

▼△▼△▼

In relatively recent years, the visual arts of the Eskimo, the American Indian, the African, and the peoples of Oceania have appeared as major elements on the international art market. Inspired by a strongly ethnocentric cultural anthropology, this appearance is the culmination of a process that began near the end of the nineteenth century and influenced even the most serious works on the history of art. Torn from their contexts and analysed in European terms, the so-called "primitive" arts have been generally treated as an annex to the European cultural tradition. The point of this article is that even now, although much more information is at hand, our attentiveness to the non-western object has not yet provoked our thoughts enough for us to decentralize our point of view concerning occidental cultural attitudes.

Today, any serious attempt to understand the contemporary visual production of non-occidentals would seem to require from the outset a systematic questioning concerning our knowledge of traditional artistic backgrounds. The occidental public tends to condemn other cultures to stagnation; change in another society is interpreted as degradation while new types of objects are treated as inauthentic. But recently anthropologists have had to revise their notions concerning the whole complex of relations that made up the structure of non-western communities. We now have facts relevant to the methods and aesthetic criteria used by artists, studies have been made concerning the non-western art market and the circulation

SOURCE: "Contemporary Arts in Non-Western Societies," *Artscanada* (Dec. 1971–Jan. 1972): 96–101. Reprinted by permission of the author and publisher.

of objects, analyses of the standards of judgment used by various members of local communities are underway. The most evident and general conclusion of these studies is that the traditional non-western community, although proud of a long tradition, was neither a closed nor a static system ruled by fixed laws. And yet, now that we can recognize the real conditions of traditional artistic production, we still find it difficult to relate to the contemporary non-western artist who works in terms of new and often excruciating social conditions.

For most people, whether they be Europeans or North Americans, a Nigerian wood sculpture, a half-animal, half-human polychrome mask from the Canadian West Coast, or even a small Eskimo ivory, are immediately classified in a vague group of things called "primitive art." Although it has a most innocent appearance, this term glosses over many ideas related to a fundamental ideological attitude: in its most immediate sense, it is rooted in an ethnocentric state of mind, a belief in the total superiority of European civilization and techniques. Bound up with the history of European economic expansion since the end of the fifteenth century, a unilateral idea of culture developed, flowered and then became fixed. Linear historicism became the means of self-justification as Europe passed from the Period of the Slave Trade to the Period of Colonization and then, with America, on to the Period of Industrial Imperialism.

The visual arts of the communities subjected to this assault were naturally situated, as were the peoples themselves, on the bottom rung of the one-way ladder of progress and evolution. Because of their position on the ladder, these peoples were thought to be devoid of the "finer" techniques of thought and expression, that is, bound up in an immediate relation with the powers of nature. Their arts were considered to be fascinating examples of the life of good (or bad, according to the case) savages, the "primitives." What one expected to find in a confrontation with the "fetishes" of Africa is what Nolde—and with him so many other Expressionists—sought in his passion for the "primitive" arts. They called it "fear and anguish." "It is in fear and trembling," said Nolde, "that man can rediscover primitive authenticity and permit to well up within himself the signs of exorcism that savages still know."

It is with this background that the "primitive" arts have acquired an international status and have been assimilated into what is so incorrectly called the universal patrimony of mankind. We have not yet attained a truly universal point of view; we see and select only what our European cultural filters permit. Happily there is a more positive side to the story. The Cubist and Surrealist movements did recognize the purely visual value of many works, and this in turn exercised some influence on the re-thinking of anthropology. André Breton was a sincere admirer of the Katchina masks and dolls of the Hopi and Zuñi Indians; his interest also centred on the masks of the Alaskan Eskimo shamans. Matisse, Picasso, Derain as well as many poets collected "l'Art Nègre."

But in spite of the sincere interest and respect so evident in a few, what most occidentals still seem to seek in the "primitive" arts is a set of qualities that correspond to their idea of traditional "primitive" life. The objects are considered valid or authentic only if they have served in religious, magic or even political functions, but the very notions of these functions lack roots in reality. Any object that does not fit the standard notions is rejected as inauthentic. In particular, any work coming from the hand of a non-occidental artist but which corresponds to criteria more or less similar to those reigning in the Occident has raised—and still raises—cries of scandal and reprobation. While we await and expect the "primitives" to offer us an unchanged and purely authentic object, we are constantly on guard to extirpate all signs of the "degradation" of a tradition. It is as if our idea of the "primitive" has been established as a norm to be imposed upon the future of all non-western peoples. Is it not time to ask ourselves very seriously what directions are open for the visual arts in living communities that have been subjected to radically new and often humiliating conditions?

Before trying to situate the problem of contemporary Eskimo artistic production, I should like to dwell upon what is happening in Africa in order to clarify a few issues. The common factor is, of course, the White Presence.

If we separate Sub-Saharian artistic production into categories—traditional and contemporary—it immediately becomes evident that the distinction is not clear and that, in a sense, these categories are not really opposed at all. Even if we exclude from consideration the rampant mass production of tourist trinkets and bad imitations of traditional African forms that Frank MacEwen has so aptly called "Airport Art," there still remain three types of contemporary production that are worthy of thorough consideration.

The first type concerns objects that, more numerous than was first thought, are produced for traditional purposes using more or less traditional methods and iconology. Their social functions have been modified for various reasons, but they clearly belong to a continuum of production oriented by local requirements. The second type includes objects that are made by Africans for trade or for sale. The organization of this trade has taken on a new market structure including the African Art Gallery, the governmental craft shop, the side street store and the market-place. The new trade structure appears to have had a direct influence on the form of traditional objects.

Whereas the first type of production is incontestably rooted in African tradition and the second poses the problem of the relationship between market methods and form, the third type raises more serious problems and will retain our attention a little longer. It concerns the production of objects, paintings in particular, that apparently have their creative and economic roots in Europe rather than in Africa. If painting on canvas or on any mobile support was imported from Europe at the beginning of this century, the first real development of African painters did not take place until between 1950 and 1960. This development took place within the framework of purely European scholastic or social institutions. But even these remarks do not seem to justify the idea that there is something non-African about painting.

The fact is that the development of painting in Africa spread so rapidly that it has acted as an incentive to re-examine many hasty statements about the absence of pictorial and painterly arts in traditional African contexts. This new investigation has abundantly shown that the step into painting taken by so many Africans was not as abrupt as formerly supposed. It was well founded in various African traditions. Figurative and geometic murals, body painting, and the painting of various supports are now well attested. These various types of work were executed by using carefully prepared and combined colors with charcoal, kaolin, clay and vegetable bases applied with a feather brush or the fingers. The White Presence has introduced three new factors: prepared commercial materials, the mobile support which corresponds to a new economic situation, and a partially new iconography.

At this point it should be repeated that the traditional African artist has never really corresponded to our idea of the primitive, non-individualized producer of communal goods guided only by the pressures of social and religious imperatives. This idea, repeated so often in scholarly books and articles, was based on our own ignorance and our inability to see personal and local stylistic differences. It has now been demonstrated that the traditional artist was and still is known by his style and that he was subjected to criticism by people using highly elaborate aesthetic norms. The traditional artist, while being very attentive to the real requirements of the community, worked with a certain margin of freedom that permitted creative stylistic innovation. The emergence of the contemporary African artist does not then reflect some kind of treason to the community; his relation with his people remains much the same as before. His problem does not concern his passage from the role of the blacksmith-sculptor, inheritor of a long and weighty social and mythological tradition, to the role of artist superstar in the occidental mode. The problem is much more ours than his, for we are being slowly forced to revise our ideas both of art and tradition. The basis of this revision cannot be our own cultural heritage, so bound up in exotic illusion. It must centre upon the realities of the present time, the problems of real people and the actual conditions of art production.

Since 1960 an increasing number of African artists have participated in both individual and group shows, mostly in large European cities and in the United States. Certain of these artists were enabled to develop their talent only with the help of interested individuals who provided them with the material means that permitted them to keep on working. Valente Malangatana from Mozambique was more or less adopted by a European architect, Hezbon Owiti was promoted by an African novelist and Thomas Mukarobgwa got his start while working at the National Gallery in Rhodesia. Without help, the possibility of a serious formation is closed to many young artists, but this does raise a problem. The patron system tends to create an exceptional if not artificial climate for the young artist.

It was this state of affairs that encouraged Frank MacEwen to found a self-supporting workshop school in conjunction with the National Gallery of Rhodesia. This workshop has greatly stimulated the production of soapstone sculpture by artists mostly of Shona origin. The visual imagery of these carvings appears to be deeply rooted in the Shona mythological tradition, but, strangely enough, many pieces are not unlike certain works of the Canadian Eskimo. This coincidence would seem to be due to more than mere chance; a deeper study of both Shona and Eskimo works will be necessary before any plausible theory can be formulated.

Other artists have been trained in Art Schools founded by Europeans in Africa; recently most of these schools have been taken in hand by African teachers. The best two examples are the School of Design of the Khartoum Technical Institute in the Sudan and the Zaria School of Art in Nigeria. Ibrahim El Salahi and Ahmed Shibrain were both trained at Khartoum. Although Salahi's preferred medium is oil, he works within the rigorous Islamic calligraphic tradition; even his more figurative works have the strong rhythmic character of the Arabic written word. Ahmed Shibrain, remaining even closer to pure calligraphy, has taken up a whole program of investigation of the visual possibilities of the written word. In a conversation, Salahi, who has studied extensively outside his own country, was asked if he had gained anything from his studies at the Slade School of Art in London. He answered that the knowledge and the experience he had acquired did not help him to express himself in his own way.

Among the many African artists who have been exiled, often for their success in expressing their point of view, one of the most remarkable is Mhalaba Dumile from Cape Province, South Africa. Although he exhibited his work in Johannesburg in 1963, he was not recognized as an artist and was forced to leave his country. He now lives in London, England. His work, particularly his ink drawings, centre on the sufferings of his people in South Africa.

Whether our brief overview of the African contemporary situation can help us in our approach to the artistic production of the Canadian Eskimo remains to be seen. What appears to be certain is that, in terms of western cultural attitudes, Eskimo arts are lumped together with the African arts in the vague category called "primitive art," or worse, "handicrafts." The cultural base of this category is the imposition of the White Presence during the colonial period.

The visual productions of both Eskimos and Africans struggle under the disadvantage of having been the object of a semi-scientific literature in which factual information, hypothesis and value judgments are hopelessly entangled. In particular, contemporary Eskimo arts are frequently presented in terms of a mono-linear historical model which, while relating the past to the present, makes constant reference to the "stone age" and the "primitive." Even if temporal differences are sometimes recognized, spatial differences are usually forgotten or put aside. The result is that the contemporary arts are seen either as the result of a homogeneous evolution in one time-space context or they appear as a totally artificial phenomenon with no relation to the past, traditional life of the Eskimo. In spite of the careful work of authors such as George Swinton, it is still necessary to analyse the contemporary Eskimo arts with reference both to date and region as well as in terms of the internal structure of each community and the social and economic pressures brought to bear on it from the outside.

It is no more reasonable to speak of "Eskimo Art" than it is to speak of "African Art," as if these expressions had a precise meaning when used in the singular. Each of these terms covers a multiplicity of art forms, styles and conditions of production. As was once the case concerning African visual production, only the sculpture of the Eskimo seems to be considered a valid "high art" form. Every kind of visual expression, from the arts of the body to the aesthetic of the environment, including embroidery, applique, ceramics, printmaking and drawing will have to be given systematic attention.

In order to give future studies a solid basis, it would seem necessary to discover in precise terms what the contemporary Eskimo has adopted from occidental artistic techniques and the reasons for this adoption. Before the "Houstonian" period of organized development, which began in 1948–49, there had already been an important period of contact and exchange with the European world. Beginning with the scientific explorations of the early nineteenth century, the arts of the Eskimo had already adopted certain new orientations, notably that of the scrimshaw. The signification of these new orientations cannot be grasped without a new look at the traditional pre-contact Eskimo context. But here, even more than with Africa where many communities still live in terms of their traditional ways, a study of pre-contact contexts—the discovery of the precise use and meaning of objects, the technical processes employed in their making and the place they assumed in the total structure of the community—seems nearly hopeless. Unfortunately most studies to date have been made on the premises of a religious and magic functionalism that neatly obliterates any social or economic facts that don't fit the theory.

If the promotion and development of a contemporary artistic production would seem to be common to Africa and the Arctic, it is nevertheless true that the character of these developments is radically different in each case. Both sociological and ecological differences need to be taken into consideration.

The encouragement given to Eskimo sculptors in the regions of Povungnituk and Port Harrison around 1949 had little or nothing to do with the discovery and recognition of an artistic movement that needed to be fostered from the outside. The hard truth of the matter is that a new means of subsistence had to be found for whole communities whose traditional economy had been destroyed. After the organization of a specialized market, it now appears that the source of artistic production is found not in traditional communities, but in various centres formed by the artificial regrouping of the Eskimo population. It is regrettable that we have little access to information concerning the organization of these centres in order to have a clear idea of the real working conditions of the artist. We need documented facts concerning the foundation of the various Eskimo centres in the Arctic, and it would be well to clarify the role of both private and official experts in the promotion of the Eskimo arts. This documentation, the records compiled by the various federal authorities, artistic advisers and commercial interests involved in the creation of programs designed primarily in terms of economic needs, should be made available through publication. But even this is not enough. Are the Eskimo now totally dependent on the market machine? Have they been permitted to direct their own affairs? Are they involved in a great economic adventure rather than in a mode of aesthetic expression?

. . . . .

One more important problem needs to be raised. The available information concerning the attitudes of Eskimo artists towards their own, and their neighbours', production seems to be very contradictory. If, as some say, certain Eskimo sculptors find deep satisfaction in their work, others quote Eskimos as saying that they force themselves to produce art works for purely economic reasons and that they would prefer to do other things to live—if they could. The amazing thing is that, under these conditions, apparently so artificial and geared to mass production for a non-selective market, numerous works of undeniable excellence, showing creative innovation both on the level of materials and of form have been produced. To take these facts into account, it is not at all sufficient to explain away reality by saying that the European concept of ART does not exist in the Arctic. The Eskimo does have reasons for producing his sculpture and he does reflect on what he is doing. What inevitably happens to us as we enter this area of study is that we begin to doubt our own notions of what art is about.

Due at least partly to the challenge presented by contemporary non-western arts, our old stereotyped image of "primitive" societies is rapidly fading out. One of the major conditions of this artistic production has been the rapid and strong movement of colonized peoples toward self-determination, frequently involving a brutal passage from one life-style to another. If we do not force these people to die—or if they do not choose to die rather than live in a way not worth the bother—they will continue to create new forms in a constant reinterpretation of life.

35

THE ROLE OF MUSIC IN WESTERN APACHE CULTURE

DAVID P. McALLESTER

There is little I can say to introduce the final essay in this section, a lovely little paper that is not particularly concerned with explorations into theory but has the goal of crossing cultural boundaries in the hope of achieving understanding of a different mode of musical expression. This paper does offer an opoprtunity, however, to comment on one of the major continuing contributions of anthropology—a contribution often given mere lip service when not snobbishly derogated. I refer to the fact that cultures are different and continue to be different. Understanding and communication among cultures will continue to be a major desideratum for as long as we can see into the future. Even when cultures are united by similar political systems, or intertwine in mutually dependent economies, there is ample ground for conflict and hostility. One of the most shocking phenomena of the present century has been the outbreak of violence in the relations between states claiming to be socialist—a development of profound significance that will not be overcome by denials or avoidance.

What all of this means is that the old function of anthropology, to describe different cultures to themselves and each other, will not disappear. While a major portion of that work must go into the description and analysis of diverging economic, social, and political systems, a very important part must be devoted to clarifying different ideologies, again each to the others. Nor does this have to be a rather grim task for it also has its own rewards as we expand our own appreciations, broaden our tastes, and whet our appetites for artistic expressions beyond those we presently know.

▼△▼△▼

The discipline of the ethnomusicologist is comparative musicology in its broadest sense. It is obvious that music is a highly integral part of the culture in which it is found. This means that comparative musicology should be, and in our case necessarily must be, comparative culturology. This is why ethnomusicologists are drawn largely from the field of anthropology or at least have had extensive anthropological training.

This insistence on the relationship of music to culture should be unnecessary and would be if it were not for a peculiar trait in our own Western European culture: the bifurcation of the concept of culture. We *can* think of culture in the anthropological sense of the total way of life of a people, but we also think of culture in the sense of "cultivated," with a particular emphasis on art forms and art for art's sake. The result of this cultural trait of ours has been a separation of art from culture-as-a-whole. We are more likely to discuss the creative periods of Picasso than Picasso as a manifestation of the social, religious and economic pressures of his times, or, in other words, Picasso as a manifestation of his culture.

Similarly, in music, we are very prone to a consideration of music *qua* music outside of its cultural context. We are most likely to discuss a song as an art form, as pretty or ugly and why, and in many other ways outside its principal cultural function.

In recent years the functional, whole-cultural emphasis has been brought—I could say "has been brought *back*"—into our intellectual discourse by, among others, the ethnologist. And the ethnologist learned this whole-cultural perspective from his contacts with small homogeneous groups. Such cultures, as we have heard since the days of Herbert Spencer, have not compartmentalized art, religion, earning a

SOURCE: *Men and Cultures: Selected Papers of the Fifth International Congress of Anthropological and Ethnological Sciences*, Anthony F. C. Wallace (ed.), Philadelphia, September 1–9, 1956. Philadelphia: University of Pennsylvania Press, 1960. pp. 468–72. Reprinted by permission of the publisher and the author.

livelihood, social organization and the other aspects of their lives. They live their lives whole and their cultures can be seen as wholes by the intelligent visitor.

The other anthropological perspective, the cross-cultural perspective, the comparison of custom across the wide gamut of diverse cultures, is less unique with us, but it has a special dimension when used by anthropologists. In our discipline as we learn the range of variation in human behavior, and, on the other hand, study the great unifying similarities, our comparative view is steadied and controlled throughout by the great lesson we have learned from our less sophisticated subjects, who are also our instructors, that cultural manifestations are meaningful only in their cultural context.

Let me illustrate these few words with an anecdote: I asked an American Indian if he thought a certain song, unfamiliar to him, was beautiful and his reply was: "I don't know. I don't know what the song is for." It was a question no one would have asked him in his culture and an answer I never would have received in mine. I saw then as never before why my teachers demanded that an anthropological education must include first-hand acquaintance with customs and attitudes different from my own.

In this paper I will try to apply the two perspectives, whole-cultural and cross-cultural, to the music of the Apache Indians of Arizona. I should say here that my remarks will apply only to the White Mountain Apaches, since I did not visit the other group of the Western Apaches on the San Carlos reservation, and these observations are based on only one summer's field study.

To get as far into Apache music as I could in a short period of time, I used the familiar techniques of the participant observer. I camped with Apache families, attended ceremonies and even assisted a medicine man in singing over a sick child. I learned some Apache songs since I have found elsewhere that even one or two songs, imperfectly rendered, are tremendous rapport builders. I secured the permission of the tribal council to make recordings and found the recording sessions invaluable with their long discussions of origin, use and meaning of songs. The questions that I asked centered around the following:

How the Apaches "felt" about their music

What musical instruments they used

How old children were when they began singing

Whether there was special effort to teach songs to children

What the different kinds of songs were

Was it a common thing to make up new songs

Were there happy (sad) and pretty (ugly) songs

Whether there were tabus of various kinds in music

What Apaches thought of non-Apache music

I attempted to ask the more general questions first in any interview in order to avoid suggesting specific answers by specific questions.

By such methods I made at least a start toward learning the various kinds and uses of Western Apache music and attitudes toward music. In trying to present some of these I will use the cross-cultural perspective by comparing Apache music with our own, and I will attempt to provide the whole-cultural perspective with ethnographic detail and excursions into various aspects of Apache culture.

Differences

One of the first differences to strike me was the difference in function. With us a principal function of music seems to be as an aid in inducing attitude. We have songs to evoke moods of tranquillity, nostalgia, sentiment, group rapport, religious feeling, party solidarity and patriotism, to name a few. Thus we sing to put babies to sleep, to make work seem lighter, to make people buy certain kinds of breakfast foods, or to ridicule our enemies. To the Western Apaches, music has a more direct function. For example in curing, the music is not to *predispose* the patient to getting well but is the direct cure. Taken so directly we call such a conception of music superstitious or magical and a confusion of cause and effect. Perhaps when our knowledge of music therapy progresses beyond its present infant stage we may get over feeling so superior in this matter.

Certainly one of the principal functions of Apache music is healing, and many aspects of Apache attitude towards music and healing are different from ours. I will list some of these:

1. *Healing is social.* It is performed at a large gathering, the larger the better, by the medicine man, and all who know the chant even partly join in. There are drummers, dancers and many on-lookers. The whole community, men, women, children and dogs are present, all participating, if only by being there. Healing is also social in another sense: social misdemeanors of the patient may be uncovered by the medicine man by the power of music. In the course of the chanting the practitioner may go into a state of trance. Everyone stops singing. The drummers go on beating the drums softly in unison (called "thunder drumming"). Emerging from the trance, the medicine man may reveal some selfish or other kind of antisocial act of the patient and pray to the supernatural for forgiveness and general blessing for all present.

2. *Healing music is fun.* Drinking is considered necessary for the right feeling of group empathy and in order that the singing will be free and enjoyable. The atmosphere is not like that of our hospital or sick room but one of boisterous good spirits with shouting, clowning and flirtation going on. In the music itself, hearty yells are frequent and the parodying of words and music may occur. The songs may be interspersed with jokes and *double entendres.*

3. *Healing music contains great power.* The words in the chants bring power to the patient and blessing to all who attend. Certain types of song are specific to certain ailments. In his trance the medicine man may discover that deer songs should be added at a certain time to a sing made up largely of lightning songs. These powerful songs can also be dangerous if misused. The sanction is the danger of being struck by lightning or bitten by a snake or spider. As presented in the literature, such tabus are often stated as absolute. They may be so among certain groups, though we are beginning to learn a good deal about the difference between ideal culture and actual culture. For the Western Apaches I witnessed the results of a broken tabu. A medicine man sang very special songs for my recording in conditions of some secrecy and with the warning that it might bring lightning, since these matters should only be discussed in the winter. A very severe lightning storm did come up and five people in the community were so frightened by near misses that they had to have the help of a ceremonial practitioner. My medicine man was busy for some time healing one of these cases, and then came back and resumed recording with me. He went on recording the same dangerous songs. There is no doubt in my mind that he felt that they *were* dangerous songs, but it was a danger he could handle. This is certainly not the abject terror of the native before supernatural forces that we heard about from the early missionaries.

4. *Healing music is not learned in an ordinary way.* Instead of being learned by ordinary memorization, healing chants are learned by ordeal and supernatural help. Putting himself under the tutelage of a ceremonial practitioner, the student listens to the songs for four nights without sleep. Then, perhaps several years later, the songs come to him in his sleep and he is ready, himself, to become a practitioner. Actually, of course, he hears these songs many times at ceremonials during this

period, but this is the Apache interpretation of how healing songs are learned.

Other differences are:

1. *Absence of certain types of songs* seems to correlate with striking differences between Apache culture and our own. There are no *lullabies* as such, though a mother might croon "baby, baby," over and over. Child training is, in general, more relaxed than ours, and Apache mothers do not seem to have to tell their children either to sleep or to eat. Babies are soothed and made much of but the whole attitude, as far as I could see it, was permissive: in fact the Apache from infancy to adulthood seems to be on a self-demand schedule. This may well relate to the absence of *work songs*. In general such songs seem to go with group labor, and Apaches do not go with group labor. In a real sense they have not learned to submit to what has been called "alienated labor." They do not desire property enough to gain it by working at a tedious job they are not interested in. Nor do Apaches have anything like our large literature of *romantic songs*. Love songs tend to be joking and boisterous. The court of love is not an Apache tradition; men do not dream of the ideal woman.

2. The Apaches do not have the concept of the artistic song performer. Anyone who can make himself heard is considered to have a good voice. A bad singer is one who does not know the song.

3. The Apaches are parochial in their musical interests. They are not curious about songs from other cultures nor do they know them except for (*a*) very active converts to Christianity, (*b*) some of the younger men who know a few Navaho songs with English words, and (*c*) the children in school who all seem to know "Davy Crockett." In the mission services I attended, the lusty singing of the evangelist and his team and the very weak participation or silence of most of the congregation afforded a notable contrast.

4. The small inventory of musical instruments seemed congruent with the Apache attitude towards property in general. They make a one-stringed fiddle (one of the few instances of a stringed instrument in the native New World), one type of drum, a water drum of buckskin over an iron pot, a flute with three or four holes made of a bamboo-like reed, and the bull-roarer (a flat stick whirled at the end of a cord to make a humming sound). The latter was said by some of my informants to be used in the Crown Dance, but there was none in the Crown Dance I saw at Cibecue in 1953. I had contradictory reports about the use of rattles but did not see any. These instruments are not kept on hand as prized possessions, though the makings of a drum are present in many households. But if a fiddle or flute is to be used, it is made and then quickly gets lost or broken. This is very like the Apache treatment of property in general: it is not something to take trouble over. Even a comparatively wealthy man lives in the same shack and thatched *wickiup* as his poorer neighbors—the only difference seems to be that he feeds more relatives. Livestock is an exception in this general attitude: horses and cattle are greatly prized.

5. There is little conscious musical training of children. There seem to be no special inducements offered to children to teach them to sing. There are few special inducements offered to children in any area. They grow up to be like their parents without special urging. There is prestige and wealth to be gained by becoming a medicine man, but this is for young men. Children are not supposed to deal with sacred music. There are no songs which are specifically *children's songs*. Children sing simplified versions of the choruses of drinking songs or social dance songs.

6. There is little singing done by the women. Those few who can join in a healing chant may do so. It seems to be much appreciated by the men but rather rare nevertheless. This is congruent with the general fact that religion is organized and practiced by the men, and relates

very well with the fact that more women than men are converts to Christianity and sing in the mission services.

7. There is little esthetic discussion in our sense. Appreciation of a song is nearly always phrased in terms of understanding it—of knowing what it is for. One or two informants did speak of preferring songs with long choruses and short verses since these are easier to learn, but the usual preference was for the important healing songs or the sacred songs in the puberty ceremony. This "functional esthetic" is found very widely among preliterate peoples.

Similarities

Every similarity between cultures contains also its differences and, in the case of music, reminds one that music is far from being a universal language that communicates across linguistic and cultural barriers. For example, there is music with a specifically *recreational* function, as with us. But such songs have sacred phrases in them, and the singing is usually done by men only with women looking on or dancing but not joining in the singing. Love songs, which are also called drinking songs, are most used in a drinking party, and this is the usual recreational situation.

There are songs that *children* sing, as mentioned above, but they are not children's songs as such. There is no literature of nursery songs: there is no nursery.

There are a few *obscene* songs, but they are very few as compared with our enormous body of such material. I was able to record only one which had reference to a man who ate too many cedar berries, had diarrhea and soiled his breech clout. There were similar references in some of the clowning that goes on during almost any kind of singing.

There are *gambling* songs intended to ensure success in the game, but they are either brief comical songs about the various animals that participated in a mythical gambling contest or are cast in the form of sacred chants.

Our spell-binding man with the guitar who is irresistible to the ladies has his counterpart in Apache folklore in the man with the flute. Butterfly songs and the flute are supposed to ensnare the senses of women. The element of magic may be said to be present in both cultures in this case, perhaps to about the same extent. However, among the Apaches almost nobody plays the flute today, and I could find no one who knew butterfly songs.

In this brief sketch I have attempted to give a picture of music in the life of the White Mountain Apache Indians. I have compared and contrasted Apache usages and attitudes with our own and I have tried to include enough ethnographic detail to supply the context in which the music is performed. I hope I have given the impression of a people who have much music and who love music as much as we do, but who come at it with strikingly different values and attitudes.

EIGHT

ANTHROPOLOGY LOOKS AT ITSELF

36

AS OTHERS SEE US

NANCY OESTREICH LURIE

The good old days. For some who use the phrase it conjures up the time when men were men and women knew their "place." Prices were low and maybe there was slavery; anyway, there were no goddam unions. Everybody worked and pulled their own weight, especially the children of the rich and privileged. Anthropologists could go anywhere to do their field work and they were properly welcomed as great white fathers; the good they did was clear to see, residing in their work. Science was good because knowledge was good; in any case, science was neutral, dedicated only to truth.

As the song says, things are changing. Not totally, there is still a very long way to go before even some of the minor excrescences in the world are obliterated. But some things have changed or are in flux and anthropologists are involved in those changes not merely as observers and analysts but as subject and object too. There are some places in the world where anthropologists are unwelcome. Peter Gutkind already called this to our attention (see selection 31) and warned his colleagues that certain changes had better be made before it is too late. His cautionary remarks were mainly addressed to the situation in Africa, but we in the United States do not have to look so far afield. Listen to the way Nancy Lurie tells it.

▼△▼△▼

The August, 1969, issue of *Playboy* magazine carried an article, "Custer Died for Your Sins," excerpted from the then forthcoming book of the same title by Vine Deloria, Jr. The book covers the nature of federal Indian administration, aspects of the contemporary Indian scene, Deloria's ideas of needed policy reform, and a chapter each on the alleged eccentricities and iniquities of missionaries, officials of government and anthropologists. For still unexplained reasons, it was Deloria's excoriation of anthropologists which was featured in *Playboy*, thus giving the widespread impression for the many who will not read the book that the biggest thorn in the Indian side is anthropologists.

Particularly distressing is that among the supposedly factional American Indians, to date not only has no one come forth to defend anthropologists, but even some of Deloria's critics among Indian activists, with whom he deals harshly in the book by implication if not by name, have applauded his stand on anthropologists (personal communications). If we are hurt and indignant about the specific charges Deloria makes, we should not be surprised at his bitterness or the fact that he has evoked a strong kindred response from other Indian people. It would be easy to refute everything Deloria says about us point for point, but in so doing we would miss the really important things he and other Indians are trying to tell us (Deloria, 1969).

First, it is worth noting that Deloria considers us one of three similar targets for Indians to shoot at. Although at the very end of the book he relents, saying he is hardest on the very groups in which he has the greatest hope for the Indians' future, it is curious that anthropologists are mentioned in the same breath with church and state. We always thought we were *different!* We always agreed with Indians that their difficulties derived from pious and political knuckleheadedness. Our peculiar distinction was that we came to learn from Indians on their terms, not lean on them like those other fellows. But Indian people have become wise to the fact that we always really worked in our own interests, which were those of science, and if we did not lean on Indians we also had little inclination to lean on people who *were*

SOURCE: "As Others See Us," *New University Thought*, Vol. 7 (1971):2–7. Reprinted by permission of publisher and author.

leaning on Indians. No matter how self-serving the individual clergyman or bureaucrat, their concern, institutionally speaking, was the Indians' interests, at least as they defined it.

Through the years, neat categories have become blurred. Religious groups and occasionally government agencies have sought enlightenment from anthropology, and anthropologists have put their skills at the disposal of these agencies for change. There is real potential for good in these relationships, and there may be potential for harm. It is worth noting that Americanists have always been proud that they were never resented by Indians in contrast to Africanists who have had to live down the fact that many of their founding fathers began their careers in colonial service. Applied anthropology in the service of American government and religion may smack of the same kind of colonialism the Africanists have outgrown and it evokes understandable suspicions from any administered people. Obviously Deloria does not believe his own conclusion that the only difference between applied anthropologists and pure anthropologists is that the latter use footnotes and the former do not. Deloria still thinks Indians can use our help, and ridicule is at least a disarming tactic to make us reveal our intentions.

Over the last decade or so, a few anthropologists have engaged in programs of the kind Deloria suggests as acceptable to Indians, that is, getting wherewithall, power, and any necessary empathic expertise into Indians' hands and letting them decide what their interests are and go after them in their own way with whatever support they can use from the anthropological sidelines. Deloria does not credit anthropologists with any actual cases, but after all his negative ranting he must have some positive evidence to consider anthropologists significant to the Indians' future. I am inclined to believe that it is such relatively recent evidence rather than our old reputation as the Indians' long time friend which inspires any grudging respect for us today.

Anthropologists are faced with a problem of impression management and ought to begin analyzing how they really appear from the Indian point of view. The American Indian population is weighted on the young side and certainly youth characterizes the activists who are influential whether we want to admit it or not. Their views of the Indian-anthropologist relationship go back no more than twenty years. Our views go back much further because they are perpetuated in the traditions of the discipline and for some of us the old relationship persists if only in regard to particular informants cultivated years ago.

The anthropologist's impression of himself is strongly influenced by the period of field work from roughly the First World War to the early 1950's. At that time there were not many anthropologists. They were about the only "establishment" whites with whom any rank and file Indians dealt as equals; and the wise old Indians often held the stronger cards. Anthropologists were sympathetic if not very effectual allies in regard to Indians' interaction with other whites. Field research was usually an enterprise of mutual intellectual interest to both Indian and anthropologist. Furthermore, the anthropologist was perceived as unique, an individual guest to the tribe which happened to harbor him. Some tribes did not even know of the existence of anthropologists. Psychically, at least, the anthropologist had a certain utility for the Indian people he worked with in regard to their own self-esteem. Although most anthropologists did not get into the field until they began data gathering for the doctorate, they had the benefit of knowing their professor's experiences, what to expect generally, what was expected of them, and what horrible examples of bad field technique of the more distant past to avoid. Each trip was expected to be a revelation and usually was. There was not a great deal of grant money; the anthropologist was lucky to get a grub-stake. Thus he had to give generously of himself in time and effort as reciprocation for cooperation in his research. Money was seldom paid directly in informants' fees, but the anthropologist observed local etiquette of gift exchange in goods, services, and sometimes even cash. His novelty value was also an asset the anthropologist traded on in still quite isolated Indian communities, albeit this was often done unconsciously, and considered evidence of achieving empathy and good rapport.

If an anthropologist proved a nuisance or an insufferable bore, the Indians lost nothing in withdrawing from him. A real menace could be driven out by enlisting the power of the mission or the Bureau in devious ways, since Indian people sensed that these institutions were by nature antithetical to anthropology. While there were hazards and some real psychic agonies for a person to begin serious research while also learning field techniques, the Ph.D. candidate was at least deeply committed to his chosen field and motivated by the fact that his professional future depended on his success. It was the Indians who held the power whether he would survive intellectually in the field and be able to return. They knew it and he knew it. Everyone enjoyed the game.

We can mark the beginning of deteriorating relationships between Indians and anthropologists when, about twenty years ago, a joke came out of the Southwest which had already become a mecca for a great many anthropologists. The average Navajo family, it was said, consisted of father, mother, three children, and an anthropologist. In the last few years the joke has been repeated by Indians all over the country to describe any average Indian family. Furthermore, while more anthropologists have sometimes begun to mean more money for the Indian community, they do not necessarily mean more fun and sometimes they are no fun at all but a source of hurt. They are not so easily gotten rid of today as in the past as there are always fresh reinforcements from our growing ranks. A lone stranger can be dealt with but when the ratio approaches 1:100 as I am told it does in some places, e.g., Hopi and Pine Ridge in the summer of 1969, Indians are hard put to decide what to do about such an invasion. It is also hard to just withdraw when working for the anthropologist helps put bread on the table.

Of course Deloria and others overstate the case of the anthropologist as economic asset, but economics certainly plays an important part in Indian grievances. Where the rest of the country got out of the Depression during the Second World War and stayed out, wartime prosperity for Indian communities was short-lived. The war had been a tremendous educational experience for Indians in giving them new skills and knowledge of economic alternatives to survive and prosper. However, policies set in motion after the war were completely inimical to using their new knowledge to improve the lot of their communities. Meanwhile, not only anthropologists but scholars in general enjoyed more federal support for research than at any time in our history. The ethnographer was no longer hard up and he could use cash and probably did so quite benevolently, to pay informants or pay them more than was previously possible. This was not bad in itself and continued the tradition of reciprocating as one is able, but it gave the ethnographer the upper hand. He can hire people who produce and fire those who do not. Much of the really esoteric information has been collected and either the old timers are now dead or remaining esoterica may be uncollectable as the folks on old age assistance can still withdraw from anthropologists they do not like. We have turned our attention to more relevant, contemporary problems where any hard up sample of Indians will do to answer questions on alcoholism, suicide, juvenile delinquency, educational problems and the like. I do not deny the value of such research, I merely point out how it has contributed to our changed image.

I would also like to point out that people who are hungry and frustrated in efforts to carry out the kinds of community development they desire find it hard to appreciate the value of grant supported research when the same money could be used to alleviate the problems whose symptoms are being so assiduously studied.

Other things happened as younger scholars found the advice conveyed by their professional mentors ever less realistic and useful. Indians could be hired for cash more easily than cultivated sincerely as friends. Other data collecting methods became more appropriate to our new interests than participant observation and direct or hidden interview. We also reacted against the sink or swim method of learning to do field work and tried to teach our students the techniques with texts, role playing sessions, methods courses, and, above all, team research and field schools where students work under supervision. These are not simply doctoral students but include beginning graduate students who may never make it through their "comps" and even, heaven help us, undergraduates with no more serious commitment to anthropology than the cost of tuition for a summer's lark that will also provide credits toward fulfilling their majors. Some team projects and field schools have serious objectives—maybe all of them can be justified as ultimate contributions to knowledge. But it is hard to avoid the fact that Indians are more conveniently and economically at hand for field schools than other still unstudied peoples. The team student does not have to be terribly interested in the substantive data he gathers. He only has to be sure he gets it right. He seeks evidence of his success from the professor in charge and finds social outlets among his peers rather than having to depend on the community for psychic and social support. If people identified as anthropologists or even students of anthropology do not appear to take seriously what Indians have to tell them, seeing their words as so much cash on the line and their persons as mere challenges to practice methods and techniques, why should Indians take anthropologists seriously and accord them respect?

There are other problems not exactly of our own making but which contribute to the impression of anthropologists. Once we only had to worry about the aggressive Indian buff who collected relics and palmed himself off as an anthropologist. Today, there is a huge host of outsiders from academic and professional disciplines who have discovered Indians for their own purposes. We could easily unmask the buff and keep our own role pure but what are we going to do about these others who come armed with tape recorders, cameras, notebooks, questionnaires, and projective texts; who have research credentials from universities or government and private foundations; and who use methods and techniques we also employ? Indians find it hard to tell them from the new breeds of anthropologists of all ages. It does no good to tell Indians that no matter how much our behavior resembles that of the others there is a *tradition* that Indians should like anthropologists. We can rail all we wish about the scholar's sacred right to freedom of inquiry, but we should understand why Deloria proposes that "Anthropologists and Other Friends" (the actual title of his chapter in the book) should register their projects with tribal governing bodies and justify them in terms of benefits to the people studied.

Of course, I am pointing up the very worst situations. However, just at the time when we are mass producing field training on a commercial basis across the country and paying small attention to all the duplication of work being done with Indians by both anthropologists and non-anthropologists, Indians themselves are developing widespread networks of communications to promote widespread inter-tribal fellow feeling. The anthropologist's role is no longer that of unique visitor who always had to justify his presence if not his practical relevance to the tribe he worked with. The anthropologist is now known to all Indians as the representative of a class of people who, like missionaries and Indian Bureau personnel, come and stay unbidden and who exploit Indians and can be exploited for Indian purposes. We are resented as a category for what we are allegedly doing to Indians, even by members of tribes which have not been studied or where a resident anthropologist still enjoys good, old fashioned relationships with the people.

Deloria may have done us a real favor in publicizing the bad impression we now make, whether it is of our own or others' doing. Others may not be so eager to trade on our formerly good reputations and we can stand forth as the real anthropologists, only having to put our own house in order.

Nor do I think all anthropologists have to confine themselves to action programs to be acceptable to Indian people, despite all the Indian grumbling about using them only to get our Ph.D.'s or engaging in costly, pointless research in order to publish to avoid perishing. Indians can figure out as well as anyone else that if we were motivated solely by considerations of income and having the equivalent of academics' hours, we would have gone into journeyman trades and spared ourselves inconveniences of field work and all the paperwork. We need have no embarrassment in admitting to Indians that we are motivated by intellectual curiosity and a desire to further our understanding of the nature of man. This outlook is probably more acceptable to Indian people than it is to much of the non-Indian public which finds it downright suspect. Indian people understand the concept of knowledge for its own sake if one pursues questions that really capture one's own curiosity. They do not even have to be obviously practical questions as long as one is polite and respectful and assumes Indians can still teach us things rather than simply be used to test or train students in methods in regard to questions to which we already think we have the answers.

What really rankles Indians is our fetish of scientific purity as being above considerations of the practical Indian interest, while at the same time we have little difficulty in finding ways to benefit our own practical interests without compromising our purity. We obtain data and publish our results, and if these are marketable we collect royalties, serve as paid consultants, hit the lecture trail, or simply move on to ever more prestigious academic institutions at higher pay. In this regard we are no different from any other scholars. But let us not go on saying we thus fulfill any obligation we may owe Indians because we have preserved their history and culture for posterity or are performing a public relations function for them with accurate data as opposed to popular stereotypes. These are not only feeble rationalizations, they are insulting. Indians can speak for themselves and we do not even listen. When Indians really can use our informed clout to avoid threats to their social life or property or to get programs they feel would really help them, we sit on our hands and raise our eyes to the pure scientific clouds. Since 1951, untold numbers of anthropologists have acted as expert witness in Indian Claims cases, taking pious pride in serving the interests of justice and the Indians as impartial scientists —for a fee. During this same period the Menominee and Klamath were terminated by outrageous legal and political tactics and their problems continue to mount. The waters of Kinzua dam rise over a good part of the Allegheny Seneca Reservation. Northwest Coast tribes fight a running battle against the interests of sportsfishing in order to preserve their rights to salmon runs which they depend upon for their livelihood. Recently, a supposedly liberal senator, Gaylord Nelson of Wisconsin, has pushed strenuously to wrest the Apostle Islands and surrounding shoreline on Lake Superior from their Ojibwa owners to create a national park on the arguments of conservation and benefiting the region economically. There is no concern for the obvious facts that this scheme will work to the direct detriment of the Ojibwa who have conserved the land very well thus far and really will only benefit whites. Oil and other mineral interests, with governmental cooperation, threaten to run roughshod over the social and property rights of Eskimos and northern Indians in Alaska and Canada. Canada is trying to move down the road to termination with the same misguided liberal rationalizations of "desegregation" and total lack of understanding of Indians' problems as were shown in the 1950's in the United States.

If we respond to these and a host of similar cases which could be cited with the view that these problems are not the business of anthropologists, that there is nothing we can do, that these problems do not concern "my tribe" or "my theoretical orientation," then we must be prepared to take the consequences in our relationships with Indians in the future. It is as simple as that.

Let us find out what Indian people think anthropologists can do, whether to donate money, write to appropriate senators or congressmen, volunteer as expert consultants, engage in research or set our students on research Indian people desire which could still provide valuable learning experience for the students.

Bibliography

DELORIA, VINE, JR. *Custer Died for Your Sins,* 1969, New York, Macmillan.

37

TOWARDS A NATIVE ANTHROPOLOGY

DELMOS J. JONES

Pandora's box is open. No longer passive, the subjects of anthropological inquiry are on the move, agitating, and escaping. The concept of benign, neutral science has come under increasingly heavy attack. It is by no means clear that anthropology, or other social sciences presently constituted, will survive. Anthropology has ceased to exist as such in the People's Republic of China; on the other hand, it survives in Cuba, Poland, Hungary, and other socialist states, and is expanding in the Soviet Union. In the United States, anthropology continues to gain ground as a discipline; but, as we have already seen, some of its salient aspects have come under critical scrutiny.

One suggestion has been to broaden the ranks of anthropologists by encouraging more people of different cultures to enter the field. This is by no means a new idea, as Professor Jones indicates in the selection that follows. But the "natives" who became anthropologists in the past often suffered a markedly invidious treatment, being valued perhaps more as super-informants than as participants in the analysis of the phenomena of culture.

However the "native" anthropologists of the past felt about their roles and status, they generally kept to themselves their views of their own treatment. That, too, is changing, as we see in Delmos Jones's candid

---

SOURCE: "Towards a Native Anthropology," *Human Organization,* Vol. 29, No. 4 (1970):251–59. Reprinted by permission of the Society for Applied Anthropology and the author.

This paper is based on two research projects: one in Northern Thailand under a fellowship granted by the Foreign Area Fellowship Program of the Social Science Research Council and the American Council of Learned Societies, the second in Denver under a small grant from the National Institute of Health (MN-16242-01). The conclusions, opinions, and other statements in this paper are those of the author and not necessarily those of either of the above agencies.

discussion of his experiences as both insider and outsider in the course of anthropological field work.

▼△▼△▼

Field methodology is currently a much-discussed subject in anthropology.[1] As usually conceived, research is a task carried out by an "outsider" or "stranger" who enters a society and attempts to learn about the way of life of its people. Thus, most discussions center on problems encountered by the outsider. But there is another vantage point from which research can be conducted—that of "insider," the person who conducts research on the cultural, racial, or ethnic group of which he himself is a member. The goal of this paper is to explore some of the problems of field work faced by such inside researchers.

The paper does not, however, focus entirely on the subject of field methodology; the epistemological dimension of field research will also be explored. I will attempt to show that the insider and the outsider do face different problems in the field situation. But as far as theory is concerned, there is as yet no set of theoretical conclusions generated from the point of view of native anthropologists. By a "native anthropology," I mean a set of theories based on non-Western precepts and assumptions in the same sense that modern anthropology is based on and has supported Western beliefs and values; for, as Maquet has pointed out:

> . . . it seems clear that the existence of a particular discipline dedicated exclusively to the study of non-Western cultures reflected the Victorian sense of superiority of the 19th century Europe and was perfectly consistent with, and useful to, the colonial expansion of that period. Is it not striking that this situation persisted in Africa as long as did the Colonial system and had to wait the decolonization process to be questioned? [2]

So long as the use of native anthropologists does not lead to the development of a native anthropology, I disagree with the statement that "the science of anthropology has been greatly enriched by those informants who were influenced by anthropologists to become anthropologists." [3] This is a process not yet achieved; its occurrence will benefit anthropology as a whole and may well prevent the "death" of anthropology predicted by some current writers.[4]

Field research is of course a process of finding answers to certain questions, or solutions to certain theoretical or practical problems. As such, it involves a series of steps from a definition of the problem to be studied through the collection of data to the analysis of data and the writing up of the results. The general philosophy in anthropology is that a graduate student should do field research for his Ph.D. dissertation. Furthermore, it is thought that his research should take place in a culture other than his own. Students are generally taught that a person working among his own people cannot maintain the degree of objectivity desirable, hence research experiences must be gained initially in another culture. Thus, a philosophical element enters into the research process. Interestingly enough, however, the rule that the student should not work in his own culture seems to be reversed when it comes to the foreign student, the "native" who is studying for a Ph.D. in the United States. It is an undeniable fact that most African students in American universities are Africanists who have conducted field work in their own society and are specialists in their own people. The philosophy concerning the field training of foreign students, therefore, is opposite to that which pertains to training American students. This discrepancy can only be explained in terms of the way in which the native anthropologist is seen by the field as a whole—not as a professional who will conduct research and develop theories and generalizations, but as a person who is in a position to collect information in his own culture to which an outsider does not have access. There is, then, the expectation that the insider will know things in a different, more complete way than will the outsider.

A basic aim of anthropological field research

is to describe the total culture of a group of people. This description, as much as possible, should be made from the point of view of the people—i.e., the inside view. For the anthropologist to obtain such a description, he must become actively involved in the life of the people, communicate with them, and spend a considerable period of time among them. With these general goals as the primary emphasis, it seems obvious that the trained native anthropologist can produce the best and most reliable data, since he knows the language, has grown up in the culture, and has little difficulty in becoming involved with the people.

According to Lowie, Boas encouraged the training of native anthropologists on the assumption that in describing the total way of life of a people from the point of view of the people themselves, it was the trained native who could best interpret native life from within. Materials collected by the trained native had "the immeasurable advantage of trustworthiness, authentically revealing precisely the elusive intimate thoughts and sentiments of the native, who spontaneously reveals himself in these outpourings."[5] In the same spirit that Boas encouraged natives to become anthropologists, he also encouraged women because they could collect information on female behavior more easily than a male anthropologist. This attitude strongly implies that native and female anthropologists are seen as potential "tools" to be used to provide important information to the "real," white male anthropologists.

It is undoubtedly true that an insider may have easier access to certain types of information as compared to an outsider. But it is consistent to assume, also, that the outsider may have certain advantages in certain situations. For example, in 1969–70, I conducted a research practicum for Health students at Denver General Hospital. The students, mostly white, were sent into the black community to inquire about health practices. One student returned with the information that some women had a craving for a particular type of dirt during pregnancy. On checking further, I found this to be quite a general practice, especially in the rural South. Although I was born and grew up in the rural South, I was unaware of the practice. None of the informants volunteered this information to me, probably because it did not occur to them that I did not already know about it, since I could be readily identified as both black and Southern. The crucial point is that insiders and outsiders may be able to collect different data; they also have different points of view which may lead to different interpretations of the same set of data.

The Problem of Point of View

As an outsider, I have done research among the Papago Indians of Southern Arizona and among the Lahu, a hill tribe of Northern Thailand. As an insider, I have done research in a black community in Denver, Colorado. In this paper I wish particularly to compare my experiences in Denver and Thailand. In both places, as a researcher (whether insider or outsider), I began with the formulation of the problem to be investigated. In Thailand the problem was to study intracultural variation among six villages of a hill tribe. In Denver the problem was to study the relationship between social structure and black self-concept. The logical processes of formulating a research problem were similar; however, the factor of point of view entered very strongly into the formulation of the Denver study, whereas it was virtually absent in the Thailand study. In Thailand, the questions relating to cultural variation were derived from the literature on the concept of culture and from the tendency of anthropologists to speak of a total population in terms of a study of one segment of that population.[6] The goal was to determine and to measure the range of variation in cultural behavior among villages of the same tribal (cultural) group.

The problem formulation for the Denver study, on the other hand, involved much more than logic. It involved intuition, experience, and self-interest (or more properly speaking, group interest). Current literature is filled with discussions concerning black self-image, and the conclusions are that in general blacks have a more negative self-image than whites.[7] First of all, there is some resentment over having one's own group described in this manner, although as a scientist, one must allow for the possibility that the findings are indeed correct. But as a skeptic, one can also consider the possibility that there may be something in the situation that other people are missing. For example, when I looked at my own experience of relating to other blacks within a black social context, I could not see the general conclusion of a negative self-image as being consistent with these experiences.

Before one can begin collecting data, it is necessary to gain access to the community. In this, the insider is faced with a much different set of problems than the outsider. But unless the insider returns to the same community in which he grew up, he still has the problem of developing contacts. Since I was new to the Denver area, I had to begin there (as I began in Thailand) with someone who knew someone, who in turn knew someone else in "a chain of introduction which leads at least to the threshold of his group."[8]

In the Thailand and Denver experiences, one of the biggest differences in gaining access to the community and establishing a continuing role for myself was the nature of the two social situations. In Thailand I was dealing with a small, close-knit village; but in Denver I was dealing with an urban neighborhood with little or no neighborhood-wide social organization. Once an anthropologist is accepted into a nonurban community, he takes a role for himself within the context of the community. In the urban situation, however, the researcher may have to establish a role for himself with each individual that he meets.

In Thailand I went through a chain of introductions: a friend in the city of Chieng-mai introduced me to a person who lived in one of the outlying districts where I wanted to work. This second person took me to a Shan village where people lived who knew the Lahu villages. People from this Shan village, who were on friendly terms with the Lahu, took me to the Lahu village and introduced me. Once I had been introduced to the village in this fashion, everyone there knew who I was.

In Denver I went through a similar chain of introductions. I knew someone at the University who knew one of the leaders of the black community. After several such contacts, however, I still had not been introduced to the people I wanted to work with—the hard-core poor. One of the community leaders introduced me to people who worked for the Office of Economic Opportunity program in Denver. These were people who worked with the poor people that were the object of my investigation; but this was still not the same as being introduced into a community, for the neighborhood workers could at best only introduce me to individuals. Thus, my first step was to obtain from the community workers the names of people whom I could interview. In this manner, when I knocked on someone's door I could tell them that their name was given to me by a friend of theirs. For a while this process worked very well. But problems arose. I could not get enough names. More importantly, other researchers were using the same technique; and a small group of people were becoming professional informants. Eventually I was forced to go out into the community to make my own contacts on a more or less random basis.

Thus, where I had to go through the process of establishing a role for myself only once in Thailand, in the urban setting where people must be met family by family, I had to explain myself anew to each family. This process was somewhat eased when one informant recommended a friend for an interview; but in both field situations, the problem of establishing a role for myself was closely related to the types of strangers that the people customarily met.

The Lahu had seen only three types of outsiders: traders, missionaries, and government agencies of various sorts. When I first arrived in the village, there was immediate suspicion that I was a missionary since most of the Americans they had seen were missionaries. This suspicion was easily overcome by pointing out that many of the things that I did with them, such as dancing in their "pagan" rituals, would be considered sinful by a missionary. The ghetto dweller, on the other hand, is faced with many different types of outsiders, many of whom are greeted with a great deal of hostility. Among the types of people who may knock on their door are social workers (perhaps checking up on the behavior of welfare recipients), bill collectors, salesmen, researchers, and representatives from various agencies such as the Office of Economic Opportunity, Department of Health, local hospital, and the like. Most of these are white. Because I am black and did not wear a white shirt and tie, I was not viewed immediately as an undesirable stranger. I could just be someone looking for a friend. Thus the reaction to me was perhaps much less hostile than it would have been to a white anthropologist. Although I have no comparison of people's reaction to a white researcher, not a single person refused to be interviewed by me.[9]

This is not to say that conducting research in the black community of Denver was without problems. Sometimes people were a bit suspicious. On occasions I was suspected of being a Black Panther; alternatively, I was sometimes suspected of being connected with some of the agencies of the Establishment. Thus, the problems of establishing rapport involved similar elements in both Thailand and Denver. But convincing the few people in Denver who objected to the Panthers and thought that I might be one was much easier than convincing the Lahu that I was not a missionary. In the Denver case the problem arose when I said something about political and economic oppression. People would ask, "Are you one of those Panthers?" They always accepted my reply of "No," and we got on with the interview. In Thailand, when the Lahu thought that I was a missionary, I had to demonstrate that I was not a missionary by pointing out that I participated in village activities which no missionary would ever do.

In order to collect data one has to communicate; but communication involves more than verbal exchanges. There are also facial expressions, hand movements, body movements, and tone of voice, to name just a few of the subtleties of communication. In my research experience among the Lahu of Northern Thailand there were certain mannerisms which I was able to understand only after a considerable amount of time. After about three months with the Lahu I discovered that I could tell when they were not telling me the whole truth by the way they answered questions. When I tried to collect information on a topic which people did not want to tell me about, such as religion, they would answer the question very softly; and on further checking, I would find their answers to be untrue. In most situations the good researcher reaches a point at which he is able to read meaning into the way a person says something as well as to record what is said. But where this was a level of understanding that I had to achieve as an "outsider" anthropologist, it was something that I began with as an "inside" anthropologist. That is, I have a core of common understanding with most black people: I grew up in a poor black community; I have experienced discrimination; and I can speak and understand the "dialect."

One task which most researchers face is how to explain what they are doing. A stranger coming to a remote village in Thailand has to have a reason for being there. How does he explain his research? Since the Lahu had not seen many outsiders and knew nothing about research, the problem was solved by simply stating that I wanted to learn all that I could about their way of life. Although they could not understand why anyone wanted to know about their life, they accepted the explanation. In contrast, most people in the urban black community *do* know what research is and are familiar with some of the implications and results of research. As stated previously, various types of research have taken place in Denver. Some of the people that I interviewed had been interviewed by other researchers as well, and some researchers have appeared on local television to discuss what they have discovered about the Denver community. In addition, many people have read descriptions of black behavior and do not like what they have read. More importantly, many persons see research as a process which takes the place of political action.[10] It is understandable, therefore, that explaining research in a context such as this takes on a different complexion than explaining the purpose of research to hill people in Thailand.

Negative feelings toward research are becoming more and more common among minority groups in the United States. Still, I found no single attitude towards research in the black community of Denver. Rather, I encountered three general reactions: The majority of the people I interviewed had no opinion or commitment toward research. The problem of explaining the purpose of research to this group was minor. The only real problem with them was that some felt that answering my questions would somehow harm them. There was no specific bit of information which seemed threatening—merely the task of giving answers. This was solved by not requiring names. The second general reaction was a feeling that research among black people by a black social scientist was a very good thing. This attitude was common among people who had read sociological discussions of blacks. They felt, for example, that the information contained in works such as the Moynihan report is distorted because reports written by whites cannot reflect an understanding of black people. Since people of this type felt that the record should be set straight and could only be done so by a black person, they were the most cooperative. The third reaction was the feeling that enough research has already been done, period. People with this attitude think that action is what is needed now; consequently, they were the least cooperative. However, because I am black, they did submit to an interview; but by and large, they made poor informants since they did not take the interview seriously.

One dimension of the Denver research experience which was completely absent in the Lahu experience was the very personal way in which many people reacted to me and the research itself. I have already explained that many people with whom I talked felt that information in the currently available literature about black people is untrue, and it is untrue because it was written by whites who were unable to understand black behavior. The desire to set the record straight, therefore, was very strong, as evidenced in one of my first encounters with a woman living in the housing project. After explaining the nature of my research project, she replied, "Finally!" And there were other ways in which people reacted to me in a very personal manner; I was, to many of them, not a social scientist but a black man who had overcome the barriers of American society and made good.

Data Analysis and Publication

A common problem confronting anthropologists when compiling their data is whether or not to withhold certain information from publication. Many who have done research in the Third World countries have withheld from their reports information which they thought would displease or embarrass the host country and jeopardize their chances of returning. As an inside researcher, I felt this emotion even more keenly than I did as an outsider. As an outsider, you work with people who, because of cultural, racial, or language differences, are always aware that you are an outsider. As an insider, people often do not look upon you as a researcher. You may be a friend, someone who is trusted.[11] In this capacity, people have revealed deeply personal things to me; and in this context also, I am in a position to learn many specific things about the people. Such revelations may be related to the research, but I would be both dishonest and disloyal to reveal such information.

Thus, the researcher doing field research among his own people may feel that there are private things which should not be made public. Paul warns of the anthropologist who becomes so involved in native life that he ceases to be an observer and can no longer be considered an anthropologist; he was referring specifically to Frank Cushing, who lived among the Zuñi and became a Zuñi priest. Cushing eventually became so emotionally identified with the people that he refused to continue publishing his Zuñi data.[12] A native researcher may begin at this point. A black man in this century cannot avoid identifying emotionally with his people. I am an intrinsic part of the social situation that I am attempting to study. As part of the situation, I must also be part of the attempt to forge a solution.

Because of my emotional involvement, I am also inclined to question certain conclusions which have been reached concerning the behavior of black people, such as the conclusion that blacks have a negative self-image or that Africans were easily enslaved compared to the New World Indians whose nobility led them to prefer death to slavery. It might not occur to an outsider to question this theory about slavery because these conclusions do not involve his own identity. For example, in a conversation at one time with a white historian, it was apparent that he had never considered the high rate of suicide or the high death rate in general among the early African population as an indication of resistance to slavery.

The fact that I may question many existing ideas about black people with which the white anthropologist might not be concerned is not in itself an argument for the advantages of either the inside or outside view.

> To observe a way of life best, it seems, involves living that way of life. This assumption invites two criticisms, each of which has both a theoretical and a practical aspect. First, is "the inside" a privileged observation point? There is nothing especially privileged about the observations of a parade made by those in it. Spectators may be in a better position, television viewers in a still better one. Which vantage point you choose must surely be a matter of what you want to observe and why.[13]

One vantage point cannot be said to be better than the other. There are logical dangers inherent in both approaches. The outsider may enter the social situation armed with a battery of assumptions which he does not question and which guide him to certain types of conclusions; and the insider may depend too much on his own background, his own sentiments, his desires for what is good for his people. The insider, therefore, may distort the "truth" as much as the outsider. Since both positions involve the possibility of "distortion," which is better? I will address myself to this question in the following observations.

Anthropological Theory and Native Anthropologists

One of the first articles in anthropology which I read was V. F. Calverton's introduction to *The Making of Man,* "Modern Anthropology and the Theory of Cultural Compulsives." [14] Calverton speaks of the vested interest involved in the development and acceptance of sociological theory. According to him, the evolutionary theory of the nineteenth century was not "merely an error in scientific approach," [15] but "afforded a new vista of human development . . . [and] provided a new justification of world progress in terms of Western civilization." [16] He explained that Morgan had great influence in anthropology until the Marxists took over Morgan's ideas and used them for their own purposes. Then Morgan's views became "repugnant" to the conservative bourgeois mind, but not to the radical mind. "What I am trying to stress," he concludes,

> . . . is that all social thought is colored by such compulsives, reactionary as well as radical, and that those who think they can escape them are merely deceiving themselves by pursuing a path of thought that is socially fallacious. . . . The liberal sociologist has merely been deceived by the myth of neutrality—the belief that he can be above the battle. . . . The very fact that the liberal sociologist in most instances is connected with a university, and is dependent upon a middle-class environment for his survival, is sufficient reason why such aloofness in the social sciences must of necessity rest upon false premise.
>
> The existence of cultural compulsives . . . makes objectivity in the social sciences impossible. Indeed, the actual claim to objectivity in the social sciences has been largely a defense-mechanism, and attempts unconsciously to cover up the presence of compulsive factors and convictions. No mind can be objective in its interpretation and evaluation of social phenomena. . . . Interpretation necessitates a mind-set, a purpose, and end. Such *mind-sets,* such purposes, such ends, are controlled by cultural compulsives. Any man living in any society imbibes his very consciousness from that society, his way of thought, his prejudice of vision. The class he belongs to in that society in turn gives direction to his thought and vision.[17]

Anthropology is a Western science. It is a science developed in the West primarily to cope with a Western problem: how to explain the diverse variety of people with whom Europeans came into contact during the Age of Exploration. The concepts, the theories, and the approaches are based on Western precepts. Stated simply, anthropology would be something entirely different if it had developed in Asia or Africa. Since anthropology was developed by representatives of the colonizing groups, the concepts are by necessity related to the scientific and other needs of this group.[18]

According to Calverton, anthropology became of value not because it began to collect facts about primitive people, but because those facts began to have meaning to Western civilization.[19] These facts about primitive people have had various meanings to the West, one of which was to foster the feelings of superiority of Western man, since evolutionary theory placed him at the apex of the evolutionary process. But a more practical use of this information is evident: It is clearly implied that slave traders and slave owners had a considerable amount of knowledge of the various cultures of Africa and modified their treatment of African slaves according to their captives' cultural differences. If one considers the important activities which brought Europeans into contact with non-Western peoples—activities such as trade and colonial conquest and administration—the practical services which anthropology has offered to its society are evident.[20]

Theories and concepts in anthropology are, for this reason, formulated from the point of view of Western ideology, Western needs, and a Western style of life. The idea of sociocultural integration or harmony among the various parts of a culture is an example. A theory of society which sees the parts of a social system working in harmony like the organs of the body could never have been developed by an anthropology founded by slaves or by any group whose position is in the lower strata of a social system. Anyone who has experienced the many institutional barriers which are constructed to keep members of one's own group in their places is more apt to view the various parts of a system as being at war with each other than as working in harmony.

Many anthropologists feel that the native's view of his own culture reflects the most accurate view. The aim of anthropological research, we are often told, is to see things from the point of view of the native. Although the inside view is loudly proclaimed by anthropologists, few go so far as to consider the belief in magic and witchcraft as an element of absolute truth. There is no escape from the idea that outsiders and insiders view social reality from different points of view and that no matter how hard each tries, neither can completely discard his preconceptions of what that social reality is or should be. From this point of view, neither is any more or less trustworthy than the other. Both have room for distortions, inaccuracies, half-truths. A social anthropologist who claims to have acquired a complete understanding of another culture stands self-condemned.[21] A lesson that most anthropologists have failed to learn is that a subsequent researcher will always find errors in one's data, no matter how many years one remains in the field, no matter how well one speaks the language, and no matter how far one thinks he has got under the skin of the native.

Since both the inside researcher and the outside researcher face the same empirical problems, is there any advantage to the native anthropologist at all? My answer is yes, potentially. The problem at this point is that there are native anthropologists, but there is no native anthropology. By this I mean there is little theory in anthropology which has been formulated from the point of view of tribal, peasant, or minority peoples. Thus, the whole value of the inside researcher is not that his data or insights into the social situation are better—but that they are *different*. Most of the few black anthropologists operating in this country are looking for something new, questioning old assumptions about social processes, developing new ones, exploding old myths, and in the process developing new ones. The work of the white anthropologist among non-Western people is not bad because he is white, but because the field of anthropology as a whole was dull and uncreative in the 1960's. Our concepts and theories, our way of looking at people have lost their relevance.[22]

Lehman, in an article on the problem of minority relations in Burma, concludes that social science theory has played a major role in generating the problem of majority/minority relations in Burma or "at least [has played a part] in obscuring the conditions required for their solution." [23] This is no less true of the situation in the United States. The theory to which Lehman refers is the consensus model of society which is the basis of much anthropological thinking about social problems.

In anthropology the conception of a primitive society has been one in which there is structure, function, and equilibrium. Consensus on values is the basic element which holds a society together. This means that the society operates without conflict, competition, or resentment. Everyone agrees upon the values, internalizes those values, and voluntarily follows the proper forms of behavior. Force is seldom needed to get this conformity. Everyone in the society does exactly as he is supposed to do at all times. This basic assumption about society leads to a description of the caste system of India as

> . . . an organic system with each particular caste and subcaste filling a distinctive functional role. It is a system of labor division from which the element of competition among workers has been largely excluded.[24]

Thus, the elements of oppression, frustration, resentment, aspirations, and hostility are not seen in most anthropological descriptions of social organization. The lower castes never rebel against the higher, nor do they resent their position in the system.

There is an alternative to the notion of primitive societies being held together by value consensus. Dahrendorf has written:

> From the point of view of coercion theory, . . . it is not voluntary cooperation or general consensus but enforced constraint that makes social organizations cohere. In institutional terms, this means that in every social organization some positions are entrusted with a right to exercise control over other positions in order to ensure effective coercion; it means, in other words, that there is a differential distribution of authority. . . . this differential distribution of authority invariably becomes the determining factor of systematic social conflict of a type that is germane to class conflict in the traditional (Marxian) sense of the term.[25]

Another important dimension to this problem involves the extremely high regard with which anthropologists tend to hold the traditions of other people. Sometimes anthropologists seem more attached to traditional behavioral patterns of a group than the people themselves, though as Maquet notes:

> I do not mean that anthropological writings, by enhancing African traditional values, have had a significant bearing on the upholding of the colonial system. . . . What matters is that anthropology was oriented as though it wanted to preserve the existing situation.[26]

Robert Redfield also recognized this in his *Peasant Society and Culture*.[27] He wondered whether differences reported about peasant values might be due to choices made by observers and writers as to which aspects of the social situation they chose to stress. He asserted that the observer of a people's values must answer such questions as "What do these people desire for themselves and for their children? To what kind of life do they attach highest esteem?" Many anthropologists never ask these questions. They assume that peasants find rural life to be just as romantic as they do. Lopreato, who did deal with this subject, found that the Italian peasant had an intense dislike of his life-situation and a strong desire to leave the inferno of his peasant community. It is unlikely, he writes, that the Italian peasant represents a special case.[28] Indeed, the concept of a culture of poverty deemphasizes the fact that poverty groups are concerned with their marginal economic position and have a strong desire for something better. This is one of the strongest elements which has come through in the interviews I have had with poor people.

It should be clear from the above that the native anthropologist should be one who looks at social phenomena from a point of view different from that of the traditional anthropologist. I feel that this point of view should be admittedly biased, in favor of the insider's own social group. Thus, when I seek to "set the record straight" about some of the things which have been written about black people, this is not only justified but necessary. It is unfortunate that Third World students who are trained in American Universities have, in the past, been *unable* to do this. This came about because the process of training itself eroded what could have been a distinctive native point of view. But this is rapidly changing. The students that are now being trained are becoming aware of the biases in social science and are not bound by the old values of objectivity and neutrality. This change in mood may disturb many people. But if anthropology is to survive it must respond to the changing social and technological realities of the present. It is well known that part of the process of colonization involves the distortion of social, cultural, and historical facts about a colonized people. The emergence of a native anthropology is part of an essential decolonization of anthropological knowledge and requires drastic changes in the recruitment and training of anthropologists.

Notes and References

1 See, for example, Thomas Rhys Williams, *Field Methods in the Study of Culture*, Holt, Rinehart and Winston, New York, 1967; Ake Hulkrantz, "The Aims of Anthropology: A Scandinavian Point of View," *Current Anthropology*, Vol. 9, No. 4, 1968, pp. 289–296.

2 JACQUES J. MAQUET, "Objectivity in Anthropology," *Current Anthropology*, Vol. 5, No. 1, 1964, p. 51.

3 ALLAN R. HOLMBERG, "The Research and Development Approach to the Study of Change," *Human Organization*, Vol. 17, No. 1, 1958, p. 12.

4 GERALD D. BERREMAN, "Is Anthropology Alive? Social Responsibility in Social Anthropology," *Current Anthropology*, Vol. 9, No. 5, 1968, p. 391–396.

5 ROBERT LOWIE, *The History of Ethnological Theory*, Holt, Rinehart and Winston, New York, 1937, p. 133.

6 E. R. LEACH, *Political Systems of Highland Burma*, Beacon Press, Boston, 1954, p. 3.

7 See, for example, D. L. Noel, "Group Identification among Negroes: An Empirical Analysis," *Social Issues*, Vol. 20, No. 2, 1954, pp. 71–84; Ralph M. Dreger and Kent S. Miller, "Comparative Psychological Studies of Negroes and Whites in the United

States: 1959–1965," *Psychological Bulletin Monograph Supplement,* Vol. 70, No. 3, Part 2, 1968, pp. 32–33.

8 B. D. PAUL, "Interview Techniques and Field Relationships," in A. L. Kroeber (ed.), *Anthropology Today,* University of Chicago Press, Chicago, 1953, p. 430.

9 There does not seem to be complete agreement on whether the race of the interviewer is an important element of bias in the interview situation. Williams concludes that the race of the interviewer "is an important variable related to bias but . . . this is only under certain conditions with certain types of interview questions." Weller and Luchterhand, on the other hand, write: ". . . our findings indicate that . . . Negro respondents gave higher quality responses to white interviewers than to Negro interviewers in a personally sensitive research area." J. Allen Williams, Jr., "Interviewer-Respondent Interaction: A Study of Bias in the Information Interview," *Sociometry,* Vol. 27, No. 3, 1964, pp. 338–352; Leonard Weller and Elmer Luchterhand, "Interviewer-Respondent Interaction in Negro and White Family Life Research," *Human Organization,* Vol. 27, No. 1, 1968, pp. 50–55.

10 See, for example, Robert K. Merton and Daniel Lerner, "Social Scientists and Research Policy," in Daniel Lerner and Harold D. Lasswell (eds.), *The Policy Sciences,* Stanford University Press, Stanford, California, 1951, p. 299.

11 *Cf.* I. C. Jarvie, "The Problem of Ethical Integrity in Participant Observation," *Current Anthropology,* Vol. 10, No. 5, 1969, p. 505, who observes that the complete participant observer conceals his character as observer. There is the problem of striking a balance between being a "good friend" and a "snooping stranger." On the one hand is the aim of participating fully, or identifying entirely with the alien way of life; on the other is the danger of betraying "trust."

12 Paul, *op. cit., loc. cit.*

13 Jarvie, *op. cit.,* p. 506.

14 V. F. CALVERTON, *The Making of Man: An Outline of Anthropology,* Modern Library, New York, 1931.

15 *Ibid.,* p. 5.

16 *Ibid.,* p. 3.

17 *Ibid.,* pp. 28–29.

18 Maquet, *op. cit.,* p. 47.

19 Calverton, *op. cit.*

20 LISA R. PEATTIE, "Interventionism and Applied Science in Anthropology," *Human Organization,* Vol. 17, No. 1, 1958, p. 5.

21 JOHN BEATTIE, *Other Cultures,* The Free Press, New York, 1964, p. 90.

22 GUTORM GJESSING, "The Social Responsibility of the Social Scientist," *Current Anthropology,* Vol. 9, No. 5, 1968, p. 400.

23 F. K. LEHMAN, "Ethnic Categories in Burma and the Theory of Social Systems," in Peter Kunstadter (ed.), *Southeast Asian Tribes, Minorities, and Nations,* Vol. I, Princeton University Press, Princeton, New Jersey, 1967, p. 103.

24 E. R. LEACH, *Aspects of Caste in South India, Ceylon and Northwest Pakistan,* Cambridge University Press, Cambridge, Massachusetts, 1960, p. 5.

25 RALF DAHRENDORF, *Class and Class Conflict in an Industrial Society,* Routledge and Kegan Paul, London, 1959, p. 165.

26 Maquet, *op. cit.,* p. 50.

27 ROBERT REDFIELD, *Peasant Society and Culture,* The University of Chicago Press, Chicago, 1956, p. 140.

28 JOSEPH LOPREATO, "How Would You Like to Be a Peasant?" in Jack M. Potter, May N. Diaz, George M. Foster (eds.), *Peasant Society: A Reader,* Little, Brown and Company, 1967, p. 436.

38

SKELETONS IN THE ANTHROPOLOGICAL CLOSET

WILLIAM S. WILLIS, JR.

Anthropology has always been surrounded by a romantic nimbus. Eric Wolf, an anthropologist whose work we encountered earlier (see selection 29) has remarked in another context that anthropologists suffer a peculiar kind of romanticism that seeks to fuse dream and reality. The anthropologist delights in pointing at "the nightside of human nature." In Wolf's cadenced words, the anthropologist "has escaped from the humdrum world of his civilization to walk among headhunters, cannibals, and peyote-worshippers, to concern himself with talking drums, magic, and divine kings." Wolf took such an imaginative walk in his *Sons of the Shaking Earth,* a reconstruction of Aztec civilization and history; yet he was never so deeply into that nightside of human nature as when he spearheaded an attack on the involvement of anthropologists in Southeast Asian counterinsurgency, intelligence operations and the war.

Because many anthropologists accept the century-old remark of Edward Tylor, that "the science of culture . . . is essentially a reformer's science," because they empathize deeply with people of other cultures and sometimes with the downtrodden, exploited, and despised, and because most of them spend long class hours cleaning out the trash of racist biological and psychological theories, they often have believed that their beloved profession was detached from its own nurturing society and culture. By the analytical precepts of anthropology itself this would be an astounding thing, but there is a dialectic here as elements of myth contend with elements of scientific process to create the ideology of anthropology. How can anthropology be racist?

Racism is not a casual set of vicious slogans compounded by happenstance, nor a theory constructed in a conspiratorial way by a corps of conscious villains. We are taught by the social sciences, among which anthropology plays a prominent part, that racism is the predictable outcome of specific sets of conditioning factors. It is a doctrine that continues to play a strong functional role in the ordering of social behavior, starting with the determination of who gets what, when, and how.

William Willis is an anthropologist who has specialized in ethnohistory. A good deal of his energy has gone into painstaking studies of the sociocultural relationships among Indians, blacks, and whites in the colonial period of the Southeastern United States. Recently he has been exercising his anthropological privilege to look deeply into another ethnohistorical problem. This time he is focusing on American anthropology itself. Here is his mordant view of that history. However unpleasant it may be, and though we may differ with the author at various points, the controversy here advanced must be faced for the sake of what we hope for the world as well as for our discipline.

SOURCE: From *Reinventing Anthropology,* edited by Dell Hymes. Pp. 121–52. Copyright © 1972 by Random House, Inc. Reprinted by permission of Pantheon Books, a Division of Random House, Inc., and the author.

This article is a small part of a larger investigation in which I am now engaged. For essential help, I thank Morton H. Fried, Robert F. Murphy, and my students: Shirley Achor, Joi Anne Garrett, Ashley Marable, Maria Luisa Urdaneta, and David M. White. However, the responsibility for any infelicities of style or errors in content is mine.

▼△▼△▼

"Do you not see how facts change their aspects, their meaning, under the pressure of oppression? So strong and widespread is this tendency for facts to be seen by the oppressed from a special point of view that I've called this a Metamorphosis of Facts." [RICHARD WRIGHT, *White Man, Listen!*]

Anthropology is in trouble, especially since World War II. The trouble arises essentially from the emergence of black and other colored peoples around the world. This emergence demands drastic changes in anthropology; even if such changes are made, the survival of anthropology is not insured. To meet the crisis, we need to know the actual conditions in which anthropology has developed and to know what anthropology has been. This knowledge is only partially attained from the perspectives of white people (Maquet 1964). We must also view anthropology from the perspectives of colored peoples, and this means from Richard Wright's "frog perspectives" of looking from below upward (1957:27–29). When we do this, the importance of color erupts, and the world of E. B. Tylor, Franz Boas, and A. R. Radcliffe-Brown becomes articulated with the world of W. E. B. Du Bois, Richard Wright, and Frantz Fanon. The "frog perspectives" reveal surprising insights about anthropology, and these insights are the skeletons in the anthropological closet.

A Minimal Definition of Anthropology

At the end of the fifteenth century, whites in Europe began expanding all over the world. They conquered, dominated, exploited, and humiliated colored peoples in America and Asia, in the South Seas, and in Africa. They established their rule by force and maintained it by force: this expansion is steeped in violence, bloodshed and deceit. The military defeat of the colored world enhanced self-confidence among white people. This confidence and the pillage of the colored world brought new prosperity and power to the white world. White superiority in technology has been increased, and superiorities have developed in other institutions in white societies. On the other hand, white rule has brought death and distress to colored peoples: some colored societies have been destroyed whereas others have been pathologically distorted. White rule has simplified the colored world by reducing its diversity and has complicated this world by creating these pathological distortions. It has simplified this world in another way: white rule has created a new generalization of worldwide inequality of colored peoples. One explanation for this inequality has been the postulation of innate biological inferiorities of colored peoples, and this explanation has achieved an uncritical acceptance that is remarkable (Worsley 1964: 1–49; Lévi-Strauss 1966; Gough 1968).

White rule with its color inequality is the context in which anthropology originated and flourished, and this context has shaped the development of anthropology. The formalization of anthropology in the nineteenth century coincided with the shift from "booty" colonialism to imperialism, which stressed profit from the control, exploitation, and preservation of cheap colored workers and consumers. The persistent distinction between "primitive" and "civilized" has been made falsely to coincide with the pervasive color bar. This distinction has ignored colored individuals and societies that satisfy the criteria of civilization; on the other hand, this distinction has ignored white individuals and societies not meeting these criteria. That these flaws existed was a major defect in the racist explanation.

The context of white rule provides a conception of anthropology that emphasizes what it actually has been. *To a considerable extent, anthropology has been the social science that studies dominated colored peoples—and their ancestors—living outside the boundaries of modern white societies.* This minimal definition of anthropology avoids key deficiencies in prevailing descriptions of anthropology as the science of man, as the science of culture, and as the science that employs field work methodology. At best, these descriptions are aspirations of contemporary anthropologists seeking design in a historical development; at worst, they are ways to avoid admitting that anthropology has been an instrument of white rule. This minimal definition reveals the hyperbole in the assertion by anthropologists that their discipline is the science of man. Indeed, realization of the preoccupation with the dominated colored world should shake this self-image and reduce confidence in the "global" visions of anthropology. The minimal definition avoids the dilemma posed by nineteenth-century anthropologists, and many British social anthropologists, who did not subscribe theoretically to the concept of culture. Similarly, this definition does not exclude anthropologists, such as James Fraser, Herbert Spencer, and Tylor, who did not engage in field work. Further, by recognizing the division of labor among the social sciences of the white world, this definition separates anthropology historically from sociology and other social sciences. These latter sciences deal diachronically and synchronically with sociocultural data of individuals and groups in white societies. In this context, sociology is seen as the study that concentrates on the poorer segments in white societies; therefore, the torturous distinction between human society and human culture becomes unnecessary in order to distinguish sociology from anthropology.

Anthropological Perceptions and Projections

The concept of the primitive is a construction created by white people from their racist perceptions of contemporary colored peoples. It is a sad fact that this concept has been accepted uncritically by many white anthropologists and used extensively in studying the colored world. Stanley Diamond is one of the few anthropologists to examine the primitive concept as a construction, but he does not then challenge the ethnographic validity of anthropology (1964). Since distortion by white rule preceded anthropologists into the colored world, it follows inexorably that no anthropologist has ever seen a real primitive. Many anthropologists disagree with this conclusion; for instance, even Marvin Harris declares that it is "undeniable" that primitive cultures have survived into the contemporary world (1968:154). But, I stress that the perceptions that anthropologists have of contemporary colored peoples as primitive peoples are mainly projections of two longstanding needs among white people. One need is to approve the conditions that have developed in white societies in the wake of capitalist industrialism and to approve the actions of white people as they dominated colored peoples around the world. The other need is to condemn some conditions in white societies and some aspects of white domination of the colored world.

In principle, the need for approval leads to negative perceptions of colored peoples and their cultures whereas the need for disapproval leads to positive perceptions. In reality, these opposing needs coexist in most anthropologists and contradictory perceptions are the rule. (The diachronic projection of this dilemma is analyzed by Diamond 1964). The emphasis on one kind of perception or the other varies among anthropologists, especially according to the century in which they live. The perceptions were more negative among 19th century evolutionists than among Boasian anthropologists, although Tylor made some comparisons favorable to colored peoples whereas even Boas believed that colored peoples were less sensitive to suffering, more cruel, and less forgiving than white people (Tylor 1891 1:29,31; Boas 1928:223–224; Stocking 1968a:110–132). Apart from the exploitation of some white people by other white people, white exploitation of colored peoples has been crucial to the prosperity of white societies. This cruciality is the key to the persistence in anthropology of negative perceptions of colored peoples, and it has insured that positive perceptions have been seldom, if ever, devoid of some kind of negativism; for instance, paternalism. In addition, it helps explain the limited acceptance of positive perceptions among white people outside of anthropology. This cruciality has operated especially in perceptions of black people, since the exploitation of these people has been cumulatively more profitable—and more crushing—than the exploitation of other colored peoples. This being the case, a worldwide racial hierarchy has developed under white rule in which black people are placed consistently at the bottom, and the black man has seldom been regarded as the "noble savage."

The projection of needs of white people

means that realities in the colored world are often distorted by anthropologists. Since the effects of white rule were often ignored in seeking aboriginal conditions, the subjective distortion by anthropologists has compounded the objective distortion created by colonialism and imperialism. This compounding of distortions within the racist organization of the modern world has prevented most—if not all—white anthropologists from seeing contemporary colored peoples as real human beings enmeshed in their intricate depths. Instead, anthropologists have constructed imaginary counter cultures to serve white needs and thereby obtained reaffirmations. In the nineteenth century, anthropologists used an explicit racist ideology to make colored peoples into different human beings than white people. Later, when scientific racism became less popular, anthropologists achieved almost the same result with the concepts of culture and of cultural relativism. The enculturation inherent in the culture concept was seen as having the power to mold most human beings into accepting and internalizing almost any kind of sociocultural arrangement. These arrangements, whatever their nature and political and economic basis, were then justified by the "dignity" that was accorded them by cultural relativism. Thus, colored peoples, having been construed as simply culturally different, could be manipulated as things in the "laboratory" of the colored world. Hence, Du Bois described the black man as the "football of anthropology" (1939:ix).

This sleight of hand, whatever the liberal intent involved in the culture concept, avoids the distress and misery of colored peoples, cringing and cursing at the aggressive cruelty of white people. This avoidance helps explain the lack of outrage that has prevailed in anthropology until recent years, and this lack of outrage made neutral inaction more tenable. This intellectual exploitation by anthropologists parallels the economic exploitation by imperialists. Indeed, anthropologists have been "penny" imperialists in making modest profits from studying dominated colored peoples and from stealing their possessions but not sharing profits with these peoples (Deloria 1969:97–100). Finally, the compounding of distortions suggests that ethnographic monographs are simply novels and that theoretical concepts are but daydreams.

Anthropologists have been worried about methodological inadequacy for a long time; they have usually seen this inadequacy in the same simple way. Both Tylor and Boas held that reporting by untrained persons led to erroneous concepts and that improved reporting by trained persons must precede theorizing (Tylor 1889:464–471; Lowie 1937:131–142). Many anthropologists have been unaware of subjective distortion via projected perceptions on the part of even trained persons, but hope now appears that intensive methodological reexamination will overcome this pitfall (cf. Scholte, 1972). The goal of Boasian anthropology to see a culture as its members see it was indeed an impossible dream, since the differences in specific enculturations precluded anthropologists from viewing the world as now an adult Crow Indian, now an adult Blackfoot Indian. In recent years, Harris has insisted upon an outside observer's ("etic") approach as a correction to the distortion inherent in an exclusive pursuit of the Boasian goal (1968:568–604). However, another kind of "inside view" at a different level of enculturation is possible, although difficult, and it is essential: the "inside view" that has arisen from being colored under white rule and is shared by Blackfoot, by Crow, and by Ibo alike. White anthropologists, guided by their colored colleagues, should be able to project their own humanity into this transtribal milieu created by white rule everywhere in the colored world and thereby achieve a new empathy with the oppressed. In addition, there is an equal need for anthropologists to reject the posture of neutral scientists and accept that social scientists can not avoid "leaning to one side." Until these steps are taken, an observer's approach is premature and runs the dangerous risk of rationalizing white chauvinism.

More anthropologists now recognize the distortion by white rule; for instance, Charles Wagley now sees most Latin American Indians as peasants and not as primitives (1968:84–90). The tradition of ignoring white rule dies hard as shown by Robert Redfield's belief that real primitive societies can be re-created after centuries of white rule (1953:48,70–72). However, some anthropologists are beginning to reappraise themselves and the history of their discipline, and a major stimulus to this reappraisal is provided by liberation movements among contemporary colored peoples. This reappraisal should end in a general recognition of the ways in which white rule and its effects have been distorted in representations commonly found in the works of anthropologists.

The Uses of Anthropology (Abroad)

That anthropology has been used for the benefit of white societies is shown by persistent efforts of anthropologists to aid imperialism (Foster 1969:180–217).[1] Early and throughout the nineteenth century, some British anthropologists tried to convince imperialists of their usefulness, stressing that knowledge of sociocultural differences among colored peoples was important to imperialist success. However, imperialists then felt too secure to need anthropologists. About the beginning of the twentieth century, the structure of imperialism began to change, and perhaps it began to weaken. Then imperialists responded to the pleas of anthropologists, and this response played a big role in the development and present organization of anthropology. In addition to collecting data on temporary assignments, some British anthropologists became permanent employees of imperialism as Government Anthropologists. Money from imperialists meant not only more anthropological societies and journals, but the establishment of anthropological institutes and the introduction of anthropology into many university curricula. There was a mutual understanding that anthropologists had one essential service as repayment: provide data that might assist the imperialists.

The story in the United States is about the same. The vast majority of anthropologists in the late nineteenth and early twentieth centuries concentrated on North American Indians, defeated victims of white expansion now placed in reservations. A tiny minority of anthropologists turned to Pacific islands acquired after the Spanish-American War. However, United States anthropologists generally gave less assistance to imperialism than British anthropologists since the United States was not then a major imperialist power, but World War II reversed this situation as the United States replaced England as the imperialist behemoth. Acquiring big grants from government and private foundations, anthropologists flocked to Latin America, then to Asia, and finally to Africa. They were enthusiastically following the new imperialist priorities of the United States government. In addition to collecting sociocultural data on colored peoples, they served as diplomats, most often in an unofficial capacity, and as public relations experts; moreover, an indeterminate number engaged in espionage. Finally, some anthropologists cooperated with the United States government in its relocation program that placed the Nisei in detention camps during World War II. This enthusiasm at mid-century for aiding imperialism contrasts with the diminished enthusiasm then appearing among some British anthropologists, but it coincides neatly with the shifting imperialist roles of the United States and England.

Until mid-century, most anthropologists accepted the inevitability of the imperialist system even when they did not accept its legit-

[1] The evidence for this discussion of anthropologists and imperialism can be found in Foster (1969). However, my interpretations are not necessarily identical with those of Foster.

imacy and permanency as well. Whatever their attitudes, they certainly operated within the framework of imperialism, and they did not agitate for the overthrow of imperialism. Indeed, nineteenth-century evolutionists and then British social anthropologists subscribed to imperialism as the "white man's burden." Since colored cultures were seen as lacking competitive innovative potential, then Boasian anthropologists also subscribed—although more covertly—to imperialism as the "white man's burden." Perhaps the acceptance of this function of imperialism is one deep reason for diffusionism in twentieth-century anthropology (see under *Boas* below), which also served as a way of masking from liberal social scientists their underlying evolutionary biases. Moreover, numerous twentieth-century anthropologists were satisfied with their participation in one-shot, piecemeal projects sponsored by their governments in the colored world. Their satisfaction in particular was in conflict with some theoretical concepts that prevailed generally in anthropology, namely, the continuity of culture, the interrelationship in culture, and the integration of culture. George Foster has concluded that the goal of "efficient and humane" administrations was one main reason for employing anthropologists in the British colonies of Africa (1969:193). In addition to the significant precedence of efficiency, making imperialism a more efficient and humane system was merely a desire for an imperialism without atrocities. This aim was consistent with the aim of imperialism: after initial subjugation via terrorization, imperialists wished to preserve colored peoples as producers and consumers. Since nineteenth-century anthropologists were racists (cf. Harris 1968), they had no quarrel with the color bar. Indeed, the main annoyance of twentieth-century anthropologists with imperialism was that they were relegated to being technicians, devoid of initial decision-making functions.

Toward the mid-century, some anthropologists began condemning the color bar. Then there was some advocacy of more sharing of the wealth of the colored world with colored peoples, and this new posture was consistent with their scientific antiracism. It was also consistent with new imperialist aims adopted to parry the threat posed by colored liberation movements. Put another way: as these anthropologists were subscribing to a policy of partnership between colored and white peoples in the colored world, the imperialists were adopting a similar policy in order to salvage white economic interests in a revolutionary colored world. But, these anthropologists and the imperialists were out-of-step with colored nationalists: Malinowski offered partnership via peaceful negotiation whereas Fanon demanded replacement via violence (Harris 1968:556–558; Fanon 1968:35–41, 46).

Anthropologists in the United States are now losing their enthusiasm for aiding imperialism. This diminished enthusiasm might mean that the militant opposition of the United States government to intensified colored liberation movements has made clearer the moral bankruptcy of serving imperialism. This interpretation flatters anthropologists and augurs well for the future of their profession. But, is this the whole story? Perhaps the diminished enthusiasm is a convenient way to avoid painful confrontations of political liberals, and sometimes even radicals, with anthropology operating under the umbrella of white rule.

The Uses of Anthropology (At Home)

To anthropologists, the study of dominated colored peoples was not merely exoticism nor even only service to imperialism. The ultimate aim of anthropology was the improvement of white societies everywhere. Indeed, anthropologists have boldly proposed solutions to social problems in white societies. I will give attention first to Tylor, the so-called "father" of British anthropology, who has been praised by Boasian anthropologists, and then attention to Boas, the so-called "father" of modern anthropology in the United States. In doing so, I will consider the scientific functions of their views on racism.

Tylor and the Use of Scientific Racism

To Tylor, anthropology was relevant to many problems besetting white societies in the late nineteenth century. Tylor believed that reconstructing white history provided general laws that were essential for guiding sociocultural change in white societies; hence, he explained that anthropology was an "important practical guide to the understanding of the present and the shaping of the future" and that the study of "savages and old nations [is] to learn the laws that under new circumstances are working for good or ill in our own development." That Tylor was not equally concerned with providing similar assistance to contemporary colored peoples is shown by his candid admission that "for matters of practical life these people may be nothing to us." Since progress in white societies meant eliminating some old customs as well as adding new ones, Tylor was greatly concerned with the persistence of survivals in these societies. These survivals were seen as resembling sociocultural patterns found in the colored world. Tylor advocated the selective elimination of these survivals; specifically, he advocated the selective elimination of those that failed the logical and functional tests of anticlerical middle class Englishmen like himself. Thus, Tylor declared that the "practical office of ethnography [is] to make known . . . what is but time-honoured superstition in the garb of modern knowledge . . . [and] to mark these out for destruction." These survivals were widespread in white societies and impeded clear thinking that was necessary for progress. Indeed, survivals were especially dangerous since they might suddenly develop into active revivals, as had happened with witchcraft and spiritualism (Tylor 1891 1:2, 16–17, 24, 159; 2:445, 453; Harris 1968:137, 140–179). That Tylor's anthropology was a frank intellectual exploitation of colored peoples for the benefit of white people is shown by his arrogant couplet: "Theologians all to expose, 'Tis the mission of Primitive Man" (Kardiner and Preble 1963:68).

The danger from religious survivals was one main reason that Tylor studied the animistic religions of colored peoples, and Christianity is predominantly animistic. Tylor declared that since this "investigation . . . bears very closely on the current theology of our own day, . . . I have set myself to examine systematically, among the lower races, the development of Animism." This danger gave a sense of urgency to Tylor toward his work, since he believed that the "oft-closed gates of discovery and reform stand open at their widest [in late nineteenth-century England]. How long these good days may last, we can not tell." Indeed, this urgency was an additional reason for using sociocultural data from the colored world, especially "innocuous" sports, games, and popular sayings. Tylor hoped that their apparent remoteness and insignificance would make his advocacy of reform, especially religious reform, more palatable (Tylor 1891 1:23, 158; 2:452). Advocating religious reform was necessary and even courageous in view of the resurgence of theological fundamentalism that had occurred earlier in the century. Nevertheless, it was political timidity in approaching social problems: it avoided the crucial problem of the private ownership of the means of production and provided an alternative prescription to the Marxian solution via violent class warfare. Finally, Tylor's preoccupation with trivia to avoid provocation helped establish a dissemblance that prevails too frequently in twentieth-century anthropology.

The desire to improve white societies guided decisively Tylor's research strategy, and was one main reason for the importance of historical reconstruction. It was another main reason for using so much sociocultural data from the colored world, since white peasants and ancient whites provided insufficient information about early white history. This led to the comparative method and equating contemporary colored peoples with white ancestors. This equation required the concept of psychic unity as modified by scientific racism: colored peoples shared only the "most elementary processes" with white people. This version of psychic unity established just the right amount of pertinency of colored peoples. Since it established the humanity of colored peoples, the comparability of their customs was acceptable; indeed, the need to fix this comparability sometimes led Tylor to make statements that approximate the scientific antiracism of Boasian anthropology. Nevertheless, scientific racism was predominant in Tylor's thinking. Indeed, scientific racism was essential to Tylor in order to establish the mental inferiority of colored peoples and thereby explain the progress of the white world over the colored world. That Tylor's scientific racism had this heuristic origin does not deny that racism had important uses as justifications for imperialism as well as for class exploitation and national aggrandizement.

Boas and the Use of "Scientific Antiracism"

The improvement of white societies was as much the aim of Boas as it was with Tylor, although the mature Boas rejected the comparative method, general laws, and scientific racism while adopting a more thoroughgoing cultural relativism (cf. Harris 1968). Believing that anthropology illuminated contemporary social processes, Boas prescribed solutions to many social problems in the white world (Boas 1928; Boas 1945). Since he posed as a neutral scientist, these prescriptions are masked in his scholarly publications beneath an apolitical surface; for instance, anti-Marxism is behind the emphasis on irrational customs among colored peoples and the incongruity between their technology and sociology. However, these prescriptions are explicit in his popular writings; but, anthropologists read *Race, Language, and Culture* and not *Anthropology and Modern Life*.

The basic prescription of Boas was the extension of individual freedom, unrestricted by the "shackles" of tradition and the merging of individuals into social categories (Boas 1938a). Hence, the high premium on deviant individuals and the opposition to class, racial, and religious discrimination. Socioeconomic changes were necessary to allow a degree of social participation in white societies that matched the participation that had been observed in small communities in the colored world. Moreover, these changes were necessary to provide more constructive leisure, and to provide much more than existed in these small colored communities (Boas 1928:218–220). The need for these socioeconomic changes became so compelling that the elderly Boas, despite his long-standing anti-Marxism, moved ever closer to the communist movement (Rohner 1969:296).

Since individual freedom was at odds with the nationalism in the white world, Boas became increasingly anti-nationalistic, and advocated pluralism within white societies and pacific internationalism among them. Indeed, his ideal prescription was world federation as the ultimate extension of the in-group ethic of brotherhood, but he compromised for the more practical federation of white nations (Boas 1928:97–101). This compromise was only an old dream of white Europe: the dream of Napoleon, Kaiser Wilhelm, Hitler, and De Gaulle. Imagine what this white federation would do to nationalist aspirations in the colored world! Thus, instead of calling for the liberation of colored peoples living in imperialist colonies in 1919, Boas saw the "true solution of the colonial problem" in a direct and kindly governance by an international organization of the nation states (1919). Finally, pluralism and pacific internationalism are distinctive of a segment of Jews living in Europe and the United States in the nineteenth and twentieth centuries.

In the Boasian strategy, diversity among colored peoples permitted an objective appraisal of white societies, and this objectivity was crucial for the rational solutions of social problems. In 1939, Boas stated that "conditions of life fundamentally different from our own can help us to obtain a freer view of our own lives and of our own life problems (1940:vi)." The desire for objectivity is another main reason for field work, since emancipation from ethnocentric blindness was obtained by immersion in an unfamiliar colored society. This meant that field work was for the immediate benefit of anthropologists and the ultimate benefit of white societies. It was not an experience to help colored peoples. On the contrary, field work was conceived in one way that was dangerous to colored peoples living under white rule: except for protecting the anonymity of individual informants, anthropologists were expected to report fully to the white world on what they had seen and heard while visiting among these colored peoples. Moreover, conversion to colored life-styles was not a goal of field work, since anthropologists were expected to return to white societies and live again as middle class white people. Some Boasians were opposed to full participation in the lives of colored peoples while engaged in field work: Alexander Goldenweiser believed that such participation should be only "on the surface" while Paul Radin considered it a "delusion and a snare" (Paul 1953:438). Melville Herskovits' position coincided with the worldwide racial hierarchy established by white rule when he admitted that "going native" might be feasible in the South Seas but that it was "neither possible nor of benefit among West African Negroes and their New World descendants." Indeed, his reason was similar to one frequently advanced by segregationists in the southern United States: the failure to observe "caste" distinctions will offend blacks and subject the white anthropologist to ridicule (Herskovits 1937:326–327). Finally, field work is always a calculated experience and it is sometimes superficial and transient as well. Therefore, it probably does not provide emancipation from ethnocentrism, and it might confirm cultural bias.

Diversity among colored peoples constituted alternative answers to some social problems in white societies. However, the Boasians seldom, if ever, advocated that white societies borrow the particular answers found in the colored world.[2] Instead, the Boasians used this diversity to show that sociocultural change was feasible in white societies. To do this, they needed to show that cultural behaviors were not determined by biology. Since they were committed to change, they needed to show that change was both rapid and widespread. These needs account for the Boasian preoccupation with human nature vis-à-vis cultural conditioning, and for pushing cultural conditioning as far as possible, as against an immutable human nature. These needs help explain why scientific antiracism replaced the racial determinism of nineteenth-century anthropology and why emphasis on cultural relativism grew. These needs were crucial in establishing the centrality of the culture concept in Boasian anthropology. Finally, these needs required the adoption of an antievolutionist position in order to deny also the inevitability of sociocultural patterns, and that psychic unity become a perfunctory concept, similarities in culture being minimized.

This strategy posed a considerable dilemma. Enculturation led to the belief in the tenacity of culture; hence, Herskovits' African survivals among New World blacks. Logically, the tenacity of culture placed unacceptable limits on the feasibility and rapidity of sociocultural change, although less than scientific racism. Therefore, the need arose to restrict the power of enculturation in order to provide more leeway for change. The first step was to show that extensive and rapid change did occur, and this was done by diffusionism and historical reconstruction. The second step was to show how change occurred. This was done by the shift to studying individuals in relation to their societies and thereby underscoring the inevi-

[2] It is possible that polygyny has been recommended by some male anthropologists.

tability of deviation. Inventors as deviant individuals produced new cultural traits and opened the way to sociocultural change via individual free will. This is one main reason for the anti-determinism in Boasian anthropology.

Since colored solutions were seldom recommended to white people, diffusionist studies were concerned with the transmission of culture among colored peoples. Acculturation studies were similarly concerned with the impact of white culture on colored peoples, however incomplete this impact was conceived. *The transmission of culture from colored peoples to white people was largely ignored, especially when studying North American Indians.* Indeed, the main exception to this generalization was the study of the diffusion of Chinese cultural traits into the white world. To Boasians, improvement in white societies depended overwhelmingly—if not completely—on deviant individuals who were white people. The implication is clear: white societies deserved something better from their deviant individuals than was offered in the colored world.

Historically, scientific antiracism was *not* conceived primarily to defend colored peoples. As applied to these peoples, scientific antiracism has been really a misnomer. This intellectual tradition increasingly minimized—but never completely excluded—the possible influence of racial factors on the sociocultural behavior of colored peoples, especially the black people. Indeed, Boas entertained consistently the hypothesis that the smaller average brain size of black people precluded them from producing as many "men of highest genius as in the other races." There is a need to recognize that scientific antiracism has been a heuristic device, sometimes used by nineteenth-century evolutionists but especially by Boasians, to increase the pertinency of colored sociocultural patterns. Also, Boasians used scientific antiracism to attack racial discrimination among white groups, especially Nordicism and antisemitism. Intermingling as well as internal variation, overlapping, and instability of physical traits among white populations in Europe and the United States were used to establish the irrelevancy of race as an explanation for the differing sociocultural patterns existing among these white groups. The minimal role assigned to race in regard to sociocultural patterns among colored peoples was also used to establish the irrelevancy of racial explanations in regard to white groups. Hence, Boas concluded, "there is no need of entering into a discussion of alleged hereditary differences in the mental characteristics of various branches of the white race (1911:268; 1934:34; 1938b: 135, 226–231, 238, 240)." Since Boasians were mostly European Jews, they suffered antisemitic discriminations first in Europe and then in the United States, and they were outraged by Hitler's atrocities. Indeed, Boas emigrated from Germany to escape antisemitism, and he admitted that most scientific antiracism was an "effort to combat the antisemitic drift" in the white world (Rohner 1969: 295; Boas 1925:21). Since most native-born white Protestant anthropologists were racist and antisemitic, scientific antiracism was used by Boasians as an intellectual weapon in their struggle for the domination of anthropology in the United States, especially against those anthropologists centered in Washington (Stocking 1969a:270–307).[3]

Scientific antiracism was only secondarily concerned with colored peoples. Yet, it was strategic to use them and their sociocultural patterns: another exploitation of colored peoples for the benefit of white people. This helps explain why Herskovits' initial work with New World blacks dealt with problems in physical anthropology: it was designed to confirm antiracist conclusions in the physical anthropology of Boas, who had dealt mainly with white immigrants (Herskovits 1928). It helps explain the detachment of many Boasians from the civil rights movement; even Herskovits as late

[3] This "power struggle" is one of the major research problems in United States anthropology.

as 1951 excluded the ending of discrimination against New World blacks as a goal of Afro-American studies (Herskovits 1951:32). Scientific antiracism has shifted more to colored peoples in recent years. This shift coincides with the muting of racism between white groups under the shock of Hitler's crimes and the remarkable economic and political advances of white Catholics and Jews. It also coincides with the increasing threat from black and other colored liberation movements.

Scientific antiracism does not mean the absence of color prejudice and discrimination. "No inherent connection between race, language, and culture" often becomes a mere catechism, devoid of personal commitment. Malinowski's secret diary shows that scientific antiracism can coexist with vicious color antipathies and suggests that color prejudice is more prevalent than white anthropologists admit (Malinowski 1967). Hence, the futile attempt to explain away Malinowski's racism as well as the silence and even hostility to this revealing diary (Firth 1967: Introduction; Hogbin 1968:575; Stocking 1968b). Manuscripts of other dead white anthropologists and life histories of the few black anthropologists will reveal additional evidence. These revelations should not be surprising: white anthropologists are members of racist societies. This color prejudice and discrimination must be incorporated into any history of anthropology. This evil helps explain the lily-white composition of anthropology and the lack of recruitment of colored anthropologists until very recently. Even Herskovits did not develop a program to train United States blacks as professional anthropologists and utilize them in African and Afro-American research. It helps explain why Boasians so largely avoided the study of United States blacks (Willis 1970). In view of the long-standing partisanship for white interests, color prejudice is one main reason for the present outcry against "relevant" anthropology.

With more information about field experiences, it becomes clear that anthropologists have not practiced what they preached, and color prejudice is one reason why. Malinowski exaggerated his separation from white people while in the field as well as his participation in Melanesian life. His periodic vacations were as much an escape from annoying colored people as an escape from aggravating customs; indeed, he confessed a "need to run away from the niggers" (Malinowski 1967:167). A double standard clearly pervaded field procedures; for instance, Boas robbed graves for skeletons and commandeered Indian prisoners for anthropometric measurements (Rohner 1969). These deceptions and bullying tactics were unthinkable toward white people in New York City. Color prejudice even in Boas (so hard to believe!) becomes a distinct possibility.

The tiresome professions of friendship for colored informants now become suspect. Real friends are not treated in such unjust ways. Moreover, the concealment of color prejudice now appears as one reason for the puzzling secrecy of anthropologists about their field experiences. Indeed, their discussions of methodological difficulties concentrate on intercultural problems and neglect interracial problems (Freilich 1970; Pelto 1970). This concealment is short-sighted: white anthropologists cannot operate successfully among angry and suspicious colored peoples unless racial arrogance is purged, and the first step is candor.

Anthropology as an Entertainment

Anthropology for the benefit of white societies is also shown by providing education and recreation to white people, and these functions were prominent in Boasian anthropology. Ethnographic museums served these functions earlier than teaching in the history of anthropology, and the demand for the possessions of colored peoples played a crucial role in the development of the profession and its structure in university curricula. Recreation has been at least as important as serious education, perhaps more so. This is obviously true of museums, especially on idle Sundays. Thus, Boas declared that the "museum as a resort for popular entertainment must not be underrated" and estimated that the "majority [of museum visitors] do [sic] not want anything beyond entertainment (1907:1)." Since anthropologists have generally presented harmless "aboriginal" customs while avoiding the frightful contemporary realities, recreation has been prominent in the teaching of anthropology, especially at the undergraduate level. This entertainment of white people at the expense of colored peoples has been widened as the teaching of anthropology now occurs in primary and secondary schools as well as on television. Anthropology for pleasure also applies to many professional anthropologists: the distant colored world is often perceived as an exotic place offering temporary escape from the familiarity and monotony of middle class society in the white world. In the nineteenth century, considerable satisfaction with middle class society existed among anthropologists; therefore, most anthropologists then were able to ease their discontent by reading accounts of the faraway colored world. However, disenchantment with middle class society deepened in the twentieth century, and this disenchantment is one main reason for the popularity of field work in twentieth-century anthropology. In this way, field work is a kind of tourism; West Indian nationalists now decry tourism as whorism.

Anthropology and the Aspirations of the Colored World

Bona fide political freedom via viable national consolidation and rapid economic development is the main nationalist aspiration in the colored world. There is need then for strong governments, but the persisting Boasian premium on individual freedom and the position of anti-nationalism oppose the development of such governments. Moreover, strong governments and violence go together. Indeed, terrible violence is predictable in the emergence of colored peoples, since this emergence is comparable to white expansion around the world and dwarfs modern revolutions in white societies. Some colored nationalists now advocate violence as a positive good, politically and psychologically; and violence has been the stock-in-trade of imperialists (Fanon 1968:35–106). However, anthropologists have been generally committed to progress via reason and opposed to sociocultural change via violence. Since anthropologists are white people, they are especially opposed to colored peoples using violence to overthrow white rule. Despite fascination with tribal warfare, anthropologists neglect brutal conquests by white people and desperate resistance by colored peoples. If understanding leads to social control, then anthropologists are derelict in not studying violent interracial conflicts. Moreover, they have missed a decisive chance to help repair the damaged self-image of colored peoples, for there is heroism in the struggle against white rule.

Some important theoretical concepts in twentieth century anthropology are inimical to the nationalist aspirations of the colored world. The ahistoricism of functionalism simply ignores the very existence of white rule, and thereby absolves white people of their crimes. The model of the isolated society does more than evade: by stressing sociocultural differences, it facilitates the imperialist policy of divide and rule. In addition, it provides colored peoples with an easy excuse for failure: they can readily point to insurmountable tribal differences. In conjunction with the search for aboriginal cultures, this model precludes the discovery of sociocultural links wider than tribal allegiance and more realistic than Pan-Africanism. Similarly, functional ahistoricism precludes the discovery of wider links in a past more meaningful than near-forgotten medieval kingdoms. Yet, the discovery of these wider links is essential to viable national consolidation and rapid economic development. To an African nationalist, tribalism is heresy.

There is now some recognition that cultural relativism is logically incompatible with advocacy of sociocultural change and that it complements Lord Hailey's "Indirect Rule" (Bidney 1967; Hartund 1954; Northrup 1955; Kluckhohn 1955). Significantly, the initial impetus to this recognition was the dilemma posed by Hitler's Germany and the Soviet Union, and not the evil of imperialism. Since relativism is applied only to "aboriginal" customs, it advises colored peoples to preserve those customs that contributed to initial defeat and subsequent exploitation. It is really advising them to preserve the crippling distortions that white rule has made of traditional customs. By applying relativism in this way, new sociocultural patterns that arise in urban settings have been frequently ignored as worthless: like imperialists, anthropologists have condemned these new patterns and warned against "detribalization." Hence, relativism defines the good life for colored peoples differently than for white people, and the good colored man is the man of the bush. Yet, the demand for liberation and modernization originates among the new men of the towns. Colored nationalists want so much more than pleasant words about traditional customs; indeed, they are suspicious that white men bearing these words are condemning colored peoples to eternal poverty and powerlessness (Wright 1957:93; Fanon 1968: 224). In revolutionary situations, the realities of fighting for liberation and modernization supersede the opiate in negritude.

Most anthropologists are at best committed only to gradual sociocultural change. Since institutions are considered interrelated, anthropologists believe that innovations may have unforeseen consequences, some of which could be harmful. This being the case, prolonged investigation must precede innovations. The meaning of "taking social factors into consideration" is clear: wisdom is to proceed slowly (Foster 1969:73–89; 108). Is the anticipation of harm from unforeseen consequences so justified? If harm is in disturbing traditional patterns, then I remind that these patterns are already crippling and pathological distortions of an older way of life that countenanced defeat. If harm is in upsetting colored peoples psychologically, then I remind that nothing has upset colored peoples more than white rule. Moreover, trauma is an inevitable concomitant to change. Perhaps the real harm is in disturbing imperialist domination and thereby upsetting white people.

It is clear that anthropology postpones the end of imperialism to the distant future. But something more: a strong bias against sociocultural change is persistent in anthropology, and some concepts defend the status quo (Myrdal 1956:171–173). This defense is now recognized in the equilibrium model of functionalism (Harris 1968:516–517). The model of the isolated society locates the causes of change inside artificial boundaries of small communities and not in the worldwide system of capitalist imperialism. This misplacement of causation in less significant conditions means that anthropology has provided an inadequate guide to change, and inadequacy is no way to achieve anything. Moreover, the premium on individualism means that sociocultural change is dependent upon previous changes in the thinking of individual persons. Even if true, the priority on changes in individuals has been historically a conservative doctrine. Finally, the Boasian position that culture is complex and that causation is fortuitous means that causes cannot be found and that the search for them is a useless procedure. The failure to seek and to find causes means the absence of any scientific basis for a program of sociocultural change.

The End of Anthropology?

The end of anthropology is an old fear. Anthropologists have been afraid of the disappearance of "aboriginal" cultures in the wake of depopulation and sociocultural change, and this fear helps explain the priority of data collection over theory and the recent shift to studying development (Worsley 1966). Ironically, anthropologists have been afraid of increasing specialization that has arisen with the expansion of ethnographic information (Mead 1964:7). Finally, they have been afraid of totalitarian repression in white societies (Linton 1936: 490). These fears have been unrealistic. Many colored populations are increasing, and their enlarged sociocultural inventories can now be studied from the point of view of development. Increased specialization has not so far disturbed the formal organization of anthropology. Finally, totalitarian success in white societies is not incompatible with the study of dominated colored peoples. Yet, there is now real reason to fear for the future of anthropology.

The end of imperialism is a probable contingency. Its end will mean the end of what has been anthropology, since this anthropology has been based on the subordination of colored peoples. Imperialist domination has now been overthrown in some parts of the colored world, and it has been weakened in other parts. In many places, anthropologists are having a hard time with the new outward anger and suspicion of colored peoples. Moreover, most conventional anthropological preoccupations are irrelevant for solving the increasing poverty in the colored world, and colored nationalists in the early years of independence turned to economists for help (Onwichi and Wolfe 1966; Myrdal 1968 1:8–10). It seems now that colored nationalists are becoming disenchanted with the economists. Will they now turn to the anthropologists? Whatever happens, anthropologists no longer have the colored world to themselves.

There is still some hope for anthropology. The present disarray among colored peoples and the still immense power of the imperialists mean that the end of imperialism is only a probability. Even if the end of imperialism is certain, it will not end quickly nor at the same time around the world. Even if imperialism does not end everywhere, new conditions in the colored world mean that anthropologists cannot proceed in the old way. It is time for anthropologists to make drastic changes. If they make these changes, then perhaps a new kind of anthropology can survive in a new world in which colored peoples enjoy *bona fide* freedom and equality.

What Is To Be Done?

Urban ethnography is one crucial proving ground to forge this new kind of anthropology. White anthropologists must get along with black and other colored peoples of the ghettos, and these peoples are now angry, literate, and politicized. Moreover, they are no longer awed by the mystique of the white man. The new terrorism in the ghetto is not only dangerous but plays upon deep-seated fears and guilt feelings, the legacy of slavery and slave revolts. It is clear that color prejudice has no place in the ghetto. If anthropologists succeed in the ghetto, then they probably can succeed with colored peoples anywhere. This requires a new kind of anthropologist, to which old standards of professionalism are impediments needing change.

The ghetto will not tolerate only white anthropologists. There is an immediate need to develop active and creative programs to recruit, train, and employ many young black and other colored anthropologists. If these programs are successful, then the new colored anthropologists will become articulated with the ghetto poor. They will not be so isolated in white academia like the few colored anthropologists of the past and thereby as derivative in their anthropology. The numerical increase and the new articulation will encourage colored anthropologists to initiate distinctive approaches (Jones 1970).[4] Perhaps they and white anthro-

[4] Jones presents a stimulating discussion of some problems facing black anthropologists.

pologists working together in the ghetto can achieve a new identity in political ideology that can overcome the divisiveness of the uniform of color. But, white anthropologists must make the first moves, and one such move is to refrain from any kind of demand for ideological subservience. Perhaps even then, this new kind of identity is a pipe dream.

Successful urban ethnographers will become a separate force in anthropology, distinctive in personality, race, and especially politics. Sociopolitical significance will become the main criterion in selecting research problems. Out of the crucible of the ghetto, a new perspective of black people as real human beings will emerge. This new perspective is consistent with the emergence of a new kind of partisanship, one that advances the political demands of the ghetto poor. Since urban blacks are structurally the most revolutionary segment in United States society, political radicalism must then replace the older liberalism. If this is not the path of urban ethnography, then it will wither away, sooner than later.

Some innovations are already occurring. Urban ethnographers are realizing that the holistic concept of culture, developed from the model of the isolated "primitive" society, does not fit ghetto sociocultural institutions. They are realizing that field work must be changed: frankness instead of deception, courtesy instead of insult, and participation in partisan politics instead of only in pathetic ceremonies. The ghetto demand for continuous accountability of outside institutions requires periodic publications while still living in the ghetto instead of publishing only when safely home from the field; indeed, urban ethnographers are never safely home, since the ghetto is so near academia. Finally, self-censorship replaces the conceit of total investigation: urban ethnographers must agree readily to the boundaries of investigation as decided by ghetto nationalists (Valentine 1970).

What else is to be done? Anthropologists can reevaluate the development of their profession from new perspectives, exposing skeletons as I have attempted.[5] By using ethnographic data already collected, to expose skeletons, anthropologists can emphasize the total impact of white rule on colored peoples (Fried 1967:52–107).[6] Like Harris, they can seek more adequate theories of sociocultural change and more rigorous methodologies. These two endeavors are closely linked. Exposing skeletons provides clues for developing better theories and methods, and both endeavors derive crucial momentum from urban ethnography and from the ferment in the colored world. Exposing skeletons has one immediate advantage: it provides effective propaganda to colored nationalists in their fight against white rule. In view of the atrociousness of this rule, exposing skeletons for this kind of propaganda poses no great threat to objectivity. However, developing better theories of sociocultural change has the potential advantage of enabling colored peoples to improve their levels of living as they move toward *bona fide* freedom and equality. This advantage is only a potentiality, since colored peoples might reject these theories for valid and/or invalid reasons. In any case, anthropologists must not try to force their theories upon colored peoples. At the same time, they must not let appeasement of colored peoples influence the development of theory, except to the extent that the goal of anthropology is the end of poverty and powerlessness among colored peoples. In correcting white middle class bias, urban ethnographers must not romanticize ghetto patterns; instead, they must evaluate these patterns by the criterion of this goal of anthropology. Finally, anthropologists must give no credence to the vicious theory that poor people are responsible for their poverty.

---

[5] The skeleton of racism in nineteenth-century anthropology has been exposed by Harris (1968) and Stocking (1968a). Fried reveals racism in twentieth-century anthropology in *The Study of Anthropology* (1972).

[6] Fried exposes some fictions about small egalitarian societies.

Urban ethnography, exposing skeletons, and developing better theories are less expensive than the old field trips to distant colored peoples; therefore, big grants from the United States government and the foundations are not needed. Also, there is less need to get involved in international politics. All this means more freedom to pursue the goal of anthropology, a goal inimical to the present foreign policy of the United States. One final point: urban ethnography, exposing skeletons, and developing better theories must incorporate a new sensitivity toward black and other colored peoples everywhere. This sensitivity will make anthropology more acceptable among colored peoples, even in Africa and Asia; but, more importantly, it will help colored peoples accept themselves as equal human beings and thereby undo the damage of centuries of white rule.

References cited

BIDNEY, DAVID (1967) Theoretical anthropology. Introduction to 2nd ed. New York, Schocken.

BOAS, FRANZ (1907) Some principles of museum administration. Science 25:921–933.

——— (1911) The mind of primitive man. New York, Macmillan.

——— (1919) Colonies and the peace conference. The Nation 108:247–249.

——— (1925) What is race? *In* Race and democratic society. Ernst P. Boas, ed. New York, J. J. Augustin. 1945 ed.

——— (1928) Anthropology and modern life. New York, W. W. Norton.

——— (1934) Race. Encyclopaedia of the Social Sciences 13:25–36.

——— (1938a) An anthropologist's credo. The Nation 147:201–204.

——— (1938b) The mind of primitive man. Rev. ed. New York, Free Press.

——— (1940) Race, language and culture. New York, Macmillan.

DELORIA, VINE, JR. (1969) Custer died for your sins: an Indian manifesto. New York, Macmillan.

DIAMOND, STANLEY (1964) Primitive view of the world. Introduction. New York and London, Columbia University Press.

DU BOIS, W. E. B. (1939) Black folk: then and now. New York, Henry Holt.

FANON, FRANTZ (1968) The wretched of the earth. New York, Grove Press.

FIRTH, RAYMOND (1967) Introduction. *In* Malinowski, Bronislaw. A diary in the strict sense of the term. New York, Harcourt, Brace and World.

FOSTER, GEORGE M. (1969) Applied anthropology. Boston, Little, Brown.

FREILICH, MORRIS (ed.) (1970) Marginal natives: anthropologists at work. New York, Harper and Row.

FRIED, MORTON H. (1967) The evolution of political society. New York, Random House.

——— (1972) The study of anthropology. New York, Thomas Y. Crowell.

GOUGH, KATHLEEN (1968) New proposals for anthropologists. Current Anthropology 9:403–407.

HARRIS, MARVIN (1968) The rise of anthropological theory. New York, Thomas Y. Crowell.

HARTUNG, FRANK (1954) Cultural relativity and moral judgments. Philosophy of Science 21:118–126.

HERSKOVITS, MELVILLE J. (1928) The American Negro: a study in racial crossing. New York, Alfred A. Knopf.

——— (1937) Life in a Haitian valley. New York, Alfred A. Knopf.

——— (1951) The present status and needs of Afroamerican research. *In* The new world Negro. Frances S. Herskovits, ed. Bloomington, University of Indiana Press, 1966. Pp. 23–41.

HOGBIN, IAN (1968) *Review:* Bronislaw Malinowski, a diary in the strict sense of the term. American Anthropologist 70:575.

JONES, DELMOS J. (1970) Toward a native anthropology. Human Organization 29:251–259.

KARDINER, ABRAM, and EDWARD PREBLE (1963) They studied man. New York, New American Library.

KLUCKHOHN, CLYDE (1955) Ethical relativity: sic et non. Journal of Philosophy 52:663–677.

LÉVI-STRAUSS, CLAUDE (1966) Anthropology: its achievement and future. Current Anthropology 7:124–127.

LINTON, RALPH (1936) The study of man. New York and London, D. Appleton-Century.

LOWIE, ROBERT H. (1937) The history of ethnological theory. New York, Farrar and Rinehart.

MALINOWSKI, BRONISLAW (1967) A diary in the strict sense of the term. New York, Harcourt, Brace and World.

MAQUET, JACQUES J. (1964) Objectivity in anthropology. Current Anthropology 5:47–55.

MEAD, MARGARET (1964) Anthropology: a human science. Princeton, D. Van Nostrand.

MYRDAL, GUNNAR (1956) An international economy. New York, Harper.

——— (1968) Asian drama. New York, Pantheon.

NORTHRUP, F. S. (1955) Ethical relativity in the light of legal science. Journal of Philosophy 52:649–662.
ONWICHI, P. CHIKE, and ALVIN W. WOLFE (1966) The place of anthropology in the future of Africa. Human Organization 25:93–95.
PAUL, BENJAMIN D. (1953) Interview techniques and field relationships. *In* Anthropology today. A. L. Kroeber, ed. Chicago, University of Chicago Press. Pp. 430–451.
PELTO, PERTTI J. (1970) Anthropological research: the structure of inquiry. New York, Harper and Row.
REDFIELD, ROBERT (1953) The primitive world and its transformations. Ithaca, Cornell University Press.
ROHNER, RONALD P. (ed.) (1969) The ethnography of Franz Boas. Chicago and London, University of Chicago Press.
SCHOLTE, BOB (1972) Toward a Reflexive and Critical Anthropology. *In* Reinventing Anthropology. Dell Hymes, ed. New York, Pantheon Books. Pp. 430–457.
STOCKING, GEORGE W., JR. (1968a) Race, culture, and evolution. New York, Free Press.
——— (1968b) Empathy and antipathy in the heart of darkness: an essay review of Malinowski's field studies. Journal of the History of the Behavioral Sciences 4:189–194.
TYLOR, E. B. (1889) On a method of investigating the development of institutions: applied to laws of marriage and descent. *In* Source book of anthropology. A. L. Kroeber and T. T. Waterman, eds. New York, Harcourt, Brace, 1931. Pp. 464–471.
——— (1891) Primitive culture. 3rd ed. London, John Murray.
VALENTINE, CHARLES A. and BETTY LOU (1970) Making the scene, digging the action, and telling it like it is: anthropologists at work in a dark ghetto. *In* Afro-American anthropology: contemporary perspectives. Norman E. Whitten, Jr. and John F. Szwed, eds. New York, Free Press. Pp. 403–418.
WAGLEY, CHARLES (1968) The Latin American tradition. New York and London, Columbia University Press.
WILLIS, WILLIAM S., JR. (1970) Anthropology and Negroes on the southern colonial frontier. *In* The black experience in America: selected essays. James C. Curtis and Lewis L. Gould, eds. Austin and London, University of Texas Press. Pp. 33–50.
WORSLEY, PETER (1964) The third world. Chicago, University of Chicago Press.
——— (1966) The end of anthropology? Mimeograph. Sociology and social anthropology working group, 6th world congress of sociology.
WRIGHT, RICHARD (1957) White man, listen! Garden City, Doubleday.

39

A CLOSING WORD

MORTON H. FRIED

> I sat in the sunset shade of their Bastille, the
> Pentagon, . . . and heard, alas, more speeches
>
> [ROBERT LOWELL]

It is the nature of any discussion of ethics to be a speech. I prefer to say it that way. Influenced by Lowell's lines, I might have written that it is the nature of any discussion of ethics to be, *alas*, a speech. But the added word implies an alternative that I think does not exist. May and Abraham Edel remark about ethics that

> we do not find specialized groups to carry it out, nothing to correspond to a priesthood or a police force. There are no buildings for ethics, nor visible tokens of it like shell money or a witch's herbal bag. Apart from education, it is hard to find common institutional forms peculiarly dedicated to it. [1968:7]

Ethics, then, is manifest in speeches, in finger-pointing, in gossip, in sublime poetry and irritating doggerel. It concerns decisions about good and bad, about the desirable and undesirable, and above all relates exclusively to human relations. A dog that takes another's bone or chases a cat or messes on the rug cannot by any stretch of the imagination be said to have commited an unethical act, no more or less than a breach of ethics is to be seen in a guppy eating its young.

The study of moral and ethical systems for-

SOURCE: *The Study of Anthropology*, Morton H. Fried. New York: Thomas Y. Crowell Company. 1972. Chapter 13. Reprinted by permission of the publisher.

merly pertained, for the most part, to philosophy, and indeed, philosophers are still to be found who make this their prime area of concern. But certain aspects of the inquiry into moral and ethical questions have become more closely associated with social scientists and anthropologists in particular. Dorothy Emmet (1968:157), a specialist in these areas, tells us, for example, that the attempt to distinguish ethical components of a sociocultural system, as distinct from political, religious, or legal aspects, or even from etiquette, crested in the late nineteenth and early twentieth centuries in the work of anthropologists like Edward Westermarck (1862–1939). In more recent decades, however, the primary interest of anthropologists in a technical sense has been devoted to the comparative study of values, including moral and ethical concepts and precepts. Paralleling this to some degree is strong sociological interest in the analysis of ethical codes as the normative charters of specialized sectors of a larger society. Thus, in the work of Talcott Parsons, ethical codes are seen as the strictures controlling role playing among such professionals as doctors and lawyers, both in terms of relations among themselves and between themselves as professionals and other portions of the larger society (e.g., patients, technicians, drug salesmen, clients, and so on). Beals, in his survey of ethical problems in contemporary anthropology, calls attention to Parsons' suggestion "that ethical problems in science arise primarily at the intersection of the various subsystems in which the individual scientist participates" (Beals 1969:n. 8, p. 82, citing Parsons 1967). Beals then goes on to identify three loci at which ethical questions appear in conjunction with professional problems: (1) with regard to professional responsibility—maintaining integrity and high working standards; (2) observing one's responsibility to others—proper treatment of associates, fellows, informants, nonprofessional associates, the subjects of research, the public; and (3) observing a responsibility to oneself—"considering one's personal background and psychological needs" (Beals 1969:83). I think that the sharpest attack on Beals could be expected to develop from left activists. I suspect that they would find that with these strictures he would have covered the waterfront—that in providing for just about everything, he has provided for nothing; he has, instead, avoided the biggest question, which asks what anthropologists should be doing in these critical times.

Having staked out some of the difficult terrain we will have to traverse, let us move first to the easiest ground, to speak briefly about matters of an ethical nature relating to anthropology, yet of such nature as to be minimally controversial or universally accepted. There is, for example, the ethical matter of standards that cuts across all subdivisions.

Whether one is linguist or archeologist, physical or cultural anthropologist, there is a presumption of craftsmanship that has ethical overtones. Most obvious are the restraints on misrepresenting credentials. The Ph.D. must be in hand before it is appended symbolically to one's name. Obvious as this may be, it is unfortunate that there have been tragic cases to the contrary. Furthermore, there is a certain low frequency of semimisrepresentations, for example, in the tendency of candidates to present themselves (or be presented by their departments) as having completed their doctorates when they are still pending. To assume, as sometimes is done, that this matter of the Ph.D. is mere elitist snobbery is to completely miss the point of the certification of competence. It is obvious, however, that concepts of competence, its standard, and the means of assessing it are subject to continual review. In the past, it has been common for students to be excluded from the process of standard setting. During the height of student activism in 1968 and 1969, there seemed to be movement in some departments toward greater student participation at this level of determination of professional competence. In the subsequent period, however, interest in such reform seems to have waned, although some examination changes were accomplished at certain institutions.

There is a set of ethical problems that have to do with the initial determination of certain types of competence and with the maintenance of a previously demonstrated competence. The latter refers to the difficulty of ascertaining in advance whether any particular individual will be a reasonably good teacher. The overwhelming majority of anthropologists are engaged in teaching as their primary activity; yet, as we have also seen, little effort is expended during their periods of training to make them competent instructors. Indeed, we have only rather haphazard and primitive means of determining how good a teacher someone is. Some of the means have dubious ethical overtones by our present values—I refer to the visits to a junior colleague's classroom of some inspector or group of inspectors (whatever they may be called). On the other hand, using the evaluations of students, a very necessary part of determining the competence of a teacher, brings up another batch of ethical questions, such as the relations between differential standards of grading and student reaction to a teacher's personality. It is evident, however, that such a problem touches anthropology only as one of many academic subjects and is exacerbated only to the degree that anthropologists are capable of looking objectively at their own social structure, however painful that may be.

Even in such relatively mild ethical considerations one finds the materials of very deep and difficult problems. There is an acceptance of a certain very general pattern of social organization in the larger society which embodies formal hierarchy, the cultivation of esoteric specializations, and elitism. There is an alternative that deplores all of these things and asserts that a counterculture can be built on opposite principles. The contrast between these systems is usually discussed in ethical as well as political terms. It is appropriate to note here that a major complication facing anthropologists who consider such problems is the latent, and frequently manifest, conflict between their moral preference for one set of solutions, and the professional ideology of objectivity.

Comparable in difficulty to the detecting of teaching competence in the young instructor is the determination of continued competence in older ones. A common method of attempting this has disturbed several generations of students and young professionals. Usually referred to as "publish or perish," placing great reliance on the volume of published work has obvious ethical implications in addition to practical drawbacks. Consider merely two aspects: the draining of some instructors' energies such that they shortchange their students in order to maintain certain levels of publication, and the burden of such publication on their science as the volume of junk and trivia swells to flood proportions. Yet, alternatives for assessing competence later in the development of a career have potentially alarming ethical consequences, particularly in suggesting some form of "thought police," or intellectual coercion.

Moving to a more general consideration of ethical problems in anthropology at large, it seems to me from my vantage point in the cultural portion of the discipline that linguists have the fewest problems of professional ethics. (This is not to say that linguists may not play vanguard roles in the moral and ethical struggles of their day, as the activities of Noam Chomsky so brilliantly illustrate.) However, even linguistics has sometimes been placed in the service of colonialist and racist ideology, as when theories of the evolutionary superiority or functional superiority of certain languages have been offered.

Archeologists have somewhat more frequent possibilities of encountering ethical problems. To suggest just one or two, let us take the once common situation in which the ancient treasures of a defenseless society were removed with neither consultation nor permission from their native locales and placed in a museum in

Europe or North America. Many of the countries in which international archeological projects are carried out have since placed an embargo on the export of antiquities. Yet, there is a substantial residue of heritage materials, ranging from such famous objects as the so-called Elgin Marbles to the uncounted precious objects of art from China, which are held in public and private collections around the world. A new case has come to the pressure point. Representatives of at least a portion of the Iroquois people (Onondaga), plus Indian leaders representing a wider spectrum of peoples, have successfully demanded the return from New York State of an extensive collection of wampum gathered into the custody of the Regents of the University of the State of New York by donation and purchase about three quarters of a century ago. In line with the ongoing political revival among American Indians is a religious revival, and the wampum is being demanded on grounds similar to those being presented the government in the case of the sacred Blue Lake near Taos Pueblo in New Mexico. Anthropologists and archeologists are becoming involved, pro and con, in such demands and are finding that what started out as professional questions are becoming more and more entangled in ethical considerations.

Archeologists also become enmeshed in ethical problems through their conduct surrounding a dig. I cannot erase from my mind a certain film supplied graciously and gratuitously to me by the French consulate for use in a class many years ago. I was teaching a survey of the cultures of Southeast Asia, and the film showed the temples of Angkor. In one segment, running perhaps a couple of minutes, an old, white-bearded, and very dignified, if anonymous, professor was shown conducting another seemingly academic person about a portion of the ruins. A fallen piece of sculpture attracted the older man's eye and he brought it to the attention of his companion. Unfortunately, at that very moment a Khmer workman was bending in front of the object, possibly at some task. Without thought or hesitation, the old archeologist poked the Cambodian away with a long fan he was carrying. So commonplace was the event that it obviously never occurred to anybody in the French information service to excise that bit of colonialist by-play.

The day has gone by, in some countries at least, when the archeologist was the great white god with clean, soft hands. My archeologist friends assure me that this image never really applied to the anthropological archeologist, who has always (it is said) been accustomed to come into first-hand contact with the dirt. In any event, labor relations can present problems with ethical reverberations, just as can the proper securing of legal rights to dig at particular sites.

A final note about archeological matters that have ethical aspects. The archeologist is no longer involved in abstruse affairs. Some of his digs are seized upon for political significance, perhaps as an additional source of legitimacy for a new or shaky state, or to place or refute some territorial claim. One example must suffice:

> Archeologists have been under attack in Rhodesia for their findings at Zimbabwe and similar ruins near Salisbury. Zimbabwe has been identified as the remains of a medieval Bantu city, dated by radiocarbon between the 11th and 15th centuries with occupation possibly as late as the 17th. These dates have undercut previous held beliefs that the city was a settlement of Egyptians, Phoenicians or Indians rather than the creation of the immediate ancestors of Rhodesia's black population.
>
> Recent discovery of a similar ruin at Bindura in the same area has stimulated attacks on the archeologists and even an Information Department pamphlet by white citizens of a new nation dedicated politically to white supremacy. It is psychologically almost impossible in the present intellectual environment for the white critics to ascribe to native Bantu technical skills that could produce the masonry buildings, gold figures, sculptures and pottery that are uncovered at the ruins. Rather, it is more comfortable to view such suggestions as black African nationalist movement propaganda. [*Newsletter of the American Anthropological Association* 11:2 (1970):11]

The ethical involvements of physical anthropology are related to those implied in the paragraphs just cited. They are also among the oldest and best known of those faced in the anthropological discipline. It is instructive and perhaps a source of relief to realize that physical anthropology played an important role in one of the decisive moral turns in the history of not only Western but world civilization. I refer, of course, to the place of physical anthropology in demonstrating the soundness of the evolutionary approach, in producing the evidence of man's evolutionary ancestry, and in driving religion and supernaturalism from this area of knowledge. But equally old, if less decisive, have been the ethical implications of the physical anthropological study of race.

Although there is no dearth of racist literature that seems to have emanated from physical anthropologists, very little of the current crop has actually been produced by scholars who have specialized in physical anthropology. Yet there are a few such specialists who join a heterogeneous group of anthropological amateurs in spreading a compost of old and new lies, half truths, innuendos, and hypotheses about race. Some physical anthropologists, who easily could do otherwise, make little or no effort to limit the use of their work by others for patently antisocial ends. Indeed, I think the most important ethical issue that faces physical anthropology concerns the basic question of the social responsibility of the scientist. I see no reason to revise an indictment that I offered some years ago. I began by noting that excellent work had already been done for years by scientists to counter what I call the pseudoscientific proclamations about race:

> I do not say that they failed in their intentions; certain ameliorations have occurred. But one thing they did not do is stop the nonsense. The pseudo studies go right on. What is more, some fine scientific journals throw open their pages to serious discussion of this nonsense. Those who oppose the pseudo study of race are called "equalitarians," and this term has been skillfully manipulated to make it appear as if there are two valid camps participating in a normal scientific exchange. But this is not a question of digging the "Mohole" or not, or whether *Homo habilis* is or is not an *Australopithecus*. It is more like dividing on the question of whether or not to exterminate six million Jews: one side says no and presents its arguments, and the other side says yes and presents its arguments, and this too becomes a debatable scientific question. . . .
>
> Science has no social responsibilities, but scientists must accept social responsibility or face the consequences. Racial problems are as fraught with danger and potential disaster as problems of nuclear proliferation. . . . What I am suggesting is only a slight extension of the element of social responsibility from the individual subject to the larger social aggregates whose futures are just as much influenced by this work. [Fried 1968:129–130]

The mounting gradient of ethical responsibility in anthropological work crests in the various subfields of cultural anthropology. Here ethical problems become so abundant and are so pressing that the present brief chapter cannot hope to do justice to them. . . . Before taking a final plunge into the most serious and controversial, we should briefly consider some of the less complex questions that arise.

Consider first the ethical problems that beset relations with informants. We already warned about potential cruelties that might arise in dealing with aged informants from whom we obtain historical, biographical, or other kinds of information. The return to the informant is likely to be limited to the transient companionship that such interviews bring. What happens when the interviews are concluded? The young and busy anthropologist goes off and forgets; the old person has been deserted yet again. Nor are such problems confined to relations across generational chasms. Most informants come to believe that they are developing a viable human relationship when they spill out confidences or help gather materials. Some make elaborate plans to use the relationship for other social purposes. After all, the anthropologist is frequently regarded as a representative of the ruling class, or the powerful metropolitan country. Usually, the anthropologist is correctly considered to be wealthy beyond local dreams. Surely such a friend will help in various emergencies throughout life. Yet, at the time of departure from the field, the anthropologist frequently disappears into a void and is never heard from again.

I have no sure remedies for these types of situations. Different anthropologists handle the matter in different ways. Let this mention of the problems, however, stand as a warning. The ethnographer had better do some thinking about these possibilities before he is swamped by events that may damage others and leave very heavy psychological burdens of guilt.

There are so many problems that revolve about the relation of anthropologists with their informants that several volumes could be devoted to them. Consider, for example, the word "informant," which carries an unwanted freight, not the least portion of which is its tendency to convert persons into things. But there are other aspects as well. Few go deeper into the ethical morass of our field than the problem of maintaining scientific verity while protecting real people from the dangers of exposure. It is commonplace now to remark that the day is long past when the anthropologists' monographs existed in a completely different world from the one in which lived their sources of information, their subjects. Now literacy is growing and communications approach the instantaneous. Write about a Minnan community in any portion of Taiwan and the people will soon know exactly what is in the book. What may be worse, the government will also know about it. In many cases this will not matter, but what if sections of the book deal candidly with political values and raise questions about the loyalty of some Taiwanese to the existing Nationalist Government? What complicates matters further is the fact that the anthropologist cannot know what may become a sensitive issue. His book may be a time bomb for decades. To avoid this possibility, or to reduce its potential, a variety of devices of concealment are utilized. But concealment is a form of secrecy and, as we shall see, anthropologists are usually opposed to secrecy and have held secrecy against various sponsoring agencies, particularly those associated with the military. Of course, it is a big leap from obfuscation to preserve privacy to total classification that leads a study to be withheld indefinitely from the scrutiny of other scientists and from the public at large.

There is also a problem concerning financial arrangements between an anthropologist and those whose information he must utilize. There are a few instances, very few, in which the anthropologist has made rather considerable sums from the books that have resulted. Should the author split the profits with his informants? To determine how equity is to be arrived at in such cases remains essentially a matter of ethics involving the conscience of the principal researcher. As we have seen, however, suggestions have been made that amounts equal in size to the grant supporting the research should be paid to the community being studied. This might be contrasted with a once rather prevalent view that condemned the paying of informants as a source of corruption in field work.

Additional ethical problems concern the relation of the anthropologist with the government of the society he chooses to study. From one point of view, the anthropologist must be considered a guest of the country he journeys to in carrying out his research. He is, of course, legally bound to observe the laws of that country. Does he have additional obligations? Some anthropologists seem to think not; they perceive their obligations to lie with some segment of the society other than the government. Many who hold such views are never called upon to translate them into any kind of action. Their field experiences pass without friction or at least without overt manifestations of such friction. There are some, though, whose activities openly fly in the face of the host government's desires. Whatever value such activities may have for whatever constituencies, the fact that they are associated with an anthropologist is likely to have decided effect on subsequent anthropological work in that country. The most obvious, of course, is that anthropologists applying to do work in that society in the future are liable to be turned away or receive less than full cooperation. It is the threat of the former eventuality that concerns so many anthropologists, raising, as it does, serious ethical questions requiring some balancing of obligations within the discipline of those that individual practitioners feel they have as citizens, or simply as members of the human race. It reminds us of Talcott Parsons' suggestion that the ethical bind is to be found precisely at the point where the individual is subjected to the clash of codes for two or more of the subsystems in which he is involved.

Since this is not a book about ethical problems in anthropology, but merely a chapter, it is time to get into some of the major controversial issues. None is more central than the question of selecting a focus of interest for anthropological teaching and research. Involved, on the one hand, is the entire battery of problems known as relevance. On the other are fundamental questions of individual decision, still very much a part of the culture in which this book will take its place.

As we have seen, one bit of advice is that anthropologists should abandon, at least for the time being (until the revolutionary transformation), all ideas about working in other cultures. They are advised, instead, to stick to their own and, in fact, concentrate even there on revolutionary activities. I am not sure how beneficial this scheme may be for any practically based concept of revolution, but it would be the death of anthropology. Anthropology came close to dying in the Soviet Union when this attitude prevailed there. Now there is some anthropology, but it is not synonymous with Marxist-Leninist theory. Similarly, in Cuba there remains an independent anthropology, although its role and contributions are not quite clear. Anthropology, however, can scarcely be said to exist in the People's Republic of China, although it is too early to consider its demise permanent. (I will argue in the sequel that at certain levels of sociocultural complexity the social sciences, and anthropology in particular, will be reintroduced, even reinvented, many times, each time in response to the need for real information as opposed to ideological eyewash.)

Concentrating once again on selecting a focus for anthropological work, let us note that the discipline is somewhat more relaxed in its attitudes about area specialization than some of its relatives, especially in adjacent social sciences. To some extent, however, it is true that the biggest kudos is reserved for those whose reputation is primarily associated with anthropological theory in general; it does not hurt to be associated *also* with some particular culture or culture area. Eric R. Wolf, pointing out that the more talented fieldworker, Malinowski, lost out in influence to the greater theoretician, A. R. Radcliffe-Brown, nonetheless underlines the significance of ethnography to the anthropologist who thereby "has escaped from the humdrum world of his civilization to walk among headhunters, cannibals, and peyote-worshippers, to concern himself with talking drums, magic, and divine kings" (1964:11). What must be added, because it enhances contrast, is that this has been done in cold blood, without patronization. As Radcliffe-Brown commented:

> the anthropologist is not concerned, as an anthropologist, with whether such things as slavery and cannibalism, or the institutions of the United States or Russia, are or are not right, good, reasonable, or just. [1949:321]

It must be realized that there were many who disagreed with that stand at the time of its writing, as there are today. Before we return to consider the dispute that this position entails, a few more remarks about the issue of problem selection in its ethical setting may be appropriate.

Let us consider first the recommendation that anthropologists place a moratorium on working in foreign cultures until the problems of their own cultures are solved. Most particularly, this stricture is aimed at anthropologists in the United States, although it is applied to those coming from other metropolitan and colonialist or imperialistic powers as well. Earlier in this chapter I wrote that observance of this stricture would destroy anthropology. A colleague, reading the draft, noted at first that if this were so, he would have no regrets. Then he continued, reflecting that a "new anthropology" might arise from the wreckage, an anthropology that had severed its links with the exploitative past. What is more, my friend suggests, the limitation of the purview of United States anthropologists to their own country does not necessarily herald the destruction of cross-cultural methods and studies, since this country contains a variety of cultures within its borders.

I can agree with my colleague, but only up to a point. I change my charge from "destroy" to "cripple." The limitation of anthropologists' research purview to the bounds of their native countries would cripple anthropology, possibly to such an extent that it would cease to exist as we know it, although not necessarily perishing as a demarcated area of knowledge and inquiry, if that were a goal in itself. What is more, there are grounds for believing that the restriction of inquiry to one country is but the leading edge of a larger restraint. We have already heard assertions that only members of a particular subculture are competent to study it.

The essence of cultural anthropological discipline is cross-cultural analysis. Since, as we have seen, one aspect of ethical behavior is conformity with high standards of technical competence, the suggestion that we abandon work in alien settings is tantamount to a professionally unethical proposal. Anthropology requires a cross-cultural setting for its most basic theoretical operations. Rather than urging anthropologists to dwell within their own cultures, the needs of the discipline are best served by encouraging all anthropologists to maximize their experiences outside their own cultures. This obviously requires that optimum support be given to ventures that would place foreign anthropologists in sensitive research niches in the United States. It also requires that anthropologists continue to press for frequent and easy international exchange of qualified research persons. But these things in turn require some understanding of the real world in which, on the one hand, codes of ethics are proposed to increase trust, and conversely, governments regard all citizens as servitors, thereby vitiating the effects of such formal ethical statements. Although this theme will reappear before the end of this chapter, let me say here simply that the matter is completely open and unresolved and a veritable cockpit of struggle. As the struggle is waged, however, it will be helpful to keep in mind the words of the 1967 Statement on Problems of Anthropological Research and Ethics by the Fellows of the American Anthropological Association:

> The human condition, past and present, is the concern of anthropologists throughout the world. The study of mankind in varying social, cultural, and ecological situations is essential to our understanding of human nature, of culture, and of society.
>
> Our present knowledge of the range of human behavior is admittedly incomplete. Expansion and refinement of this knowledge depend heavily on international understanding and cooperation in scientific and scholarly inquiry. To maintain the independence and integrity of anthropology as a science, it is necessary that scholars have full opportunity to study peoples and their culture. . . .

We must recognize, however, that the choice of subject made by an anthropologist in the United States, while free in certain respects, is often the result of certain subtle pressures.

Outstanding among these are the sources and quantity of available funds for research support. The matter is given fairly extensive treatment in the recent book by Ralph L. Beals (1969:85–146, *passim*); let us take up a few of the main points and one question not raised by Beals.

Treating the last matter first, it should be noted that legitimate efforts of scholars to delve into the workings of the foundation world (e.g., the Ford Foundation, Foreign Area Fellowship Program, Social Science Research Council, and the like) have sometimes been rebuffed. Quite often, the refusal to cooperate has been based upon an implicitly ethical response: the files to which access is requested contain information relating to the evaluation of individual scholars and their projects, evaluations that are usually collected with the explicit proviso that their contents will not be divulged. The matter is both sticky and sensitive. The reason for the investigations I have in mind is the fear in certain circles that the foundations have acted deliberately to direct the development of United States scholarship along certain lines while keeping it away from others; this, it is asserted, has been done by careful selection of projects for funding not so much by merit as by the conformity of projects with the desires of the foundation in question.

Those of us who have served on various boards and panels connected with the making of research grants are often baffled by such charges. They do not conform to our experience, which tells us that, indeed, individual merit of researcher and proposal is the outstanding, if not the only, focus of judgment. Yet none of us has experience of more than a limited arc of the total spectrum of grants. On the other hand, it seems possible to erect certain procedures that would make public a great deal of the inner workings of foundations, including the details of their grant-bestowal machinery, without violating the privacy of individuals. Since this is a problem that torments cultural anthropology at large, there is no reason for avoiding it at home in our own operations.

Taking another tack, the fellows of the American Anthropological Association have recommended that "when queried by individuals representing either host countries or groups being studied, anthropologists should willingly supply evidence of . . . their sponsorship and source of funds." The phrasing of 1967 now seems a bit narrow. One of the main constituencies that wish to know such details consists of the students who attend such researchers' classes. I can see no reason why they, and the researcher's colleagues, and indeed his public, should not also be granted such information if they desire it.

Left untouched is the question of accepting government funds for any particular research. There is a wide range of such support. We assume that large sums are available for espionage and that some anthropologists will join others in claiming them. I don't think that anything can be done to stop such activities. Traditionally, when such individuals have been exposed, the government concerned has denied any connection with them. Can any self-respecting, organized discipline do less?

What we are concerned with, however, usually comes in more complex packages, such as in the shape of a Project Camelot. There are still quite a number of social scientists who feel that the mistake was in the stopping of Camelot, which they believe put the brakes on the development of "big social science" in the United States. Most recently the center of attention has been on certain aspects of anthropological research in Thailand and elsewhere in Southeast Asia.

Although the American Anthropological Association is perhaps more deeply riven over such matters than ever in the past, this is not the first time that such issues have arisen. Half a century ago Franz Boas denounced the use of the anthropological research role as a cover for espionage. Subsequently, additional issues of an ethical nature occupied the attention of the profession. World War II, however, saw a general diminution of sensitivity. Anthropologists were called upon to serve the war effort by placing their distinctive skills at the service of the military. With few, if any, exceptions, they responded with pride and proved eager to assist in the conduct of the war, whether by serving directly in intelligence, compiling area background handbooks, or providing other applications of the discipline. After the war, sentiment remained high for assistance to certain kinds of projects, particularly those associated with the United Nations, especially in such subdivisions as UNESCO. Quite soon after the end of the war, the Executive Board of the AAA was given a mandate by the membership to draft a Statement on Human Rights. It appeared in 1947 (*American Anthropologist* 49:539–43), but by this time opposition was again more vocal and the publication of the Statement precipitated an interesting although inconclusive debate. Homer G. Barnett summed up one view when he wrote:

> The import of the statement is that anthropologists, as trained students of human relations who maintain a disciplined attitude toward their materials, have something scientific to say about the requirements for a charter of human rights. Unfortunately this is not so; and the reason is as obvious as it is well known; namely, that there is no scientific approach to the question of human rights, nor to any other problem that calls for an appraisal of human relations in terms of some absolute value system. [1948:352]

Julian H. Steward offered similar views and expressed them more forcibly:

> The conclusion seems inescapable that we have gotten out of our scientific role and are struggling with contradictions. During the war, we gladly used our professional techniques and knowledge to advance a cause, but I hope that no one believes that he had a scientific justification for doing so. As individual citizens, members of the Association have every right to pass value judgments, and there are some pretty obvious things that we would all agree on. As a scientific organization, the Association has no business dealing with the rights of man. I am sure that we shall serve science better, and I daresay we shall eventually serve humanity better, if we stick to our purpose. Even now a declaration about human rights can come perilously close to advocacy of American ideological imperialism. [1948:352]

For another side of the argument we can deliberately take an anachronistic jump of twenty years, to the words of Gutorm Gjessing:

> Ethically, the social sciences should serve humanity—no more, no less; but in a world filled with conflict between classes, ethnic groups, nations, etc., it would seem to be impossible to serve the interests of all simultaneously. If we must choose between the immediate interests of the oppressed and those of the oppressor, there can be no doubt that our responsibility is first and foremost to the former; for it is here that our special competence lies. [1968:402]

Leo S. Klejn, a Soviet anthropologist, applauds the view that "a neutral science is an illusion, cultivated because of its advantages for the ruling circles of capitalist society" (1968:415). Klejn reminds us that "the scientific truth is not always easy to discover," and is sometimes perceived differently by different scientists because of the differences in their social positions. Klejn is amused by Gjessing's tendency to seek truth through self-searching. Instead, he points out, "The Marxists believe that the most progressive scientific position . . . , that the most fruitful methodological conception is dialectical materialism" (*ibid.*).

To pursue the implications of Klejn's remarks, I will jump to a very interesting book, one that Kathleen Gough has mentioned on several occasions as favorable to the "newer socialisms," and which she says has consequently suffered the fate of being "neglected or scoffed at in the United States" (1968:404). I refer to William Hinton's *Fanshen,* a well-written, detailed, and by no means entirely uncritical account of the coming of the Chinese revolution to one particular village. There is no question, however, of Hinton's involvement in what he is describing. One of the main things that disturbed him was the demand of the poorest peasants for egalitarian distribution of just about everything that could be divided. Although quite understandable, such demands threatened the development of a viable socialist economy. The problem, however, was that egalitarian demands were viewed by the Chinese Communist Party as appropriate in certain contexts, but counterrevolutionary in others. Hinton discussed the matter with one Comrade Lai, the Subregional Communist Party Secretary. The peasants could not understand, complained Secretary Lai, that egalitarianism "was revolutionary when applied against the power and the property of the landlords and the rich peasants, but it became reactionary as soon as it was applied against the middle peasants" (Hinton 1966:606). Comrade Lai continued his analysis, "Many peasants do not understand about this turning point, and so they make mistakes. . . . It is just for this reason that the peasants need proletarian leadership" (*ibid.*:606–607). It is Hinton's comment at this juncture that deserves our sharpest consideration, for at its heart is every question relating to determinations of truth in all of social science, including anthropology:

> Obviously one aspect of "proletarian leadership" was an ability to define and anticipate turning points. The Chinese Communist Party, through a grasp of history as process, through diligent study of all pertinent social phenomena, through never-ending analysis and review of all actions undertaken, had developed this to a remarkable degree. It was therefore able to prepare its adherents in advance for major shifts in the spiral of events or to adjust policies quickly whenever events outran foresight. [Ibid.:607]

Whatever lies within Hinton's remark, it is not science. To me it sounds like some not altogether unfamiliar blend of religion and politics. At the least, it is a surrender of the essential responsibility of individuals to make their own determinations, as far as that is possible, given access to data and theory. It may be anticlimactic on my part to suggest that the Chinese Communist Party, that very same organization which Hinton clearly believes had developed "to a remarkable degree" the "ability to define and anticipate turning points," was caught completely off balance by the Red Guards and was almost destroyed in the middle 1960's during the Great Proletarian Cultural Revolution.

I certainly have no intention of denying the generally coercive character of a specific sociocultural setup, much less of the institution we know as the state, which evolved as an instrument of political repression. It is with full recognition of the forms and degrees of compulsion that may be brought to bear in matters of this kind that a contrary statement must be made. In making such a statement, I am painfully aware, to paraphrase the recently quoted remark of Julian Steward, that I have no scientific justification for doing so. Nonetheless, I exist as citizen as well as scientist, worker as well as anthropologist, in short a human being. Hopefully, it is in the last-mentioned role that I would like to say that one should not voluntarily resign the initiative in making crucial decisions, and it does not matter if such relinquishments are made to a political party or to a religious organization or body.

On the other hand, there is no quibble about the reality of racism, exploitation, and war. What is more, not to oppose these phenomena and the societal and cultural institutions which maintain and reinforce them is tacitly to support them. The political events of our own century have forced many of us to bite into another apple of knowledge, and with that bite we have lost every claim to innocence. The numbing truth is that neutrality has been abolished and everyone is seen to lean to one side. Given this burdensome vision, what should an anthropologist do? At this point the field is wide; nonetheless, though some anthropologists tend to be much more active than others, out and out revolutionaries are very few among them.

At present, anthropologists in large numbers, considering the yet small size of the profession, are vocal in protest, as behavior at recent annual meetings shows. In a break with the past, resolutions bearing on current social problems are passed on with increasing frequency to the Executive Board for appropriate action. Activity has not stopped there. In growing numbers anthropologists are becoming increasingly cautious about participation in various types of programs. Not all options are open, it is true, nor is there anything like agreement on proper courses of action. Wherever choices appear, the ethical questions are reasserted and take predominance. Into the breach have stepped some volunteers who would show the way. Gerald Berreman, for instance, puts it this way:

> we must demand of ourselves and our colleagues a sensitive, responsible interest in the ecology of scholarship; a conservationist point of view and behavior consistent with that view. Herein lies the ultimate commitment to the scholarly profession. Its essential ingredients are a deep respect and concern for the people we study, responsiveness to their values, claims and perspectives, trust in them, and commitment to the truth as we discover it. This means avoiding even the appearance of mission-oriented, politically or economically colonialist research. A crucial step in achieving this is to avoid all funds from mission-oriented agencies of government or neo-colonialist private agencies, to avoid any hint of secret or clandestine activity, and to coordinate closely and reciprocate fully with [foreign] colleagues at every step of the way. [1970:9]

When I first wrote this, I intended to close with these words of Berreman, allowing him to express shared feelings of disgust and revulsion against unwanted war, racism, and complicity with a social system and an economy that mandate such atrocities. But neither the world nor the issues are that simple. Berreman's ideas, like many of those expressed by Kathleen Gough, Gutorm Gjessing, and others who have cried out to our consciences, are rich in humanity and good feeling, but romantic and enmeshed in philosophical idealism. Forget the unadjudicated claim of the culturologists, that the cultural process brooks no interference by the actors, that humans' assertions of control over culture are boastful and illusory. What remains inescapable is the realization that Berreman's notions are never so true as when we agree with them, when we as anthropologists see eye to eye with the people whose culture we are studying. But seeing eye to eye with the people an anthropologist studies is not a prerequisite for nor a necessary accompaniment of good anthropology. It may lead to the worst kind of anthropology imaginable.

At the heart, the core, of anthropology is the requirement that people and their cultures be viewed dispassionately. Anthropologists must be able to see their own culture for what it is, but they must also see other cultures for what they are. Anthropologists may not be unflinching, but they cannot turn away their gaze if they see human sacrifice, slavery, a cult of torture, the glorification of war, degradation of women and men, racism, exploitation, or a thousand other garden-variety cultural predilections. This does not mean that they approve of what they see, but they should not confuse their task of analysis with the act of judgment. Nor does this discrimination in any way curtail the anthropologist's personal exercise of ethical decision in rejecting certain kinds of research, certain kinds of funding, certain kinds of employment.

Anthropologists must confront the distribution of realities. In today's world, this means that they cannot attribute all the evil to one social system, one form of economic organization. More basically, anthropologists, as anthropologists, cannot transfer their scholarly responsibilities to anyone else, not to the president of their country, or the chairman of their party, or the head of their department or even their research assistant. One cannot, as an anthropologist, subscribe to a code of ethics that vacillates between science and politics. Just as it is true that science is never neutral in a political sense, so politics can never be objective in a scientific sense. I said earlier that a basic incompatibility exists between the roles of anthropologist and revolutionist. No one can carry out both simultaneously without betraying one or the other.

Whatever it may be for others, ethics for the anthropologist turns out to be a miserably charted sea in which one makes a personal way, like a frail craft that lacks slick navigational devices. Terrifyingly enough, there is no infallible helmsman at the wheel. In lieu of precise azimuths, we lecture each other, interminably. Alas! This puts us back to where we started at the beginning of the chapter. Unfortunately, that's exactly where I think it is. You take it.

References

BARNETT, HOMER G. (1948) "On Science and Human Rights." *American Anthropologist* 50:352–355.

BEALS, RALPH L. (1969) *Politics of Social Research. An Inquiry into the Ethics and Responsibilities of Social Scientists.* Chicago: Aldine.

BERREMAN, GERALD M. (1970) "Ethics, Responsibility and the Funding of Asian Research." Expanded version of "The Funding of Asian Studies: Needs, Opportunities, and Ethics." Paper presented to Presidential Panel: 22nd Annual Meeting, Association for Asian Studies. Mimeographed.

EDEL, MAY, and ABRAHAM EDEL (1968) Anthropology and Ethics: The Quest for Moral Understanding, rev. ed. Cleveland: Press of Case Western Reserve University.

EMMET, DOROTHY (1968) "Ethics: Ethical Systems and Social Structures." *International Encyclopedia of the Social Sciences* 5:157–160.

FRIED, MORTON H. (1968) "The Need to End the Pseudoscientific Investigation of Race." In Margaret Mead, Theodosius Dobzhansky, Ethel Tobach, and Robert E. Light (eds.), *Science and the Concept of Race.* New York: Columbia University Press, 122–131.

GJESSING, GUTORM (1968) "The Social Responsibility of the Social Scientist." *Current Anthropology* 9:397–402.

GOUGH, KATHLEEN (1968) "New Proposals for Anthropologists." *Current Anthropology* 9:403–407, 428–431.

HINTON, WILLIAM (1966) *Fanshen; A Documentary of Revolution in a Chinese Village.* New York: Monthly Review Press.

KLEJN, JEO S. (1968) "Comments [in 'Social Responsibilities Symposium']." *Current Anthropology* 9:415–417.

PARSONS, TALCOTT (1967) "The editor's column." *American Sociologist* 2:138–140.

RADCLIFFE-BROWN, A. R. (1949) "Functionalism: A Protest." *American Anthropologist* 51:320–323.

STEWARD, JULIAN H. (1948) "Comments on the Statement on Human Rights." *American Anthropologist* 50:351–352.

GLOSSARY

This glossary has been provided to help the reader with the terminology in this book that may be difficult. The definitions, therefore, are appropriate for the context in which the terms are used here. However, the reader should realize that in many cases the definitions are not necessarily the only ones or the most complete that could accurately define the terms, and therefore they should not be considered as absolute. This glossary was prepared by Stephen Kaufman.

aboriginal: Native, original; pertaining to the original inhabitants of a country or place.

acculturation: The process of massive change based upon borrowing as a result of contact with another culture.

acephalous society: A categorization of societies whose organization lacks an acknowledged head or leader.

acoustic phonetics: The study of the actual physical properties of sounds produced by a person during speech.

adaptation: The process by which organisms or cultures change to meet shifting environmental conditions. The environmental pressures may also involve interactions with other organisms or cultures.

affinal: Relationship or relative through marriage.

agnatic: Common descent or relationship through the male or paternal line.

allele: Alternative genes possessing some value for a particular trait, usually occurring in pairs.

allomorph: A variant of a morpheme restricted to certain linguistic environments. For example, *is* is an an allomorph of the morpheme*be* restricted to environments following the third person singular.

allopatric: Refers to species (or other taxa) that occupy distinct non-overlapping territories, or the same territory at distinct and non-overlapping time periods.

animism: A belief in individual spiritual beings.

anomie: The condition during which people within a society have poorly integrated ties to one another and to society in general.

anthropoid: The infraorder of primates including man, apes, and monkeys.

articulatory phonetics: The study of how different sounds are produced by changing the shape and air flow of those parts of the body involved in the production of speech sounds.

Australopithecus: Genus designation for the first hominids found in the late Pliocene and Lower Pleistocene.

avunculocal: The practice whereby ego lives with mother's brother.

balanced polymorphism: Refers to the presence of two or more phenotypes in the population and usually reflecting the selective advantage of the heterozygote.

band: A grouping of several related families into a nomadic or semi-nomadic collective which lacks a permanently institutionalized leader who makes and enforces decisions. Usually bands are associated with specific territories. Additionally all people according to age and sex have equal access to strategic resources.

bifurcate merging: The terminological arrangement of relationships that distinguishes between maternal and paternal kin (bifurcation), but ignores the distinction between lineal and collateral kin (merging). Thus, in a bifurcate merging kin terminological system one term applies to mother and mother's sister but a distinct term is used for father's sister.

biogenetic: Refers to the production of living organisms from other living organisms.

biogeography: The study of the distribution of organisms in the physical environment.

brachiation: Locomotive pattern of swinging hand over hand through the trees found amongst certain apes, the gibbon in particular.

brachiators: Animals that use brachiation as a means of locomotion.

breccia: A rock composed of pebbles and pebble fragments embedded in a matrix.

butchery site: The location where an animal was butchered after it was killed. It may or may not be the same place where the animal was killed. A kill site.

carbon 14: Absolute dating technique useful for organic materials up to about 60,000 years old.

carnivore: Predominantly or exclusively a meat eating organism.

carrying capacity: Refers to the number of people that a particular ecological niche can support relative to the technological complexes being employed.

Ceboidea: A taxon; the superfamily including New World monkeys.

Cercopithecoidea: A taxon; the superfamily including Old World monkeys.

cerebral cortex: Outermost layer of nerve cells in the brain which is greatly expanded and marked by convolutions in the primates.

chinampas: Agricultural fields that have been produced by filling a lake with soil. They are crosscut with canals and the ever present water supply insures that farming can proceed throughout the year without depending upon rainfall.

chromosomes: Refers to the strands of genetic material on which genetic loci are located. Man has 23 pairs of chromosomes.

clan: A group of people claiming, but not necessarily able to demonstrate unilineal descent from, a common ancestor.

cognate: Refers to the presence of identical words in different languages having the same meaning. This indicates either the borrowing of the word from one language to the other or, in examples where cognates are frequent, a common ancestor.

cognatic descent: The tracing of one's descent through both the mother's and the father's sides of the family.

cognition: Refers to the possession of or the ability to acquire knowledge.

coitus interruptus: The practice of the male removing his penis from the female prior to ejaculation. Very commonly used as a birth control method with varying degrees of success.

compound family: Consists of two or more, usually related, nuclear families residing together, sharing a common budget and food preparation.

concord: Agreement between words according to gender, number, etc. that must be used when constructing a sentence, e.g., she *is*, they *are*—the change in the verb showing concord with the number of the subject.

codominance: Refers to the case when neither allele is dominant for a particular genetic locus and the resulting phenotype is a blending of the two characteristics, but not of the genes themselves.

consanguineal: Refers to relatives said to be determined by genetic or "blood" ties.

copula: Linking words which connect the subject and predicate.

cranial: Refers to the head and its constituent parts.

crossing over: *See* recombination.

cultural relativism: The idea that there is no single or absolute set of values or standards by which all cultures can be judged because of each culture's uniqueness.

culture core: Those activities and institutions that are directly related to the economic survival of a culture.

deep structure: Refers to the abstract output of semantic rules that are then transformed into phonological output or surface structure.

demography: The study of population.

diachronic: Literally, across time; refers to the study of phenomena with temporal change a major variable. *See* synchronic.

dialect: A subdivision of a language upon the basis of observable differences in the way the language is spoken in one area, locale, or social class. The differences in the dialect, however, are not so great that it would warrant classification as a different language. Analogous to species and race.

diploid: Refers to twice the number of chromosomes found in the sexual cells, gametes, and is designated by the sign 2N.

discriminant function analysis: A mathematical technique whereby many variables are compared simultaneously and those that correlate with one another are grouped together.

DNA (deoxyribonucleic acid): The organic compound that makes up the chromosomes and that the genetic instructions are encoded on.

dominant allele: An allele that is expressed in both the homozygous and heterozygous states.

double cropping: The practice of planting a particular piece of land twice during the course of one year.

dry season farming: Farming that occurs during the season when the natural rainfall is insufficient for the natural growth cycle of the plants.

dyad: A set consisting of a pair.

ecological niche: A delimitable portion of the environment characterized by a certain mix of inorganic and organic features. Ecological niches tend to be more or less hospitable to certain bioforms, and similarly to certain cultures and cultural developments.

ecology: The study of the complex interactions among various components of the environment, its populations of bioforms and its cultures including the organic and inorganic components.

ectogenetic: Genetic changes induced directly by the environment.

edaphic: Refers to conditions created by particular soil conditions or features.

egalitarian society: A society in which all individuals have equal access to status and to strategic resources.

elision: Refers to the omission of a vowel or syllable in the pronunciation of a word. Can also be applied to cases where part of the word has been omitted for literary purposes, as in poetry.

embryology: The study of prenatal development.

emic: Behavioral research domains or operations whose validity depends upon distinctions that are real and meaningful to the "natives" themselves. *See* etic.

enculturation: *See* socialization.

endogamy: Refers to the practice of marrying within one's own village, band, clan, etc.

endogenetic: Genetic changes induced by a variety of intrinsic forces.

Eocene: The second epoch of the Cenozoic era, covering the time span of 60 to 42 million years ago.

epistasis: The interaction of one or more gene pairs which mask the expression of another gene pair or in some way influence the expression of the gene pair.

estrus: *See* oestrus.

ethnocentrism: Refers to the evaluation of another culture's practices or morals on the basis of the standards of one's own culture; usually associated with the belief that the observer's culture is the best.

ethnography: The description and analysis of a particular delimited culture or society.

ethnomusicology: The study of musical expression, including the role of music in the society and the comparison of musical forms cross-culturally.

ethology: The study of animal behavior.

etic: Behavioral research domains or operations whose validity does not depend upon the demonstration of conscious or unconscious significance or reality in the minds of the "natives." *See* emic.

eugenics: Speculative attempts to improve human varieties by the deliberate selection of hereditary characteristics.

exogamy: Refers to the practice of marrying outside of one's own village, band, clan, etc.

extended family: Any domestic unit larger than a nuclear family. Joint families are one type of extended family.

factor analysis: A mathematical technique that groups together variables correlating with one another.

fallow: Refers to the period during which a particular piece of land is not under cultivation and is permitted to rest from the pressures of agriculture.

fecundity: Refers to the biological capacity for reproduction.

fellaheen: Arabic word for a peasant or agricultural laborer.

femur: The upper leg bone positioned between the pelvic girdle and the knee.

fetish: An object thought to have supernatural power, sometimes associated with a supernatural being.

formal economics: The analysis of the economic transactions of a society according to the doctrines of scarcity, supply and demand, maximization of value, market exchange, etc.

gene flow: Changes in the gene pool of a population through the influx of alleles from another population. The mechanisms most commonly referred to are migration and cross-fertilization among neighboring populations.

gene pool: The totals and frequencies of alleles within a Mendelian population.

genealogy: A listing, written or oral, often diagrammatic and showing specific linkages of individuals bearing kinship ties to one another. Genealogies may span a few or very many generations. They can be unilineal or bilateral. They are often used as charters of group membership and may underlie access to power and property.

genetic isolates: Populations separated from others by a variety of geographical or nongeographical barriers to interbreeding.

genetic isolation: Refers to the maintenance of some boundary, either physical or behavioral, between two populations of the same species resulting in little or no gene flow.

genetic locus: The location on the chromosome of a particular gene.

genetics: The study of the chemical makeup, organization, and role of genes in individual development and phylogenetic evolution.

genotype: The genetic constitution of an individual which interacts with the environment to produce the phenotype.

graminivorous: Refers to a diet consisting almost exclusively of seeds.

Günz: The first of the major Alpine glaciations occurring during the Pleistocene.

Halafian period: A prehistoric cultural period during which settlement of the Mesopotamian Plain occurred around 5000 BC.

haploid: Refers to the number of chromosomes found in the sexual cells, gametes, and is designated by the sign N.

heterozygous: The condition where the alleles for a single gene are not identical.

heuristic: Practice serving to guide research or analysis for the purpose of gaining further understanding or insight.

homeostasis: The tendency of organisms and cultures to reach a condition of equilibrium.

hominid: A taxon; the family Hominidae, which comprises man and direct fossil ancestors classified as man.

hominoid: A taxon; the superfamily Hominoidea, comprising the Hominidae (man), the Pongidae (all apes except gibbons and siamangs), and Hylobatidae (gibbons and siamangs).

Homo economicus: An aphorism for a hypothetical person behaving strictly according to formal economic doctrines.

Homo erectus: Fossil human ancestor of the Middle Pleistocene period. Formerly known as *Pithecanthropus;* also *Sinanthropus, Atlanthropus,* etc.

Homo habilis: Fossil human ancestor; probably australopithecine but said by L.S.B. Leaky to be transitional between *Australopithecus* and *Homo erectus.*

Homo sapiens neanderthalensis: A subspecies of *Homo sapiens* which was present during the Middle Paleolithic times, 100,000 to 40,000 years ago.

Homo sapiens sapiens: Subspecies of *Homo sapiens* to which we, modern people, belong.

homozygous: The condition of identity between the paired alleles for a single gene.

horticulture: A form of agriculture where the mode of technology includes only simple tillage with digging stick or hoe.

HRAF (Human Relations Area Files): A composite collection of ethnographies from cultures found throughout the world including some now extinct. This file has greatly facilitated cross-cultural studies.

humerus: The long bone of the upper arm positioned between the shoulder and the elbow.

hybridization: The crossing of populations representing different gene pools, resulting in a new mixture of genes.

hydraulic model: Sees the rise of complex or stratified societies as the result of the organizational requirements of maintaining large and elaborate water control systems of drainage and/or irrigation.

hypodescent: Refers to the idea that in cases where the offspring is the product of parents of two different social aggregates, the offspring is assigned to the one that is socioeconomically and politically subordinate.

hypostasis: The effect that one gene has in inhibiting the expression of another.

iconology: The historical analysis of art forms including symbols, images, and context.

immunological index: A scale of differences in the reaction of various serums from different animals to a common foreign substance which are then ordered. The assumption is that those who show similar reactions are more closely related than those who show dissimilar reactions.

infanticide: The practice of deliberately killing some newly born infants.

interglacial: The period of warmer climate found between different glacial periods when the glacier has retreated.

intermembral index: The ratio

$$\frac{\text{length of humerus} + \text{length of radius}}{\text{length of femur} + \text{length of tibia}} \times 100$$

This ratio is usually employed to show the elongation of the forearm of brachiators.

interstadial: The short term warm period (geologically speaking) found during one glacial period.

knuckle-walker: An animal that tends to rest weight on the knuckles of the hands as it moves about, as among gorillas.

level of phenomenological integration: a conceptual division of phenomena comprising all those things understood in terms of a particular set of rules and laws. (*See* superorganic.)

lexicon: The set of linguistic signs including words and morphemes used in a language.

lineage: A group of people claiming and able to demonstrate descent from a common ancestor. Lineages may or may not be found as parts of clans.

linguistics: The study of language in its broadest sense. This includes the analysis of how a language works, how it developed, what other languages it is related to, and the reconstruction of past unwritten languages.

Lower Paleolithic: First part of the Old Stone Age which includes the cultural materials of the australopithecines and *Homo erectus.*

mana: A supernatural impersonal force thought to pervade the universe. Though dangerous, it may be manipulated by skilled practitioners. *Mana* is a Polynesian word; many other unrelated languages also have words for the concept, like *wakan, orenda,* and *manitou.*

mandible: Lower jaw.

Mandrillus: Genus designation given to a baboonlike monkey known as a mandrill.

marriage: The various systems of bonding two or more people, usually of opposite sexes, into a more or less permanent association, most generally for the production and rearing of children. Monogamy, polygyny, polyandry, are examples.

matrifocal: Household in which the dominant position and central point of reference is held by a female, usually the mother or grandmother (mother's mother).

matrilineal: The tracing of one's descent through the mother or female side of the family.

mazeways: The set of goals, both positive and negative, present at any one time within the cognitive framework of an individual.

meiosis: Division of sexual cells which results in the production of two sex cells with the haploid number of chromosomes.

Mendelian population: A population of organisms characterized by a high degree of intrabreeding showing gene frequencies in conformity with Mendelian expectations.

Mesolithic: Term applied to the cultures found between the end of the last glaciation and the beginnings of food production. The term is applied to hunters and gatherers who have adapted to the environmental conditions found after the glacial period, though this has come under recent criticism.

Mesopotamia: The flat plain area between and adjacent to the Tigris and Euphrates rivers in Iraq and Iran.

Middle Paleolithic: The prehistoric period during which *Homo sapiens neanderthalensis* and/or certain lithic cultural materials are placed. Usually covers the period 100,000–40,000 years ago.

millennial movements: An attempt by a culture that has undergone major cultural changes in a short time to return to older and more traditional lifeways. The people at the head of these movements usually claim visions that advise them of future actions.

Mindel: The second of the Alpine Pleistocene glaciations.

Miocene: The fourth epoch of the Cenozoic era covering the time span from 30 million to 14 million years ago.

mitosis: The division of cells that results in the production of two cells containing the same number of chromosomes as the original cell.

monistic: The idea that change can best be seen as the result of the operation of single forces.

morpheme: The smallest discrete linguistic sign having meaning. For example, *car* consists of one morpheme *car,* but *cars* has two morphemes: *car* and *-s.* The latter is a bound morpheme indicating more than one.

morphology: The study of form or structure. It can be carried out in various realms, for example, in biology or in linguistics.

Mousterian: Flake tool industry associated with the Middle Paleolithic.

mutation: Refers to the change in the code of the genetic material at a locus, resulting in a different allele, hence ultimately perhaps in a different phenotype.

myth: An explanatory story based on or incorporating unverifiable or imaginary elements.

myth charter: A story that enables the tellers (presumably the people to whom the myth applies) to claim some rights, for example, over property or people.

N-achievement: Term introduced by social psychologists to express the factor of motivation in economic or social development. N-achievement or the need for achievement is said to vary in frequency in different cultures.

natural selection: The differential survival and reproductive success of diverse elements of a population in interaction with the environment.

Neanderthal: *See Homo sapiens neanderthalensis.*

Neolithic: Term applied to the first food producing cultures. Original definition referred to the appearance of polished stone tools.

neolocal: Post-marital residence at a new location; i.e., with neither bride's nor groom's relatives.

network analysis: The location and identification of all people contacted or interacted with by tracer individuals and the analysis of the groups thereby constituted.

niche dominance: Refers to the idea that the position or seat of power will develop in the area where the population potential is greatest and the land most productive.

nomadic: Descriptive of a society or social aggregate that moves about in quest of life's necessities rather than remaining in one fixed location. Most nomads, however, occupy relatively set territories.

nomothetic: The idea that general laws can be established to explain similar phenomena.

nuclear family: A domestic group consisting of a husband, wife, and children, if any.

numinous emotions: The basic emotional states of dependence, surrender, and love.

oestrus: Refers to the period when the female of the species has ovulated and the egg is ready for fertilization. This is usually accompanied by a set of behavioral and physical signals for the males.

Oldowan: Refers to the stone tool culture, pebble tools, associated with the australopithecines.

Oligocene: The third epoch of the Cenozoic, covering the time span from 42 to 32 million years ago.

omnivorous: Relating to diets comprising all kinds of foods, vegetable and nonvegetable.

ontogeny: Refers to the development and history of a single organism.

ontology: The branch of philosophy that concerns itself with the nature of existence.

Oreopithecus: An anthropoid form of the Pliocene.

organization of diversity: The processes involved in organizing the different individual behavioral and structural frameworks to a common and acceptable pattern of integration.

orographic: Refers to the study of physical geography concerned with mountains.

orthogenesis: Refers to the idea that things change according to predetermined outlines for their growth irrespective of changes in the conditions of which the things are a part.

Paleocene: The first epoch of the Cenozoic era, covering the time span from 75 to 60 million years ago.

Paleolithic: Old Stone Age divided into 3 parts: Lower, Middle, and Upper. See respective designations for more information.

paleontology: The science devoted to the evolution of life forms through time and to the recovery of its fossil remains.

paradigm: A theoretical model used as a framework to examine data or attempt to explain phenomena.

Paranthropus: A genus designation for some of the earlier hominids. This term is now generally replaced by the designation *Australopithecus robustus.*

participant observation: A method of ethnographic fieldwork whereby the anthropologist collects data by taking part in as much of the life of the subject society as is permitted.

patrilineal: The tracing of one's descent through the father or male side of the family.

patrimony: Refers to inheritance from one's ancestors, usually on the paternal side.

pebble tools: *See* Oldowan.

phenotype: The physical expression in a specific individual organism of the encoded genetic material as it is modified through interaction with the environment.

phoneme: A set of acoustic sounds that are equivalent regardless of the environment in which they are found and which do not change the meaning of the morpheme.

phonology: The study of the sound system of a language.

phyla: Taxa of a high level of abstraction comprising aggregates of organisms that show a high degree of structural similarity suggesting a common ancestor. We are in the phylum Chordata.

phylogeny: Refers to the development and evolutionary history of groups of related organisms.

pithecanthropines: Former designation of a genus of fossil types now termed *Homo erectus*.

Pleistocene: Refers to the epoch during the Quaternary that begins approximately 3 million years ago and ends 10,000 years ago. It is during this epoch that much of human physical and cultural evolution took place.

Pliocene: The fifth epoch of the Cenozoic era covering the time span from 14 to 3 million years ago.

pluperfect: A past perfect tense of a language.

polygene: Refers to a characteristic that is under the influence of two or more genes simultaneously for its expressive character.

polytypic: Refers to the presence of easily recognizable subspecies within a single species.

pongid: A taxon; the family which includes all living apes and their apelike ancestors, but not gibbons or siamangs or their ancestors. Gorillas and chimpanzees are among the pongids.

post-cranial: Refers to the skeletal parts below the head or cranium.

post-partum abstinence or taboo: Refers to the prohibition of sexual intercourse with a female for a specified period of time after she has given birth.

potassium argon: A technique that dates the formation of certain rock formations by measuring the ratio of argon to potassium.

potlatch: A ritual during which great amounts of food and/or material items are exchanged. Term is usually applied to the rituals found along the Northwest coast of North America.

praxeology: Refers to the application of knowledge, use of skills, or general behavior as seen in customs.

preformism: Refers to the idea that there is a miniature preformed adult ready to develop in the egg and sperm cells.

prescriptive: Refers to situations where individuals are obliged by custom or law to behave in some way.

preterite: Refers to actions that have taken place in the past and therefore appropriate linguistic terms must be used.

primate: An order of mammals that includes man, apes, monkeys, and prosimians.

pristine states: State-level organizations that develop independently of contact or pressure from other state level organizations.

proconsul: Term given to a group of Miocene hominoid forms.

progeny: Offspring.

projective technique: An analytic procedure used to obtain certain personality characteristics.

proletariat: The working class, whose members have no property and must sell their labor to insure survival.

prosimian: The taxon that includes tree shrews, lemurs, tarsiers, and lorises. This is the taxon that in the Paleocene probably provided the link between insectivores and primates. Some question whether they should or should not be included in the primate order.

quadruped: An animal that moves on four feet.

race: An arbitrary subdivision of a species based upon observable biological characteristics.

radius: The shorter of the two forearm bones on the thumb side.

Ramapithecus: A late Miocene early Pliocene hominoid which on the basis of teeth evidence suggests an ancestral relationship to the hominids.

recessive allele: An allele that is only expressed phenotypically in the homozygous condition.

recombination: Refers to one part of the meiotic process during which paired chromosomes exchange genetic material resulting in increased variability.

replication of uniformity: The processes involved in the socialization of individuals within a society which provide for a common behavioral and structural framework.

revitalization movements: *See* millennial movements.

rhythm method: A birth control technique that is based upon abstinence from sexual intercourse during certain phases of the menstrual cycle in the female.

ribosomes: Small particles of cytoplasm in cells that are active in the synthesis of proteins.

Riss: The third of the Alpine Pleistocene glaciations.

rites de passage: Ritual behavior that changes the

status of a person, usually marking a juncture conceived of as very important in given societies. Examples include confirmation ceremonies, weddings, funerals.

ritual: Behavioral displays where the content and sequence of the acts are established by tradition.

RNA (ribonucleic acid): The material that takes the encoded messages found on the chromosome to other parts of the cell.

Romer's Rule: A general proposition named for the paleontologist who first stated that evolutionary change is essentially conservative since it comprises changes that attempt to preserve established patterns of adaptation.

sacred: Those elements that have their established values based upon unverifiable truths and are accepted as such by the followers.

sanctity: *See* sacred.

secondary state: Refers to the development of a society with a state level organization from pressures created by an already existing state-level society.

sedentary: Established in permanent settlements.

segmentary lineages: A descent group that experiences internal division and separates into two or more lineages.

semantics: Refers to the meanings attached to the various elements of the lexicon.

serological: Pertains to matters concerned with analyzing the content of blood.

sexual dimorphism: Sexual differences in body size and structure within a given species. Homo sapiens displays moderate sexual dimorphism.

sibship: A state of group composition whereby membership is based upon the recognition of a common ancestor.

simian: Ape- or monkey-like.

slash and burn: An agricultural practice whereby a field's natural vegetation is cut down and burned. The burned residues form a fertilizer for the subsequent planting. Fields worked in this manner usually have limited fertility and must be abandoned after several plantings. Now often called *swidden.*

socialization: The process by which an individual learns to become a member of the society in which he or she was born.

sociolinguistics: Refers to the study of language acquisition, language change, and other linguistic phenomena having sociological inputs or consequences.

Solutrean: A subdivision of the Upper Paleolithic during which special care was taken by the toolmakers in the production of pressure flaked points.

sororal polygyny: The practice of a man marrying his wife's sisters.

speciation: Refers to the formation of species and the separation of one species into two or more different species.

species: Organisms are said to belong to the same species if they can produce fertile offspring. A taxon based on the grouping of animals according to this criterion.

state: A level of political development in which stratification is maintained by a special apparatus of rule.

stem family: A family comprising two or more nuclear units, each at a different generation level.

stratification, social. Division of a society into two or more population components, each with different rights of access to strategic resources.

substantive economics: Refers to the analysis of economic transactions within the framework of the larger societal setting where formal economics may not apply.

superorganic: Three "levels of phenomenological integration" comprise all known phenomena. The inorganic refers to matter, time, space, and energy; the organic refers to living phenomena; and the superorganic refers to culture. *See* level of phenomenological integration.

surface structure: The phonological output of the semantic rules governing the formation of sentence structure.

swidden: *See* slash and burn.

symbiosis: The mutual interdependence for survival of two different organisms, usually species.

sympatric: Overlapping in geographic distribution, as exemplified by two or more species sharing a territory.

synchronic: Literally, at the same time; it refers to the study of phenomena holding time constant. *See* diachronic.

syntax: Refers to the rules underlying the organization of sentences in a language.

synthetic theory: The modern theory of evolution which is a synthesis of post-Darwinian biology, genetics, and mathematical statistics.

systematics: Refers to the classification of objects or

organisms on the basis of similarities and differences into a heirarchical arrangement.

taxon: A group in any hierarchical system of classification; a category in taxonomy.

taxonomy: The classification of objects on the basis of their similarities and differences.

tell: A mound that is the result of the accumulation of cultural debris over long periods of time.

Teotihuacan: The name of one of the largest pre-Columbian cities in the New World occupied from 250 BC to 700 AD.

Tertiary: Geologic period that includes the following geologic epochs: Paleocene. Eocene, Oligocene, Miocene, and Pliocene.

Theropithecus: Genus designation for the gelada monkey.

tibia: The inner of the two lower leg bones.

unilineal descent: Descent that can be traced either through the male or female side of the family but not both.

Upper Paleolithic: Term given to those cultures showing the use of specially prepared blade tools. Cultures of this kind existed in some parts of the world during the period 40,000–12,000 years ago.

uxorilocal: A residence pattern where the married couple resides with the wife's kin group or family.

variation: Alternative characteristics in genotype and/or phenotype in an evolving species.

vernacular: Common everyday speech.

Villafranchian: The first part of the Pleistocene (prior to the glaciations) during which certain modern animal forms appear.

virilocal: A residence pattern whereby the newly married couple resides with the husband's kin group or family.

wickiup: A house built with grasses or reeds in the shape of a beehive found in the Western part of the U.S.

Zinjanthropus: A genus designation for some of the earlier hominids. Now generally included under the designation *Australopithecus robustus.*